STUDIES IN EARLY MODERN CULTURAL,
POLITICAL AND SOCIAL HISTORY

Volume 28

BRISTOL FROM BELOW

Studies in Early Modern Cultural, Political and Social History

ISSN: 1476–9107

Series editors
Tim Harris – Brown University
Stephen Taylor – Durham University
Andy Wood – Durham University

Previously published titles in the series
are listed at the back of this volume

BRISTOL FROM BELOW
Law, Authority and Protest in a Georgian City

Steve Poole and Nicholas Rogers

THE BOYDELL PRESS

First published 2017
The Boydell Press, Woodbridge

ISBN 978-1-78327-244-0

The Boydell Press is an imprint of Boydell & Brewer Ltd
PO Box 9, Woodbridge, Suffolk IP12 3DF, UK
and of Boydell & Brewer Inc.
668 Mt Hope Avenue, Rochester, NY 14620–2731, USA
website: www.boydellandbrewer.com

A catalogue record for this title is available
from the British Library

The publisher has no responsibility for the continued existence or accuracy
of URLs for external or third-party internet websites referred to in this book,
and does not guarantee that any content on such websites is, or will remain,
accurate or appropriate

This publication is printed on acid-free paper

Printed and bound in Great Britain by
TJ International Ltd, Padstow, Cornwall

Contents

List of Illustrations

Acknowledgements

This book has been a long time in the making; a collaborative product of several decades of independent work by each of us on various aspects of Bristol's eighteenth-century past. We should probably thank one another first and foremost for the cooperative and friendly scholarship we have both enjoyed as we've worked together, albeit, for much of the time, on opposite sides of the Atlantic. In the process, we have each incurred many debts of gratitude to myriad colleagues, students, librarians and archivists who have discussed with us our shared interest in the city's history 'from below'. Listing all of them here would require a feat of memory too great to contemplate, but one or two debts should certainly be honoured.

The ready availability and steady growth of digitised archival collections, from newspapers to pamphlets and manuscripts has, of course, transformed the ways in which scholars research the eighteenth century. We have made full use of those resources, but the physical archives and libraries from which so much of that material is drawn continue to play a vital role. So we'd like to thank the friendly, approachable and efficient staff at the Bristol Archives, the National Archives and the British Library in particular, for helping us face to face with enquiries as our research progressed. Jenny Gaschke, curator of fine art at Bristol Museum and Art Gallery, was as helpful as ever, and special thanks are due to Dawn Dyer and the local studies staff at Bristol Reference Library. Dawn helped us with countless references, rooted things out that we didn't know were in the local collection, and invariably offered us the peace and quiet of the book-lined special collections rooms to work in. Madge Dresser and Jonathan Barry generously shared references of their own, and James Bradley was kind enough to send us a full version of the *Bristol Contest* of 1781: a good example of a resource otherwise available digitally only in an incomplete form. Liverpool University Press generously allowed us to reuse sections of an essay in Adrian Randall and Andrew Charlesworth (eds), *Markets, Market Culture and Popular Protest in Eighteenth-Century Britain and Ireland* in the composite of our Chapter 7. Jonathan Barry and Roger Leech kindly offered us their 1668 parish map of Bristol, which will soon appear in their Bristol Record Society edition of the 1670 hearth tax. In Canada, the librarians in the Media Commons of the Robarts Library,

ACKNOWLEDGEMENTS

University of Toronto offered invaluable help with microfilm copies of British newspapers. We're grateful too to our anonymous readers at Boydell, whose constructive promptings made us tighten up the argument and structure of the book, and to Tim Harris, who, as one of the editors of the Studies in Early Modern Cultural, Political and Social History series, encouraged us to send the proposal to Boydell in the first place. Thanks, too, to Megan Milan at Boydell for efficiently and discreetly keeping us on schedule and getting this book to press.

Steve Poole & Nicholas Rogers, February 2017

Abbreviations

BA	Bristol Archives (previously Bristol Record Office)
BL	British Library
BRL	Bristol Reference Library
CSPD	Calendar of State Papers Domestic
FFBJ	*Felix Farley's Bristol Journal*
GRO	Gloucestershire Record Office
HC	House of Commons
JHC	Journals of the House of Commons
Latimer	John Latimer, *Annals of Bristol*, reprint (3 vols, Bath, 1970)
ODNB	*Oxford Dictionary of National Biography*
TNA	The National Archives, Kew, London

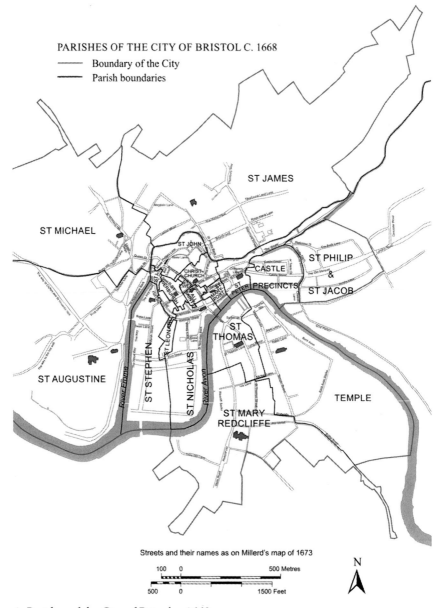

PARISHES OF THE CITY OF BRISTOL C. 1668
——— Boundary of the City
——— Parish boundaries

ST JAMES

ST MICHAEL

ST JOHN

CHRIST-
CHURCH

ST PHILIP
CASTLE
&
PRECINCTS
ST JACOB

ST PETER

ST THOMAS

ST AUGUSTINE

ST STEPHEN

ST NICHOLAS

River Frome

River Avon

ST MARY
REDCLIFFE

TEMPLE

Streets and their names as on Millerd's map of 1673

100   0   500 Metres

500   0   1500 Feet

N

1 Parishes of the City of Bristol, c.1668.

Introduction

At the beginning of our period, Bristol was the major Atlantic port, poised to lead the slave trade and become England's 'second city'. At the end of our period, the city was in flames. When the ultra-Tory Sir Charles Wetherell came to open the assizes in October 1831, having contemptuously dismissed Bristol's enthusiasm for political reform, he was met by protests and an escalating momentum of unrest that resulted in the burning and pillage of large sections of Queen Square and the opening of the gaols. Bristol's burgeoning middle class, thoroughly alienated from the corporation and its allies in the Merchant Venturers, stood by and watched. The more broadly based Bristol Political Union, the political arm of Reform, offered its help, but on condition that its institutional status be recognised. That offer was rejected by the closed corporation, and this rejection paved the way for dragoon repression more savage than that at Peterloo in 1819.

To a considerable extent this narrative frames our book. The broader context charts how a prosperous port with a civic identity strong enough to survive the politico-religious purges of the Restoration degenerated into a narrow, introspective oligarchy that failed the city politically and economically. This means that the book is in part about the power and limits of paternalism, or patron–client networks. Bristol's hierarchical structures worked as long as the economy was buoyant and certain rules about civic responsibility were respected. But Bristol's economy began to lose momentum after the American war and revealed significant structural weaknesses after the Napoleonic, when it proved difficult to tap into the new enterprises of industrial change. And Bristol's politics was a chequered story of new possibilities and arrested development, of the stifling effects of caucus agreements and compromised elections that debased civic freedoms and prompted oscillating bouts of cynicism and hope among the excluded. We found elements of radicalism in Bristol politics: during the American war, the French, and under the banner of Henry Hunt as the Napoleonic wars came to a close. But it proved impossible to fashion a coherent cross-class alliance for radical political reform. The hallmark of Bristol radicalism in this era was ultimately one of impotence. The late appearance of the Bristol Political Union in the crisis of 1830–32 and its often defensive tone – it promised to defend the conscientious voter from the reprisals of the 'local aristocracy' as much as fashion a platform for reform – spoke to the difficulties of popular mobilisation.[1] These were difficulties that would not be quickly overcome, as the problems faced by Bristol's Chartist movement demonstrated only too well a decade later, when its leaders tried to bring working-class trades unionists and parliamentary reformers into progressive political alignment. Chartism at Bristol never made as robust an impact as one might have expected from a city of its size, despite the proximity of militant centres in the coal and iron districts of south Wales and the distressed textile towns of western Wiltshire.[2]

Four of our chapters address the popular politics of the period in some detail. Three zone in on the period after 1770 when the issues of imperial and commercial policy, and of loyalism and political liberty, were forefront in the minds of Bristolians. One, an investigation of popular Jacobitism and its resilience as an idiom of political blasphemy, harks back to the party strife of the period 1680–1720 that gave it such meaning. One element of discordance on which Jacobitism fed, the intrusive power of the state in wartime, is explored more fully in a chapter on naval recruitment, a matter that concerned a wide range of Bristolians who might be pressed into his majesty's navy because they 'used the sea' or 'worked on rivers'. In the period 1738–1815 Britain was at war two in every three years, and so the possibility of being shipped off for the duration of fighting was very real. Resistance to impressment was often extremely violent, especially in the years when the Admiralty attempted to secure a more permanent footing in the ports, but over time Bristol-bound seamen found it easier to evade the press-gangs by landing before their vessels reached the Avon estuary. On balance this strategy proved successful, thanks to the pilots of Pill and to Bristol's merchants, who were prepared to shelter their topmen from the searches of the gangs; although it eventually forced the Admiralty to insist on quotas of qualified seafarers from coastal workers, whether shipwrights, trowmen or pilots.

Impressment was often a triangulated affair, with merchants attempting to mediate between seamen and the Admiralty, on their own account and for the general commercial interests of the city. One of their main arguments against heavy-handed impressment was that it would disrupt essential food supplies, particularly the shipments of grain from the upper Severn. These, the merchant elite were very keen to protect, as our chapter on food provision reveals. Here we suggest that for much of the century the corporation appreciated the need to alleviate food shortages, and as far as possible it sought commercial solutions to dearth by encouraging new shipments of grain and subsidising existing ones rather than enforcing the statutes against

---

[1] *British Mercury*, 21 June 1831.

[2] For the problematic assimilation of trades organisations into the Chartist programme for radical parliamentary reform in the 1840s, see David McNulty, 'Bristol Trade Unions in the Chartist Years', in *British Trade Unionism, 1750–1850: The Formative Years*, ed. John Rule (Harlow, 1988), pp. 220–37.

profiteering. By and large this was successful. It adds a new dimension to the copious literature on the moral economy of the crowd in recognising that the bourgeoisie of large cities were not insensitive to the customary expectations of the poor, as is sometimes assumed. The imponderables in the Bristol context were the miners, with those in the Forest of Dean disrupting lines of supply in the Severn, and those in nearby Kingswood quite prepared to march on the city, confront magistrates, prevent exports and press for a fair price for food or grain. Over time, the corporation became increasingly swayed by the maxims of the market economy, and in 1801 refused to intervene, remonstrating with crowds with the military in waiting. The turn of the century, in fact, marked a tougher stance against plebeian expectations altogether, not only in the politics of provision but in the enforcement of tolls on Bristol Bridge, where disagreements flared over whether the bridge had been adequately financed.

One area where the corporation and its allies took an early stance against customary expectations was over turnpikes, where tolls helped those with economies of scale but not small producers bringing goods to market. Without a modern police force, the corporation and the turnpike trustees were largely helpless to prevent the destruction of turnpikes by colliers and country people, precipitating an escalating round of confrontations between turnpike projectors and rebellious outliers that in turn generated tougher legislation against turnpike wreckers and examples of judicial terror at the gallows. This solution to the conflict proved unsatisfactory. Plans for a special commission to try rioters in Bristol faltered and trials in neighbouring jurisdictions largely backfired. Moreover, the disposition of the trustees to employ vigilantes to handle crowds in 1749 left a legacy of mistrust between the trustees and turnpike users, and unleashed the threat of reprisal against noteworthy merchants, one of whom was forced to lay low outside of Bristol for several months.

The turnpike troubles revealed how vulnerable the city elite was to direct action of crowds from outside. A series of episodes in the 1730s revealed how difficult it was to control similar threats to the peace and self-confidence of the city as it entered its golden age. First, there was a series of labour disputes in the weaving trade that spilled into the city at Temple and Lawford's Gate, culminating in the trial for manslaughter of Stephen Fechem, a well-known drugget-maker at Castle Ditch, and his subsequent effigy-burning and mock execution. Then there were threats from arsonists to the houses of prominent merchants in St Augustine's Back and Queen Square, accompanied by demands for money that were laced with denunciations against the rich. This was followed by a Tory riot against the dominant Whig faction on coronation day, 1735, and a series of sodomy trials that resulted in uncharacteristically low conviction rates. The impression that these seemingly unrelated incidents produced, we argue, was that Bristol was besieged by alien forces: Irish Catholic Jacobites, 'Dutch' or Scottish pederasts, anonymous arsonists, lawless weavers on the fringes of the city. At a time when Bristol had just overtaken Norwich as England's 'second city' and supplanted London in the African slave trade, these 'dark' forces unsettled the equanimity of the mercantile elite and its capacity to bring peace with commercial prosperity.

In writing our history 'from below' we have steered a fairly conventional path in that we address the passions and dispositions of the plebeian or subaltern classes in their collective contests and negotiations with authority. We make no apologies for this: the meta-narrative of the city in the long eighteenth century demands it. This does not mean we are writing a triumphal history of working-class advance, or one that necessarily valorises politically correct resistance. Part of our story is about degeneration, perhaps apt for the years 2016–17. Part of it is about the hold and social purchase of clientage, about empty, extravagant civic rituals, lumpen-voters, the cynicism that comes from political compromise and the rage and recalcitrance of the powerless. We might have said more about the social space of the city and the way it was appropriated. We might have said more about the social dynamics of defamation suits and the way lower-class women used the church courts, but we leave that to others to explore. We could have quarried for black seamen and servants in a city known for transatlantic crossings and the slave trade. In the broader social canvas of the city they are important, though not crucial for our purposes here. Our interest in the slave trade is largely contextual, as a way of understanding the *mentalité* of an important fraction of the Bristol elite and as a significant register of Bristol's economy.

'Every event, however brief', wrote Fernand Braudel, 'lights up some dark corner and even some wide vista of history.'[3] In exploring the dark corners and wide vistas associated with the Bristol riots, we have done some heavy contextualisation in the opening chapters, and here we should acknowledge our debt to those historians who have helped us: David Richardson and Kenneth Morgan on the slave trade and the Atlantic economy; Jonathan Barry on civic culture; Madge Dresser on the relationship between urban gentility and slavery; James Bradley on nonconformity and radical politics, to name just a few. We hope our book will be an inspiration to those historians of Bristol who have participated in the talks and conferences of the Regional History Centre and have found a voice in Redcliffe Press and in the industrious events and publication programme of the Bristol Radical History Group.[4] As far as we know this is the first urban history from below of the long eighteenth century. The methodological problem it poses is one of coherence and scale, for histories from below are generally short-span incident

---

[3] Fernand Braudel, *The Mediterranean and the Mediterranean World in the Age of Philip II*, trans. Siân Reynolds (2 vols, London, 1973), II, 901.

[4] The Bristol Radical History Group, a history from below initiative, entirely conceived outside the academy, was founded in 2006. It has grown and prospered since that date to become one of the most energetic and active provincial history organisations in the country, producing nearly forty original pamphlet essays, two books, and a regular programme of talks, workshops and events. It is living proof that history from below did not expire with the winding down of the History Workshop movement but reseeded itself in the local and regional identity culture of the twenty-first century. See <http://www.brh.org.uk>.

histories covering a specific form of protest and, in the founding decades in particular, revolution. Long-term histories from below, such as those written by Keith Wrightson and David Levine, for example, had the serial backbone of demography. *London Lives*, the recent venture by Tim Hitchcock and Bob Shoemaker, has its own digital archive based on the printed Old Bailey Proceedings and an abundance of parish examinations.[5] We don't have any series that approximate theirs, and in any case, Georgian Bristol disposed us to write more categorically at the interface of social and political history.

---

[5] Keith Wrightson and David Levine, *Poverty and Piety in an English Village: Terling, 1525–1700* (Oxford, 1995); Tim Hitchcock and Robert Shoemaker, *London Lives. Poverty, Crime and the Making of a Modern City, 1690–1800* (Cambridge, 2015).

1

Bristol: Prospects and Profiles

In 1725 Daniel Defoe completed the second volume of his *Tour*, in which he took his readers down the Great West Road to Bristol. He had been to Bristol before and had contacts in the city, so his literary visit was not something he simply cobbled together from histories and travel books. Defoe was well aware of Bristol's reputation: 'the greatest, richest, and the best port of Trade in Great Britain', he declared, 'London only excepted'.[1] This was a pretty accurate assessment. Bristol had just surpassed Norwich in the provincial league tables, and was certainly the leading western port. With its expanding commerce to North America and the Caribbean it had surged ahead of other prominent early modern cities, such as York and Exeter, and remained the foremost provincial centre in England for the next half-century. The statistics for transatlantic trade also reveal that Bristol was well ahead of its rival ports. At the time Defoe was writing, Bristol's tonnage from mainland America was conspicuously higher than Liverpool and Glasgow. In 1725 fifty-five ships entered Bristol carrying 4417 tons of merchandise. The corresponding figures for Liverpool were fifteen and 1175, and for Glasgow, which was making strong inroads into the Chesapeake tobacco trade, twenty-six ships carrying 1625 tons.[2] Bristol's trade in the Caribbean was even more impressive. Its cargoes of rum, sugar, indigo and logwood were greater than Liverpool, Whitehaven and Glasgow combined. And in the slave trade Bristol had outpaced London as the premier slave-trading port, sending forty-eight ships annually to Africa and delivering over 10,000 slaves to the West Indies. In the 1740s, Bristol's ships delivered 36,700 slaves to the plantations compared to Liverpool's 21,500 and London's 4800.[3]

---

[1] Daniel Defoe, *A tour thro' the whole island of Great Britain*, 2nd edn (4 vols, London, 1753), II, 292.
[2] Kenneth Morgan, *Bristol and the Atlantic Trade in the Eighteenth Century* (Cambridge, 1993), p. 17, tables 1.2 and 1.3.
[3] Morgan, *Bristol and the Atlantic Trade*, p. 133, table 5.1; Kenneth Morgan, 'Liverpool's Dominance in the British Slave Trade, 1740–1807', in *Liverpool and Transatlantic Slavery*, ed. David Richardson, Suzanne Schwarz and Anthony Tibbles (Liverpool, 2007), p. 25, table 1.2.

Visitors to Bristol were very aware of the hive of activity on the streets and quays. When Alexander Pope approached the city on his way to take the waters at Hotwell, he noted

> the River winding at the bottom of the steeper banks to the Town, where you see twenty odd Pyramids smoking over the Town (which are Glasshouses) and a vast Extent of Houses red and white. You come first to the Old Walls, and over a bridge built on both sides like London bridge, and as much crowded with a strange mixture of Seamen, women, children, loaded Horses, Asses, Sledges with Goods dragging along, without posts to separate them. From thence you come to a Key along the old wall with houses on both sides, and in the middle of the street, as far as you can see, hundreds of ships.[4]

At low tide, cranes were used to load and unload cargoes, the vessels themselves stranded in the mud. The 1785 depiction of Broad Quay illustrates this activity, although it also seeks to capture the inherent sociability of trade. Merchants converse, children play on a makeshift see-saw, workers chat as they unload cargoes. In the painting, commerce seems leisurely.[5]

Not everyone was so amiably disposed to trade or to Bristolians. Their criticisms were not levelled at the slave trade, which seldom came under attack until the American Revolution underscored the contradictions of liberty coexisting with slavery.[6] The earlier charge was that Bristolians were rather too mercenary to aspire to noble sentiments and gracious living. 'People give themselves to Trade so entirely that nothing of the Politeness and Gaiety of Bath is to be seen here', remarked Thomas Cox in *Magna Britannia*.[7] Others agreed. John Macky found Bristol a 'large, opulent and fine City', but compared to the gaiety and politeness of Bath, he saw 'nothing but Hurry, Carts driving along with Merchandizes, and People running about with cloudy Looks and busy Faces'. Even the clergy 'talk of nothing but trade and how to turn the Penny'.[8] Macky was not heavily critical of this. He luxuriated in the comedy of manners he found at Bath – it made better copy for his polite readers – yet he found Bristolian 'diligence' commendable

---

[4] George Sherburn (ed.), *The Correspondence of Alexander Pope* (5 vols, Oxford, 1956), IV, 204–5.

[5] The painting used to be attributed to Peter Monamy, but is now attributed to Philip Vandyke. There are two versions, one in the Bristol City Museum, the other in the mansion of the Society of Merchant Venturers. The see-saw can only be found in the first.

[6] Christopher Brown, *Moral Capital: Foundations of British Abolitionism* (Chapel Hill, NC, 2006).

[7] Thomas Cox, *Magna Britannia antiqua & nova* (6 vols, London, 1738), IV, 744–5, cited in Peter T. Marcy, 'Eighteenth Century Views of Bristol and Bristolians', in *Bristol in the Eighteenth Century*, ed. Patrick McGrath (Newton Abbot, 1972), p. 30.

[8] John Macky, *Journey through England* (London, 1724), pp. 123–6. See also Rosemary Sweet, *The Writing of Urban Histories in Eighteenth-Century England* (Oxford, 1997), pp. 127–34.

when compared to Bath 'indolence'. Samuel Simpson was more negative. He chided Bristolians for 'their too eager Pursuit after filthy Lucre'.

Even Defoe, the apostle of trade and enterprise, thought Bristol's merchants could do with a good dose of politeness. The narrowness of their vision was replicated in the narrowness of the town, which still resembled its medieval forebear. Bristol retained its old walls and gates, which were locked at night, and were only dismantled in the 1760s. Its inhabitants carried goods on sleds not carts, which smoothed out the cobblestones and made the ground slippery in wet weather. Many of the houses had overhanging upper floors, patched up rather than renovated, which made side streets in particular dark and narrow. With a population densely crowded at a riverine confluence, plagued by the effusions of sugar and glasshouses, the acrid smell of a ropewalk fire, not to mention to flotsam and jetsam of low tides, Bristol did not have a pleasing prospect. One writer claimed the pollution from the glasshouses covered the city in 'a continual cloud of smoke'.[9] To Londoners who admired the squares and walks of Westminster and the grandeur of buildings by Wren or Hawksmoor, Bristol was a polluted trading port given over to making money. It needed an urban renaissance.

There were a few signs of this in the residential housing that had emerged after 1660, especially in King Street and College Green, and further afield on St Michael's Hill, where the rich merchants sometimes had weekend retreats or garden houses.[10] But the physical geography of the city, its centre a low spur at the confluence of the Rivers Avon and Frome, did not make this immediately apparent to visitors. It was not long, however, before the Georgian squares and buildings made their presence felt. Queen Square was completed in 1727, not long after Defoe wrote; the Exchange was erected in 1742; a new Assembly Room appeared nine years later in Prince Street, after a significant absence of good halls of entertainment. Pleasurable places were still attentive to business though. Prince Street and Queen Square did not bypass trade for gentility; their design included warehouses and lofts, not simply terraced houses. Prince Street was also the site of the Africa House, a tavern or coffee house for neighbouring merchants, many of whom were involved in the slave trade.[11] It was principally during the second half of the century that new residential squares appeared in the suburbs; some of the more prestigious, like Portland and Berkeley, came after the American war.

---

[9] John Stuckey, *A compleat history of Somersetshire* (Sherborne, 1742), p. 29. A few authors were more complimentary of Bristol's prospect and buildings. See James Brome, *Travels over England, Scotland and Wales* (London, 1700), pp. 27–30. Brome commended Bristol for the 'stateliness' of its buildings and the 'Commodiousness of its Harbour'.

[10] See Roger H. Leech, *The Town House in Medieval and Early Modern Bristol* (Swindon, 2014).

[11] Madge Dresser, *Slavery Obscured* (London and New York, 2001), pp. 101–11.

By that time Clifton was well on the way to becoming a fashionable suburb, Royal York Crescent being completed in 1791.[12]

In the first half of the eighteenth century Bristolians were not especially concerned with the views of genteel outsiders and were quite prepared to take their time conforming to fashionable taste. They would have stressed the antiquity of the trade, their pride in opening up the Newfoundland cod fishery and deepening their contacts with Ireland and the Iberian peninsula, and latterly their new enterprises in the Atlantic. The early association of the city with the Society of Merchant Venturers underscored the links between civic identity and trade, and this was enriched by the energy and earnestness that the Nonconformist or dissenting sects brought to Bristol's economic development in the mid to late seventeenth century, particularly in the more open sectors of industrial and commercial enterprise.[13] Alexander S. Catcott, the rector of St Stephen's, sought to capture this spirit in a sermon he delivered to the Merchant Venturers in 1744. He showed how embedded trade was in biblical history, and how useful, raising populations above the grind of subsistence. In an island like Britain trade was especially esteemed. 'Our island has put on quite a different face since the increase of commerce among us.'[14] Trade stimulated manufacture, brought employment to thousands, and was essential to colonial development. Countering the aristocratic disdain for trading fortunes, Catcott assured his mercantile audience that commerce 'renders a people polished in their manners'. It cured 'self conceit and roughness both of temper and behavior'.[15] In the eyes of another admirer, the merchant was the 'true practical Philosopher' who taught moral virtue 'by an experimental knowledge and practical display of its necessity and usefulness in Society'.[16]

The possible melding of trade, civic identity and urbanity was an engaging topic to commentators on Bristol in the second half of the eighteenth century. Some writers would still insist that Bristol was 'renowned for dirt and commerce'. R. J. Sullivan in 1780 wrote that 'when we consider Bristol as a place of trade and riches we are greatly surprised to find the houses so meanly built, and the streets so narrow, dirty and ill paved. This is in some measure owing to an ill-judged parsimony.' Edward Clarke was more complimentary. He believed Bristol recaptured 'the throng and bustle of the metropolis'.

---

[12] Leach, *Town House*, p. 45. The main terraces and crescents of Clifton were constructed during the building boom of 1783–93.

[13] On this see David Harris Sacks, *The Widening Gate. Bristol and the Atlantic Economy, 1450–1700* (Berkeley and Los Angeles, 1991). On civic consciousness, see Jonathan Barry, 'Bristol Pride: Civic Identity in Bristol, c. 1640–1775', in *The Making of Modern Bristol*, ed. Madge Dresser (Bristol, 2005), pp. 25–47.

[14] Alexander S. Catcott, *The antiquity and honourableness of the practice of merchants* (Bristol, 1744), p. 14.

[15] *Ibid.*, p. 16.

[16] Andrew Hooke, *Bristolia, or Memoirs of the City of Bristol, both Civil and Ecclesiastical* (Bristol, 1749), pp. iv–v.

It's 'busy faces, crowded streets, carts, coaches smoke, and noise, represent so exactly the hurry and confusion of London'.[17] Yet wealth was bringing a welcome urbanity to the streets of the city. The Reverend George Heath, who certainly had an eye for Bristol's commercial and industrial enterprise, waxed eloquently on Bristol's parades, parks and promenades that offered some respite from the bustling business of the quays. Writing in 1794, he was impressed by the newly built Berkeley Square, on the north-east side of Brandon Hill, which commanded impressive views of the city. And like others before him he thought Queen Square had a 'magnificent appearance, the walks and grass being rolled and kept in the neatest order by an officer who has an annual salary'.[18] Bristol's inhabitants might have been 'early addicted to Trade and Manufactures', he averred, but the profits of business were now decanted to taste. By this time Bristol's commercial success had been surpassed by Liverpool, but one beneficial consequence of this eclipse was a decline in the 'melancholy traffic' in slaves. The 'ardor for the Trade to Africa for men and women, our fellow creatures and equals, is much abated among the humane and benevolent Merchants of Bristol'.[19]

Whether benevolence had much to do with it is moot. Modern experts would attribute Liverpool's takeover of the slave trade to better shipbuilding facilities, lower insurance rates, and a thriving culture of risk and rapacity among the city's marine and shopkeeping class, not to any principled concession by Bristolians, who had themselves displaced Londoners in the trade in the 1720s.[20] Yet Heath certainly thought Bristol's measured commerce in the last quarter of the eighteenth century, and the declining importance of slave trading, conducive to gracious living.

> The gentry, merchants, capital traders and medical men are generous, live well, keep elegant carriages and country houses. The ladies, gentlemen and decent ranks in Bristol dress fashionably, having Bath almost at their gates and a great resort of nobility to the Hotwell. Literature and genteel education are more celebrated here than ever, and there are circulating libraries in the various parts of the Town.

Even the notorious local dialect had been ironed out of the diction of the merchant, the professional, and their families, so that 'polite, well bred and well informed people pronounce with propriety'.[21] Artisans and mariners might mouth uncouth Bristolese, merchants less frequently.

---

[17] Edward Daniel Clarke, *A tour through the south of England* (London, 1793), p. 148; R. J. Sullivan, *Observations Made During a Tour Through Parts of England* (London, 1780), pp. 91–2, cited in Marcy, 'Eighteenth Century Views', p. 24.
[18] George Heath, *The new history, survey and descriptions of the city and suburbs of Bristol* (Bristol, 1794), p. 52.
[19] *Ibid.*, p. 38.
[20] Morgan, 'Liverpool's Dominance', pp. 18–19. See also David Richardson, *Bristol, Africa and the Eighteenth-Century Slave Trade* (4 vols, Bristol, 1986–96).
[21] Heath, *New History*, p. 90.

Heath's fleeting observations suggest a gentrification of the Bristol elite, a shift away from earlier decades when merchants identified strongly with the city, its governance and commercial hierarchies.[22] How did this shift affect the spatial setting of the city? Did it result in conspicuous social zoning, in new contrasts of genteel suburbs with crowded, industrial enclaves or over-flows? And what impact did gentrification have on Bristol's entrepreneurship? Bristol grew threefold in the course of the eighteenth century, from just over 20,000 in 1700 to 63,000 by the time of the first census in 1801. Yet this steady growth was eclipsed by the industrial towns of the north, relegating Bristol to fourth place in the urban provincial hierarchy by the end of the century, after Birmingham, Manchester and Liverpool. The dynamic quality of Bristol's economic development paled accordingly, but to what was this attributable? To a retreat from business among old mercantile families, to entrepreneurial conservatism or complacency? Or to structural factors that linked city to hinterland? These questions must now be addressed.

The Social Ecology of Bristol

We might start with maps, of which three are particularly pertinent: James Millerd's *Exact Delineation* of 1673; John Rocque's *Survey* of 1743; and Benjamin Donne's *Plan* of 1773. Urban maps are of course representations, imaginative projections of a cityscape on a horizontal plane. They are not always to scale and the marginalia often hint at what the cartographer saw or wished to convey to his customers. Millerd's map breathes civic pride. It connotes busyness; there are vessels docked and sailing the two rivers; it is a city of improbably broad streets, with grand terraced houses and some impres-sively large back gardens. A seal is thrown in for good measure, swimming merrily at the junction of the Frome and Avon, as if Millerd aspired to the lineage of ancient Atlantic maps. The grandeur of the city is also conveyed by its magnificent churches in the margins, even if the civic and commercial buildings pale by comparison. It is an ancient, thriving town, beginning to spill over the old walls to the south in Redcliff and Temple and to the east along Old Market, Broadmead and Horsefair, a development that followed hard on the demolition of the castle in the 1650s.

What is particularly instructive, when the three maps are compared with one another, is how much of Bristol's growth in the eighteenth century was largely contained within the city's boundaries. The only exception was the parish of St Philip and St Jacob, whose buildings had absorbed about 95 per cent of its parochial space and stretched a long way from Lawford's Gate.

---

[22] For the strength of this civic identity and its durability, see Jonathan Barry, 'Bristol Pride' and 'Civility and Civic Culture in Early Modern England: The Meanings of Urban Freedom', in *Civil Histories. Essays Presented to Sir Keith Thomas*, ed. Peter Burke, Brian Harrison and Paul Slack (Oxford, 2000).

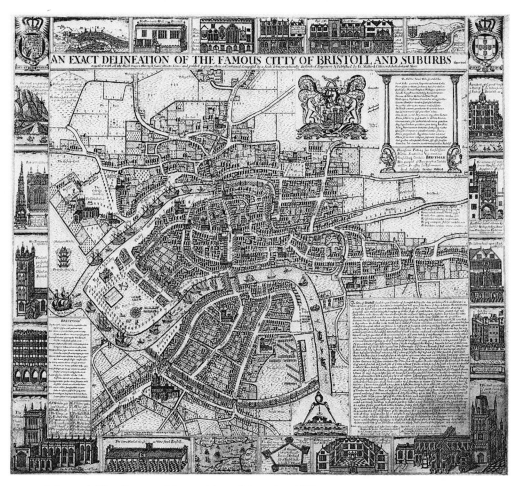

2 James Millerd's map of the parishes of Bristol, *c*.1673.

Between 1673 and 1773 Bristol's population tripled, and yet there is little evidence of urban sprawl at the mid century and not much in the next two decades.

In John Rocque's map there is some build-up beyond St James and towards St Michael's Hill, but relatively little to the south and east. This is consistent with calculations based on the number of houses, which show a dramatic increase in St James between 1712 and 1735, and more modest increases in Redcliff, Temple and St Augustine's.[23] By 1773 there is further development towards Kingsdown and Stokes Croft, and the parks to the south of Brandon Hill have given way to some new streets around College Green and Park Street. But essentially the strenuous growth of the city in the first

[23] BL, Add. MS 5811, fol. 87b.

13

three-quarters of the eighteenth century was accommodated within the 738 acres of the city, of which 450 (61 per cent) were still unsettled in 1700. Bristol's expansion was a matter of intensification not sprawl. Green spaces were filled in and existing lots were subdivided. Inner-city houses were given new facades, or they were demolished to make way for remodelled residences, new civic buildings, wider thoroughfares to the quays, and higher rents. This meant, until Bedminster became part of the Bristol conurbation, there was a distinctly definable city, set apart from the villages within ten or so miles, which had densities of five to fifteen acres per person at a time when one acre of city land housed sixty-five or more.[24]

It could be argued that the social morphology of Bristol in the late seventeenth century roughly corresponded to the classic 'pre-industrial' model advocated by Gideon Sjoberg.[25] Its richer citizens lived in the centre of the town and the poorer at the periphery. According to the hearth-tax return of 1670 and the marriage-tax return of 1696, the wealthiest parishes were in the central inner city: All Saints, Christchurch, St Ewen and St Werburgh. Over a quarter of their inhabitants were servants. Correspondingly the poorer parishes, whether measured by tax exemptions or paupers or the paucity of servants, tended to be on the fringes of the city as it then existed. They included St Philip and St Jacob, Temple, St Michael, St James, and St Mary Redcliff. In three of these parishes, less than 4 per cent of the inhabitants were servants; in Redcliff, under 7 per cent.[26] The Sjoberg model however, presumes the elite derived its fortunes from non-urban sources and was singularly distant from the rest of the population, whereas in Bristol wealth was derived from trade, and many prosperous merchants still lived in riverside parishes where trade and manufacture coexisted, such as St Thomas, St Nicholas and St Augustine.[27] The latter was known in this period for its shipbuilding and cooperages; the two former for their distilleries and soap manufacture. None of these parishes had many paupers in the late seventeenth century, but they did have a fair number of houses that were exempt from the hearth tax: 15 per cent in St Thomas ward; 13 per cent in St Nicholas. The same was actually true of All Saints, described at the time as the 'chief place of tradesmen for mercers, silkmen and linen

---

[24] Carl B. Easterbrook, *Urbane and Rustic England* (Manchester, 1998), pp. 43–6.

[25] Gideon Sjoberg, *The Pre-Industrial City, Past and Present* (Glencoe, IL, 1960).

[26] These observations are based on the 1670 Bristol hearth tax in TNA, E 179/116/541; E. Ralph and M Williams (eds), *The Inhabitants of Bristol in 1696*, Bristol Record Society, 25 (Bristol, 1968), and David Souden, 'Migrants and the Population Structure of Later Seventeenth-Century Provincial Cities and Market Towns', in *The Transformation of English Provincial Towns 1600–1800*, ed. Peter Clark (London, 1984), pp. 133–68.

[27] For criticisms of Sjoberg, see John Langton, 'Residential Patterns in Pre-Industrial Cities: Some Case Studies from Seventeenth-Century Britain', *Transactions of the Institute of British Geographers*, 65 (1975), 1–27. Cf. Gary Nash, 'The Social Evolution of Preindustrial American Cities, 1700–1820. Reflections and Directions', *Journal of Urban History* 13:2 (1987), 131, who assumes the model holds for the urban centres of the Atlantic basin.

drapers'.[28] As a ward, which also took in part of St Werburgh parish, its houses had 3.5 hearths on average, and yet over 18 per cent were also exempted from paying any tax on account of their poverty or small dwellings.

So outside some small inner-city parishes and the one that did sprawl beyond the gates, St Philip and St Jacob, there was actually considerable social mixing. In only two parishes did roughly 8 per cent of inhabitants pay surtax; in the others the percentages were 3.2 and below. Of the twelve wards assessed for the hearth tax only one had fewer than 10 per cent exemptions. Most of them exhibited central tendencies in which the average hearth size was close to the median, in most cases in the 2.8–3.5 range. Sjoberg's model was built on contrasts. Bristol's social topography in the late seventeenth century reveals social mixing and middling prosperity. The 'middle-ness' of Bristol is underscored by a comparison with Newcastle and Exeter, both of which had a few wards where the number of fireplaces per house averaged six or more. Bristol's most affluent ward averaged 4.4 hearths per house.[29] The middling stature is also replicated in the hearth-tax exemptions, which tended to be in the 11–18 per cent range; only two wards, Temple and St James topped 20 per cent, although St Philip and St Jacob would have joined this group had it been part of the city's assessment. By contrast, industrial Staffordshire had an average exemption rate of 45 per cent, with no town or hamlet under 37 per cent.[30] To put it another way, Wolverhampton's nailers and buckle-makers were very poor; Bristol's artisans were generally not.

How, then, did this social mosaic change as Bristol grew and matured as an Atlantic port? In trying to answer this question we encounter a problem of sources. Tax rolls for the eighteenth century are historically bleak, almost intractable as windows to evolving social structures. They have only been used in conjunction with poll books and trade directories for the period 1774–75 by the historical geographer Elizabeth Baigent. We shall refer to her results, and offer some impressionistic observations from earlier poll books, which give some hints to occupational clusters and distributions over time.

In the 1671 hearth-tax returns only one of the central wards of the city, St Ewen, lacked a forge. This was illustrative of the mix of industry and trade that characterised the inner-city parishes. A third of the forges were to be found in the northern and western wards of St Michael and St James, but the highest concentration was in St Stephen, where the two rivers met. This was a parish that serviced Bristol shipping. It featured sailmakers, anchor-smiths, shipwrights, turners and joiners, and many coopers or hoopers who

---

[28] Elizabeth Ralph (ed.), *Inhabitants of Bristol in 1696*, Introduction. Wards are not coterminous with parishes, which sometimes makes comparisons between the 1670 hearth tax (organised by ward) and the 1696 marriage tax (organised by parish) confusing. Thanks to Jonathan Barry and Roger Leech for alerting us to this problem. They are preparing an edition of the 1670 hearth tax for the Bristol Record Society.

[29] Langton, 'Residential Patterns', 7; TNA, E 179/116/541, Hearth tax 1670.

[30] John F. Ede, *The History of Wednesbury* (Wednesbury, 1962), p. 99.

provided the containers, the barrels and chests for Bristol's cargoes. It also had some soap-makers, for soap manufacture was a long-standing local industry, which in the seventeenth century successfully fought off Stuart monopolies and was poised to produce high-grade toilet soap for the nation as a whole. Remarkably the transpontine parishes, the ones on the other side of Bristol Bridge, had very few forges at this time, or perhaps more accurately, very few that were noted by the assessors. St Thomas had three, Temple one, and St Mary Redcliff none at all, although a sugar house worth £1000 had burned down in Redcliff Street in 1669.[31]

Even so, these three parishes were noted for their industrial activity. Samuel Seyer remarked that when Bristol Bridge was first built in the mid fourteenth century, a city wall was erected to enclose the southern parishes 'given over to the manufacture of soap, cloth and glass'.[32] The long association of the transpontine parishes with these industries was very apparent in 1722, judging from the parliamentary poll book of that year. Temple was the pre-eminent parish of weavers, along with St Philip and St Jacob. Two-thirds of Bristol's resident weavers who voted in 1722 came from these parishes. St Thomas and St Mary Redcliff also had a smattering of weavers among their electors, but they were better known for the other two trades; glass-making in the case of Redcliff, and soap-making in St Thomas. This industrial topography would change as the Atlantic economy kicked in and the West Country woollen trade foundered in the face of competition from Yorkshire. Cheap brass and ironware was needed for the slave trade. The staple products of America and the Caribbean were tobacco and sugar, and these imports opened up opportunities for tobacco-processing shops and sugar refineries. Consequently these parishes diversified, along with St Philip and St Jacob, the first parish to sprawl beyond the walls. By the end of the American war, there were more glassmakers than weavers in these three outer parishes, not to mention brass founders and sugar bakers. By 1790 sugar refiners could be found in Redcliff Street, Temple Backs, but also in Lewin's Mead, Old Market, St John's bridge and Bridewell Lane. William Barrett remarked that St Philip had even become 'a large town of itself full of inhabitants; and the large distilleries, plate and bottle glass works, the iron foundries, smelting works and the like, have contributed to the increase'. On the Redcliff side of the river he observed that 'the erection of several glass-houses, sugar-houses, the brewery and distillery, pottery and other manufactories have made a great accession'.[33] Not all of the heavier industries were in these parishes. The 1812

---

[31] Samuel Seyer, *Memoirs historical and topographical of Bristol* (2 vols, Bristol, 1823), II, 513. For the complexities of decoding the hearth tax, see P. S. Barnwell and Malcolm Airs (eds), *Houses and the Hearth Tax: The Later Stuart House and Society* (York, 2006).

[32] Seyer, *Memoirs historical and topographical of Bristol*, II, 51.

[33] William Barrett, *The history and antiquities of the City of Bristol* (Bristol, 1789), pp. 94–5. See also William Matthews, *Matthews's New Bristol Directory for the year 1793–4* (Bristol, 1793).

poll book suggests that St James also had a number of sugar refineries and soap manufacturers, and along with St Michael and Castle Precincts, some iron and brass founders. Yet one could say that compared to the late Stuart Bristol, where the concentration of heavier industries was in the centre of the city, there had been a significant shift to the southern, eastern or north-eastern peripheries by the time of the American war. Elizabeth Baigent's research reveals that by 1775 there was a definable ring of predominantly artisan parishes circling the centre of the city: St Michael and St James (within the city limits), Temple, St Mary Redcliff, and St Philip and St Jacob.[34]

Was there a corresponding change in the urban topography of wealth? In 1670 the wards with the highest concentration of large houses, that is, with six or more hearths, were in the central city parishes. The same was largely true in 1696, although St Augustine, now assessed separately rather than part of St Michael's ward, enters the list as well. Judging from the poll books, St Augustine and inner-city parishes like St Werburgh, had staying power. They are high in the rank order in 1722, 1754 and 1781; if, that is, one measures wealth by the proportion of resident merchants and gentlemen voters. St Stephen also enters the list with the building of fashionable streets like Prince Street and Queen Square, and there are quite a few wealthy men in contiguous parishes like St Leonard at the mid century. So merchants in particular showed no urgent disposition to fly to the suburbs in a century of growth. There were still merchants who lived cheek by jowl with riverside workers of various kinds, or at least within a stone's throw of them. Many of the city's cheapest and more disreputable taverns and lodging houses could be found in Marsh Street and Fisher Lane, close by the Quay and Queen Square, and in Tower Lane, a narrow and curving thoroughfare following the line of the old medieval wall from St John's Gate to the Pithay and pitching its poor residents close to respectable property owners in Broad and Wine Streets. Merchants who wanted to walk from the Drawbridge to the Exchange or Council House had to negotiate streets and lanes notorious for their poverty and sexual disorder, at least until 1774 when a local Improvement Act was acquired and much of the area around St Stephen's church bulldozed to create Clare Street. What remained of Fisher Lane was remodelled to form the new St Stephens Street. Moral and material improvements of this kind were not repeated in Tower Lane however, except in piecemeal form, despite frequent complaints about it in the newspaper press. 'What can be said of the unhappy prostitutes who inhabit this miserable place?' demanded a correspondent in *Felix Farley's Bristol Journal* in 1792. Indeed, the Lane's 'wretched, tottering dwelling houses' threatened the respectable reputation of the entire city; a 'silent reproach and stigma on the general character of Bristolians,

---

[34] Elizabeth Baigent, 'Bristol Society in the Late Eighteenth Century' (Unpublished DPhil Thesis, University of Oxford, 1985), figures 4.1, 5.27. Table 5.3 does show that some inner parishes like St John and St Leonard had low modal scores for rateable houses, comparable to St Mary Redcliff and St Philip and St Jacob.

whose charities and benevolent institutions may vie with any place of its size and population in the kingdom, if not the world'.[35] Various proposals were entertained for improvement, but although odd houses were pulled down and rebuilt after about 1795, the sheer length of the Lane and the scale of the problem mitigated against planned reconstruction. Christchurch vestry, which owned much of it, lent on tenants to refurbish so that rents could be raised and the area improved, but the houses were in too dilapidated a state and wholesale rebuilding too prohibitively expensive, so many remained well into the following century.[36]

Some merchants were prepared to stomach streets notorious for their poverty and the sex trade, but there was a discernible movement to suburban enclaves by the 1780s. In many respects this was an acceleration of an earlier movement from the centre, for Roger Leech has established that wealthy merchants from rich parishes like St Werburgh were already occupying 'garden houses' around Park Row and St Michael's Hill in the post-Restoration decades. What was then a trickle became a flood during the building boom of 1782–93, when 3000 more houses were added to Bristol's existing stock of 5000.[37] The fashionable squares and terraces that began to appear in the mid-century decades, were nonetheless enclaves, for they were situated in large sprawling parishes that also had industry and sometimes what snobby Londoners would have called noxious trades. Redcliff Parade, built by the shipbuilder, owner, and slaver Sydenham Teast in the 1770s, overlooked glassworks, distilleries and Wapping's dry docks. In John Baptiste Malchair's view of St Mary Redcliff, the smoke from the cones of the glassworks obscures the spire.[38] St James's Square, built as part of the suburban development of the out-parish, was essentially on the fringes of an increasingly artisan parish where tailors, in particular, had several houses of call.[39] Several prestigious developments were predictably a fair way from the bustle of the port. Lower Clifton may have had its shipbuilding trades, as did St Augustine Backs, but genteel wealth was gravitating to the more salubrious parts of the upper city: to the crescents of Clifton Hill, to Park Street, St Michael's Hill and Kingsdown. The process was well under way by 1781, the year of a snap

---

[35] FFBJ, 10 Nov. 1792.

[36] BA, Chamberlain's accounts, 00228/6, Report on the ruinous state of sundry tenements in Tower Lane, 28 February 1799; Christchurch Vestry Minutes, P/XCh/1/17/7, entries dated 30 May 1798, 2 Nov. 1802, 28 Aug. 1807, 17 March 1810.

[37] J. R. Ward, 'Speculative Building at Bristol and Clifton, 1783–1792', Business History 20:1 (1978), 3–19.

[38] Leech, Town House, p. 143. On Teast, see Joseph E. Inikori, Africans and the Industrial Revolution in England (Cambridge, 2002), p. 245.

[39] Julian Paul Davies, 'Artisans and the City: A Social History of Bristol's Shoemakers and Tailors, 1770–1800' (Unpublished PhD Thesis, University of Bristol, 2003), p. 56, table 2.2. On St James Square and other developments on the St James plain, see Archibald Robertson, A topographical survey of the great road from London to Bath and Bristol (2 vols, London, 1792), II, 171.

by-election in Bristol. There were still a few pockets of wealthy people living in inner-city parishes like St Werburgh, and of course, in St Stephen, with its Queen Square and Prince Street; although slums in Marsh Street and Tower Lane disposed many merchants and gentlemen to gravitate to the Georgian terraces and squares of the upper city. Of all the merchants and well-to-do who voted in the by-election, 67 per cent lived in St Augustine, St Michael, Clifton and St James Barton. For those still active in trade and commerce, this was a growing separation of home from work.

We can take a different kind of snapshot of the rich at this time, one that allows for more gender and occupational diversity. This is from the 1780 tax on male servants, introduced by the North government to help pay for the American war.[40] Early tax impositions are not without their problems as rudimentary censuses. Given the serious possibilities of evasion, we have no guarantee that they are comprehensive. Not all of the super-rich families listed in *Bonner and Middleton's Bristol Journal* of 1785, for example, are mentioned in this tax register.[41] One doubts they lacked butlers and valets, although it is conceivable that they considered their domestic slaves exempt from the tax. Even so, the two hundred-odd names that are noted offer some clues to the profile of the wealthy living in Bristol and its environs, a quarter of whom had two or more male servants.

Eleven per cent of the people who bore the tax were female. A few were spinsters, but most were rich widows, the beneficiaries of mercantile fortunes. They included a Mrs Hassell, whose son became a councillor after the Napoleonic war, and a Mrs Ames, whose family owned slaves and founded one of Bristol's first banks. There were two Elton spinsters among the group and Mrs Abraham Elton, the widow of a former mayor. Their family's fortune was also rooted in slavery and the plantation economy; as a consequence the Eltons owned one of the largest mansions in Queen Square and also Cleveland Court. In 1780 Mrs Elton lived in Clifton with five male servants, as did Edward Elton, also with five. Edward is a complete unknown in this prominent Bristolian family, but he inherited a fair share of the Elton wealth through father Isaac and his aunt Mary, enough to make him a man of leisure who eventually gravitated to Bloomsbury in London.[42]

Among the men on the list, 18 per cent were described as esquires or gentlemen. Presumably they were rentiers or retired businessmen. Nearly a quarter can be identified as active merchants from Sketchley's 1775 directory. Many were sugar or tobacco importers, sometimes combining these trades with a proprietary interest in plantations. Others illustrated the diversity of Bristol's commerce. John Noble ran a successful trade in the Newfoundland cod fishery; Dietrick Meyerhoff imported timber from the Baltic. Joseph Harford sent brassware to Africa in return for slaves. Along with Levi Ames, John Cave

[40] TNA, T 47/8, register of tax on male servants, 1780.
[41] For the list, Latimer, II, 462–3.
[42] TNA, PROB 11/1191/198, will of Mary Elton, 4 Oct. 1789.

and George Daubeny, he helped found the New Bank of 1786.[43] To this list one should add sugar refiners, glass manufacturers, distillers, shipwrights, the owner of a large cooperage, 'society' physicians and surgeons, and a surprising number of clergymen, eleven in all. Forty-five per cent of these men had civic affiliations, if we include the Merchant Venturers, the clergy and the charitable societies in that cohort. They testify to the strong link between wealth and civic governance in the last quarter of the century. The links to slavery, which Madge Dresser has so ably detailed, are clear as well.[44] At least 10 per cent of the tax payers can be directly identified with the slave trade, including some of the leading slavers: John Anderson, Evan Baillie, Thomas Deane, John Fowler and Thomas Jones. Indirectly one might hazard that a fifth of those in this select tax bracket serviced or profited from the traffic in slaves.

Most of these affluent taxpayers lived in predictable places. Nineteen lived in Clifton, eighteen in Queen Square, eleven on College Green, eight in King Square. Some had moved beyond the city altogether: to Sneed Park and Stoke Bishop on the other side of Durdham Down, to Westbury, Henbury, Mangotsfield and rural Stapleton. One named Peter Capper, who may have been related to affluent London linen drapers, lived in Stoke Gifford. There were still a few men who lived in the centre of the city, such as Thomas Hobbs, a linen merchant who lived in Shannon Court, Corn Street. But within this wealthy cohort, inner-city addresses more often than not turn out to be businesses, not residential properties. An aspiration to genteel living had become fashionable, and social zoning within the city was more evident. It was symptomatic of the partial retreat of the city elite from active commerce, and its increasingly introspective nature. The days when the Bristol elite identified with civic life and its institutions were disappearing.

The City Elite and its Critics

The Bristol building boom of 1783–92 was built on easy money; it ruined quite a few builders and creditors. By 1793 there were many bankruptcies and a corresponding dent in business confidence. As one shipping firm wrote to Captain Haitier: 'Bankruptcys happen almost every day and God knows where it will end.'[45] Yet the fact that building stock increased by 60 per cent in the space of a decade does testify to a robust demand for housing. The strong economic growth of Bristol in the early to mid-century decades, when Bristol dominated the slave trade and established strong roots in the Caribbean and North America, helped to spread wealth around, and non-elite

[43] Latimer, II, 468. All of the partners, or members of their families, are listed in the 1780 servant tax register.
[44] Dresser, *Slavery Obscured*.
[45] Walter E. Minchinton, *The Trade of Bristol in the Eighteenth Century*, Bristol Record Society, 20 (Bristol, 1957), 176.

businessmen in the distributive trades had clearly benefitted. Prosperity gave the middling classes in Bristol more heft, and culturally this was enhanced by an expansion of the public sphere, as defined by Jürgen Habermas. In the first half of the century respectable Bristol had been dominated by church and chapel; its sectarian rivalries resonated through its politics and its literary endeavour.[46] Such associations remained strong during the American war when the dissenting congregations were generally pro-American, or at the very least in favour of peace talks with the colonists. Twenty-five per cent of West Indian or American merchants in the 1770s were members of the powerful Lewin's Mead Presbyterian chapel, and that congregation dominated the aldermanic bench and council, often blocking loyalist resolutions in favour of the North ministry. As we shall see later, in Bristol the ideological battle over America was fought between a prominent Anglican and a Baptist, between John Wesley and Caleb Evans.

At the same time the parameters of public debate were widened by the existence of a healthy crop of local weekly newspapers. Bristol was one of the first provincial towns to have a weekly newspaper, the *Post-Boy of 1702*. During the accession crisis of 1713–16 it ventured two, only to fall back to one in the years 1727 to 1742. Thereafter Bristol was well served by rival and often partisan papers: two by the mid 1740s, three by 1775, and as many as five by the turn of the century, offering readers a broad spectrum of political views.[47] There were also six circulating libraries and quite a few booksellers servicing this expanding reading public, something that caught the eye of the *New Bristol Guide*. In addition there were coffee houses and pubs where politics, local and national, might be discussed. Sketchley's directory of 1775 mentions four coffee houses: the Exchange; the West India on Prince Street; Mary Darvil's Foster coffee house on Corn Street; and the Assembly on the Key. The latter catered to the Hotwell clientele as well as Bristolians, and was the favourite haunt of the local poet Robert Collins, a customs officer.[48] These four were joined by the American Coffee House opposite the White Lion on Broad Street. Sketchley also lists fifty-eight victualling houses around the city where conversations could turn on politics as much as trade, not to mention

---

[46] Jonathan Barry, 'Chatterton, More and Bristol's Cultural Life in the 1760s', in *From Gothic to Romantic. Thomas Chatterton's Bristol*, ed. Alistair Heys (Bristol, 2005), pp. 29–30; Jürgen Habermas, *The Structural Transformation of the Public Sphere*, trans. Thomas Berger (Cambridge, MA, 1989).

[47] The five were the *Bristol Mercury* printed by Bulgin in Broad Street, the *Bristol Gazette* by Pine and Son in Wine Street, *Sarah Farley's Bristol Journal* by Routh in Bridge Street, *Bonner and Middleton's Bristol Journal* by Bonner on College Green, and *Felix Farley's Bristol Journal*, by Rudhall in Small Street. On these and the expanding reading public, see Rev. George Heath, *The New Bristol Guide* (Bristol, 1799) pp. 143–4. Papers from London, Bath, Gloucester and Sherborne were also in 'common circulation'.

[48] Jonathan Barry, 'Chatterton', p. 26. See also his 'The Press and the Politics of Culture in Bristol 1660–1775', in *Culture, Politics and Society in Britain, 1660–1800*, ed. Jeremy Black and Jeremy Gregory (Manchester and New York, 1991), pp. 49–81.

the four hundred or so alehouses scattered throughout the city.[49] In 1771 a visitor to Bristol commented on the 'oratorical publicans' who were 'amusing their customers by railing at the government'.[50] The widening range of discussion can be detected in the records of the Bristol Library Society, which show that by the 1770s history, geography and travel literature were more popular than religious topics. A hefty 45 per cent of all books borrowed hailed from these categories, compared to just 4.5 per cent in theology.[51] Clergymen were quite prominent in this rather select society of letters, but the intellectual horizons of the merchants and professionals who subscribed were widening. It meant that the intellectual authority of the clergy, still formidable in the 1770s, was not necessarily paramount or incontestable. This is registered in the richer variety of books published in Bristol after 1756.[52]

The changing prospect can also be gauged by the emergence of new voices in the 1780s and by reconfigurations within elite society. After the American war, the demand for the abolition of the slave trade intensified. Initiated by the Quakers, who had often opposed slavery even if some of their members happened to be slavers,[53] a committee was formed to petition parliament for the total abolition of the slave trade, or at the very least, substantial reform.[54] The composition of the committee was occupationally professional or mercantile and religiously non-denominational: it included Anglicans and Dissenters; divines, doctors and merchants. It featured men who had been at loggerheads over the American war and issues of parliamentary sovereignty, notably Josiah Tucker, the rector of St Stephen's and Dean of Gloucester, and Caleb Evans, the Baptist preacher of Broadmead. Together with John Wesley, who had crossed swords with Evans over America's right to regulate its own taxation, they were prepared to put aside former political differences and campaign for changes that potentially struck at the heart of Bristol's economy and its continuing investment in the slave trade. As Madge Dresser has shown, the groundwork for such as challenge had developed since the 1760s with the staging of Thomas Southerne's *Oroonoko* at Jacob's Wells and with literary contributions by Thomas Chatterton and William Combe,

---

[49] Patrick McGrath and Mary E Williams (eds), *Bristol Inns and Alehouses in the Mid-Eighteenth Century* (Bristol, 1979). For a major provincial city Bristol could accommodate a lot of guests, more than Norwich in the 1686 survey, even though its population was smaller. See TNA, WO 30/48, cited by Phil Withington, 'Intoxicants and the Early Modern City', in *Remaking English Society. Social Relations and Social Change in Early Modern England*, ed. Steve Hindle, Alexandra Shepard and John Walter (Woodbridge, 2013), p. 142.

[50] *Town and Country Magazine*, 3 (1771), p. 698.

[51] John Brewer, *The Pleasures of the Imagination: English Culture in the Eighteenth Century* (London, 2013), p. 181.

[52] See Barry, 'The Press and the Politics of Culture', table 1, pp. 54–5.

[53] Dresser, *Slavery Obscured*, p. 131. Eight of the twenty principal contributors to the new meeting at Quaker Friars turned out to be members of the Society of Merchants trading to Africa.

[54] *Bristol Gazette*, 1 Feb. 1788; *Bath Chronicle*, 31 Jan. 1788. The resolutions did talk of 'total abolition', but also of reforms that parliament might see fit to pass.

who in *The Philosopher in Bristol* condemned the 'inhuman traffic' in slaves.[55] Harry Gandy, a Bristol lawyer who had spent some time as a seaman and then a slave captain, added his experience to the growing disquiet, if not outrage about the slave trade.[56] This followed hard on Thomas Clarkson's fact-finding visit to Bristol concerning the overcrowding and cruelty on slave ships, and the heavy mortality of both slaves and sailors. By early 1788 the anti-slavery committee was able to mount a public petition against the trade, which was tabled in the Commons in February.[57]

The reaction of the pro-slavery lobby was relatively muted at first. Bristol's slave trade was in decline, outshone by sugar and associated trades, although the combined transatlantic commerce in and out of Bristol was still formidable. Bristol's merchants were never happy about the Dolben Act of 1788 that sought to regulate the command of slave ships and the size of slave cargoes, but when it became clear that the anti-slavery lobby intended to push for the total abolition of the trade, the slavers and associates showed their teeth. In May 1789 Bristol submitted no fewer than six petitions against Wilberforce's motion to ban the trade. These hailed from the Bristol corporation, from the Merchant Venturers, the African merchants, the West India planters and merchants in Bristol and its environs, the shipbuilders and associates, and the merchants in the Newfoundland cod trade.[58] The committee set up to defend the trade included five aldermen, several MPs, past, present and future, and a familiar roster of Bristol merchants and bankers, including representatives of the Bright, Cave, Pinney, Protheroe and Vaughan families.[59] Its pitch was that a total ban on the slave trade would undermine the labour supply so necessary to the plantation economy; it would ruin the many trades that provisioned the islands, provided manufacturing wares to Africa and the Caribbean, and serviced the shipping industry. Other matters were added: the potential dearth of seamen for the royal navy if shipping lanes contracted or disappeared; the international repercussions of evacuating a trade from which other imperial powers like France and Spain would profit. Even so, the central issue was the dire consequence of abolition to the Bristol economy, a crucial matter since at the mid century roughly 40 per cent of all trades had been linked in some way to the traffic in slaves. The West Indian faction put it even higher, at 60 per cent.[60]

[55] Dresser, *Slavery Obscured*, pp. 130–41.
[56] Gandy's account can be found in Anthony Benezet, *Some historical account of Guinea* (2nd ed. London, 1788), pp. 125–31.
[57] JHC, 43 (1788), 243, 20 Feb. 1788; Thomas Clarkson, *The History of the Rise, Progress and Accomplishment of the Abolition of the Slave Trade* (2 vols, London, 1808), I, 293–367.
[58] JHC, 44 (1789), 352–4, 12 May 1789.
[59] Latimer, II, 477.
[60] David Richardson, 'Slavery and Bristol's "Golden Age"', *Slavery and Abolition*, 26:1 (2005), 35–54; Roger Hayden, 'Caleb Evans and the Anti-Slavery Lobby', in *Pulpit and People. Studies in Eighteenth-Century Baptist Life and Thought*, ed. John H. Y. Briggs (Eugene, OR, 2009), p. 162.

The pro-slavery lobby prevailed and the slave trade persisted in an era of wartime patriotism and black revolution in St Domingue, where race war and atrocities fuelled apprehensions about the consequences of giving ground on slavery. In Bristol itself, abolitionism remained a minority movement, seldom voiced at the hustings, and not as popular as in Manchester and Sheffield. However, scholars suspect that artisans who were not directly involved in the African and Caribbean trades were likely to be abolitionist, especially if they were non-conformist in religion.[61] Their distaste for a merchant elite who endorsed slavery was compounded by the fact that after the American war pre-arranged elections once more became the norm, with pro-slavery parliamentary candidates firmly in the saddle, at least until 1830. Freemen were denied the opportunity to vote, and often had nothing to show for their freedoms but a bumper supper financed by rival caucuses. In a city where so much had been made of civic patriotism, this state of affairs rankled. It manifested itself in renewed demands for electoral independence, for the right to exercise the vote and to do so without interference from masters or local political bosses. The debate over slavery, in fact, occurred at a time of increasing restlessness among the trades, very apparent in the summer of 1792 when there was an epidemic of strikes among Bristol's artisans.

Bristol's merchant elite and their wealthier clients were coming under increasing scrutiny, from mechanics and abolitionists, from disaffected businessmen outside the privileged circle. This occurred at a time when Bristol's momentum of growth was stalling. After the American war, Bristol's consignment merchants were seldom able to recover their debts in the North American trade, nor their hold on it. Fifty-nine ships had cleared for America in 1775 at the outset of the war, despite the inhibitions of non-importation agreements in the colonies. The corresponding figure for 1789 was twenty-five, and for 1790, twenty-two ships.[62] Bristol's participation in the slave trade was also on the decline, despite the fact it paradoxically received a fillip from the early abolition movement because West Indian planters panicked and bought extra slaves in anticipation on a ban of the trade. That brief revival, from 1788 to 1792, did nothing to disrupt Liverpool's dominance of the trade, which was four times as large as Bristol's in 1789 and dramatically larger during the French wars.[63]

Within the larger context of the transatlantic trades, Bristol's commerce was now heavily reliant on West Indian sugar, the amount of which grew five-fold 1750–1800, when nearly 500cwt of sugar entered the port. The trade was also concentrated in fewer firms, eighty-five in 1790 compared to

---

[61] Dresser, *Slavery Obscured*, p. 187; Seymour Drescher, *Capitalism and Antislavery* (London, 1986), pp. 68–77.

[62] Minchinton, *Trade of Bristol*, nos 32 and 39, pp. 48–50, 53–5. On debts, see no. 73, pp. 174–5.

[63] Peter Marshall, *The Anti-Slave Trade Movement in Bristol* (Bristol, 1968), p. 22; Morgan, 'Liverpool's Dominance', pp. 17–32.

six times that number thirty years earlier.[64] This helps explain the hyper-reaction of the mercantile elite to abolition and subsequently slave emancipation. The return on the Caribbean trade was still substantial, nonetheless. There was no inevitable decline of sugar in the last three decades of the century. Production remained strong and prices buoyant. Domestic demand remained high in a period of demographic growth, and European demand increased because the French sugar industry collapsed in the face of British victories in the Caribbean and black revolution in St Domingue, soon to be known as Haiti.[65] This unique set of circumstances boosted the Bristol sugar trade and reinforced the inherent conservatism of its merchants. As a group they remained remarkably complacent about their position in society and unwilling to move outside the well-worn routes that had secured their families fortune and civic status. One visitor to Bristol remarked that the leading traders were 'principally rich respectable West India Merchants who do not go out of their usual line of business & [are] averse to speculation'. As the Nevis planter and merchant John Pinney confided to James Tobin in 1793: 'You had better have a snug little business and safe than an extensive one which may produce the contrary effect.'[66]

After the Napoleonic war, however, Bristol's hold on its share of the Caribbean trade became more precarious. Liverpool competed vigorously for a larger share of sugar imports, especially from the new plantations of Trinidad and British Guiana; it also dominated the new trade in raw cotton from the British colonies and America. Bristol's conventional links were to the older islands in the Antilles, whose sugar production and profits declined after 1807, Barbados excepted.[67] Whereas the Bristol elite benefitted from the wartime boom in sugar, it was in trouble after 1815 – constrained, even encumbered, by assets in old plantations and poorly equipped to deal with the changing landscape of world sugar in which there were new players such as Brazil, Cuba, Java, Mauritius, and a rejuvenated French colonial industry after 1825. The impact was felt in Bristol's associated industries. Brass and iron founding gravitated to the Midlands; sugar refineries declined in number, from twelve at the end of the eighteenth century to four by 1830. Bristolians were losing the overseas markets they had comfortably penetrated three decades earlier.

[64] Kenneth Morgan, 'The Bristol West India Merchants', *Transactions of the Royal Historical Society*, 3 (1993), 186–7.
[65] Seymour Drescher, *Econocide. British Slavery in the Era of Abolition*, 2nd edn (Chapel Hill, 2010), chs 3–6.
[66] *Ibid.*, p. 204.
[67] See J. R. Ward, *British West Indian Slavery, 1750–1834* (Oxford, 1988), figure 2, table 3. On overall trends in Caribbean trade from 1783, see Drescher, *Econocide, passim*. Of the seventy-two Bristolian claimants for slave compensation in 1834, only 17 per cent had investments in Trinidad, Tobago and British Guiana. The great majority owned slaves or shares in slave plantations in Jamaica, Barbados, St Kitts and St Vincent. See University College London, Legacies of British Slave-Ownership, <http://www.ucl.ac.uk/lbs>.

According to some critics, this state of affairs was attributable to the narrow oligarchy of predominantly West India merchants who were entrenched in the corporation and the Society of Merchants, and who dominated the boards of various statutory bodies. They were undermining Bristol enterprise through the continued imposition of arcane levies and high port dues, shutting the city out of the new economies of industrial textiles and hindering the coastal trade in important resources such as coal. 'The spirit of clique', remarked John Barnet Kington in a series of letters to the radical *Bristol Mercury*, 'overpowers the spirit of improvement.'[68]

There was certainly some substance to the overlapping membership and cousinage within the Bristol elite. It was a long-standing phenomenon, but it came under closer scrutiny as Bristol entered a period of slow, if not stagnant growth. Of the sixty-nine members of the Common Council between 1820 and 1835, twenty (29 per cent) were members of the Society of Merchant Venturers. Over one-third had close relatives who had preceded them to civic office in the previous two generations, and some of the most powerful men on the council were linked by marriage, a predictable strategy for businessmen in the age before limited liability. After 1820 only five members of the council actually owned plantations in the Caribbean, but a further fourteen depended on the West Indies for their sugar-refining or merchandising. So at least 28 per cent of all council members in the final years of the old corporation had direct business connections to the Caribbean economy.[69] If we add bankers or bank directors who had some stake in Caribbean property, as assignees or mortgagees, the proportion would likely rise to a third, slightly less than in the mid-century decades, but significant nonetheless.

This self-elected, closed elite arrogated to itself much of the formal and informal power in the city. It dominated the charitable societies associated with the slaver philanthropist Edward Colston. It was well placed on trusts associated with Bristol's turnpikes and toll bridge. It decided when and where new gaols should be erected and resented the intrusion of public scrutiny. As we shall see, the refusal to make a full public disclosure of the debts associated with Bristol Bridge sparked riots and deaths in 1793. Critics like Kington and Thomas Lee saw the elite's activities as exemplary of Old Corruption. In their eyes this commercial patriciate was ruining the city through political and economic cronyism.

Particularly galling was the story of the floating dock. The idea of expanding Bristol's port facilities with a floating dock at Canon's Marsh had been around for decades. Finally, in 1802, years after Liverpool had improved its dock facilities, a coterie of merchants and bankers decided to propose one. The scheme encountered a lot of opposition, however, because it was to be

---

[68] John Barnet Kington, *Thirty letters on the trade of Bristol* (Bristol, 1834), p. 223.
[69] Graham Bush, *Bristol and its Municipal Government 1820–1851*, Bristol Record Society, 29 (Bristol, 1976), pp. 24–6. Our calculations for 1700–69 are that 38 per cent of the Common Council had links to the slave trade and Caribbean economy.

financed by a group of subscribers in a separate Dock Company, with ex-officio representation from the corporation and the Merchant Venturers. In reality the three groups were interlinked, at least among the core subscribers: 40 per cent of the corporation and 50 per cent of the Merchant Venturers subscribed to the scheme.[70] This did not prevent a degree of backbiting among the elite concerning the funding, with some of the leading West India merchants unhappy that they would be obliged to pay extra port dues for a facility they might not use.

The Bristol Dock Company was resented on a number of accounts. It was cliquey; it was not open to public scrutiny; it was a sweet deal for the corporation and Merchant Venturers, who sloughed off the financial responsibility of improving a public facility and ultimately acquired it without spending a penny. It was untimely and expensive, costing almost twice as much (£594,000) as projected. It also imposed heavier dues on Bristol's overseas and coastal traffic than any other port in the country. Bristol's dockside dues surpassed London's by 65 per cent, Hull's by 56 per cent and Liverpool's by 42 per cent.[71] Among other things, that meant more expensive food for the city, because provisioning merchants would pass on their costs to the consumer. Thomas Lee dubbed the dock tax a *corvée*, by which he meant a forced tax on the poor. In his estimation the dock scheme was nothing more than 'a mode of realizing speculation, and of legalizing an usurious interest upon otherwise idle capital'.[72]

Lee's comment raises a question that historians have yet to resolve satisfactorily. What happened to Bristol money after the abolition of the slave trade, when the old plantation complex was running into difficulties? Just how much divestment from the West Indies was there and how quickly? Historians have often argued that third-generation merchants or entrepreneurs veered into gentility, preferring the life of the gentleman to the active man of commerce. Certainly there is evidence of this among the Bristol elite. Bristol merchants appear in the lists of those qualified to shoot game; some had gaming parks in the country, including the Society of Merchant Venturers at Beer.[73] Active merchants were followed by genteel sons. Henry Cruger's son, Samuel, inherited his grandfather's estate in Tockington Court, adopted his name, and set up as a country gentleman.[74] His cousin Philip John Miles established Leigh Court in 1814, although he also carried on his father's business and gravitated to banking. That sort of move, from merchanting to banking, was quite typical of some of the more prosperous West Indian families, allowing them

---

[70] Peter Malpass, 'The Bristol Dock Company and the Modernisation of the Port', in *A City Build upon the Water: Maritime Bristol 1750–1900*, ed. Steve Poole (Bristol, 2013), p. 132.

[71] Bush, *Bristol and its Municipal Government*, p. 9.

[72] Thomas Lee, *White Lion Club, late Riot and Dock Tax* (Bristol, 1807), p. 26.

[73] *Bath Chronicle*, 9 Oct. 1800; *Gloucester Journal*, 8 Sep. 1805.

[74] On the grandfather, Samuel Peach, see Dresser, *Slavery Obscured*, p. 115.

to invest in new local enterprises and diversify their assets over time. Even so, some of the prominent mercantile families stayed the course in the West Indies. Ken Morgan has identified six merchants who applied for compensation in 1834, largely for estates in Barbados, St Kitts and Jamaica. Two of these, Thomas Daniel and Evan Baillie, had investments in the newer plantations in Trinidad and British Guiana, although they were exceptions rather than the rule. Bristol's interest in Trinidad and British Guiana was modest compared to that of Liverpool. Almost 40 per cent of the ninety-two Liverpudlians who applied for slave compensation had a stake in those two territories, Guiana in particular.[75]

A more typical route to continued affluence was to invest in industrial enterprises with which the elite had some contact or familiarity, such as gunpowder, ironworks, cooperages, glassworks and breweries.[76] And of course, land, which was not only the classic marker of gentility but a safe investment in the wake of the corn laws and a surge in population, offering tenant farmers profitable returns and landowners handsome rents. Philip Protheroe owned an estate at Overcourt in Gloucstershire; Jeremiah Innys a manor and lands in Somerset; the Harfords bought lands in Cardiganshire. Richard Bright used his surplus capital from the Jamaica trade to venture into banking, canals, sugar refineries, copper, iron and rope works. He had a stake in the Great Western Cotton works on Barton Hill and he became the first deputy chairman of the Great Western Railway. To cap his business career and gentrify, he bought land around his ancestral home in Colwall, Herefordshire.[77]

Bright was among the most entrepreneurial of his generation, especially with his ventures into cotton manufacture and railways. Most merchants stuck to familiar local industries affiliated to their overseas business.[78] If they moved beyond that, they seem to have capitalised on their civil privilege or insider knowledge, investing in property development or urban infrastructure such as bridges, turnpikes, and canals. The 250 or so subscribers to the Dock Company adopted this strategy. The shares, dividends and promissory notes associated with the project offered a stable investment. So, too, did civic bonds, short-term loans to a corporation that had overspent the money it received from rents, rates and various town dues, partly because it had leased wharf-side dues to the Merchant Venturers on ludicrously generous terms

---

[75] Figures derived from UCL, <http://www.ucl.ac.uk/lbs>.

[76] See Morgan, 'The Bristol West India Merchants', 183–208.

[77] Kenneth Morgan (ed.), *The Bright-Meyler Papers: A Bristol–West Indian Connection, 1732–1837* (Oxford, 2007), pp. 63–6; and UCL, <http://www.ucl.ac.uk/lbs>. Richard Bright was initially active in the development of the Floating Harbour, but along with his cousin Lowbridge Bright and other West Indian merchants, he opposed the more ambitious plan that surfaced in 1802. See Malpass, 'The Bristol Dock Company', p. 125.

[78] B. W. E. Alford, 'The Economic Development of Bristol in the Nineteenth Century: An Enigma?', in *Essays in Bristol and Gloucestershire History*, ed. Patrick McGrath and John Cannon (Bristol, 1976), p. 263; Morgan, 'The Bristol West India Merchants', 183–208.

and was reluctant to renegotiate them. In the 1820s in particular, the city's indebtedness to bondholders doubled, reaching £89,300 in 1835.[79]

Not all local investments were stable. Some speculators were burned by the building bubble of 1782–93, when easy credit swamped a fragile property market and led to a significant spike in bankruptcies. Bristol was high among the towns and cities that experienced business failures in 1793, the year of the crash. The failures among Bristol merchants and their associates were especially severe, including a conspicuous number of slavers active in the years 1790–92. According to Henry Thornton's account, of the losses sustained by the leading sixty firms in the country, Bristol's contribution was over £1 million of the total 6.4£ million.[80]

Bristolians not only speculated in property development after the American war. They were also caught up in the canal mania of the early 1790s, when over £7 million was authorised to build some fifty canals or canal extensions.[81] In November 1792 large sums were subscribed at Guildhall for a projected canal from Bristol to Gloucester, which it was hoped would link Bristol more securely to the West Midland industries and avoid the heavy and sometimes unpredictable costs of shipping down the turbulent Severn. A second project linking Bristol to Taunton was launched a few days later, and quickly subscribed. And when it was rumoured that a canal was projected linking Bristol to London there was a frantic rush to subscribe in Devizes. A flotilla of hackney carriages trundled off to Wiltshire via the Bath road, much to the delight of the satirists.[82] Romaine Joseph Thorne lampooned these speculators in his popular poem, the *Mad Gallop*, in which 'high and low, rich, poor and bad,/ Were justly reckon'd Canal mad'.[83]

In fact, the speculators had been sent on a wild goose chase by Nehemiah Bradley, a distiller in Temple Street, who wanted to divert attention away from the Bristol subscription to the Kennet and Avon canal. Along with alderman and former MP George Daubeny, he was a member of the 'White Lion junto' who bought up the available shares to this project amounting to £264,000. Subsequent pressure, not least from the disappointed investors in Devizes, raised that subscription to £945,000, and a proposal was launched to link the Kennet and Avon to a canal running from Southampton to Salisbury.[84] This subsidiary project came to little; enthusiasm waned and the money dried up. The Gloucester canal reached Berkeley Pill; the Southampton stopped at Salisbury and Andover; the Taunton terminated at Bridgwater, where it

---

[79] Bush, *Bristol and its Municipal Government*, pp. 76–9.

[80] TNA, PRO 30/8/183, cited by L. S. Pressnell, *Country Banking in the Industrial Revolution* (Oxford, 1956), p. 546, appendix 28; Hayden, 'Caleb Evans and the Anti-Slavery Question', p. 164.

[81] Charles Hadfield, *British Canals*, 5th edn (Newton Abbot, 1974), pp. 107–8.

[82] Latimer, II, 498–9.

[83] Charles Hadfield, *The Canals of South and South Eastern England* (Newton Abbot, 1969), p. 239.

[84] *Ibid.*, pp. 235–41.

hooked up to the River Parrett. The only successful canal was the Kennet and Avon, which linked Bristol to London in 1810 and enabled coal from the South West coalfields to compete with Newcastle in the London market. In its heyday it carried 300,000 tons per annum, although within three decades it faced severe and devastating competition from the railways.[85]

The canal mania underscored Bristol's inability to tap into the industrial enterprises of the Midlands and the north. Bristol was simply unable to compete with Liverpool as the principal western port for manufacturing exports, and while it was able to import slave-grown cotton from the American south, the Great Western Cotton Company was no match for Cottonopolis, the textile complex of Manchester and its nearby townships. In fact, Bristol's participation in canal construction proved largely speculative; it fell off rapidly after the commercial crisis of 1793. Liverpool's pattern of investment, by contrast, was measured and pragmatic, related to its immediate economic interests.[86] In the one Bristolian venture that made economic sense, the Kennet and Avon, the mercantile elite of largely Tory persuasion monopolised the best shares. Its tactics reinforced the impression that this mercantile elite was simply interested in feathering its own nest when it came to developing a new course for the city. Self-interest trumped civic responsibility.

Bristol's Declining Fortunes

'With regard to opulence and importance', intoned a writer in the *Gentleman's Magazine* at the end of the eighteenth century, 'Bristol has long been esteemed the second city in the Kingdom: in extent and population, however, it must yield to Birmingham; in commerce and commercial liberality to Liverpool.'[87] This was a polite way of saying that Bristol's golden age was over. Although Bristol's population topped 100,000 in 1831 and enjoyed a rate of growth comparable to the national trend, it was flagging by the standards of the great industrial towns. Liverpool, Manchester and Birmingham had all surpassed Bristol by 1801 and had extended their lead by 1831. In terms of trade, Bristol had long been eclipsed by Liverpool, whose tonnage exceeded that of its southern rival as early as 1772, and grew substantially larger thereafter. In 1791, the tonnage berthing at Bristol was 28 per cent of Liverpool's. Within three decades it had fallen to 14 per cent, for Liverpool's annual tonnage in the years 1816–25 averaged a massive 871,713 tons. By the early 1830s Bristol was fifth in the port hierarchy, behind London, Liverpool, Hull and Newcastle in terms of tonnage, behind London, Liverpool, Hull and Greenock in value. An average of 392 British and foreign ships entered Bristol in the

[85] *Ibid.*, pp. 251–9.
[86] J. R. Ward, *The Finance of Canal Building in Eighteenth-Century England* (Oxford, 1974), pp. 138–40.
[87] *Gentleman's Magazine*, 64 (1799), p. 1039.

years 1830–32 carrying 71,235 tons. The corresponding outward-bound figure was 284 ships carrying 64,170 tons. The estimated value of Bristol's exports in 1833 was £375,442, a fraction of Greenock's, which had soared to £1.4 million, and of Hull's exports, which had surpassed £5 million.[88]

Bristol's flagging fortunes owed a lot to structural factors. The west of England was de-industrialising in crucial areas like textiles, and Bristol lacked the communications networks that linked Liverpool to the new industrial heartland. Although Bristol had valuable coal resources nearby, it was not as favourably placed for industrial take-off as its Lancashire counterpart. Even so, its modest performance was a telling indictment of the mercantile elite, which still strove to dominate civic and parliamentary politics, yet provided little economic leadership. Efforts were certainly made to emulate Liverpool's success and cash in on the trade of the early American republic. In the railway age rich Bristolians renewed efforts to link the port to Midland industry and to the London market. In 1832 a committee of deputies from the corporation, the Society of Merchants, the Dock Company and the decade-old Chamber of Commerce issued a statement on the importance of connecting Bristol to the metropolis. It was a crucial factor in revitalising local industries and overseas trade, the city being 'more favourably situated than any other Port in this island for the commerce of the whole civilized world'.[89] Such bombast scarcely touched reality. The Great Western Railway ran into gauge problems. Its terminal at Temple Meads was not adequately linked to the quays until 1870, and by then it benefitted ports like Milford Haven rather than Bristol. Other grandiose schemes projected for the port in the 1830s foundered as well. The most ironic was the Great Western steamship, which brought a cargo of cotton back on its maiden voyage from New York, but was too large to enter the floating dock.[90] That cotton was intended for the Great Western factory on Barton Hill, which employed 1800 workers and ran six steam engines on a weekly quota of 150 tons of coal. Its list of partners read like a 'Debrett of Bristol capitalism', including representatives from some of the well-known West Indian families such as the Pinneys, the Brights and the Miles. Yet with the failure of the steamship line it had to draw its raw cotton from Liverpool, and this inevitably impaired its competiveness. What the 'Great Western' projects underscored was the 'desultory entrepreneurship' of the Bristol elite, if not its commercial incompetence.[91] John Wesley thought

---

[88] House of Commons, *Parliamentary Papers*, vol. 115 (1847), A return of the number of vessels entering and clearing the 12 principal ports of the United Kingdom, 1816–1845; see also Bush, *Bristol and Its Municipal Government*, p. 4 and Gordon Jackson, 'Ports 1700–1840', in *The Cambridge Urban History of Britain 2: 1540–1840*, ed. Peter Clark (Cambridge, 2000), p. 709, table 21.1.

[89] B. J. Atkinson, 'An Early Example of the Decline of the Industrial Spirit? Bristol Enterprise in the First Half of the Nineteenth Century', *Southern History*, 9 (1987), 75.

[90] *Ibid.*, 79–80.

[91] The phrase is from Kenneth Morgan, 'The Bristol West India Merchants', 206.

Bristol's 'besetting sins' were 'love of money and love of ease'.[92] Clearly the Bristol elite didn't know how to juggle the two in formulating a practical strategy for Bristol in the early nineteenth century. It could not reconcile itself to the fact that Bristol's 'golden age' was over.

Bristol's Deepening Poverty

Bristol's economy flagged but its population grew at a faster rate than the national average. Its population in 1821 was 87,779 for the city and suburbs, a 15 per cent increase over 1811. Ten years later Bristol topped 100,000; 117,000 if Bedminster is included. This increase was not simply the result of in-migration as in the early modern era, when infants constituted 30 per cent or more of all burials in any year.[93] All the evidence suggests that Bristol was reproducing itself by the early nineteenth century, if not before, with a healthy excess of baptisms over burials.[94] This produced a younger society in which 56 per cent of the population was minor (under twenty-one). It also meant that Bristol had a high dependency ratio of 825 per 1000 working adults, a little less than the national figure in a period of extraordinary demographic growth, but one in which many children had to take on dead-end jobs to help their families.[95] Bristol was also a predominantly female society, with an overall sex ratio of 81 males to every 100 females. In the poorer working-class districts, the sex ratio was more evenly balanced because of the paucity of female servants, who made up 10 per cent of the population. Thus for every 100 females in Bedminster, there were 92.3 males, and in Temple, 93.4. In more affluent areas such as St Augustine the ratio was skewed, with 69.7 males per 100 females (not so very different from what it had been in 1696), while in Clifton the proportion of males was 60.8.[96]

What also comes across in the early-nineteenth-century parliamentary enquiries is the deepening poverty of some parts of Bristol. Kington did not attribute this to surfeit of population in the manner of Malthus, nor indeed to high prices. He laid the blame on the oligopolistic policies of the elite, which

[92] John Wesley, *The Journal of the Reverend John Wesley*, ed. Nehemiah Curnock (8 vols, London, 1909–16), VII, 209.

[93] BA, JQS/BW/1–2, Burials in wool. In the years 1708–10, 1719–21, 1730–32, infants constituted 30 per cent or more of all recorded burials on 6 of 9 occasions.

[94] HC, *Parliamentary Papers*, vol. 502 (1822), 46.

[95] *Ibid.*, pp. 118–19; for dependency ratios over time, see E. A. Wrigley and R. S. Schofield, *The Population History of England 1541–1871* (Cambridge, 1981), pp. 445–6. The dependency ratio is taken as the number of those aged 0–14 and 60 or over per 1000 persons aged 15–59. The peak nationally was in 1826 with 857 per 1000. See also Martin Gorsky, *Patterns of Philanthropy. Charity and Society in Nineteenth-Century Bristol* (Woodbridge, 1999), p. 23.

[96] HC, *Parliamentary Papers*, vol. 502 (1822), 115. David Souden, 'Migrants and the Population Structure', p. 153, table 18.

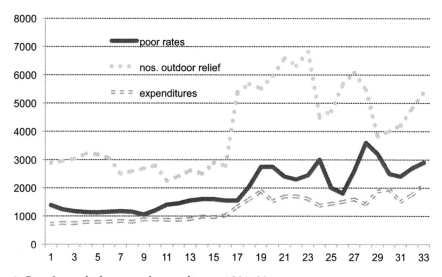

3 Poor Law relief, rates and expenditures, 1801–32.
Source: Kington, *Thirty letters on the trade of Bristol*, p. 311.

rendered Bristol uncompetitive and undermined its long-standing ranking as the metropolis of the west. He pointed to lost opportunities in developing Bristol's extensive networks and industrial resources and to the resulting lack of employment for many 'mechanics and labourers'.[97] Economic stagnation was merely an inconvenience to the 'upper classes of society', he observed, but it 'gathered force' as it descended down the social scale until 'it crushes poverty into one wretched mass of want and pauperism'.[98] Kington too easily ascribed Bristol's failures to the exclusivity of its elite, yet it was clear that post-war retrenchment and economic stagnation pressed hard on the poor. As the figures for outdoor relief revealed, Bristol's pauperism rose dramatically after 1815 and continued to do so on the resumption of cash payments in 1819. It spiked again after the speculative boom of 1825 when half the Bristol banks failed.[99] What is also noteworthy is that poor-law rates and expenditures lagged behind indigence, expenditures especially, and it was this form of social provision rather than philanthropy that was crucial for survival.[100] The poor rates were responsive to the poverty crisis, although not without considerable complaints from the middle-class ratepayers in the richer parishes who resented subsidising the poor.[101] The actual amounts spent on relief, however, did not track need, particularly as poverty surged.

[97] Kington, *Thirty letters on the trade of Bristol*, pp. 321–9.
[98] *Ibid.*, p. 2.
[99] On that speculation, see Boyd Hilton, *A Mad, Bad and Dangerous People? England 1783–1846* (Oxford, 2006), pp. 300–5.
[100] Gorsky, *Patterns of Philanthropy*, figure 4, p. 57.
[101] *Bristol Mercury*, 4 May 1820.

Outdoor relief to the able bodied was officially given only to those who were prepared to work. Usually paupers repaired roads or broke stones for the turnpike at Hotwell, although as the numbers escalated it was clearly impossible to maintain this policy, as the assistant overseer to St Philip and St Jacob admitted to the 1834 commissioners.[102] Beyond the aged or infirm, moreover, welfare provision was niggardly and intrusive, subject to review and after 1826 denied to any who had struck for higher wages.[103] Deputy Governor James Johnson reported cases where male heads of households were ordered to bring their daughters to the workhouse to head pins for a Gloucester manufacturer. They were to be paid a meagre four pence for heading a pound of nails. Fathers who refused to put their daughters to such drudgery were denied relief. Johnson was convinced the casual poor included 'numbers of idle and dissolute men who would never exercise any industrious habits if they could be otherwise maintained'.[104] He thought the threat of starvation was the only way they could be disciplined.

Pauperism was so rife in parts of St Philip and St Jacob that mean-spirited poor-law overseers campaigned to raise the rateable value of houses so that fewer families could apply for settlements in the parish. In Bedminster, where the job market for labourers and miners was highly unstable, the overseer feared that the banning of outdoor relief would produce a 'revolution'.[105] Officials were also troubled by the high incidence of common-law marriages and by the social consequences of family breakdown. They struggled to control the constant influx of migrant workers from Ireland who came to work in the summer harvests. The expense of removing these workers skyrocketed, doubling between 1815 and 1830.

The 1820s' depression and the poor-law crisis suggested that Bristol society was coming apart at the seams. John Ham of the Bristol General Union talked of growing class cleavage: 'The master manufacturer ... is frequently too high for those in his employ – there is no cordiality of feeling among them.' Thousands of children in the city were neglected street urchins, he mourned, whose survival skills made them 'pests and scourges to society'.[106] The contrast between rich and poor was more glaring and no longer capable of being mediated by charitable doles. When it was decided to adopt a forty-eight-hour week for the stone-breaking at Hotwell rather than allow poor-law applicants the chance to complete their assignments by piecework, there was a riot at St Peter's Hospital, the workhouse of the Corporation of the Poor.

[102] In answer to Town Query 35, House of Commons, *Parliamentary Papers*, vol. 44 (1834), appendix B2.
[103] E. E. Butcher (ed.), *Bristol Corporation of the Poor*, Bristol Record Society, 3 (Bristol, 1932), p. 24.
[104] HC, *Parliamentary Papers*, vol. 44 (1834), 81.
[105] HC, *Parliamentary Papers*, vol. 44 (1834), 397d; vol. 502 (1822), 46.
[106] *Bristol Mercury*, 21 June 1831.

Angry paupers menaced officials, and the deputy governor had to call on the magistrates to commit the troublemakers to jail.[107]

A month later, an outbreak of cholera revealed Bristol to be a class-fractured society. Between July and October there were over 1500 reported cases of cholera and over 580 deaths, with St Peter's Hospital bearing the brunt of the disease because of the wretched overcrowding of its wards, its high incidence of frail people, and its proximity to the fetid waters of the Frome which discharged twelve tons of sewage every day.[108] In the first month over one hundred people died there, fuelling fears that the guardians were suffocating the poor and quite possibly burying them alive. More realistically, relatives of the deceased suspected their bodies might be handed over to the surgeons for medical research under the terms of the new Anatomy Act, an act of desecration for the many who believed souls would never rest if cadavers were not buried whole. As a consequence mobs broke into the burial ground of nearby St Philip's and began digging up the recently interred bodies to ensure their integrity, a macabre ritual that was repeated at Temple churchyard, another area where the disease was virulent. Two days later mobs gathered at St Peter's, threatening to pull the old poorhouse down. One sailor accused the guardians of 'burking the people' and offered to lead the wrecking party.[109]

Thereafter, dead paupers were moved discreetly by water to an unmarked burial site near the cattle market.[110] Meanwhile the health authorities looked for plausible sites for cholera wards, only to encounter stiff resistance from neighbourhoods. Redcliff and Temple blocked proposals for 'pesthouses' in their area, and Clifton, having initially agreed to house one on Hotwell road, agitated to have it transferred to Bedminster on the other side of the river. Nimbyism was alive and well in the summer of 1832, and ultimately the authorities settled for a hospital on the Cut. In what the *Mercury* described as a 'novel and distressing' ritual, the infected were transported there in long baskets affixed to poles.[111]

Despite its reputation for charitable relief, respectable Bristol was slow to respond to the crisis. As the epidemic spread, some of the Clifton rich simply left town. Well-known families like the Eltons, the Harfords and the Ames chipped in a token £5 apiece to relieve cholera victims in the slums of St Philip and St Jacob. Mrs Daniel, whose husband and son made huge fortunes out of slavery, offered a meagre ten shillings, perhaps because some of her family's property had been wrecked in the Bristol riots the previous year.[112]

---

[107] *Bristol Mercury*, 2 June 1832; Butcher, *Bristol Corporation of the Poor*, p. 9.

[108] *Bristol Mercury*, 17 July 1826.

[109] *Bristol Mercury*, 11 Aug. 1832; on the rituals of burying the dead and the afterlife, see Ruth Richardson, *Death, Dissection and the Destitute*, 2nd edn (Chicago, 2001).

[110] Latimer, III, 186–7.

[111] *Bristol Mercury*, 18 Aug., 1 Sep. 1832.

[112] *Bristol Mercury*, 8 Sep. 1832.

The reluctance of the well off to contribute generously was noticed. The *Mercury* sardonically remarked that far more attention was being paid to the Bristol–London railway project than to helping the cholera-ridden poor, as if the latter were disposable and had no future. 'How can you think of proposing any plan for future advantage', asked Ignotus, 'when death is stalking around us in every direction?'[113] Eventually some 6000lb of boiled rice were distributed from designated shops, but the relief committee quickly realised it was feeding more than the sick, for between four- and six hundred families were being turned away every day in what was becoming a squalid working-class run on the kitchens. As the *Mercury* pointed out, the vulnerability to cholera was class specific. No outbreak was recorded in Clifton, only in the crowded districts by the two rivers and the poorer out-parishes, areas where many were 'deprived of wholesome food and the common necessaries of life … huddled together in crowds, in noxious and unwholesome places of abode'.[114] As Bristol entered the Reform era it was a class-divided city in which the civic motto of *Virtute et Industria* sounded decidedly hollow.

---

[113] *Bristol Mercury*, 18 Aug. 1832.
[114] *Bristol Mercury*, 18 Aug. 1832.

2

Voices in the Crowd

In our first chapter we delineated some of the broader frameworks for contextualising a history from below in Bristol during the long eighteenth century. We mapped out a social topography of the city in a period of solid demographic growth, and the slow emergence of elite suburbs in the upland areas. We suggested there was a conspicuous fusion of political and economic privilege at the centre of Bristol society, enough to make it a genuine urban patriciate, something we develop in our next chapter. And we offered some thoughts on whether the corporate privilege of that patriciate and its gentrification were responsible for the relative economic decline of Bristol after the American war, or whether Bristol's fortunes were determined by more impersonal structural factors in a rapidly changing industrial era. After the Napoleonic war, Bristol's loss of competitive advantage was visibly inscribed in bankruptcies, higher poor rates and deepening pauperism that generated critiques of the patricians who ran the city.

In this chapter we move to the voices in the crowd and its rules or conventions of engagement with authority. Pioneering studies of the crowd tended to ignore the interplay with authority. They were more interested in the faces of the crowd than the manner in which power was exercised.[1] It was Edward Thompson's study of the 'moral economy' of provision that opened up investigations of the dialogue between rulers and ruled in a relatively unpoliced society: one that addressed not only the customary expectations of the poor but the theatre of the great, whose studied paternalism and spectacle strove for consensus rather than conflict, or at the very least, legitimations of rule.[2] That model of eighteenth-century relations, of a field of force whose

---

[1] George Rudé, *The Crowd in History. A Study of Popular Disturbances in France and England 1730–1848* (New York, 1964); *Paris and London in the Eighteenth Century* (London, 1970). Rudé's *Ideology and Popular Protest* (New York, 1980) did address power more comprehensively.

[2] E. P. Thompson, 'The Moral Economy of the English Crowd', *Past and Present*, 50 (1971), 76–136; 'Eighteenth-Century English Society: Class Struggle without Class?', *Social History*, 3 (1978), 133–65; Peter King, 'Edward Thompson's Contribution to Eighteenth-Century Studies: The Patrician–Plebeian Model Re-Examined', *Social History*, 21 (1996), 215–28.

radiating centres were patrician and plebeian, has come under criticism for ignoring third-party middling players. Yet in Bristol's social formation, where the merchant class was patrician, where political and economic power over-lapped conspicuously, it works rather well as an organising model of social action. While it does not ignore those middle-class actors who as voters, peti-tioners, jurymen, employers or charitable-aid professionals played their part in the life of the city – and we are alert to their contribution, as readers will discover in the chapters on politics in particular – it proves particularly perti-nent to those visible social dramas where power, authority and reputation were at stake.

Early modern elites hoped to bedazzle and awe their audiences. They might have taken their cue from Richard Hooker, who reminded Puritans in the late Elizabethan era that no nation ever tolerated 'public actions which are of weight ... to pass without some visible solemnity, the very strange-ness thereof ... doth cause popular eyes to observe and mark the same'.[3] The value of symbolic authority, of generating a sense of grandeur, was not lost on the Bristol elite, which sustained a robust ceremonial year. Quite apart from the national anniversaries such as the martyrdom of Charles I (30 January), Restoration Day (29 May), the discovery of the Gunpowder Plot and William's landing at Torbay (5 November) when there would be sermons and processions to the Cathedral, the civic elite would have been visible at the inauguration of mayors and sheriffs in late September, at the entry of the Recorder for the Bristol assizes, and on the king's accession, coronation and birthday. When John Scrope entered the city as Recorder to open the summer assize in 1732, he was escorted by forty coaches and chariots and 'vast numbers' of 'well-equipped' horsemen. 'The cavalcade was truly pompous', declared *the Daily Journal*, 'and conducted with great order, and the evening concluded with the ringing of bells and other demonstrations of joy.' The elite would have been present, too, at the shire feasts, of which there were five, mostly concentrated in late August and early September, and at the anniversaries of the Colston societies on or around the benefactor's birthday on 13 November. This meant there were at least a dozen occasions every year when the civic elite processed the streets or gathered for dinners at company halls and Assembly rooms. And this excludes celebrations of military and naval victories, of which there were many in the mid-century decades, in particular. The churchwarden accounts of St Stephen's, for example, noted that bells were rung on nine occasions in 1757 and 1758, in each year cele-brating a victory of Britain's ally Frederick of Prussia. In 1760 the parish bells pealed Britain's victory against the French in Montreal when Bristol enthusi-astically celebrated the news with a general illumination.[4]

The Colston Society dinners were designed to impress upon the public the charitable disposition of the elite, which used the bequest and membership

---

[3] Richard Hooker, *Of the Laws of Ecclesiastical Politie* (London, 1594–97), p. 7.
[4] BRL, Weare MS 19841 (3); Latimer, II, 339–40; *Daily Journal*, 2 Sep. 1732.

subscriptions to finance apprenticeships and lying-in facilities. Royal anniversaries and military victories gave the city authorities an opportunity to roll out the barrels of beer and fire *feux de joie*. On the thanksgiving of the suppression of the Jacobite rebellion in 1716, the conduits may well have run with wine, for the corporate audit details the purchase of eight and half gallons of French wine, twenty-six gallons of claret, and thirteen gallons of sherry.[5] Not all of that, surely, could have gone down the gullets of merchants and their hangers-on at the Society Hall. At the proclamation of George III in 1760, six barrels of ale were purchased for the populace; at his marriage to Charlotte of Mecklenburg-Strelitz a few months later, another four. There were also payments for dragging the cannons to Brandon Hill and discharging them. Celebrations such as these offered the poor a little festive cheer, although the civic bills suggest token munificence compared to the massive wine and sherry consumption of the elite. No wonder a visitor to Bristol remarked that the 'laced waistcoats and clumsy carcasses' of the merchants 'ought to be drawn by Hogarth'.[6]

An indication of how grandiose and time-consuming some of these ceremonies could be is revealed in the account of the proclamation of the peace of Aix-la-Chapelle in 1749.[7] The whole city council turned out on this occasion, sometimes travelling in thirty-seven coaches to the seven sites where the peace was proclaimed, which included the former site of the Holy Cross, St Peter's Pump, Thomas Pipe, Temple Cross, the Exchange and the equestrian statue in Queen Square. Led by the marshal and a troop of soldiers, and accompanied by a band of music playing 'God save the King', the procession wound its way around the proclamation circuit in a ceremony that lasted four hours. Wine was distributed to the spectators at each proclamation point, where a 'prodigious Concourse of People' saw the sheriffs declare the war at an end and symbolically sheath their swords. The afternoon's ceremonies were then concluded with the mayor and council repairing to the Council House to drink the health of the king and royal family.

On coronation day constituent parts of the 'crowd' might be invited to participate in the formal ceremonies. In 1761, for example, various trades joined the mayor and corporation in the procession from the Council House to the Cathedral. The shipwrights carried models of two ships built in the harbour; the wool-combers offered Bishop Blaize and a worker finishing a cloth; the printers a press from which verses on the king's marriage and coronation were presented to the populace. Charity boys followed, with a sprig of gilt laurel tagged to their uniforms. In the evening there were fireworks at Queen Square, St John's and Lawford's Gate, lighting up the coronation bunting on church towers and ship masts. Several barrels of beer were given

[5] BA, F/Au/1/85 [1716]; F/Au/1/131 [1761].
[6] Cited by Reginald James, 'Bristol Society in the Eighteenth Century', in *Bristol and its Adjoining Counties*, ed. C. H. MacInnes and W. F. Whittard (Bristol, 1955), p. 234.
[7] *Bath Journal*, 13 Feb. 1749.

away to the populace at Brandon Hill, and at Temple Meads a gentleman provided an ox, roasted whole. This convivial gathering sought to incorporate the crowd, as spectators, as actors, as the recipients of elite hospitality, although the festivities were carefully calibrated by rank; trades before merchants in the procession; fireworks and beer for the plebs, a coronation ball for the merchants and their ladies.[8]

Civic celebrations were not necessarily moments of munificence, however, nor did they always express the mutuality that Jonathan Barry has seen as epitomising Bristol's civic traditions.[9] Sometimes they were flashpoints for unruly crowds, who could easily disrupt the formality of the occasion with irreverence, laughter, violence and sullen disrespect. On the thanksgiving of the Peace of Paris in 1763, for example, the crowd largely ignored the celebrations planned by the corporation, sensing that the peace had been a sell-out to the French. Some churches concurred, decorating their porches with crepe and apples, an acid rebuke of the presumed architect of the treaty, John Stuart, Earl of Bute. In the evening the mob paraded a jackboot, a pun on the courtier's title, and also an effigy wrapped in Scottish plaid, which they ceremoniously burnt.[10]

By contrast, crowds could be dictatorial, enforcing public recognition of celebrations by insisting upon lit candles in the windows. Citizens who were averse to such public displays of loyalty, like the Quakers, would soon learn their ratings with the crowd. So, too, would political dissidents. Indeed, in the early decades of the century, when the battle between Whig and Tory was fierce and sometimes fearless, political anniversaries were highly contentious events that the authorities found extremely difficult to contain, especially when they featured provocative acts of effigy-burning and symbolic desecration. A 'crowd' might seem evanescent. Like the Cheshire cat, Richard Cobb once remarked 'it is there, it is almost there, then it is not there, and then it is there again'.[11] But the 'crowd' populates the shadows cast by captains of industry, commerce and social influence, lining the streets to cheer or jeer civic celebrations, to witness public punishments, or rising inexplicably in riot when roused in protest. The crowd is ever-present in the narrative, sometimes passive, frequently troublesome, but rarely approached in its constituent parts.

It was in the late eighteenth and early nineteen century that the Bristol crowd developed a reputation for unpredictable, explosive violence. In the aftermath of the Bristol Bridge riots, *Matthews' Guide and Directory* remarked

---

[8] BRL, Jefferies MS, XII, 270.

[9] Jonathan Barry, 'Bristol Pride: Civic Identity in Bristol, c. 1640–1775', in *The Making of Modern Bristol*, ed. Madge Dresser (Bristol, 2005), pp. 25–47; see also his 'Bourgeois Collectivism? Urban Association and the Middling Sort', in *The Middling Sort of People*, ed. Jonathan Barry and Christopher Brooks (London, 1994), pp. 84–112.

[10] Latimer, II, 357.

[11] Richard Cobb, 'Overcrowding', *Times Literary Supplement*, 30 Dec. 1965, p. 1205.

that 'The populace are apt to collect in mobs on the slightest occasions.'[12] This point of view was reasserted *a fortiori* in 1831, after thousands of the city's poorest and most marginalised workers had taken command of the streets and systematically invaded, looted and burned prominent structures of privilege and authority. So complete was the loss of public deference on this occasion, and so abject the failure of the corporation and civil power to control the crowd, that only the most robust and deadly use of military force was able to disperse it. Thomas Babington Macaulay's much quoted belief that Bristol's 'mob' was 'the fiercest in England' was certainly built upon recollections of the riots of 1831,[13] and other commentators were prompted by the riots to trace its historical roots to a lengthy legacy of disorderly behaviour. 'The lower classes of Bristol and its neighbourhood have always been a turbulent race', reflected the *Observer*. 'So far back as the reign of Stephen, the place was characterised as "a volcano whence the kingdom was deluged with fire and sword".'[14] In a more retrospective account of the upheavals of 1831, the nineteenth-century chronicler, William Hunt, traced the city's rioting tradition back as far as 1714, when partisan violence marred coronation day, as we shall see later.[15]

Some nineteenth-century observers saw deep and long-standing divisions in Bristol society underpinning and enabling the 1831 disturbances. One liberal-radical pamphleteer addressed the problem in terms of 'Ignorance', 'Want' and class 'Disunion'. He urged that the working class should have 'a sufficient supply of the comforts of life without that hard and incessant labour which now wears them out prematurely'. With this in place, educational reform and cooperatives would give the lower orders a stake in society and inhibit the degraded behaviour so visible in Bristol, which was an affront to the civilised world.[16] 'Whilst the West Indies were cultivated by slaves and Virginia partly by transported criminals', reflected the anarchist French geographer, Élisé Reclus, 'the wealth generated in Bristol by intercourse between them produced, on the one hand, an upper class singularly haughty and unsympathetic, and on the other, a mob exceptionally rough and violent.'[17] General Sir Richard Jackson, sent by the War Office to take command of military operations against the Bristol crowd in 1831, took much the same view. These inherent social divisions were dangerously aggravated he thought, by

---

[12] *The New History, Survey and Description of the City and Suburbs of Bristol or Complete Guide* (Bristol, 1794), p. 90.

[13] Thomas Babington Macaulay, *The History of England from the Accession of James II*, 12th edn (2 vols, London, 1856), II, 99.

[14] *The Observer*, 6 Nov. 1831.

[15] William Hunt, *Historic Towns: Bristol* (London, 1887), p. 200.

[16] Anon., *Thoughts on education, union of classes and co-operation suggested by the late riots in Bristol* (London, 1831). This pamphlet was in the collections of Joseph Hume and Francis Place.

[17] Élisée Reclus, *The Earth and its Inhabitants: The Universal Geography* (6 vols, London, 1878–94), IV, 115.

the weakness of the civil power, the alienation of the magistrates from their responsibilities as governors and the growing inefficiencies of the unreformed corporation. But he added a refrain that had been commonplace in 1714, when Whig pamphleteers pointed the finger at Tory–Jacobite agitators. 'The composition of the populace of Bristol is of a description very easily worked upon by mischievous persons and the means of inflicting great injury to property are always ready to hand', he noted. 'Mobs are speedily collected from a population so ill-composed and so uncontrolled by authority as that of Bristol and there are persons here endeavouring to keep up popular excitement.'[18]

These were the varied narratives of degeneration that flew off the press in the wake of the 1831 riots. Yet some authors went back in time and saw the problem in terms of the incursions of outsiders. They pointed to the proximity of the city to large communities of coalminers and weavers on the peripheries of South Gloucestershire to the east, who lived outside the jurisdiction of the mayor and magistrates. These communities, who supplied essential materials for the city's economy, had developed a reputation for disorder, coming into Bristol in disorderly crowds on a number of occasions to protest against turnpike charges, high bread prices or their conditions of service. They were notoriously difficult to control. Figuratively at least, their reputation placed them at the centre of virtually every disturbance, for, as one St Georges' landowner put it in 1795, 'the infatuated people called colliers who abound in the said parish stick at nothing for the accomplishment of their purposes. Reasoning is not only lost but Dangerous, for the disclosure of one's sentiments is attended with hazard.'[19]

To property-owning Bristolians, the colliers of Kingswood negated everything that a hierarchically ordered economy stood for. 'They have played such mad Pranks that one would think they had forgot there were ever any Laws in Being for the Government of a People, and to secure the Peace and Property of the Subject', complained a broadside after an invasion of the city in 1738, during a wage dispute. The account continues with a detailed exposition of the colliers' impertinence. They had stopped the pits, demanded money from passers-by 'with heavy strokes on refusal', then marched through Brislington and Totterdown, threatening pub landlords and taking drink without payment. They 'enter'd what Houses they pleas'd; ate and drank every Thing they could come at, without paying any money; and so turn'd towards the City', where they marched through the centre with 'bravadoing Halloos and shouting Clamours'. They advanced as far as Castle Gate, searching for coal waggons and pack saddles, breaking the wheels and

[18] TNA, HO 40/28 Jackson to Lord Melbourne, 15 Dec. 1831; John Dunton, *The Shortest Way with the King* (London, 1715), pp. 67–71; Anon., *An Account of the Riots, Tumults and other Treasonable Practices since his Majesty's Accession* (London, 1715), p. 2; *Flying Post*, 2–4 Dec. 1714.
[19] GRO, Blathwayte Papers, D1799/C170, Rev. Dr Small to William Blathwayte, 28 March 1795.

spilling coals about the streets, before spotting an unpopular bailiff named Purnell and chasing him back to Totterdown. Britain's second city endured several days of disruption like this, the limited jurisdiction of its JPs making effective interference with communities beyond the city boundaries all but impossible. The watch and the military guard were doubled, patrols maintained throughout the night, and a further party of soldiers kept under arms in Queen Square, but the magistrates were understandably wary of directly engaging the colliers in combat at times like these.[20] Even after the 1831 riots a century later, in which there is little evidence of their participation, rumours of the colliers' presence were gamely peddled by the press. *The Observer's* reflections are worth quoting at some length:

> The colliers, who are said to have taken an active part in the late riots, occupy a district of country a few miles out of the city, called Kingswood, and until they were in some degree civilised by the Wesleyan Methodists, a few years since, these people were in a state of moral degradation scarcely above that of barbarians. In times of public commotion, they have always been the most important auxiliaries of the town mob, whenever the latter have, from any cause, been excited to rise in opposition to the laws; and in 1793, they assisted the city malcontents in their opposition to a bridge toll ... In old times, the city was often besieged by the colliers. During the last thirty years, it has frequently been found necessary to call in the military to repress the violence of the mob at elections ...[21]

As we shall see, colliers played an important role in a medley of popular interventions in eighteenth-century Bristol, particularly over provisions and turnpikes. But they could hardly serve as a metonym for the Bristol mob or disorder *tout court*. In the vortex of reform agitations, contemporaries were a little bewildered by the riots of 1831, which seemed to either justify the notion of a degraded populace unworthy of the vote, or a regrettable regressive eddy in the popular tide of reform. We shall assess these claims later, and the degree to which the 1831 riots departed from eighteenth-century norms of crowd behaviour.

Voices on the Street

One of the difficulties in trying to capture the milieu from which crowds emerged is the paucity of the sources. British historians are not blessed with the judicial and police records that Arlette Farge used in reconstructing street life in eighteenth-century Paris. There is no *procès-verbal*, the interrogatory records of suspects and witnesses that illuminate the lives of the poor: where they lived, what they earned, whether or not they were married, and so on.

---

[20] *The Colliers of Kingswood in an Uproar, Or, an Account of their present Mobbing, and Preventing Coal being brought to this City* ... (Bristol, 1738).
[21] *The Observer*, 6 Nov. 1831.

Nor are there forty-eight police commissioners monitoring the pulse of the street.[22] From these sources Farge was able to detail neighbourhood quarrels that are impossible to replicate in the British context, even using the depositions for sexual defamation and assault in consistory courts and quarter sessions. These offer some insights into the language of insult, but they only hint at deeper tensions.

For example, a street quarrel in 1760 resulted in a defamation suit before the church courts.[23] It was launched by Jane Banfield, the wife of a soap-boiler in Hallier's Lane, in one of Bristol's central parishes, St John the Baptist – a crowded and noisy thoroughfare, home to several busy sugar refineries and poor lodging houses. Indeed Jane and her husband Warren ran a lodging house as well as the soap business and there were suspicions that it was a house of ill repute. Jane sent her servant, Mary Brewer, to collect some sticks from the yard of a brewer opposite. The brewer's wife, Sarah Norman, did not take kindly to this scavenging and told the servant to go back to the 'whorehouse' where she belonged. She added that Mary had only been sent over to entice her son into her neighbour's den of iniquity, just as her servant had been inveigled into the house when he should have been working. These remarks prompted a war of words between the two wives in the middle of the street that lasted for half an hour. In the course of this quarrel, which was watched by numerous spectators including a smith and a tiler/plasterer, Norman allegedly told Banfield, 'Thou art a whore, thou keeps a bawdy house and I'll prove it.' These words were clearly intended to discredit the reputation of the house, some of whose lodgers testified on Banfield's behalf, believing her to be a woman of 'good fame and reputation'. What this quarrel disclosed were the simmering tensions between two neighbours, the source of which remains murky. Was petty pilfering the real source of the quarrel? Did Sarah Norman think Jane Banfield was taking advantage of the piles of wood in her yard? Was she anxious about the company her son was keeping? Did she see Banfield's rooming house as a tonic to sin and idleness? After all, lodging and beer houses in Halliers' Lane did have a reputation for sexual disorder; indeed the city quarter sessions heard cases against the Lane's 'lewd women' and bawdy-house keepers in 1749, 1760, 1772 and 1799.[24] Moreover, Sarah Norman's husband, Onesiphorous, was a freeholder in the parish, a man of some standing, who likely smarted at the sight of unruly, disreputable neighbours, if that is what the Banfields were. Whatever the reason for the quarrel, the deeper story eludes us.

[22] Arlette Farge, *Fragile Lives. Violence, Power and Solidarity in Eighteenth-Century Paris*, trans. Carol Shelton (Cambridge, MA, 1993), p. 11.

[23] BA, EP/J/2/1, 1760, bundle 12.

[24] BA, JQS/D/11, Quarter Session docket book, 1748–53; *FFBJ*, 15 Aug. 1772. For Onesiphorous Norman, see *The Bristol poll-book* (Bristol, 1754), p. 58, where he is listed as having a freehold in the parish.

Within England, London sources are better than Bristol's for capturing the texture and pulse of street life. The Old Bailey Proceedings, now available online, offer a rich vein of information on subjects like tavern life, working hours, street prostitution and theft, even if some of the *parole* of the Cockney is written out of them. Together with parish examinations and the Bills of Mortality, it is possible to get some insight into the life chances of the poor, sexual encounters, plebeian unions, and the fragility of family life in an age of war and hardship. None of these sources is available in the Bristol archive. The records of the Corporation of the Poor were largely destroyed during the war. There are no Bills of Mortality, just fragmentary lists of those taxed for woollen shrouds. What Bristol does have is a fairly comprehensive run of pre-trial informations and depositions for the quarter session and assize courts from 1748. Although different in form to the records of actual trial proceedings we have for the Old Bailey, and somewhat opaque in their coverage of misdemeanours like assault, this large archive of manuscripts does offer valuable insights into plebeian experience in relation to indictable crime. They have been used to good effect by Matt Neale for example, to explore crime on Bristol's boats and wharves, and the circulation and disposal of stolen property in the city,[25] and we have used them where practical in this chapter. We are conscious however, that one consequence of using legal papers and newspaper reports of crime to reconstruct the life experience of labouring men and women is that their lives might appear to be framed by little else but brushes with the law. Newspapers are invaluable sources, of course, and Bristol was extremely well served by them from the 1720s onwards, but editors tended to see the plebeian world as antagonistic and socially dysfunctional, and problematic in its opposition to civic norms. Overused descriptive nouns in the press, like 'gang' or 'mob' overrode any suggestion that labouring communities were made up of individual actors, and restoring their voices today is made difficult by a relative paucity of source material.

One lucky windfall in the Town Clerk's papers concerns a parish survey in 1816 relating to post-war poverty, a period when the competition for employment grew as thousands of demobilised soldiers returned home from the continent. A total of 3195 people were estimated to be wholly or partially dependent on poor relief in December of that year, 1214 of them from St James's parish alone and where, 'from the peculiar nature of their usual occupations', claimed parish officers, 'it will be an arduous undertaking to find adequate employment'. Many families were, as the vestry of St Philip and St Jacob succinctly put it, 'in a truly wretched state'. As the corporation pressed parishes for a solution, some suggested putting the poor to work laying the foundations for the new gaol, others that they should be made to break stones

---

[25] Matt Neale, 'Crime and Maritime Trade in Bristol, 1770–1800', in *A City Built Upon the Water. Maritime Bristol 1750–1900*, ed. Steve Poole (Bristol, 2013), pp. 76–93; Matt Neale, 'Making Crime Pay in Eighteenth-Century Bristol: Stolen Goods, the Informal Economy and the Negotiation of Risk', *Continuity and Change*, 26:3 (2011), 439–59.

for road building or be pressed into service as night watchmen. Officers in Temple suggested they do sewerage work, 'to draw off a quantity of the filth which now accumulates upon the surface of the water' in the Floating Harbour.

The nature of the record makes it easier to see Bristolians in statistical terms than as human beings. The only parish to trouble the mayor and magistrates with the personal circumstances of individual claimants was St Nicholas. From this we learn a little about some of the city's poorest men and women. For example, William Humphreys was a thirty-year-old seaman renting a room with his wife in the Rackhay. Illness had prevented him working for the last three years so he was dependent on the parish for his rent. His wife 'endeavours to get washing or sell fruit but has not earned more than 3/– a week for the last three months'. Margaret Morgan had lodgings in the same house, with her fifteen-year-old daughter. Both were out of work, and since her husband was drowned in the harbour seven years ago, they were in a severe state of distress. The daughter would try going into service but 'her clothes are nearly all pawned so as to be almost unfit to offer herself for another place'. William Brown was an American seaman who a year earlier had been cast adrift off the coast of Scotland and been rescued with severe frostbite. Brown came to Bristol in search of his brother but was soon on the street in a destitute condition, and sleeping rough, as many others did, in lime kilns for warmth. 'This poor wretched man was taken from the lime kiln in Limekiln Lane by his sister-in-law who is herself a poor distressed woman … and seems to have saved him literally from starvation and made him as comfortable as her little means can afford. He is very ill and weak in bed.' Joseph James was a thirty-year-old brazier. He had been laid off two years earlier and had since tramped through several midland counties to Lancashire and Yorkshire in search of work but had been unable to find any.[26]

Then, as now, gnawing poverty was apt to beget intolerance and scapegoating. Black and ethnic minority workers were by no means strangers in a cosmopolitan port like Bristol. Many were assimilated into the wider workforce with little outward sign of antagonism from their white neighbours. In this economic climate, however, pecking orders might be established, even amongst the vagrant poor. 'It is painful to the community to witness the number of Blacks who are begging about the city and suburbs', observed 'A Friend to Humanity' in an anonymous letter to the mayor in 1817. He hoped the magistrates would 'send them to their own country' for 'it is not to be

---

[26] The comprehensive survey of 1816 is preserved in BA, TC/Adm/Box/67/9. Most parishes responded by counting male claimants of relief but noting that many had families dependent upon them. The overall figure presented here has been arrived at by multiplying the number of reported male claimants by three; smaller perhaps than the average working-class family but a rough figure that tries to take into account those men who did not have families. Redcliff parish broke their figure down as 94 men supporting 58 wives and 167 children; St James parish as 342 men supporting 225 wives and 647 children.

supposed they will get employment here whilst there are so many of our own countrymen out of employ'.[27]

These brief glimpses of personal poverty may sound exceptional, but they reflect the conditions in which many poor people lived throughout much of the period covered by this book. Certainly some parishes were less impoverished. The parliamentary commission of 1845 considered Redcliff a very mixed parish, home to 'families of independence, opulent merchants, and professional men in small numbers, tradesmen and persons of more moderate means numerous, minor tradesmen, artisans and labourers very numerous, poor numerous'. But even relatively well-heeled parishes like St Augustine and Castle Precincts could not shrug off their indigent enclaves: Host Street, Trenchard Street and 'the tenements between Lime Kiln Lane and the Floating Harbour which are somewhat densely peopled' with poor families.[28]

In such an environment, allegations of public disorder were frequent. Any attempt to assess 'from below' the collective social experience of the labouring population in an urban centre like this is inevitably heavily dependent on sweeping and impersonal aggregated data on the one hand, and on the other, those voices that shout the loudest, if somewhat anecdotally, from a limited and fragmented archival record. We recognise that these voices may not be fully representative of the streets, courts and alleys from which they came, but neither should they be discounted, for the vicissitudes of daily life were not merely stacked, weighed and measured by those at the sharp end of them, but felt.

Riotous Bristolians: Disorder and the City Crowd

George Grigg ran a public house in the Shambles, called the Leg. One February evening in 1756, Charles Parfitt came and stood outside and demanded the release of his brother, who he believed was being held inside as a prisoner. If his brother was not released, shouted Parfitt, he would 'fetch the mob'. What does this phrase mean? Who were 'the mob', from where might they be raised with such certainty, and what did they think? Charles Parfitt was not much troubled by questions like these. When he got no response from Grigg, he ran up St Peter's Street and came back a few minutes later with 'the mob', 150 strong. A plebeian army now laid into Grigg's house with sticks and stones, breaking doors, windows and shutters. Grigg and his customers barricaded themselves in. Abraham Lewis, a gentleman drinker, went outside and ordered the attackers to disperse, but they beat him with bludgeons and he was forced to retreat back inside, his social authority ignored. Two shoemakers and a weaver then ventured out, and tried to reason with the crowd.

[27] BA, TC/Adm/Box/67/20, A Friend to Humanity to mayor of Bristol, 29 Aug. 1817.
[28] *Second Report of the Commissioners for Inquiring into the State of Large Towns and Populous Districts* (London, 1845), p. 68.

Parfitt hit one of them with a stick but they managed to drag him into the pub in the hope that his removal would encourage the crowd to disperse. It did, but soon returned to renew the attack, now leaderless and demanding the release of both Parfitt and his brother. The siege finally ended only when some constables arrived and took Parfitt into custody.[29]

The issues over which this battle in the Shambles was fought are no longer a matter of record. Major disturbances, associated with forms of protest, election rivalry or marketing, are extensively dealt with in this book, but crowd disorder often took forms that defy categorisation of this kind. Evidence of minor affrays or promiscuous gatherings unconnected with standard forms of protest are not always easy to locate or to interpret, and contemporary reporting, however descriptive, was not always concerned with issues of cause and motivation. Often they were neither reported nor prosecuted; such brief moments of antagonism were accepted perhaps as part of the warp and weft of everyday life. Clearly, contentious crowds gathered easily and frequently in densely populated urban areas like Bristol and not always for progressive causes.

For instance, take events on Shrove Tuesday in 1752, or on Trafalgar Day in 1811. Both were annual celebrations and neither was intrinsically contentious. Yet street violence erupted in 1752 when customary processions of the apprentice shipwrights and coopers clashed in King Street. Constables intervened to restore order but the two trades decamped to Durdham Down, beyond the mayor's jurisdiction, and settled the conflict there. They then marched triumphantly back into the city where they were opposed once again by constables and a number were taken up and lodged in Bridewell for disorderly behaviour.[30] In 1811, a crowd gathered spontaneously outside the Exchange to celebrate the anniversary of Trafalgar. They let off fireworks, fired guns into the air and hissed the constables sent out to police them. 'There was a general cry among the mob for a Ring', one of the constables testified (a space in which to fight and a command well understood by all those present). Several were later charged with riot and James Cole, who had been heard shouting 'a Ring, a Ring' more loudly than anyone else, was sent to Bridewell for a month.[31] These two apparently random outbursts of contention are typically opaque. The scrappy surviving record (a newspaper in the first case and a quarter session deposition in the second) reveals almost nothing of the circumstances, intention or argument of either dispute. Had rivalry between apprentice shipwright and coopers broken the peace before? What was the cause of it? Was the issue laid to rest or did it re-emerge in 1753? Had Trafalgar celebrations got out of hand before? Why did the crowd call for a ring, who was to fight in it and what was at issue?

[29] BA, TC/Adm/Box/10/3, Information of Samuel Bonnell, Abraham Lewis and Thomas Williams, 25 Feb. 1756.
[30] *Bristol Intelligencer*, 15 Feb. 1752.
[31] BA, JQS/P/281, Information of William Phillips, 22 Oct. 1811.

Occasionally, contexts in outbursts like these can at least be guessed at. One evening in 1770, a stick-wielding mob of fifty people, led by two men armed with swords, ran through Temple Street, Thomas Street, Baldwin Street and Marsh Street, breaking the windows of a glasscutter, a shoemaker and a former sheriff, William Weare. This disturbance was unrecorded in the newspaper press and although witness statements were taken with a view to prosecutions for riot at the quarter session, no evidence of either intention or context has survived. But the answer may possibly lie in the contentious reputation of John Wilkes. Public bonfires on Brandon Hill to celebrate Wilkes's victory in the 1768 Middlesex election had already indicated strong support for his cause amongst Bristol's more independent Whigs. A day before the Bristol riot in 1770, Wilkes had been released from prison in London, a liberation prompting boisterous celebrations all over the country, although none are recorded in Bristol. This may have been a Wilkite disturbance, but no further clues survive in the archive and, critically perhaps, none of the surviving depositions record anything that was said during the course of the evening.[32]

Crowd activity was not always representative of collective and abstract aspirations like 'Wilkes and Liberty'. Often it was personal and sometimes it was brutal. In 1781, Alice Mead complained to a magistrate about a man she knew, one Thomas Blandford. For nine months Blandford had been following her 'through the streets of the city, greatly abusing her and raising mobs or great numbers of persons about her', frequently waylaying her and 'concealing himself in the porches of houses … and suddenly jumping out behind her' so that she was 'greatly terrified' and an object of public derision.[33] Moves towards the better regulation of public behaviour during the early years of the following century reflected a growing unease amongst the respectable middling sort for lower-class 'disorders'. 'The language used by the women renting the Oyster Shed is at times dreadful in the extreme and shocking to every modestly disposed person', complained householders close to Bristol Bridge in 1803, in an unsuccessful bid to have them removed from sight. They wanted action too against boys bathing naked in the horse pool at the bottom of Castle Street, so that 'not a female of any delicacy or modesty can pass without being put to the blush'. Boys who disturbed the public peace on Sundays were equally troublesome. 'On the afternoon of the last Sabbath', wrote A Respecter of Morality, 'nearly 100 boys of various ages were playing in the most vociferous manner possible to the great annoyance of all moral and sedate people who have occasion to pass that way to places of worship.'[34]

[32] BA, TC/Adm/Box/24/4, Information of John Judge and others, 20 April 1770; FFBJ, 2 April 1768.

[33] BA, TC/Adm/Box/33/18, Calendar of prisoners, 23 Oct. 1781.

[34] BA, TC/Adm/Box/56/23, Petition to the mayor and magistrates, n.d. [1803]; TC/Adm/Box/69/6, A Respecter of Morality to the mayor, 22 July 1816.

Calls like these for a reformation of manners were effectively calls to reform the city police. Before the establishment of a city-wide paid constabulary in 1836, Bristol's policing was reliant upon an assortment of part-time ward constables and watchmen, recruited in numbers proportionate to the size of each ward, but demonstrably insufficient as a preventive force. They wielded little authority and Bristolians were rarely shy of confronting them. In 1750, constables on patrol secured 'the noted Thomas Summers of Kingswood', at an inn in Temple Street, but as they tried to take him away, they were set upon by a party of 'countrymen' who took objection to the arrest. After a 'smart skirmish', Summers was freed from his captors and 'march'd off in triumph'.[35] The authority vacuum necessarily left by inefficient policing like this was sometimes filled by popular agency, especially where social mores were outraged and community values undermined. In 1818, it was believed in the streets around Temple Back that Charles Fenning was in the habit of beating his wife. He was taken up for suspected assault, but not before a crowd of women gathered outside his house, kicked down the door, broke furniture, hurled saucepans and tubs of water at his head and swore they would murder him. 'They were more like furies than women', thought Fenning's mother, who witnessed the riot.[36] Language of this kind effectively robbed women of legitimate agency by treating their leadership of crowds as unnatural to their sex. Contemporary commentators were not always entirely blind to women's prominence, as the anonymous engraving of a crowd seen attacking Bristol Jail during the reform riots of 1831 clearly demonstrates (figure 4), but the recovery from the official record of women as participants is rarely easy.

Incidents like these are difficult to accommodate within a narrative of protest, resistance and progressive politics; indeed they have a tendency to challenge the structured ways in which mass social phenomena are conventionally represented. Mark Harrison's work on the city's election crowds is a case in point. At Bristol, where the interests of a large freeman electorate were frequently frustrated by no-contest pacts between the Whig and Tory clubs, 'contested elections usually involved major disturbances'. These disturbances have been characterised as having 'a strong carnival element' where a 'ritualised format … facilitated maximum popular participation'. For John Belchem, the Bristol election of 1812, for example, was typically 'rumbustious' and both he and Harrison have discussed its theatrical and counter-theatrical features.[37] These approaches mostly imagine crowd behaviour at election times in Hogarthian terms. Party crowds broke windows and fought on behalf of agreed party interests in an agreed 'electoral theatre' between the Bush

[35] *Bristol Intelligencer*, 28 April 1750.
[36] BA, TC/Adm/Box/69/6, Martha Jenning to mayor of Bristol, n.d. [1818?].
[37] Mark Harrison, *Crowds and History: Mass Phenomena in English Towns, 1790–1835* (Cambridge, 1988), pp. 202–33; John Belchem, *'Orator' Hunt: Henry Hunt and English Working-Class Radicalism* (Oxford, 1985), p. 29.

4 Detail from *Life, Trial and Execution of the Four Unfortunate Men for the Bristol Riots.*

tavern and the Exchange and between the White Lion and the Guildhall. But elections were not always fought by the mob according to agreed rules and the Bristol election of 1812 was no exception. As the clothier William Sheppard revealed in a letter of complaint to the mayor, rough crowds, 'idle fellows of the very lowest class in society', began to gather in the street outside the Exchange before the polls had even opened. Although they were there 'on account of the approaching election', they were not much interested in party politics.

> These gatherings do nothing but mischief, such as insulting passengers by hustling and ill-treating them, throwing mud, throwing a large basket – with the bottom out – which sometimes catches an unwary passenger – when he gets tossed about in a thousand directions – and at last is rolled in the mud ... There are some hundreds now before the door, tossing a basket – and from their shouts, have just catched someone passing, making such a horrid noise of screaming, whooping and yelling, enough to make one think they were from the Infernal Regions ... They have just been rolling a large hogshead against my door with such force as I expected would have broke it in. Nor do I dare to go out and speak to them, if I were, my windows would be broke in.

This was a crowd that did not play by the rules and it has not been noticed by previous historians of Bristol's electoral politics. 'What a pity that 2–300 of the greatest miscreants should govern the interior of so large a city as this', Sheppard reflected. 'I want to go out of the city on business but am deterred, fearing all my property would be destroyed in my absence, by a set of villains who think they have license to do what they please during an election.'[38]

Our intention here is to take a broad and less prescriptive view of the crowd, of the disorders associated with crowds, and of their various interactions with structures of authority. We'll start with an overview of one aspect of street life where crowd participation, albeit within customary rules of regulation and engagement, was actively encouraged by the city's elite: the administration of public punishment. Other sites of contention will then be considered – relations between the vagrant or 'disorderly' poor and the civil power, relations with billeted soldiers, and relations in the workplace. The chapter concludes with a case study in intersecting social relationships, in the experience of three figures from divergent backgrounds, whose fates became intertwined at the beginning of the nineteenth century.

Crowds and Public Punishment

The corporation's judicial and executive powers were far reaching. In addition to the quarter sessions, the city's court of Oyer and Terminer was empowered to hear capital cases before the Recorder and aldermanic bench, by which arrangement the magistrates were, in the words of one critic, 'the only judges of all disputes between citizen and citizen and of all crimes committed or pretended to have been committed within the city'. Such an incestuous jurisprudence, it was sometimes objected, was not always exercised in the best interests of civil liberties. The radical solicitor, Charles Holden Walker, was particularly scathing. It was bad enough that a full gaol delivery often occurred only once a year instead of twice yearly in line with the assize circuits in the rest of the country, but worse still was

> the manifest injustice of magistrates having a chartered interest in the conviction of those who happen to be tried before them for misdemeanour. This privilege the Corporation of Bristol has – a privilege that enables its members to reap all pecuniary advantage and to receive into their own coffers all fines and amendments inflicted upon others by a portion of themselves![39]

But city elites well understood the advantages of introspective surveillance. In 1733 for example, the Recorder, Sir John Scrope, publicly confirmed an unshakable confidence in 'the diligency of the magistrates and that he had

---

[38] BA, TC/Adm/Box/64/27, William Sheppard to the Town Clerk, n.d. [July 1812].
[39] Charles Holden Walker, *Letters on the Practice of the Bristol Court of Requests on Judicial Sinecures in Bristol* (London, 1820), p. x.

often reflected with pleasure how they could keep so numerous a people in subjection'.[40] One effect of all this judicial diligence was that citizens had plenty of opportunities to witness not only the use of locally ordered public whippings and the pillory, but executions on the St Michael's Hill gallows. Exemplary hangings might also be ordered by the Gloucestershire assize on ground close to the city and county boundary near the turnpike on Durdham Down, and the Somerset assize on the city's southern fringes at Totterdown and Bedminster. The corpses of Somerset and Gloucestershire felons hanged in these places were usually left there in gibbet cages, and would have been a familiar site to anyone travelling in or out of the city from the north or south.[41] In addition, visitors to Bristol arriving by water had to pass the mouldering corpse of the murderer, Matthew Mahoney, consigned to a gibbet cage at the mouth of the Avon in 1741, and then the body of Patrick Ward, gibbeted beside the river at Broad Pill in 1761. A proposal that several pirates executed in London in 1762 should also be brought up and gibbetted beside Mahoney was only rejected on grounds of cost.[42]

These grisly warnings were not just highly visible but, by design at least, permanent markers on the landscape. Mahoney's gibbet cage had collapsed into the sand by 1784, but the pole did not fall until the middle of the following century and the stump was still visible in 1880. A visitor by boat in 1772 noted his passage past the Avonmouth gibbets in his diary, his memory for the detail a little confused, but the impact plain enough even after the passing of several decades:

> Just as we had nearly approached ye mouth of ye river ye Ladies were not a little alarm'd at two very disagreeable objects viz a couple of gibbets on ye left hand whereon Captn Goodere and a foot solider had been formerly suspended. The first for murdering his uncle ye latter a farener. When we had passed these the rest of ye way was made more agreeable, sailing thro' verdant groves and glowery gardens till we arrived at ye Hotwells.[43]

Gallows and gibbets were both practical and symbolic structures; their looming presence at the city's jurisdictional boundaries a permanent reminder that the criminal justice system was locally robust. But the relationship between these markers and the plebeian poor who passed them and lived in their shadow was not always straightforward. Footpads and highway robbers were not dissuaded from committing serious crimes within sight of them; indeed

---

[40] *The Parliamentary History of England* 15: *1753–1765*, cols 477 and 493, debate on the Bristol Nightly Watch Bill; *Daily Courant*, 11 Sep. 1733.
[41] For Somerset cases, see the executions of Cornelius York and John Millard, *London Evening Post*, 6 Sep. 1740 and Richard Randall, *FFBJ*, 10 Aril 1784. For Durdham Down see the hangings of Richard Payne and Andrew Burnett, *Gloucester Journal*, 1 May 1744, and Joseph Abseny, *Whitehall Evening Post*, 26 Aug. 1749.
[42] *St James's Chronicle*, 22 April 1762.
[43] BL, Add. MS 27951, 'Itinerarium Bristoliense', 3 Aug. 1772. Our thanks to Madge Dresser for this reference.

the open country of Bedminster and Durdham Down remained dangerous to travellers throughout the century, and public disregard for the gallows as a deterrent was occasionally commented upon. Disorderly gatherings had been 'entertained at about seven or eight unruly public houses near the gallows on St Michaels' Hill, and many dangerous insults and robberies have been committed on the market people and others travelling thereabout (as suspected) by the persons harbour'd in those houses', noted the *Intelligencer* in 1749. Even as a man was being executed on Durdham Down in 1764, a mounted highwayman reportedly robbed two women 'within sight of the gallows' and 'in the midst of some thousand spectators'.[44]

The top of St Michael's Hill remained the regular place for executions at Bristol until the New Gaol on the southern side of the Floating Harbour opened in 1821. Condemned felons were taken 'in slow procession'[45] from Newgate by cart or by mourning coach, depending upon the depth of the prisoners' pockets. Even by the most direct route, the gallows lay almost a mile from Newgate and the journey could take over an hour to negotiate.[46] Conveying prisoners through the congested city centre, with halters round their necks and leaning upon their own coffins, made these processions highly visible. The route customarily taken is unrecorded, but the way selected in 1810 for William Lewis's public whipping from Newgate to the gallows went through Broadmead, North Street and Upper Maudlin Lane to St Michael's Hill, so avoiding the busiest streets and the tricky incline of Steep Street, and it may be that hanging processions took this route as well. Bristol's last gallows procession was staged in 1816; remarkable in itself because elsewhere, processions to the gallows tended to survive into the nineteenth century only where the customary journey was a short one from county gaol to rural hinterland and where congestion was unlikely to give rise to disorder. The two-mile cavalcade from London's Newgate gaol to Tyburn was abandoned on these and other grounds as early as 1783. But Bristol's – despite the necessity of taking prisoners right through the city from south to north, on narrow roads and up a very steep hill – was not. It seems likely then that the execution process at Bristol was relatively well managed and a far cry from the confused, bestial and bacchanalian excesses claimed by the many critics of the Tyburn ritual.[47]

---

[44] *The Lives and Trials of Cornelius York, George Masters and John Millard* (Bristol, 1740); *Bristol Intelligencer*, 16 Dec. 1749; *Oxford Journal*, 19 May 1764.

[45] *Oxford Journal*, 20 Oct. 1781.

[46] In 1772, Jonathan Britain 'left Newgate between eleven and twelve and arrived at the Tree about one o'clock': *FFBJ*, 20 May 1772.

[47] For the debate over the ending of gallows processions in London and provincial England, see Steve Poole, 'For the Benefit of Example: Crime Scene Executions in England, 1720–1830', in *A Global History of Execution and the Criminal Corpse*, ed. Richard Ward (Basingstoke, 2015), pp. 72–8; Simon Devereaux, 'Recasting the Theatre of Execution: The Abolition of the Tyburn Ritual', *Past and Present*, 202 (2009).

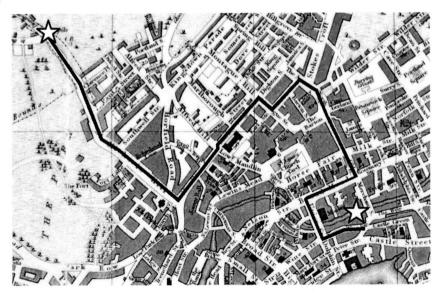

5 The only recorded route taken for a punishment procession from Newgate gaol to the gallows on St Michael's Hill (starred): William Lewis's public whipping for assaulting a child in 1810. This route is traced onto Benjamin Donne's *Plan* of 1773. The route of most public whippings is unrecorded.

Bristolians were certainly willing witnesses and most executions were carefully managed as public spectacles. Condemned men and women who arrived on the Hill still insisting on their innocence could expect sustained attempts by the Sheriff to extract a dramatic and crowd-pleasing last-minute confession. Patrick Sheppard, hanged for sodomy in 1761, firmly maintained his innocence beneath the gallows, but 'at the point of being cast off, the Sheriff questioned him touching the crime he died for. He was now already half strangled and eternity full in his view when for the last time he testified his innocency.'[48] Performance of this kind demanded witness and audiences were often large. The sensational hanging of Captain Samuel Goodere and two accomplices for the murder of his own brother on board the *Ruby* in 1741 drew 'the greatest crowd as ever was known in Bristol', including 'people for some miles round the country', who looked on, 'with great concern, and many tears were shed on this sad occasion'.[49] Gallows crowds grew increasingly large as hangings became less frequent in the early years of the nineteenth century. An estimated 30,000 people, a third of them women, 'travelled on foot from distant parts of the country', to see the forger William Carter die in 1816. It was the first execution since 1805, and the last before the procession

[48] *Some Particulars Relating to the Life of William Dillon Sheppard* (Bristol, 1761).
[49] Samuel Foote, *The Genuine Memoirs of the Life of Sir John Dinely Goodere* (Bristol, 1741), p. 36; *Daily Post*, 24 April 1741.

was abandoned and all hangings relocated to the roof of the gatehouse at the New Gaol.[50]

If contemporary reporting is to be believed, disorder at the gallows was rare; the atmosphere at most executions seems, if anything, to have been quietly sympathetic to the condemned.[51] And the condemned, for their part, generally behaved in an approving manner. At Samuel Goodere's hanging, according to the murdered man's nephew, the condemned man conversed politely with spectators and 'many of the audience sent up their good wishes and prayers for his eternal welfare'.[52] Some convicts deliberately curried favour and affected to die game. Sarah Barret, convicted for a robbery in 1743, 'behaved very boldly as she passed along and about the middle of Wine Street she pledged the hangman out of a bottle of liquor'. So fortified, Barret prepared a final gesture for the crowd on the hill. She called for a bowl of water beneath the gallows and demonstratively washed her hands in it, 'as a Token of her pretended Innocence'.[53] Matthew Daley came out of Newgate, 'drank almost a pint of ale in one draft', then 'mounted the cart himself (in his sailor's dress) and shook hands with a great many people over the sides of the cart'.[54] Clothing mattered. The forger, John Barry, 'appeared dressed in a blue Camblet coat, black velvet waistcoat and breeches, white wig, white stockings, and new pumps, and seemed as cheerful (or rather hardened in natural boldness) as if he had been going to a wedding'.[55] And some, like the highwayman Nicholas Mooney and the forger Jonathan Britain who 'sung and prayed and exhorted the people with much fervour and affection', made an elaborate show of their own guilt and contrition. Mooney went so far as to request that nobody pulled on his legs to quicken his death, because he wanted to feel the pain of his own demise.[56]

These displays can only have been effective if crowds were quiet enough to acknowledge them, and sheriffs prepared to permit a degree of agency to the convict. If prisoners asked how long they might be allowed to stand in prayer or to speak with spectators, they would generally be told that it was up to them to give the sign when ready. The soldier Thomas Kitchingman, hanged for murder in 1734, delayed his death for more than an hour, first by making a detailed declaration of his innocence and then by requesting a lengthy series of prayers and devotions.[57] Signalling readiness was usually done at Bristol by dropping a handkerchief, although in the case of Benjamin Loveday and John

[50] *Bristol Mirror*, 27 April 1816.

[51] For a full discussion of the complex relationship between audience, institutional authority and the condemned at London's Tyburn, see Andrea McKenzie, *Tyburn's Martyrs: Execution in England, 1675–1775* (London, 2007), pp. 21–9.

[52] Foote, *Genuine Memoirs*, p. 36.

[53] *General Evening Post*, 14 May 1743.

[54] *General Advertiser*, 30 Sep. 1746.

[55] *Old England*, 24 May 1746.

[56] *Bristol Intelligencer*, 25 April 1752.

[57] *London Evening Post*, 1 Oct. 1734.

Burke, hanged for consensual sodomy in 1781, it was a posy of flowers, some two and a half hours after leaving Newgate.[58] Edward Macnamara, executed for forgery in 1790, left Newgate at noon and only when 'the hour of two had arrived, on which he had fixed for his departure, he took leave of this world saying, "God bless you all"'.[59] Agency of this kind was scarcely possible in London because, as Andrea McKenzie has pointed out, 'a signal was impracticable when many people were hanged at the same time'.[60]

But the efforts of the condemned to maintain a measure of dignity were sometimes hampered by the incompetence of the authorities. John Vernon and Joshua Harding, hanged together in 1736, both recovered after being taken away by their friends, partly perhaps because they were left to hang only for eight minutes before being cut down. Vernon died within a few hours in the care of his friends who, in order to keep him from the surgeons, then took his body secretly to Kingroad for burial in the sands. Harding survived and was unexpectedly reprieved. Three years later, John Kimmerley had to be hanged four times because the ropes kept breaking,[61] and the man charged with hanging Carter in 1816, 'who appeared to be but little skilled in the duties of his vocation', was so severely pelted for his incompetence as he left that he was forced to take shelter at a house in Maudlin Lane.[62]

Unsurprisingly, when disorder did occur, it was generally aimed not at the convict but at representatives of the law. The hangman who tried to claim Nicholas Mooney's shoes in 1752, 'very deservedly had his head broke' for his trouble by the crowd, and Thomas Boon used his last speech from the platform to name a woman whom he claimed had tricked him into committing the thefts for which he was now hanged. This performance 'had such an effect that a little time after he was executed, a mob got about the woman's house on the Weare, battered it with dirt and stones, broke all the windows and hung out a parcel of rams horns at the shop windows'. The mayor read the Riot Act to disperse them and the following day an anonymous note arrived at the Mansion House, warning him, 'not to trouble yourself about what you call a riot on the Weare ... We think it justice to serve her so and your Worship worse if you doth not hold your Peace.'[63]

Between 1733 and 1835, the Bristol gallows accounted for the deaths of seventy-one men and seven women. However, excepting one sharp rise at the beginning of the nineteenth century, use of the gallows at Bristol declined slowly over the period considered here and by the early years of the nineteenth century, hangings had become something of a rarity. Indeed, between 1805

[58] *Bonner & Middleton's Bristol Journal*, 13 Oct. 1781; FFBJ, 13 Oct. 1781.
[59] *The Life of Nicholas Mooney* (Bristol, 1752); FFBJ, 21 May 1772; 13 May 1790.
[60] McKenzie, *Tyburn's Martyrs*, p. 17.
[61] *Daily Post*, 14 Sep. 1736; *Daily Gazetteer*, 7 Sep. 1736; *Country Journal*, 12 May 1739.
[62] *Bristol Mirror*, 27 April 1816.
[63] *Daily Gazetteer*, 19 April 1738; *London Evening Post*, 22 April 1738; *London Gazette*, 18 April 1738.

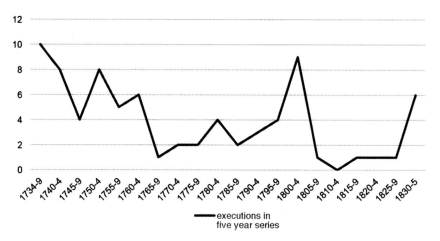

6 Bristol executions, 1733–1835.

and 1831 only five capital sentences were carried out. A brief 'peak' in 1832 was caused by the anomalous execution of the four reform rioters, but there were only another two after that (in 1835 and 1849) before public execution was ended for good in 1868. The Bristol courts were not much inclined to order the gibbeting of felons after death either. Eighteenth-century gibbet cages on Durdham Down, at Totterdown and at Brislington were ordered not by the city sheriffs but by the assize courts of Gloucestershire and Somerset. Gibbets were ordered just twice by the authorities at Bristol, for the seamen Matthew Mahoney in 1741, and Patrick Ward in 1761, both for murder and both set up close to the mouth of the Avon. Gibbets were expensive; Ward was hanged for just 3 guineas, but gibbeting him cost a further £20.[64] In line with the national trend, capitally convicted offenders were increasingly likely to have their sentences commuted to transportation. Some 750 people in total were transported from Bristol to the colonies during the half-century between 1727 and the outbreak of the American war alone, roughly a third of them women, although not all were sent by the Bristol courts. Some were sentenced by the Gloucester assize and sent down to Bristol by waggon.[65]

Physical punishments for lesser offences included public exposure in the stocks and pillory or a whipping at the carts tail. In the early years of the eighteenth century, stocks set up on the quay and in St James's churchyard were used to punish anyone defaulting on the payment of fines summarily imposed for minor moral offences, predominately drunkenness and swearing.

[64] TNA, T90/154, Bristol Sherriff's cravings, 1761; BA, F/AC/Box/73/12, City Chamberlain's accounts.
[65] Gwenda Morgan and Peter Rushton, *Eighteenth-Century Criminal Transportation: The Formation of the Criminal Atlantic* (Basingstoke, 2004), p. 178, ft. 55; for twenty-three Gloucester convicts conveyed to the Quay at Bristol see *Bristol Oracle*, 30 Sep. 1749.

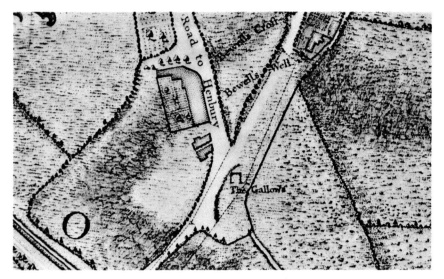

7 The site of the Bristol gallows, from John Rocque's *Survey*, 1750.

Between 1729 and 1731, 26 men and 2 women spent between one and four hours sitting in stocks for these misdemeanours, but they were used far less frequently after that date. In common with the pillory, the stocks' effectiveness was dependent upon interactivity between offender and spectators, but public disapproval for these very common and minor offences was unlikely to be great and magistrates seem gradually to have decided that a levy of distress to recover the value of fines was a better option. As petty session records make clear, the stocks were used exclusively for the public exposure and correction of the labouring poor; they featured porters, basket-makers, shoemakers, mariners, carpenters, tobacco-cutters, blacksmiths, glass-men, coachmen, wool-combers and general labourers.[66]

Crowd reactions were conditional on the nature of the crime however. In 1737 an informer who had tried to frame a gin-seller under the unpopular act of 1736 was put in the stocks for a vexatious prosecution. While he was there a mob brought a pitch kettle, covered him in tar, and rolled him in feathers, making him 'a most Grotesque Figure'. [67] In the same year an itinerant fiddle player named Elliot was placed in the stocks for falsely reporting the landlady of a Marsh Street inn for giving him short measure. Elliot's status as both a perjurer and an informer ensured rough handling from spectators, not just during his official punishment, but after it. As soon as he was released,

---

[66] BA, JQS/C/2, Summary Convictions register 1728–95.
[67] *Three letters upon the subject of the Gin Act and common informers* (London, 1738), p. 12. On hostility to the Gin Act, see Jessica F. Warner and Frank Ivis, '"Damn you, you informing Bitch": Vox Populi and the Unmaking of the Gin Act of 1736', *Journal of Social History*, 33:2 (1999), 299–330.

his tormentors led him 'through several streets, pelted him with kennel dirt, flung ashes in his eyes, and otherwise bedaubed him, that no Pillory Chap could be worse served; to make him clean they afterwards flung him into the common horse pond on the weir'.[68]

Crowd punishments like these, much like the parading and hanging of unpopular figures in effigy, or traditions of rough music and charivari, mimicked official forms of punishment and drew a degree of legitimacy from them. They would re-emerge in mock executions of Tom Paine in the 1790s, and in the use of skimmington, or 'horsing' in nineteenth-century labour disputes. Indeed, when magistrates convicted Rachel Isoll, John Morris and Edward Daley for 'lewdness' after they were 'found in bed together' in 1729, they ordered them to be 'put on horseback and ride, according to the ancient custom of the city'.[69] Two years earlier, a couple caught fornicating in St Phillips were 'Carted through the Town, and were severely pelted by the Populace for being catch'd in their Amore'.[70] Whether their punishment was ordered by magistrates or decreed by popular demand is uncertain, but clearly, the line between official and popular forms of justice-making in the city was sometimes a fine one. William Elliot's public ordeal in 1737, then, may be understood as a reflection of judicial attitudes to shaming, procession and exposure. And Margaret Davis, convicted for stealing meat in 1750, was not merely ordered to be exposed in a fixed position, but led through the market 'with a label of her crime affixed to her breast and the meat hung around her neck'.[71]

The pillory was essentially a variant on the stocks, another public punishment in which, theoretically, offenders were shamed through exposure but not physically harmed. It was used for more serious misdemeanours and usually ordered at quarter sessions in the presence of a jury. Its most frequent use was for the public shaming of sexual offenders, and for this reason it invariably attracted large and active crowds. Victims stood for an hour at midday with heads uncovered and sometimes with a note pinned above them to denote their crime. As we shall see, popular violence against men convicted of attempted sodomy peaked at Bristol during the 1730s when some were pelted so badly in the pillory that they only narrowly escaped death. Robert Hull and Thomas Rawlings were placed in the pillory for attempting consensual sex in 1737. 'Never were two wretches worse pelted', it was reported,

> especially old Hull, who was stunned several times, and so deprived of his senses that he hung some time by the wrists in the iron handcuffs of the pillory; after which the mob pulled down his breeches and continued pelting with such fury

[68] *Gloucester Journal*, 22 Feb. 1737. Very occasionally in later years, the stocks were revived. See *Bristol Mirror*, 21 May 1821, for one late instance of their use for drunk and disorderly behaviour.

[69] BA, JQS/C/2, Summary Convictions register 1728–95.

[70] *Farley's Bristol Newspaper*, 21 Jan. 1727.

[71] *Bristol Intelligencer*, 18 Aug. 1750.

that, had not the pillory broke down, tumbling them backward over head and heels on the street, and the magistrates with some constables intervened, they certainly would have been killed on the spot.[72]

By the second half of the century, the pillory was better guarded by constables,[73] but even in the nineteenth century suspected sodomites could expect harsh and exemplary treatment at the hands of hostile spectators. Two labourers, Thomas Carter and John Wellington, were convicted, gaoled for two years and sent to the pillory in 1810. As a former thief-taker, Carter was 'not very popular with the mob', as *Felix Farley's Journal* put it, and the tone was set by handbills pasted onto the walls of the Exchange, urging attendance at, 'A Grand Exhibition by Signor Carter and Signora Wellington, two Celebrated Performers from the City of Sodom'. An 'immense' crowd pelted them hard with vegetables, 'dead cats, dogs, rats and other objects of annoyance' until Carter was 'shockingly cut and bruised about the head, but both escaped with their lives'.[74]

By contrast, crowd behaviour at the pillory when either men or women were sent to it for keeping a bawdy house was rarely recorded, but it is unlikely to have inspired levels of violence on this scale. The tolerance of crowds to other kinds of offender in the pillory varied, but it may have been influenced by the circumstances in which an offence was committed or by the language in which it was advertised in the press. In 1727 for example, Thomas Huxley, a customs officer, was placed in the pillory for a forgery. This was no ordinary offence however, for Huxley had been 'making seizures of run [smuggled] goods from sailors and converting them to his own use'. Consequently, he was roughly handled, and 'the sailors were pretty busy about his Peepers'. *Farley's Bristol Newspaper* then reminded its readers that another man, Richard Skelton, was to be pilloried the following week for an unspecified perjury, during which 'he may find some part of his Punishment'. Indeed he did, but opinions as to his culpability appeared sharply divided. 'There happened a great scuffle at the Tolzey', reported the paper, during which Skelton was 'severely pelted and several received hard stripes and wounds in the fray'.[75]

But the most frequent means by which convicts were subjected to exposure was by public whipping. Like the stocks and the pillory, this was another punishment whose impact would have been nullified without an audience to witness it, but one in which, although crowds were invited to watch, they were not permitted to participate. We have very few accounts of responses

---

[72] *Read's Weekly Journal*, 24 Sep. 1737; BA, JQS/D/8 1733–7, Quarter Sessions docket book, entry dated 7 Sep. 1737; *Sherborne Mercury*, 20 Sep. 1737; *Gloucester Journal*, 20 Sep. 1737.

[73] TNA, T/90/153 Sheriff's cravings 1761: the city spent two guineas on the protection of two men set in the pillory that year.

[74] BA, JQS/P/265, Printed calendar, 16 April 1810; JQS/P/257, Information of William Edwards, Mary Thomas and Joel Couzens, 8 July 1809; FFBJ, 5 May 1810.

[75] *Farley's Bristol Newspaper*, 11, 18 Nov. 1727.

to public whipping, but it was frequently laid on by the courts and, in the early years of the eighteenth century at least, women were as likely to be subjected to it as men. Indeed, between 1735 and 1737, ten women and five men were put to the whip by the city courts.[76] Although some men (and all women by mid century) were whipped in private, the sessions invariably ordered at least one public flogging, most often for petty larceny. Few Bristolians perhaps would claim never to have seen one. Between 1782 and 1786 alone, 31 men were whipped in the open street at the cart's tail, or occasionally outside Bridewell or Newgate, and 109 felons of both sexes whipped privately as part of a custodial sentence. How hard they were whipped, or how many lashes they received, is open to question. Occasionally, severity was hinted at in the language of sentencing. Mary Sorter, publicly whipped for theft in 1736, was to be 'whipped onto until the blood issues', but no such instruction was laid down for other men and women sentenced that year.[77] Severity was also contingent upon the distance to be travelled. There was no set route for whipping processions, but the most common ran from the Drawbridge to Newgate via Clare High and Wine Streets. Some offenders were subjected to longer ordeals. In 1793, John Freeman was taken through three different parts of the city for an unspecified misdemeanour, and in 1810 William Lewis was whipped twice, at either end of a gaol sentence, from Newgate to the St Michael's Hill gallows and back, a journey of more than two miles in total. Lewis's exceptional punishment reflected the seriousness of his offence, sexual assault on a child, and it is one of the few occasions when the presence of spectators was noted by the press. 'An immense crowd was assembled', reported the *Mirror*, 'and it was with much difficulty that the constables succeeded in protecting the culprit from the rage of the populace.' Ironically, Lewis was one of the last men to be whipped at the cart's tail, but public whippings at a post erected beside the Wine Street pump continued into the 1820s, when the punishment was most frequently used against juvenile offenders for petty offences and persistent cases of vagrancy.[78]

Until the New Gaol was opened in 1820, the men and women we have been discussing here would have spent at least a little time either in Bridewell

[76] BA, JQS/D/8, Quarter Sessions docket book, 1733–37.

[77] BA, JQS/D/8, Quarter Sessions docket book, 1733–37, entry dated 5 July 1734; BA, 11168/70/a–b, Bright Papers, Returns of prisoners in Newgate, with their punishments recorded, 1777–89.

[78] Public whippings of women at the cart's tail are noted in *Farley's Bristol Newspaper*, 17 Dec. 1726, 18 May 1728. A route used on at least two occasions ran from Broadmead to Stokes Croft turnpike, *FFBJ*, 14 June 1755; and Lewis's route went from Newgate, to Union Street, Broadmead, Barr's Lane, North Street, Earl Street, and Maudlin Lane to St Michael's Hill: *Bristol Mirror*, 13 and 20 Jan. 1810. For other routes see cases of Charles Jones and Thomas Webber (1784) and John Freeman (1793), in G. Lamoine (ed.), *Bristol Gaol Delivery Fiats, 1741–1799*, Bristol Record Society, 40 (Bristol, 1989), pp. 60, 83. For later cases, *Bristol Mirror*, 26 Sep. 1818, 4 Dec. 1819, 19 Aug. 1820, 18 Nov. 1820, 21 May 1821, 8 and 15 April 1826.

or, more probably, in the city's ramshackle old prison, Newgate, at the eastern end of Wine Street. For some it was a more than passing acquaintance. Robert Hamilton, living evidence, if any were needed, that eighteenth-century prisons served the needs neither of deterrence nor reform, endured two spells in Bridewell, and four in Newgate (including one stay of two and a half years while awaiting transportation), before finally succumbing to the hangman on St Michael's Hill in 1793. He was then just twenty-two years old.[79] Newgate, built in 1689 and in a deplorable state by the middle of the eighteenth century, was as insecure as it was unhealthy. Too small to serve its purpose, overcrowding meant that male prisoners were often crammed into a damp and barely lit dungeon known colloquially as the Pit. 'This gaol ... is very antique and much too small', wrote the prison reformer James Neild in 1807. Neild interviewed the turnkey about the state of the Pit and was told 'that in a morning when he unlocked the door, he was so affected by the putrid steam issuing from the dungeon, that it was enough to strike him down'.[80] Women fared no better. 'Frequently', admitted a former governor in 1763, the turnkeys had been obliged to put twelve women together in an eight-foot-square cell, making it impossible for all of them to lie down to sleep at the same time.[81]

Despite the appalling conditions, prisoners found their own ways to assert themselves. In 1736, a gang of gaoled housebreakers challenged the governor by making a 'shouting noise' one night in the Pit, and 'rung changes with their fetters in imitation of bells', to warn him of 'what they would do if he came near them'. Two months later, some of the same men, still confined in the Pit and now awaiting transportation, acquired several files, a crow bar and a chisel and managed to make a small hole in the outer wall before their escape attempt was discovered by the governor.[82] Breakouts were not uncommon. John Phillips, a 56-year-old man partially disabled so that he walked with a stoop, was nevertheless able to break out after four months in Newgate as an illegally returned transportee earlier in the same year, and four men escaped by breaking a hole in the wall in 1750. Later that same year, a number of iron bars were discovered, presumed to have been brought in to furnish further escape attempts, and in November male prisoners managed to saw through their fetters. When the turnkey came to check on them that evening, they 'rose in a body' and grabbed the key to the outer door. More turnkeys arrived and a struggle ensued but the guards 'soon quell'd them, after having well drubb'd some of the most daring ones with Pokers, Tongs,

[79] *Bristol Gazette*, 9 May 1793.

[80] Trevor Pearce, 'A Divided Elite: Governance and Prison Reform in Early Nineteenth Century Bristol' (Unpublished PhD Thesis, University of the West of England, 2009), p. 35.

[81] BA, TC/Adm/Box/20/1, Thomas Cantle to Christopher Willoughby, 19 May 1763.

[82] *London Daily Post*, 20 July 1736; *Daily Gazetteer*, 19 Sep. 1736.

etc'.[83] In such an insecure environment, the smuggling of tools and weapons into Newgate's cells by visiting families and friends was not difficult. In 1757, five prisoners furnished themselves with pistols, iron bars and a set of iron tongs, forced their way into the kitchen and began demolishing the wall under the window, 'declaring the day was their own, that they were determined to make their escape that night'. They made too much noise however, and were discovered by a soldier, who opened fire and shot one of them dead.[84] Violent confrontations like these were clearly an occasional feature of social relations between the Bristolian poor and the city authorities, but they were not reserved exclusively for conflicts over overt forms of criminality as the case of one poor woman was to prove in 1755.

Vagrancy and the Disorderly Poor

One night in November, seven constables were observed by a number of bystanders, manhandling a pregnant young woman named Mary Wheeler and beating her with their staves. She was 'a very bad disorderly woman', one of them asserted, 'a drunken bitch of a whore', and she must be taken to Bridewell. According to Mary Nelson, an ironmonger's servant who witnessed the scene from her window,

> She consequently fell to the ground and on her rising again … (they) repeated the blow and felled her again to the ground and after she rose, one of the three … gave her a hard push or thrust whereby she was again brought to the ground and on her getting up the three men came to her and forcibly laid her on a pair of trucks that stood near and hauled her a small distance where she sprung up herself from off the trucks and cryed out, You'll kill my child.

Wheeler was eventually subdued by having a length of cloth tied around her neck to secure her to the trucks, and then pushed along in spite of her protests. When they arrived at the Bridewell, she was found to be dead.[85] Mary Wheeler's case may have been exceptional in its outcome, but in its circumstances it was less so. Constables were not just accustomed to dragging 'disorderly' men and women to the Bridewell if they chanced upon them; it was a requirement of the job.

If Mary Wheeler's voice speaks uncharacteristically loudly across the centuries, it is perhaps not because her experience at the hands of the city watch was unusual but because it resulted in her death and so became a matter of public record. It could not pass without an inquest, and since there

[83] *Farley's Bristol Newspaper*, 6 April 1736; *Bristol Intelligencer*, 12 May 1750, 18 Sep. 1750, 10 Nov. 1750.

[84] BA, TC/Adm/Box/13/2, Information of Richard Watts, Danish Collins and Ann Harris, servant to gaoler.

[85] BA, TC/Adm/Box/10/3, Inquest into the death of Mary Wheeler, 20 Nov. 1755, and bundle of notes marked 'For the Town Clerk immediately'.

were a large number of independent witnesses, the hearing was relatively well informed. Although Wheeler had 'contusions to one of her eyes, her face and other parts of her body', cause of death was judged to be strangulation from the cloth tightly tied about her neck. Magistrates had little option but to arraign the seven constables for murder, and at the subsequent assize, three were convicted on the reduced charge of manslaughter. They were gaoled for six months and burnt in the hand.[86]

A wide variety of people frequently preoccupied both the city bench and the Corporation of the Poor, simply as 'vagrants'. In 1750, the Grand Jury demanded action against the 'abundance of vagrant young people, boys and girls, wandering up and down the streets and whose nightly refuge is the Glasshouses, houses uninhabited etc. and appear destitute of any employment for maintenance'.[87] In common with other British towns, significant concerns over both the levels and effects of vagrancy were raised at Bristol in the aftermath of the Gordon riots and in the economic downturn that came with mass demobilisation after the American war. As Tim Hitchcock and Robert Shoemaker have noted, during the 1780s rising efforts were made to clear London's streets of men and women without either settlement or regular employment. But the apprehension, whipping and incarceration in Bridewell of exemplary numbers of beggars had financial consequences which, in the capital at least, prompted a change in policy by mid decade. In London after 1786, suspected vagrants were still taken up and examined in numbers, but then passed to their parish of settlement without either a whipping or a spell of confinement and hard labour.[88] Bristol did not immediately follow suit.

Under its unique Act of Incorporation in 1696, the Bristol Corporation of the Poor was empowered to seek out vagrants and commit them to labour in the poorhouse (St Peter's Hospital) for up to three years; a right the guardians rarely exercised for practical reasons of space and expense. But shorter terms before passing were common throughout the eighteenth century. A Bristol clampdown can be detected during the severe winter of 1785–86 when a 'great number' of 'disorderly persons' were apprehended, whipped and passed to their parishes after a night in Bridewell. Handbills, first produced in 1782 and now vigorously republished and circulated, advertised rewards for anyone apprehending as many 'beggars, ballad singers, minstrels or other vagrants' as they could find, so that they might be 'corrected' at St Peter's. Paid officers were appointed by the Committee of Guardians, 'with a cap made for that purpose, on which shall be placed the following words in legible characters, St Peter's Hospital Officer for Apprehending Vagrants, Beggars etc.' These

---

[86] *Public Advertiser*, 25 Nov. 1755; *London Evening Post*, 1 May 1756; BA, TC/Adm/Box/10/3, Inquest into the death of Mary Wheeler, 20 Nov. 1755.

[87] BA, TC/Adm/Box/4/14, Presentment of the Grand Jury, 15 Feb. 1750.

[88] Tim Hitchcock, *Down and Out in Eighteenth-Century London* (London, 2004), pp. 166–7; Tim Hitchcock and Robert Shoemaker, *London Lives: Poverty, Crime and the Making of a Modern City, 1690–1800* (Cambridge, 2015), pp. 385–9.

men were tasked with patrolling the streets by day, equipped with a length of netting stretched between two long poles, on which suspected vagrants offering resistance could be carried to St Peter's, secured by their wrists and ankles with ligatures.[89] Described variously and interchangeably in the press as vagrants, thieves and prostitutes, nightly hauls of twenty to thirty men and women were typical, and on one night alone, 'no less than 26 unhappy females devoted to prostitution'.[90] Most victims were taken up after dark, just as Mary Wheeler had been, but instead of being taken straight to Bridewell, they were confined in 'the Pen' at St Peter's, then examined by the governor, deputy governor and the committee in the morning.[91] St Peter's kept a careful record of the tallies brought in by these officers and forwarded them to the city press, who published them to assure readers that action was being taken.

Between 1786 and 1787, at least eighty-one suspected vagrants were named, examined, whipped and passed at St Peter's. Many had not far to go. Although the home parishes of twenty of them are unrecorded, twenty-four were Bristolians, taken up for being in the 'wrong' parish and unable to give a good account of themselves when an officer came by. A further fourteen came from parishes less than twenty-five miles distant; just six were Irish. Another six were described as ballad singers, including Ann Waters, who was whipped twice for the offence in the space of two months, and eight were 'desperate ill-looking fellows', but we learn little more of most of them. The severity of punishment is equally difficult to assess. Sarah Rogers pleaded her belly and was so spared the lash, but the only concession made to most vagrants in the 1780s was that it was laid on behind closed doors. In the 1760s, by contrast, annual expenses had been claimed by the city sheriffs for 'the hire of carts and horses for whipping felons and vagrants' in the open street. It is not clear how many lashes vagrants were usually given at St Peter's, although in one case at least, it was twelve, the most typical number aboard naval vessels. This was the punishment ordered for four young women from St Phillips, all adjudged 'on the town' and all subjected to twelve lashes. The youngest of them, Elizabeth Sibbol, was just twelve years old.[92]

If poor women became stigmatised as prostitutes and vagrants, it was circumstance and low status, not choice that drove them to it. At port cities like Bristol, where so many men made their living at sea, families were often left destitute for months at a time, for the Jamaica run could take eight months and a slaving expedition a year or more, not to mention absences in the Caribbean because of a discharge or desertion.[93] Ann Smith was taken

---

[89] E. E. Butcher (ed.), *The Bristol Corporation of the Poor*, p. 124.

[90] *FFBJ*, 3, 24 and 31 Dec. 1785; 7 Jan. 1786.

[91] *Bonner and Middleton's Bristol Journal*, 7 Oct. 1786.

[92] *Bonner and Middleton's Bristol Journal*, 6 May 1786, 29 July 1786, 5 and 12 Aug. 1786, 7 Oct. 1786, 16 Dec. 1786, 6 Jan. 1787, 3 Feb. 1787; TNA, T90/150 Sheriff's cravings, 1767.

[93] For examples, see Bristol's muster rolls, BA, SMV 9/3/1/1, 29 Sep. 1750 to 29 Sep. 1751.

up by officers from St Peter's as she walked the streets of St Nicholas, seeking work in January 1773. She had settlement by marriage in the nearby village of Brislington, but her husband 'went to sea, since which she has never seen him or heard from him, nor does she know whether he is living or dead'. Left with two illegitimate children from earlier relationships, and another now a year old, Ann Smith picked up casual work, mostly in domestic service, wherever she could and had drifted into the city because Brislington offered her only agricultural labour.[94] For women like this, selling sexual favours may not have felt much different to any other means of selling their labour. But rhetorical prostitution conjured communities of women economically and exclusively dependent upon their own promiscuity. Susanah Smiley for instance, 'a very low and disorderly person', often seen 'walking the streets late at night with men', was regarded unequivocally by *Felix Farley's Bristol Journal* as having no means of support beyond 'being a common street walker',[95] but that is not to say it was true, or that she traded in sex by preference if alternative forms of work were available. In 1759, Prescilla Colner became involved in the sex trade more by chance than design. As a speculative incomer with few obvious skills to offer the local economy, she first tried to scratch a living as a ballad singer, but drifted into prostitution when a Fisher Lane bawdy-house keeper heard her singing in the street and persuaded her to come inside to earn money having sex with sailors instead.[96] A similar entrée was provided for Lucy Yeats, daughter of a Bristolian jeweller, who'd been propositioned several times by John Bayley, a bawdy-house keeper in Lewins Mead, as she passed by running errands for her father in the summer of 1790. Bayley finally got her into the house with the offer of a drink and when a potential client came by she agreed to go upstairs with him for money.[97]

Colner and Yeats told their stories by becoming informers against keepers of disorderly houses. Susannah Milledge told hers when a magistrate questioned her about the theft of £130 from a farmer in a house on St James's Back while the fair was in full swing in 1785. She had been seen with her 'left hand round his neck and his head was in her bosom'. Born in Stapleton and brought up in the parish poorhouse, Milledge was apprenticed to an aunt in Kingswood for three years but tired of it and ran away to Bristol. There she picked up whatever work she could, most often as a carrier of meat and vegetables in the market, but she augmented her meagre and uncertain pay by selling sex and picking pockets. In 1786 she described herself as twenty-one, and in 1789 said she was thirty; she was sometimes Milledge, sometimes Miller, but to her

---

94 BA, P.St LB/OP/13 (St Lukes, Brislington, vagrancy examinations), Examination of Ann Smith, 22 Jan. 1773.
95 BA, JQS/P/30, Information of Archibald Owen, 16 Jan. 1770 and Francis Bourne, 28 Jan. 1770; FFBJ, 27 Jan. 1770.
96 BA, TC/Adm/Box/13/4, Information of John Roach and others, 22 Jan. 1759 and 19 Feb. 1759; and of Priscilla Colner, 2 March 1759.
97 BA, JQS/P/123, Information of Lucy Yeats, 7 June 1790; Information of Joseph and Joshua Gardener, 24 June 1790; *Sherborne Mercury*, 2 Aug. 1790.

friends she was 'Shuke'. Like many women classified simply as 'prostitutes', Milledge was an economically and socially marginalised adoptive Bristolian who took whatever opportunities for survival she could. Before the magistrate she vigorously denied theft but talked freely if a little ambiguously about her prostitution when he pressed her about the coins and silver buckles found on her when she was taken up at Salisbury. She earned them in Bristol and Bath, she said. 'I had then in my pocket twelve or thirteen guineas, given to me by several gentlemen at a great many times ... the silver buckles I had were given me at Warminster by a gentleman.' And why had she gone to Bath? 'I went there to see a boy flogged; I know him at Bristol. I went into the prison and gave him half a guinea.' Milledge was convicted in 1786 but then spent a year in Newgate awaiting sentencing, during which time a second charge was laid against her (later dropped) for a robbery in the prison. She was sentenced to death in 1787 but reprieved when some undisclosed 'favourable circum-stances' emerged about her, and transported instead for fourteen years after a further two in Newgate.[98]

In Bristol's frequently violent social and economic margins, women like Milledge sometimes risked their lives. Eleanor Dillard in 1748, and a woman known only as Pye Moll in 1762 were both murdered by men they had agreed to have sex with in Fisher Lane. Sarah Smedley was stabbed and wounded by another in 1768. In 1806, Sarah Brown died while being taunted and chased over Brandon Hill by local boys for going with soldiers. 'The damned bitches', one had shouted, 'we'll hunt them out!'[99] Plebeian women, assumed promiscuous by their very class, could not always expect protection from the law. In 1757, Mary Wright went on board the Johnson privateer, then lying in Kingroad, to visit her husband, the ship's steward. He warned her not to go below, but three officers, the surgeon and the ship's owner, John Griffiths, 'pulled and hauled' her down a ladder, made her drink with them and ordered her to 'make herself easy' while her husband was secured on deck. Declaring that 'she was a whore and her husband had consented that they should lie with her', they abused and probably raped Mary Wright for half an hour or more before she could escape. She and her husband both later testified to the assault before magistrates, but the ship sailed for Ireland before anything could be done and there were no prosecutions.[100] Women like these lived rough and precarious lives and may have died young, but they did not always pass unmourned. When one renowned Fisher Lane woman, 'the infamous

[98] BA, JQS/P/101, Information of James Sisney and others, and Examination of Susanna Milledge, 9 Sep. 1786; TNA, HO 42/14, D. Burgess to E. Nepean, 18 April 1789, encl. list of female transports at Newgate; *Bath Chronicle*, 18 Sep. 1787; BA, HO 47/6, Richard Burke to ?, 15 Sep. 1787.

[99] *Bristol Mercury*, 27 Feb. 1815, 6 March 1815; BA, JQS/P/110, Information of Thomas Cole, Thomas Chilcot and Samuel Bryant, 24 Sep. 1787; JQS/P/228, Depositions at inquest on the body of Sarah Brown, 7 Oct. 1806. *Bristol Oracle*, 26 Aug. 1749; FFBJ, 12 June 1762, 12 Dec. 1767, 7 May 1768.

[100] BA, TC Adm/Box/13/2, Information of Mary and James Wright, 23 Sep. 1757.

queen of that neighbourhood, commonly known by the name of Sal Clogg', died in 1757, her funeral drew a large and sympathetic crowd, derided in the press as a 'mob of bullies and cullies'. And when Pye Moll was buried five years later, 'the virtuous sisterhood' as *Felix Farley's Bristol Journal* mockingly called the mourning party, turned out in force, finely dressed in gowns and jackets and sporting a 'profusion of ribbands'.[101]

Unsurprisingly, measures taken by the Corporation of the Poor and the law courts, however formative on the experience of individuals, could make little impact on the broader picture. Early-nineteenth-century public rhetoric was, if anything, even less tolerant in tone. Among the voluntary associations generated during the war was the Prudent Man's Friend Society. Sponsored by some of the leading lights in Bristol society such as Thomas Daniel and Charles Harford, it sought to encourage 'prudence and economy' in the 'labouring classes' and cracked down on the mobile poor, believing many of them to be improvident, work-shy impostors. In its first report in 1813 the Society was pleased to report that while it had ticketed 150 persons for relief, it had convicted and passed 289 others as vagrants.[102] Such hostility to the down-and-out was shared by the social reformer, James Johnson, who considered both casual and vagrant poor posed a significant threat to the city's stability in the years following the Napoleonic wars. The casual poor who habitually 'look up to the parish for relief', were 'exceedingly numerous ... We cannot be mistaken in them – they are clamorous, impudent, lazy and prove a great burthen on the city.' Worse still, he calculated, there were around 380 vagrants regularly begging on the streets, the responsibility for which he placed squarely with the magistrates' failure to properly police and regulate disorderly plebeian premises. 'Places exist *in this city* where young and old, male and female, meet at night (after receiving their daily contributions in the streets) and promiscuously mix and sleep together', he believed. 'It is in these houses that their plans of systematic begging are duly arranged.'[103]

Magistrates did sporadically make raids on suspected disorderly houses, but with mixed success. Even when every ward in the city was systematically investigated in 1752, only thirteen 'lewd women' were captured. Twenty 'girls' were taken up from two houses one evening in 1762, and thirty in a sweep of houses in the out-parish of St Phillips in 1789. In the best recorded search, at St Stephens in the summer of 1767, houses on Temple Back, Marsh Street and Fisher Lane were raided over several weeks, yet only twenty women were taken up, all either discharged the next morning or ordered to a month's hard

---

[101] *FFBJ*, 16 April 1757, 12 June 1762.

[102] *First report of the Prudent Man's Friend Society* (Bristol, 1813), pp. 7–8.

[103] James Johnson, *An Address to the Inhabitants of Bristol on the Subject of the Poor Rates with a View to their Reduction* (Bristol, 1820), pp. 16–22.

labour in the Bridewell.[104] Sometimes attempts to arrest them were foiled by onlookers who appeared not to share the Corporation's zeal for moral reform. One was 'carried off in triumph by a Gang of Fellows, whom she treated well for their pains',[105] and several jumped from upstairs windows during a raid in Marsh Street to be caught and borne away by local men as constables forced an entrance through a rear door.[106] Houses like the one kept by Elizabeth Davis in Lewins Mead, where 'four or five men would come out together and throw stones and break her windows' while those inside shouted and swore back at them, might advertise themselves for suppression, but obtaining evidence against quieter properties was not always easy. In 1749, officers contrived a 'stratagem' to enter a suspicious house but left it without obtaining any evidence of disorder, and in 1760, constable Richard Trevett burst into some bedrooms in a Marsh Street house and found four women 'in a very indecent and disorderly manner, crying and swearing', but did not believe he had witnessed sufficient evidence of prostitution to recommend prosecution. Another constable tried spying on a house from the outside. 'I have seen the men and women go upstairs together as I look through the key hole', he told magistrates, but he could offer no further evidence of unlawful activity.[107]

Nevertheless, a total of 166 prosecutions were recorded against suspected disorderly houses at Bristol between 1720 and 1820, and in the process, an unknown number of women hauled to Bridewell, put to hard labour or whipped as vagrants. Those charged with theft by men who had lost watches, money and pocketbooks while in their company, could expect a spell of one to two years in Newgate or transportation. The keepers of disorderly houses might be placed in the pillory in Wine Street, with papers pinned to their breasts denoting their offence. Between 1740 and 1760 alone, fourteen people were pilloried as keepers of disorderly houses. Labouring women deemed promiscuous and regarded as prostitutes did not only suffer at the hands of the judiciary however. Two men were sent to Bridewell in 1770 for 'chasing' women in Fisher Lane and Tower Lane,[108] and on at least four occasions, hostilities turned into destructive rioting. In Fisher Lane and Marsh Street in 1758, 1762 and 1768, bawdy houses were ransacked and damaged, clothing and bedding stolen or slashed with cutlasses, and women violently attacked

---

[104] *Bath Journal*, 27 Nov. 1749. BA, Town Clerk's letter box, 1748–50 box, bundle 1, Information of John Sheldon and others, 23 July 1750; 1788–89 box, Dr Small to mayor of Bristol, 3 Sep. 1789. FFBJ, 16 Sep. 1752, 20 Feb. 1762, 20 and 27 June 1767, 4, 11 and 18 July 1767, 8 Aug. 1767.
[105] *FFBJ*, 6 June 1752.
[106] *FFBJ*, 20 and 27 June 1767, 4, 11 and 18 July 1767, 8 Aug. 1767.
[107] BA, JQS/P/63, Information of Matthew Good, William Painter and others; *Bath Journal*, 27 Nov. 1749; BA, Town Clerk's box, 1759, bundle 10, Information of Chas Wedmore and others, 18 March, Information of Richard Trevett, 3 April and 23 April 1760.
[108] *FFBJ*, 23 June 1770.

by crowds of sailors and soldiers settling petty differences with them.[109] In the most serious explosion of crowd violence, on bonfire night at Tower Lane in 1792, three bawdy houses were seriously damaged by a crowd shouting 'damn the whores; let us kill them'. Their furniture and even a staircase were pulled onto the pavement outside the Exchange, piled up and ceremoniously set alight.[110]

Civil–Military Relations

Sailors awaiting passage, or carousing between voyages, and soldiers either posted to Bristol or pausing in the course of a march, posed particular problems for the local authorities, and not only because of their relationship with the city's young women. Sailors were always difficult to handle. When a party of them were taken up for disorderly behaviour and lodged in Bridewell in 1745, their comrades simply armed themselves with cutlasses in 'a great Mob', descended on the place, and demanded the prisoners' release. In the ensuing conflict, the Bridewell governor was stabbed and more sailors taken up.[111] We consider the perennial problem of resistance to impressment into the Royal Navy elsewhere in this book, but Bristol was rarely without a military complement of some sort, partly because of the city's convenience as a port of embarkation to Ireland and south Wales, but also because soldiers were required for guarding French POWs at Stapleton during the war years of the 1780s and 1790s.[112] Bristol had no regular barracks and soldiers were therefore billeted upon pubs and lodging houses throughout the city.

For very obvious reasons, access to trained troops was useful to the mayor and magistrates when civil disturbance threatened, but popular antagonism to military interference in civil affairs invariably made their deployment difficult. As the corporation discovered when it sanctioned their use against protesting civilians on Bristol Bridge in 1793, the repercussions could be long-lasting and damaging. In 1770 a brief panic was created by the return to Bristol of several merchant ships from Danzig, where there had been an outbreak of plague. The mayor was determined to quarantine them at King Road, and to ensure that none of the crew found their way overboard and into the city he requested two troops of infantry to patrol the shoreline. The War Office rebuffed him. In such instances it was always preferable to use the civil power, he was told, but if that should prove insufficient, he should call

---

[109] BA, Town Clerk's box, 1758, bundle 6, Information of Chastity Fidoe, Sarah Bird and Francis Bourne, 7 Dec. 1758; *FFBJ*, 25 Oct. 1762 and 19 July 1768.

[110] *FFBJ*, 10 Nov. 1792; 13 April 1793; BA, JQS/P/129, Information of Alice King, Isabella Hines, Sophia Taunton, Mary Davis, Elizabeth Nelson and others, 10 Nov. 1792.

[111] *Daily Gazetteer*, 10 Sep. 1745.

[112] For example, in March and February 1783, the East Devon militia and the 61st and 75th Regiments of Foot were all billeted in Bristol on POW guard duty. See *FFBJ*, 1 March 1783.

upon cavalry as 'the most effectual for that purpose, with less danger to the lives of individuals than is to be apprehended from Foot using musquets or bayonets'.[113]

But all soldiers, whether mounted or on foot, were widely regarded as lawless, violent, prone to heavy drinking and criminality, and a drain upon provisions; traits bad enough in themselves but aggravated by easy access to weaponry. Violent incidents involving soldiers and unarmed civilians recurred frequently throughout the period but particularly during the first half of the eighteenth century.[114] In 1734, three sentinels in Colonel Montague's regiment beat a shopkeeper to death at Pithay Gate and one of them, identified as a 'Scotchman' to boot, swung for it on St Michael's Hill.[115] In 1737, two drunken recruits from Brigadier Handasyde's regiment were committed to Newgate after running amok on St James's Back, swinging their swords at passers-by, cutting one man's finger off, hacking another across the head and slashing the clothes of a third.[116] The following summer, an officer from Brigadier Harrison's regiment waited on the mayor and demanded billets for his men who would be arriving the next day. The mayor refused. It was too short notice, the assize was about to open and it would be inappropriate and unprecedented to have armed soldiers in the city at the same time. When the officer marched his men into Bristol regardless, the mayor prevailed upon the assize judge to persuade the regiment to leave, but only after requiring the mayor to welcome them back as soon as the assize was over.[117] Trouble erupted once again three months later. Soldiers protesting the eviction of an unruly private from the Fountain Tavern in High Street, retaliated by dragging an inn servant to the Guard House and threatening to shoot any townsmen that interfered. Magistrates arrived and demanded they release him. 'We are not to be governed by a standing army and I hope we never shall be', declared one, leaving the *Gloucester Journal* to comment that the mayor and aldermen had 'acted like men of spirit' in defending the rights of the town.[118]

At the heart of the issue here was the right of the civil power to control the number of soldiers being lodged in the city at any one time and to police them once they had arrived. The mayor and magistrates were frequently at odds with innkeepers without Lawford's Gate over whether the economic burden should fall upon the city or the Gloucestershire out-parishes.[119] During the

---

[113] BA, TC/Adm/Box/24/15, Craggs Close to Thomas Deane, 17 and 18 Oct. 1770.

[114] For example, soldiers were associated with a violent series of robberies around Totterdown and Bedminster in May 1740, and suspected of a murder on Durdham Down in July. In 1755, a drummer recruiting men to the marines was taken up for cutting people with his sword near the Drawbridge. *Sherborne Mercury*, 25 May 1740, 8 July 1740; *FFBJ*, 6 Dec. 1755.

[115] *London Journal*, 21 Sep. 1734.

[116] *Sherborne Mercury*, 8 Nov. 1737.

[117] *Sherborne Mercury*, 29 Aug. 1738.

[118] *Gloucester Journal*, 28 Nov. 1738.

[119] BA, Mayor's letter book, John Foy to Henry Fox, 5 Dec. 1747.

Revolutionary wars, troops might disembark from Ireland with little prior notice, putting a high demand on billets. In the harsh winter of 1794–95, the mayor appealed to the War Office for better regulation. Some 16,000 regular soldiers had recently been sent through Bristol from Ireland, he claimed, their officers often assuming powers of governance in direct competition with the civil authorities. In recent weeks, men of the 83rd Regiment had only been prevented from ejecting the resident militia from the Guard House by a direct intervention from the magistrates, who reminded them the building was corporation property.

> The 17th merely in passing through the place, gave such orders as would, if they had not been disobeyed by the troops here, have thrown the city into the greatest confusion, and would probably have occasioned the worst of consequences. The orders were for the militia here to beat to arms against some few troublesome people who had been drinking and who had in some measure interrupted the Officer of the Regiment. The drums of the 17th Regiment actually beat to arms, but happily for the tranquillity of the place, the commanding officer of the militia … did not obey their orders.

Sudden influxes of soldiers returning from foreign service also sparked fears of infectious diseases spreading amongst the civilian population. When the 110th arrived from Cork in 1794, they were so wracked with fever that a quayside warehouse had to be requisitioned as a temporary quarantine hospital. Within days, 13 of the 122 men who disembarked were dead and a further 80 had absconded into the city in an attempt to avoid the fever. Many of them were now 'wandering about the town in a wretched condition, without hats and badly clothed', and the mayor charged the War Office with abandoning them and threatening the stability of the city. In such cases, he wrote, 'men of almost every regiment have been left behind, who are constantly making application for relief and are left for some time a nuisance on the town, no one knowing where their regiment are gone to'.[120] Of greatest concern were the large numbers of demobbed Irish recruits who became stranded at Bristol while trying to obtain passage home. After a serious mutiny of Irish Fencibles at Pill in 1795 over the alleged non-payment of bounties, district military commander, General Rooke, urged the army to expedite the removal of Irish soldiers in transit, 'as by repeating their situations and distresses to the common people here, I fear may produce a riot as I assure you I find the mob of this city too much inclined to'.[121] The War Office had already been warned by one of its recruiting captains that the labouring poor at Bristol were proving hard work. Twenty-two of the fifty men signed up by Captain Wilmott in 1794 deserted before he could muster them, and those that remained were in 'such a turbulent, rioting, mutinous state, up to every Jacobin principle, which compelled me to dispose of them to the Bristol Regiment – or I do

120 BA, TC/Adm/Box/46/9, Mayor of Bristol to William Wyndham, 22 Dec. 1794.
121 TNA, WO/1092, General Rooke to Lewis, 19 July 1795; *Bath Journal*, 20 July 1795.

suppose the rascals would near all have deserted, being determined against going to Chatham'.[122]

Military commanders repeatedly accused the civil power of discriminating against their men. After a series of fights between townsmen, watchmen and soldiers from the Royal Lancashire militia in 1810, five soldiers were arrested and committed to Newgate to answer charges of assault. No townsmen were taken up. After spending several weeks in the cells, the soldiers were brought into court but immediately dismissed for want of prosecution. Their furious commanding officer demanded their accusers be named and made to forfeit their recognisances, only to discover that none had been taken. Stiff letters of protest were fired off to the War Office and an explanation demanded from the mayor by the secretary of state. 'The watchmen of this city have insulted soldiers and even sergeants when going quietly along the streets at night in hopes of making them retaliate', concluded the CO, 'that they might have opportunities of taking them to the watch house for no persons are released from thence or from the gaol of this city, although proved innocent, without paying fees.'[123]

One of the most serious breakdowns in relations between the civil and military authorities took place two years later when, once again, public hostility to Irish regiments played a critical role. In August 1812 Edward Irwin, a sergeant in the Leitrim militia, was attacked in St James's church-yard by two men, one of whom shouted 'Damn you and your Irish regiment', while the other cut him in the back of the legs, hamstringing him so that he was unable to walk. Irwin's CO criticised the magistrates' lukewarm attempts to catch the perpetrators and warned the mayor that 'a considerable degree of irritation has been produced in the minds of the men by insults and prov-ocations received by them from the inhabitants of Bristol'. Despite a £50 reward being offered, no suspects could be found. When a witness finally came forward with an allegation that two men from the East Middlesex militia had seen Swain on the ground but offered him no assistance, the mayor suppressed it for fear it 'might tend to cause a dispute between the two regiments'.[124] Sidmouth wrote to the mayor, reminding him of his respon-sibilities and to enquire 'whether there are any indications ... amongst the lower orders of people in Bristol, of such a spirit as that which seems to have led to it'. The mayor assured him that there was not, and that Addington's reminder that it was the responsibility of the magistrates to 'promote a good understanding between all descriptions of persons belonging to that city', was unnecessary.[125]

---

[122] TNA, WO/1081, W. C. Wilmott to Lewis, 5 July 1794.

[123] BA, TC/Adm/Box/62/7, Lieutenant Colonel J. Plumbe to Secretary of State for War, 13 June 1810.

[124] BA, TC/Adm/Box/64/22, Information of Edward Swain and others, 14 Aug. 1812.

[125] BA, TC/Adm/Box/63/15, Addington to John Wilcox, 16 Sep. 1812; TC/Adm/Box/64/22, Wilcox to Addington, 23 Sep. 1812.

Simmering discontent amongst the soldiers escalated in November when a Leitrim ensign named McRobin became involved in an altercation with a townsman on the Drawbridge one evening, and then proceeded to beat a young boy unconscious with a stick for singing an offensive song and not leaving quickly enough when ordered. McRobin was taken into custody for the assault and lodged in the Bridewell by a constable who loudly expressed his delight at locking up an Irishman. 'You had better mind what you're at', the constable is supposed to have told him, 'you're now in a Christian and peaceable country … if you can't do without fighting, you had better go over to Ireland among the rebels.' The following morning 'near two hundred' militia men with drawn bayonets in their hands forced their way into the Bridewell, seized the keys from the warden's wife and rescued McRobin. He turned himself in again ten minutes later, and after agreeing to recompense the boy he had assaulted, was freed by the mayor with a promise that he would not be prosecuted. This expedient decision was not universally welcomed. A few days later as the Leitrim's drummers were beating a tattoo, they were,

> most wantonly attacked by the mob and grossly insulted, such as in the vilest terms calling them damned Irish Rebels etc. The Guard of the town was likewise attacked and in such a violent and abusive manner that unless the officers had interfered, and the men themselves had been unwilling to hurt the populace, very serious consequences might have ensued.[126]

The Labouring Crowd

Collective forms of disorder were not conceptualised solely in terms of riot and affray. Labouring people also found themselves at odds both with their employers and the city authorities in their workplaces. Collective bargaining over the terms and conditions of labour was one aspect of daily life in which workers were able to go on the offensive, and in which we might see them less as the subjects of authority and more as active agents in shaping power relationships. Later in this book we discuss major industrial disputes amongst the weaving and mining communities, mostly centred without Lawford's Gate in the out-parish of St George and in Kingswood. But in Bristol's broadly based economy, workers' combinations were by no means confined to these key industries. In the one hundred years between 1726 and 1826, it is possible to trace at least sixty-nine trade disputes serious enough to come to the notice of either the newspaper press or the law courts. As Malcolm Chase and others have demonstrated, the 1790s saw the most 'prodigious increase in the incidence of strikes' in the country as a whole, and Bristol is no exception to this

[126] BA, TC/Adm/Box/64/14, Proceedings of a court of enquiry, 4 Nov. 1812; Major General J. Gordon Cuming to the Secretary of State for War, 8 Nov. 1812; Postmaster General to mayor of Bristol, 14 Nov. 1812.

rule. The incitement was there. In the opinion of the shipwright John Gast, Bristol was 'notorious for overbearing and despotic masters'.[127]

Discounting the riotous incursions of weaver and collier crowds in the 1720s and 1730s, Bristol's most assertive workers in the first half of the century were those connected to seafaring and its related trades. In 1746, 2000 sailors marched to the top of Brandon Hill to protest an attempted wage reduction, then 'came in a formidable body into the city and patrolled the streets with their colours flying, armed with bludgeons, and huzzaing in a very loud manner'. Key trades like these, able to quickly mobilise large numbers of workers, were in a powerful bargaining position, and in this case prevented four privateers from leaving the harbour until a settlement was reached. In May 1768, encouraged by similar actions on the Mersey, the Tyne and the Thames and at the height of the national agitation for 'Wilkes and Liberty', the sailors struck again, this time for a rise of five shillings a month. At least one West Indies merchantman was boarded and detained at the quay, but since they were able to rally only forty men to join them, they were successfully resisted, 'the merchants being determined not to submit to such illegal proceedings'.[128]

Illegal or otherwise, magistrates were wary of taking such hugely supported trades as these to law. They suffered no such reticence when it came to smaller groups of artisan journeymen however, and they moved confidently against the city's tailors when they struck work in 1755. Declaring an intention to fine and gaol all striking workers under the conspiracy laws, at least one journeyman tailor was committed to the quarter session for assaulting blackleg labourers during a later wage dispute in 1762. The gunpowder manufacturer, William Dyer, nipped in the bud a combination amongst his workers by threatening them with prosecution in 1760, yet despite suppression, trade organisations continued to flourish; indeed the tailors union came out again in 1773, 1775, 1777, 1781 and 1790 before more widespread stoppages affected the city later in the decade.[129]

The watershed came in 1792: the first year in which the city could be said to have experienced a cross-trade strike wave. Painters, tilers, plasterers, sail-cloth dressers, masons, bricklayers, pipe-makers, plumbers, staymakers,

---

[127] Malcolm Chase, *Early Trade Unionism: Fraternity, Skill and the Politics of Labour* (Aldershot, 2000), p. 74; Iorworth Prothero, *Artisans and Politics in Early Nineteenth-Century London: John Gast and his Times* (London, 1979), p. 16.

[128] *FFBJ*, 14 May 1768. See also Richard Sheldon, 'The London Sailors' Strike of 1768', in *An Atlas of Industrial Protest in Britain, 1750–1990*, ed. Andrew Charlesworth et al. (London, 1996), pp. 12–17.

[129] *FFBJ*, 3 and 10 May 1755, 15 Oct. 1762, 17 April 1773, 1, 22 and 29 May 1773, 17 July 1773; BRL, Manuscript diary of William Dyer, 2 vols, 1744–1801, 3 Oct. 1760; Latimer, II, 404; Steve Poole, 'Introduction', in *A City Built Upon the Water*, p. 26. Journeyman curriers, wig-makers and bakers also struck work during the 1760s: C. R. Dobson, *Masters and Journeymen: A Prehistory of Industrial Relations, 1717–1800* (London, 1980), p. 159; *FFBJ*, 25 Jan. 1766, 8 Feb. 1766.

bakers, shoemakers and tailors all struck work that year with varying degrees of success, but it was the impact made by these disputes on the Kingswood colliers that most caused the authorities alarm. In August the colliers rose, stopped the pits and demanded a wage increase of two shillings, 'encouraged as is supposed, by the success of the shoemakers and other tradesmen'. The military commander, George Munro, was concerned that 'this alarming combination' had 'met with no opposition from the magistrates of the county of Gloucester, nor has the Corporation of this city apparently taken any measures', and that if the colliers were successful, mine-owners would use the dispute as 'a pretence to raise the price of coals'. If that happened, 'the consequences for this city will really be alarming; very numerous and extensive glass houses, very large copper works, lead works, distilleries, and other concerns that consume an immense quantity of coal', might face 'a total suspension of their business ... One glass house will stop work this morning and as the colliers will suffer no coal to be brought into the city, three more will stop on Monday should this combination continue.'[130]

No legal action was taken against the colliers, but the mayor, John Noble, placed the blame on 'the great employ that is afforded to all labourers in this city from the vast undertakings at New Buildings'. A buoyant economy and the high demand for labour had given artisans unaccustomed levels of confidence. The colliers had 'paraded through the city', causing general alarm, and now 'the journeyman bakers have also refused to work and I hear many other trades will follow so that I fear the civil power may eventually stand in need of the aid of the military'.[131] Repressive legal action, when it came, targeted the less volatile artisan trades. Two cases, one against three brick-moulders, for breach of contract, and the other against six tailors, reached the assize in September, but although convictions were secured, no exemplary sentencing followed. The brick-moulders were bound over, ordered to return to work at their old rate of pay and threatened with two years' hard labour if they reoffended, while the tailors were released in exchange for a public apology in the press to their master, Fortunatus Hagley. Almost simultaneously, a confederation of master shoemakers who had been threatening legal action against their own workers unexpectedly gave way, drawing howls of protest from the newspapers. *Felix Farley's* chastised them for not going to law. If they had, 'the alarming spirit of combination which now so universally prevails in this city amongst workers of every description would have been completely prevented'. For *Sarah Farley's* journal the masters' failure was critical, for 'in consequence of this circumstance, other journeymen are made uneasy and threaten a combination for the like purpose'.[132]

[130] TNA, HO 42/21, Evan Nepean to George Munro, 9 Aug. 1792.
[131] BA, Common Council letter book, John Noble to Henry Dundas, 13 Aug. 1792.
[132] FFBJ, 14 April 1792, 5 May 1792, 18 Aug. 1792, 20 Oct. 1792; *Sarah Farley's Bristol Journal*, 25 Aug. 1792.

In many instances, disputes were fought politely but assertively by both sides through the placing of paid advertisements in the newspaper press. This practice was developed during the later years of the eighteenth century as the newspaper press itself became increasingly influential in the framing of opinion in an expanding public sphere. The terms under which the tailors' strikes of 1773 and 1796 were played out, for example, can be traced in some detail from the very public argument of masters and journeymen in the city's papers. For more than four months in 1773, the two sides argued over the profitability of the trade, the ability of the masters to pay a fair price for labour, and the rights and wrongs of exposing profit margins in public. In 1796, the dispute was over the imposition of piecework, an issue laid before the public by the journeymen as one of value for money:

> In regard to an offer of piece work from the masters in our trade, we well know a discerning public will never suffer it for these reasons: when a man works by the day, duty is done both to the customer and the employer; when done by the piece, the employer receives every advantage that hurry can give him, the customer every disadvantage from the work being slighted.[133]

Journeymen's language in disputes following the politically charged years of the 1790s bridged a divide between obsequious courtesy and robust egalitarianism. 'We approach you with diffidence and respect, becoming the station we hold', began the carpenters as they pressed a wage claim in 1806, but 'permit us to speak the free and undisguised language of MEN'.[134]

In the early years of the nineteenth century, broader languages in which trade specificities were submerged in the shared interests of social class began to find voice. When a bill was introduced into parliament in 1806 to suppress unions amongst shoemakers, the language of the journeymen in organising against it was clearly intended to unite the interests of all skilled workers in the city. Shoemakers urged 'journeyman mechanics at large' to contest any proposed legislation that might 'materially affect the whole class of working mechanics in the Imperial kingdom and utterly subvert their rights and privileges as Britons'. A similar appeal was launched by London unionists in 1816 'To all Mechanics and Artisans in the City of Bristol', and pledged to oppose the introduction of 'all machinery by which manual labour is dispensed with'. A delegate meeting of united trades was proposed, and a nationally coordinated petitioning movement against labour-saving machinery, 'exercising the charter of your birthrights as Englishmen'.[135]

---

[133] *FFBJ*, 17 April 1773, 1 and 29 May 1773, 17 July 1773, 7 Aug. 1773; *Bristol Gazette*, 17, 24 and 31 March 1796, 5 May 1796; *Sarah Farley's Bristol Journal*, 26 March 1796, 2 April 1796.

[134] *Bristol Mirror*, 21 June 1806.

[135] *Bristol Mirror*, 19 April 1806; BA, TC/Adm/Box/66/23, 'To all Mechanics and Artisans in the City of Bristol', handbill (Bristol, Nov. 1816).

These public exhibitions of rational and reasoned argument should not persuade us that disputes in the artisan trades were orderly in all respects. Strikers were occasionally prosecuted for assault and riot, particularly when attempts were made to enforce unity and prevent the introduction of black-leg labour. Incidents of this kind sometimes made use of traditional and customary shaming rituals: rough music and 'horsing', 'riding the cow-tang' or cool-staffing – that is, exposing transgressors to public ridicule. In 1738, the Kingswood colliers enforced trade solidarity by giving strike-breakers 'a sound Drubbing and riding the Cow-Tang', then attacking the house of one of the city sheriffs, where they caught hold of a servant and 'put him on a Cow-Tang' too.[136] Eleven sawyers were committed to the quarter session in 1752 after they made a public spectacle of a strike-breaker, 'put him upon a string and carried it about in triumph'. But charivari was not restricted to 'pre-modern' disputes, as another would-be strike-breaker, the shipwright James Tuckfield, discovered during a bitter strike in the dockyards in 1826. Tuckfield was picked up one morning on his way to work when the union had been in dispute for three months, forcibly hoisted onto a pole, and paraded through the principle streets and then a number of shipyards between Queen Square and the Hotwell. Bruised and mocked at every turn, and with the word 'Black' scrawled across the back of his jacket, Tuckfield's disgrace was richly symbolic. In the Hotwell Road, 'they met a chimney sweeper carrying a soot bag which one of the mob seized and immediately rubbed the bag upon [his] face and back so as completely to disguise his person'. This performative ritual only ended when his two hundred tormentors carried him up onto Pile Hill where they made him 'promise them that he would stick to the society and not to go to work again unless they all went together'. The severity with which the case was pursued at the quarter session may reflect the compara-tively large number of magistrates who either owned shipyards, like George and Abraham Hilhouse, or had direct interests in shipping as the Merchant Venturers. A number of striking shipwrights, all identified by Tuckfield in court, received gaol sentences of up to nine months with hard labour. And it was, one suspects, the disorderly nature of the offence as much as the fact that it arose from a combination, which ensured conviction.[137]

The use of the courts against artisan unions was piecemeal under the Combination Acts between 1799 and 1824, and in the years immediately following repeal. However, in common with other parts of Britain, the rela-tive ease with which unionists could be prosecuted under these consolidating

---

[136] *The Colliers of Kingswood in an Uproar, Or, an Account of their present Mobbing, and Preventing Coal being brought to this City* ... (Bristol, 1738).
[137] BA, JQS/P/588, Information of James Tuckfield and others, 30 Sep. 1826. The case is analysed in detail in Martin Gorsky, 'James Tuckfield's "Ride": Combination and Social Drama in Early Nineteenth-Century Bristol', *Social History*, 19:3 (1994), 319–38. For other disputes involving quayside and dockyard trades, and particularly the shipwrights, see Poole 'Introduction', in *A City built upon the Water*, pp. 26–30.

laws tended to ensure conviction whenever they were used. In 1806, a carpenter Edward Symons was fined and sent to Bridewell for two months with hard labour following conviction by a single magistrate sitting in petty sessions and on the evidence of a single witness. The same fate befell three coopers in 1809. In 1818 eight journeyman potters were sent to Bridewell for a month when they struck work to demand the reinstatement of a dismissed colleague. Workers convicted under these laws might take their cases on appeal to the quarter sessions but were unlikely to meet with success.[138] As employers became more sophisticated in combatting artisan unions, often forming associations of their own to present a more united response, journeymen occasionally tried using the courts themselves to prosecute masters for forming illegal combinations. The plasterers met with limited success when they tried this tactic in 1815. Magistrates were sympathetic to the charge that employers had formed a 'combination to reduce wages', but did not prevent them from imposing one. The days in which magistrates felt comfortable in fixing fair levels of pay under a moral economy of industrial relations were clearly long gone.[139]

Mary Milford, Henry Lippincott and Charles Houlden Walker

In our previous chapter, we alluded to the close proximity in which both wealthy and poor Bristolians were still living at the start of the nineteenth century. Common access to Bristol's crowded public streets, taverns and open spaces meant that the divergent lives of all the city's classes and interests intersected regularly. Often these intersections passed without incident, but on occasion they did not, and it is then that some of the inequalities of agency and influence that characterised daily life in the city were most graphically exposed. We'll conclude this section with a short exploration of some of the ways in which these overlapping social relationships were experienced, by taking a measure of the intersecting lives of three early-nineteenth-century Bristol residents, Mary Milford, Henry Lippincott and Charles Walker.

Milford was a Welsh migrant, seventeen years old in 1809 and recently arrived with her father on the packet boat from Cardiff. Before her mother died five years earlier, Mary had received some elementary schooling in Taunton, but her father's quest for work in subsequent years kept them on the move to London, Cardiff and Bristol, where the family had relatives on her mother's side. After a few weeks living with her father, first in lodgings in Earl Street and then in Trenchard Street, Mary took lodgings of her own with a Mrs Evans on Welsh Back. Here she shared a room with Mary Jones, a young woman who had come to Bristol from rural Gloucestershire

---

[138] FFBJ, 19 July 1806, 4 May 1809; Bristol Mirror, 5 Dec. 1818.

[139] The progress of this strike and the legal arguments connected with it can be traced in FFBJ, 7, 14 and 28 Jan. 1815.

six weeks earlier seeking work as a nurse maid. Although allegedly Jones had a reputation as 'a woman given to the town',[140] Mary Milford befriended her and spent time with her circle of acquaintants in some of the city's many open spaces, taverns and coffee houses.[141] As independent young women with few employable skills, Jones and Milford's experience of life in early-nineteenth-century Bristol was far from unique. Like many others before and after them, they were drawn to the city by the economic and social opportunities it appeared to offer. They lived on their wits, with little property, in bare rooms at temporary addresses, taking work where they found it, and leaving little record of their lives, loves and struggles.

Life at the opposite end of the social spectrum was somewhat different. Sir Henry Camm Lippincott was thirty-three in 1809, the only son of a prosperous tobacco merchant and former MP for Bristol. Through his father's death when he was just four years old, Lippincott inherited a baronetcy, a fine town house in Portland Square, and another, his main residence, in Clifton, Stoke House. There he devoted his time to breeding racehorses, acting as a turnpike commissioner and commanding the North Gloucestershire militia. Although Lippincott's social experience of the city was about as far from Mary Milford's as it is possible to imagine, many of the public spaces in which each of them moved were common.

Our third character is Charles Houlden Walker, a Clare Street solicitor who acquired a reputation for defending some of the city's less privileged men and women in the city's law courts. In 1802, Walker had taken the case of a young basket-maker's daughter named Mary Ellis, a young woman seduced, made pregnant and smartly abandoned by the Broad Street auctioneer, Samuel Alexander. To ensure the case came to trial, Walker arranged to have Ellis taken into protective custody, but Alexander sent a servant, Snelling, to prevent it. There was a violent altercation after which, at the city sessions, Snelling managed to get Walker, Ellis's legal guardian John Morgan, and her brother and father all fined and gaoled for assault. Walker protested that it was Snelling who had assaulted them, but the magistrates dismissed the charge on a technicality. Walker next appealed to the Tory MP, Bragge-Bathurst, to use his influence to secure their release, but the city bench, led by Mayor James Harvey and Alderman John Noble, stood firm in their defence of Alexander's interests. As soon as his six months in Newgate were up, Walker successfully laid charges against Snelling for assault and perjury, in Kings Bench rather than the Bristol courts, 'in order to obtain an impartial trial'. While Snelling absconded to evade punishment, Walker turned his attention to the aldermanic bench, applying to them for compensation and the repayment of his fine. However, they refused to accept any mistake had

---

[140] *Evening Mail*, 27 April 1810.
[141] Details of Mary Milford's life have been taken from Charles Houlden Walker, *A Report of the Trial of Sir H. C. Lippincott, Bart., on a Charge of Rape Committed on the Person of Mary Milford, Spinster, Aged 17 Years* (London, 1810).

been made and when Walker appealed to the Recorder, Vicary Gibbs, he was rebuffed once again, 'because it was incompatible with his situation to interpose in any manner that might tend to control the decisions of magistrates at their sessions'. This experience was formative in Walker's development as a staunch critic of the exclusive privileges of the corporation and the practice of 'a *local* jurisprudence where private prejudices are but too often gratified under the veil of an administration of public justice'.[142]

Milford, Lippincott and Walker may be said to illustrate something of the divergent social strength and agency of the classes who made up Bristol's population at a moment in time. Although none of them appears personally in standard histories, the cultural and political interplay between the interests they embodied – the rarely encountered yet numerous labouring poor, the propertied elite, and the radical/liberal meritocratic middling sort – is a central concern of this book. By chance in April 1809, this trio were thrown together as key protagonists in a courtroom struggle that tested the influence and reputation of each of them.

On a Sunday afternoon shortly before Christmas, Mary Jones and Mary Milford set out across College Green to visit Jones's sister who was in service at a house adjoining the cathedral.[143] They were held up briefly near the mayor's chapel by Sir Henry and a fellow soldier, Captain Gregory, who had met Jones before and wanted them to call in at Gregory's nearby lodgings. Once there, Jones went into an adjacent bedroom with Gregory 'to help him dress', leaving Lippincott and Milford alone together in another room. According to Milford, Lippincott locked the door, offered her money for sex (which she refused) and then pinioned her wrists behind her and raped her on the couch. Milford testified to the assault before the mayor, John Wilcox, ten days later and was then examined by three surgeons who confirmed injuries consistent with a violent sexual assault. Wilcox issued warrants for the arrest of Lippincott for rape, Gregory as his accomplice, and Mary Jones 'on a violent suspicion of aiding Sir Henry in perpetrating the crime'. Charles Houlden Walker took the case for the prosecution.

Wilcox and his fellow magistrates were conscious of the implications however. If they charged Lippincott with the capital offence rather than a mere suspicion of felony, it would be difficult to grant him bail, leaving them no alternative but to incarcerate him in the damp and draughty cells of Newgate until the assize opened in April. The socially inferior Mary Jones, moreover, had already been admitted to bail. Town clerk Samuel Worrall wrote to Vicary Gibbs, the Recorder, 'The public are of course very much interested in this unfortunate affair and my wish is the magistrates should

---

[142] C. H. Walker, *An Appeal to the Public on the Conduct of David Evans Esq, late Mayor, and John Noble and James Harvey Esqs, Aldermen of Bristol* (Bristol, 1807); *Gloucester Journal*, 31 Oct. 1803.

[143] Unless otherwise stated, this account of Lippincott's trial is taken from Walker, *Report of the Trial of Sir H. C. Lippincott*.

so conduct themselves as not to be open to any reflection as to either the severity or lenity of their conduct.' Gibbs told him they had little choice but to commit Lippincott on the capital charge, and if they felt bail was appropriate, they should put it before a judge in chambers. Their blushes were spared however because Lippincott absconded for four months, then surrendered himself to the court as the assize opened. Only Charles Houlden Walker appears to have made any effort to find him.[144]

By the time the trial began, the cases against Gregory and Jones had been dropped, and Jones had agreed to appear as a witness for the defence. Lippincott did not deny locking the door and admitted he and Milford had been 'playing together' in the room. Mary Jones insisted that she and Gregory had heard no sounds of a struggle and the surgeons agreed that Milford's injuries could not have been ten days old when examined. Worse still, the defence counter-charged Milford with attempted extortion; that she had only brought the prosecution in revenge for Lippincott's refusal to pay for her silence. Gregory did further damage to Milford's reputation by claiming she had allowed him to 'put my hand in her bosom' and that Lippincott had not wanted to have sex with her anyway because she 'stank of herrings and tar like the devil'. Some of Walker's witnesses could not be produced (he suspected they had been paid off) and others had changed their initial statements before the magistrates and, like Mary Jones, appeared instead for the defence.

After seven hours of evidence, the Recorder directed the jury. Milford's allegations were unconvincing, he suggested, on a number of counts. First, she had initially tried to aggravate the offence by claiming to be two years younger than she actually was; second, if she had cried out, somebody would surely have heard her, so close to College Green; third, Lippincott had surrendered himself voluntarily to the court; fourth, Milford had recently been in London where a scandalous extortion case concerning the Duke of Gordon was the talk of the town; and fifth, she had gone voluntarily to Gregory's lodgings. If it were not that Lippincott's life was now at stake from Milford's allegations, Gibbs averred, 'I should be induced to treat the idea as ridiculous'. The jury acquitted Lippincott in a matter of minutes and without leaving their seats. In the days that followed, Walker was incensed by assertions in a number of local and national newspapers that he had been party to a 'conspiracy to extort money' from Lippincott, a man of unimpeachable reputation. The idea that a poor young woman like Milford should have thought such a charge practicable was absurd, he maintained. 'Let it be remembered who the acquitted baronet is – a man resident on or owner of a large estate scarcely two miles from the spot where he was arraigned for his life – arraigned in the

---

[144] For correspondence with Gibbs, see BA, TC/Adm/Box/62/7, Samuel Worrall to Vicary Gibbs, 29 Dec. 1809; Gibbs to Worrall, 4 Jan. 1810.

very heart of his connexions, and this too by a poor girl having nothing but her presumed conscious truth to support her in the conflict.'[145]

Lippincott's friends were not yet done. While Lippincott retreated quietly back to his estate, Captain Gregory publicly confronted Mayor Wilcox in the lobby of the Theatre Royal, twice calling him 'a damned blackguard and a dirty scoundrel' for ordering their arrest. Assuming he was being challenged to defend his honour in a duel, Wilcox wisely complained to Gibbs that Gregory had slandered the collective reputation of the entire judiciary. Gibbs obtained a ruling in the Court of King's Bench that Gregory must make a full apology to Wilcox and Gregory agreed to do so, but only after prevaricating over the venue for the hearing and having it removed to Somerset. Gregory had no more confidence in the impartiality of the city courts than Walker had felt in 1802, and argued that he should not have to defend himself again in them. But since he was, in any case, unable to pay the corporation's £600 legal bill, he was obliged to serve two months in the Marshalsea for debt.[146]

Charles Houlden Walker, now more confirmed than ever in his conviction that the unaccountable interests of Bristol's elite classes should be challenged and reformed, would be a prominent critic of the corporation for the next twenty years. He will reappear in this book as an advocate of electoral independence, local government reform, and as defence counsel for the Reform Bill rioter, William Clarke, on trial for his life in 1832. Of Mary Milford and her ruined reputation, we will hear no more.

[145] Walker, *Report of the Trial of Sir H. C. Lippincott.*
[146] *Kentish Gazette*, 1 Feb. 1811; *Bristol Mirror*, 11 May 1811; *The Times*, 3 July 1811; *Taunton Courier*, 29 Aug. 1811; *Hampshire Telegraph*, 18 Nov. 1811.

3

Authority, Class and Clientage
in Bristol Politics

Writing to the Quaker merchant Joseph Harford in April 1780, Edmund Burke talked of his chances of again representing Bristol in the forthcoming general election. He was reluctant because he stood 'merely upon publick ground' and did not have 'what is called a natural Interest in that City'.[1] By this he meant his appeal rested solely upon his reputation in the public sphere, what he achieved in the 'Business of Parliament' for his country and his constituents. In the short time he had been involved in Bristol politics he had been unable to build up the networks that were so useful in eighteenth-century politics: close contacts with important intermediaries in Bristol, links to clubs and associations, a familiarity with those channels of government patronage that would favour his friends and build up dependencies. 'My circumstances', Burke explained, 'have prevented me from cultivating the private regards of the Citizens so much, as in common Course, might have been expected from me.'[2] In a hierarchical society in which whom you knew and whom you could influence mattered, such contacts were often the fabric of parliamentary politics. At the very least they undergirded the more turbulent shoals of political favour generated in the public domain.

Burke's comment encapsulates one of the central issues that have engaged historians of eighteenth-century politics *tout court*: the degree to which those politics might be regarded as intensely oligarchical, client based and local in orientation; the extent to which changes in the public sphere, in the modes of communication and culture, created extra-local identities that themselves had political traction.

Sixty years ago the convention was that British politics were intensely oligarchical and elite directed, and Bristol was offered as a classic case. In *The Structure of Politics at the Accession of George III*, Sir Lewis Namier used Bristol to repudiate the notion that the larger urban constituencies were ideologically independent and hostile to oligarchy. In his view Bristol politics was so dominated by merchant groups and their clubs that they were able to carve

---

[1] John A. Woods (ed.), *The Correspondence of Edmund Burke* (10 vols, Cambridge, 1958–1978), IV, 221.
[2] *Ibid.*, IV, 221.

up the political representation of the city to their own satisfaction, frequently agreeing to share the representation of this two-member constituency city in ways that denied voter choice. This view persisted well into the 1980s. 'Control was securely in the hands of the long-established political clubs, led by a comparatively small number of men from the propertied and mercantile classes', wrote Doug Fisher of turn-of-the-century Bristol.[3] The thousands of freemen and freeholders eligible to vote, some 3500 in 1713 and over 6000 a century later, largely adhered to this arrangement for the venal benefits it would bring, in terms of electoral treats, freemen fees, jobs and charity.

There is a lot to be said for this view, at least in terms of the ordained results of Bristol elections. Of the forty general or by-elections that were held between 1690 and 1832, seventeen (43 per cent) were uncontested, the majority of them falling in the mid-century decades or in the forty years after the American war. If we add token contests to the list, for sometimes a third candidate did half-heartedly stand against the nominations of the big clubs, if only for a few days, then the number of elections where the result was entirely predictable was roughly half. This is a large number for a free-man constituency of Bristol's size, the third-largest urban constituency after London and Westminster. It reflected the dominance of the merchant elite, who as members of the Society of Merchant Venturers, the corporation and other select groups, could avoid the expenses of heavy contests by means of gentlemanly agreements. Those expenses, the wining and dining of freemen, the purchase of new freedoms to boost one's chances of election, the cost of transporting out-voters to the hustings, could be formidable – routinely in the region of £5–10,000 for each candidate in the mid-century decades and £12–15,000 in the early nineteenth century, sometimes as high as £30,000.[4] Elite subscriptions were the only way such costs could be managed, even with the thousands of pounds of secret service money that found its way into the pockets of ministerial candidates. This predicament disposed the main caucuses, for much of the century the Tory Steadfast Society and the Whig Union, to share the seats and minimise expenses.

Electoral compromises of this nature were possible because of the tight weft of oligarchic power at the apex of Bristol society. Unlike London, which elected its officials, in the case of common councillors on an annual basis, Bristol had a closed corporation of forty-three councillors, twelve of whom were internally chosen as aldermen to serve the wards of the city. Most of these men were co-opted from the mercantile elite. Merchant representation among mayors increased in the late seventeenth and eighteenth century, from 43 per cent in the Jacobean years, to 52 per cent in the post-Restoration decades, to 56 per cent in the period 1702–39. By the early

---

[3] R. G. Thorne (ed.), *The History of Parliament. The House of Commons 1790–1820* (4 vols, London, 1986), II, 167; Sir Lewis Namier, *The Structure of Politics at the Accession of George III*, 2nd edn (London, 1957), pp. 88–91.
[4] For early nineteenth-century expenses, see Latimer, III, 52–3.

nineteenth century it was still around half, especially if one includes merchant bankers in the cohort.[5] The link between the corporation and the Society of Merchant Venturers, who were responsible for the economic management of the port, was particularly tight. The proportion of councillors who were at some point officers of the Merchant Venturers, not simply members, was substantial.[6] It ran at 33 per cent in the period 1680–1710, despite the turn-overs prompted by quo warranto actions in the 1680s, when the Stuarts purged the Bristol corporation to make it politically more amenable. In the period 1730–50 the figure rose slightly to 36 per cent, declining to 25 per cent in the decades after 1770 when the Venturers became a more inbred introspective group devoted to West Indian trade. Even so, the core of West India merchants continued to be well represented at Merchants' Hall and Guildhall.[7] In the period after 1750 twenty-seven of the fifty in this select circle (54 per cent) joined the Merchant Venturers; twenty-four were common councillors (48 per cent) sixteen of whom stood for twenty years or more.[8] A few in the late eighteenth and early nineteenth century held office for as many as fifty years. One, Thomas Daniel, whose plantation holdings were second to none in the city, was colloquially known as the 'King of Bristol'.[9] Ten of the group became aldermen, twenty sheriffs. They were a tight interlocking group who domi-nated the economic and political life of the city from 1730–1830.

So for much of that century there was a significant concentration of political and economic power at the apex of Bristol society. The Society of Merchant Venturers was an active lobbyist on matters that affected Bristol's trade and expected MPs to do its bidding. Edward Southwell, the member from 1739–54, complained that 'the Duty of a Representative of Bristol requires every hour of the day a constant attendance in Parlt., an extensive and regular correspondence, an attention to every Branch of trade, an univer-sall solicitation in all Offices & with all persons in power'.[10] As a country gentleman in Kings Weston with significant landholdings in Ireland, where he also held high office, he found it all a bit much, as did Edmund Burke,

---

[5] Graham Bush, *Bristol and its Municipal Government 1820–1851*, Bristol Record Society, 29 (Bristol, 1976), appendix 4; Mark Harrison, *Crowds and History. Mass Phenomena in English Towns 1790–1835* (Cambridge, 1988), pp. 66–7.

[6] By high standing, we mean masters, treasurers and wardens of the Society. The figures are derived from Alfred Beaven, *Bristol Lists. Municipal and Miscellaneous* (Bristol, 1899), pp. 275–315. See also Nicholas Rogers, *Whigs and Cities. Popular Politics in the Age of Walpole and Pitt* (Oxford, 1989), pp. 261–7.

[7] Kenneth Morgan, 'The Bristol West India Merchants', *Transactions of the Royal Historical Society*, 3 (1993), 201–2.

[8] This length of service was not untypical. In the period 1715–34 the length of service on the corporation averaged 20.3 years. For 1735–54 it was 22.6 years and 1755–74, 28.5 years. See Ronald H. Quilici, 'Turmoil in a City and an Empire: Bristol's Factions 1700–1775' (Unpublished PhD Thesis, University of New Hampshire, 1977), p. 225.

[9] Latimer, II, 455.

[10] BA, MS 44785/7, Southwell Papers, Southwell to William Berrow, 11 Dec. 1741.

who considered the demands of Bristol business to be 'vexatious and some-times humiliating'.[11] This explains why the Bristol elite often nominated one of its own kind as a potential MP, a merchant who would not cavil at the time-consuming, arcane matters of commercial regulation. Of the twenty-five MPs who represented Bristol in the period 1714–1832, sixteen (64 per cent) were merchants, bankers or industrialists with strong local roots. A further four were men whose commercial experience commended them to the Bristol elite: Robert Hoblyn, the son-in-law of Thomas Coster and a mining magnate from Cornwall, whose tin and copper was made up into slave-purchasing hardware; Robert Nugent, who first attracted the atten-tion of Bristol merchants for his robust defence of outport interests; Richard Beckford, one of the richest planters in Jamaica, whose agent on the island was a Bristolian; and the political economist John Baker Holroyd, Baron Sheffield, who seemed at first politically unpalatable to the Whigs because he had supported Lord North, but was expected to 'please them well in the end by his assiduity and attention to their business'.[12] Several commended them-selves because of their potential influence in the corridors of power, but in each case they had commercial contacts or local affiliations that might bene-fit Bristol: John Scrope, a close adviser of Robert Walpole, was the Recorder of Bristol; Burke, the protégé of Lord Rockingham and a major player in the repeal of the Stamp Act, was the colonial agent of New York; Charles Bragge, a close ally of Addington, was the treasurer of the navy in 1801 and subse-quently Secretary at War, important posts when commercial lanes had to be protected. Aristocratic influence upon Bristol's representation was minimal after the seventeenth century, when the Duke of Beaufort was able to sponsor Tory candidates. To be sure, Beaufort's son, Henry Charles Somerset, was elected in 1790 when the Steadfast Society was running short of potential candidates. He and Charles Bragge could be considered Beaufort's nominees, but this was the first aristocratic representation since 1685 and it proved temporary. Somerset lasted one term before moving to Gloucester; Bragge, a former MP for Monmouth, only a little longer. During the last twenty years of the unreformed parliament, Bristol's MPs were either merchants or bankers.

Bristol's political representation represented the dispositions of its mercan-tile elite, which was not especially deferential to the galaxy of aristocratic interests nearby, despite the fact they rubbed shoulders at the annual dinners of the county societies. The merchant elite could be bitterly divided on party and sectarian lines, but when it came to business there was always room for negotiation. If one looks at the partnerships that launched wartime priva-teers, for example, one discovers men making financial ventures with their erstwhile enemies. During the Seven Years' War, for example, the *Southwell*, a 300-ton ship with 24 guns and a crew of 200 men, was fitted out by two Whig

[11] *Correspondence of Edmund Burke*, IV, 274.
[12] Douglas R. Fisher, 'John Baker Holroyd, Ist Baron Sheffield, MP Bristol 1790–1802', in *History of Commons 1790–1820*, accessible <http://historyofparliamentonline.org>.

aldermen and two stalwarts of the Tory Steadfast Society, William Berrow and Michael Miller. Berrow also had an interest in the *Phoenix*, a 150-ton sloop that he shared with his fellow Steadfast colleague John Brickdale, and one of the leading lights of the rival Union Club, Richard Farr.[13] Partnerships such as these were tonics to electoral compromise. Lowbridge Bright, a Bristol merchant active in privateering during the American war, reflected this viewpoint when he talked of 'the bad consequences attending a contested election in a commercial city'.[14]

Despite the concentration of political and economic power that enhanced oligarchy, Bristol did not conform to the general pattern of growing political sclerosis mapped by historians like J. H. Plumb and Bill Speck, the vitality of Augustan contests giving way to Georgian placidity and electoral management. Nor did it quite conform to the profile of the larger boroughs, where there was a significant revival in the number of seats contested after 1761.[15] The Bristol experience is one of two short cycles of electoral compromise, in the 1740s and the 1760s, and a longer one after 1790. Generally electoral deals between the parties lasted no more than three, possibly four elections, each time collapsing under the weight of inveterate factionalism among the elite and broader voter dissatisfaction. It is only in the period after 1790 that electoral deals really dominate the political landscape, and even then, as the interventions of Henry Hunt, Samuel Romilly and a few idiosyncratic Tories reveal, such deals were resented.[16] Namier's analysis does not take this chequered history into account.

This is because Namier presumed that oligarchical political structures meant political apathy, myopia or deference on the part of ordinary voters. Influenced by the elite theory of Vilfredo Pareto and the politics of interest advanced by Charles Beard,[17] he was quick to disparage popular political participation. The kinds of sources he used, the private papers of large landowners, lent credence to that view. Yet one of the significant features of Bristol politics was the coexistence of oligarchic power with a terrain of vibrant political debate. It is the toxic mix of these factors that accounts for the timbre of its politics.

---

[13] TNA, HCA 26/30/147, 26/32/45.

[14] Kenneth Morgan (ed.), *The Bright-Meyler Papers: A Bristol-West Indian Connection, 1732–1837* (Oxford, 2007), p. 470.

[15] John A. Phillips, ' The Structure of Electoral Politics in Unreformed England', *Journal of British Studies*, 19:1 (1979), 79–100, especially 91, figure 2; J. H. Plumb, *The Growth of Political Stability in England 1675–1725* (London, 1967); W. A. Speck, *Tory and Whig: The Struggle in the Constituencies 1701–1715* (London, 1970).

[16] For more details, see chapter 11.

[17] David Hayton, who is writing a biography of Sir Lewis Namier, alerted us to Namier's interest in Charles Beard following Beard's *Economic Interpretation of the United States* (1913). For Beard's English influences, see Richard Drake, 'Charles Beard and the English Historians', *Constitutional Commentary* 29:3 (2014), 313–22.

Bristol was the second provincial town to have a newspaper, the *Bristol Post-Boy* of 1702. From then on, as we have already seen, the city was served by a succession of local newspapers, the longest ventures emerging from the presses of two branches of the Farley family. In periods of political excitement Bristol was able to field two, three and in the 1790s, as many as five weeklies. They did not simply echo news from London and entertain readers with amusing anecdotes and digressions; they were vigorously partisan. By the mid century these newspapers imparted a provincial perspective to local readers as well as filling them in on events in London and aboard, especially news from ports such as Dublin, New York and Boston, with which Bristol was in regular commercial contact. The earliest editions of the *Post-Boy* contained no local news at all, but *Farley's Bristol Newspaper* carried a regular column of Bristol news from 1726. These papers lacked editorials, but their partisanship came through in the way they appropriated material from the London press, producing what Jonathan Barry has described as prompts or stimulants for discussion.[18]

There were many venues for such discussions. A lot of social life in Bristol revolved around church and chapel. Alongside the seventeen main parish churches and the Cathedral cloisters, the Methodists created their first permanent chapel in 1739, the New Room, which became a rendezvous for itinerant preachers and a distribution centre for the many Methodist tracts that were printed in the mid-century decades. Bristol also sustained an actively political set of Dissenting congregations. The Pithay Baptist Church, still bustling in the 1770s, had been deeply implicated in the Monmouth rebellion of 1685. Whig in politics in the early eighteenth century, it was joined by two other Baptist churches, one of which, at Broadmead, was at the epicentre of opposition to the American war. Bristol also featured two of the largest Quaker meeting houses in England, whose collective wealth at the Hanoverian accession was said to be in excess of £500,000.[19] Almost as wealthy and certainly as influential was the Presbyterian chapel at Lewin's Mead, whose 1400 strong congregation produced a significant number of aldermen, councillors and sheriffs in the period before 1780. Well represented in the parishes of St James and the suburban parish of St Philip and St Jacob,

---

[18] Jonathan Barry, 'The Press and the Politics of Culture in Bristol 1660–1775', in *Culture, Politics and Society in Britain, 1660–1800*, ed. Jeremy Black and Jeremy Gregory (Manchester, 1991), pp. 49–81. Cf. G. A. Cranfield, *The Development of the Provincial Newspaper, 1700–1760* (Oxford, 1962); Carl B. Estabrook, *Urbane and Rustic England: Cultural Ties and Social Spheres in the Provinces, 1660–1780* (Manchester, 1998), pp. 206–13. Estabrook emphasises the focus of Bristol's earliest newspapers on London and 'the urban network and areas abroad' at the expense of news from the city's own immediate hinterland.

[19] Dr Williams Library, London, John Evans MS 34.4, fol. 147; William Braithwaite, *The Second Period of Quakerism* (Cambridge, 1961), pp. 100–8. On Nonconformity in early-eighteenth-century Bristol, see also Jonathan Barry and Kenneth Morgan (eds), *Reformation and Revival in Eighteenth-Century Bristol*, Bristol Record Society, 45 (Stroud, 1994), pp. 63–74.

the Nonconformists made up roughly 20 per cent of Bristol's population and a large section of the local bourgeoisie. In 1715 it was thought that about 700 Nonconformists voted in Bristol elections, and 'many of these by their Estates and Interest in trade can make many 100 more votes'.[20] This meant that at the Hanoverian accession the Dissenters and their allies constituted approximately a quarter of the electorate. Fifty years on they were still a force to be reckoned with. 'Dissenters are numerous in Bristol', remarked the *Bristol Gazette* in 1771, 'in elections their votes chiefly preponderate, and those who canvass are not a little assiduous to gain their favour.'[21] By 1820 there were twenty-three Protestant nonconformist chapels in Bristol, including eight Methodist, which by then had broken its affiliation with the Church of England. At this point in time they just outnumbered the twenty-two Anglican churches and chapels in the city.[22]

Alongside church and chapel, Bristol had many taverns and alehouses where politics might be discussed, not to mention coffee houses, where 'wise Remarkers on the Church and State/ O'er Turkish Lap and smoky Whiffs debate'. [23] Judging from the port books, which reveal just how many small investors dabbled in trading ventures, Bristolian conversations were heavily weighted towards commerce, a bias that led cynics to suggest that Bristolians were money-grubbing philistines. Yet this did not mean they were parochial, or as one commentator put it, that 'Bristol was never a hot-bed of politics; it minded its business and that business was trade.'[24] Quite apart from the fact that commercial issues were political, especially in the mid-century decades when governmental policy influenced the fortunes and future of the transatlantic economy, nationwide political conflicts continually intruded on the Bristol scene. This is patently clear from the extra-parliamentary petitions and instructions that voters signed and agitated for throughout the century. Taking just those from 1733 to 1784, from the Excise crisis to the furore over the East India Bill, Bristol participated in every petitioning campaign save one, namely the demand for parliamentary reform in 1783.[25] From 1769

[20] Elizabeth Ralph, 'Bishop Secker's Diocese Book', in A *Bristol Miscellany*, ed. Patrick McGrath, Bristol Record Society, 37 (Bristol, 1985), pp. 28–56; Dr Williams Library, John Evans MS 34.4, fol. 147.

[21] *Bristol Gazette*, 31 Oct. 1771.

[22] Martin Gorsky, *Patterns of Philanthropy. Charity and Society in Nineteenth-Century Bristol* (Woodbridge, 1999), pp. 32–3.

[23] William Goldwin, *A Poetical Description of Bristol* (Bristol, 1712), cited by Latimer, II, 97.

[24] Derek Robinson, author of a number of popular books on Bristol, on BBC Radio, 16 January 1980. For a condescending look at Bristol tradesmen, see William Combe's characterisation of 'Timothy Plodman' in *The Philosopher in Bristol* (2 vols, Bristol, 1775), II, 68–70.

[25] Of the eleven petitioning movements 1769–95, Bristol participated in eight. Only London and Newcastle were more active. See Joanna Innes and Nicholas Rogers, 'Politics and Government 1700–1840', in *The Cambridge Urban History of Britain 2: 1540–1840*, ed. Peter Clark (Cambridge, 2008), table 16.2, p. 564.

onwards many of these petitions were signed by large numbers of local inhabitants and dug deep into the population, sometimes encompassing non-voters
as well as voters. They frequently involved a fifth of the adult male population. In terms of participation rates this is a remarkable record, arguably
matched only by London in its monster petition against Catholic Relief in
1780.

One of the crucial political audiences in Bristol was, of course, the voters
themselves. Bristol was a freeman borough that also allowed local freeholders
to vote, the latter constituting about 12–15 per cent of the resident electorate. In a large commercial city this generated an urban electorate that was
third in size only to those of the cities of London and Westminster. In the
130 years before the Reform Act of 1832 this electorate grew by 350 per cent,
from approximately 1800 in 1698, to 6385 in 1830. This increase did not
keep pace with population growth, which grew five-, almost six-fold over the
same period, from 20,112 in 1696, to 103,886 in 1831 (117,016 if one adds
Bedminster). So, proportionate to the adult males living in Bristol, the electorate actually shrank over time. Taking into account the changing demographic profile of the city and the numbers of voters actually resident there,
our calculations suggest that roughly two in three males were eligible to vote
at the beginning of the eighteenth century and one in five on the eve of the
Reform Bill.[26] In practice this is not such a radical decline if one considers the
rudimentary nature of electoral organisation in the unreformed era. Managers
and agents of the major parties struggled to court and marshal thousands of
voters. At every election Bristol was awash with political denunciations and
vindications of the rival candidates. Ballads, poems and open letters paraded
their virtues and vices before the voters, detailed and caricatured their positions. In the hotly contested by-election of 1781, to give one example, the
electoral ephemera generated enough material for a memorial collection of
over 150 pages.[27] At the same time, scores of party managers scoured their

[26] The calculations are complicated by three factors: the eligible number of voters rather
than the number who actually voted, the former often imponderable; the changing
proportion of resident to out-voters; and the proportion of male adults over twenty-one
in populations where there were subtle changes in the age and gender ratio. John Phillips
and Frank O'Gorman's figures for other constituencies are predicated on a rising proportion of adult males, from 21.5 per cent in the late seventeenth century to 25.5 per cent
in the early nineteenth. Yet the demographic evidence suggests the proportion of adult
males shrank over time, from 29 per cent in 1690 to 24.5 per cent in 1831. See E. A.
Wrigley and R. S. Schofield, *The Population History of England 1541–1871* (Cambridge,
1981), pp. 528–9, appendix 3. See also J. A. Phillips, *Electoral Behavior in Unreformed
England 1761–1802* (Princeton, 1982), pp. 202–3 and Frank O'Gorman, *Voters, Patrons
and Parties. The Unreformed Electoral System of Hanoverian England 1734–1832* (Oxford,
1989), pp. 178–82. O'Gorman's conclusion that the decline in the unreformed electorate
has been exaggerated is one we would accept, but in Bristol participation seems unpredictable, with a turnout of 84 per cent in 1754 and 66 per cent in 1812.

[27] *The Bristol Contest* (Bristol, 1781). The first edition, found in Eighteenth Century
Collections Online (ECCO), contains only seventy-seven pages. A second edition was

area for eligible or vulnerable voters. Seventy-eight agents were so mobilised by the Tories in 1812.[28] They included two linen drapers, a currier, a tin-plate worker and a brush-maker in Castle Precincts. In the out-parish of St Philip they featured two gentlemen, a lead merchant, a maltster, an ironmonger and a baker, and at Gloucester Road a rope, twine and sack-maker. Their job was to arrange for the electors to be entertained in local taverns and to escort them to the hustings to cast their open votes at the appropriate time. In 1781 we know this was an orderly affair; at least orderly enough, because for seventeen days that winter the two candidates were absolutely neck and neck, with George Daubeny only surging ahead of the American Henry Cruger on the eighteenth day.[29]

The interaction between oligarchic and participatory politics is in fact crucial to understanding the Bristol experience. This emerges clearly from the first electoral compromise attempted in Bristol, during the 1740s. In the early decades of the century Bristol politics were riven by party strife, and driven by a politics of sectarian rivalry that harked back to the bitter struggles of the Clarendon Code when thousands of Dissenters were threatened with prosecution for practising their religion. So much so that in 1734, in the wave of popular opposition to Walpole's Excise Bill, Tory voters overwhelmingly plumped for their candidate, Thomas Coster, rather than pair him with the anti-Excise Whig, but Dissenting magnate, Sir Abraham Elton, thereby forfeiting one of their two votes.[30] In spite of this the Tories held one seat in 1734, for Coster edged out the Secretary of the Treasury, John Scrope, by little more than two hundred votes. High Church Toryism, however, was in decline in Bristol as more clergymen veered to the Whig establishment, and so five years later, upon Coster's death, the Tory party in Bristol revamped its image. Under the leadership of the newly formed Steadfast Society, it built upon Walpole's unpopularity in Bristol, first over the Excise, then over Spanish interference with transatlantic traffic, to develop a more broadly based opposition that encompassed Country Whigs as well as Tories. In the by-election of 1739 this did the trick, for the independent Edward Southwell was returned over the corporation candidate Henry Combe, with a significant middling vote opting for the independent.[31] Southwell's victory took some of the sting out of sectarian rivalry. This development, and the increasing expense of elections, was enough to force Bristol's premier factions to some

<hr />

produced with more broadsides, numbering 152 pages. It can be found in the Bristol Reference Library. We thank James E. Bradley for providing us with his copy of the second edition. *The Bristol Contest* (Bristol, 1754), another compilation of electoral ephemera, ran to seventy-four pages.

[28] BA, 12144, 'Steadfast Society: election proceedings, 1806–1812', pp. 127–9.

[29] *The Bristol poll-book, being a list of persons who voted at the election of a Member to serve in Parliament with Matthew Brickdale, Esquire* (Bristol, 1781), p. 214.

[30] To plump is to forfeit one vote in a two-member constituency by opting for one candidate only.

[31] For these developments see Rogers, *Whigs and Cities*, pp. 268–89.

sort of entente throughout the forties. Indeed, while Southwell was originally sponsored by the Tory Steadfast Society, his attention to overseas trade quickly won him support from the influential Society of Merchant Venturers and the Whig-dominated corporation. He proved a useful mediator on local issues like the Street Lighting Bill of 1748, when party rivalries flared. His partner from late 1742 was Robert Hoblyn, a Cornish industrialist and son-in-law of Thomas Coster. Technically a Tory, he stayed out of the limelight on controversial issues like the Naturalization Bills of 1751 and 1753 and was enough of a trimmer to be considered a plausible candidate in the Whig interest, certainly someone who 'would act agreeably to the ministry'.[32]

This disposition to electoral compromise did not last. The emergence of more Tory-minded candidates in the mid-1750s, including the reputedly Jacobite Sir John Phillips, once again stoked the embers of sectarian rivalry and saw a revival of the old partisan rhetoric of Whig and Tory. The elections of 1754 and 1756 were fought at ruinous expense and exhausted the coffers of both the Steadfast and Union clubs. It spawned fresh overtures for compromise. What also helped was the fact that the leaders of the Steadfast Society, who were initially outside the Whig-dominated corporation oligarchy, became increasingly associated with it: commercially, socially, and even politically. Indeed during the Minorca crisis of 1756, which deeply embarrassed the Duke of Newcastle and his Bristol allies, the Steadfast Society showed no disposition to flaunt its former Tory radicalism and discredit its opponents locally. Moderation became the name of the game.[33]

Again, this state of affairs did not endure. Quite apart from the fact that the major clubs had allowed their political machines to run down, the American war bitterly divided Bristolians. This is very evident in the run of addresses and petitions that accompanied the drift to war in 1775, in which the conservative faction defended Lord North's policy of coercion while the more progressive Whigs pleaded for conciliation. The differences over America, within the mercantile elite and without, were too great to forge another electoral agreement to share Bristol's two seats, although overtures were certainly made. The result was a spate of contested elections during the American war and its aftermath that were fiercely fought and fiercely expensive. In 1774 over 2000 new voters were enrolled after the dissolution of parliament, 900 of them while the polls were actually open. And while both parties agreed to restrain the inflation of voters, at least in terms of admitting new burgesses, the numbers kept rising: 5384 in 1775, 5914 in 1781 and over 6000 in 1784. The last of these elections continued for a remarkable thirty-one days and prompted legislation to restrain the duration of a poll to three weeks. The expense of entertaining voters and bringing non-residents into Bristol was formidable. In 1781 and 1784 there were roughly two thousand out-voters, who constituted a third of the active electorate. They were given travelling

[32] Romney Sedgwick (ed.), *House of Commons 1715–1754* (3 vols, London, 1970), II, 143.
[33] Rogers, *Whigs and Cities*, pp. 292–303.

money to get to the poll, which for the six hundred or so voters from London and Middlesex, could take three to four days.[34] The expense could be enormous, so much so, that Matthew Brickdale, who contested three of the four elections between 1774 and 1784, destroyed an inheritance in his bid to represent the city. On his last debut in 1784, some freemen were furious that he did not treat them to a chairing once elected.[35]

One aspect of this state of affairs is worth stressing: that is, the decline in the civic identity that Jonathan Barry has emphasised for the period 1660–1775. In the late seventeenth century Bristol still had over twenty active guilds, a civic militia, and a healthy influx of apprentices who took up the freedom, infusing new blood into the city's commercial community. These features, together with a strong tradition of endowed charity, strengthened the bonds of civic affiliation within Bristol despite the ferocity of its politico-religious divisions during the Interregnum and its aftermath.[36] Yet *pace* Barry, who wants to stress its durability, Bristol's civic identity started to fragment quite early in the eighteenth century. Bristol's trained bands, the hallmark of the arms-bearing citizen in early modern politics, cherished by Machiavelli and his English emulators as the foundation of civic republicanism, disappeared. This city militia was last mobilised in 1709 to handle bread rioters; within a few years all that was left was a ritual muster involving a handful of militiamen.[37] A few decades later the guild structure had also collapsed, and the consequence was that fewer apprentices joined the ranks of Bristol's burgesses. In the first decade of the century the apprentices constituted 65 per cent of burgess admissions; after 1740 they seldom surpassed half. Indeed, apprentice admissions shrank conspicuously in election years, when the number of hereditary or nuptial enrolments soared, and it was these occasions that really drove admissions.[38] In 1727, 778 new freemen were created; in 1739, 878. In 1774 the number spiked at over 2000, on this occasion taking in more than a third of the total electorate.[39] This practice continued down to 1830, when over 1800 new freemen were enrolled prior to and even during the election.[40]

In effect, the civic freedom was prostituted for political gain by rival factions. Every election saw surges in admissions as rival factions sought the

---

[34] The stagecoach from London to Bath took three days in the mid century. See *The tradesman's and traveller's pocket companion, or the Bath and Bristol Guide* (Bath, 1753), p. 7.

[35] Latimer, II, 457.

[36] Jonathan Barry, 'Bristol Pride: Civic Identity in Bristol, c. 1640–1775', in *The Making of Modern Bristol*, ed. Madge Dresser (Bristol, 2005), pp. 25–47, and his 'Bourgeois Collectivism? Urban Association and the Middling Sort', in *The Middling Sort of People*, ed. Jonathan Barry and Christopher Brooks (London, 1994), pp. 84–112.

[37] Latimer, II, 79, 85.

[38] Quilici, 'Turmoil in a City', table 10, p. 191.

[39] Rogers, *Whigs and Cities*, pp. 287–8; G. E. Weare, *Edmund Burke's Connection with Bristol, From 1774 till 1780* (Bristol, 1894), p. 84. Newly enrolled voters constituted 18 per cent of the total in 1739, and 20 per cent in 1754.

[40] Bush, *Bristol and its Municipal Government*, p. 21.

political advantage. And on one notable occasion, in 1734, a disappointed Whig party thought of reshaping the freeman electorate by halving rather than increasing it, insisting that all voters should pay 'scot and lot', that is local taxes. Had this occurred, it would have been a flagrant abnegation of the civic freedom, the right of all burgesses to cast their ballots. Voters were reminded of this 'iniquitous measure' of trying to disfranchise 2400 voters some twenty years later, in a handbill to the 'Free and Independent Electors of Bristol'.[41]

Bristol's burgesses did not suffer a legal proscription, but they were marginalised and debased by electoral compromise and deals from the top. Elite politics degraded the urban freedom, frustrated middling voters, and introduced a new cynicism to political representation. One reflection of this was the emergence of a lumpen-electorate in Bristol politics, voters and indeed non-voters who took advantage of the eat-and-swill character of Bristol elections to fill empty stomachs and indulge briefly in the festivities that accompanied elections. Writing to the Duke of Portland in September 1780, Edmund Burke asserted that the 'dreadful prospect of stopping the Aletap has as much Effect in this City as in any other you are acquainted with'.[42] James Thistlethwaite would have concurred. In the same year he depicted a Tory plebeian participating in the chairing of the members 'With dirty shirt, blue-wig and hungry face/ The miserable emblem of disgrace,/ Shewing his master's *hospitable* cheer/ Under the meagre type of sour small beer'.[43] This plebeian figure was titillated by the sexual licence that accompanied Bristol elections, where the right to vote could be obtained by marrying a freeman's daughter or widow, a provision that prompted a surge of mock unions upon the dissolution of parliament and reputedly something of a whore's holiday.

As it was, the batch of new voters provided neither party with a large permanent electoral interest, for there is little evidence that they voted with much consistency or regularity. In the by-election of 1781, for example, which left little time for canvassing, the two candidates mustered 697 new freemen in the final month.[44] Of these, 35 per cent secured their freedom by patrimony, 28 per cent by apprenticeship and 38 per cent by marriage; in the latter category, to a significant number of widows and daughters whose freemen husbands and fathers had died, which made the legitimacy of their burgher claims difficult to trace. In these circumstances it was hardly surprising that a significant proportion of new freemen were out-voters. Roughly a third of these new freemen hailed from outside of Bristol, some as far afield as Portsmouth, Salisbury, Bewdley and London, a strong recruiting ground for

---

[41] *The Bristol Contest* (Bristol, 1754), p. 12.

[42] *Correspondence of Edmund Burke*, IV, 269.

[43] James Thistlethwaite, *Corruption* (London, 1780), canto iv, lines 253–9.

[44] See the Burgess Book (1780–1785). We took a 7 per cent random sample (N=50) of the new freemen from 24 January–24 February and traced their voting record in the Bristol polls of 1781 and 1784.

the radical Whig, Henry Cruger. Nearly a quarter (24 per cent) of these free-men, however, evaded voting altogether, for they do not appear on the 1781 poll. Some must have used the by-election as a free trip to Bristol, expenses paid. Of the newly enrolled freemen, a further 30 per cent failed to vote in the following election three years later. Three voters in our random sample actually switched sides in 1784, so the investment of money in these new voters in effect produced a relatively modest (40 per cent) phalanx of 'loyal' supporters. In some earlier elections the return on investment was meagre. Only 8 per cent of the 1734 new freemen voted in the by-election five years later.[45]

The elusive character of these new voters certainly troubled the campaign managers. Electoral agents were asked to keep copies of freemen certificates to check that they voted for the candidate who paid for their freedom (the equivalent of a week's wages in the mid century) and only then to provide them with 'polling money' for a tavern supper. A directive in the minutes of the Tory club for the 1806 election suggests some vigilance on this matter.[46] Older, resident voters were doubtless subject to ongoing pressures, especially if they were dependent on charitable aid, which was often distributed in a partisan fashion. As one merchant reported 'it would not do for poor men to fly in the face of those who could do them good.'[47]

The importance of such aid is reinforced when we consider that charitable societies sometimes sponsored 30 per cent of all apprentices in any one year, a boon for fatherless applicants, in particular, who at the turn of the eighteenth century constituted 30 per cent of those offered indentures. Demographic fortunes likely reinforced the sinews of clientage, especially when we recog-nise that 24 per cent of all households in Bristol in 1696 were headed by widows or widowers, with 30 per cent in Temple and 26 per cent in St Mary Redcliff.[48] The proportion of orphans likely shrank over time, but not enough to vitiate the ability of charities to influence the life chances of more vulner-able Bristolians.

Yet despite these webs of clientage, the distinct impression is that the new lumpen-voter secured the better bargain: the right to work in the city without harassment, at least until the mid century when guild regulations

---

[45] Rogers, *Whigs and Cities*, p. 288n.

[46] BA, 12144, 'Steadfast Society: election proceedings, 1806–1812', p. 13.

[47] *House of Commons, Parliamentary Papers*, 8 (1835), Select Committee on Bribery, p. 382. For an example of Tories using the Colston charity to muster votes early in the century, see *An Account of the Riots, Tumults and other Treasonable Practices since his Majesty's Accession* (London, 1715), pp. 25–6.

[48] J. R. Holman, 'Orphans in Pre-Industrial Towns – The Case of Bristol in the Late Seventeenth Century', *Local Population Studies*, 15 (1975), 42–4. The number of appren-tices financed by charities is calculated from the Register of Apprentices 1724–40 (BA, 04353/5) for the years 1735–40. The Colston Society was the largest sponsor (31 per cent). The county societies together made up roughly the same proportion and Queen Elizabeth's Hospital (12 per cent). Minor charities made up the rest.

were relaxed; the opportunity to bypass long apprenticeships; the right to send children to free schools in the city, to partake of charities reserved for burgesses and their families, and perhaps move a step up the social ladder; an exemption from town dues if one happened to invest in maritime trade. According to the parliamentary select committee on municipal government, £16,895 was distributed annually in the form of money, clothing, schooling, and provision for paupers and widows. Over £5000 was available in the form of free or cheap loans.[49] The electoral clubs, by contrast, gained a one-off vote at considerable expense and an imponderable constituency for the future.

Mannaseh Dawes, the lawyer who represented Henry Cruger in the post-election enquiry of 1784, was pretty appalled by the state of affairs in Bristol where 'power, wealth and corruption' determined elections. He thought the practices 'burlesqued the name of liberty', particularly the flagrant creation of last-minute, dependent voters, which 'wants only time to establish it into immemorial custom'.[50] Dawes found the laws regarding new freemen opaque and ambiguous, for it appeared that there was no consistent agreement about whether new freeman could be admitted after the issue of the writ to hold an election. He thought the situation could only be clarified by some ruling whereby only those who obtained their freedom a month before the election could be eligible to vote. This sort of proposal would have appealed to the independent journeymen who deplored the way in which voters were 'bought and sold like cattle at Smithfield market'.[51] Such men emerged as a viable force championing electoral independence in the decades of Wilkes and the American Revolution.

Electoral independence was a hallmark of the older civic identity, but the emergence of self-conscious journeymen demanding a political say was a new aspect of the landscape and indicative of a shift from civic mutuality to a politics of class struggle. It grew in part out of a growing restlessness among the trades whose work was disrupted by the American conflict and the colonists' policy of non-importation, and by rising prices, which cut into working-class budgets. In June 1777 journeymen shoemakers complained that their families were living on 'potatoes and salt'. And while real wages recovered briefly the next year they fell once again in 1779 and 1780, at critical points in the American war.[52] Struggles to maintain a living wage manifested themselves in what Julian Davies has called a 'rhetoric of need', self-conscious appeals to the public arguing for a modest 'competence' consonant with their skill

[49] *House of Commons, Parliamentary Papers*, 8 (1835), pp. 379–88, 24 (1835), pp. 1161–3, cited by Terry Jenkins, 'Bristol', in *House of Commons 1820–1832*, accessible <http://www. historyofparliamentonline.org >.

[50] Mannaseh Dawes, *Observations on the mode of electing representatives in parliament for the City of Bristol* (Bristol, 1784), pp. iii, 4, 26.

[51] *FFBJ*, 12 Feb. 1781.

[52] Julian Paul Davies, 'Artisans and the City: A Social History of Bristol's Shoemakers and Tailors, 1770–1800' (Unpublished PhD Thesis, University of Bristol, 2003), pp. 113, 119, 127–34.

and standing in the civic community. In the opening years of the war such strategies were also accompanied by pleas, even demands, to reconcile with the Americans. Many artisans supported conciliation over coercion in mass petitions of 1775. And as the war intensified and political positions hardened, the more radical came to realise that a more proactive stance on local political representation was necessary. 'The poor man has an *equal* right but *more* need to have representatives in the legislature than a rich one', declared one in 1781.[53]

This assertiveness was accompanied by efforts to create an independent platform in Bristol self-consciously distanced from the major clubs and factions. In 1769, in the wake of the controversy over the Middlesex election brought about by the election of the technically outlawed John Wilkes, a number of citizens formed an Independent Society 'unconnected with party and uninfluenced my ministerial power'.[54] In subsequent years these independents welcomed Wilkes to Bristol and sent instructions to their MPs to support John Sawbridge's motion for shorter parliaments. They indulged in the kinds of Wilkite sociability that characterised the metropolis. One group celebrated the anticipated release of Wilkes from King's Bench prison with a dinner that commemorated his infamous *North Briton* number 45, the publication that brought the political adventurer and libertine to notoriety. Forty-five men were invited to share 45 lbs of beef, 2 legs of veal weighing 45 lb, 45 tankards of ale, 45 pipes of tobacco and 45 bowls of punch.[55] Whether they managed to survive this *grande bouffe* is unknown. One suspects it was really a canard designed to keep Wilkite signifiers at the forefront of the political imagination.

The leaders of this radical group were patrician, richer than most of the middling professionals associated with the Wilkite Bill of Rights Society. Samuel Peach, a linen merchant and subsequently a banker, hailed from a Gloucestershire family who had made a fortune in textiles; his brother was a silk merchant and director of the East India company. Peach's son-in-law, Henry Cruger, was the Bristol factor of a well-heeled New York merchant dynasty. A lot of his import–export business was associated with the Caribbean slave economy. This did not stop Cruger from bringing some of the breezy, open politics of New York's waterfront to Bristol. Elected to parliament in 1774 on a wave of pro-American sentiment, he attracted a popular following restless and resentful of the electoral deals of Bristol's elite clubmen.

---

[53] *The Bristol Contest* (Bristol, 1781), p. 104. See also Peter Marshall, *Bristol and the American War of Independence* (Bristol, 1977), p. 24; James E. Bradley, *Religion, Revolution and English Radicalism. Nonconformity in Eighteenth-Century Politics and Society* (Cambridge, 1990), p. 380.

[54] *FFBJ*, 11 March 1769.

[55] *FFBJ*, 14 April 1770. On Wilkite sociability, see John Brewer, 'The Number 45: A Wilkite Political Symbol', in *England's Rise to Greatness, 1660–1763*, ed. Stephen Bartow Baxter (Berkeley and Los Angeles, 1983), pp. 349–80.

As Bristol opinion hardened against the Americans, Cruger found himself fighting for political survival. Yet many independent-minded journeymen stuck by him. In 1781, a thousand journeymen who met at the Three Queens tavern in St Thomas Street pre-empted an agreement between the Steadfast and the Union Clubs to share the representation of the constituency by once again promoting Cruger.[56] As journeymen outside the orbit of privilege, they declared it was 'a high infringement of the privileges of the freemen and free-holders ... for any club or combination of men to declare who shall or who shall not become candidates to represent us in Parliament'. Mobilising the discourse of freemen civility that defined the vote as a birthright, they protested against deals from the top and asserted the virtues of political independence.[57] This stance was sharpened by a class antagonism against masters who tried to bully them into political subservience. Some of this was captured by the radical printer, William Pine, in his edition of the electoral ephemera for the 1781 contest. Analogies were drawn between the elite clubmen and 'imperious masters'.[58] Journeymen were reminded that Bristol merchants lived in luxury and 'get Fortunes besides by the sweat of our brows', a line of argument that anticipated the producerism of later decades where a distinction was drawn between the useful and useless classes. Journeymen were advised to strike if their masters tried to dictate political choices to them, or seek employment on privateers.[59] The phoney affability of mercantile candidates like George Daubeny was mocked, their gentility ridiculed. The purported qualifications for a Bristol MP were reeled off with bitter irony: 'Easy of address, elegant and modest in his carriage and manners, an affluent fortune, an extensive knowledge of the commercial interest of the kingdom (particularly of this great city) and above all, a man of unshaken, inviolable integrity.'[60] The adjectival emphasis of the last phrase said it all. Smarmy merchants simply could not be trusted. Better to leave the representation to coppersmiths, ribbon-weavers, even jappaners, artisans who varnished wood, metal or glass.

'It is time for us to know our Consequence', one journeyman declared; that is, realise our collective importance or weight. A 'true friend of the people' even considered moving out of a discourse of freeman rights towards manhood suffrage: 'every man in the commonalty (excepting infants, insane persons and criminals) is of common right, and by the laws of God, a freemen and entitled to the full enjoyment of liberty' – something that could only be achieved by the vote.[61] Despite these aspirations, Bristol's radical vanguard failed to mobilise its artisans. In the 1781 by-election the great majority

---

[56] *The Bristol Contest*, p. 7.

[57] On freeman values, see Jonathan Barry, 'Civility and Civic Culture in Early Modern England: The Meanings of Urban Freedom', in *Civil Histories. Essays Presented to Sir Keith Thomas*, ed. Peter Burke, Brian Harrison and Paul Slack (Oxford, 2000), pp. 182–99.

[58] *The Bristol Contest*, pp. 10–11.

[59] Tailors were on strike in 1773, 1777, 1781 and 1790. See Latimer, II, 404.

[60] *The Bristol Contest*, pp. 18–19.

[61] *The Bristol Contest*, pp. 10, 104.

opted for the politics of interest over class. This was particularly the case in the maritime trades. Whereas the mariners, shipwrights and ropemakers had voted decisively for Cruger in 1774, in 1781 they switched to Daubeny – partly under pressure from merchants, no doubt, but also because they were persuaded by the Tory argument that the Americans and their fellow travellers, such as Cruger, were responsible for the economic dislocations of the war. The shift to the Tories was even evident among allied trades to whom the radicals had appealed, such as the coopers and hoopers. They had strongly supported the Whig candidates in 1774, but in 1781 the journeymen were more evenly divided, more so than the masters who were clearly for the Tory candidate.[62] The same was true of the journeymen shoemakers and tailors, groups noted for their labour militancy. Among this cohort, Daubeny scored narrow victories, at least among those resident in the city.

In any case, Cruger's leadership proved disappointing. Despite his early enthusiasm for Wilkes, he did not create the space for a vibrant journeymen politics. Thomas Chatterton satirised him as a haughty libertine whose allegiance to radical politics was superficial.[63] Defeated in 1781 but returned three years later, he devoted his time to rebuilding his family's fortune and reputation after a disastrous war. Standing as a Pittite in the 1784 election, he involved himself in those commercial issues of keen interest to the Bristol elite and defended the city's investment in the plantation economy. In tune with the powerful West India interest in Bristol, he believed a comprehensive abolition of the slave trade would be 'ruinous in the extreme'.[64] Towards the end of his parliamentary career, before he returned to New York to try to repair his family's fortunes, Cruger even angled for a consular appointment in the United States, largely on the basis of advice he had communicated to the government on US matters.

Bristol politics during the American Revolution turned out to be one of lost opportunities, of arrested radicalism, and a reassertion of alignments where narrowly construed economic interest and factionalism mattered. Unlike Norwich and Newcastle, where freemen radicalism generated spaces for a genuinely democratic politics in the 1790s and beyond, Bristol relapsed into a client-dominated regime that choked movements for change. This is not to suggest that Bristol was immune from the political ferment of the French Revolution, when the political horizons of artisans on the margins of parliamentary politics were dramatically widened by the publication of Paine's *Rights of Man* and related tracts. The Society for Constitutional

---

[62] The voting for all resident coopers and hoopers was 71 for Daubeny and 66 for Cruger. Among those that can be identified as masters the voting was 11 for Daubeny and 3 for Cruger, which meant among journeymen the voting was 60 for Daubeny and 63 for Cruger. Among the out-voters Daubeny won 17 votes to Cruger's 10. In making this calculation we have assumed that all coopers noted in *Sketchley's Bristol Directory* of 1775 were masters. For shoemakers and tailors see Julian Davies, 'Artisans and the City', table 6.9.
[63] [Thomas Chatterton], *The Squire in his Chariot* (London, 1775).
[64] FFBJ, 21 May 1789.

Information encouraged such aspirations, publishing its positive recommendations of Paine's book in the Bristol newspapers.[65] Such activity was enough
to prompt the secretary of state, Henry Dundas, to ask the mayor John Noble
about 'the number and extent of seditious Associations which have formed
in Bristol'.[66] Yet, as we shall see later, radical clubs were few on the ground,
nothing compared to places like Sheffield and Norwich.[67] Bristol did sponsor
a Corresponding Society that liaised with its London counterparts in early
1794. Its only known address stressed the growing inequalities of rank incident upon the war and the absence of a genuinely democratic Commons to
counteract the entrenchment of oligarchy and class privilege. Adopting the
plan of the maverick radical the Duke of Richmond, it advocated universal manhood suffrage, equal electoral districts, single member constituencies and one-day elections, the later two designed to erase the power of big
money over large freemen boroughs like Bristol.[68] It insisted that the conservative rallying cry of 'King and Constitution' inhibited 'true loyalty' to an
ancient constitution that in principle at least, vindicated the sovereignty of
the people. No doubt the society was troubled by the mobilisation of anti-
republican sentiment by magistrates and merchants, who helped finance
and stage the well-publicised effigy-burnings of Tom Paine in surrounding
towns and villages and possibly in Bristol itself.[69] These events signalled that
supporters of Tom Paine were not to be tolerated. As Bristol mobilised for
war and sponsored a regiment of infantry, loyalist voices drowned out radical
aspirations for a new order.

The upshot was that popular radicalism did not undermine the ongoing
conventions of electoral management and compromise that were becoming
Bristol's hallmark. Early-nineteenth-century commentators talked more of
the same: elections dictated from above; electors forfeiting their vote for the
cheap thrills of a booze-up and the raucous chairings of the so-called victors,
whose mock pageantry and bombast invaded the streets and taverns at enormous expense, sometimes to the tune of over £2000. In the seven elections
between 1790 and 1807 the White Lion Club and its rival, then called the

---

[65] TNA, TS 11/961/2567, fols 223–4.
[66] BA, Lord Mayor's Papers, box 1791, Henry Dundas to John Noble, 12 Sep. 1792, cited
by Mark Harrison, *Crowds and History*, p. 274.
[67] Sheffield's Constitutional Society had between two and three thousand members, and
Norwich had a confederacy of radical clubs. See TNA, HO 42/22/218, and C. B. Jewson,
The Jacobin City (Glasgow and London, 1975).
[68] *Address of the Bristol Corresponding Society for Parliamentary Reform, to the people of Great
Britain* (Bristol, 1794).
[69] *Bath Journal*, 4 March 1793; *Bristol Gazette*, 7 March 1793. There were loyalist
associations formed in virtually all of the surrounding towns to Bristol and effigy-
burnings of Paine in Gloucester, Mells, Saltford, Wells, Shepton Mallet, Bath Easton and
Kingsdown. See *Bath Journal* and *Gloucester Journal*, Dec. 1792–March 1793. See also
Nicholas Rogers, 'Burning Tom Paine: Loyalism and Counter-Revolution in Britain,
1792–3', *Histoire sociale/Social History*, 32:64 (1999), pp. 139–72.

Independent and Constitutional Club, dictated the outcome on five occasions without even moving to a poll. Only in 1790 and 1796 was there token resistance to the caucus nominations, and on both occasions it lasted no more than a day, despite the fact that in 1796 the Whig merchant Benjamin Hobhouse had attempted to mobilise the anti-war sentiment that was gathering momentum nationally.[70] The fact that corporation Whigs openly discouraged a contest in 1796 riled some of Hobhouse's supporters. After the nomination meeting and first day of polling, they broke the windows of the Bush tavern, the Council House and the Mansion House in protest.[71]

Caucus politics was none the less coming under new pressures. Political clientage worked in periods of economic buoyancy, when the incidental benefits of trade could be distributed more widely and when the maritime population could be assured of some protection from the press-gangs. Yet Bristol was entering a period of relative decline, surpassed by Liverpool as a premier Atlantic port, and losing industrial enterprises to the Midlands and the north. The controversy over the floating dock revealed a parasitism of interests at the apex of Bristol society that was stifling its growth and shaping its politics.

The stage was thus set for a further challenge to caucus politics, this time from a gentleman farmer turned radical named Henry Hunt. Hunt had honed his radical politics in conversations with Samuel Waddington and others at King's Bench, where he was briefly imprisoned.[72] Struck by James Paull's dramatic debut in Westminster in 1806, where he ran a successful campaign without treating, Hunt was determined to break the stranglehold of the big clubs in Bristol, where he had been winding down an unsuccessful brewery. In the election of May 1807 Hunt was disgusted to witness the pseudo-nomination of the Irish barrister, Sir John Jarvis, in an effort to placate the popular demand for a real contest.[73] Two months later he chaired a meeting that passed resolutions condemning caucus politics in Bristol. Those 'that arrogate to themselves the power of returning as representative for this city', one resolution ran, were acting in 'direct opposition to the sound principles of the British constitution'.[74] Consequently the motion was passed to launch the Bristol Patriotic and Constitutional Association, whose successes, it was hoped, would emulate radical advances in Westminster. It was given a publicity boost by William Cobbett in his *Weekly Political Register*, a periodical with a widening circulation, reaching 40,000 in 1816 when its price was reduced.

As we shall see in Chapter 10, where the Hunt phenomenon is analysed in more detail, the first test of the new Association came in the summer of 1812

---

[70] O'Gorman, *Voters, Patrons, and Parties*, p. 297n.

[71] *Bath Herald*, 4 June 1796.

[72] John Belchem, *'Orator Hunt': Henry Hunt and English Working-Class Radicalism* (Oxford, 1985), p. 21.

[73] Henry Hunt, *Memoirs Of Henry Hunt, Esq.* (3 vols, London, 1820), II, 234–55, 260–3, 275–81. Hunt subsequently realised Jarvis was little more than a lackey of the White Lion club, the Tory caucus.

[74] *Cobbett's Weekly Political Register*, 8 Aug. 1807.

when Bragge Bathurst vacated his seat on becoming chancellor of the Duchy of Lancaster. The banker Richard Hart Davis was nominated by the White Lion Club to take Bragge Bathurst's place, and the two rival Whig groups in Bristol declined to contest it on the understanding that the seat belonged to the Blues. Hunt, however, was determined to force a contest. He arrived from Sussex in a post-chaise to which a long pole was attached, topped by a huge loaf of bread and the motto 'Hunt and Peace', a clear criticism of the war machine that was intensifying scarcity, and evocative of the hopes Bristolians nurtured at the Peace of Amiens after two hard years.[75] It pointedly hailed the more recent protests against rising food prices, which resulted in at least two popular interventions to fix the price of provisions and calls from the mayor for troops to contain angry crowds.[76]

The 1812 by-election was unusually violent, with the Tories hiring muscle from the Kingswood colliery, the shipyards, the coastal trows, and even ten boxers, to attack Hunt's supporters at the hustings.[77] Hunt's supporters responded by sacking the White Lion Inn, the Tory headquarters, and later launching forays on the Council House and the mansion of the Tory candidate, Richard Hart Davis. Given the huge resources at the disposal of the Blues such bruising confrontations were unnecessary and counterproductive, but it is likely that a slightly disorganised Tory party, which had really wanted Bragge Bathurst to stand once more for Bristol, was unnerved by Hunt's sudden candidature. The violence certainly did not intimidate Hunt, who was a courageous street politician, adept at dealing with hecklers in the crowd. Determined to keep the poll open against overwhelming odds of winning, for the Blues wined and dined their voters at prodigious expense, Hunt processed to the hustings each day with a man 'bearing the Cap of Liberty before him à la Française'.[78]

Hunt mustered a mere 235 votes in the by-election, and a further 447 in the general election three months later. This meant some 10 per cent of the Bristol electorate, largely petty artisans, braved ostracism and intimidation to vote for the radical candidate. Judged by electoral standards, this was a failure, although it did reveal the possibilities of an unchained mechanic vote. Yet Hunt was as interested in the politics of provocation and constitutional defiance as laying the foundations of an electoral machine equivalent to that of Francis Place in Westminster.[79] Here he did score, for the Tories overstepped themselves in provoking violence and flouting the constitutional

[75] Mark Harrison, *Crowds and History*, pp. 235–45; Steve Poole, 'Scarcity and the Civic Tradition: Market Management in Bristol 1707–1815', in *Markets, Market Culture and Popular Protest in Eighteenth-Century Britain and Ireland* (Liverpool, 1996), pp. 91–114.
[76] Harrison, *Crowds and History*, p. 207.
[77] BA, 12144, 'Steadfast Society: Electoral Proceedings, 1806–1812', pp. 102–3.
[78] Cited in John Belchem, *Hunt*, p. 38. See also Harrison, *Crowds and History*, pp. 211–19.
[79] On constitutional defiance and its signifiers, see James Epstein, 'Understanding the Cap of Liberty: Symbolic Practice and Social Conflict in Early Nineteenth-Century England', *Past and Present*, 122 (1989), 75–118.

conventions of keeping the electoral arena free of military interference. Quite apart from the free use of maritime muscle, the minutes of Steadfast Society reveal quite clearly that the Tories used the press-gang to beat up Hunt's supporters. The recruiting officer, Captain John Phillips, was accused by one of Hunt's attorneys of a 'gross dereliction of duty', although the Steadfast Society predictably defended him.[80]

If Hunt succeeded in exposing the Tory's nefarious tactics in intimidating his supporters, he must have realised that he needed a critical threshold of 2000 votes to launch a realistic challenge to the two caucuses who ran the constituency. Their hold on Bristol remained formidable, reinforced by parochial jobbery and charitable dependency.[81] It was made stronger by the fact that Tories and Whigs of the old school were ideologically compatible with one another, or, as in the case of Henry Bright, had sufficient business interests in common to allow for a play of small differences. In the event of a contested election, caucus supporters would likely share their votes, as in the general election of 1812 where the vast majority of the Tory voters paired Hart Davis with the old-time Whig Edward Protheroe, and vice versa.[82] In fact only 86 freemen (2 per cent) voted for the official Whig candidates in this election, out of a total of 4386 voters. Among Protheroe's supporters, voters opted for the Tory Hart Davis over the well-known Whig lawyer, Sir Samuel Romilly, by a ratio of twenty-five to one, a preference that can be explained in part by Romilly's unfortunate endorsement by John Noble, the aldermen held responsible for the Bristol Bridge riots.[83] This pattern of caucus voting was repeated in 1820 when Henry Bright was adopted by the Whig Loyal and Constitutional Club even though he was more liberal than Protheroe. Once again the majority of Bright's voters opted for the Tory Davis and vice versa. Although Bright received more plumpers in 1820 than did Protheroe in 1818, over 70 per cent of his supporters paired him with Hart Davis. The third candidate, James Evan Baillie, nominated by dissident Whigs, was effectively marginalised.

Caucus politics underwent some adjustments at the top, the Tory Steadfast Society giving way to the less exclusive White Lion. Even so, the grip of caucus politics on Bristol was not effectively undermined until the 1830s, when Edward Protheroe junior, an abolitionist, was elected against the wishes of a West Indian dominated elite. That victory was not without its ironies. Edward Protheroe junior disagreed with his father over abolition, but he was compensated for seventy-two slaves on the Endeavour plantation in Jamaica

---

[80] BA, 12144, 'Steadfast Society', p. 98.
[81] Gorsky, *Patterns of Philanthropy*, pp. 91–101, which reveals strong attachments to the main caucuses and their electoral deals among vestrymen, lessees and charitable recipients.
[82] David R. Fisher, 'Bristol', in *History of Parliament 1820–1832*, accessible <http://www.historyofparliamentonline.org>.
[83] Harrison, *Crowds in History*, pp. 210–11.

in the emancipation settlement.[84] Before his victory, reform politics in Bristol was always heavily mediated by the power of the two clubs, with liberal-radical politicians like Thomas Stocking and Charles Houlden Walker angling to break their hold by promoting other Whig candidates, in an effort to open up formal politics to wider social and political movements. Such movements were never entirely absent from the Bristol scene, and it is misleading to characterise the port as a Tory bastion in which radicalism was without a voice. While the city never had the radical presence of a Norwich, Sheffield or industrial centre like Manchester, it was not immune to broader national movements for change.

For example, in 1820 Bristolians also evinced considerable sympathy for Queen Caroline, who was subjected to a trial and Bill of Pains and Penalties for allegedly having an adulterous affair with her Italian secretary while her husband, George IV, was openly gadding about with a series of mistresses in London and Brighton. Approximately 24,640 inhabitants signed an address to the Queen lamenting her ordeal, and there were two other petitions sent from Clifton and Kingsdown by females who deplored the double standard so visibly displayed in George IV's actions. They wished to defend the rights of women and familial domesticity from laws that perpetuated patriarchal constructions of marriage. One of them, penned by Elizabeth Cranidge, the daughter of the radical schoolmaster and attorney, John Cranidge, collected 14,000 signatures.[85] This broad-based opposition did not face corporate harassment, as had other aspects of the mass platform. It proved difficult to mobilise the armoury of repression for meetings in favour of royalty. When the bill against the Queen was abandoned by the ministry, Bristol rejoiced for two nights despite efforts by the Tory magistrates to curb the celebrations.

As long as the Caroline affair remained before the public, liberal-radicals like C. H. Walker were exempt from prosecution, although the corporation did attempt to stifle some printers. At the same time, it proved difficult to mobilise a radical platform around the very disparate issues that brought Queen Caroline sympathy, which had as much to do with the politics of

---

[84] See University College London (UCL), Legacies of British Slave-Ownership, accessible <http://www.ucl.ac.uk/lbs>.

[85] *Bristol Mercury*, 18 Nov. 1820; *Cobbett's Weekly Political Register*, 21 Oct. 1820; Harrison, *Crowds and History*, pp. 246–8; Jeremy Caple, *The Bristol Riots of 1831 and Social Reform in Britain* (New York, 1990), p. 120. One came from the Married Females of Bristol, but there was also one from the females of Clifton and Kingsdown, Bristol. On the sexual politics of the Queen Caroline Affair, see Leonore Davidoff and Catherine Hall, *Family Fortunes: Men and Women of the English Middle Class 1780–1830* (London, 1987), pp. 149–55; Anna Clark, 'Queen Caroline and the Sexual Politics of Popular Culture in London, 1820', *Representations*, 31 (1990), 31–88, and her *The Struggle for the Breeches: Gender and the Making of the British Working Class* (Berkeley and Los Angeles, 1997), pp. 164–74. John Cranidge helped seamen in their legal battles with the Admiralty. See Nicholas Rogers (ed.), *Manning the Royal Navy in Bristol: Liberty, Impressment and the State, 1739–1815*, Bristol Record Society, 66 (Bristol, 2013), p. 296.

domesticity as it did with parliamentary reform and public space. Queenite sympathies certainly sullied the coronation festivities, especially the civic procession to the Cathedral. 'From the time the procession started from the Council-House till it returned', remarked the *Mercury*, 'no one cheer of approbation from the *people* marked its progress.' [86] On the death of the Queen a few months later, the newspaper attempted to mobilise opinion against the 'disgraceful outrages' inflicted by the army on those Londoners who insisted her funeral cortege should pass through the city. It talked of the people's victory in defying the authorities' efforts to divert the procession, calling it 'a new, and important aera'.[87] But nothing came of it.

Over the long term the corporation and its social allies lost credibility because it spent too much time defending its privileges and insulating itself from wider discontents. For example, since the publication of John Howard's *State of the Prisons* in 1777, there had been a growing concern over the condition of Bristol's Newgate and Bridewell, a situation made more pressing by a growing crime rate at the end of the century. In an effort to clean up the jails on a Howard model, segregating debtors from felons, and young offenders from old, money was needed. Many citizens believed it was the responsibility of the corporation to find the money from its own funds, as its charter decreed, but when a bill was drafted in 1790, it was discovered that the new prison was to be financed in perpetuity from the county rate, by a tax set by the aldermen and administered by the Common Council. There was a ratepayer revolt against this recommendation, and to the idea that the new prison should be built in the crowded Castle Precincts. In the face of these middle-class protests, the corporation backed down, both in 1790 and again the following year, but in 1792 the corporation sneaked a bill through parliament before an opposition could be organised. The upshot was that the mayor and several aldermen were insulted in the streets and a legal challenge to the bill launched and financed by parish ratepayers. This delayed the building project until the end of the Napoleonic wars, when the corporation again revived the plan to construct a new prison. This time the parishioners decided to take over the project themselves and have elected commissioners administer it. Members of the corporation attempted to block this by flaunting their chartered rights, but the predominantly middle-class parishioners prevailed. In 1816 an act declared the new prison was to be administered by a new statutory body at a cost of £60,000. In deference to the 'nimbyism' of central city ratepayers, the site for the new jail was moved to a poorer district near the Cut.[88]

The prison episode revealed that Bristol's citizens disliked the way in which the corporation and its allies on the Merchant Venturers arrogated to itself the right to determine the future of the city without consulting broader

[86] *Bristol Mercury*, 21 July 1820.
[87] *Ibid.*, 18 Aug. 1821.
[88] Caple, *Bristol Riots*, pp. 117–19; Latimer, II, 488–9; III, 65–7.

interests or delegating responsibilities to public, non-elite bodies. The same issue dogged the corporation over the building and maintenance of Bristol Bridge. Under the terms of the 1785 act, the trustees, most of whom were councillors, were supposed to remove the tolls once the loans were paid off and a balance secured for general repair. Initially it was determined that the tolls should end in September 1793 when the lease to manage the bridge expired, but the trustees decided to continue the tolls for another year without explaining their reasons for so doing. This precipitated, as we shall see, a serious riot in the interval between the two leases of the bridge which resulted in eleven deaths and forty-five injuries.

As we have seen, the willingness of the corporation and its close allies to retain control of city development emerged once more over the building of the Floating Harbour. The radical Thomas Lee believed the whole enterprise scandalous because there had been no open and satisfactory discussion of the potential benefits of modernising the port. He thought it was 'legalizing an usurious interest upon otherwise idle capital' and feared, because some of its principal supporters were members of the Tory White Lion Club, that it would be a measure designed 'to create and to preserve influence, dependence, patronage and monopoly'.[89] This was a politically overdetermined vision of the project, but it did signal the passion such enterprise evoked and the deepening distrust of the mercantile-banking elite among the rank-and-file citizenry, who at the hustings in 1807 allegedly assailed the Blue candidate, Bragge Bathurst, with the cry 'No Dock Tax! No Peculation!'

The commercial oligarchy that controlled the port of Bristol came in for increasing criticism for its sharp practice and lethargy. In 1807, hard on the formation of the Bristol Dock company, the Merchant Venturers successfully lobbied for a wharfage act that clarified their title to various port dues and secured them on a lease of £10 per annum from the corporation. The return on these dues was estimated at £4000 per annum, none of which was ploughed back into the port in the shape of improved facilities.[90] It looked as if the corporate-mercantile elite was profiting from civic privilege, and no doubt entertaining itself to turtle dinners on the side. Certainly the Merchant Venturers were sensitive to criticisms that their profits were poured down their own throats. One member protested to John Matthew Gutch, the editor and proprietor of Felix Farley's Bristol Journal: 'We have no allowance, no equipage, lacqueys or perquisites, a dinner once a year.'[91]

---

[89] Thomas Lee, *White Lion Club, late Riot and Dock Tax* (Bristol, 1807), pp. 15, 28.

[90] B. W. E. Alford, 'The Economic Development of Bristol in the Nineteenth Century: An Enigma?', in *Essays in Bristol and Gloucestershire History*, ed. Patrick McGrath and John Cannon (Bristol, 1976), p. 260.

[91] J. M. Gutch, *Letters on the impediments which obstruct the trade and commerce of the city and port of Bristol* (Bristol, 1823), p. 61.

Insider profits were compounded by a tight grip on corporate privilege. Town dues and wharfage fees remained high, although breaks were given to freemen and to the sugar trade in which so many of the elite had an interest. Such taxes drew the ire of a wide spectrum of opinion, from radicals like Lee to free-trade conservatives like J. M. Gutch, who attacked the corporation and Merchant Venturers for crippling trade through uncompetitive dues. Unless this 'commercial aristocracy' associated itself with new entrepreneurs, he protested, unless it aligned with what he called 'the Democracy and Plebeian interests' of Bristol, there would be a 'chilling blight' on the city's fortunes.[92]

Gutch's diatribes were welcome words to the Chamber of Commerce. Created in 1823, it served as a counterpoint to the commercial aristocracy and began a series of legal challenges to its regulation of the port. In the light of Gutch's critique the corporation made some concessions, reducing dues for the coastal and Irish trade in 1825. Yet Bristol's elite held on to its privileges and continued to plough the familiar pathways of overseas trade. To be sure, there would be some gestures towards arresting Bristol's evident economic decline. A few wanted to develop the industrial resources of south Wales to boost Bristol's fortunes, and as we saw in Chapter 1, there was a move to develop rail links with London and the Midlands.[93] Yet prior to the reform crisis of the early 1830s, the Bristol elite as a whole remained entrepreneurially complacent. Most merchants hesitated to venture from the paths that had brought wealth and civic standing to their families. Some adopted a more passive rentier existence, living in Clifton, Redland or perhaps on a neighbouring estate. Together they formed an introspective patriciate, comfortably situated in their own clubbable world, unwilling to relinquish their corporate privileges, and poorly equipped to deal with the reformist waves that would confront them, beyond resorting to the more blatant forms of repression.

Some members of the elite clearly hoped that a bond of unity might be carved out of the royal celebrations staged by the corporation and the charitable societies, but in the 1820s, in particular, the rather empty effusions of loyalism betrayed real differences in patrician, middling and plebeian responses to these events and generated very little consensus.[94] In 1831 the Bristol corporation was so lethargic in its preparations for the coronation of William IV, perhaps because it knew its days were numbered by the irrepressible waves of reform striking the country, that it was pre-empted by the trades. With their banners and symbols they dominated the event, although

---

[92] *Ibid.*, p. 7.
[93] B. J. Atkinson, 'An Early Example of the Decline of the Industrial Spirit? Bristol Enterprise in the First Half of the Nineteenth Century', *Southern History*, 9 (1987), 70–89. On south Wales, see A. H. John, *The Industrial Development of South Wales, 1750–1850* (Cardiff, 1950), pp. 8, 25, 31–2, and *The Bright-Meyler Papers*, p. 660.
[94] Harrison, *Crowds and History*, ch. 10.

the cordwainers chose to boycott the ceremony on the grounds that 'idle pageantry' could 'only afford the rich and powerful of an opportunity of displaying the wealth that they have wrung from the pockets of the suffering people'.[95] Bristol's elite may have soldered the electoral representation of the city to its advantage, but by 1831 – if not decades earlier – it had lost the ability to command the allegiance of Bristol's citizenry.

[95] *Bristol Mercury*, 13 Sep. 1831; *FFBJ*, 10 Sep. 1831, cited by Harrison, *Crowds and History*, pp. 257–8.

4

Wreckers from Without: Weavers, Colliers, Arsonists and Sodomites, 1729–34

At the end of September 1729, the corporation filed into the Mayor's Chapel on College Green to hear the customary sermon from the Bishop's chaplain, Carew Reynell, at the swearing in of the new mayor. Reynell's themes were equally customary. In January, he had reminded them that 'little jealousies bred discontents, that discontents occasioned murmurings, and murmurings ripened into faction', and in November he would remind them of 'the just sense (they) must have, as a Rich and Trading City, of the Benefits of Government'.[1] Yet as the corporation listened to Carew's sage advice that day, events were unfolding in another part of the city and in its hinterland to the east to ensure the poignancy of his message for several weeks to come. At seven o'clock that morning the weaving community beyond Lawford's Gate had mobilised en masse and set off in a crowd to the house of a Bristol drugget maker, Stephen Fechem in Castle Ditch. Within a day or two, eight would be dead and Fechem in hiding.[2] This chapter considers the often complex relationship between corporate governance, economic hubris and a series of threats to Bristol's stability emanating, or so it was presumed, from 'without the Gate' – not only from marauding weavers and colliers but from criminal extortionists and 'gangs' of sodomites. The self-confident reputation of the merchant elite would be severely tested by challenges of this kind over the next five years, culminating in the unexpected defeat of one of the oligarchy's sitting MPs, the Walpolean minister and the city's Recorder, Sir John Scrope.

Bristol's continued pre-eminence as the nation's second city, it was frequently said, required constant vigilance against factional discord and weak local government. Nourished by two decades of peace, Bristol's economy thrived in the 1730s, as the city finally outgrew Norwich as Britain's second-largest urban centre, and came to dominate the tobacco, sugar and

---

[1] Carew Reynell, *Two Sermons Preached Before the Mayor, Aldermen and Common Council of the City of Bristol* (Bristol, 1729), p. 24.
[2] The death toll, originally estimated at eight, was revised to nine in December. The dead were: John English (a soldier), Christopher Horroway, Andrew Hall, John Rogers, William Hampton, William Terry, John Dyer, John Newton and William Thompson, BL, Add. MS 36192, Duke of Newcastle to the Attorney General, 2 Jan. 1730.

slaving trades.[3] Suggestions from detractors that its culture was materialistic and unrefined were countered by a self-confident corporation, who fondly ordered the publication of sermons like Carew's that elevated merchants to the status of local and national heroes. By 1744, Bristol had become the modern Tyre, counselled A. S. Catcott, rector of St Stephens, 'the crowning city whose merchants are princes and whose traffickers are the honourable of the Earth'. Trade was the *cause* of cities, ran another locally published sermon, 'and cities are as well the nurseries of learning and schools of politeness as the centre of trade and the seat of magnificence'.[4] Pride in their commercial inheritance led the corporation logically to a parallel sense of satisfaction with the libertarian benefits of Whiggery. 'We, who have so much at stake (as a trading city) can never too warmly acknowledge what tends to secure us a free people', proclaimed the mayor in a speech on that theme in 1734. The promotion of conditions under which trade and commerce might continue to thrive was a frequent talking point in the city's pulpits and press, where magistrates were frequently found 'vigilant and active in the suppression of faction and in the promotion of unity and concord'. For the MP Robert Nugent indeed, there were no magistrates in the kingdom with a 'more disinterested concern for the peace and prosperity of the city they have under their care'.[5]

This was well and good, but it was to prove a difficult decade. Three times during the 1730s, Bristolians were shaken from their collective reverie by the unprecedented and unwelcome arrival of gangs of extortionists, threatening (and attempting) wholesale arson against mercantile property. These attacks spread later to adjacent counties and finally to London, but the significance of their first appearance at Bristol was not lost upon the local community, nor the intense frustration of their fruitless attempts to tackle it. And while fruitlessly chasing the shadowy perpetrators, the corporation, by chance or design, launched a vigorous campaign of its own to prosecute men suspected of sodomy. Moreover, they did so as the first press reports arrived in English towns of the sweeping and vicious pogroms then being carried out against sodomite 'clubs' in the Dutch republic, together with exaggerated rumours that hundreds of Dutch suspects were on their way, under cover, to claim sanctuary in English ports.[6] In fact, a rhetorical association between the

---

[3] In a little over two decades of continuous growth, the population within the city liberties had escalated from about 23,000 in 1712 to 30,000 in 1735; Latimer, II, 194.

[4] A. S. Catcott, *The Antiquity and Honourableness of the Practice of Merchandize: A Sermon Preached Before the Worshipful Society of Merchants of the City of Bristol* (Bristol, 1744). See also the arguments presented in Andrew Hooke, *Bristollia, or Memoirs of the City of Bristol* (Bristol, 1748).

[5] *Samuel Farley's Bristol Newspaper*, 30 March 1734; Rev. William Batt, *Union and Loyalty Recommended: A Sermon Preached at the Mayor's Chapel, 15th September 1754* (Bristol, 1754).

[6] For the Dutch pogroms, which caused a considerable moral panic in the Low Countries and an enormous number of executions, see L. J. Boon, 'Those Damned Sodomites:

arsonist and the sodomite had been noted a few years earlier by Daniel Defoe. Both arson and sodomy were non-clergyable offences, historically associated with Catholic otherness and intrigue, perpetrated (or so it was thought) by secretive and shadowy figures, and in practice inextricably linked to criminal extortion. As we shall see, at Bristol, the mental journey between imagined gangs of incendiaries and imagined sodomite coteries was negotiated without difficulty, so that by 1734 sodomites too 'caused great uneasiness in that ancient and prosperous city' and had regrettably become 'the talk of the town'.[7]

Not all of Bristol's imagined enemies were shadowy and anonymous however. Some gathered openly in destructive crowds; weavers, colliers and 'country people' from the city's peripheries and across the county border at Lawford's Gate to the east. These tensions were felt all the more strongly at Bristol because despite retaining control of the corporation since 1696, the Whigs, many of whom as Dissenters were barred from holding office, had never been able to secure steady Whig representation in parliament. The Tories romped home with both seats in 1710 and held them until the accession of George I in 1714. By that time, the city's Whig oligarchs had become practised in passing the Kingswood colliers off as Tory hirelings and Jacobite mercenaries, the blunt instruments of civic destabilisation. 'Four in five of the sober, honest, thriving part of the magistrates and citizens of Bristol are Whigs', boasted a pamphleteer after disturbances during the 1713 election and at the coronation a year later. 'And the Torys could never have carry'd any point here ... These High Church colliers hardly ever heard of religion till Cheverel was the word, given them by the faction, and as they will do anything for a drink, the faction take care to give them enough of it when they are wanted.'[8] The Whig elite paraded their Hanoverian loyalism as openly as possible during these years, signalling their Walpolean opposition to Tory Jacobitism with grand public gestures. When the notorious London Jacobite, Nathaniel Mist, used his weekly newspaper to compare George I's administration with the corrupt court of Persia, the Bristol Grand Jury quickly publicised their 'utmost indignation and abhorrence' in the loyalist press, putting the names of each member to a public demand for Mist's prosecution for 'a

Public Images of Sodomy in the Eighteenth Century Netherlands', and Theo van der Meer, 'The Persecutions of Sodomites in Eighteenth-Century Amsterdam: Changing Perceptions of Sodomy', both in *The Pursuit of Sodomy: Male Homosexuality in Renaissance and Enlightenment Europe*, ed. Kent Gerard and Gert Hekma (New York, 1989).

[7] Allegations of a popish plot to burn Bristol to the ground were revealed in 1679. For Defoe, see Ian McCormick (ed.), *Secret Sexualities: A Sourcebook of 17th and 18th Century Writing* (London, 1997), pp. 49–50. For civic distress over sodomy, see *Gloucester Journal*, 17 Feb. 1732; *London Journal*, 24 Sep. 1734.

[8] *The Bristol Riot, containing a full and particular account of the riot in general ...* (London, 1714). See also John Miller, *Cities Divided: Politics and Religion in English Provincial Towns, 1660–1722* (Oxford, 2007), pp. 272, 279–83.

libel that must be detested by every British subject that hath any regard for our present Happy Establishment'.[9]

In Carl Estabrook's estimation, the weavers, most of whom resided beyond the Gate, were a good deal more Bristolian by inclination than the colliers.[10] In fact, however, the relationship between cyclical agricultural work, mining and weaving in the economy of Kingswood Forest is not so easy to pick apart, and all three forms of employment certainly served communities living in close proximity and quite possibly in shared housing. Weavers had the capacity to collectively defend craft skills that colliers had not, but we might also differentiate them by their geographic dispersal on both sides of the Gate and in Bedminster to the south, and their interdependent relationship with Bristol-based masters. In this sense, weavers straddled, and were influential in, communities both in and outside the city boundaries. While the colliers carried a reputation as Jacobites moreover, weavers were usually regarded as Protestant and inclined towards Whiggish Dissent. Whatever the intricacies of the polity, the Gloucestershire bench came frequently under fire from Bristolian interests for neglecting its duty in this far-flung corner of the county. 'Mobbing' would prosper and grow, it was feared, 'unless the Justices who have power outside Lawfords Gate, the place of the rendezvous of the mob (and is a bad as the Mint was in London), exert themselves more to hinder it for the future than has been done in time past'.[11]

As we shall see in Chapter 6, the colliers of Kingswood rose in numbers against the introduction of turnpikes on the city's main approach roads in 1727 and developed a well-earned reputation for both industrial action and the enforcement of moral economy in Bristol's markets. Their reputation as Jacobite hirelings became pertinent once again during the 1730s, when the determination of the Whig elite to steer a course independent of Walpole's government allowed the corporation to take a leading role in provincial opposition to the 1733 Excise Bill. This divided the electorate to such an extent that the Recorder Sir John Scrope, one of the city's two Whig members and a minister under Walpole, unexpectedly lost his seat to the Tory, Thomas Coster, in the election of 1734. The corporation had done its best to minimise party considerations in its objections to the bill, but was powerless to prevent the burning of Walpolean effigies, including of Scrope, in several parts of the city. Its position was somewhat ambivalent. Although the stated intention of the public celebrations it sponsored was to toast and eulogise the king rather than castigate his ministers, at least one effigy-maker was taken up on the mayor's instructions. According to one openly hostile report, 'most

[9] Daily Courant, 25 Sep. 1728.
[10] Carl B. Estabrook, Urbane and Rustic England (Manchester, 1998), pp. 67–8. Estabrook's conclusions rest on the assumption that the marriage registers for St Phillip and St Jacob give the birthplaces of the registrants. In fact, the places named could simply be the residences at the time of marriage.
[11] London Journal, 11 Oct. 1729.

of the considerate people were greatly disgusted' by this action. Indeed, it was rumoured 'a new set of Healths' was being drunk in the Council House, and the mayor had become 'principal promoter' of 'riots and tumults'.[12]

These events took place against a background of bullish political posturing, most notably in the corporation's lavish commissioning of Rysbrach's equestrian statue of William III as a centrepiece for Queen Square – a target for further Jacobite rioting – and, importantly in 1737, the establishment of the Tory Steadfast Club as a focal point for organised opposition. Jacobitism provided a context for a good deal of division and disorder in the city after Scrope's dismissal, with Lawford's Gate frequently a symbolic presence in the divide, and these incidents illustrate something of the complex social relations between and within the Lawfords Gate community. On the king's birthday in October 1735, a Tory mob disrupted official celebrations by seizing and destroying the corporation's loyal illumination, but there had been worse trouble earlier in the summer. In June, the annual Coronation Day celebrations prompted rumours that weavers beyond the Gate were to parade effigies of the pope, the Pretender, and Tory MP Thomas Coster. Fighting broke out when a Tory mob 'out of the City', but supported by colliers, 'supposed to be hired for that purpose', surrounded and then broke into the weavers' houses. Shouting 'Coster for ever!', they seized and destroyed weaving equipment, cloth and some fireworks. No effigies were discovered and they had to be forcibly dispersed by magistrates, who made a number of arrests. The majority were acquitted at the March assize in Gloucester, but one, Nathan Pick, who had been cleared of loom-breaking in George Street, was issued with a second warrant for a misdemeanour. The four men selected as bailiffs to re-arrest him – a publican, a baker and two soap boilers – clearly identified themselves with the weaving community, and one at least had suffered damage to his property. They armed themselves with staves and set about their task with some enthusiasm. In the mêlée that followed, Pick escaped but his sister, Sarah Williams, was badly beaten, and she was taken up for rescue along with her husband. When she subsequently died of her wounds in Gloucester gaol, the four bailiffs found themselves committed to the assize for her murder, but they were acquitted. Contrary to the findings of the inquest, the court ruled Williams's wounds to have been caused by a beating administered by her husband sometime earlier. No charges were laid against him for causing her death but he was arraigned and fined one shilling for the rescue.[13]

Given their scapegoat status and association with Catholic/Jacobite politics, it is perhaps surprising that the colliers were not suspected of involvement in the arson extortion panic of 1730, although the oligarchy certainly

[12] Kathleen Wilson, *The Sense of the People: Politics, Culture and Imperialism in England, 1715–1785* (Cambridge, 1998), p. 127; *Daily Courant*, 19 April 1733; *Read's Weekly Journal*, 21 April 1733.
[13] *Grub Street Journal*, 19 June 1735; Latimer, II, 193; *Read's Weekly Journal*, 17 July 1736; *Daily Gazetteer*, 9 July 1735, 9 Sep. 1736.

convinced themselves that foreign and Irish wreckers lay behind the plot. The colliers' occasional appearance during riots 'dressed in Women's Cloaths and high crown'd Hats', and their subsequent association with a convicted Bristol sodomite, Richard Baggs, who hired them as a protective guard at the pillory, only confirmed their alien status in the city. On that occasion indeed, the magistrates arrested and imprisoned nine of them for allegedly 'riotous' behaviour against the burgesses in front of the pillory, and 'to let them see that they were not above the Authority of the Law'.[14] Local fears that outbreaks of moral degeneracy might reflect badly upon the reputation and future stability of the whole town surfaced visibly in the wake of disturbances like these. As economic growth became increasingly tempered by competition from northern ports, Bristolians grew wary of impending decline, and conscious of the debilitating effects of self-pride and 'luxury'. These concerns are discernible, for example, not only in a resurgence of local interest in Quaker prophecies of imminent eschatological disaster, but in John Wesley's declaration of war upon the city's 'indolence, effeminacy and idleness', which 'effect trade in an high degree'.[15]

The Corporation and the Weaving Disputes of 1729–33

Trouble had been simmering amongst the weavers beyond Lawford's Gate for two years prior to the march on Stephen Fechem's house in Castle Ditch. In the autumn of 1726, textile workers in Wiltshire had managed to persuade sympathetic county magistrates and two parliamentary commissioners to mediate a dispute with clothiers over various cost-cutting measures, and despite a number of confrontations with troops, they were encouraged to petition the Commons for redress. The Privy Council found in their favour and persuaded both sides to enter into an 'Agreement', to be overseen by the county bench, to better regulate conditions of labour and settle all future disputes. It failed to hold, but weavers unsurprisingly emerged with a stronger sense of legitimate right in disagreements with their masters.

Events in Wiltshire were not without their impact in Bristol. In August 1726, two textile workers without the Gate were taken up by a Gloucestershire JP during a dispute over the size and weight of warping bars. The following day, five hundred weavers forcibly released them and attacked the houses of

---

[14] Serious incursions from the colliers occurred in 1727, 1731, 1735 and 1738. For their alleged political contexts, see Robert W. Malcolmson, 'A Set of Ungovernable People: The Kingswood Colliers in the Eighteenth Century', in *An Ungovernable People: The English and their Law in the Seventeenth and Eighteenth Centuries*, ed. J. Brewer and J. Styles (London, 1979), pp. 93–5, 105–6. For the pillory episode, see *Daily Journal*, 18 Sep. 1732.

[15] For Wesley, see Peter T. Marcy, 'Eighteenth Century Views of Bristol and Bristolians', in *Bristol in the Eighteenth Century*, ed. Patrick McGrath (Newton Abbot, 1972), p. 20. For Quaker prophecies, see *A Collection of Sundry Messages and Warnings to the Inhabitants of the City of Bristol*, 2nd edn (Bristol, 1728).

two prominent employers, Edgar on St Phillip's Plain and Fechem in Castle Ditch. After causing considerable damage, they marched through Temple Street to Bedminster, cut cloth from the looms of several weavers, burned it in the open street, and then marched back. All this was accomplished under the eye of the military, who were given no orders to interfere, although according to some accounts several were 'shot but not mortally'. Agreements for mediation by magistrates were negotiated at Stroudwater and Bristol in the coming months, although the refusal of clothiers to be bound by them remained a constant source of friction.[16]

Poor harvests and rising prices in 1727 and 1728 prompted economically squeezed employers to cut piece rates further, drawing a reciprocal response from the Lawford's Gate weavers. In October 1728, a crowd of five hundred 'pretended weavers … from Bristol, from without Lawford's Gate, Bedminster and other places', downed tools over these reductions and destroyed about thirty looms before marching into Somerset and doing the same in Keynsham, Pensford and Chew Magna. They broke windows, seized looms and cloth, and 'burnt the same in a great fire they had made in the church-yard', then 'cut their beds, destroy'd their goods, ate or carried away all their victuals so that they left them destitute either of tools or materials to work or any other means of maintaining their familys'. Although the rural victims of this incursion alleged that many in the crowd were not actually weavers but 'butchers, ropers, tylers, carpenters and other disorderly idle fellows', the only four men named in evidence were certainly weavers; John Gamer from St Phillips, and Marmaduke Holbrooke, Joseph Lewis and Abraham Jenkins from Bedminster.[17]

Trouble resumed the following year on 1 September when, at the instigation of the prominent clothier and grand jurist, Henry Tonge, some of the Bristol masters lowered piece rates on long ells (longer pieces of cloth) by sixpence. One again, looms were carried into the street and fired and the houses of offending masters surrounded. The military were called to protect buildings, which on this occasion proved a sufficient enough measure and they were not required to act.[18] According to his own later account, Stephen Fechem, whose house in Castle Ditch had been severely damaged by crowd action three years earlier, had already made it clear to his workers that he would stand by previous agreements.[19] An anonymous 'letter from Bristol' went so far as to claim that once Fechem had 'stood their friend', Tonge's confederacy was broken and the reduction shelved. Sensing their advantage, the weavers now pushed for an increase instead, stopped work, and 'would

[16] Daily Journal, 17 Aug. 1726; FFBJ, 13 Aug. 1726; Adrian Randall, Riotous Assemblies: Popular Protest in Hanoverian England (Oxford, 2006), pp. 140–1.
[17] Somerset Heritage Centre, Q/SR/296/23–4, Information and examination of John Jenkins and Arthur Peters, 22 Oct. 1728; FFBJ, 30 Sep. 1728.
[18] Gloucester Journal, 9 Sep. 1729.
[19] TNA, SP 36/16 pt 1, Deposition of Stephen Fechem, 20 Nov. 1729.

have had Mr Fechem, who had been their friend before, be the first in thus raising the price' from eight to nine shillings.[20] Fechem 'told them that was a rate or price he could not afford to give ... but assured them he would never lower their wages'. The dispute rumbled on for several weeks but reached stalemate in late September when clothiers refused to give out any more work until their men agreed to accept the lower rates first proposed by Tonge. This brought the weavers back into Bristol in force. While the local bench was busy at the mayor-making service in the Mayor's Chapel on 27 September, a crowd marched to Castle Ditch where they first confronted the clothier, Nehemiah Harris, and did some serious damage to the front of his house. They then sent a smaller deputation to Fechem and told him that unless he now agreed to pay at the higher rates, they would come back and give him 'as good a breakfast next Monday morning as they had given Harris a dinner'.

Fechem told them he could not afford it and appealed to the city bench for protection. The new mayor 'promised him help and bid him provide to stand on his own defence', an extraordinary enough piece of advice in itself, given that the Earl of Deloraine's Regiment of Foot was billeted in the city at the time. These were experienced soldiers, who four years earlier in Glasgow had been embroiled in a bloody encounter with a crowd protesting the Malt Tax, killing nine rioters and wounding a further seventeen.

So, hoping for support from some riot-seasoned troops, Fechem took the magistrates' advice, equipped himself with thirteen blunderbusses and prepared for trouble.[21] Early on Monday morning fourteen men from Deloraine's regiment, headed by two sergeants, formed up outside Fechem's house, but with orders 'not to fire anything but powder', presumably because no JP was sent with them to read the Riot Act and neither was there an officer to direct their actions. Meanwhile Fechem learned that beyond Lawford's Gate, a crowd of 140, all stripped to the waist, had gathered outside the house of a weaver called George Bidgood, and 'had bound themselves by an oath to each other, that the first that would come to this deponent should rip open his body and drag him by the guts or bowels about the street and that for that purpose they had fastened a knife with a blade crooked or bent inwards at the end of a staff'.

In fact, some complex negotiations had been taking place without the Gate that morning. According to John Skynner, a London merchant on business in Bristol that week, knots of weavers were waiting on every street corner for the return of Porch, the landlord of the White Hart, who had gone to parley with five clothiers, including Fechem, to give them one last chance to come to terms. The well-dressed Skynner was quickly suspected as a spy as he eavesdropped and was forced into a hasty retreat, but he stayed just long enough to witness Porch's return with an agreement signed by three out of five masters. Some in the crowd were for calling a truce on receipt of this

[20] *London Journal*, 11 Oct. 1729.
[21] *London Journal*, 11 Oct. 1729.

118

news, but others were interested only in what Fechem had said. Porch told them that Fechem had repeated his promise not to lower the price of labour but would not agree to raising it while threatened by weavers. According to Skynner, 'Porch did not doubt that he should bring him over likewise and exhorted them to disperse in a peaceable manner and sleep upon it.' They demanded to know whether Fechem was armed. When Porch confirmed it, some said 'All is over; its all over.' But stronger voices carried the day. 'I don't value my life of a farthing', said one, 'let us be revenged on the villain.'

So the crowd, armed with swords, clubs, sticks and stones, and including most 'if not all weavers', now advanced to Castle Ditch. There, 'assisted and attended by a vast number of women with stones in their aprons', they hurled stones at the soldiers.[22] Fechem's civilian party retreated indoors and watched as the panicking and poorly commanded guards fired powder ineffectually into the air. Realising the soldiers had no ball, the crowd grew bolder and came forward, at which one of the sergeants shouted for Fechem to open fire himself or they would be overrun. Windows were broken and a cellar door forced before an all-out assault was made on Fechem's front door. As one of the two sergeants grappled with the crowd in the doorway, live powder and ball was fired by the defenders inside, killing the sergeant and three weavers outright and wounding several others.

Further mayhem was prevented only by the arrival at last of the city magistrates, a party of constables and the rest of Deloraine's regiment 'headed by their proper officers'. The Riot Act was speedily read, some arrests made and the rest of the crowd dispersed, many of them carrying off wool, wine and other goods plundered from Fechem's cellar. They spent much of the evening carousing in and around Temple Street with 'the city in an uproar'. That night and then again over the next few days, the houses of any weavers loyal to Fechem were similarly attacked and relieved of their contents so that, the clothier complained, he lost upwards of £200 worth of stock.[23] Tonge was now ready to come to terms with his workers and began giving out work again, 'but the other Party seized and destroy'd it'.[24]

The corporation's extraordinary mismanagement of this affair caused them further discomfort in the ensuing days as coroner's inquisitions were returned on the bodies of the fallen. This was complicated by five mortally wounded weavers being carried back to Kingswood and dying beyond the jurisdiction of the city. Unsurprisingly, Fechem was exonerated of the deaths recorded in Bristol, but a Gloucestershire coroner's jury sitting on the other five returned a verdict of manslaughter after deliberating for three days. A warrant was issued for his arrest and trial at the next Gloucestershire assize. Fechem immediately fled the city and petitioned the secretary of state (the Duke of Newcastle) for a pardon. This was granted to Fechem and two of his servants

[22] TNA, SP 36/16 pt 1, Deposition of John Skynner, 20 Nov. 1729.
[23] TNA, SP 36/16 pt 1, Deposition of Stephen Fechem, 20 Nov. 1729.
[24] Weekly Journal, 17 Oct. 1729.

on the advice of the Attorney General Sir Philip Yorke in December. Yorke also urged Newcastle to pursue legal action against weavers still languishing in Bristol Newgate, 'for Example's sake and in order to deter people from the like offences'. The mayor had already forwarded about twenty-five examinations and depositions taken from these captives and Yorke considered it an easy enough matter to secure convictions on the capital charge of cutting wool from the looms.[25]

Fechem was arraigned at the Kings Bench Bar in June 1730. He pleaded the Royal Pardon and was released.[26] Despite Yorke's call for exemplary prosecutions amongst the weavers, relatively few appear to have been so treated, although cases were commenced in at least three different courts. Some were arraigned before the Somerset assize in March 1730, and at least one, John Callway, was convicted and condemned to death, although he insisted he had been an involuntary participant. He pleaded that when the weavers rose, he 'absconded from his house and business', but he was discovered, beaten and intimidated into joining the protests against the masters. Callway won a respite but remained in Ilchester gaol where he was still languishing in great distress several months later. He petitioned the crown for a pardon, 'in great misery and want, having no money nor friends to support him, nor clothes to cover his nakedness and has a wife and a large family of small children wholly unprovided with the necessaries of life'. In fact, even evading the noose, Callway was fortunate to have survived, for gaol fever amongst prisoners awaiting trial at Ilchester had swept through the courtroom during the trials, causing the premature deaths of two sergeants at law, the High Sheriff, Sir John Piggott, and even the presiding judge, Lord Chief Baron Pengelly.[27]

At Bristol's summer assize, four other protesters, including Jonathan Dye and William Osborne, were brought before the recorder, Sir John Scrope, and bailed for a year. At Gloucester, Samuel Reynolds, John Perry, George Bidgood and John Gomerfield (or Gornerson) were each convicted of loom-breaking in Temple Street in the wake of the shootings outside Fechem's house, and condemned to death. Reynolds and Perry were reprieved but Bidgood, who, it will be remembered, had earlier been singled out by Fechem as a ringleader, was ordered for execution along with Gomerfield. The latter was then also reprieved, leaving Bidgood alone to hang. The decision to execute him at Gloucester rather than at a site closer to Bristol suggests unease on the part of the crown, for a hanging so far from the community on which it was intended to make an impact cannot have been conceived as exemplary. Bidgood died 'penitent' according to press reports,[28] but – especially in the light of Fechem's exoneration – his death did not make the weavers any more acquiescent.

---

[25] *Weekly Journal*, 11 Oct. 1729; TNA, SP 36/16, P Yorke to Newcastle, 20 Dec. 1729.
[26] *London Evening Post*, 16 June 1730.
[27] TNA, SP 36/21, Petition of John Callway, n.d. [1730]; *Monthly Chronicle*, April 1730.
[28] *London Evening Post*, 18 July 1730; *Fogs Weekly Journal*, 1 Aug. 1730; *British Journal*, 12 Sep. 1730; BA, JQS/D/7, Quarter Session Minute Book, 1729–33.

The situation remained tense throughout 1731 as a further 'abatement' in the woollen trade set in, and in November Bristol's clothiers made a renewed attempt to reduce wages. Crowds of weavers withdrew their labour once again, gathering on the streets outside the Gate to protest a recession that 'has render'd those that have large families very low'. 'Should their Masters present Design take effect', reflected one observer, 'how much more miserable must those poor subjects be?'[29] By March 1732, Fechem's business was ailing. To the irritation of his workers, he ceased trading and 'absconded' from the city, quite possibly because he owed some of them money. They responded by parading his effigy through the city, in a cart with a halter round his neck, to the site of the 1729 affray in Castle Ditch. Here, 'one of them raising the hand of the effigy spoke something for him expressing his sorrow for the murders there committed', then the procession wound its way up to the gallows on St Michaels Hill for a mock execution before retracing the route back to Lawford's Gate. A large crowd 'from diverse parts of the city' witnessed these counter-theatrics, 'the weavers going two by two with long sticks in their hands to represent the constables and two of them who personated the sheriffs were mounted upon asses for, poor creatures, they could not afford a horse, not even so much as to draw the cart'. Although this demonstration took the form of a charivari, Fechem's mock hanging was considerably more exemplary and bullish than Bidgood's, and it culminated with a gibbeting at Lawford's Gate and a paid 'Watch' to prevent Fechem's friends from cutting it down over the next few days. The city bench risked interfering only to veto a route that too closely replicated the official processional way though the central streets from Newgate to the gallows. Fechem, who never returned to the city, was declared bankrupt a week or two later.[30]

The robust objections of the colliers to turnpikes in 1727 and of the weavers to wage reductions in 1729 were a timely reminder to the corporation of the city's vulnerability to attacks by large, mobile and assertive groups of workers from communities just beyond its boundaries. Both represented challenges to enterprise and to the ability of the city's mercantile and political elite to protect the interests of entrepreneurial trade. They exposed not just the frustrations of mixed and limited jurisdiction in a city whose urban form was fast outgrowing its traditional boundaries, but a good deal of uncertainty about how best to respond. Within a few short months of George Bidgood's execution in 1730 moreover, the local bench was distracted by a far more insidious and potentially damaging threat to its authority – and one characterised not by highly visible crowds of workers with a recognisable grievance but by silent, anonymous and shadowy figures, motivated entirely, it seemed, by a desire to plunder mercantile wealth.

[29] *Daily Advertiser*, 30 Nov. 1731.
[30] *Read's Weekly Journal*, 25 March 1732, 1 April 1732; Bodleian Library, MS *Gough, Somerset 2*, fol. 169, 13 March 1732.

The Bristol Firemen

Shortly after midnight on 3 October 1730, a series of brilliant 'fireballs' or hand-made grenades were seen arching through the air on St Augustine's Back and over the wall of merchant George Packer's mansion house on the Butts. There was 'a noise like the report of several guns' followed by quickly spreading flames. Within minutes, Packer's home was ablaze, his household in full flight. But for a favourable wind, the fire might easily have spread to nearby warehouses and the dense flotilla of wooden ships crowding the adjacent quay. Plunged into 'the utmost consternation', Bristolians would be gripped for several months afterwards by the fear of shadowy fire-raisers they could neither identify nor apprehend. The newspapers would dub them 'The Bristol Firemen'. George Packer had just become the first English victim of organised criminal extortion by arson, a protection racket of ingenious simplicity that required its targets either to part with their money or have their houses burnt down. It was, marvelled the London press, 'a new kind of robbery' to which 'history does not afford a parallel'. As the contemporary doggerel had it, 'What Prince in's palace can be void of fear/ While these INCENDIARYS are lurking near?'[31]

Historians have paid relatively little attention to the ways and means of urban fire-raising. The great south-western catastrophes of Tiverton (1732), Blandford (1735) and Crediton (1743) have been well documented, but these were accidents. Arson as a political weapon has also been studied, especially in the rural world, and in Bristol and Portsmouth through the activities of John the Painter during the American Revolutionary wars.[32] Historians of crime have been slower to grasp its significance. As interest developed in 'social crime' during the 1970s, E. P. Thompson briefly cited the Bristol episode as a 'crime of anonymity', but arson remained unnoticed in the painstaking typology laid out by John Beattie in 1986.[33] Nevertheless, it would be

---

[31] *The Historical Register*, 60 (1730), pp. 306–7; *London Evening Post*, 6 Oct. 1730; Richard Chapman, *New Year's Gift; Being a seasonable call to repentance, as well upon the account of some threatening incendiaries, as of the more threatening vices of the present age … in a poem, moral and divine* (London, 1731).

[32] Penny Roberts, 'Arson, Conspiracy and Rumour in Early Modern Europe', *Continuity and Change*, 12 (1997); Bernard Capp, 'Arson, Threats of Arson and Incivility in Early Modern England', in *Civil Histories: Essays Presented to Sir Keith Thomas*, ed. Peter Burke, Brian Harrison and Paul Slack (Oxford, 2000); E. P. Thompson, 'The Crime of Anonymity', in *Albion's Fatal Tree: Crime and Society in Eighteenth-Century England*, ed. D. Hay, P. Linebaugh, J. Rule, E. P. Thompson and C. Winslow (London, 1975); Carl Griffin, *The Rural War: Captain Swing and the Politics of Protest* (Manchester, 2012); Jessica Warner, *John the Painter: The First Modern Terrorist* (London, 2004); Steve Poole, 'A Lasting and Salutary Warning: Incendiarism, Rural Order and England's Last Scene of Crime Execution', *Rural History*, 19:2 (2008), 163–77; John Archer, *By a Flash and a Scare: Arson, Animal Maiming and Poaching in East Anglia, 1815–1870* (Oxford, 1990).

[33] J. M. Beattie, *Crime and the Courts in England, 1660–1800* (Oxford, 1986).

difficult to overestimate the profound anxieties felt by contemporaries when faced with the purely avaricious Firemen and their imitators in the 1730s.

A fortnight before his house was destroyed, George Packer had received a number of anonymous letters threatening to fire it and murder his family unless he left six guineas, either in a hole in the wall in Swan Lane or in the wall of St Augustine's churchyard on the other side of the river. The family fled first to the house of a fellow merchant, John Clements, and from there to Packer's country estate, but the threats continued. He might run into twenty different houses, asserted one letter, but they would burn them all, 'and pursue him till he had nothing to subsist on'. Then, on 5 October, Clements's house was also targeted.[34]

Packer did not return to the city, but the threatening notes continued. One was posted on the gates of Sir Abraham Elton's house in Queen Square, while others were received by Clements, a maltster in Temple Street, several owners of shipping anchored at Sea Mills, and a Marsh Street merchant named Boltley who was also suspected of sheltering Packer. If Packer would only agree to pay the ten guineas demanded of him, the letter ran, 'neither he nor his family should come to any further harm and that, by G_d, if he did not, they would murder him the first Opportunity that happen'd'. When letters were sent threatening a number of houses at Canons Marsh, several merchants began moving their goods to places of greater safety. 'I would not have you fill yourself with such fancies as to think you will catch us', boasted one letter, 'for you will never, as long as Bristol stands, tho' £1000 rewards shall be offered, it is past the art of man to find us out, for we give the letters to boys in the street, unknown to us and we to them'.

Rewards were indeed offered for useful information and they were not ungenerous. The crown pledged £100 and an indemnity to anyone who came forward to give evidence, the corporation added a further £31 10s, the Fire Office £50 and Packer himself £21, but the money remained unclaimed. Fireballs were subsequently launched into Teague's and Farr's warehouses in Canons Marsh but the scale of the damage is not recorded. Since the attack on Packer's house had required the Firemen only to wait until the night watch had made their first round, magistrates quickly realised that extra guards were necessary. The watch was doubled and volunteer constables enrolled. Soldiers were brought in from Lord Mark Kerr's regiment, and posted by every threatened building. Suspects against whom only the flimsiest evidence could be gathered were daily examined at the Guildhall, and an ambitious plan proposed to 'search every house in the city and suburbs'. Copies of affidavits taken in Bristol were forwarded to the secretary of state in the hope of attracting government funding for prosecutions. Boltley received two further letters demanding twenty guineas be left in the wall in Swan Alley. He complied, but on both occasions the money remained untouched, very possibly because Kerr's soldiers had the place under surveillance. In fact, a man was seen at

---

[34] *The Historical Register* (1730), pp. 206–9.

Boltley's back door one evening before running off through Marsh Street, and soldiers were quickly ordered to seal the approach roads while constables conducted a house-to-house search. Even so, the suspect could not be found.[35]

Letters with Bristol postmarks from some 'poor b'leag'd tradesmen' were delivered to the Duke of Beaufort in November. They demanded that he leave ten guineas at the sign of the Elephant in Old King Street, or they would be 'going a journey' towards his house and 'have your heart or money'. Beaufort appealed for help from William Brydges, a Gloucestershire JP, who wrote immediately to the secretary of state. 'His Lordship and family have been placed under apprehensions that can be better imagined than expressed', Brydges observed, adding for good measure, 'these villainous practices ... very much terrify his Majesty's subjects in these parts, especially when attempts of this nature are made upon persons of rank and quality'.[36]

After the Boltley incidents, much suspicion was entertained of Bristol's Irish community in and around Marsh Street, and a number of arrests made. 'Five or six Irish fellows' were initially detained and before long, 'those of the Irish nation who cannot well account for their way of life', began leaving Bristol, and 'not in a little hurry'.[37] Since actively lending support and manpower to the French since the 1690s, the Irish in England were easily cast as Jacobites, enemies of the Hanoverian regime and, as the press would have it, 'a shoal of vermin who are capable of enlisting themselves in the French or any other foreign service rather than in that of their own country'. *The British Journal* was explicit:

> You, Beelzebub, are the prince of incendiaries, and to you, in some measure, doubtless Mr Packer of Bristol and several other worthy subjects owe their late misfortunes. You give courage to those inferior beings who fire but houses while you are toiling to fire a Nation. They see with what impunity you scatter your firebrands and strive to emulate you in their wickedness.

Rumours that the Irish were implicated spread quickly to neighbouring towns, so that when a letter was discovered at Frome at the end of October, 'the Town rose in great number and ... were resolved if they found any strangers of a certain nation, that could not well account for themselves, to tear them to pieces'.[38]

John Power, the son of an Irish attorney, finally became the principal suspect. He was arrested on the Quay after a ten-year-old girl recognised him as the man she had seen throwing a letter into Boltley's shop. Two boys, already in custody for delivering a letter to George Packer, then identified

---

[35] *British Journal*, 17 and 24 Oct. 1730, 14 Nov. 1730; *London Journal*, 21 Nov. 1730; *London Evening Post*, 20 Oct. 1730.

[36] TNA, SP 36/21, Wm Brydges to secretary of state, 10 Nov. 1730, with enclosures.

[37] *Grub Street Journal*, 15 Oct. 1730.

[38] Peter Linebaugh, *The London Hanged: Crime and Civil Society in the Eighteenth Century* (London, 1991), p. 297; *British Journal*, 12 Dec. 1730; *Grub Street Journal*, 5 Nov. 1730.

Power as the man who had instructed them. If Power's presumed Catholicism was not motive enough, papers 'found about him' indicated he was 'in great necessity', and when it emerged that he had lodgings in Swan Lane, opposite the hole in the wall in which the money was to have been left, magistrates were convinced of his guilt and sent him to Newgate. Encouraged by this success, they then moved against a number of Power's suspected 'confederates'. These included his uncle, newly arrived at Bath to play the tables, and three of his friends, 'one of them Irish'. Soldiers were posted to Bristol's Irish enclave in Marsh Street, further searches made, and several more Irishmen arrested, although Power was the only one against whom a case could be built. Confined for very nearly a year on the flimsiest of evidence and repeatedly protesting his innocence, Power initially refused food and 'behaved in a very insolent manner' when questioned. Indeed, given that he was lodged at first in the gaol's 'pit' or condemned cell, chained to a staple, 'without pen, ink, paper, fire or candle, far distant from my relatives and destitute of money', Power may have felt he had much to be insolent about. 'I fear there are some clandestine dealings devised against me', he speculated.[39]

For three weeks following the fire at Packer's house, copycat notes concerning 'these new-invented black practices', proliferated in neighbouring south-western towns, including Stroud, Exeter, Tewkesbury, Barnstaple, Chepstow and Exeter, where a merchant was warned to 'remember Bristol and Mr Packer'. Local administrations did what they could, but once again evidence was difficult to gather. At Bridgwater, where guards were appointed to 'clear all suspicious persons' from the town and its surrounds, a merchant was promised, 'We will serve you as we did Packer', while at Gloucester, constables were sworn in to 'clear petty alehouses on the outskirts of the city' and take up 'all strolling people'. Two women were lodged in the gaol on suspicion. In Taunton the committal of two further suspects prompted a threatening letter to 'Mr Mare', reading 'G-d d--n you; if you don't let those persons out of Bridewell, we will set the Town and your House on Fire. We are one hundred in a Gang, G-d d--n you, chase us if you can.'[40]

The Bristol acts of arson eventually spawned a spate of similar threats in other parts of the country. In Kent and Hertfordshire two men were prosecuted under the Black Act for sending threatening letters demanding money, and at least one of them, Jeremiah Fitch, a joiner from St Albans, is known to have swung for it.[41] Threatening letters continued to appear in Bristol too; indeed, reasoned Power, since 'incendiaries were still sending out their

[39] *London Evening Post*, 8 and 20 Oct. 1730; *Daily Post*, 13 Oct. 1730, 15 Dec. 1730; *Gloucester Journal*, 8 June 1731, 21 Sep. 1731; Latimer, II, 172.

[40] *British Journal*, 7 Nov. 1730, *Evening Post*, 14 Nov. 1730; *London Journal*, 21 Nov. 1730; *Read's Weekly Journal*, 14 Nov. 1730.

[41] *London Evening Post*, 11–13 March 1731; *Daily Advertiser*, 22 March 1731; *Read's Weekly Journal*, 13 and 27 March 1731. For the Black Act, E. P. Thompson, *Whigs and Hunters: The Origins of the Black Act* (London, 1975). Thompson notes (pp. 245–6) that the act could be used against incendiaries, but he did not cite these cases.

flagitious letters for some time after my confinement', his innocence should be obvious. The mayor thought it merely proof that he had accomplices and continued questioning him. They had few other leads after all, but were momentarily diverted by the arrest of two horse thieves at Devizes, who confessed they had been in the company of two incendiaries who operated at Bath and were party to drafting no fewer than fourteen threatening letters. One of the arsonists named Ned, a plasterer and tiler, allegedly swore 'that the Rich Men had it all in their own Hands, and Damn them, He wou'd make them know that One should not have all and the others none'. Such an outbreak of class hostility alerted Bristol's mayor, who was very keen to read the depositions of the horse thieves, since Packer was mentioned as a target along with a Dr Allen of Bridgwater. Arrests were made but no evidence could be found and the suspects were released.[42]

Then, in September 1731, Power was finally put before the assize, after what he called his 'long and melancholy confinement'. He complained from the outset not only that he had been denied proper representation but that the clerk to the court, who had prepared the case for the crown and whose impartiality was essential, was 'employed as solicitor against me'. The only witnesses against him were 'the Children, who varied very much in their Depositions', and he was quickly acquitted.[43]

The inability of the corporation to settle the nerves of the merchant elite after the firing of Packer's house did nothing to repair dents in the second city's self-confidence. Coming so soon after its uncertain handling of the Fechem affair, the corporation's inability to deal with the Firemen only further exposed the city's vulnerability to hostile external threats. Bristolians were assured that 'the magistrates are as diligent in their examination as an affair of such importance requires' and were 'very assiduous in examining persons daily', yet convictions did not follow. Moreover, thanks to the continuing and extensive publicity given to the extortionists by the London and regional press, not only was George Packer's name known and cited the length and breadth of the country by November, but a damaging association between incendiarism and Bristol was clearly etched in the public mind.[44] Nor did the matter end there, for in 1734, against a background of renewed anti-turnpike rioting between Bristol and Gloucester, three letters were sent to a wealthy gentleman on St Michael's Hill. There was a further incident three years later, when 'the incendiaries begun their old game as they did in the year 1730'. This time the target was John Combes, 'an eminent merchant on College Green'. The threatening note demanded twelve guineas; it was composed 'in the usual style of fire and faggot'. As usual, a number of 'suspicious persons'

---

[42] TNA, SP 36/21, fols 9–11, John Eyles to the Duke of Newcastle, 12 Dec. 1730; *Gloucester Journal*, 21 Sep. 1731; *Read's Weekly Journal*, 19 Dec. 1730; *Echo, or Edinburgh Journal*, 16 Dec. 1730.

[43] *Monthly Chronicle*, Sep. 1731.

[44] *British Journal*, 17 Oct. 1730.

were rounded up and an attorney with similar handwriting held for questioning, but no further action followed.[45]

The Saints Backsiding: Sodomy Panic in the 1730s[46]

In 1756, the Bristol curate, schoolmaster and doggerel poet, Emanuel Collins, published an extraordinary moral vindication of the city in response to growing rumours that it was a place in which 'unmanly', 'unnatural' and unlawful sexual behaviour was both rife and tolerated. Purges against sodomites appear sporadically in the Hanoverian period in London and one or two other provincial towns, but as Collins's pamphlet made clear, Bristol's reputation was unparalleled, and its origins can be squarely traced back to the difficult years of the 1730s. 'I am not unacquainted with the many foul reflections that have been cast on my Fellow-Citizens of BRISTOL concerning this most abominable vice', Collins began, but 'tis the fate of all cities to be the conflux of bad men.' They go there 'to hide themselves in the multitude and to seek security in the crowd'. It was no more the fault of the citizens of London that the capital attracted thieves, he protested, than it was the fault of those of the second city if *it* attracted sodomites. 'Must the enormous vices of the provinces in our neighbourhood be charged to our burgesses?'[47]

The statistical evidence that underlay these concerns is worth exploring in some detail. At least fifty-eight allegations of non-animal related sodomy were made before magistrates at Bristol between 1730 and 1800, 61 per cent of them ending in conviction. It is singular enough that some 40 per cent of these prosecutions took place during the 1730s, but even more so that the decade produced only four convictions from a total of twenty-three prosecutions; a very low success rate of just 17 per cent. Moreover, this apparent failure of the courts to enforce moral virtue was reflected in several outbreaks of public vigilantism. According to accounts published in the press, one suspect was almost 'torn to pieces before he could either be examined by a magistrate or committed to prison', another had his penis almost severed with a knife, and another found himself 'well mobb'd, confoundedly pelted,

---

[45] *Daily Courant*, 25 June 1734; *Read's Weekly Journal*, 5 Nov. 1737.

[46] This section is largely based on Steve Poole, '"Bringing great shame upon this city": Sodomy, the Courts and the Civic Idiom in Eighteenth-Century Bristol', *Urban History*, 34:1 (2007), 114–26.

[47] Emanuel Collins, *The Saints Backsiding: or, The Remarkable Case of a Late Reverend, Holy, Anabaptistical Preacher belonging to Their Meeting in Bristol, Who Had Been Too Fond a Pastor of the Ram Lambs, to the Great Offence of the Young Neglected Ewes, To Which is Added an Historical Account of his Armours, Intrigues, Successes and Disappointments Amongst his Male Sweethearts* (Bristol, c.1756). Little more is known of Collins. In the pejorative verdict of the chronicler George Pryce, however, he was 'one of the strangest fellows that ever wore a cassock … scribbling for inclination and publishing for gain'. See George Pryce, 'Emanuel Collins', *Notes and Queries*, 3rd series, 8 (Sep. 1865), 214.

and beat thro' divers streets' where 'the butchers got him into their common
Beast Penn, and dragg'd him thro' the filth, till the wretch was almost suffo-
cated'.[48] Yet even when 'a devil of a blow among the sodomitical gang'
caused 'a list of those Hell Cats, with their proper names and effeminate
Titles' to fall into magistrates' hands, no suspects were prosecuted.[49] In keeping perhaps with broader concerns about secretive coteries of wreckers from
without, accusations were sometimes made against associated groups of men
rather than lone individuals and couples. Two multiple prosecutions against
a total of thirteen defendants, which made use of the additional count of
'aiding, abetting and encouraging sodomy', were approved by the Grand Jury
between 1733 and 1734, but no convictions were secured and no sworn affidavits have survived.[50]

Difficulties experienced in mounting prosecutions and securing convictions at Bristol during these years were unlikely to inspire much praise for
the alacrity of the magistrates or for the vaunted impartiality of the judicial
system. As we have seen, these were years in which it was severely tested.
Moreover, the coincidence of moral disquiet, political anxiety and hostility from without should not be overlooked. The sodomy panic of the 1730s,
in other words, was the symptom of a related series of political and administrative problems that were specifically Bristolian in origin. A second city
whose eminence had been built upon foreign trade was particularly suscep-
tible to charges of hubris and self-satisfied introspection. Bristol's economic
miracle had created fortunes but also a taste for luxury among her wealthiest
mercantile families, and 'luxury', as contemporaries were fond of reminding
themselves, was emasculating, foreign and un-Protestant. Sodomy, as the
Bristol press would later have it, was a 'vice of foreign growth imported from
abroad'. Emanuel Collins's determination to distinguish native genius from
the perversions visited upon it by contact with the outside world reflected a
local polity in which the consequences of ethnic and global dilution could
be seen and heard in the course of a morning's walk along any of the port's
teeming quays.[51] Like arsonists, sodomites were suspected of both confederacy
and secrecy. They were hard to detect because they were rarely what they
seemed. One, 'an old lecher from Leicester', convicted at Bristol in 1737, it
was alleged, 'infested this country upwards of five years lurking for his Prey

[48] Read's Weekly Journal, 22 Aug. 1730, 9 Sep. 1732; Gloucester Journal, 28 Dec. 1731,
18 July 1732, 1 Feb. 1737.
[49] Gloucester Journal, 1 March 1737.
[50] BA, JQS/D/7, Quarter Session docket book 1729–33, entries dated Aug. 1732 and
March 1733; BA, JQS/D/8, Quarter Session docket book 1733–37, entries dated 4 Sep.
1733 and 9 Sep. 1734; Gloucester Journal, 13 March 1733; Read's Weekly Journal, 3 and
17 March 1733.
[51] FFBJ, 15 Oct. 1768. The quotation is from an advertisement announcing a new edition
of Saints Backsiding.

under the different Characters and Disguises of a Solicitor, a Gentleman of an Estate, a Steward to a Nobleman, a Cook, a Tapster, and other Shapes'.[52]

The purging of sodomites at Bristol began with the successful prosecution and conviction of a man called Richard Baggs for an attempted assault on a male servant in 1732. Baggs may not have been a native of Bristol, but neither was he a typical outsider. On the contrary, he was a wealthy woollen merchant in the city and a guardian at St Peter's Hospital for the poor. His appearance in the pillory left him roundly pelted despite his mercenary guard of colliers, and the whole event was subsequently immortalised and celebrated in verse. Baggs's case, which was compounded by the simultaneous disclosure that he had been embezzling hospital funds, became something of a benchmark, helping not only to model the sodomite as a specific danger to civic virtue, and feeding concern that sodomites might *appear* to be virtuous citizens on the outside, but also confirming the diligence of the local bench in exposing and bringing them to justice.[53] The city's consequent concern over the next few decades with the uncovering and suppression of sodomites was extraordinary and unparalleled. 'The very Reason that our Town has been talk'd of', Collins thought, 'was because it always appear'd diligent and unwearied in discovering and prosecuting such Offenders, wheresoever they came from, that were found within our Jurisdiction.' The city press was in full agreement. 'If we take a survey of what had formerly passed', reflected *Felix Farley's Bristol Journal* in 1753, 'we shall soon perceive how ardent, how zealous, the magistrates of this city were in bringing every Wretch of this stamp to condign punishment. They have condemned, – they have pillor'd, – they have punished in every shape, where the least evidence appeared to convict.'[54]

If determination of this sort suggests a prejudicial legal system, impartiality was not always a popular cause in any case. When magistrates rejected the claim of Samuel Baber in 1737 that he had been sexually assaulted by a man, and instead convicted him for extortion on the evidence of his intended victim, it cut no ice with the city crowd. Instead of pelting Baber at his subsequent pillorying, they listened while he 'made an harangue to the People, desiring them to take warning by him, not to take a bribe to screen persons from justice, when a sodomitical attempt was offer'd'. Preferring to believe Baber's story, the crowd 'were so civil as to pelt themselves, and left him alone to be a spectator to their dirty sport'.[55] After another suspect, Adam Raffs, was acquitted at the same sessions following some inconclusive evidence and a string of young women who 'gave him a good character', popular frustration

---

[52] *Newcastle Courant*, 24 Sep. 1737. We are grateful to Pete Rushton for sharing this reference with us.

[53] *Gloucester Journal*, 4 April 1732; *Read's Weekly Journal*, 9 and 16 September 1732.

[54] FFBJ, 17 Sep. 1752; Collins, *Saints Backsiding*.

[55] BA, JQS/D/8, Quarter Session docket book, 1733–37, entry dated 16 March 1737; *Read's Weekly Journal*, 29 March 1737; *Gloucester Journal*, 12 April 1737; *Sherborne Mercury*, 5 April 1737.

was temporarily assuaged by the first successful conviction of two consent-ing men, Thomas Hull and Robert Rawlings, for attempted buggery. Yet, although the court sentenced them to two stints in the pillory, they were so savagely beaten on their first exposure that magistrates intervened to take them down early and the second exposure was rescinded.[56]

Matters came to a head in 1738 when the courts finally secured a capital conviction against David Reid, whose local unpopularity rested not only on allegations of sodomy, nor even upon his negative status as an outsider, but on his ethnicity as a Scot and his employment as a billeted soldier. Despite the reported readiness of the mayor to send Reid to the gallows however, the local bench was overruled by interference from central government and Reid's execution was respited on petition. Reid himself, now languishing in gaol, became haunted not only by lynch mobs goaded on by the city press, but by a mayor who remained 'determined to hang me himself if I was the last man in England'. Despite receiving clemency, he protested to ministers, 'I die hourly'. Public delight at the prospect of Reid's death is certainly reflected in much of the surviving literature. Possessed of an 'innate wickedness and malice ... the people of Bristol Repine at the Royal Clemency', the prisoner wrote. If Reid had not been reprieved, the *Sherborne Mercury* remarked, he would have been 'tucked up to the satisfaction of the whole city'.[57]

Yet this slant on events is heavily dependent upon the trail of correspond-ence passing between Reid, his regiment, the authorities at Bristol and central government. It does not seem to have been disseminated on the streets of Bristol, where, according to Collins at least, the finger of blame had come to rest on the mayor for apparently granting Reid his life, a rumour given strength by the disclosure that Reid would have hanged if the execution had not been postponed to accommodate the election of a new mayor. Reid's reprieve arrived the following day. The idea that the aldermanic bench had gone soft on sodomy at a time when the ruling oligarchy was still recovering from the loss of Scrope's parliamentary seat and the consequent revival in Tory fortunes was a further unwelcome challenge to the corporation and the influence it appeared to exercise over local affairs. Its enemies well under-stood its vulnerability. The poet Richard Savage for example, embittered at his gaoling for debt in the early 1740s and forced to share Newgate prison with the still incarcerated Reid, predicted disaster. 'Proceed great Bristol', he

---

[56] *Gloucester Journal*, 20 Sep. 1737; *Sherborne Mercury*, 5 April 1737, 20 Sep. 1737; BA, JQS/D/8, Quarter Session docket book, 1733–37, entries dated 16 March 1737, 7 Sep. 1737.
[57] TNA, SP 36/46, David Reid to the Earl of Scarborough, 6 Sep. 1738; Brigadier General Roger Handasyde to the Earl of Scarborough, 6 Sep. 1738; Abel Dagge (keeper of Newgate) to the Earl of Scarborough, 16 Sep. 1738; David Reid to the Duke of Montague, 20 Sep. 1738; and Petition of David Reid, n.d.; *Sherborne Mercury*, 3 Oct. 1738.

mocked, 'Still spare the catamite and swinge the whore/ And be whatever Gomorrah was before'.[58]

The fact that Reid's case, and the controversy surrounding it, was dredged up by Emanuel Collins eighteen years afterwards, says much about its impact on popular memory at Bristol. As Collins inferred, it was plausibly the single most damaging source of the city's sullied moral reputation amongst outsiders. Not only were prosecutions less forthcoming in the years following Reid's reprieve, press coverage declined too. It is possible, of course, that contrary to outward appearances, the rumour mill of accusations ground inexorably on. This possibility is given weight by an odd, yet unsupported remark in two newspapers that the arrest of a man in 1741 was 'the third … within these three months', and by an admission in another that 'the sound of SODOMY is so odious and offensive that we have occasionally omitted the little Thing sent us on that Topick'.[59]

---

[58] Richard Savage, *London and Bristol Compar'd – a Satire written in Newgate*, Bristol (London, 1744). For the last-minute nature of Reid's reprieve, see *Sherborne Mercury*, 3 Oct. 1738.

[59] *Sherborne Mercury*, 17 March 1741; *Gloucester Journal*, 17 March 1741; *FFBJ*, 20 Sep. 1752.

5

Popular Jacobitism and the Politics of Provocation

In March 1756 a by-election was held in Bristol to replace Richard Beckford, the West Indian planter and merchant, who had briefly represented the constituency. The previous election two years earlier had proved prohibitively expensive, especially for the Whigs, who spent over £30,000 getting Robert Nugent elected, and there was a disposition on both sides to come to some kind of compromise. A joint committee of the Steadfast and Union Clubs initially agreed that the Steadfast would choose a candidate to replace Beckford, technically a Tory, with the understanding that the Union should have the next vacancy. According to Josiah Tucker, the pamphleteer and rector of St Stephen's who was among those who tried to broker the deal, a 'club of low tradesmen among ye Dissenters' rejected it, believing it would be in their interest to have an MP of a Nonconformist denomination to represent the City.[1] The Union Club was not happy with this intervention and informed the Tories that if the well-known Bristol attorney, Jarrit Smith, stood as their candidate, it would raise no objection.

As it was, a contest could not be avoided. Jarrit Smith, a well-connected local Tory, but a reluctant candidate at sixty-four years of age, found himself facing an aristocratic outsider. He was John Spenser, a 21-year-old pipsqueak, heir to the fortune of Sarah, Duchess of Marlborough, and backed by the Sunderland family. In another electoral battle that emptied pockets, Smith edged out Spenser by fifty-two votes, a mere fraction of the 4765 cast; to date, the highest number that had ever polled in a Bristol contest and probably 90 per cent or more of the eligible electorate.[2] Spencer's friends, piqued that they had been unable to mobilise a shifting population of soldiers and sailors to prevent defeat, demanded a scrutiny. The 'Blue Mob' protested, Josiah Tucker recalled, and threatened the sheriffs with their lives unless they made 'a fair return, that is, returned Mr. Smith'.[3] The sheriffs complied, much to the jubilation of Tory supporters in town and country, where sheep were roasted whole and local dignitaries chaired in imitation of the victory parade

---

[1] BL, Add. MS 11, 275, fols 147–8.
[2] In 1754, 4738 freemen and freeholders voted.
[3] BL, Add. MS 11,275, fols 154–5.

in Bristol. In reply, the Whigs complained to parliament of an unfair return, but failed to overturn the verdict.

In early April 1756, Jarrit Smith returned to Bristol to celebrate his victory. He was met near Keynsham by three thousand supporters, many decked out in Tory blue, or at the very least sporting blue favours. Some carried streamers with the words, 'Smith and Liberty', 'King George, No Pretender'.[4] Huge crowds hailed the cavalcade, and mobs slowed Smith's own chariot by hanging on the harness of his horses. Smith's grand entry into Bristol was greeted with a cannonade and ended before a triumphal arch on College Green, where the old attorney resided. The arch was boldy inscribed 'Smith and Liberty'. On one side was Smith's family arms; on the other the arms of the late Thomas Coster, Tory MP for Bristol 1734–41, and Smith's brother-in-law. It was accompanied by a representation of Justice treading on Envy, a tart reminder of the Whigs' willingness to break the electoral deal and venture thousands of pounds to gain Bristol's second seat.

The initial arrangement of the arch had included something more controversial. Lacking the royal arms, the organisers had borrowed those of All Saints' church, which was undergoing renovations. The problem was these arms were pre-Hanoverian. They were the royal arms of the Stuart line and caused some consternation, enough to have them removed. The regulating officer for the port of Bristol, Captain Samuel Graves, locked in a dispute with the Tories over the impressment of one of their supporters, could not resist pointing this out. 'I think it my Duty to acquaint their Lordships', he wrote to the Admiralty, 'how that party shew'd themselves yesterday upon expecting the Return of their Member, Jarrit Smith. They put up a Triumphal Arch with the Arms Proper of the Royal House of Stewart before the Union, which I suppose was well understood by that party.' [5] How well understood, how deliberate, was a moot point. Some writers cast the incident off as a genuine oversight, especially in the light of the streamers that had accompanied the cavalcade; others were not so sure. The 'outrageously loyal', reported the *Public Advertiser*, put it out that it was an 'Act of Rebellion and setting up the Pretender's Standard'.[6]

The political charge of Jacobitism might seem odd. The Forty-Five rebellion was over, the insurrectionary threat of a Stuart restoration had been thwarted. In 1746 Bristol had celebrated the victory over the rebels at Culloden by burning an effigy of the Young Pretender in Prince Street and illuminating the Exchange coffee house with the motto 'King George triumphant and his Succession everlasting'.[7] Yet the language of Jacobitism

[4] *FFBJ*, 3–10 April 1756.
[5] TNA, Adm 1/1833 (Samuel Graves) 7 April 1756, cited in Nicholas Rogers (ed.), *Manning the Royal Navy in Bristol: Liberty, Impressment and the State, 1739–1815*, Bristol Record Society, 66 (Bristol, 2013), no. 37.
[6] *Public Advertiser*, 13 April 1756.
[7] *FFBJ*, 11 Oct. 1746.

continued to resonate in Bristol. White roses were flaunted on the Pretender's birthday (10 June) in 1750 and the bogey of Jacobitism spilled onto the hustings four years later in the shape of Sir John Philipps, a Pembrokeshire baronet with trading links to Bristol through Haverfordwest and Milford Haven. Sir John belonged to a club of prominent landowners in west Wales, the Sea Sergeants, which was thought to be a hotbed of Jacobitism.[8] During the Forty-Five rebellion he had tried to convince a Westminster grand jury that ultra-loyalists were bullying inhabitants into joining their associations, an argument that was bound to raise eyebrows as the Young Pretender and his army ventured as far south as Derby and panic broke out in London. Philipps also had links with the Independent Electors of Westminster, one of whom, the erratic Welshman David Thomas Morgan, was a requisitioning officer and adviser to the Young Pretender in Manchester, and was executed for his treasonable activities in July 1746. A few years later Philipps represented an Independent Elector at King's Bench, one Alexander Murray, brother to Lord Elibank, a well-known Jacobite. He had demanded a writ of habeas corpus for Alexander Murray, whom the Commons had imprisoned for libelling and abusing the High Bailiff of Westminster during the 1749 by-election and defiantly refusing to apologise before the House. Sir John Philipps of Picton Castle was in fact an independent country gentleman who was not afraid to espouse unpopular causes in the name of liberty. Within his own fiefdom in west Wales he probably felt he could do what he damn well liked, and if that meant drinking a few toasts to the 'King across the Water', so be it. Linked to the Walpoles by marriage, he even joined the Pelham administration in 1744 as a Lord of Trade, but his flamboyant libertarianism and High Anglican Toryism made him politically suspect, and he didn't last long in that position. In 1754 he was fair game for a Whig smear campaign that sought to tarnish the Steadfast Society with Jacobitism. Bristol had given clear evidence of its loyalism in 1745, raising between £30–40,000 for auxiliary troops to meet the Jacobite invasion from the north, with the corporation contributing £10,000 and some aldermen as much as £500.[9] Less that ten years later, the Steadfast Society was prepared to sponsor a man who disparaged such activities and rubbed shoulders, even conspired, with known Jacobites.

When Jarrit Smith's supporters raised the Stuart standard on College Green they were very likely joking at their opponents' expense, thumbing their nose at the Union Club and the Whig-dominated corporation. In local taverns they were said to have toasted Sir John's health along with several

---

[8] P. D. G. Thomas, 'Jacobitism in Wales', *Welsh Historical Review*, 1 (1960–63), 279–300; Francis Jones, 'Disaffection and Dissent in Pembrokeshire', *Transactions of the Honorable Society of Cymmrodorion* (1946–47), 206–31; Donald Nicholas, 'The Welsh Jacobites', *Transactions of the Honorable Society of Cymmrodorian* (1948), 467–74; Nicholas Rogers, *Whigs and Cities. Popular Politics in the Age of Walpole and Pitt* (Oxford, 1989), pp. 294–9; Eveline Cruickshanks, *Political Untouchables: The Tories and the '45* (London, 1979), p. 99.
[9] *Bath Journal*, 11 Oct. 1745, 4 Nov. 1745.

unmentionable ones, presumably seditious plaudits for the Stuarts.[10] This was quite likely, as Jacobite sympathies continued to surface in pub conversations and disputes. In late 1753 a merchant tailor named William Ball damned the corporation and professed that he would 'fight for Prince Charles against the King'.[11] In the run-up to the 1754 election a tin-plate worker flamboyantly declared at the Coopers' Arms in Tucker Street: 'George is a Cuckold and Jemmy's a King, and we shall be happy when Jemmy comes in.' He rounded off this couplet with a toast to King James.[12]

What one should make of these seditious remarks is unclear. Neither of these pub confessions prompted a prosecution, although the depositions were taken down by the Whig mayor, Abraham Elton, and could have been pursued more rigorously. Most likely they provoked exasperation rather than fear; they were solitary, intemperate denunciations by alienated artisans, not tocsins of popular revolt. Toasting Sir John Philipps and a king across the water in a by-election celebration was of the same kidney, a gesture of political defiance and impudence. It was invoking the Tory ghosts of the past, including Jarrit Smith's father-in-law, Sir John Smyth of Long Ashton, who was dismissed from the Somerset bench during the Hanoverian accession crisis for being too soft on sedition. It was recalling the debut of Thomas Coster, whose victory over the Whigs in 1734 spawned mischievous interventions on Whig anniversaries. Originally the arms of Coster and Smith were placed on either side of the arch, with the Stuart standard in the centre.[13] Contemporaries might have wondered whether they represented the Pretender's emissaries, redolent of the 'devils' that accompanied the effigy of the Pretender in the loyal pageants of the Forty-Five.

This politics of provocation had a long history in Bristol. It was founded on a bedrock of sectarian strife that stretched back to the civil war. Bristol developed a strong Nonconformist presence in that era, and once the royalists had re-established themselves after the Restoration, strenuous efforts were made to cut it down to size. The Bristol corporation was purged of commonwealth men in October 1661, most of them members of congregations outside the established church. Royalist zealots strove to enforce the laws against recusancy by imprisoning hundreds of Nonconformists. Sir John Knight, senior, MP in the Cavalier parliament and mayor in 1663, is said to have incarcerated as many as nine hundred during his year of office. This policy of harassment, dramatic in years when royalist zealots were in the civic saddle, had a mixed success. Most councillors were not interested in a rigid enforcement of the Clarendon Code, particularly the Conventicles Act of 1664. They wanted to stay on reasonable terms with Dissenting merchants and tradesmen, particularly those of a Presbyterian persuasion, who made a

[10] *Public Advertiser*, 12 April 1756.
[11] BA, TC/Admin/Box/7/1/6, 12.
[12] BA, TC/Admin/Box/7/1/4,6, 10.
[13] *London Evening Post*, 10 April 1756.

significant economic contribution to the city. Ichabod Chauncy claimed that the persecution of Protestant dissenters meant forfeiting the Bristol Customs of £2000 a year in port duties.[14] The result was that Nonconformity survived the purges of the post-Restoration era. According to the Compton census of 1676, the Nonconformist population amounted to 11.2 per cent of the Bristol population, almost certainly an underestimate.[15] By the early eighteenth century the different denominations made up approximately a fifth of the city's inhabitants, and a larger percentage of its aggregate wealth.

In the heady politics of the 1680s it was often difficult to maintain a middle ground in a city that was becoming increasingly polarised by party. The politics of the exclusion crisis and its aftermath were tense moments for Bristol. Royal zealots like Sir John Knight junior, a former West Indian factor and cousin to his namesake in the Cavalier parliament, cracked down on Dissent, convinced that these heirs to the commonwealth were bent on destroying the monarchy. Along with John Hellier, he prosecuted many radical sectaries and ordered the demolition of the Presbyterian conventicle in Broadmead and a Quaker meeting house in the Friars. He even tried to implement an old Elizabeth statute by which those who did not conform to the church and refused to leave the realm were punishable by death.[16] Richard Vickris, a Quaker merchant, was convicted under this brutal statute and lay under sentence of death in Newgate. It was only through the interventions of William Penn, the governor of Pennsylvania, that he escaped a hanging.[17] This political extremism provoked its counterpart, particularly after the failure to exclude James, Duke of York, from the throne. Radical Whigs like Colonel John Rumsey the Customs collector, John Roe the sword-bearer, and Nathaniel Wade, a lawyer and son of a Cromwellian army officer, were part of an armed insurrection to topple James. So, too, was clothier Joseph Tiley, and Joseph Holloway a linen draper and merchant. They were members of the Horseshoe Club in Bristol and also of an independent congregation in Castle Precincts; three of them, Rumsey, Roe and Tiley, rubbed shoulders with the leading Whig peers and politicians at the Green Ribbon Club in London.[18]

---

[14] Ichabod Chauncy, *Innocence vindicated* (London, 1684), p. 11. On the disposition not to persecute, see Jonathan Barry, 'The Politics of Religion in Restoration Bristol', in *The Politics of Religion in Restoration England*, ed. Tim Harris, Paul Seaward and Mark Goldie (Oxford, 1990), pp. 169–70.

[15] Barry, 'Politics of Religion', p. 181n.

[16] Latimer, I, 406–9.

[17] Tim Harris, '"Lives, Liberties and Estates": Rhetorics of Liberty in the Reign of Charles II', in *The Politics of Religion in Restoration England*, ed. Tim Harris, Paul Seward and Mark Goldie (Oxford, 1990), pp. 225–6.

[18] Melinda Zook, *Radical Whigs and Conspiratorial Politics in Late Stuart England* (University Park, PA, 1999), pp. 9–11, 21, 103–4, 111, appendix. Richard L. Greaves, *Secrets of the Kingdom. British Radicals from the Popish Plot to the Revolution of 1688–1689* (Stanford, 1992), pp. 99, 123, 154–5. There are good accounts by these authors of Rumsey, Roe and Wade in the ODNB. See also Jonathan Barry, 'Politics of Religion', p. 176.

Rumsey was the Earl of Shaftesbury's henchman; along with Robert Ferguson he was responsible for coordinating plans for a rising in the south-west. After the discovery of the Rye House Plot in which at least five Bristolians were implicated, Rumsey was captured and banished. Roe and Wade fled. Ichabod Chauncy, another Rye House plotter, a popular physician who was reputedly the 'bellwether of the phanaticks' at the independent chapel in Castle Green, Bristol, was also banished, largely on the evidence of the Bristol town clerk, who had been harrying him for Nonconformity. Finally James Holloway was outlawed, captured in the Caribbean, and executed. His dismembered body was sent back to Bristol for all to see.[19]

The exposure of these plots prompted the moderate royalists to purge the corporation once again. In July 1684 nineteen councillors were replaced and twenty-seven new men brought in. This purge did not, however, extinguish Whig extremism. Roe and Wade joined the Duke of Monmouth in his western rising; Tiley even proclaimed him king at Taunton. Many more might have joined the illegitimate son of Charles II had not the Duke of Beaufort quickly occupied the city with seven troops of cavalry and called out the militia. Historians continue to speculate what might have happened had Monmouth entered the city from the Keynsham side; some feel he erred in delaying his march to Bristol and not testing its allegiance. The Earl of Feversham believed Bristol was 'in a great ferment', strong enough for at least one Baptist minister to leave the city and meet the rebel army.[20] Lord Chancellor Jeffreys thought Bristol a 'most factious city', arguably worse than Taunton, one of the principal centres of Monmouth's support. Yet in the bloody reprisals that followed the rebellion, few Bristolians were executed or transported.[21] Although Jeffreys assured Charles II he would 'pawn my life and loyalty that Taunton and Bristol and the county of Somerset too shall know their duty before I leave them', only six were tried for treasonable practices and three hanged on Redcliff Hill. Three rebels condemned at Wells were hanged, drawn and quartered in Bedminster, however, an exemplary punishment pointedly directed at Bristolians to bring them to allegiance. One of the victims, a Bristol shoemaker named Edward Tippett, protested 'he did not more than go to see the army'.[22]

If the Monmouth rebellion tested the allegiance of the Whigs in Bristol, James's religious politics tested the resolve of the Tories. Strongly Anglican and monarchical, they were deeply disturbed by James's willingness to use his

[19] Latimer, I, 418–24; Greaves, *Secrets of the Kingdom*, pp. 246–7. On Chauncy, see the entry by Jim Benedict in the *ODNB* and Chauncy's own *Innocence Vindicated*.

[20] Peter Earle, *Monmouth's Rebels* (London, 1977), p. 95. Barry, 'Politics of Religion', p. 178.

[21] In total 250 rebels were executed, many hanged, drawn and quartered. This was roughly 7 per cent of the rebel army. Earle, *Monmouth's Rebels*, p. 175.

[22] Samuel Seyer, *Memoirs historical and topographical of Bristol* (2 vols, Bristol, 1823), II, 532; *An account of the proceedings against the rebels … tried before Lord Chief Justice Jefferies*, 2nd edn (London, 1716), p. 20.

dispensing power to tolerate Catholics. In May 1686 Sir John Knight junior alerted the mayor to a Catholic Mass and had the offending priest arrested. In celebration, a crowd staged 'a profane and indecent pageant in which the Virgin Mary was represented by a buffoon, and in which a mock host was carried around in procession'.[23] Troops tried to stop this drollery, but the crowd resisted, egged on by leading Tories. King James reacted to this affront by flooding the commission of the peace with country gentlemen and hauling Bristol's Tories on the carpet. Sir Richard Hart, the chief of the ultras, was ejected from the council. Bishop Trelawny, questioned by Lord Sunderland, only evaded censure by obsequious backtracking. Not so the irascible Sir John Knight junior, no friend to papist or Dissenter. He was brought before the Privy Council with the mayor and five aldermen and charged with 'terrorizing' citizens in the streets with his sword. To the chagrin of the Attorney General, and no doubt the town clerk who informed against him, Knight was acquitted in December 1686 by a local jury.

James responded to this setback by once more remodelling the Bristol corporation. This time he purged eleven Tories from the council on the grounds that they opposed the Declaration of Indulgence offered to both Protestant and Catholic recusants. They included John Lane, the mayor who had arrested the celebrant priest, and John Rumsey, the town clerk who had provided evidence against the errant Sir John Knight, but who was also an active campaigner against conventicles. In their stead he introduced a conspicuous number of Dissenters, one of whom, Thomas Scrope, was the son of a regicide. To the astonishment of Bristol's Tories, James replaced Rumsey with none other than Nathaniel Wade, the Rye House plotter and Monmouth supporter, a man who had sought his destruction a few years earlier. This move was impolitic and capricious. It was certainly not a reasoned effort to win over a new bourgeoisie in Bristol politics, as has sometimes been suggested.[24]

The remodelling brought James little in the way of support for his Catholicising policy, even in a city as Nonconformist as Bristol. In November 1687, following the visit of the Papal Nuncio to the city, Bristolians vigorously celebrated the anniversary of the Gunpowder Plot to signal their displeasure with court politics. In June 1688, they scarcely celebrated the news of the birth of the Prince of Wales. What little was done compared poorly with the jubilations that greeted the release of the seven Bishops from the Tower a month later.[25] Unsurprisingly, as support for James visibly crumbled from within, Bristolians expressed further displeasure with his policies. In December 1688, Catholic houses in King and Castle Street were attacked.

[23] Latimer, I, 439.
[24] By J. R. Jones, *The Revolution of 1688 in England* (London, 1972).
[25] In April 1688 seven bishops refused to publicise James II's Declaration of Indulgence towards Catholics and Dissenters. They were tried for seditious libel but acquitted on 30 June. This was a very significant setback for James's pro-Catholic policy, and indeed, for his regime.

Prompted perhaps by Hugh Speke's manifesto on behalf of William calling on the population to disarm all Catholics, a Mass house was gutted and its contents burnt in the street.[26] The Duke of Beaufort, sent in to occupy Bristol for the king, saw which way the tide was turning and declined to call out the trained bands on whose loyalty he could no longer rely. He was very troubled by the 'universall disaffection' of Somerset and presumably felt it might be contagious. Or he moved cautiously, considering his own political options. Either way, anti-Catholic crowds had a free hand dispensing rough justice until they were contained by the Earl of Shrewsbury's troops. Among those who helped restrain the crowd was Sir John Knight and Sir Thomas Earle, Tories who had hitherto been at loggerheads about the enforcement of religious uniformity but who now shelved differences in the interests of social order. The only plausible source of support for James, and it scarcely surfaced in 1688/9, was from Ireland. Hugh Speke had circulated letters disclosing 'an universal Conspiracy of the Irish and their Popish Adherents' and so a close watch was kept for Jacobite agents sailing into Bristol, intensified no doubt by rumours of imminent massacres of Protestant men, women and children by disbanded Irish soldiers.[27]

In a world that ideologically favoured the Whigs, Bristol remained Tory in the immediate aftermath of the 1688 Revolution. Hart and Knight won support for their virulent anti-Catholicism and opposition to James's religious policy, but Knight had to use dirty tactics to discredit the candidature of the moderate Tory Sir Thomas Earle with whom he had recently restrained anti-Catholic crowds. He also had to contend with a strong Whig challenge from Earle's nephew, Robert Yate, and the city Recorder, William Powlett, who both had the support of the Dissenters and the militia.[28] Earle countered the charge that he had traded with Britain's enemy, the French, by denouncing Hart and Knight as Jacobites. The accusation was not inapt because, while they personally detested James, both had voted against the offer of the crown to William and Mary and retained a residual belief in the hereditary divine right of kings. They did not waver from that path and were both arrested as potential Jacobite conspirators in the 1696 plot to assassinate William III. They were released after an inconclusive examination by the Privy Council, although Knight was recharged with treason and imprisoned in Newgate for four months, possibly to remove his factious presence from Bristol while the Whigs consolidated their hold on the corporation.

The ultra-Toryism of people like Knight had some purchase in the Bristol area. In 1718 Edward Bisse, the rector of Portbury and St George, the parish

---

[26] Latimer, I, 451; Greaves, *Secrets of the Kingdom*, pp. 324–5. John Marshall, *John Locke, Toleration, and Early Enlightenment Culture* (Cambridge, 2006), p. 134 cites attacks on chapels in thirteen towns outside London, including Bristol.

[27] Latimer, I, 452; Greaves, *Secrets of the Kingdom*, p. 325.

[28] See Andrew A. Hanham on 'Bristol 1690–1715', in <http://www.historyofparliamentonline.org >.

of the Pill pilots, ran into trouble for denouncing George of Hanover and declaring the country had 'no Laws these Thirty Years, never since the Time of King James the Second'. The post-1688 era had simply involved England 'in a bloody and expansive war' Bisse asserted, 'and instead of our lawful and rightful sovereign, we [had] a poor diminutive worm, the Prince of Orange, set up in his place'. Bisse was arrested for these seditious remarks but he was rescued by his parishioners and allowed to thunder his sedition across several counties before he was brought to trial at King's Bench. Fined £600 and imprisoned for four years, he remained an unrepentant Jacobite, for in London's Newgate he was reported as having given a printer 'a copy of verses upon the numerous attendance of the Pretender abroad'.[29] Pilloried at Charing Cross, no offal or excrement was thrown at him. A man who denounced him as a villain was berated by the crowd.

Bisse was an idiosyncratic figure, something of a self-appointed martyr. Formerly a battler at St Edmund Hall, Oxford, he was known as 'mad Bisse' by fellow Aularians. He has been improbably compared to Henry Sacheverell, the Tory cleric whose sermons and trial created such an uproar in 1710.[30] Crowds might have admired his audacity, or his ability to be indicted for sedition in three different counties, but in the West Country his unqualified commitment to the Stuart cause still placed him in a minority. Bisse repented the fact that he had sworn loyalty to William and Mary; he wished he had remained a non-juror. Yet in the West Country non-jurors were few on the ground. Of the 568 noted by John Overton, the western dioceses of Bath and Wells, Bristol and Gloucester mustered only 22 (3.9 per cent), the most important strongholds being Norwich, Lincoln and London. In Bristol itself, only Walter Hart, one of the prebendaries of the Cathedral, and three other clergymen refused to swear fealty to William and Mary. Their protests cut little ice. Over time, the Bristol clergy drifted towards the Whig establishment; the intransigently Tory core dwindled. This is evident from the electoral record. In the first two elections of the Hanoverian accession the resident clergy in Bristol were predominantly Tory; in 1722 twelve voted for William Hart, a kinsman to the non-juror, as opposed to four against. Yet by 1734 that position was reversed. Twenty years later the clerical vote was principally for the Tory candidates, partly because the sole Whig candidate, Robert Nugent, was thought to be an unscrupulous political trimmer. He hailed from an old established Irish family and had seemingly converted to Anglicanism to further his social and political ambitions. This disposed some Broad Churchmen to vote Tory and to reverse the trend. Yet if we add neutrals to the equation, the numbers even out. The plain fact is that Bristol's High Church clerical base eroded over the long term; increasingly it had to live with Latitudinarian

---

[29] *Annals of King George*, 4 (1718), pp. 351–2; *Weekly Journal*, 6 Dec. 1718; *Latimer*, II, 121; TNA, SP 35/7/214 and 35/13/93; Paul Monod, *Jacobitism and the English People 1688–1788* (Cambridge, 1993), pp. 149–50.
[30] Cf. Monod, *Jacobitism and the English People*, p. 150.

aspirations and a more confident cluster of Dissenters. This development, and the absence of strong non-juror affiliations, meant that Bristol lacked a strong ideological base for old-style Jacobitism, the kind that made Manchester such a Stuart stronghold. Lingering nostalgia for the Pretender there certainly was, although popular credulity in the magical powers of the Stuarts faced ridicule. In 1717 Christopher Lovell returned to Bristol from Avignon, apparently cured of scrofula by the royal touch of the Pretender. The curious flocked to see him, but Jacobite well-wishers had to smuggle him out of the country again when the disease returned. Thomas Carte forgot this essential fact when he revived the story in his 1747 *History of England*, only to be gleefully exposed by Josiah Tucker, the rector of St Stephen's and leading Whig cleric. Tucker derided Carte's account as 'an idle Jacobite tale, calculated to support the old thread-bare notion of a divine hereditary right of a certain house, which notion, I thought, had been long exploded by Men of Sense'.[31] Carte's error tarnished whatever credibility remained of a Jacobite *jure divino*.

In the opening decade of the Hanoverian accession the government considered Bristol a potential centre for a Jacobite rising, very possibly because the ultra-Tory-cum-Jacobite James Butler, the Duke of Ormond, was the High Lord Steward of the city and the likely military leader of a western rebellion. In the autumn of 1715, General Pepper searched Oxford for conspirators; among those arrested was one Lloyd, a 'famous Jacobite Coffee Man' from Charing Cross, whose papers revealed he had been engaged to recruit support for a western rising in Bristol and Bath.[32] Thus alerted, government troops quickly occupied both cities, arresting a few leading members of the Loyal Society in the process. Among them was William Hart, who was charged with having a secret cache of arms, and Francis Colston, who was accused of circulating Bishop Atterbury's provocative pamphlet, *English Advice*.[33] Four years later, amid fears of a Spanish-sponsored Jacobite invasion, Bristol once more came under the spotlight. Samuel Buckley, the former printer of the *Daily Courant* and now in government service, scoured the West Country for signs of a Jacobite gathering, and decided that Bristol was a likely site if the invasion fleet landed along the coast near Minehead. In conversations with several gentlemen and merchants in Bristol, he was assured there was no sign of a high-level cabal in favour of the rising, and that the magistracy and the officers of the Bristol militia were in good hands. Certainly Colonels Joseph Earle and Robert Yates were on the lookout for trouble. In July 1719 they commended the government for ditching disaffected JPs in

[31] Latimer, II, 117–18; *General Evening Post*, 14–16 Jan. 1748.

[32] Abel Boyer, *Political State of Great Britain*, 9 (1715), pp. 345–6.

[33] Latimer, II, 110–11; BA, Quarter Session docket book, 3 Sep. 1715; TNA, SP 44/118/28. *English Advice* argued that George I was mean-spirited and willing to allow the Whigs a monopoly of power. See G. V. Bennett, *The Tory Crisis in Church and State. The Career of Francis Atterbury, Bishop of Rochester* (Oxford, 1975), pp. 192–3.

neighbouring counties, an act that had 'given greate satisfaction & spirit to ye Government's friends in these parts'.[34]

Doubts were nonetheless raised about the 'vulgar in general', who were said to be 'two parts in three more inclined to the Pretender than to the king'.[35] When it was discovered that a consignment of gunpowder and arms was destined for Bristol, troops were once again marched in. A Hungarian visitor by the name of Baron Leuben was questioned by the mayor and bailed to appear at the next quarter sessions, an 'affront' for which he demanded 'satisfaction'. No duel took place, and the streets remained quiet. With troops and cavalry cruising Bristol, there were few overt signs of disaffection. This was not true of neighbouring Bath, where treasonable ballads were sung after the suppression of the 1715 rebellion and where the mayor was reprimanded for allowing the town to become 'pretty famous for riots'.[36] Bristol was also quiet during the Layer conspiracy of 1722 despite fears that it might be a citadel of revolt. The government had been alerted that arms and ammunition were travelling by water and road from London to Bristol. An informer reported there was 'great reason to suspect' it was 'designed for traitorous purposes agst. His Majesty's person and Government'. John Becher, the mayor of Bristol, was alerted, although he suspected the gunpowder was intended for slavers trading on the Gold Coast.[37] He nonetheless interrogated a husbandman named Owen Daly, who had just arrived by boat from Ireland. Daly admitted that he and his brother Eamon had been raising men for the Pretender in Ireland, although once the recruiting drive had been discovered, he had fled for his life. Becher thought the information serious enough to send it by express to Secretary of State Townshend, and complained bitterly when the postmaster at Chippenham would not allow the messenger a change of horses.[38]

How disaffected Bristol really was during these conspiracies is an open question. John Oldmixon recalled that the Pretender was proclaimed in Bristol on 27 October 1715, but he was in his fifties when he wrote this, and it is very possible he confused his stories, for Abel Boyer had suggested the proclamation was the work of a 'disloyal rabble' in Oxford not Bristol, just prior to Colonel Handasyde's entry into that city.[39] Be that as it may, with Bristol guarded like a garrison town, many must have felt discretion better than heady proclamations of King James III, or reckless denunciations of King George and his government. This did not stop someone from

---

[34] TNA, SP 35/17/31.
[35] TNA, SP 35/15/63–4, 254–6 and SP 35/16/6–8, 23; W. K. Dickson (ed.), *The Jacobite Attempt of 1719*, Scottish History Society, 9 (Edinburgh, 1895), p. 141; Paul S. Fritz, *The English Ministers and Jacobitism between the Rebellions of 1715 and 1745* (Toronto and Buffalo, 1975), pp. 56–8.
[36] TNA, SP 44/118, 15 Dec. 1715.
[37] TNA, SP 35/33/14, 21, 32–3.
[38] TNA, SP 35/33/197, 210.
[39] John Oldmixon, *The history of England during the reigns of King William and Mary …* (London, 1735), p. 611; Boyer, *Political State*, 9 (1715), p. 346.

distributing the Pretender's manifesto in the streets in early 1716 and staging a summer's night revel on the Pretender's birthday.[40] Predictably the government zoned in on the Loyal Society, the Tory club that was responsible for managing the electoral fortunes of the party, and the likely epicentre of political dissidence. The arrests in this instance were inconclusive. William Hart, a tobacco and sugar merchant, was never prosecuted; the bill against Francis Colston was not found. Indeed, the arrests themselves may well have been as much a warning to the Tories as a genuine probe. Hart, a Somerset JP and son of the High Church Jacobite who represented Bristol 1689–95, was a member of a leading Tory family in the city; Colston was a cousin of the well-known merchant philanthropist Edward Colston, MP for Bristol 1710–13, around whom the Tories had rallied. His birthday celebrations were appreciated by the Bristol crowd, especially those who gained the freedom through his charity; they served as a grand occasion for a meeting of the Tory party. In 1713, for example, Colston's birthday was celebrated by the Duke of Beaufort and ten MPs from Bristol and neighbouring counties. As many as four hundred guests and Loyal Society members attended the service in the Cathedral and the junket afterwards, where the party's fortunes and strategy were doubtless part of the agenda.[41] Yet after the prosecutions of Hart and Colston these annual meetings were abandoned.

The prosecution of Hart and Colston silenced the ultras, but there is evidence to suggest that the bulk of the mercantile bourgeoisie in Bristol were not in favour of extremist politics in any case. This can be illustrated through an examination of Joseph Earle, MP for Bristol 1710–27, who began his career as a moderate Tory but successfully made the transition to Whiggery at a time when party feelings ran high. Like his father Sir Thomas Earle, Joseph seems to have cultivated the middle ground. He was sufficiently entrenched in the Merchant Venturers to become its warden in 1709–10, just before he launched himself into the maelstrom of party politics as a Tory; he was the master in 1721–22, when he was already the Whig MP for Bristol and about to be re-elected once more. Early in his career Earle had been troubled by the extremism of Sir John Knight. Knight had not only engineered the dismissal of Earle's father from the corporation for tolerating Dissent, but his diatribes against William of Orange had alienated the government to the detriment of the city's commerce. In 1694, in a debate on a naturalisation bill for Protestant refugees, Sir John had described the court as already overrun by 'froglanders'. A printed copy of the speech, published by Sir John's Jacobite friends, was burnt by the common hangman. Had not Sir John delivered it in broad Bristolese, he might well have been imprisoned as the author of the

[40] Latimer, II, 113; *Flying Post*, 14–16 June 1716.
[41] *Post Boy*, 7–10 Nov. 1713. In 1735–40 about a third of all freedoms were subsidised by charities, and Colston's was undoubtedly the most formidable. See BA, Burgess Book, 1735–40.

cleaned-up version.[42] Such behaviour did not help Bristol's chances of receiving the appropriate attention of the Admiralty's convoys; nor did the celebrations that greeted the death of Queen Mary, when the Tory clergy tolerated merry peals in their steeples and watched people dance in the streets to the refrain of 'The King shall enjoy his own again'.[43]

Earle was one of those who tried to repair the damage, petitioning hard for extra protection for Bristol shipping and refusing to allow sectarian politics to warp his judgement of what was in the best interest of Bristol's merchants. Consequently in 1713 Earle refused to back his party's proposals for revising the trade tariffs between England and France, sensing that they would undermine Bristol's distillery trade and offer nothing to the West Country clothing industry, whose serge sector was facing stiff competition from lighter fabrics. At the same time he pushed ahead with a new bill to remodel the Corporation of the Poor, opting to once again free this statutory body from any religious tests that might exclude Dissenters. Neither of these stances endeared him to the hardliners in the Tory party, who expelled him from the Loyal Society. This affected his political fortunes, for running as a Whig in the 1715 general election, he trailed in a keenly fought contest in which a mere one hundred votes separated the four candidates. The Whig sheriffs still declared him elected, having found enough bad votes among the Tories to merit the decision, and a Whig-dominated Commons upheld his return. In the next election in 1722 Earle romped home, defeating the Tory William Hart by nearly 400 votes. In fact Earle emerged as the only national politician to top the poll as a Tory (in 1713) and as a Whig (in 1722) in the heyday of party. His success was attributable to his ability to cultivate the centre, refusing to allow the politics of religion to impair trade, and refusing to allow the party contest of Whig and Tory to collapse into a rivalry between Hanover and Stuart. It is no accident that the majority of merchants stood by him. His political position was also echoed by those merchants who petitioned the crown to prevent the Bahamas becoming a haven of piracy in 1717, backing the plan to install Woodes Rogers as the new governor of the colony.[44] Predominantly Whig, they also included a cluster of Tories, including a Hart and a Hellier.

Further down the social scale the politics of the Hanoverian accession seem to have been more volatile. In the period after 1688, years of war and hardship prompted some disillusionment with the new regime. War had brought heavier taxes, an issue that the Reverend Edward Bisse had raised in his seditious sermons, noting that it raised the bar on peacetime levies as well.[45] War also brought impressment, an issue of crucial importance to a port city like

---

[42] Latimer, I, 466–7; *CSPD* (1695), p. 241.

[43] Latimer, I, 470.

[44] TNA, CO 5/1265, fol. 187.

[45] TNA, SP 35/14/139; see also the Pretender's declaration of 1692, which promised to reduce customs and excise taxes by 50 per cent. *CSPD: William and Mary* (1692), p. 262.

Bristol, where the Customs was ordered to keep an informal register of eligible seamen and to solicit the mayor's help in taking them up.[46] For the first time in English history naval requirements topped 45,000, putting an incredible strain on existing maritime resources and prompting parliament to create a voluntary register to smooth the process of mobilisation. The experiment failed, and the Admiralty resorted to impressment to fill its crews, denying seamen the opportunity of spending the winter months with their families.[47] Indeed impressment disrupted the customary patterns of seafaring life to such an extent that a 1709 pamphlet declared that seamen 'come into the Service with as much reluctancy as if they were going to the Gallies'.[48] This issue continued to resonate with Bristolians, for during the 1715 election, one of the electoral managers on the Tory side warned freemen of the prospect of further impressments at the hands of another Eurocentric monarch.[49]

The growth of a standing army, especially the need for soldiers to fight in Ireland, also brought more landlubbers into the clutches of the state. Bristol was a departure point for forces to Ireland, and an inevitable place for last-minute recruiting. Sir Richard Hart complained to the Privy Council about the impressment into the army of three Kingswood colliers in 1691, saying their detention was not only contrary to the liberty of the subject, but dangerous to the safety of the city as it would antagonise a work force known for its tumultuous interventions. This indeed happened in 1709, when bread prices reached unacceptable levels.[50] On this occasion colliers may have even mouthed Jacobite sentiments, an understandable reaction to the fact that merchants had diverted local supplies of grain to feed the army in Flanders.[51] Ordinary people must have wondered what another foreign prince with European ambitions might bring. They were certainly not impressed with George, the Elector of Hanover, who was reviled for his cuckoldry and unflattering mistresses, his poor command of the English language and his haste to summer in Germany. It is no accident that the Pretender's declaration, which circulated London and Bristol in early 1716, traded on war weariness and the likely prospect of further military burdens under a Euro-monarch.[52]

---

[46] *CSPD* (1701), p. 277.

[47] N. A. M. Rodger, *The Command of the Ocean* (London, 2004), pp. 206–10, 636–7.

[48] *A dialogue between the Member of Parliament and a commander of a ship, about encouraging the seamen of Great Britain and the speedy manning the navy without impressing* (London, 1709), p. 3. See also *The Seaman's Groans* (London, 1702).

[49] *An Account of the Riots, Tumults and other Treasonable Practices since His Majesty's Accession to the Throne* (London, 1715), p. 25.

[50] Latimer, I, 462; II, 78–9.

[51] John Oldmixon, *The Bristol Riot* (London, 1714), p. 5. Oldmixon gets the date wrong, for the confrontation with General Wade of the militia is in May 1709. There is only a hint of Jacobitism here, for Oldmixon alleges that the Loyal Society recruited the colliers for seditious activities. See also George Pryce, *A Popular History of Bristol* (Bristol, 1861), pp. 424, 617 who corrects the date; and Seyer, *Memoirs*, II, 558.

[52] For the declaration, see *Annals of King George*, 2 (1715), pp. 61–5.

Disgruntlement with the status quo could easily flip into a denunciation of the turnip king from Hanover or a reckless toast to the Stuart across the water.

Such sentiments certainly surfaced during the abortive Western rising of 1715 and its aftermath.[53] A cabinet-maker named James Winter was whipped for shouting 'King James for ever' and sentenced to three months in Newgate.[54] Philip Somers, a sailor, was picked up for dispersing scurrilous libels against the king and royal family; he was bailed and subsequently discharged because no witnesses appeared against him. Several others were prosecuted for seditious words, although in two instances the prosecutions were thought to be malicious; the result, no doubt, of neighbourly quarrels that had escalated out of control. The following year brought a new crop of cases before the courts. Andrew Sheppard, a farrier, was indicted for drinking James III's health before King George. William Mabberly was found guilty of blessing 'King James the third and ye devil take those that will not fight for him for they are all Rogues and Villains in their hearts.' Five other cases of seditious words came before the courts in 1716, three of which were successfully prosecuted. Two of those involved women, Mary Herbert and Margaret Sharp, the latter fined one shilling and ordered to be whipped at the cart's tail from High Cross to Lawford's Gate. Most of those prosecuted were lower class, although one, William Cox, a gentleman indicted for seditious words, had two merchants as sureties. One of them was Henry Combe, a merchant planter who was famously wealthy when he died in 1752. In 1716 he was still an up-and-coming merchant, poised to enter the Bristol council in 1721, win civic honours, campaign for parliament in 1739, and entertain royalty at his house in Queen Square.[55] Since Combe was a prominent Whig, one wonders why he stood bail for Cox, or more probably, why Cox found himself in trouble. Was it another frame-up? Or perhaps it was a drunken revel, as in the case of Joseph Merryweather, a carpenter also accused of seditious words, who convinced the Grand Jury that liquor had got the better of him.[56] Since nothing more is known of the Cox case we shall never know.

Cox aside, the prosecutions of 1715–16 revealed an undercurrent of disaffection in Bristol's Tory ranks, disconcerting enough to make the government anxious about the city's allegiance in the opening years of the Hanoverian accession. Particularly troubling to the new regime was the riot on coronation day, one of about thirty that occurred across the country, including

---

[53] On Jacobite plans for a rising, see Sir Charles Petrie, 'The Jacobite Activities in South and West England in the Summer of 1715', *Transactions of the Royal Historical Society*, 18 (1935), 85–106.

[54] For these cases, see BA, Quarter Session docket books, Sep. 1715–August 1716; Tolzey Books, 1703–16.

[55] Madge Dresser, *Slavery Obscured* (London and New York, 2001), p. 103; Alfred B. Beaven, *Bristol Lists: Municipal and Miscellaneous* (Bristol, 1899), p. 283; Rogers, *Whigs and Cities*, pp. 282–5; Latimer, II, 213.

[56] BA, Quarter Session docket book, 5 March 1716.

an arc of disturbances around Bristol featuring Gloucester, Cirencester, Chippenham, Frome, Bridgwater and Taunton.[57] The Bristol riots, however, attracted uncommon attention. They were the subject of three pamphlets and considerable press coverage in these early days of the newspaper. They also prompted a special commission to try the rioters and their opponents. For these reasons, they are worth examining in detail.

The authorship of the pamphlets is not entirely clear. One of them, an account of the trials published by John Smith in 1714, seems to have disappeared.[58] The authorship of the other two was attributed to Daniel Defoe, but he had been too busy defending Harley in *The Secret History of the White Staff* and fending off slurs to his journalistic integrity to investigate the Bristol riot in any detail. In the two months prior to the coronation day riots he was actually under prosecution for insinuating in the *Flying Post* that one of the king's regents, the fifth Earl of Anglesey, had previously aligned himself with Jacobites to break up the Whig corporation of Dublin.[59] So the most likely candidate for authorship is John Oldmixon, a Whig pamphleteer whose family hailed from Hutton, near Weston Super Mare, and who lived with members of the Blake family in Bridgwater after the bankruptcy and death of his father.[60] Oldmixon had close contacts in Bristol, including the town clerk, John Rumsey; he had worked in the West India trade, and some of the pre-eminent merchants in it subscribed to his *History of England* as did Thomas Cadell, a bookseller who was also a member of the Lewin's Mead congregation at the time of the riot.[61] Like Samuel Buckley, Oldmixon hoped that his services as a Whig journalist would reap some reward, which it did in June 1716, in the shape of the office of Customs Collector in Bridgwater, where he remained something of an 'intelligenser-general', an informer or spy.[62] During the Spanish invasion scare of 1719 he complained that the Bridgwater magistrates had not arrested a suspected spy and was very troubled that 'some weak persons represent the projected Invasion as an amusement of the Government with a View of getting Money'.[63]

Whether Oldmixon actually attended the trial in Bristol is unclear. He certainly claimed as much, since the authorship is attributed to a 'gentleman

---

[57] Monod, *Jacobitism and the English People*, pp. 174–9; Nicholas Rogers, 'Riot and Popular Jacobitism in Early Hanoverian England', in *Ideology and Conspiracy: Aspects of Jacobitism, 1689–1759*, ed. Eveline Cruickshanks (Edinburgh, 1982), pp. 74–6.

[58] *The Tryals of the Rioters at Bristol* (Bristol, 1714).

[59] Paula R. Backscheider, *Daniel Defoe. His Life* (Baltimore and London, 1989), pp. 378–82.

[60] See the *ODNB* entry by Pat Rogers. For the attribution to Defoe, see J. R. Moore, *A Checklist of the Writings of Daniel Defoe* (Bloomington, 1960), p. 114.

[61] Pat Rogers, 'Daniel Defoe, John Oldmixon and the Bristol Riot of 1714', *Transactions of the Bristol and Gloucestershire Archaeological Society*, 93 (1973), 145–56. Cadell subscribed to the 1735 edition of the *History*; for his membership of Lewin's Mead Presbyterian chapel, see BA, MS 6687, Lewin's Mead minute book, 1710–14.

[62] Called so by Defoe in *Mist's Weekly Journal*, 28 July 1718.

[63] TNA, SP 35/16/37.

who attended the commission'. His opening remarks on the Bristol riots situ-
ates them very firmly in the context of the sharp polarisation of Whig and
Tory following the trial of Dr Henry Sacheverell, who was indicted for 'high
crimes and misdemeanours' for delivering a partisan sermon at St Paul's before
the London corporation on 5 November 1709. In it, Sacheverell attacked the
Dissenters as enemies of church and state and repudiated the rights of resistance that moderate-to-radical Whigs used to justify the coup d'etat of 1688.
Impeached by parliament in March 1710, Sacheverell became something of
a Tory martyr. Mobs rallied to his cause and sacked several meeting houses
in London. Although parliament found Sacheverell guilty, suspended him
from preaching for three years, and had his sermon burnt before the Royal
Exchange, the Reverend Dr became the rallying symbol of a Tory resurgence
throughout the country. After Sacheverell, the politics of commemoration
heated up, with Whig and Tory crowds vying for public space, sporting party
colours, transgressing on their opponents' territory, disrupting each other's
celebrations, and threatening the other's supporters. In Bristol party rancour
was very evident in the year before the Hanoverian accession. At the proclamation of the Peace of Utrecht in 1713, Tory mobs rampaged through the
city destroying windows that were not illuminated, a path of destruction that
must have been substantial because many merchants, manufacturers and
distillers were unhappy with the commercial policies of the government and
had sported wool favours rather than the oak sprigs of a 'Tory spring'.[64] In
the subsequent general election the same Tory mobs threatened the house
of one of the principal supporters of single Whig candidate, Sir William
Daines, and intimidated freemen who tried to vote for him. A partisan sheriff
closed the poll after little more than a quarter of the electorate had voted,
leaving Daines trailing with a humiliating 189 votes. Daines predictably
petitioned, but despite the very evident irregularities, he failed to impress a
Tory-dominated Commons.

The advent of the Elector of Hanover to the British throne in August 1714
promised to change this political landscape. The new monarch was known
to favour the Whigs, to such an extent that some leading Tories flirted with
the prospect of backing the exiled house of Stuart. In Bristol the Whigs were
elated by the accession of George and the conduits ran with wine. One cooper
in Baldwin Street decided to celebrate the event in a summer pavilion that
had reputedly been used by the Rye House Plot conspirators, only to find that
the ornamental crown suspended from the roof was hidden by a huge cobweb,
an omen that ultra-Tories welcomed.[65] That aside, Whigs renewed their celebrations in September when George made his first public entry to the capital.
The pro-Whig corporation ordered a public holiday and dispensed £84 on the
festivities. It looked forward to the coronation of the king in October, when
a ball was to be held at the Customs House in Queen Square.

[64] Boyer, *Political State*, 5 (1713), p. 248.
[65] Latimer, II, 106.

The coronation day festivities proved contentious.[66] It was rumoured that the Whigs planned to burn an effigy of Sacheverell to drive home their victory and this put Tory crowds in an ugly mood. Shouting 'Sacheverell and Ormonde', 'Down with the Roundheads', 'Down with Foreigners', they destroyed some of the celebratory bonfires and then turned their anger on the Dissenters, a group that had survived the persecutions of the 1680s and were poised to consolidate their presence on the city council.[67] Tory mobs threatened to pull down Gough's Presbyterian meeting house in Tucker Street in what would have been a symbolic re-eneactment of the Clarendon Code. Alerted that there were armed men inside the chapel, they turned their attention to one of the leading members of that congregation, Richard Stephens, a wealthy baker who lived on the same street, in whose premises the effigy of Sacheverell was thought to be hidden. Hundreds assembled before the door of the bakery at dusk and told the mistress of the house that they intended to visit it later. They also demolished the windows of Mr Jeffrey, a distiller in Tucker Street, who was also a member of the Gough's chapel; then moved on to the house of a button-maker who was suspected of contributing to the effigy's costume. Mobs also attacked the house of the under-sheriff, Mr Whiting, on Temple Backs. Whiting may have been a Quaker; he had certainly incurred the ire of the crowd for prosecuting one of the Tories for perjuring himself during the enquiry into the electoral disturbances of 1713. How much damage Whiting's house sustained is impossible to say. His windows were wrecked, but it seems he managed to buy the crowd off with wine and liquor, and had the perspicacity to note down the names of those he knew.

The main action, nonetheless, took place at Stephens' bakery. The lord mayor had been alerted that trouble might ensue and sent constables to search the house for the effigy.[68] Although he let it be known that nothing had been discovered, this did not satisfy the Tory supporters. Sometime before 6.00p.m. the mob returned there and attacked the house, beating out the shutters and windows and assaulting Richard Stephens, his apprentice and his servant Anne Baker, who sustained a serious wound to the eye. By the time the mob swung by for a third time Richard's son, Francis, the captain of a West Indiaman, had returned from looking at the illuminations in Queen Square. According to Oldmixon, he tried to parley with the crowd and even offered to allow it to search for an effigy, but there were tussles at the door

---

[66] The following account is primarily based on John Oldmixon, *The Bristol Riot* (London, 1714) and his *A Full and Impartial Account of the late Disorders in Bristol* (London, 1714).

[67] See BA, MS 6687/1, Lewin's Mead Presbyterian Minute Book. The members for 1710–14 reveal a number who would enter the Common Council in the next twenty years: John Bartlett; Michael Pope; James Hilhouse (or his son); plus Captain Matthew Wraxall, a kinsman of Nathaniel Wraxall, member of congregation 1718–22 who was a common councilman from 1721–31.

[68] See *Tryals of the Rioters*, p. 4, annexed to Oldmixon's *Bristol Riot*, but not reproduced on Eighteenth Century Collections Online. For a copy, see the BRL, B222.

of the shop when the crowd tried to surge through. Francis was beaten with a pole at the door of the house and in response drew his sword and stabbed a cooper's apprentice who was at the forefront of the mob. When the mob pressed further into the house he fired off a blunderbuss and killed one of the intruders, John Gonning. He then beat a hasty retreat through the back. Another casualty of the mayhem was a Quaker named Henry Thomas, who tried to intervene in the ruckus before Stephens' door and was trampled to death by a crowd. By this time the rioters had taken possession of the front of the house; they rifled the till, stole the plate and drank what liquor they could find. They were prevented from going any further by Francis' friends, who defended the passage to the bakehouse with a kneading trough until the magistrates and constables arrived.

The confrontation in Tucker Street was the most serious incident of the night, but by no means the only one. Crowds spoiled the merriment of the coronation ball by smashing the windows of the Customs House and shouting abuse until they were dispersed by servants and officers. The night of riot disposed the corporation to send a series of detailed depositions of what happened to Whitehall, but unfortunately they have not survived.[69] On the basis of this evidence the government decided to send a special commission to try the rioters, who over the course of the next few weeks were systematically rounded up and committed to Newgate, in almost every case by Whig magistrates.[70]

The creation of a special commission signified that the government was interested in swift exemplary justice. Precisely what that might mean was a matter of intense speculation. Kingswood colliers hailed a coach thought to contain the judges with the words 'No Jefferies, No Western Assizes'. They clearly feared a bloody assize in the manner of 1685, with gruesome hangings or worse. On the other hand, as Oldmixon recognised, the three judges assigned this task were of Tory lineage, and this disposed some to expect a measure of leniency. Sir Littleton Powys hailed from an old Shropshire family of Tories; his political allegiances were such that the government even contemplated removing him from King's Bench at the Hanoverian accession.[71] The other two judges, Baron Robert Price and Justice Robert Tracey, had been supporters of the Tory minister, Robert Harley. Price had started his career as a client of Beaufort and then switched to Harley, although he was High Tory enough to remind Dissenters in his charge to the Winchester assizes in 1705 that they owed their existence to the indulgence of the

---

[69] Rogers, 'Bristol Riot of 1714', 145n, noting a reference to the affidavits in TNA, T 54/23/2.

[70] The government took a keen interest in coronation riots elsewhere, especially at Reading. In that case informations were sent to King's Bench, and the Attorney General ordered a trial. See *Tryals of the Rioters*, p. 5.

[71] John Lord Campbell, *Lives of the Lord Chancellors* (10 vols, Jersey City, 1885), V, 221n. See also entry by David Hayton on Powys's brother, Sir Thomas Powys, MP Ludlow, 1701–13 in <http://www.historyofparliamentonline.org>.

Anglicans. Tracy was touted as Lord Keeper in 1705 and Lord Chancellor during the Tory resurgence after 1710. Yet when he presided over the trials of three ringleaders in the Sacheverell riots, he endorsed Lord Chief Justice Parker's argument that destroying meeting houses was tantamount to 'levying war' against the monarch on the grounds that it contested the Toleration Act of 1689. This was certainly a capacious definition of constructive treason, and not one that every judge would have supported. This emerged very clearly in the special verdict for George Purchase, whose basic crime was that he had waved his sword at the troops sent to prevent the sacking of a meeting house in the neighbourhood of Drury Lane. Had he not been pardoned, Purchase could have been hung, drawn and quartered as a traitor.

So it remained unclear what these three judges from 'Toryland' would do, which perhaps explains why Tories as well as Whigs attended the coach that brought judges and prosecuting counsel to Bristol. The Tories headed the cavalcade into Bristol, a tactical error, because the Whigs changed the route once inside the walls and left them high and dry on St Thomas Street while the judges moved through Redcliff Street before crossing the bridge into the old city. This partisan move was only a beginning. The trial sermon, by Samuel Coopey, the rector of Wraxall, tried to exonerate the Tory party from any responsibility in the riots, arguing that the rioters could not have been true men of the church. This sermon was followed by a fairly stiff charge from Littleton Powys on the unlawfulness of riot, one that tacitly reprimanded the ultra-Tories for inciting disorder. The fear that harsh sentences might be handed down by Powys and company prompted the defence counsel to spend a whole day challenging the jury selection. This was a politic move, as it seems the crown prosecution had wanted to indict the rioters for treason under 25 Edward III, following the precedent set in the Old Bailey trials of the Sacheverell rioters. Samuel Seyer suggests that the judges pressed for indictments of this kind, but the grand jury demurred, likely because a Dissenting meeting house had not been systematically destroyed as in the London disturbances of 1710. Indeed, they cited an anti-enclosure statute from the Marian era to suggest that pulling down property was not *ipso facto* a treasonable felony at common law.[72] The judges disagreed, and insisted that a collective attempt to pull down houses was technically levying war against the king, just as had been determined in 1710. They buttressed this by citing an Elizabeth statute and a judgement on a well-known anti-enclosure riot in Oxfordshire.

So the political stakes were high, and in the light of the disagreements over the indictment, the Tories kept up the pressure. Two were taken to task for attempting to bribe witnesses and were ordered to appear at the next Gloucester assizes. Once the trials began William Hart tried to prop up the spirits of those accused by standing unconscionably close to the dock. Colonel Joseph Earle pointed out this irregularity, and Powys ordered Hart to

[72] Seyer, *Memoirs*, II, 568–71. *Tryals of the Rioters*, pp. 6–7.

stand down. It was not a good start for the Tories, who mustered their clans in and outside the courtroom. Mobs attended the prisoners on their way back to Newgate with cries of 'a 'cheverel, a 'cheverel, down with the roundheads'. One Christopher Gay threatened to rescue them from Newgate. Some sang the ballad 'round-headed cuckolds, come dig, come dig',[73] which could have been interpreted as a barbed reference to George I's cuckoldry at the hands of Count Königsmarck, or possibly to Baron Price's cuckoldry by Thomas Neale, the 'great projector'.

On the third day of the trial, Tory mobs demonstrated outside the house of the Whig mayor, Henry Whitehead, who had ordered a £50 reward for the discovery of the murderer of the Quaker, Henry Thomas. Whether these intimidating tactics made any difference to the verdict is arguable. There is no evidence that the grand jury buckled under pressure, for it accepted virtually every indictment that was put before it. In only one instance did they conceivably downsize an indictment. This was in the case of Francis Painter, a pipe-maker from St James, who was found after the riot with two hats belonging to Mr Stephens. He was indicted for a felony and a burglary. He was acquitted of the last charge, since in the mayhem no one could conclusively prove he was in the house. As for the felony, the hats were valued at only ten pence, and so Painter received a public whipping rather than a trip to the gallows.

One defendant, William Shewell, was found guilty of encouraging the mob to pull down Mr Whiting's house in Temple Backs. He is said to have shouted 'damn it, down with the house'. For this he was fined thirty nobles (£10), sentenced to three months imprisonment, and ordered to find sureties for his good behaviour for a year. This proved to be the standard sentence for those found guilty of riot, for the judges held back from the full force of the law and elected to be merciful,[74] a tactical move in the light of the reservations of the grand jury and the highly charged political atmosphere in Bristol.

Two of the rioters committed to jail on 27 November were not tried for lack of evidence. Christopher Gay was tried for threatening to rescue those committed to prison, but he was acquitted; so too was Edward Hughes, indicted for riot, murder and burglary at Stephens' bakery.[75] Ten were found guilty of riot, most before Stephens' house rather than Whiting's, despite the fact that Whiting had taken the trouble to write down their names. Six of them were also indicted for murder and burglary, specifically for killing Henry Thomas, the Quaker cordwainer, and breaking into Richard Stephens' house. These charges did not stick. It proved impossible to determine who was responsible for Thomas's death in the mêlée before Stephens' door, or who had their hands in the till. The fact that rioters actually returned the

[73] Bodleian Library, Oxford, Harleian MS 3782, fol. 64. See also Eliot Warburton, *Memoirs of Prince Rupert and the Cavaliers* (3 vols, London, 1849), II, 7.
[74] See the judges' speech in *The Tryals of the Rioters*, p. 9.
[75] *Tryal of the Rioters*, pp. 4–5.

plate stolen from Stephens suggests they had been tipped off not to incur offences that might result in a hanging.

The majority of those indicted were artisans who lived in the riverside parishes around Tucker Street, over the bridge from the old city, or further out in the parishes of St James and St Philip and St Jacob. They featured a fairly rich variety of trades: two cordwainers, a weaver, cooper, sugar baker, sadler, a glover, barber, tailor, and a wig- and pipe-maker. They were hardly the poor 'rascally fellows' of Oldmixon's description, but local men, working in the commercial hub of the city. The only defendant not from Bristol was Evan Howell, a gardener from Back Bourton in Oxfordshire, near the crossroads of three counties, some sixteen miles east of Chippenham. How and why he came to participate in these disturbances is unknown, but we do have hints why others might have. One of the ringleaders, John Pine, the barber of St Philip and St Jacob, was known for his aggressive antipathy to Dissenters.[76] He seems to have delighted in stalking Dissenters to and from their conventicles and abusing them in the street. Perhaps Pine disliked the rather earnest, austere demeanour of the Presbyterians, for Gough's chapel had been a former theatre, bought by the congregation in 1704. Certainly the Dissenting presence in the city's Reformation of Manners movement was strong.[77] It contrasted dramatically with the Tory conviviality of the Loyal Society, subsidised by patrons like the Duke of Beaufort, who is said to have to have expended £19,000 promoting the fortunes of the party.[78]

A clash of values and intense partisanship characterised the coronation day riots. Whig writers fumed that the real authors of the riots were the Loyal Society and their clerical allies, who consistently whipped up hostility against Dissenters. Colonel Joseph Earle said as much in court when he reprimanded William Hart for his ostentatious support of the rioters. In fact whatever comfort Bristol's Tory merchants gave the rioters, it was never as conspicuous as in places like Taunton and Shrewsbury, where JPs, civic officials and their sons were actively implicated in the disorders.[79] The top-down interpretation also ignores the fact that many artisans had the vote in early-eighteenth-century Bristol, perhaps two in every three, and were politically literate. It tones down the memory of political rivalry that was played out in these riots, with Tory demonstrators seeing their opponents as heirs to the commonwealth tradition and at one point even identifying with the 'Cavaliers'.[80]

What is particularly noteworthy in October 1714 is the absence of any specific Jacobite slogans accompanying the disturbances, unless one reads the championing of Ormond as tacit support for the Stuarts. In this respect it is

[76] Seyer, *Memoirs*, II, 568; Oldmixon, *Bristol Riot*, p. 12.
[77] Rogers, *Whigs and Cities*, pp. 274–5; BRL, B10162, Minutes of the Society for the Reformation of Manners 1699–1705.
[78] Oldmixon, *Full and Impartial Account*, p. 21.
[79] TNA, SP 35/74/5–6, 12–13.
[80] Seyer, *Memoirs*, II, 569; Oldmixon, *Full and Impartial Account*, p. 25.

worth remembering that in the opening months of the succession Ormond was still a legitimate Tory hero, a military counterpoint to Marlborough, not the soldier who was later impeached by a Whig-dominated Commons and driven into a Jacobite exile. In the heat of the riot there were no cries for the Pretender, no explicit denunciations of the Elector of Hanover as there were at Birmingham and Norwich.[81] Had there been, one could guarantee that Oldmixon and company would have made something of it; yet in fact he could only claim that the cry for Sacheverell was a metonym for Jacobitism, a familiar charge by Whig partisans.[82] In October 1714 the two parties in Bristol were still battling for political space, with rumours of burning Sacheverell in effigy triggering violence against Dissenters and high anxiety that a Whig regime might be the order of the day. Whigs complained after the riots of the lenity of the judges in handing down moderate sentences; Tories were disappointed that they were unable to prosecute Captain Francis Stephens successfully. As a counter-challenge to the trials of the rioters, the Tories had indicted the sea captain for murdering John Gonning and stabbing a cooper's apprentice; but the judges brushed both prosecutions aside on grounds of self-defence. They did not want Whig or Tory martyrs, although the unfolding of the trial must have brought home to them and the government the legal difficulties of dispensing stern punishments for riot without invoking a doctrine of constructive treason, something that was rectified the following year with a new Riot Act.[83]

In the aftermath of the riot the *Flying Post* said it hoped the special commission would be a salutary warning to the Tories to desist from using mob rule to perpetuate its power, yet the general election a few months later revealed that the Tories had not been dramatically discredited by the riots. In a very tough battle the Tories claimed a narrow victory, bucking the trend of other open boroughs that had swung back to the Whigs. A scrutiny was called for by the Whig candidates, Sir William Daines and Joseph Earle. This prompted a lot of wrangling about the eligibility of voters, to a point where the sheriffs adjourned the proceedings to the Council House where they would no longer be plagued by public scrutiny from party attornies. Daines, by now a very prominent stockholder of the Bank of England, boldly declared 'let the Scrutiny go how it would, it should be a Parliament case, and ... he would

---

[81] On Jacobite slogans at Birmingham, TNA SP 35/74/14–15; at Norwich, *Annals of King George*, 1 (1714), p. 260.

[82] See, for example, John Dunton, *The Neck Adventure: or the Case and Sufferings of John Dunton* (London, 1715), p. xix: 'all the mobbing that has been made in England since you [King George] came to the throne is wholly owing to these Passive Rebels that Cant so much of Hereditary Right and the Church's Danger on purpose to make way for a Popish Pretender'.

[83] On Jacobite unrest and the creation of the Riot Act of 1715, see Nicholas Rogers, 'Popular Protest in Early Hanoverian London', *Past and Present*, 79 (1978), 73–5.

sit in the House'.[84] According to the Tory apothecary Edmund Tucker, the sheriffs signed a return for Daines and Earle before the scrutiny was formerly concluded, although one of them, Richard Taylor, was pressured into signing a double return and even tolerated the chairing of the Tory members. This chaotic and highly irregular contest ultimately worked to Whig advantage, as Daines predicted. The Whig candidates were returned, despite efforts by the Tories to reverse the decision. No fewer than three petitions were presented to the Commons, in 1715, 1717 and again in 1718, but the committee in charge of disputed elections never reported a verdict.[85]

The Tories were enraged by the electoral defeat and the subsequent impeachment of their leaders by a Whig government implacably bent on political revenge. This rage often took the form of Jacobitism, sharpened in the West Country by acts of provocation by their opponents. At Cirencester, the Whigs burnt effigies of Ormond, Bolingbroke and the Pretender on the king's birthday in 1716, and at the thanksgiving for the suppression of the rebellion on 7 June, paraded an effigy of James Stuart in a warming pan, a reference to the allegation that James II's son was really an illegitimate child smuggled into court to shore up the succession in 1688.[86] At Marlborough, the Whig corporation paraded a foppish effigy of the Pretender through every street at the thanksgiving, tempting the Tories to try to disrupt their celebrations and banning them from the belfries on the Pretender's birthday. Tories, in turn, vowed to burn a dummy of Oliver Cromwell on the following birthday of the king.

This style of denunciatory street politics, aggressively territorial, incited acts of party rage and extremism. At Frome, Tory mobs rescued effigies of the pope and Pretender intended for the bonfire commemorating Gunpowder Plot. At Bath, disaffected Tories sang treasonable songs in the streets after the defeat of the rebels at Preston. A few miles to the south, at Norton St Philip, the Pretender was proclaimed on his birthday, while at Beckington celebratory bells were rung.[87] These were acts of defiance rather than acts of insurrection, informed by general developments no doubt, but essentially generated by local rivalries.

Jacobite sentiments in Bristol surfaced after the Tory defeat at the polls and before the 1715 rebellion. Most involved seditious words against the king, and of these specific cases only William Brewer was found guilty. He

---

[84] A letter to a Member of Parliament from a Gentleman of Bristol, containing a Particular and True Account of the Extraordinary Proceedings relating to the late Election of Members of Parliament for that City, 2nd edn (London, 1715), p. 11. On Daines's stock, see P. G. M. Dickson, The Financial Revolution in England (London, 1967), p. 279.

[85] Latimer, II, 108–9; An account of the Riots, Tumults and other Treasonable Practices since his Majesty's Accession to the Throne (London, 1715), pp. 25–6. In several newspapers the Tories were declared the victors. See Weekly Packet, 19–26 Feb. 1715 and British Weekly Mercury, 5–12 March 1715.

[86] Flying Post, 2–5 and 14–16 June 1716.

[87] TNA, SP 44/118, 15 Dec. 1715; Flying Post, 30 Nov.–2 Dec. 1714, 14–16 June 1715.

was publicly whipped from the High Cross to Newgate and sentenced to prison for six months, twice the term of the coronation day rioters, a sign that the local authorities wanted to contain disaffection that might spiral out of control. The rising temperature can be gauged from the case of John Chisild, a clothier. Early in 1715 he had defended the execution of Charles I and flatly refused to regard him as the martyr of Anglican orthodoxy. This stance enraged Samuel Trevett, a house carpenter, who was also accused of assaulting three other men. The indictments do not tell us where this disagreement occurred, but one suspects it was a tavern quarrel in which political positions rapidly moved to the bottom line. Confrontations like this, in which republican sentiments were juxtaposed to royalist, make it easier to explain why party battles could generate extreme positions, why Whig–Tory rivalries could collapse into dynastic ones. Contemporaries were actually not surprised when this happened. In June 1716 the *Flying Post* reported that Bristolians expected the 'Jacks and Tories' would proclaim 'their Loyalty by some Public Token' on the Pretender's birthday. They were surprised they resisted until 10.00p.m., when they lit a celebratory bonfire on Brandon Hill, 'this being the most conspicuous Place thereabouts so that all the Country for several miles around might observe it'.[88] The correspondent added that a few days earlier, on the thanksgiving for the suppression of the 1715 rebellion (7 June), Tories nailed a 'label' to the door of Gough's meeting house in Tucker Street, a reminder, at the very least, of their continuing hostility to Dissenters, and no doubt a warning to Whigs to curb their exuberance.

Whiffs of Jacobitism continued to plague Bristol. In February 1718, early one winter morning, the watch at the Tolzey was disturbed by cries of 'Down with the Roundheads' from the mouths of a local trowman and his frolicsome company. They assaulted one of the watchmen, William Harvey, and shouted 'God damn you all, and your Mayor too, you Presbyterian dogs.'[89] Street scuffles and seditious words like this continued to crop up at the quarter sessions. A Bristolian named Peter Cumberbatch protested against an encampment of dragoons just north of Gloucester, shouting 'Down with the Roundheads' and singing 'The king shall enjoy his own again.'[90] In the mid 1720s Whig zealots singled out a Peter Hammond for special attention, believing he was conspiring to the kidnap the Prince of Wales while George II was in Hanover. Hammond was taken up and questioned, but nothing came of the enquiry. Meanwhile, seditious rhymes and emblems on royal anniversaries kept people on edge, especially since Hanoverian/Jacobite holidays were back to back. The 28 May, George I's birthday, gave way to the celebration of the Stuart restoration in 1660; the Pretender's birthday on 10 June preceded the accession of George II.[91] Such contention spilled onto the streets in 1735.

---

[88] *Flying Post*, 14–16 June 1715.
[89] BA, JQS/P/3 1718–1719, no. 3.
[90] Latimer, II, 139.
[91] Latimer, II, 164. Latimer talks of tension down to the 1750s.

In our previous chapter we examined the 1735 riots as a metaphor of disorder, symptomatic of a more general crisis of governance in Bristol that involved a spectrum of socially diverse incidents. Here we wish to say something about their political context, which grew out of the Tory victory in the general election of 1734. Briefly, the unpopularity in Bristol of Sir Robert Walpole's Excise Bill opened the door to the return of the Tories after a twenty-year absence. In a three-cornered contest, the man most identified with Walpolean Whiggery, John Scrope, the city Recorder, was narrowly defeated at the polls by the Tory Thomas Coster, a local industrialist. The Whigs protested the result, particularly the Nonconformists, who constituted over 60 per cent of the 230 petitioners against Coster.[92] One scrutineer calculated that if the bad votes were eliminated from the poll, Scrope would have won by sixty-six votes. The Whigs were so angry with the result they were even prepared to narrow the franchise to reinstate Scrope, to reduce it by two-thirds. However, Sir Robert Walpole advised Scrope to abandon the petition, offering him a seat in Lyme Regis instead, and so after a protracted enquiry in parliament, Coster's return was upheld – to much jubilation in Bristol and its environs. The celebrations continued for three days, with sheep roasts and plenty of beer. The lesson drawn by one observer was that the Whig corporation and its cohorts had misjudged the popular mood, which was potentially harmful to the exercise of power:

> however meanly some People may think about a Populace or Mob of a Country, it is certain that the Power and Strength of every free Country depends entirely upon the Populace, and by their Affections only it is, that Magistrates can be protected and supported in the Exercise of that Power with the People have entrusted them with.[93]

Whigs might well have smarted at this reassertion of radical Whiggery at the hands of the Tories. They certainly disliked their re-appropriation of public space, and so just over a month later, some Whigs outside Lawford's Gate planned to celebrate the king's accession on 11 June by staging a St George and the dragon ceremony, in which the dragon was dragged by a rope on the end of which was a large orange with a crown fixed upon it.[94] This was not simply in deference to George II; it recalled the visit of the Prince of Orange to Bristol in February 1734, when three hundred weavers joined his cavalcade as it entered the city. It also reminded Bristolians of the preparations

---

[92] A List of All the Names that Sign'd the Two Petitions against Thomas Coster, esq, n.d., no place. This list, in the Bristol Reference Library (B 15163) was probably printed in Bristol. It is annotated, noting those petitioners who were Baptists, Quakers and Presbyterians. See Rogers, Whigs and Cities, p. 273, and An alphabetical list of the freeholders and burgesses ... who polled at the election in the year 1734 (Bristol, 1734). This poll book lists the potentially unqualified voters in the margin, suggesting that Coster had 362 bad votes and Scrope 91. The Craftsmen, 10 May 1735, claimed Scrope had over a thousand bad voters.
[93] Boyer, Political State, 49 (1735), pp. 468–9. See also Craftsman, 10 May 1735.
[94] Daily Gazetteer, 10 July 1735.

launched to promote a statue of William III in Queen Square, including the unveiling of a model by Schymaker in December 1734, when the corporation 'drank prosperity to the friends of the Revolution, particularly in the City of Bristol'.[95]

According to the Daily Gazetteer, the Tories were prepared to tolerate this display of Whig exuberance, but they were not happy to learn of plans to burn the pope, the Pretender and Thomas Coster in effigy on the same day. The plan seems to have been hatched by weavers in George Street who congregated at the Red Bull and the Three Ginger Cakes taverns, although one of the leaders, John Colebrook, is also listed as a shopkeeper and tallow chandler.[96] Their efforts to mock Tories were disrupted by a crowd of four hundred people – colliers, labourers and artisans – led by Nathan Pick a mason, John Vaughan a blacksmith, John James a gardener, and two weavers, Francis Lewis and Daniel Harding.[97] They smashed the windows and shutters of Benjamin Pope's tavern, the Three Ginger Cakes, and then turned their anger on John Colebrook, who sought refuge in Anthony Farrier's Red Bull. In the affray Colebrook's wife, Elizabeth, was injured in the nose and mouth. Eventually the mob found the dragon in the room of Nathaniel Harrison, a weaver who lodged at the house of John Stephens in George Street. It was confiscated and paraded around the town in triumph. The procession halted outside Thomas Coster's door in Prince Street, before proceeding to burn dragon, orange and crown in the Old Market. Later the mob returned to George Street and forced some Whig celebrants to huzza for Coster. There were a few more visitations. Liquor was stolen, very probably from Farrier's; Stephens was stunned with a stone, his furniture destroyed.[98] Whigs were warned not to transgress Tory territory, real or symbolic.

Some of the rioters were taken up and committed to Newgate. 'There is great industry us'd in finding the rioters out', reported the London Daily Post, and so it seemed, for the authorities were still collecting informations in late July. Eventually thirty-three of the participants would find themselves before King's Bench.[99] They included six colliers, a smattering of artisans such as blacksmiths, wheelwrights and plasterers, and three weavers and a woolcomber. Some were of higher social standing. Thomas Griffith, a tiler, appears as a freeholder in the 1734 poll book. One was a surgeon, Fortune Pye, another a gentleman named Thomas Wright, and there was one woman, a spinster named Sarah Tanner who was in the crowd that attacked Farrier's.

The Whigs clearly hoped that these arrests and prosecutions would curb Tory violence. They did not. On the king's birthday in October 1735 the Whig magistrates and merchants met to celebrate the evening and symbolically

---

[95] Latimer, II, 178–9; Craftsman, 2 March 1734.
[96] TNA, KB 33/5/3.
[97] Details from TNA, KB 33/5/3.
[98] London Evening Post, 14–17 June 1735; Daily Gazetteer, 9 July 1735.
[99] TNA, KB 33/5/3.

re-enacted the St George and dragon ritual, this time with an illumination in which an orange was placed under George's name 'from which issued a spear wounding a dragon'.[100] No sooner was the illumination lit than a mob 'pelted out the lights with dirt and stones'. To conclude this defiance, a pasquinade was surreptitiously placed on the statue of King William.

The 1735 interventions were essentially triumphal affirmations of the Tories' first parliamentary victory in twenty years. They should be regarded dialogically, as a continuing battle with Whigs for symbolic space in which crypto-Jacobite imagery was juxtaposed to Hanoverian, recalling even the old battles in which the notorious Tory Sir John Knight railed against the Dutch 'froglanders'. After the exuberant celebration of the marriage of the Prince of Wales in 1736, when the Whig corporation distributed no fewer than five hundred gallons of beer to win over the populace to the Hanoverian cause, there was a further flurry of white roses on the Pretender's birthday.[101] Thereafter, Jacobite revelry declined in intensity, although some ladies continued to brandish white roses on 10 June until 1750, on one occasion as a response to the repair of the statue of King William in Queen Square.

Predictably Jacobite sentiments surfaced during the Forty-Five rebellion. A Broadmead tavern-keeper named Daniel Taylor was committed to Newgate for drinking the Young Pretender's health and asserting his right to the throne. He was fined a noble (6s 8d) and imprisoned for six months, as was John Osmotherly for the same offence. A seditious paper cursing his Majesty and all those in authority was nailed to the Cathedral door. It was hostile to Protestants in general but singled out Quakers and Presbyterians in particular, threatening to burn down the house of Richard Farr senior, a merchant and member of Lewin's Mead chapel, whose son was about to become a councillor, and eventually an alderman.[102] Threatening letters of this kind often occurred where collective resources were weak, and neither the letter nor the affirmations of Stuart loyalty were taken as seriously as they might have been earlier in the century. At least the authorities did not regard them as manifestations of a deeper plot implicating Tory leaders, as they had done during the Fifteen.

The evidence for this comes from two lengthy depositions involving a founder named Joseph Rendall. In October 1745 he had allegedly offered a local baker named Robert Burges or Burgess an interest-free loan of between £50–100 and a weekly allowance of 6–10s if he would work for the Tory Steadfast Society. According to Burgess, Rendall claimed that the Tories were hiding the Young Pretender in Bristol, passing him from house to house. He testified that Charles Stuart had stayed with Jarrit Smith, the reputed master of such operations, but more recently he had resided in Redland. Rendall

[100] *Daily Gazetteer*, 5 Nov. 1735; Latimer, II, 193.
[101] Latimer, II, 196–7, 258, 278.
[102] *Bath Journal*, 18 Nov. 1745, 14 April 1746; BA, Sessions docket book, 1741–48, sessions 5 April 1746; *Farley's Bristol Advertiser*, 16 Nov. 1745; Latimer, II, 257.

claimed the Pretender had brought in boatloads of silver for an insurrection and was expecting 10,000 men to land at Penzance any day.[103] Burgess was to act as a runner in these covert operations, but instead he reported Rendall to the city authorities, who hauled him in for questioning.

These revelations could have been momentous. They implicated a well-connected local Tory in a Jacobite plot to take the West Country, something paranoid Whigs had feared for decades. Yet the aldermen quickly discovered that Rendall's testimony was shaky. He proved to be a deranged know-it-all who even professed he could uncover the identity of the author of the threatening letter stamped to the Cathedral door. 'One of the aldermen asked me', he deposed, 'if what I said was not a dreame, or if I was not knavish.'[104] The magistrates had Rendall identify one of those accused of harbouring Charles Stuart, very likely Jarrit Smith. When Smith produced an alibi, they threatened Rendall with perjury and threw him into Newgate.

The interesting aspect of this episode is that the Whig corporation did not panic or chase down members of the Steadfast Society for treasonable activities. Since the election of Sir Edward Southwell in 1739 there had been a truce between the two parties. The Whigs found Southwell very acceptable, and also, remarkably, Coster's son-in-law Robert Hoblyn. Both proved adept at handling Bristol's business and helped remove some of the bitterness between the two parties. This honeymoon was short-lived. The Whigs came to resent the efforts of the Tories to control statutory bodies like the Corporation of the Poor and the turnpike trust, and the candidature of Sir John Philipps in 1754 revived the old divisions and memories of nefarious plotting during the Forty-Five. Did Whig aldermen remember the allegations of Joseph Rendall when Jarrit Smith became their MP two years later? In this recharged climate, flaunting the Stuart standard at College Green was a political joke at Whig expense, perhaps even a canard. As had often been the case, Jacobitism could be droll and blasphemous, a source of irritation to the Whigs, the product of a festive politics that ran to excess.[105]

---

[103] TNA, SP 36/73/357–8.
[104] TNA, SP 36/77/336–7.
[105] On the many faces of popular Jacobitism, see Nicholas Rogers, *Crowds, Culture and Politics in Georgian Britain* (Oxford, 1998), ch. 1.

6

Anger and Reprisals: The Struggle against Turnpikes and their Projectors, 1727–53

By the mid eighteenth century Bristol had firmly established itself as the 'metropolis of the west', servicing and receiving goods from a vast hinterland. Daniel Defoe foresaw this in his famous *Tour* of 1724, noting that Bristol merchants maintained carriers 'to all the principal countries and towns from Southampton in the south, even to the banks of the Trent north; and tho' they have no navigable river that way, yet they drive a very great trade though all these counties'.[1] Grain came in from the Midlands and Wales, peas and beans from Gloucestershire, butter from west Wales and Glamorgan, eggs and poultry from Somerset. As far as industrial products were concerned, timber came down the Severn from the Forest of Dean, wool from Milford and Cardiff for local weavers and the Cotswolds, metal goods from the west Midlands, tin from Cornwall, copper from Anglesey. Such was the traffic that Bristol emerged as an entrepôt for raw materials, displacing other Severn and Channel ports, who tapped into its trade networks, both regional and Atlantic.[2]

While nearly five hundred vessels linked Bristol to Africa, Europe and the New World, some nine hundred coastal vessels would sail the Avon each year by 1750. Indeed, coastal trade was very much the backbone of Bristol's metropolitan status. At the same time road traffic was important, for local supplies of coal, for the flow of goods to and from neighbouring counties, for the famers and hucksters who flocked to Bristol's two annual fairs.

In the eyes of many a civic booster, the five main roads in and out of Bristol were poor. What were needed were turnpikes, toll roads managed by boards of commissioners who would supplant the older system of statute labour whereby each parish was responsible for its section of the road. First introduced after the Restoration, turnpikes strove to make travel faster, safer, and over time substantially cheaper for commercial traffic. Bristol was among the towns that invested in turnpike trusts in the second wave of activity in

---

[1] Daniel Defoe, *A Tour thro' the Whole Island of Great Britain* (3 vols, London, 1724), II, 55.
[2] Walter E. Minchinton, 'Bristol: Metropolis of the West in the Eighteenth Century', *Transactions of the Royal Historical Society*, 5th series, 4 (1954), 69–89.

8 Samuel Hieronymus Grimm, *The Turnpike Above Cook's Folly*, 1788.

the mid 1720s. Its act followed hard on those that linked the West Country woollen trades to vital supplies and expanding markets. Bristol established turnpikes on virtually every arterial road to the north, south, and east of the city, linking it to the Mendips, to Bath, to Chippenham and the Great West Road, to the Stour valley woollen industry, and to Gloucester. This network of roads was intended to make Bristol the hub of West Country traffic and industry.

Championed by the Bristol Common Council, its merchants and the local gentry, the turnpikes did not meet with universal approval. Although it is conventional to suggest that turnpike advocates were 'modernisers', some early political economists like Josiah Tucker, the rector of St Stephen's, thought otherwise. Compared to the excellent public roads in France, financed centrally by the court, turnpikes were a 'heavy tax' upon 'trade' and quite unnecessary.[3] This hostile view of turnpikes was widely shared, among others by the Kingswood colliers, a term that in the eighteenth century included carriers as well as miners.[4] Although the Bristol turnpikes reduced

[3] Josiah Tucker, *A brief essay on the advantages and disadvantages which respectively attend France and Great Britain*, 2nd edn (London, 1750), pp. 44–5.

[4] See the *OED*, where collier means someone who worked in the coal trade, mining or delivering the coal. Hence coal ships and their sailors were also called 'colliers'. In practice, Kingswood miners were often separate from the drivers, see John U. Nef, *The Rise of British Coal Industry* (2 vols, London, 1932), I, 435–7. The drivers had as many as five hundred packhorses in 1675. In an industrial dispute in 1738, coal miners blocked wagons of coal intended for Bristol, mine owners having cut their prices for local glass- and brass

the toll on packhorses carrying coal from a penny to halfpenny a load, the coal carriers regarded turnpike fees as a troubling tax on their livelihood, raising the cost of delivering coal to Bristol. Upon the introduction of the first turnpike trust in July 1727, they remonstrated with the mayor 'whether they should not come Free to the City with their Coals without paying toll'.[5] This was the case with the turnpike at Bath, why not Bristol? In a sardonic letter to the trustees, written the same month by a likely sympathiser,[6] it was claimed that local lords of the manor had deliberately allowed the public roads around Kingswood to deteriorate so that a case could be made for a new toll road. To reiterate the point, in October 1727 the colliers actually began repairing the road from the pits to Bristol to underscore the vitality of the old system of statute labour.[7] All that was needed was the political will to make it fully operative.

Turnpike trusts have historically had a good press. They are seen as reducing the heavy costs of transporting goods to markets, one of the factors that gave Britain the edge in early industrialisation. Eric Pawson emphasises that they were not profit-making enterprises but public statutory bodies that revitalised a transport system that had fallen into desuetude and decline.[8] Such a perspective ignores the class dimensions of turnpike legislation, which benefitted the larger dealers and landlords at the expense of the smaller producers who could not compete with larger economies of scale. It also ignores the quite considerable knock-on effects of turnpikes, which raised the price of surrounding land by as much as 20 per cent over the long term, a not inconsiderable amount in an age when rates of interest were low and land values relatively stable, at least outside of London's 'commuter belt' of fashionable weekend villas and country houses.[9] Turnpike trusts also had the right to expropriate local materials for the upkeep of the roads, and even to insist parishes pay their share of statute labour or its equivalent, privileges that affected the small, customary economies of cottagers or manorial tenants. These certainly would have implicated coal miners as well as drivers, for the

producers. The waggoners in this conflict were clearly working for the large owners and ignored struggles of piece-rates in the pits. See TNA, SP 36/46, fols 163–4; Adrian Randall, *Riotous Assemblies: Popular Protest in Hanoverian England* (Oxford, 2006), pp. 131–2.

[5] *London Journal*, 1 July 1727. For the exemption at Bath, see Robert W. Malcolmson, '"A set of ungovernable people": The Kingswood Colliers in the Eighteenth Century', in *An Ungovernable People. The English and their Law in the Seventeenth and Eighteenth Centuries*, ed. John Brewer and John Styles (London, 1980), p. 95.

[6] GRO, D 15/2, 'The Colliers Letter to the Turnpike', printed in full in William Albert, *The Turnpike Road System in England 1663–1840* (Cambridge, 1972), pp. 27–8.

[7] *Evening Post*, 5–7 Oct. 1727; *Mist's Weekly Journal*, 5–7 Oct. 1727.

[8] Eric Pawson, *Transport and Economy: The Turnpike Roads of Eighteenth Century Britain* (London and New York, 1977).

[9] Dan Bogart, 'Turnpike Trusts and Property Income: New Evidence on the Effects of Transport Improvements and Legislation in Eighteenth-Century England', *Economic History Review*, 62:1 (2009), 128–52.

cottages they rented came with little land and consequently the resources of the chase were important to them.[10] The Kingswood colliers complained that the new legislation gave Bristol trustees the right to cut furze and heather on the chase, to the detriment of their everyday livelihoods. The Turnpike Act also left a lot of room for jobbery – the rewarding of fat contracts to surveyors, for instance, or discretionary exemptions to friends of the trustees, an aspect of the trusts that troubled Jonathan Swift.[11]

In the doggerel that accompanied the 'Colliers Letter' to the trustees, turnpikes were perceived as an aspect of a more ruthless age of speculative projects, epitomised most colourfully by the South Sea Bubble of 1722.

> Turnpikes are grown much in Fashion
> The hardest Tax in all our Nation
> For where Wine & Women & Stockjobbing past,
> The Turnpike must help us at last.[12]

Tory paternalist in tone, the letter saw turnpike tolls as a vexatious impost on the poor, part of a growing trend in Walpolean legislation to redistribute levies in favour of the gentry through reducing land taxes and burdening the consumer. After taxes on salt, soap, beer and candles, why not a tax on transportation? Why not give landlords a break and penalise the working poor, who spent too much time in the alehouse and really needed the stiff discipline of hardship to bring them to labour? Embedded in this rhyme is this set of assumptions, especially in the last ironic line, 'The Turnpike must help us at last.' Its tone, with its references to financial speculation and fast living – of 'Wine & Women & Stock-jobbing' – echoed Alexander Pope's barbed satire to John Donne, the Dean of St Paul's, in which a credulous widow is cheated by unscrupulous financial advisers and tolls greeted Londoners on their country excursions.[13]

The Kingswood colliers were not about to let turnpikes stand. They were a tightly-knit group whose collective solidarities grew out of their experience

---

[10] On landholdings and tenure in Kingswood Forest, see Buchanan Sharp, *In Contempt of All Authority. Rural Artisans and Riot in the West of England, 1586–1660* (Berkeley and Los Angeles, 1980), pp. 188–90.

[11] In the *History of John Bull*, Swift talked of commissioners doing favours for friends by allowing them to pass toll-free. Jonathan Swift, *Works* (12 vols, London, 1765–75), V, 96.

[12] Albert, *The Turnpike Road System*, pp. 27–8, 77. See also Randall, *Riotous Assemblies*, pp. 161–2.

[13] Fourth Satire of Dr John Donne, Dean of St Paul's, in Alexander Pope, *Works* (London, 1735), II, 153; see also Alexander Pope, *Poetical Works*, ed. Herbert Davis (London, 1966), p. 404.

> Who in the Secret, deals in Stocks secure,
> And cheats th'unknowing Widow, and the Poor;
> Who makes a Trust, or Charity, a Job,
> And gets an Act of Parliament to rob;
> Why Turnpikes rose, and now no Cit, nor Clown,
> Can gratis see the Country, or the Town:

in the pits, and they exhibited much of the truculence that characterised the cottagers of open parishes of heath and wasteland, who cherished their vagrant independence and were not under the close supervision of big landlords and their factors. Rejected by the mayor, who claimed that amendments to the legislation were now out of his control, the colliers vowed 'they would pay none of their taxes' and began pulling down the turnpike at Totterdown on the Bath road, burning it with cartloads of coals that were on their way to town.[14] As the mayor reported to the secretary of state,

> The colliers ... rose Monday last and continue still assembled in a tumultuous manner, and have burnt, pulled down and destroyed the turnpikes and obstinately persist, if any more are erected, they will serve them in the same manner. They are a set of ungovernable people, violent in their way and regardless of consequences.[15]

Together with miners from neighbouring Brislington, they formed a strong wrecking-squad that proceeded to destroy other turnpikes in the area, marching through Bristol on one occasion 'with Clubs and Staves in a noisy manner' to show the civic authorities they meant business.[16] That business included putting pressure on the city by cutting off vital supplies of coal to domestic consumers, but also to Bristol's glass and sugar refineries and brass and copper works. According to a report of 3 July, the colliers had destroyed all carts carrying coal in Bristol and, according to at least one newspaper report, sank several boatloads of coal shipped from Wales.[17] Unsurprisingly, the mayor requested troops to curb their outrageous behaviour. When the miners audaciously pulled down the turnpike on Durdham Down, in the very shadow of the Gloucestershire county gibbet pole, and started levying money from passers-by to sustain their families during these incursions, troops from Colonel Grove's regiment moved in and captured four protesters: Thomas Fry, Abraham Biggs, Thomas Bright and James Robbins, a mason from Horvil (Horfield?).[18] The colliers vowed to rescue them and the city was put on full alert, with five detachments posted a various points in the city and patrols sent out to watch the miners' movements in and around Kingwood forest. The protesters were examined by Gloucestershire JPs (Durdham Down being under county jurisdiction) at the Lamb inn outside Lawford's Gate. Two of the four, Fry and Biggs, were allowed bail; Robbins and Bright were cuffed, tied up on horses and sent to Gloucester jail to await trial at the next assizes.[19]

The authorities hoped that this show of military and legal strength might inhibit the colliers. This was not to be. No sooner were the turnpike gates and bars erected than they were destroyed. Colliers appear to have taken

---

[14] *London Journal*, 1 July 1727; *Mist's Weekly Journal*, 1 July 1727.

[15] TNA, SP 36/1, fol. 56

[16] TNA, SP 36/1, fol. 56, see Malcolmson, 'Ungovernable People', pp. 94–8.

[17] *Daily Post*, 4 July 1727; *London Journal*, 8 July 1727.

[18] *Daily Journal*, 12 July 1727; *Parker's Penny Post*, 14 July 1727; *London Journal*, 15 July 1727, *Mist's Weekly Journal*, 15 July 1727.

[19] *Daily Journal*, 29 July 1727.

advantage of a hiatus in military assistance, with companies of Murray and Grove's regiments moving off to Ireland before Kerr's regiment arrived in Bristol. The colliers certainly made short work of the turnpike commissioners' own guard at Lower Easton, but at Lawford's Gate there was a bloody affray in which one collier, Ralph Phillips, was slashed across the face with a cutlass, an act that provoked the miners to wound severely several guards.[20] By August 1727, no turnpike was operating in the Bristol region. Colliers visited them as community redressers, in women's clothes and high-crowned hats, despite the dangers of prosecution under the Waltham Black Act, which came down hard on disguised protesters of any kind.[21] Rewards for their apprehension came to nothing. As the London Journal remarked, arresting colliers was a difficult business, 'they being numerous in their Holt called King's Wood'.[22]

Even legal sanctions proved only marginally successful. Thomas Fry and Abraham Biggs were acquitted at the Gloucester assizes and the cases against the two rioters who were unceremoniously carted off to prison were not prosecuted, even though the indictments against them were found to be true. Three other protesters who attacked the turnpike at Frampton upon Severn were also pursued through the courts, but only one was successfully prosecuted. He was Ralph Phillips, a conspicuous leader in the demonstration, who had also axed the turnpike at Lawford's Gate. He was sentenced to hang at the Gloucestershire assizes in the spring of 1728 under the terms of the Riot Act of 1715, but the prosecutors requested his reprieve. This was perhaps to inhibit further protests, perhaps because prosecutions under the Riot Act were still controversial and unpopular, having been introduced in 1715 to curb a rash of attacks upon Dissenting meeting houses in the west Midlands.[23] Other rioters were given lenient punishments. Two of them, Joseph Isgar and John Wicks, were simply fined for cutting down a turnpike and sentenced to a month's imprisonment. These legal decisions underscored the difficulties of finding the right sanctions for 'crimes' that commanded considerable support. While Phillips stood in the shadow of the gallows, public efforts were made to petition parliament to exempt crucial provisions such as coal, timber and grain from the tolls, perhaps following the example of impressment protections, because they were essential supplies. 'There appears a thorough Dislike to this Toll-Duty', remarked Nathaniel Mist's Journal, and the direct action of the colliers 'mixes in all Conversations'.[24] Perhaps this was why the trustees did not press for Phillips's execution: at the August assizes, after three months in prison, he was sentenced to fourteen years' transportation.[25]

[20] London Journal, 29 July 1727.
[21] E. P. Thompson, Whigs and Hunters. The Origins of the Black Act (London, 1975).
[22] London Journal, 1 July 1727.
[23] Mist's Weekly Journal, 20 April 1728. For details of these prosecutions, see Gloucestershire assizes, summer 1727 and spring and summer 1728, in TNA, ASSI 2/9.
[24] Mist's Weekly Journal, 10 Feb. 1728.
[25] Daily Journal, 13 Aug. 1728; TNA, ASSI 2/9.

Nothing came of the move to exempt coal and other supplies from the tolls, for petitioners became mired in jurisdictional squabbles about the range and scope of turnpike trusts in the Bristol region. But efforts were made to clarify the law. In May 1728, a month after the spring assizes in Gloucestershire, the Studley Bridge-Toghill trustees petitioned parliament for a law that stand-ardised the punishment for destroying turnpikes. The result was I George II, c. 19, which allowed a public whipping and three-month prison sentence for the first offence, and transportation for seven years for the second. Subsequently, in an act that reinforced gentry control over local turnpikes, concessions were offered the colliers. Packhorses carrying coal were now exempted from tolls into Bristol, alleviating the burden on the smallest carri-ers, although as formerly, this concession would not apply to tolls levied east of Kingwood towards Chippenham.[26]

The Bristol trustees clearly hoped these carrot-and-stick measures would curb the opposition to turnpikes and began erecting new tollgates in June 1731. Colliers and 'country people' quickly rose to destroy them, specifically those to the east of Bristol where coal transported on packhorses was not exempt from the toll. On 30 June, William Blaithwayt, a JP from Dyrham and also a turnpike trustee, raised a private posse and confronted the protesters who were destroying the turnpike near his estate. Four men were taken pris-oner, but before Blaithwayt could examine them with another JP, Sir William Codrington of Doddington, colliers surrounded his mansion and demanded their release. As Blaithwayt reported to the Duke of Newcastle in London, he was told at two o'clock in the morning that he must discharge the prisoners or else his house would be burnt down. Blaithwayt refused to concede until he was 'overpowered with numbers', principally pitmen from Kingswood, in spite of the fact that Codrington had come to his aid with twenty of his own servants and tenants.[27] Blaithwayt and Codrington tried to placate the colliers with beer, but they were soon reading the Riot Act at fresh outbreaks of violence in Marshfield. The two JPs complained of the colliers' 'impu-dent Defiance to Authority'. They asked Newcastle for further military aid, noting that the current troops in Bristol had restricted orders and could not be mobilised outside of the city. Together with other JPs in the region, some of whom had significant holdings in the Kingswood 'liberties' where coal was mined, they impressed upon the secretary of state the fact that rioters had burnt down another turnpike at Yate and had sent threatening letters to leading landowners, and to Alderman William Hart, a Bristol merchant and Tory candidate in the 1727 city election. Further troops were essential, they maintained, 'to protect us in putting up the Turnpikes again, the Insolence of the Rioters being now greater, their having cut down some other gates even at noon day'.[28] Two months later, learning that Lord Cadogan had no

[26] 4 George II, c. 22; Malcolmson, 'Ungovernable People', pp. 98–9.
[27] TNA, SP 36/23, fols 206–7, 257–8.
[28] SP 36/23, fol. 250.

orders to move troops out of Bristol, Codrington and Blaithwayt reiterated their vulnerability. 'The License these Rioters have taken makes it difficult to execute any process or Warrant of the Law at present.'[29]

Blaithwayt and Codrington may have exaggerated their difficulties. They had no wish to appear ineffectual magistrates before the leading patron of the country. Committals and convictions were made in the next round of confrontations. In March 1732 the Toghill trustees and other JPs and gentlemen to the east and north-east of Kingswood joined forces with those of Hereford, where opposition to turnpikes had also been rife.[30] They asked for tougher legislation against turnpike rioters and secured an act that made transportation for seven years a punishment for first, not simply second offenders.[31] The sponsors anticipated that this would intimidate turnpike protesters, but the Kingswood colliers swore they had 'enter'd into Articles not to suffer any Turnpikes to be erected'.[32] They were true to their word, for when two more toll gates were erected by the Toghill trustees between Marshfield and Chippenham, a large party of Kingswood colliers 'armed with hatchets and axes' descended on Ford, four miles east of Chippenham, and proceeded to cut down the gates. Notice of their movements had been given to Rogers Holland, MP for Chippenham, an enthusiastic trustee and a warm supporter of the increasingly tough legislation against turnpike demolition. He mustered two gentlemen and his servants to meet the colliers, but arrived to find the colliers cutting down the gate. Holland ordered the colliers to stop; they defied him and so Holland's party dispersed them with small shot. Three rioters were apprehended and taken the following morning to Salisbury gaol, under guard.[33] Holland, who had received a threatening letter warning him not to proceed, managed to secure a crown prosecution of the three men. One, a seventeen-year-old named Stephen Crow, was acquitted of pulling down turnpikes, but the two others, Isaac Smith and John Harding, were found guilty and sentenced to seven years' transportation.[34] In a letter of 14 April 1733, Holland wrote to a fellow trustee, Thomas Haynes, that he had received from one of his tenants a petition of the Kingswood colliers to the king, begging a pardon for the two convicted men. They promised 'to oppose any Attempt for destroying Turnpikes for the future' if their plea was granted, he noted, a matter he thought worth considering.[35] In the event no pardons were made, and colliers continued to confront the trustees. It was widely reported that every turnpike was destroyed on the Bristol–Gloucester

[29] SP 36/24, fol. 115.
[30] On the Hereford disturbances, see William Albert, 'Popular Opposition to Turnpike Trusts in Early Eighteenth-Century England', *Journal of Transport History*, 5:1 (1979), 1–17.
[31] 5 Geo II, c. 33.
[32] *Gloucester Journal*, 30 May 1732, cited by Malcolmson, 'Ungovernable People', p. 101.
[33] *London Evening Post*, 19–21 Sep. 1732.
[34] *St James's Evening Post*, 13–15 Feb. 1733; *London Evening Post*, 13–15 March 1733.
[35] BA, MS 09701/26, noted in Malcolmson, 'Ungovernable People', p. 103.

road in the early summer of 1734 and the crown issued a proclamation offering a reward of £50 for every rioter taken up and convicted.[36] At the end of the decade Ralph Allen, the postmaster of Bath, remarked: 'the Colliers have pulled down, and do constantly pull down any Turnpikes that have been at any time erected'.[37] By that date parliament had made the destruction of turnpikes a capital felony. In just seven years, from 1728–35, MPs had increased the punishment for first-time offenders from three months' imprisonment, to seven years' transportation, to death by hanging.[38] Yet extreme legal sanctions and military force had not curbed popular opposition to turnpikes in the West Country. However determined, Bristol's trustees had failed to put their projects into effect. The wrath of the colliers seemed implacable and their affront to authority total, save that they avoided any accusations of Jacobitism by insisting that they were for King George even if they despised turnpikes – a canny line in an age when the government was quick to ferret out such disaffection and blur the lines between political and social protest.[39]

In 1749 the turnpikes around Bristol had lain dormant for a decade, but in July of that year a new effort was made to revive them. The grants of the previous trusts had lasted for twenty-one years and they had to be renegotiated. The Commons Journal reveals that this renewal was very much a regional enterprise, with the Bristol MPs, Edward Southwell and Robert Hoblyn, and the MPs from Somerset and Gloucestershire active on the committee.[40] The commissioners for the new trust were weighted towards the Tories rather than the Whigs, largely because country gentlemen from the two predominantly Tory counties outnumbered merchants from the city. The Whig-dominated corporation complained of this imbalance to their MPs. Southwell and Hoblyn retorted it was an oversight. They said they had been very preoccupied with fighting the monopolies of the Royal Africa and Hudson's Bay companies on behalf of the city. They marvelled that the Whig corporation should be so upset by their representation on the turnpike trust when matters of the slave and fur trade were at stake, 'wch are surely of more consequence to the Trade of the City'.[41] In fact Southwell and Holblyn appear to have followed the recommendations of the Tory caucus at the Steadfast Society, who did not want the corporation to 'dictate to two Countys & the whole City of Bristol'. Instructively, when the two Bristol MPs agreed to increase urban representation on the trust, they added the governors of the Corporation of

[36] *London Evening Post*, 22–25 June 1734; *London Gazette*, 16–20 July 1734.

[37] JHC, 23 (1737–41), 258–9, 273–4, 333; Malcolmson, 'Ungovernable People', p. 104.

[38] In 1735 under 8 Geo II, c. 20.

[39] For the slogan 'King George and no Turnpike', see *Mist's Weekly Journal*, 1 July 1727; for the uses of Jacobitism as an idiom of defiance and the government's preoccupation with it, see Nicholas Rogers, *Crowds, Culture and Politics in Georgian Britain* (Oxford, 1998), ch. 1.

[40] JHC, 25 (1745–50), 737, 806, 828.

[41] BA, Southwell MS 44785/10, Letter of Hoblyn and Southwell to Francis Fane, June? 1749.

the Poor, not eligible members from the corporation.[42] This amendment was consonant with the Tory policy of trying to make the city more accountable, for governors of the poor were elected officials, not part of a self-perpetuating oligarchy. The powers of the corporation had been a point of disagreement between the two parties over the Street Lighting Bill of 1749, and fears about the exorbitant powers of urban oligarchies also framed the discussion of the turnpike trust.[43] In the final bill the trust could be subdivided into sections to allow for a greater degree of local participation over particular roads, subject to approval from a general meeting of the trustees at Guildhall.[44]

Party politics certainly complicated the propertied response to the revival of the turnpikes. Before the meeting at Guildhall was held, the Whig-dominated corporation withdrew their subscription of £500 towards the administration of the turnpikes, an action that was seen in Tory quarters as a retaliatory move against the Tory majority on the trust. The Steadfast Society was consequently forced to lend the trustees £1000 to promote the trusts, the bulk of it coming from John Brickdale.[45] By January 1754 the Steadfast Society had invested over £1700 in the turnpike trust, making it very much a Tory enterprise.[46]

In July 1749 the immediate challenge was how the populace in general would react. Five new tolls had been added to the original twelve, three of them in Somerset. This might prove troublesome, as the trustees were well aware. They sought to neutralise the opposition of the colliers by making further concessions on coal delivery. Under the new legislation coal on waggons was also exempt from tolls into Bristol, not just coal carried by packhorse. So, too, was the carriage of firewood, limestone, hay and grain, concessions that would appeal to small farmers. At the same time the trustees publicly reminded the populace at large that pulling down turnpikes was a capital offence. An extract of the 1735 act was inserted in the regional press.[47]

Trouble began soon after the tolls opened on 19 July. Two days later there was an attack on the Toghill road at Don John's Cross, about a mile from Bristol, which 'greatly exasperated the commissioners', who were resolved to prosecute 'all Delinquents they can discover'.[48] The following week there was a second attack on this turnpike by men stripped to the waist with their 'faces black'd'. They bored holes in the posts and blew them up with gunpowder – the work, one suspects, of colliers or smithies from Kingswood, although the *Bath Journal* talked of a 'Body of Country People', an ascription that did not

---

[42] BA, Southwell MS 44785/10, July 1749.
[43] On the politics of the Street Lighting Bill, see Nicholas Rogers, *Whigs and Cities. Popular Politics in the Age of Walpole and Pitt* (Oxford, 1989), pp. 280–1.
[44] Albert, 'Popular Opposition to Turnpike Trusts', 9.
[45] BA, SMV/8/2, Steadfast Society, Rules and Orders 1737–1802, p. 47.
[46] BA, SMV/8/2, Steadfast Society, Rules and Orders, pp. 52, 55, 62.
[47] *Bath Journal*, 3 July 1749.
[48] *Bath Journal*, 24 July 1749.

necessarily exclude industrial workers.[49] The tollman was threatened and his wife was told 'if she did not go home, her Bones should be sent in a Bag'.[50]

A day earlier, 'a great Body of the Country People' from Somerset descended on the turnpike at Bedminster on the Long Ashton road. Making prodigious shouts that could be heard for miles around, they made swift work on the turnpike with hatchets and axes and destroyed it within thirty minutes. The turnpike commissioners attempted to counter these outbreaks of violence by erecting a barrier across the Ashton gate and by continuing to collect the toll. They even appeared in person, twelve at a time, in an effort to overawe the demonstrators. Farmers and labourers retaliated by driving cattle and colts through the cordon on their way to the Bristol fair. One demonstrator, Charles Wilmot of Congresbury, was charged for this infraction; another, Thomas Hardwicke of Clapton, near Radstock, a coal-mining area, was indicted for assaulting the collector.[51] But these arrests and charges did not deter the rioters. On their return, they threatened the commissioners with a horse-whipping. Three men, John Waich or Walsh, George Hickes and John Old (sometimes Ould), were seized in this confrontation and examined before two local JPs, John Hippisley Coxe and George Hedges.[52] Two of them were released upon the payment of a fine of £5 for deliberately evading tolls, the standard punishment for such an offence, but they were bound over to face more serious charges at the next quarter sessions. The third was sent to the gaol in Shepton Mallet.

These arrests only raised the tempo of protest. A 'prodigious body' of country people once again converged on Ashton gate, this time with drums beating, shouting 'Down with the turnpikes! Down with the turnpikes!'. Wielding 'cutting instruments fixed on long staffs' and with some dressed as women, they prevented the tollhouse from being rebuilt and threatened anyone who dared to do so.[53] They also attacked the house of a gentleman whom they mistakenly thought was a commissioner, ripping out his sash windows. A few brazenly asserted that if gentlemen did not like their treatment 'they would come and pull down the EXCHANGE', or perhaps burn it to rubble, as one threatening letter warned.[54] Others mocked the commissioners by suggesting that the protesters might take their place and receive the toll.

Another party of protesters attacked the toll-house on the Dundry road and signalled that they would return the following day to finish off the job. Tipped off that this might happen, the commissioners marshalled a posse of

---

[49] See Andrew Charlesworth et al., 'The Jack-a-Lent Riots and Opposition to Turnpikes in the Bristol Region in 1749', in *Markets, Market Culture and Popular Protest in Eighteenth-Century Britain and Ireland*, ed. Adrian Randall and Andrew Charlesworth (Liverpool, 1996), pp. 46–68.

[50] *Bath Journal*, 31 July 1749.

[51] Somerset Heritage Centre, Q/SR/317/2/19–20, Indictments dated 26 July 1749.

[52] *Bath Journal*, 31 July 1749.

[53] *Bath Journal*, 31 July 1749.

[54] *Bath Journal*, 31 July 1749; BA, TC/Adm/Box/3/7, 1749, bundle 7–39.

constables and demobilised sailors to confront them. The posse even ventured eight miles into Somerset in an effort to arrest the ringleaders, picking up one man at Backwell and bringing him back to Bristol strapped to a horse. A couple of drummers were also arrested at Ashton gate, and, to the dismay of the country people, they divulged the names of other rioters, some of whom were taken up.

Protesters once again swung into action, once again converging on Bedminster under the leadership of two men on horseback, one 'with his face black'd', the other a young gentleman farmer from Nailsea who carried a standard. According to one newspaper report, this group styled themselves 'Jack-a-Lents' and had 'JL' on their caps and hats, a reference to the effigy that was traditionally stoned and burnt at the end of Lent, but that possessed satirical power to criticise the authorities.[55] Within the carnivalesque conventions of misrule, the protesters saw themselves as an army of redressers, revenging themselves on the social 'traitors' who had affronted community norms and threatened to undermine their standard of living. Their immediate task was to tear down the Long Ashton gates that had been quickly rebuilt. But they also directed their anger on Stephen Durbin, the tithingman of the hundred, who had turned the three rioters over to the commissioners. They demolished his house, even breaking a chain while struggling to pull down some of the main timbers. One rioter, William Pearce of Dundry, was subsequently indicted at the Somerset quarter sessions for assaulting Durbin.[56] Crowds also raised contributions for their fellow rioters and moved towards Redcliff Hill with the intention of entering Bristol to free their comrades from Newgate. A city shoemaker warned them that if they went any further they would 'receive harm', but they told him 'they would for that the Town would not hurt them, being all of their sides'.[57] The authorities had anticipated their move, however, and closed all the gates to the city, so the Jacks moved on to Totterdown where they began levelling the gates and sentry boxes of the turnpikes on the Bath and Pensford roads. There the Jacks were confronted by the posse of the commissioners, who had hired fifty demobilised sailors and a handful of city artisans to assist them. The sailors violently attacked the protesters with cutlasses and badly wounded several, including one farmer Barnes, who was armed with two pistols, but who was cut through the skull and wounded in the hand. Many demonstrators retreated over Knowle Hill. The Riot Act was read and around twenty-five to thirty turnpike rioters were arrested.[58]

[55] *Bath Journal*, 7 Aug. 1749; *Western Flying Post*, 14 Aug. 1749; *London Evening Post*, 5–8 Aug. 1749; Charlesworth *et al.*, 'The Jack-a-Lent Riots', p. 59.
[56] Somerset Heritage Centre, Q/SR/3172/21, Michaelmas session, 1749.
[57] BA, TC/Adm/Box/3/7, Informant of John Maddocks, 8 Aug. 1749.
[58] BA, Southwell MS 44785/10, William Berrow to Southwell, 1 Aug. 1749. Barnes later died of smallpox in Bristol Newgate: *Bristol Oracle*, 18 Nov. 1749.

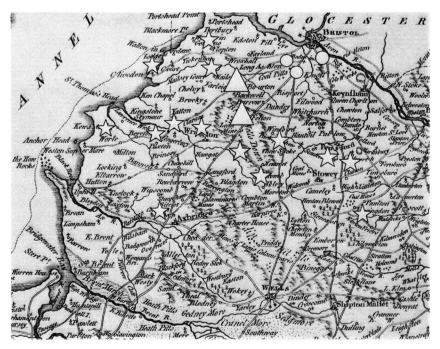

9 The popular mobilization against turnpikes in Somerset, 1749. Stars = places of origin of turnpike protesters; Triangles = meeting points; Circles = turnpike gates.

The survival of the depositions relating to these arrests allows us to map the Somerset protests in some detail.[59] The people who converged on Ashton gate and Bedminster came from a twelve or more mile radius from Bristol encompassing Clevedon, Congresbury, Wrington, Redhill, Chew Stoke, Sutton Wick [or Week] and Radstock, and further in, Nailsea and Backwell and Dundry. Two men, Richard Taylor and James Lovell, the drummer who helped mobilise the rioters into a wrecking battalion, came from Worle, on the fringes of Weston-super-Mare. Most were described as husbandmen in the depositions, although several were rural artisans, including a blacksmith and at least two carpenters. They may well have been recruited for their wrecking skills. A number emphasised they were servants to particular farmers: Samuel Hewlet was the servant of Joseph Cooke of Week, near Sutton Court; James Waich was servant to Peter Old, a yeoman farmer of Congresbury, whose brother James Old was seized at Ashton gate on a return visit to the turnpike. Waich's testimony, and that of Aaron Cross, servant to farmer Halstone of Broadways Down, reveal that some arm-twisting did take place to muster the turnpike phalanx, whose epicentres appear to have been Congresbury to the west and Chew Stoke to the south of Bristol. The general rendezvous was at Broadways Down and Backwell, where they were marshalled by four men on

[59] The depositions are in BA, TC/Adm/Box/3/7, bundle 6.

horseback, including the young farmer, Mr Bullock of Nailsea, who carried the standard. From Backwell, with their colours flying and drums beating, they descended on Long Ashton.

Curiously, no mention of Jack-a-Lent is made in any of these detailed depositions, which at least raises the possibility that the description was a journalistic invention of the *Bath Journal*, where it first appeared.[60] This does not compromise the notion that the turnpike protests were ritually charged, with many elements of rough music: discordant music, drums, flags, smutty faces, cross-gendered dressing. Carnivalesque mock violence, familiar enough to Somerset villagers, gave some unity to the protest and very likely helped to coordinate the different reasons why people joined. At its core the protesting was against the new tolls that affected small farmers bringing products like milk, cheese, fattened calves or sheep to market. North-east Somerset was an area of mixed farming, predominantly dairy, that serviced Bristol and Bath. But the threatening letters that surfaced during these protests also point to broader social grievances. One, purportedly written by a Bristol labourer, saw turnpike tolls as yet another oppressive tax on urban 'workin'men', for 'Our Sety [City] is very much imposed upon' and 'we are ye sufferers by it'. The net effect of higher transport costs would be higher prices on meat and butter, but 'we will not pay deare for our me[a]t to plese a parsell of por broken Shentlmen [gentlemen]', declared the writer. If the farmers were determined to destroy the turnpikes, 'we will help them'. Another saw turnpike tolls as little more than highway robbery. 'I can call it no better than Rob[b]ing the Poor of Town & Country by Authority', wrote the anonymous author, 'I wish Every poor man in Town & Country may be of my Mind.'[61]

After the defeat at Totterdown at the hands of the commissioners' vigilantes, the country people called on the colliers, who collectively had remained aloof from the protests, partly no doubt because they had received significant concessions from the turnpike trustees. Labourers toured the smelting works and coal pits around Kingswood in an attempt to rustle up some aid. While the colliers were divided on whether to join the agitation or not, some certainly did, despite efforts by the commissioners and local industrialists to dissuade them.[62] Miners helped demolish the Toghill turnpike once more and started raising contributions for the campaign against the turnpikes. Some called for the assistance of their fellow colliers in the north Somerset coalfield around Paulton and Clutton.[63] The liaison between the two groups was badly coordinated; it led to some accusations of treachery from the Somerset group, who felt they had been needlessly mobilised. Nonetheless, further turn-pikes were threatened. Some protesters declared not one would stand 'in the

---

[60] Cf. Charlesworth *et al.* 'The Jack-a-Lent Riots', pp. 59–61; Randall, *Riotous Assemblies*, pp. 161–4.
[61] BA, TC/Adm/Box/3/7, bundle 7–39.
[62] *London Evening Post*, 5–8 Aug. 1749.
[63] *London Evening Post*, 12–15 Aug. 1749.

Country', that is, in the Bristol region. One newspaper reported that the Yate (Chipping Sodbury) and Bath turnpikes were under attack 'if not already down', and that rioters were demanding that those arrested be released.[64] The threat of a combined force of approximately seven hundred country labourers and colliers descending on the jails was enough to put Bristol on an emergency footing.[65] For two or three days city residents anxiously awaited the arrival of troops, with demobilised soldiers recruited for guard duty and many citizens enrolling as special constables. Meanwhile the remaining turnpikes were exposed. In fact, the turnpike at Yate was demolished before the arrival of the second regiment of dragoons, and another at Stokes Croft, close to the city, was only saved by the intervention of demobilised soldiers and sailors.[66]

The presence of the troops swung the balance of force in favour of the authorities. Certainly it emboldened the local dignitaries to seek reprisals. The Whig mayor of Bristol, Buckler Weekes, had been reluctant to intervene in the riots, which he felt were inflamed 'not only from the inveteracy of the Country People but from the indiscreet warmth and precipitate measures of the acting Trustees', many of whom belonged to the Tory Steadfast Society.[67] He was upset by an advertisement published by the trustees that advised citizens to defend themselves and rendezvous at the Exchange should a general alarm be given.[68] Clearly he felt the predominantly Tory trustees had usurped his responsibilities for order.[69] Indeed, he believed the 'great forwardness, warmth and severity of the acting trustees' and the inactivity of the JPs had forced him to take prisoners of turnpike protesters who should have been examined and committed to county jails, not Bristol Bridewell and Newgate.[70]

Upon the arrival of the troops, however, the mayor believed peace would soon be restored and eagerly reported that the 'gentlemen in the country' were keen to have a quick trial of the rioters who had been arrested.[71] Since the Bristol assizes were about to begin, an effort was made to try the turnpike rioters expeditiously. But this plan was postponed at the request of the commissioners because the prosecuting witnesses were not ready. Equally important was that discontent over the turnpikes was far from over. Letters were sent to

[64] *Worcester Journal*, 10 Aug. 1749.

[65] *Ipswich Journal*, 12 Aug. 1749.

[66] *General Advertiser*, 8 Aug. 1749; *Whitehall Evening Post*, 5–8 Aug. 1749; *Worcester Journal*, 10 Aug. 1749.

[67] TNA, SP 36/111/14; Rogers, *Whigs and Cities*, p. 291. Weeks voted for Nugent in the Bristol election of 1754, see *The Bristol poll-book* (Bristol, 1754), p. 2.

[68] TNA, SP 36/ 111/15, dated 28 July 1749.

[69] BL, Add. MS 32719, fols 161–2, 182. The Earl of Hardwicke thought that one of the problems was the mistrust that existed between the Tory-dominated trust and the Whig corporation.

[70] BA, Mayor's letter book, 28 Aug. 1749.

[71] TNA, SP 36/111, fol. 77v, Weekes to Newcastle, 19 Sep. 1749, cited in Philip D. Jones, 'The Bristol Bridge Riot and its Antecedents: Eighteenth-Century Perception of the Crowd', *Journal of British Studies*, 19:2 (1980), 79.

the mayor of Bristol threatening arson if the turnpikes were rebuilt. Further arrests were made. On 17 August 1749, Alderman Day committed John Riddle (otherwise Riddler), Samuel Durbin and Reece Davis for cutting down the turnpikes on the Brislington and Whitechurch road, near Totterdown.[72] Bailiffs strove to track down some of the Kingswood colliers who were active in the riots. They attempted to arrest one of the 'underground men' named Harborough, alias Reynolds, who barricaded himself in the upper room of his house and kept them at bay with large stones and a pitchfork.[73] After this incident, armed colliers patrolled Kingswood every night and were quite prepared to confront other officers of the law who ventured into the forest to arrest them. To make the point, the patrols fired slugs into the turnpike lodge on the Toghill road.[74] As on previous occasions when the colliers fell foul of the law, they used their muscle to keep officers away. Their reputation as 'a set of ungovernable people' remained intact.

As late as mid September the turnpike trustees were pressing the Duke of Newcastle for a full regiment of troops in the Bristol area. According to John Brickdale, the JPs among the trustees had been 'intimidated & discouraged from doing their duty in both respects by the Insurrections, Insults and Threats of their Riotous Countrymen'.[75] By September the newspapers were speculating that a special commission would be called to deal with the rioters. The Recorder of Bristol, Sir Michael Foster, concurred with this idea. He thought a special commission the appropriate court for 'such heinous and aggravating Offences'.[76] The Attorney General, Sir Dudley Ryder, at first agreed. He wondered 'whether in a Case of such open publick insult upon government and the Laws, and where the Gentleman of the Country [were] immediately concerned', there was not the need for a 'speedy and solemn Trial, in order to strike a Terror in the most effectual manner'. It was best, he thought, to hold a special commission in a county adjacent to Somerset, where there might be a 'disinterested jury'.[77]

By November, however, Ryder had second thoughts. He seems to have been troubled by the quality of the evidence against the rioters, quite possibly the large number of informations by itinerant sailors, some of whom might not be available as witnesses in court. He decided that instead of a special commission the law should take its course in the normal way.[78] Those charged with destroying Stephen Durbin's house in Bedminster would be tried at the Somerset assizes, as already planned. Those taken at Totterdown, the great

---

[72] *Bath Journal*, 21 Aug. 1749.
[73] *Bath Journal*, 18 Sep. 1749.
[74] *London Evening Post*, 23 Sep. 1749; *Whitehall Evening Post*, 23 Sep. 1749.
[75] BL, Add. MS 32719, fol. 171.
[76] *Bath Journal*, 14 Aug. 1749.
[77] TNA, SP 36/111, fols 77–8. See also BA, Southwell MS 44785/10, Robert Hoblyn to Edward Southwell, 2 Oct. 1749.
[78] TNA, SP 36/111, fols 180–1, 188.

majority, would be sent to the Wiltshire assizes under a clause in the 1735 act that allowed turnpike rioters to be tried in a neighbouring county.[79]

Attacks on toll collectors continued up to and beyond the spring assizes, when the great majority of rioters stood trial.[80] The men charged with destroying Durbin's house were tried at Taunton in early April 1750. Several bills were not found, notwithstanding the fact that Joseph Derrick, active at Bedminster and Totterdown, had turned king's evidence. Some were acquitted. Sympathy for the rioters ran deep.[81] The crown had solid evidence against Thomas Cox, who was considered one of the principal agitators at Bedminster, but he was presented as a 'lunatic' and discharged.[82] In the end, the crown was only able to successfully prosecute two men, Thomas Perryman and John Roach. They were charged under the Riot Act with pulling down Stephen Durbin's house and sentenced to be hanged, although the principal witness against them, Aaron Cross of Ubley, was regarded as devious and untrustworthy. It was widely anticipated that they would be reprieved at the intercession of some local gentlemen. Some newspapers actually reported they had been pardoned, but in fact they were executed at Ilchester on 19 April. At the gallows, both refused to admit their guilt.[83]

During their long imprisonment several turnpike rioters had died of small pox in Bristol gaols. Eighteen were sent to be tried at the Wiltshire assizes in Salisbury, again in April 1750. There the grand jury declared three indictments to be ignoramus, including that of John Waich or Walsh, who had been arrested during the early confrontations between rioters and trustees at Bedminster.[84] With the other fifteen that went to trial, the crown prosecution encountered some difficulty. The trial of the first turnpike protester, Isaac Coles, took up the best part of the day. The evidence seemed watertight. A constable from All Saints, Bristol, swore he saw Coles swinging a pick and iron bolt at the turnpike, and in captivity Coles had declared at the Council House 'that if he was hangd he shd not be ye first'.[85] John Brickdale, a leading Tory trustee, also gave evidence against Coles. He was one of three men Brickdale had identified cutting down the turnpike on the Whitchurch road. Yet the jury acquitted him. A new jury was empanelled to hear the next case, that of William Denmead. Two depositions identified Denmead at Redcliff

---

[79] 8 Geo II, c. 20, clause 3. Offenders could be tried in an adjacent county for 'a better and more impartial trial'.

[80] See Somerset Heritage Centre, Q/SR 318/2, Midsummer 1750. The cases of Samuel Smith of Clapton, and William Andrews of Cross, both fined for assaulting turnpike collectors.

[81] *London Evening Post* and *Whitehall Evening Post*, 14 April 1750; *Bath Journal*, 9 April 1750.

[82] BA, Town Clerk's letter book, 1749, 6–83.

[83] *London Evening Post* and *Whitehall Evening Post*, 21 April, 8 May 1750; *General Advertiser*, 10 May 1750; *Old England*, 21 and 28 April 1750.

[84] *Whitehall Evening Post*, 14–17 April 1750.

[85] BA, Town Clerk's letter book, 1749, 6–85 and 87; *Worcester Journal*, 19 April 1750.

gate and then at Totterdown, where he attacked one of the commissioners' aides, a cordwainer named John Maddocks, with a hay-knife. Once again the defendant was acquitted; perhaps because Denmead had managed to destroy the knife by tossing it into the burning timbers of the turnpike as he was taken up, and perhaps too, as Robert Hoblyn hinted to Southwell, because the trustees appeared overzealous in prosecuting protesters.[86] At this point the crown counsel abandoned the other prosecutions, sensing that the jury would be overly sympathetic to the turnpike rioters, and so thirteen further defendants were discharged. The best that the crown could do was to bind eleven rioters over to the Taunton assizes to answer for other offences.[87]

The hangings of Perryman and Roach left a bad impression, and did nothing to improve relations between the Bristol elite and the populace at large. The trustees finally succeeded in establishing turnpikes in the Bristol area, but at a considerable price. When Sir Michael Foster arrived in Bristol to begin the assizes in August 1749 he found the city in a state of panic, 'not unlike that of a town taken by storm'.[88] He thought the trustees needlessly provocative in re-establishing turnpikes so as to not lose face in the light of successive humiliations. And he believed their use of demobilised soldiers and sailors had caused unnecessary bloodshed and aggravated frictions between the Whig corporation and the Tory opposition in the city. One index of these tensions was the prosecution of John Brickdale for his role in suppressing the riots in November 1750, a suit that the Steadfast Society felt obligated to defend and finance on Brickdale's behalf.[89] These frictions, and the bad blood over the suppression of the riots by a private force unregulated by the civic authorities, would linger on into the 1750s.

They surfaced dramatically in 1753, a year in which the harvest was not particularly bad but in which there was a regional scarcity in the West Country, prompted, it was popularly thought, by farmers holding back grain from market, or selling it to exporters in order to force up the price. At Taunton several hundred women descended on the town mill and demolished the weir, egged on by many men who applauded them for the 'dexterity with which they carried out the task'.[90] A month earlier, Mendip miners had been active in their local markets. Five to six hundred colliers descended on Shepton Mallet and had a crier proclaim that goods should be sold at a 'reasonable price'. They searched all the inns and supervised the sale of corn, meat and butter 'as they thought proper and delivered the money to

---

[86] BA, Southwell MS 44785/10, Hoblyn to Southwell, 2 Oct. 1749; BA, TC/Adm/Box/3/7, Information of John Maddocks, 8 Aug. 1749. Both of the deponents against Demeade lived at the Cradle in the Horsefair. One, Benjamin Cox, was a mariner.

[87] *Worcester Journal*, 19 April 1750; TNA, Assizes 23/6, Western Circuit 1749–50; Randall, *Riotous Assemblies*, p. 163; Jones, 'Bristol Bridge Riot', 79.

[88] BL, Add. MS 32719, fols 161–2.

[89] BA, SMV/8/2, Steadfast Society, Rules and Orders, pp. 48–9.

[90] FFBJ, 7–17 July 1753.

ye farmers that owned it, if they would receive it'.[91] Before leaving they gave notice that they intended to do the same at Warminster and Wells within the week.

Kingswood colliers, whose hardships intensified when a local outbreak of the staggers hit their livestock, were also party to these efforts to drive down the price of provisions.[92] Ten days after the rising of the Mendip miners, the Kingswood colliers gathered together and declared they were determined to visit the city to discuss the high price of corn with the authorities. The mayor, John Clements, was apprised of their movements by a scout, a bright-smith named John Jones.[93] When the colliers entered the city with their colours flying, attracting the support of some country people on the way, the mayor was prepared to meet them. He agreed to talk to a deputation of four miners and informed them that the aldermen had agreed to settle the price of grain at 5s 3d a bushel. He added they would consider altering the price if there was any good reason to do so.[94] This seemed to satisfy the deputation and some miners, but not all. Some lingered around the Council House and proved threatening enough for the Riot Act to be read. One group of malcontents headed for the quay and boarded the *Lamb*, which was about to transport seventy-four tons of wheat to Dublin. As the colliers cleared the deck of the boat and started unloading the sacks of grain from the hold, they were attacked by armed constables who had been sent to protect the vessel. There were brawls in which the constables appear to have gained the upper hand and apprehended several rioters. Consequently an angry mob of demonstrators returned to the Council House and began smashing the windows, injuring the town clerk and one alderman. It threatened to return with more men and arms. For their part the mayor and aldermen sought to defuse the situation by releasing most of those arrested on promises of good behavior. One or two were retained in custody as some sort of surety.[95]

Mayor John Clements wrote to the Duke of Newcastle asking for military support, as 'we have a great reason to dread some very bad consequences'.[96] He also organised the internal defence of Bristol. Special constables were sworn in to deal with possible reprisals; the militia was mobilised; the city remained under arms all day and night, awaiting the arrival of troops from Gloucester some forty miles away. For two days there was no sign of the colliers, but on Thursday 24 May, a large group of colliers, weavers and country people appeared at Lawford's Gate and there was another brief confrontation in which the city authorities held their position and prevented

---

[91] BL, Add. MS 32,731, fol. 446.
[92] *Bath Journal*, 6 Nov. 1752.
[93] TNA, SP 36/122/31, 33.
[94] TNA, SP 36/112/31.
[95] *FFBJ*, 19–26 May 1753; Malcolmson, 'Ungovernable People', p. 119.
[96] TNA, SP 36/122/31.

the demonstrators from entering the city. Some were even taken up and admitted to bail.[97]

On Friday 25 May the violence escalated. A large party of between one- and two thousand circumvented the city's secured gates by entering Bristol through Milk Street, and made their way to the Bridewell where riot- ers were held. 'The inhabitants were in great consternation', recorded the diarist, William Dyer, 'the Drawbridge drawn up, the shops shut, making a gloomy appearance at noon-day.' The mayor mustered forces to meet the colliers, 'and with a constable's staff in his hand, tho a very nervous man and unavoidably agitated', he led a small party of fifty Scots Greys, just arrived from Gloucester, on a circuitous route towards Bridewell via the Pithay and across the river Frome to St James's Back. The soldiers' commanding officer would not order his men to open fire without clearance from Clements, and since the mayor was clearly nervous of doing so, no shots were fired.[98] From this position the officer could only witness the advance on the prison, leav- ing volunteer units of tradesmen and gentlemen to confront the colliers. According to some accounts, the volunteers were led by Charles Lysaght, a future captain of infantry; according to others, by the off-duty Lieutenant Paget, a Flanders veteran. Echoing the events surrounding the defence of Stephen Fechem's house during the weaving dispute of 1729, these specials had the mayor's approval to disperse the crowd forcibly and accordingly armed themselves with guns, cutlasses and clubs.[99] By the time the volunteers reached Bridewell, the mob had already broken into the gaol and had rescued the demonstrators taken four days earlier, but the volunteer force opened fire as the demonstrators made their way out. According to William Dyer, the posses were overzealous in dealing with the 'poor, misguided colliers', who only had stones with which to defend themselves. The miners fled as best they could, along with a party of their womenfolk who had gathered in St James's churchyard 'with a supply of stones in their aprons with which they made a mighty clatter' as they ran from the gunfire.[100] Two colliers were shot dead as they retreated across Bridewell bridge, several others were wounded and about thirty were taken prisoner. In retaliation, the crowd took several townsmen hostage as they pulled back, most of whom managed to escape at Lawford's Gate. They included John Brickdale, badly bruised from 'many a severe stroke from sticks and clubs'; Michael Miller and Thomas Knox, prom- inent citizens in Bristol's two rival factions; and the West Street jeweller Mr Millard, and Samuel Worrall, both of whom received serious head wounds.

[97] *FFBJ*, 19–26 May 1753.

[98] Steve Poole, 'Scarcity and the Civil Tradition: Market Management in Bristol, 1709– 1815', in *Markets, Market Culture and Popular Protest*, p. 97; BRL, Manuscript diary of William Dyer, 2 vols, 1744–1801, 25 May 1753, 33–4.

[99] J. F. Nichols and J. Taylor, *Bristol Past and Present 3: Civil and Modern History* (Bristol, 1882), p. 191; BL, Add. MS 32,732, fol. 152.

[100] BRL, Diary of William Dyer, 25 May 1753, 33–4.

An impetuous haberdasher's apprentice named Brown was less fortunate. Passing through Lawford's Gate without any support, Brown chased after the retreating colliers as far as Baptist Mills, firing his musket at them as he went. The colliers surrounded him, took him prisoner, and secured him in a nearby public house. According to Dyer, Brown was taken from there by two colliers who feared their comrades might harm him, and hidden in a mineshaft for his own protection. He was eventually freed by the intercession of Lord Berkeley and managed to make his way back to Bristol after eight days in captivity. If Samuel Seyer's memoirs are to be believed, Brown was not the only hostage taken by the colliers, although we do not know what happened to them.[101]

The confrontation of May 1753 was as serious as the Totterdown affair of August 1749. From the perspective of authority, it was more significant in that it occurred within the city walls. The episode revealed just how difficult it was for the Bristol authorities to handle large demonstrative crowds without adequate military support, and how gentlemanly militias could spiral out of control, switching from panic to vengeful violence when confronting groups like the Kingswood colliers, who so frequently served as the shock troops of popular insurgency. They had led bread riots in 1709 and 1740, turnpike riots in 1727 and 1731, and their muscle and collective strength was called upon once more in 1749. In 1753 they again led the demand for lower grain prices, although they arguably miscalculated the determination of the authorities to resist physical intimidation and disavow the theatre of popular solidarity, the huge musters of people with flags, horns, cockades and guisers, cross-dressed or otherwise. In 1749 the threat of popular invasions of the city put the authorities into a veritable panic; in 1753 Bristol was again said to be in the 'greatest confusion'.[102] In 1753 the threat was contained, but clumsily and bloodily. The bodies of four colliers, William Fudge, Jonathan Crew, James Bryant and Richard Gunning, all shot by the posse as they tried to retreat, lay at St Peters Hospital awaiting an inquest.[103] Yet a coroner's enquiry resolved little. While Mayor John Clements was trying to negotiate the return of the hostages, angry insurgents were mobilising in Wiltshire for another invasion of the city. The anger over scarcity, moreover, did not abate. A baker's shop was razed outside Lawford's Gate, and in Bristol itself, Clements sensed 'a strong inclination ... among the lower sort of our citizens to join them [the rioters]'. Resisting this disaffection, he concluded, 'may be too hard a task for our present forces'.[104]

The aftermath of the 1753 riots was messy. The mayor cancelled the celebrations on Restoration day (29 May) fearing they might serve as a pretext for further violence. Gestures were made to placate the colliers by agreeing to

[101] Samuel Seyer, *Memoirs historical and topographical of Bristol* (2 vols, Bristol, 1823), II, 599; BRL, Diary of William Dyer, 55; *Gloucester Journal*, 5 June 1753.
[102] *Public Advertiser*, 25 May 1753.
[103] *Gloucester Journal*, 5 June 1753.
[104] TNA, SP 36/122, fols 34–5, 45.

provide medical aid for their wounded men in Kingswood, where as many as fifty were said to be nursing serious injuries from the affray. Colliers awaiting trial in Newgate were less fortunate. By 26 June, three of them were dead from untreated wounds: Job Phipps who had been shot in the thigh; James Cains, shot in several parts of his body; and Emanuel Evans who had been beaten about the head with a club.[105]

Earlier that month, on 6 June, the city elite had celebrated a sanitised interpretation of the riot and its suppression.[106] A great number of citizens 'of the best credit and reputation', numbering it was claimed two thousand, processed from the Exchange to the Guildhall where the mayor and members of the corporation were assembled. There William Berrow, a linen draper, merchant and key member of the Tory Steadfast Society,[107] thanked them for their efforts and hoped Bristol would be rid of the 'like illegal and daring insults' in the future. The speech overlooked the dubious way in which the mayor personally handled the threat of disorder; his actions in this regard might have been considered pusillanimous. Certainly William Dyer thought so. But the speech did accord with the relief of the propertied that order had been restored. The mayor for his part thanked them for their recognition of civil zeal, and assured them of 'his utmost Endeavours to promote a continuance of the present Harmony and Union among them'.[108]

The mayor's message here is noteworthy. In 1749 the incumbent mayor, Buckler Weekes, had railed at the ingratitude and treachery of the Tories in subverting civil authority. In 1753 John Clements preached union. The change in tone was made more startling because it ultimately centred around the fate of John Brickdale, a very rich woollen draper and leading member of the Tory Steadfast Society. Brickdale had been critical of the Whig corporation's handling of the 1749 crisis. He led the posse at Totterdown; he acted without reference or deference to the mayor; he personally pressed the Duke of Newcastle for more troops, believing the mayor had not really appreciated the gravity of the crisis. Indeed, his disagreements with the corporation were such that the Steadfast Society was forced to foot the bill for the defence and reconstruction of the turnpikes in 1749.[109] In 1753 he was again very active in the suppression of the riots, and along with John Chivers and Michael Miller, the latter another member of the Steadfast Society, had been indicted for murder at the coroner's inquisition into the death of the collier,

---

[105] BA TC/Adm/Box/6/6, Inquests, 1753.

[106] FFBJ, 26 May–2 June 1753, 2–9 June 1753.

[107] Berrow is listed as one of the members of the Steadfast Society in 1741, and he was one of the caucus who arranged a political compromise with the Whigs in 1754. See BRL, *Jefferies Collection*, 10:10 and BA, SMV/8/2. In the late 1730s he was sending linen to Jamaica and also cider to Ireland, see TNA, E 190/1214/3.

[108] FFBJ, 2–9 June 1753.

[109] BA, SMV/8/2, Steadfast Society, Rules and Orders 1737–1802, p. 47; Rogers, *Whigs and Cities*, p. 291.

William Fudge, during the fight close to Lawford's Gate.[110] This happened not once, but twice, for there were two inquests that reached the same verdict, notwithstanding the fact that the leaders of the posse all claimed that Fudge menaced them with a pick and pitchfork and that they acted in their own self-defence.[111] With these verdicts in their favour, the colliers were out to get Brickdale, who, sensing the danger, very sensibly remained in London. Indeed, travellers were stopped at Pickwick on the London road by searchers looking for the draper and threatening 'to put him in a Pitt'.[112]

The Whigs could have left Brickdale to stew in his own juice, but they didn't. They actually petitioned the government for a nolle prosequi or a pardon to stay any prosecution of him and his companions, which included not only Tories but a member of the Whig Union Society, the merchant Thomas Knox, who had also been part of the citizen posse. The Attorney General Dudley Ryder favoured the first course, since he believed the first inquest had been very partial and might serve as a precedent for more. He advised that the indictment against Brickdale and company be removed to the Court of King's Bench and emphatically laid to rest. He also advised an information against the coroner, Edward Webb, 'as it is now become necessary to put a final issue to this affair, as otherwise the Riotous Colliers may find Means to procure new inquests as fast as the old ones shall be quashed'.[113]

The 1753 crisis revealed that the Bristol elite was prepared to shelve political differences in the interests of law, order and property. It was an important precedent that would frame patrician–plebeian relations in the future. But what of the rioters? How did they fare in the legal aftermath of the disorders?

In late July a reward of £200 was offered for the apprehension of Sampson Phipps, one of the ringleaders in the riot. A further £100 was offered for the apprehension of any of four other leading rioters, Samuel Britton, John Woods aka Woody, John Summers and Hezekiah Hunt. None of these men was ever apprehended, and no one informed on them, even when the full battery of the law was directed at Phipps and Britton, for two bills of high treason were laid against them and any who harboured them.[114] In this respect the authorities failed to get the men they really wanted. A conspiracy of silence among miners and their associates confronted them.

At a special commission before Mayor John Clements, Sir Sidney Stafford Smythe and Sir Richard Adams, the crown lost some cases. Eight men charged with riot-related misdemeanours were acquitted because townsmen decided

---

[110] TNA, SP 36/122, fols 87–8.
[111] Add. MS 35,413, fols 220ff.
[112] TNA, SP 36/122, fol. 45; BL, Add. MS 32732, fol. 43.
[113] TNA, SP 36/122, fols 42–3, 87–8. BL, Add. MS 32,732, fol. 10. The letter reveals that steps were taken to quash the inquest before the end of the term at King's Bench in early June 1753.
[114] *FFBJ*, 1–8 Sep. 1753.

to withdraw charges.[115] Yet the crown did successfully indict eight colliers for riot, offences for which they received a fine of two nobles (13s 4d) and a prison sentence of two years. In January 1754 they begged for clemency, citing the distress to their families and the rather lame excuse that they had been swept up in the riot by angry weavers.[116] This request was denied. In reviewing the evidence John Sharpe, Solicitor to the Treasury, recommended to the Duke of Newcastle that their convictions stand, 'to make a deeper Impression on the minds of the Colliers and operate in terrorem, so as to deter them the more from Joining in the like Attempts for the future'.[117] Sharpe noted, rather pointedly, that examples had to be made here because no protester had gone to the gallows. The crown prosecution had tried to get some capital convictions. Two of those imprisoned, John Paviour and William Jefferies, had also been prosecuted for stealing a hogshead of sugar from the *Lamb*, a charge that carried the death penalty. But no one could conclusively prove sugar was in the caskets and so they were acquitted of a felony.[118]

In other words, the crown and corporation did not get the real terror it desired. At the special commission in Wiltshire in 1750, so in Bristol three years later, the sympathies of many were with the crowd. The man who felt this most keenly was John Brickdale, who fled Bristol after the Bridewell riot. He was very troubled by the reports of colliers stopping people on the London road looking for him, and quite startled by the fact that one looka-like, a gentleman named Benson Earle, was attacked and stoned while riding through a village in a post-chaise with his son. When he ventured back into Bristol from London in early June, he had to be escorted for twenty miles by his wealthier 'Fellow-Citizens'.[119] There were many fugitives from justice in 1753. Wealthy Bristolians had suppressed a food riot, but members of the propertied class faced reprisals for the zeal of their repression.

The fragile and uneasy equilibrium between patrician and plebs in the early eighteenth century came unstuck in 1749 and 1753.[120] Political division within the Bristol elite was one reason for this; another was civic lassitude if not ineptitude – a disposition to panic when large crowds entered the city and only act decisively when troops were behind magisterial backs – which was not conducive to building trust when dealing with popular grievances. In the next food crisis Bristol's corporation would adopt a more proactive approach, complaining to parliament of shortages created by the distillery industry, demanding tax incentives to import foreign grain, and arguing for

---

[115] BA, Sessions docket book, 1748–1753, entry dated 31 Aug. 1753. These were Francis Britton, Thomas Andrews, Francis Flew, Moses Aubrey, James Roach, John Pearce, John Carter, Samuel Cox. See also *FFBJ*, 8 Sep. 1753.

[116] TNA, SP 36/125, fol. 25; TNA, Assizes 23/6, Western Circuit Gaol Book, 1 Sep. 1753.

[117] TNA, SP 36/125, fol. 97.

[118] *FFBJ*, 1–8 Sep. 1753.

[119] BL, Add. MS 32,732, fol. 51.

[120] On this model of eighteenth-century social relations, see E. P. Thompson, 'Patrician Society, Plebeian Culture', *Journal of Social History*, 7 (1974), 382–405.

national uniform measures so that the assize of bread was properly admin-istered.[121] Bristol also distributed subsidised food to the working poor of its parishes and its magistrates implemented the laws against grain specula-tion and profiteering. As a result, the city managed to avoid the riots that surrounded it, in Bath, Gloucester, and in the textile towns of Wiltshire, east Somerset and the Midlands.[122]

One way in which the status of Bristol's elite was enhanced was by rewrit-ing history. It created a fiction of its victory over riot and disorder in 1753. It began with William Berrow's speech on 6 June 1753 and crystallised in Samuel Seyer's *Memoirs*. 'This attack of the colliers afforded matter of mirth and conversation for many succeeding years', Seyer recalled, especially the 'conduct of well-known citizens' and the 'folly and strange dialect of the assailants'. Much was made of the resolution of the gentlemen citizens and of the lethargy of a 'whig government, which out of too nice a tenderness for popular liberty had taken no care to restrain the licentious insolence of the vulgar by proper laws and regulations'.[123] Colliers were burlesqued; elite Bristolians were brave citizens battling libertarian licence from above and below. The reality had been more complex.

[121] JHC, 27 (1753–7), 652, 847.
[122] *FFBJ*, 27 Nov. 1756; *Northampton Mercury*, 30 April 1757; *Bath Journal*, 23 and 30 May 1757, 6 June 1757; *Gentleman's Magazine*, 27 (1757), pp. 185, 235. See also Andrew Charlesworth (ed.), *An Atlas of Rural Protest in Britain 1548–1900* (Philadelphia, 1983), pp. 86–8.
[123] Seyer, *Memoirs*, II, 599.

7

'It is better to stand like men than to starve in the land of plenty': Food Riots and Market Regulation in Bristol[1]

The Food Riots of 1801

On 6 April 1801, in the midst of the most serious subsistence crisis of the Napoleonic war years, four or five hundred Kingswood colliers struck work in an attempt to persuade city magistrates to reduce the price of provisions in Bristol market. Two days earlier, disturbances had broken out in the streets of the city over the price of meat, butter and potatoes; indeed the whole south-west region had been gripped by marketplace rioting, chiefly over bread supplies, for a number of weeks, leaving civil and military authorities severely stretched.[2] It was not the first time the colliers had taken collective action over the price of food. Similar tactics had been used in 1709, 1740, 1753 and, to a lesser extent, in 1795, but the 1801 dispute marked a watershed in relations between the Bristol crowd and the corporation over the principle of marketplace intervention. Quite simply, magistrates were no longer disposed to cooperate.

However, the colliers' confidence was initially strengthened by knowledge that a customary mix of mobbing and formal parleying had earned crowds in Bridgwater, Taunton and several other regional centres, substantial market reductions. A list of these 'agreed' Somerset prices were accordingly drawn up by the colliers into a petition to the mayor of Bristol, and pressure put upon farmers in the region to add their signatures to it. 'Our whole intention is peace', insisted the colliers, but 'through hard living, many of us are not able to perform the labour we wish to do'.[3] But the mayor had no intention either of receiving the petition or adopting Somerset prices.

---

[1] Parts of this chapter originally appeared in Steve Poole, 'Scarcity and the Civic Tradition: Market Management in Bristol, 1709–1815', in *Markets, Market Culture and Popular Protest in Eighteenth-Century Britain and Ireland*, ed. Adrian Randall and Andrew Charlesworth (Liverpool, 1996), pp. 91–115, and are reproduced here by permission of the publisher.

[2] For the full regional context see Roger Wells, 'The Revolt of the South-West, 1800–01', *Social History*, 6 (1977) and republished in R. Wells and J. Rule, *Crime, Protest and Popular Politic in Southern England, 1740–1850* (London, 1997).

[3] TNA, HO 42/61, Statement of the Bristol magistrates, J. A. Small to Duke of Portland, 14 April 1801.

The so-called Bridgwater agreement had been brokered after crowds forced dealers to accept price reductions at Wellington and Taunton at the end of March, then walked from Stogursey to Nether Stowey, Goatchurch, North Petherton, Bridgwater and Otterhampton, in search of a magistrate to sign a petition of endorsement for lower prices. Although magistrates consistently refused to do so, they had been unable to disperse the crowd by persuasion or military force, without promising assistance. A day later they called together the farmers, gentlemen and principal inhabitants of the district and contrived a public agreement to relieve the markets with plentiful supplies of cheaper food the following week. This victory for public intervention was widely reported.[4] But the Somerset agreement had flown in the face of the Home Secretary's (the Duke of Portland) strict instructions that local authorities should resist attempts at popular regulation, however strong the customary belief that magistrates could and should regulate the profits of producers and retailers in times of shortage. As if to clarify the position, the Somerset assize condemned two men to death on 3 April for robbery at Old Cleve. By purchasing bread at the village bakery at a price lower than the baker's asking price, it was judged, they had 'entered the house where they took the bread and paid their own price for it, which is in fact the same as if they had taken it without paying anything because no person has a right to fix the price and take another's property'.[5] This important trial took place just one day after the publication of the Bridgwater agreement and a day before the riots at Bristol.

Trouble at Bristol began early in the morning of 4 April when butter jobbers and potato, beef and bacon farmers were waylaid as they approached town to sell produce in the market and obliged to slash their prices by more than half. Crowds appear to have outwitted city magistrates by waiting for the dealers on the approach roads and forcing price reductions before anything could be done to stop them. Some products, particularly butter, were largely bought up by this popular method of forestalling, leaving little for sale in the market. 'Inflammatory' notices causing 'very serious alarm' were posted by unknown hands on city walls. As the gunpowder maker and occasional special constable William Dyer noted, 'The rioters were for some time without opposition; the public mind rather countenancing than otherwise. The farmers have long been exorbitant in their prices.'[6] At 11.00a.m. magistrates ordered the Volunteers to muster at the Exchange, then sent them with parties of regular troops and militia under General Rooke, to secure

---

[4] This extraordinary sequence of events is poorly reported in the newspaper press but recorded in minute detail in correspondence between the magistrates John Evered, David Davies and John Acland. See *The Times*, 2 and 3 April 1801, and Somerset Heritage Centre, Acland Papers, DD/AH/59/12/1–16, Evered to Acland 1 April 1801, Davies to Acland 28 March 1801.

[5] *The Trial of Samuel Tout and Robert Westcott for Forcibly Breaking and Entering the Dwelling House of Richard Griffey, Acting Riotously Assembled with Diverse Other Persons and Stealing Fifteen Loaves of Bread … At Taunton Assizes in Friday 3rd April 1801* (Taunton, 1801).

[6] BRL, Manuscript diary of William Dyer, 2 vols, 1744–1801, 4 April 1801.

the approach roads. In the early afternoon, the Riot Act was read in the High Street and a handbill published 'to admonish the inhabitants of this city to keep at home this evening, as the military will be ordered to suppress further riot'. A number of people were taken up and lodged at Bridewell and Newgate and the Volunteers ordered to remain on parade at the Exchange to ensure no further disturbance broke out.[7] Many retailers shut up their shops, according to one report, 'and very little business was done during the whole of that day'.[8]

The situation became more serious in the evening as crowds gathered outside butcher's shops. One man, Samuel Nash, went into Thomas York's shop and tried to buy a neck of mutton priced at six shillings for just four. York managed to eject him but the crowd outside prevaricated: "'Ah you fool, why has thou not took it?" He replied, "Damn you, why had you not come in and helped me?"' When Nash tried to force his way back in, York threatened to 'chop his hands with a knife', but the issue was resolved by the arrival of the Inniskilling dragoons, who rode up and dispersed the crowd. Rooke complemented the 'measures adopted by the magistrates and the steadiness of the troops in support of the civil power' and thought further trouble unlikely.[9]

The magistrates, fearful that their ability to control popular regulation was now in question, were unequivocal. A second batch of notices was quickly issued that evening, assuring 'all Farmers and Others, usually bringing provisions to the Bristol market, that they are determined to preserve THE FREE MARKETS of the CITY and that the CIVIL POWER will be exerted to the utmost and if necessary a MILITARY FORCE will be called out to protect the property of ALL PERSONS bringing provisions to the markets'.[10]

The rising of the colliers on the city's eastern fringes on 6 April was thus doubly unwelcome and magistrates resolved to deal with it firmly and speedily. General Rooke, Charles Harford and several other magistrates immediately led two parties of Inniskillings to Kingswood to oppose them. They seized the petition and ordered the miners to disperse or face the cavalry. There was nothing the magistrates could do to reduce prices, they insisted, but if the colliers agreed to go home peaceably, they would hear their complaints in Bristol in two days' time, and payments of parochial relief would be increased. After 'much persuasion and some threats', the colliers agreed to terms, but did not return to work.[11] A day later, they were joined by three hundred north Somerset miners and Nailsea glass-men. They gathered at the Star Inn in Bedminster and with the assistance of the Redcliff shoemaker and Methodist preacher Joseph James, drew up a petition of their own. James and

[7] *Courier*, 11 April 1801.
[8] *Hampshire Chronicle*, 13 April 1801.
[9] BA, JQS/P/169, Information of Thomas York, 5 April 1801; TNA, HO 42/61, Lieutenant General Rooke to Duke of Portland, 5 April 1801.
[10] *FFBJ*, 11 April 1801.
[11] TNA, HO 42/61, Joseph Small to Duke of Portland, 14 April 1801.

a small delegation of community representatives then walked into town and presented it to magistrates. With equally respectful language, they too prayed for the adoption of the Somerset agreement: 'Your humble Petitioners Trust that your Goodness and Superior Knowledge will take the Earliest opportunity in Redressing the Present Distress of the Labouring Poor that now Petitions your Worship.'[12] The magistrates sent them away with the same promises they had made in Kingswood.

Rooke notified the Duke of Portland for a second time that although 'the colliers and lower class inhabitants of this city and neighbourhood have endeavoured to intimidate the farmers', the situation was under control.[13] On 9 April, the Kingswood crowd, now doubled in size, reassembled as planned and, accompanied by a supportive constable and a sergeant from the Henbury Volunteers, marched into Bristol with a fresh petition. They were politely heard but once again rebuffed. There was deadlock. Magistrates refused to make further relief payments unless the colliers called off the strike, but they 'said that they would not return to their work till their terms were complied with and they could die but once'. The colliers refused to leave and so the Inniskillings were summoned once again, to disperse them at sword point.[14]

When the assize opened a few days later, Vicary Gibbs, the Recorder, used his opening address firstly to repudiate the popular notion that forcing prices down would effectively combat scarcity. On the contrary, he maintained, the actions of the mob would only deter the farmers from coming to the market in future weeks. According to some reports, very few farmers had come into market when it reopened on 6 April, two days after the first disturbance, 'and the consequence was that scarcely any article of provision was to be purchased at any price'. Secondly, he reiterated the judgement of the Somerset assize in the death sentences handed down to Tout and Westcott for regulating bread prices at Old Cleve. Gibbs was, after all, one of four eminent counsel retained at the end of March to advise the Somerset bench on the use of lethal force to repel rioters.

> He exposed with much perspicuity, the danger the rabble exposed themselves unto who were engaged in any of these outrages, for whoever forced people to sell their property at reduced prices committed the same act of felony as he who should put his hand in their pockets and robbed them of their money; and all persons who stood by and abetted such measures were, in the eyes of the law, considered as accomplices.[15]

These words were doubtless intended to fray the nerves not only of Samuel Nash, now awaiting his trail for the riot at Thomas York's butcher's shop on

[12] BA, JQS/P/169, Annotated petition dated Bedminster 7 April 1801.
[13] TNA, HO 42/61, Lieutenant General Rooke to Duke of Portland, 8 April 1801.
[14] TNA, HO 42/61, Joseph Small to Duke of Portland, 14 and 15 April 1801, with enclosures.
[15] *Courier*, 11 April 1801; *Hampshire Chronicle*, 13 April 1801.

4 April, but of three colliers and four men of the Monmouth and Brecon militia, taken up for breaking into a building and carrying off several bags of potatoes without payment in the days that followed. Yet capital examples would have been awkward to make from these cases. Nash had not actually taken anything, and any order to hang soldiers and miners at Bristol was unlikely to be effected without controversy at best and further disorder at worst. Gibbs had previously tried to hang a man for meat rioting in 1796, but the sentence caused a public outcry and a spirited campaign to have him reprieved, and so the Recorder had thought it wise to back down. The ends of justice would be no better served by exemplary hangings at Bristol in 1801 than in 1796, and all eight defendants were acquitted.[16]

In Kingswood the strike continued until 15 April, broken partly by military protection given to blackleg labour at some of the pits, partly by the taking up of colliers for picketing and localised bread seizures, and partly by a steadfast refusal to offer poor relief to strikers. Handbills were circulated throughout the coalfield reminding the colliers that for every day they remained on strike, they lost two shillings in wages, and so, 'If five hundred men do no work for a whole week, their wives and children will be deprived of the enormous sum of Three Hundred Pounds.' Relief payments, it was emphasised, would only be forthcoming to individuals recommended by the pit owners.[17]

This complex sequence of events in April 1801 cannot simply be explained as 'food rioting'. The several attempts of the colliers and others to negotiate intervention by magistrates over the price of basic foodstuffs suggest a customary belief in the integrity of the 'moral economy' and the duties of the aldermanic bench towards poor consumers. Yet, while the colliers clung to these customary beliefs, encouraged no doubt by news reports of the Somerset agreement, the corporation were now equally clear that markets must find their own level and that 'artificial' price regulation was out of the question. The events of 1801 represent something of an impasse over the status of a negotiated moral economy. But how and why did it arise?

Regulating the Market, 1709–53: Repelling Force with Force

In years of plenty, Bristol was well supplied with provisions in its various markets. Corn and flour arrived in trows from the producing districts of Herefordshire, Gloucestershire, Worcestershire and Monmouthshire; there was a twice-weekly fish market, first at the bottom of Fisher Lane on the quay, and later in Union Street; and separate markets for Welsh produce (on Welsh Back) sold hay, dairy products, livestock and vegetables. These markets often became particularly busy during scarcity periods, as dealers arrived

---

[16] *Bonner and Middleton's Bristol Journal*, 11 April 1801.
[17] TNA, HO 42/61, Joseph Small to Duke of Portland, 14 and 15 April 1801, with enclosures.

from less well-supplied landlocked towns like Birmingham, as well as from smaller ports like Bridgwater.[18] At these times, the dependence of surrounding regions only stiffened the resolve of the corporation to ensure uninterrupted avenues of supply, but the free movement of goods could be disrupted not only by war but by the interference of local communities resentful of Bristol's magnetic attraction. Forest of Dean miners blockaded the Severn and Wye waterways during the scarcities of 1709, 1757, 1766, 1795 and 1800 for instance, severely disrupting the movement of grain barges, and by 1801, corn merchants were beginning to feel the pinch of the port's relative uncompetitiveness. The deteriorating state of the city docks contributed to Liverpool's success in attracting more grain supplies than Bristol in that year, when it was even proposed that Bristol merchants should purchase grain in Liverpool and ship it back down.[19] Charitable provision in the shape of soup kitchens and Provision Committees selling cheap rice alleviated the worst of the distress in most years, but for the markets to run smoothly, the civil power needed to be confident of its ability to prevent rioting. Serious disturbances were few in the first half of the eighteenth century, but when trouble did break out, the colliers were invariably the instigators. When prices escalated in 1709, they sacked the city's granaries but were quickly brought to heel by a combination of threats, promises and arrests. Magistrates turned a blind eye when several detainees 'escaped' from the Council House, then dipped into the public purse to subsidise grain sales and arbitrarily lowered the assize of bread without reference to the market value of corn.[20]

In 1740, miners again parleyed with the mayor over bread prices, but he believed he had deterred them from forcing reductions by parading Colonel Blakeney's regiment of Foot, who made a public show of loading live ball outside the mayor's house.[21] A ready supply of billeted militia, ready at a moment's notice to support the civil power when necessary, buoyed magistrates and usually gave them the upper hand. However, they were often nervous about committing troops to action and unclear about the legal position, as the conduct of negotiations with the miners in 1740 demonstrated. The regiment's CO, Francis Leighton, reported back to Whitehall on the short-term success of their armed presence in Queen Square. But he also

[18] For concerns about the increase in outside purchasers during scarcity years, see for example TNA, HO 42/35, Greville to Duke of Portland, 19 June 1795, and Stamford to Duke of Portland, 27 June 1795. For the dependency on markets in Bristol of smaller outlying towns like Bridgwater see responses to the Home Office survey in HO 42/54.
[19] For blockades see BL, Add. MS 61609, Blenheim Papers, Bristol magistrates to Earl of Sunderland, 26 Oct. 1709; Information of N. Harrison, 10 Oct. 1709; *FFBJ*, 19 Feb. 1757, 7 May 1757, 8 Nov. 1766, 5 April 1800; BA, Corporation Letter Book, Joseph Smith to Duke of Portland, 17 Oct. 1795.
[20] BL, Add. MS 61609, Blenheim Papers, Bristol magistrates to Earl of Sunderland, 21 and 23 May 1709; Savage to Earl of Sunderland, 24 May 1709.
[21] TNA, SP 36/52 pt 2, Clutterbuck to Duke of Newcastle, 23 Sep. 1740; SP 41/12, Francis Leighton to Wade, 24 Sep. 1740; *Gloucester Journal*, 30 Sep. 1740, 7 and 14 Oct. 1740.

noted that when the colliers arrived, 'they did not bring so much as a stick with them' and were clearly not expecting the soldiers to trouble them if they remained orderly.

> They marched by our guard in a body to the Town House where the mayor and magistrates were sitting in court. One of them was admitted into the room, who told the mayor that they desired the assize of bread may be settled. His answer was that he would take care about it; upon which they departed peaceably, complimenting the court with Huzzas. But the colliers, on finding that their Orator had mistaken settling the Assize of Bread for lowering the price of corn, have threatened to come into this place a second time in a different manner.

Realising that his attempt to confuse the colliers with careful language had gone awry, the mayor sent for Leighton and quizzed him about the legal situation should the colliers return and troops be asked to oppose them. Leighton told him he could not 'repel force by force' without an order from government and written instructions from the magistrates, for 'Captain Porteous's unhappy fate was too fresh in my memory not to make me act with the utmost caution and security.' All he could do for now, he explained, was to 'keep the soldiers out of the way of mischief and, by being under arms, deter the colliers from their rash attempt'.[22]

The mayor responded with an express to Whitehall, advising ministers that Bristol had been 'infested with a great number of colliers', that they had arrived 'in a tumultuous manner', but that he had found 'means to disperse them'. But since it would not be practicable to reduce the assize of bread any further than its current setting while the price of corn remained so high, he did not expect to be able to trick them into leaving empty-handed a second time. He therefore requested permission for Leighton to use force if magistrates required him to do so in the event of the colliers' return. A reply was accordingly sent directly to Leighton that he assist the magistrates in apprehending the offenders if any riot should occur, but not to repel force with force 'unless in case of necessity or being thereunto required by the civil magistrates'. This was standard language but it was as carefully phrased as the mayor's had been to the colliers, for the instruction to use military force was dependent upon the magistrates' judgement of 'necessity'. Any arising fatalities were therefore most likely to be blamed on the magistrates as much as the soldiers, if not legally then certainly in local memory. Fortunately for the mayor, the colliers did not return that year and so his judgement was not put to the test.[23] In 1753 however, it most certainly was. The catastrophic riots of that year demonstrated just how fragile the corporation's hold on public order had really become by mid century, given a growing population and determined opposition.

[22] TNA, SP 41/12, Francis Leighton to Wade, 24 Sep. 1740.
[23] TNA, SP 36/52 pt 2, Clutterbuck to Duke of Newcastle, 23 Sep. 1740; SP 41/12, Arnold to Francis Leighton, Instructions, n.d.

As we show in the detailed analysis of this disturbance in Chapter 6, the stress lines exposed by the 1753 riots severely shook the self-confidence of the city bench. Things began conventionally enough as the colliers arrived en masse at the Council House to lobby the mayor for cheaper bread. But as the dispute escalated from polite negotiation to physical intervention, magistrates lost their grip. The corporation had done nothing to prevent merchants from shipping grain out of the city for profitable sale elsewhere, arguing that it was essential 'for the British plantations', in which many of its members had substantial interests.[24] But exportation in times of dearth was extremely unpopular. The use of stave-wielding constables to prevent colliers unloading grain barges on the quay and restore calm had the opposite effect and the later introduction of soldiers was ineffectual because magistrates dithered over permitting them to act. Coalfield community leaders were taken up, but rather than release them at the end of the day, the mayor opted to commit them for trial, a decision that raised tempers further. When the colliers vowed to return and forcibly free the prisoners, the city was forced into lockdown, the markets closed, and magistrates were powerless to prevent either the chaotic gunfight that followed, or the consequent legal repercussions. The limitations of *force majeure* as a means of containing discontent had been demonstrated in dramatic fashion.

The very fact that the most persistent threat to the city's peace came from communities of outsiders, over whom the city had only limited jurisdiction, only emphasised the problem. Moreover, the riots showed that straightforward bargaining between consumers, retailers and magistrates over the price of bread and the adjustment of the assize would not always be enough to address consumer demands for intervention against the perceived injustice of exportation amid deficiencies in the home market. It was in this period of reappraisal that more positive and paternalistic initiatives for alleviating scarcity first emerged. Between 1740 and 1753, magistrates had been cracking down hard on short-weight bread and meat with the full cooperation of the Companies of Bakers and Butchers. Convictions were secured against forty 'dishonest' bakers and twenty butchers in this period.[25] Put simply, as well as making a public show of upholding fair trade, magistrates believed the key to averting disorder was the maintenance of supply and the control of cost. This was approached in several ways. First, the corporation repeatedly manipulated the assize of bread in an attempt to keep it within the reach of the poor. Second, they used their influence with the merchant community to create incentives and encouragement for the purchase and importation of large shipments of grain from foreign ports. And third, charitable provision from public sources and the creation of non-profit-making provision committees funded by popular subscription, was promoted as a public good.

[24] *FFBJ*, 26 May 1753.
[25] BA, Petty Session convictions, 1728–95.

Regulating the Market 1757–84: 'Our magistrates were so generous and careful'

Provision shortages in 1757 put to the test a number of interventionist strategies that would later become commonplace. With domestic supplies in constant jeopardy from blockades on the Wye and Severn, the corporation first set £123 aside to pay for the exemplary prosecution of the culprits. Secondly, it exploited its own intimate connections with the Society of Merchant Venturers and appealed to them for help. After successfully petitioning parliament for an end to import duties on foreign grain, bounties to a total value of £200 were offered on any consignments 'sold ... to the citizens and other inhabitants for their immediate use and consumption'. Considerable sums were set aside for additional poor relief payments: £200 in January and a further subsidy in June. Select vestries raised subscriptions to augment their own relief funds, and the Cathedral chapter house was turned into a depot for the distribution of cheap rice to the poor. These measures had a positive impact. While rioting was reported at Worcester, Tewkesbury, Hereford, Taunton, Devizes, Frome, Castle Cary and South Wales, Bristol remained calm and, most importantly, the Kingswood colliers, amply relieved with donated bread, stayed at home.[26]

Success was consolidated in the next serious scarcity period, 1766–67. In January, months before shortages in the south-west became critical, and to the vociferous approval of the local press, the corporation championed public over private interests by petitioning parliament for a complete ban on corn exports. However, it was not until September, with crop failure a certainty and the surrounding countryside convulsed by rioting, that the corporation took any positive steps of its own. Unlimited bounty payments of £20 on every 300 quarter load were promised on all grain imports pledged to local sale and Lord Clare, one of the city's two MPs, personally added a further £8 to the tally. Several merchants and even the corporation itself made successful bids for corn cargoes arriving in other British ports during November and December 1766, moving the Grand Jury to conclude that 'the care of the magistrates has greatly contributed to the public tranquillity'.[27] Apart from framing petitions of their own to parliament, the Merchant Venturers set up a standing committee to import corn for local consumption in 1767, voting 'all monies necessary' and purchasing six thousand bushels at Danzig.[28]

Corn soon began to arrive in quantities, significantly improving availability, but to ensure prices remained low, magistrates agreed in October to

[26] *Bristol Weekly Intelligencer*, 30 April 1757, 14 May 1757; *FFBJ*, 1 and 15 Jan. 1757, 5 and 19 Feb. 1757, 28 May 1757, 4 June 1757.
[27] *FFBJ*, 20 Dec. 1766; BA, Common Council proceedings, 1762–72, resolutions of 18 Oct. 1766.
[28] BA, Proceedings of the Society of Merchant Venturers, resolutions of 28 Nov. 1767.

deliberately set the assize of bread below the recorded market value of corn and flour.[29] This drew indignant protests from the bakers, but they were indulged:

> Our magistrates were so generous and careful for the interest of the poor that, sooner than the bread should be made less, agreed with the bakers to satisfy them for the loss they should sustain till next Spring.[30]

However, relations between the corporation and the Company of Bakers were rarely cordial. In setting the assize, magistrates calculated an allowance to the bakers for covering costs and permitting moderate profits, but the Company complained of its members' poverty and that theirs was the only trade subject to such strictures. According to the Company's petition of grievance to the mayor, the assize had 'Greatly Distressed Every person in our trade, many it has intierly Ruined and obliged to leave their famielies in want'. One disgruntled baker put it plainly: 'att this time I can't by my trade alone gert Bread for my children ... [or] journeyman's wages by baking which is raley a Great hardship'.[31]

The corporation actively encouraged the establishment of new corn mills, but were disappointed by the number of millers who instead abandoned corn production and converted their premises for the more profitable manufacture of snuff and copper. By 1766, the decline of public corn-milling in Bristol had left the distressed poor and the bakers dependent upon market-priced flour for making bread. The corporation invited entrepreneurs to build public mills on its lands under terms and conditions laid down by the city surveyors, but it took a loan of £200 from the Merchant Venturers to persuade one James Walters to take the risk. Despite the Venturers' support for the 'public utility' of the project, Walters was in debt within a year and only spared eviction by a disastrous fire in the building'.[32] Landowners of private means took steps of their own however. In January 1767, Norborne Berkeley paused from making improvements to his landscape gardens at Stoke Park to build a windmill and a range of bread ovens, ordered all his corn to be threshed immediately, and began supplying cheap bread to the Kingswood colliers.[33] Unsurprisingly, the mining district remained a constant source of anxiety. 'They are in great expectation here of seeing the colliers come to Bristol to plunder the bread', reported a correspondent in the London press. 'They say there are about 5000 of them that intend coming.' But although 'the soldiers are all under arms expecting the mob', Kingswood remained quiet.[34]

[29] *FFBJ*, 18 Jan. 1766, 27 Sep. 1766, 8 Oct. 1766.
[30] *FFBJ*, 27 Sep. 1766, 2 and 25 Oct. 1766.
[31] BA, Petty Session convictions 1728–95; BA, TC/Adm/Box/20/3, Petition of five Bristol bakers, n.d. [1766]; BA, TC/Adm/Box/21/8, 'A Baker' to mayor of Bristol, 12 Feb. 1767.
[32] *FFBJ*, 29 Nov. 1766; BA, Proceedings of the Common Council, 1762–72, resolutions passed 18 Nov. 1766; Proceedings of the Society of Merchant Venturers, 9 Dec. 1766.
[33] *Salisbury Journal*, 19 Jan. 1767.
[34] *Public Advertiser*, 2 Oct. 1766.

Besides measures aimed at keeping the markets well stocked and bread prices pegged to affordable levels, magistrates used the courts to uphold the statutes against forestalling, regrating and engrossing, though not extensively. As the most visible and easiest form of malpractice to prosecute, regrating was the most frequently targeted, and often under the strictest terms. It was not the scale of illicit profit that mattered, but the principle. In October 1766 for instance, a butcher was successfully prosecuted for purchasing and then reselling meat in the market at a mark-up of just one halfpenny a pound, but these old statues were never upheld as forcefully at Bristol as they were in several other West Country towns, including Winchester and Worcester. At Bath, a public subscription fund headed by Jefferys, the Town Clerk, was set up in 1765, specifically to pay for the detection and prosecution of fore-stallers and regrators, and was active throughout the 1766–67 crisis. But the corporation at Bristol approached things differently, preferring commercial to judicial solutions.[35]

Within the limits imposed by free-market practice then, corporation and merchant initiatives successfully averted public disorder and famine in Bristol during the crisis of 1766–67 and established a pattern for contain-ment in future years. Bounties from the public purse were extended to fish – a commodity blissfully secure from harvest failure and plentiful enough to attract hauls away from such riot-prone ports as Padstow – in 1772–73, 1795–96 and 1800–01. Almost £3000 was paid out in bounty money to fishermen in 1800 alone.

Caught between the continuing complaints of the bakers about the corpo-ration's interference, and the pressing hunger of the poor, magistrates trod a difficult line during scarcity periods and their efforts at regulation were not always appreciated. 'They enjoy fullness of bread and therefore care very little about those who have none', declared one man as prices rocketed again in 1772, 'or why do they suffer the bakers to be filling their purses at the expense of the poor and needy?' One baker made a name for himself by unilaterally slashing his own prices. John Jenkins claimed he, 'would rather lose money than be the cause of oppression to the poor', but he was soon selling between seven- and eight thousand loaves daily and unlikely to have been in much financial trouble. While the press praised him for his 'truly patriotic' moral economy, the Company was less enthusiastic; it bankrolled two prosecu-tions against him, one for irregularities in the labelling of his loaves, and the other for an infringement of the apprenticeship laws. Both were ruled vexatious and thrown out.[36] Jenkins was unrepentant; indeed he believed himself responsible for lowering the price of bread all over the city. 'I feel a peculiar satisfaction in reflecting that it is entirely owing to my example that

[35] *Bath Chronicle*, 9 May 1765; *Derby Mercury*, 17 Oct. 1766.
[36] The case for and against Jenkins's initiative was extensively played out in the news-paper press throughout 1772: *FFBJ*, 17 Oct., 28 Nov., 5 Dec.; *Bath Chronicle*, 23 July, 4 Nov.

this wonderful change is effected', he proclaimed on an elaborately illustrated broadside (Fig. 10).

> But what is very remarkable, some of those Men who rancorously prosecuted me with every species of litigiousness their malice could invent, or rage suggest, for baking LARGE BREAD, now eagerly contend with each other which shall give most for the Money, and by it lay open their former unfeeling extortions... but least those Gentlemen should relapse into their former ill Habits of making an artificial scarcity and grinding the Face of the Wretched, I shall from time to time use such stimulations as I hope will effect a thorough Reformation, being determined to exert every Endeavour in my Power to render to the POOR all sorts of CORN SUSTENANCE on the lowest rates possible.[37]

In keeping with the practice adopted in 1766, the price of corn was repeatedly assized a full shilling per bushel below the official market return during the serious scarcity of 1795–96, and the price of the quarter loaf held down accordingly. From June 1795 to March 1796, the standard quartern loaf never once rose beyond a shilling and was often slightly less. This caused a good deal of confusion in surrounding districts where the price of bread was based on the prices millers and bakers were paying for corn in Bristol and other regional markets. At the nearby Somerset village of Keynsham for instance, the magistrate Francis Adams was stopped by a bewildered crowd as he returned from Bristol market in 1795 and quizzed about prices. Why, they wanted to know, were they paying so much more for bread than the people of Bristol? Adams did not entirely understand it himself, and wrote to the Home Office for advice.[38]

Even when Bristol bread prices spiralled wildly upwards during the subsistence crisis of 1800–01, they remained cheaper than at Bath, where by March 1801 the assize was fixed solely on market returns from Bristol. The mayor of Bath sent a string of letters to his Bristol counterpart, seeking an explanation, but remained puzzled by the discrepancy. The Company of Bakers at Bristol raised their customary objections and were particularly aggrieved when the mayor stepped up supervisory checks on bakers' weights, a tacit suggestion that he suspected them of under-weighing loaves. Strike action was threatened as magistrates fined a number of bakers for using false measures, and in May 1801, when the mayor refused to raise the price of the quartern loaf beyond 1s 4d despite a sudden steep rise in the cost of corn, the bakers unilaterally raised their prices and ignored the assize. The mayor, who felt that by holding prices down he was effectively offering protection to the bakers from uncontrolled regulation by the crowd, finally washed his

---

[37] John Jenkins, *An Exact Representation of the Manner of Conducting the Scheme for Supplying the Poor with Bread in the Cheapest and Best Manner* ... (Bristol, May 1772).
[38] TNA, HO 42/36, Francis Adams to Duke of Portland, 19 Oct. 1795.

10 John Jenkins, *An Exact Representation of the Manner of Conducting the Scheme for supplying the Poor with Bread in the Cheapest and Best Manner…* (Bristol, May 1772).

hands of them and abandoned the assize altogether, 'leaving the bakers to themselves'.[39]

The previous scarcity of 1795–96 had come at a critical juncture in the war with revolutionary France. In February 1795, supplies of British grain to the port were wholly cut off by a government embargo on coasting vessels, introduced to ease naval impressment. Blockades of the Wye and Severn by starving colliers in Gloucestershire compounded the problem until 'we are deprived of having a supply ... and therefore nearly left to the quantity already in the city'. Mayor Joseph Smith felt besieged and begged the Privy Council, already inundated with similar requests from other towns, to divert some shipments into Bristol by government order. Smith was warned not to expect special treatment, but managed to secure a single consignment of grain from Yarmouth after personally pleading the city's case to the Duke of Portland. It was not a long-term solution. Smith asked for more a week later but was turned down as, 'present circumstances render it impossible'.[40]

Forced to find solutions of its own, the corporation despatched two agents to Southampton, along with the merchant and alderman, John Noble, to purchase grain with money from the city treasury. More than £20,000 was spent in this way over the next few months, and the bulk of the grain sold to Bristolians at cost price. Millers from outside the city were prevented from purchasing any of it by order of the mayor, although a surplus was retained for sale at a comfortable profit in neighbouring markets to regain the investment.[41]

Profits from corporation-sponsored flour sales were donated to the city's charitable Provision Committee, which also doled out soup to the needy. This relationship worked reasonably well in principle but was not always managed effectively in practice. In September, the corporation purchased what turned out to be 'a large quantity of stale flour' for cheap sale to the city's bakers. However, neither they nor the Provision Committee seemed able to prevent its being sold to the factors 'and by them mixed with fresh flour and then sold on to the bakers at £4 10s a sack, with the bakers assizing to the first cost which ... was no more than 54s a sack'. This injustice was recalled

[39] BA, Assize of Bread Grain returns 04351, 1790–1823; BA, Assize of Bread books, 04350/5 and 04350/6, 1795–6 and 1800–01, Clark to Ludlow, 5 March 1801, Ludlow to mayor of Bath, 7 March 1801 and entry dated 21 May 1801; BA, TC/Adm/Box/53/8, Company of Bakers petition and statement of bread prices; Attwood to mayor of Bristol, 14 April 1801; Bath Guildhall Record Office, Assize of Bread records, 23 and 30 May 1801; *Bonner and Middleton's Bristol Journal*, 21 Feb. 1801. Magistrates abandoned the assize again in similar circumstances in 1815: *FFBJ*, 2 and 16 Sep. 1815.

[40] TNA, HO 42/35, Joseph Smith to Duke of Portland, 8 July 1795, with minutes of the Privy Council; TNA, HO 43/6, Duke of Portland to Joseph Smith, 7, 11 and 22 July 1795; PRO 30/8, Chatham Papers, Joseph Smith to William Pitt, 21 Feb. 1795; BA, Corporation letter book, Joseph Smith to Duke of Portland, 10 July 1795.

[41] *Bristol Gazette*, 22 Feb. 1795; *FFBJ*, 18 Feb. 1795, 4 and 11 March 1795; TNA, HO 42/35, James Harvey to Duke of Portland, 15 July 1795; Roger Wells, *Wretched Faces: Famine in Wartime England, 1793–1801* (Gloucester, 1988), p. 45.

some thirty years later as a pernicious attack on 'the fair tradesman's legitimate profit'. The bakers demanded regular market hours for the sale of freshly landed cargoes so that they might stand a better chance of attending sales and bidding for flour and grain Otherwise, 'when there is any goods come to the Back, it cannot be called a market for it is nearly all promised before it comes to those persons who grasp all into their own hands'.[42]

The Press, the Middling Sort and the Politics of Boycott

So far, this chapter has been considering responses to scarcity among three broad sections of Bristol society: the corporation and merchant elite who possessed the capital and authority to manage a crisis, squeezed retailers in the baking and allied trades, and the labouring poor who experienced dearth at the sharp end. But the wider public sphere and the representation of 'public opinion', especially among the middling sort, constituted a fourth arena of influence rarely considered in studies of moral economy. As consumers with a greater capacity than the poor to exercise choice in the marketplace in fact, the activities of the middling sort were vital to resolving issues of supply and demand, and certainly went far beyond their occasional role as an adjunct to the civil power when called upon as special constables. Some organisational responses may be divined from a study of the city press, for Bristol's large, literate and politically sophisticated freeman electorate ensured a ready market for printed polemics and pamphlet doggerel. By the end of the century, the city could boast five competing weekly newspapers, all of which took a lively interest in debating issues of local and national importance, inviting consensus through appeals to common sense from correspondents calling themselves 'Bristoliensis', or 'Civis'.[43]

But newspaper attitudes to riot were often underscored by ambiguity: popular disorder and regulation amounted to unacceptable interference with the principle of free trade, yet challenges to the extortionate prices of retailers and middlemen were considered both proper and necessary. 'The case of the poor has become so desperate that it demands some immediate redress', asserted *Felix Farley's Bristol Journal* in 1766. When rioting broke out in Devon a week later, the paper thought the crowds 'behave remarkably well, taking only the corn and leaving the value of it in money, at a moderate price'. But what might have been excusable in Devon, argued the paper, was quite unnecessary in Bristol where the poor had 'prudently' awaited the

---

[42] BA, TC/Adm/Box/47/33, Petition of thirty-two master bakers to the mayor, 28 Sep. 1795; *FFBJ*, 4 March 1826.

[43] For an appraisal of the impact of the city press on the life of the city, see Jonathan Barry, 'The Press and the Politics of Culture in Bristol 1660–1775', in *Culture, Politics and Society in Britain, 1660–1800*, ed. Jeremy Black and Jeremy Gregory (Manchester, 1991), pp. 49–81.

intercession of the elite: 'Far preferable is it thus for the poor to await the proceedings of those who have inclination and power to redress their griev-ances than rush headlong into riots.' Yet, in the face of the frequently stated opinion that forestallers and other villains were operating with impunity, remarks like 'riots owe their growth and continuance not so much to any real want or defect of the laws as to the pusillanimity of such of those whose Duty it is to put them into execution' effectively shifted the blame from the shoulders of the riotous poor.[44] Moreover, by carrying letters like the one published in 1784, pressing magistrates to combat speculation by regulating prices, *Felix Farley's* played on popular mythologies of distress in the midst of plenty and public irritation at the inability of market prices to reflect every twist and turn of the weather.[45]

In the same year, colliers in Kingswood began seizing provisions bound for Bristol market in the very week that *Felix Farley's* declared, 'We trust ... considering the abundance of potatoes that have been grown this year, the public will see that there are no grounds for advancing their price and will accordingly resist any such attempt.'[46] The key word, 'resist', may have been intended to inspire a consumer boycott rather than a riot, but the distinction was far from clear. No paper openly countenanced riot. Indeed by 1800, *Felix Farley's* had adopted a policy of silence when faced with the reality of disorder at Bristol. The nearest it came to acknowledging a flour riot in September was the editorial announcement that the paper had hitherto 'scrupulously avoided entering into the particulars of riots in other places for fear it might rather spread the evil than allay the ferment, and we shall continue to perse-vere in the same line of conduct'. This may have been so, although a week earlier, the paper had not shied from printing a letter boldly predicting that unless something was done to reduce prices in this 'alarming present period ... heaven knows what may be the consequence'. The disturbance was also ignored by all of Bristol's other newspapers, but revealed nevertheless by an insertion from the magistrates, appealing for calm. The *Gazette* would not have reported an isolated and unexpected disturbance over butter prices in 1811 at all, 'thinking the sooner it was forgotten the better', but for the necessity of refuting the colourful version of events reported in the London *Courier*.[47]

For all its fierce hostility to 'popular commotion', there was nevertheless some correlation between press scapegoating of hoarders and hucksters, deni-als of genuine scarcity and the incidence of crowd activity. Rumours and innuendo were relentlessly paraded as scandalous fact. *Felix Farley's* blamed corn dealers and distillers for the shortage of 1757, and avaricious retailers in 1784. Greedy grain-exporting merchants were singled out in 1772 and

[44] *FFBJ*, 9 and 16 August 1766, 4 Oct. 1766.
[45] *FFBJ*, 7 Aug. 1784.
[46] *FFBJ*, 7 Nov. 1795.
[47] *FFBJ*, 13 and 20 Sep. 1800; *Bristol Gazette*, 28 March 1811.

Bristol's export conscious cheese factors in 1773. In 1795, the *Mercury* blamed flour shortages on hair-powder makers and illegal wartime trading with the French after an 'uncommon plentiful harvest'. By repeatedly denying the reality of dearth and ascribing inflation to 'alarm alone', newspapers offered a natural platform for public demands that prices be lowered. Having judged the harvest of 1810 to be 'plentiful', for example, *Felix Farley's* impatiently compared Birmingham and London's more favourable prices with Bristol's and called for a substantial reduction since, 'it cannot be much longer deferred'.[48] Through the use of such simple rhetoric as this, the newspaper press encouraged public action.

The type of action the press preferred and actively endorsed, the consumer boycott, was more likely to be organised by the middling sort than the labouring poor. Boycotts were a 'respectable' and extremely effective form of popular price control, and their relationship to rioting was sometimes close. A butter boycott agreed by respectable householders at Godalming, Surrey, in 1800, led directly to rioting in the market there as well as at Midhurst, Sussex, when a printed agreement was read out like a proclamation by marketplace crowds.[49] Newspapers played a leading part in suggesting, publicising and legitimising butter boycotts at Bristol in 1796 and 1801. Boycotts may have been respectable but, as the angry stallholders who assaulted two boycotters in 1772 were to demonstrate, they were not necessarily non-violent. When, as in 1797, the price of butter was reduced because 'the people would not purchase it', but also because 'some of them began to be riotous', the distinction between boycott and riot became even more tenuous in real terms. The *Bristol Gazette* would not countenance disorder, but was convinced nevertheless that a price reduction had been 'very prudent'.[50]

Felix Farley's greeted the 'fair prices' agreed by boycott committees in 1801 with evident approval, but toed the line in voicing sharp criticism of the prices demanded by plebeian crowds and imposed upon farmers by magistrates in Taunton and Bridgwater. The impropriety ... is too obvious to require elucidation', commented the paper, 'for it is a measure which cannot possibly be complied with'. Rioting had a legal definition of course, but in practice the difference between a collective agreement to publicly withhold custom from retailers until prices were lowered, and a collective congregation in the marketplace in which the same demands were made in a 'disorderly' manner by labouring people, deserved greater 'elucidation' than newspaper editors were prepared to offer. In many ways, boycotts represented as great a challenge to the free market the Bristol corporation had pledged itself to protect as were 'riots', but their legitimacy was founded in the class prejudice of the middling sort towards certain forms of social action and

---

[48] *FFBJ*, 15 and 22 Jan. 1757, 7 Aug. 1784, 20 Oct. 1810.
[49] TNA, HO 42/52, Milford to Duke of Portland, 8 Oct. 1800.
[50] *FFBJ*, 27 June 1772, 15 Aug. 1801; *Bristol Gazette*, 1 June 1797; *Bristol Mercury*, 25 Jan. 1796.

economic freedom. A Bristol tradesman who witnessed the disturbances of 1801 put it this way:

> The magistrates, it is true, are not authorised by law to compel the farmer or butcher to sell at a certain price; but the purchaser has as clear a right to determine what he will give as the seller has to fix what he will ask – But it would be of no avail for any individual to stand out and pretend to fix the price of the market. No, that must be the work of many. Let then the principal inhabitants of this City (if they would wish to prevent tumult and confusion), come forward – let them meet by public advert at some Tavern ... Let them appoint a committee to fix a proper price on each different article of provision and let every person who attends such meeting subscribe his name to an agreement not to give more than the price so set down ... and I think there can be no doubt that this disagreeable business will be peaceably and properly settled without any intervention of the military.[51]

A vestry meeting in St John's parish a week later condemned the 'ill-judged conduct of purchasers ... in giving whatever price has been asked', and drew up fair-price restrictions on all meat, potatoes and dairy products in the market by agreement with 'nearly every householder in the parish'. Other vestries were more circumspect and a delegate meeting soon afterwards agreed a more moderate form of words. While 'preference' would be shown to traders offering the lowest prices, the free market would not be interfered with.[52] Surely but equivocally, in Bristol and in many other urban centres, the philosophy of laissez-faire that so characterised public debates over market relations at the close of the century, struggled to define its own terms of reference. Organised boycotting marked not the death of the moral economy, but its evolution.

Political Economy and Intolerance, 1795–1801

Despite the difficulty of maintaining regular channels of supply in the face of objections from the baking trade on the one hand and threats of interference from the colliers on the other, the corporation and its wealthy allies were able to prevent serious disorder in Bristol's markets in most scarcity periods after the debacle of 1753. Rumours of the colliers' imminent arrival circulated readily enough during the dearth of 1766, but troops were 'all under arms expecting the mob' and the threat did not materialise.[53] However justified the Bristol crowd's violent reputation, the city enjoyed relative calm in 1766–67 and 1772–73, during months in which many neighbouring towns and villages in Gloucestershire, Wiltshire and Somerset experienced serious rioting.

---

[51] *FFBJ*, 11 April 1801.
[52] *FFBJ*, 18 and 25 April 1801, 15 Aug. 1801, 30 Jan. 1802.
[53] *Public Advertiser*, 2 Oct. 1766. Walter Shelton alleged 'particularly serious disorder' at Bristol in 1766, but there is no evidence for it. Walter Shelton, *English Hunger and Industrial Disorders: A Study of Social Conflict During the First Decade of George III's Reign* (Toronto, 1973), p. 37.

The situation became more difficult as the century drew to a close, although the only rioting experienced at Bristol in 1795–96 was sparked off not by the cost of bread but of meat and fish. As in a number of other urban centres, the relative success of the authorities' efforts to regulate the provision of bread had begun, by the end of the eighteenth century, to stimulate demands for price control on commodities that had never been subject to regulatory legislation and which were, in any case, increasingly sold in shops rather than openly in the public markets.[54] Although the Kingswood colliers remained within their parish in 1795, they struck work in May, withheld coal from the city's dependent industries, and soldiers were sent out to subdue them. But magistrates felt obliged to parley over bread prices and discuss terms in exchange for a 'promise' from the colliers that blockades on the approach roads and river would not be resumed.[55] However, in June, as prices of butter, fish and meat began to rise, the *Gazette* railed indignantly against the 'exorbitant' price of beef, called for a consumer boycott of city butchers' shops and demanded the arrest of all hucksters.[56] Crowds gathered at the city markets and shops, and magistrates struggled to decisively tackle them. The fishmongers and butchers endured sporadic attacks on their premises and produce for two days, before soldiers were called upon to restore order. By that time, at least one house and shop, belonging to the butcher Samuel Kindon, had been badly damaged by rioters and all his meat carried away without payment.

Butchers called on the corporation to defend them. Their prices were high, they argued, because no action had been taken to prevent profiteering middlemen from controlling the supply of meat and livestock. They now found themselves at the mercy of

> the description of men called *Jobbers*, who attend most of the fairs and farm houses and buy up all they can lay their hands on, and by those means oblige us to purchase from them at such great and advanced prices that we are necessarily prevented from selling the same at the fair and customary rate our inclinations would lead us to were such practices discontinued and prevented.

Magistrates knew they were powerless to actively prevent jobbers from forestalling meat supplies in places beyond their jurisdiction but responded by seizing a quantity of underweight butter and offering generous bounties on any fish brought into the market, 'with the laudable intention', it was reported, 'of lowering the exorbitant price of beef and other meat'.[57]

There are various possible explanations for the failure to contain disorder in 1795. It was the first time magistrates had been tempted to use the

---

[54] This point is enlarged upon by John Bohstedt, *The Politics of Provisions* (Farnham, 2010), pp. 187–8.
[55] TNA, HO42/34, Lieutenant General Rooke to Duke of Portland, 10 May 1795; BA, Corporation letter book, Joseph Smith to Duke of York, 5 May 1795; *Bristol Gazette*, 14 May 1795; *FFBJ*, 14 Nov. 1795.
[56] *Bristol Gazette*, 14 May 1795, 4 June 1795.
[57] *Bath Chronicle*, 11 June 1795.

military for crowd control since their disastrous deployment against bridge-toll protesters two years earlier in 1793, and they may have been anxious not to stage a repeat performance. Secondly, the billeted East Devon militia were considerably under strength through illness and were in any case severely stretched by being repeatedly called upon to police crowds in the surrounding districts. Thirdly, relations between regular soldiers and the host population had allegedly been on edge for several weeks and there are indications that the militia had proved unreliable during the colliers' strike. On the eve of the June disturbances, a magistrate heard a butcher refusing to serve two soldiers, whose 'reply was fierce and menacing, saying that they would have meat for the poor and for themselves – at a fair price!' Although the local press made no mention of it, two anti-ministerial dailies insisted that rioting had been led by men from the East Devon regiment. The troop was certainly reposted immediately afterwards, and it was the Northamptonshire militia who turned out to quell a mutiny of new recruits at Pill dock in July. Finally, the coincidence of the 1795–96 scarcity with the emergence of a radical Jacobin reform movement invites speculation that Bristol's military rank and file was suspected of harbouring 'political' views about scarcity, and was no less outraged over market prices than civilian consumers. City radicals were certainly accused of pressing handbills 'of a most treasonable kind' upon the Hampshire Fencibles when they arrived to subdue renewed outbreaks among the colliers in October. The people were arming, declared an anonymous letter-writer, 'a body of colliers is already prepared and we have also three regiments of soldiers on our side'.[58]

Whatever the explanation, magistrates were in no mood for leniency. Three men were taken up and one of them, the brewery worker William Gage, singled out for exemplary punishment, but the case was not well handled. Gage was held for almost a year before being tried at the spring assize in 1796, charged not with riot but the capital felony of robbery. But the only evidence against him, given in court by another butcher, was that he was seen in the crowd, throwing stones at Kindon's windows. Gage's employer had been ready to testify that he was at work the whole time, but was not called by the defence and so the prosecution evidence went unchallenged. Gage's presence made him a legal party to stealing Kindon's meat and he was accordingly convicted and sentenced to death in the same month that two more local food-rioters, Thomas Yemm and Thomas Rosser, were hanged at Gloucester. The verdict was not popular in Bristol where Gage was widely regarded as a scapegoat for magisterial incompetence. Popular outcry on a local scale threatened to develop into a national scandal as the opposition

---

[58] TNA, WO 1/1083, Walker and Haynes to Yonge, 8 May 1795; TNA, 1/1092, Lieutenant General Rooke to Wyndham, 23 March 1795; Walker and Rooke to Lewis, 11 June 1795; PRO, 30/8, Chatham Papers, Grenville to Pitt, 31 May 1795; TS 11/944, The king against John Vint for a libel; BA, TC/Adm/46/19, Anon to mayor of Bristol, 31 Oct. 1795; *Bristol Mercury*, 8 and 15 June 1795; *Courier*, 11 June 1795.

press – particularly Coleridge's *Watchman* – elevated Gage to martyrdom, and three of his fellow workers trooped into the Guildhall to swear affidavits on the prisoner's behalf. Now concerned about possible reprisals, Mayor Harvey sought advice from the Recorder, Gibbs, who was clearly irritated. If these witnesses had been heard at the trial, he told the mayor, 'it is probable that Gage would have been acquitted'. Gibbs had actually learned of Gage's uncalled witnesses 'within half an hour of the conviction' the previous year, and although ready to admit that a reprieve would be politic, 'the production of such evidence after the trial is very irregular and if often permitted would lead to bad consequences.' News that Gage might at last be reprieved soon provoked noisy demonstrations outside the prosecutor's house as celebratory songs and papers were hawked about by 'ballad singers and other rabble'. In such an atmosphere, Harvey was determined not to have Gage liberated and appealed successfully to the crown for a transportation order rather than a pardon. Despite a petition appealing for a pardon, signed not only by his wife but by every member of the jury that originally convicted him, Gage was transported in 1797 and he was dead by 1808. It was a pyrrhic victory for the city bench. With policing and other expenses arising from the riots costing the corporation at least £500, this exercise in exemplary justice had proved something of a disaster.[59]

Nevertheless, the 1795 riot and its aftermath illustrated some key changes in attitudes to the customary moral economy. Crowds were as likely now to demand controls over the price of meat, dairy produce and vegetables as the only foodstuff traditionally associated with regulation, bread. Changes in retail practice meant that they were as likely to stage protests at shops as at market stalls, and this was important because it invited prosecution for the capital offence of breaking and entering private property rather than plain riot. Meanwhile, the clear signal now being sent to plebeian crowds by the corporation was that, apart from the setting of the assize of bread, there would be no artificial adjustments made to prices, and anyone arrested for rioting would find the full weight of the law ranged against them. There were occasional prosecutions of regrators, but no concerted policy of prevention, and cases were not generally instigated by the magistrates but by private individuals. At the August sessions in 1796, a prosecution was begun against one of the city's still deeply unpopular butchers for regrating lamb in the city market, but the expenses were met by the 'celebrated' and 'truly patriotic' landlord of the Bush Tavern, John Weeks. He was loudly congratulated for this public-spirited gesture by the Grand Jury but the corporation did not offer to pay for it.[60]

[59] BA, Proceedings of the Common Council, 1791–96, entries for June and July 1795; BA, TC/Adm/Box/48/8, Affidavits 4 April 1796; Vicary Gibbs to mayor of Bristol, 9 April 1796; Lewis to Gibbs, 9 April 1796; Corporation letter book, Joseph Smith to Vicary Gibbs, 17 April 1796. *Bristol Gazette*, 31 March 1796, 17 April 1796; *The Watchman*, 6 and 11 April 1796; John F. Mackeson, *Bristol Transported* (Bristol, 1987), p. 146.
[60] *Gloucester Journal*, 5 Sep. 1796.

These trends set the agenda for the more serious and prolonged shortages that followed the poor harvest of 1799. A corporation-backed Provision Committee began canvassing for subscriptions to pay for a soup kitchen in January 1800, well before the situation became critical, while the corporation made plans of its own to secure supplies. An unprecedentedly ambitious scheme was launched between the Merchant Venturers, city bankers and the corporation, sufficiently well endowed to make unbeatable bids for cargoes in friendly international ports. It was a major enterprise. With each Bristol banking house investing £1000, and the corporation giving £500, this new merchant-led committee was soon able to announce a preliminary budget of £15,500 and place an immediate order for three cargoes at Hamburg and another at Milford Haven.[61] Shipments of wheat and rice continued to arrive throughout the spring and summer, earning praise for the committee from the local press, for 'even if the price be high, the having it at any price, compared with the total deprivation of it, should induce our gratitude'. With accumulating profits for investors, the local market thrived as dealers from all over the south-west vied for a share. By mid May, the city's soup kitchen was able to close despite an 'increasing exigency of circumstances' at nearby Bath. When the West Indian fleet returned home 'fully laden' in July, there was 'general joy' in the streets.[62]

People were therefore 'somewhat suspicious' when prices continued to rise. Rumours abounded that 'the late joyful importation of corn into this port is, in a large measure, locked up till the price is higher'.[63] Merchants do not appear to have begun selling their foreign grain to the poor at reduced cost until mid July when, following early expectations of a successful harvest, regional prices briefly tumbled. To discourage forestalling and to hold these prices steady, the corporation now let market stalls to local farmers at a greatly reduced rate. Although corn prices did rise again after a month, Bristol alone amongst south-western market towns successfully avoided any major public disturbance until the colliers rose in April 1801. Even this might perhaps have been avoided if the merchants' committee had not ceased trading in October 1800, just as the soup kitchens were reopening on an extended plan.[64]

When crowds did briefly take matters into their own hands, disrupting a warehouse 'cheap' flour sale in September 1800 during a protest over its price and quality, Rooke acted swiftly, assumed command of the situation and forcibly dispersed them without a word of negotiation. Having witnessed the consequences of magisterial dithering in 1795, the frustrated General may

---

[61] BA, Corporation letter book, Morgan to Duke of Portland, 26 Feb. 1800; *FFBJ*, 4 Jan. 1800, 1 March 1800.

[62] *FFBJ*, 17 May 1800, 11 Oct. 1800. For reports of grain arrivals, see 21 June, 26 July, 9 Aug., 6 Sep. 1800.

[63] *FFBJ*, 19 July 1800. See also J. Ayers (ed.), *Paupers and Pig Killers: The Diary of William Holland, a Somerset Parson, 1799–1818* (Gloucester, 1984), p. 41.

[64] *FFBJ*, 26 July 1800, 11 Oct. 1800; *Sherborne Mercury*, 15 Sep. 1800.

have felt fully justified in taking decisive action now. 'Lest false reports should reach your Lordship of a riot that took place here last night', he advised the Duke of Portland the following day, 'Troops were in readiness to receive them and without waiting for the presence of a magistrate, the constables being obliged to retire, I gave orders for the Cavalry to charge, which dispersed them and all remains perfectly quiet.' The peace of the city, he added, was 'not likely to be disturbed again'. If not entirely unlawful, it was certainly unusual for an army officer to order military action against unarmed civilians without the presence of a magistrate and without recourse to the Riot Act. Indeed, Rooke's action pre-dated by more than six months the controversial ruling by the Somerset Grand Jury and magistrates that independent military intervention against food-rioters was admissible 'in cases of great necessity'. But Portland was clearly delighted for he wrote to the king, praising Rooke's initiative as an example to be emulated. Such 'judicious and spirited conduct ... has had the best possible effect and, supported as the Duke of Portland is persuaded he will be, by the Magistrates of that city, he trusts that it will be attended with very salutary consequences, not only in that large and populous place but throughout the district'.[65]

The Bristol strategy was now perfectly clear. On the one hand, elite and entrepreneurial groups would ensure a regular supply of grain to the market, charitable initiatives would maintain soup kitchens for the poor, magistrates would tacitly regulate bread prices through the assize while doing their best to keep the price of other commodities relatively low by offering subsidies and bounties, and consumers of the middling sort would apply pressure to retailers through organised price boycotts. However on the other hand, popular commotion and regulation would not be tolerated. There were political as well as economic imperatives behind this strategy. As noted by Roger Wells, Adrian Randall and others,[66] by the close of the 1790s traces of Jacobin rhetoric were beginning for the first time to find their way into the language of subsistence crowds, an unwelcome development in the popular rhetoric of moral economy at a time when the moral economy itself was under attack from the ideologues of laissez-faire. Indeed, Rooke had reported some early signs of this at Bristol in 1795, when the loyalty of the East Devon militia was in question and the mayor received an anonymous warning that 'a body of colliers is already prepared and we have also three regiments of soldiers on our side'. The poor, he was told, were ready to 'bodily take up arms ... to compel those extortioners to comply'.[67]

---

[65] *FFBJ*, 20 Sep. 1800; TNA, HO 42/51, Lieutenant General Rooke to Duke of Portland, 19 Sep. 1800; Portland to the king, 20 Sep. 1800, in A. Aspinall (ed.), *The Later Correspondence of George III, Vol III, 1798–1801* (Cambridge, 1967), pp. 414–15. For the 1801 ruling see *Bonner and Middleton's Bristol Journal*, 11 April 1801.

[66] See especially, Wells, *Wretched Faces*, p.144 and Adrian Randall, *Riotous Assemblies: Popular Protest in Hanoverian England* (Oxford, 2006), pp. 226–9.

[67] TNA, WO 1/1092, Lieutenant General Rooke to Windham, 13 Nov. 1795; BA, TC/Adm/Box/48/8, Anon to James Harvey, 31 Oct. 1795 .

Anonymous notes demanding 'Peace and a large Bread, or a King without a Head' were received at Bath in November 1800, shortly before a spectacular incendiary attack on one of the city's grain-hungry distilleries, and at Bristol, blood-soaked loaves carrying similar threats had been impaled upon the railings around the statue of William III in Queen Square in February. In December, an anonymous letter to the 'Right Worshipfool' mayor asked, 'are the labourous people to be starved this winter?', then launched a withering critique of 'the Rich men of the Nation' and their selfish use of land. 'Let us take a view of France and see what a united people have done; the labouring people have sum little share in the Good things of that land', claimed the writer. If all land currently enclosed for game and pleasure was put to food production, prices would fall and

> the poor working man would get a pint of good working ale for 1d as formerly, but then the Farmer and the Landlord will not be able to a Ford to ride about on sutch Gay Horses as they do at present ... Every poor man have a right to put his hands in the Rich Merchant, Rich Millers and Rich Farmers pockets and say Give Back what you have acquired by the Extortions that you have a practices for the last Ten Years ... The present race of Farmers must be turned out of the Farms and Large Farms Divided into smaller; the Parks woods and Pleasure Grounds must be Destroyed and converted into Potato and Corn Fields and all useless horses Destroyed and there ought not to be so many Carrages kept ... I hope you will aulter it in time before obligations take place ... It is better to stand like men than to starve in the land of plenty.[68]

The language of political discontent coloured popular demands once again in March 1801, during the closing stages of the scarcity. Another anonymous letter, purportedly penned by billeted Somerset militia men, was mailed to Major General Andrew Cowell, temporarily in command at Bristol while Rooke was trying to suppress the riots in Devon and Somerset. The writers would have provisions at 'the Old Price', or

> there shall not a Parliament exist on this island. We are Determind one and all not to see our Families and the People at large Starve in a Plentiful Country through a Tyrant and a Damned Infernal Imposing Lords and Commons, a Republic must ensue and we will fight for our Rights and Liberties to the last Moment. France has succeded in her grand undertaking and got Every Article Cheap and Reasonable, and we will follow her example, so we wid advise you to communicate it as soon as possible else it be too late.

Cowell forwarded the note to Portland, with an assurance that he had already 'taken every step to detect the villain and have solicited the assistance of the mayor and have had spys upon the military'. He was not convinced the letter was genuine but he will have known about the trouble caused by the East Devon regiment at Bristol in 1795 and also that the reliability of militia

---

[68] BA, Corporation letter book, Morgan to Duke of Portland (with enclosures), 26 Feb. 1800; TC/Adm/Box/52/20, Anon to mayor of Bristol, 6 Dec. 1800; *Bonner and Middleton's Bristol Journal*, 11 April 1801.

regiments elsewhere in the region had been in question for several weeks. So the final sentences, 'Let the mob do as they please. Peace and a Large Loaf. We will not Interfere', could hardly be ignored. Relations between the Bristol Volunteers and the militia were not in any case good at this time, and according to William Dyer the fault lay with the latter. 'Today as well as Saturday, the Volunteers assembled at the Exchange, a riotous disposition appearing', he noted during the disturbances that broke out in the marketplace in April. But, 'tis said the Somerset Militia rather give countenance than otherwise and do even insult our Volunteers'.

The extent of military complicity in these disturbances is uncertain, partly perhaps because the disorder was underplayed in the newspapers for fear of encouraging further action, but four militia men were certainly put to the assize for complicity with the colliers for stealing potatoes.[69] A local poet noted only the active role taken by the Volunteers. Like many other contemporary commentators, he was as much amused as impressed by Bristol's part time Volunteer regiments, but in *The Recontre*, no hints are dropped about the behaviour of the militia:

At length the mob impatient grew,
To Shambles did repair;
And at the meat transported flew,
Resolved to have a share ...

Short is your reign, ye rabble-rout,
For hear a noise like drumming!
And see advance the dreaded scout –
The Soldiers are a-coming!

They form in terrible array
Amid the horrid din;
Old Women shrieked with dire dismay,
And drowned their fears in gin!

The children cry'd – and Maids looked glum,
And married Dames had fits; –
Again loud beats the calling drum! –
To arms! Ye valiant cits! –

With horse and foot the streets were fill'd;
Tis lucky 'twas no worse;
Thank Heaven, no human blood was spill'd,
All RIOTS *are a curse!* [70]

[69] TNA, HO 42/61, Major General Cowell to Duke of Portland, 20 March 1801 (with enclosure: anonymous letter dated 17 March 1801); BRL, Diary of William Dyer, 4 April 1801: 'It seems some of the rioters and even some of the soldiers were taken before the magistrates.'
[70] The poem then takes amusement in the adaptation of simple tradesmen – cobblers, tailors, barbers – to military activity. That the poem is about the Volunteers is also signalled by their description as 'cits'. R. Paddock, *The Rencontre: A Poetic Tale (Founded on Fact) descriptive of the late violent Proceedings in the City of Bristol* (Bristol, 1801).

As we showed in the examination of the 1801 disturbances at the beginning of this chapter, Bristol's magistrates were not prepared to follow some of their counterparts elsewhere in the region, in ignoring Portland's strict instructions to uphold laissez-faire dealing at all costs. If the Bristol and Kingswood poor believed they could persuade the city bench to lean on producers and retailers to lower their prices in accordance with the Somerset agreement, it was because they had failed to understand the approach magistrates had been taking to market regulation since 1753. Ensuring adequate supply and moderate prices through the encouragement of charity, subsidy, a fixed assize and commercial entrepreneurism was not the same thing as instructing producers to supply the market or permitting the poor to enforce their own agenda through riot. Adrian Randall rightly refers to the efforts of the Bristol bench as reflecting 'an essentially paternalistic ideology',[71] but it was paternalism with a contemporary feel, at ease with government support for the free market but antagonistic to a moral economy that blamed producers for greedily inflating prices and creating false scarcity.

The soup kitchen, which would become an annually recurring institution during the 1820s, set its face against both cheap-bread schemes and the prosecution of monopolists and forestallers, who unwittingly rendered the poor an essential service' by conserving stocks. By 1821, *Felix Farley's* had assimilated enough Malthusian wisdom to praise speculators for raising prices to levels which 'discourage consumption' and 'encourage thrift and good management' among the poor.[72] Increasingly in nineteenth-century Bristol, the 'unjust' prices of retailing cartels were met by competition not from organised boycotts, but from gentlemen's cooperatives and joint-stock provision companies. These had their origins in the corporation-backed Flour and Bread Concern of 1800, which, by mid-century, faced mounting criticism for being 'the head of a monopoly', dictating artificially high bread prices and reaping enormous benefits for its shareholders. Nevertheless, the corporation's early encouragement of this 'modern' business structure is significant; a similar venture at Bath was scrapped for want of corporation support. A rival Bristolian Bread Concern, established in 1829 by the political reformer James Acland, attracted some four thousand members through a populist campaign against the Company of Bakers, and organised a mass march through the city. This was a peaceful enough crowd however. No attempt was made to forcibly regulate prices despite much hooting outside the shops of unpopular bakers.[73]

---

[71] Randall, *Riotous Assemblies*, p. 233.

[72] *FFBJ*, 23 and 30 Nov. 1816, 14 Dec. 1816, 22 Sep. 1821; *Bristol Mirror*, 14 June 1817.

[73] *FFBJ*, 6 and 20 Sep. 1800, 1 and 8 Dec. 1821, 10 July 1847; BA, Corporation letter book, Mayor of Bristol to Edward Protheroe, MP, 14 May 1813; BA, Abstract of the Articles of Agreement of the Bristol Flour and Bread Concern (1801). The rise and fall of the Bristolian Bread Concern may be followed in Acland's newspaper, *The Bristolian*, between

After the unhappy experience of 1753, the corporation was keen to have soldiers on hand in times of difficulty as a visible show of force. However, after the even more unhappy experience of the military massacre on the Bridge in 1793, magistrates were equally keen to avoid using them whenever possible. Bristol was quite different from Oxford for example, whose magistrates had lobbied for the removal of soldiers from the town in 1800 and whose apparent sympathy for the crowd deeply irritated Portland.[74] As we have seen, military crowd-dispersals were effected at Bristol in 1795 and 1800 and in Kingswood in 1801, though not always with magistrates visibly present. More often, however, soldiers were paraded but not called upon. They were not used against butter-rioters in 1797 or 1811, nor against potato-rioters a year later, although the mayor had several regiments of infantry at his disposal. What he wanted, he told the Home Office, was 'a few regiments of Horse', unobtrusively stationed, 'in order that the public may not be unnecessarily alarmed'. Their presence alone, he hoped, would 'very much tend to reserve the peace'. And as it turned out, 1812 was the last time Bristol was disturbed by food-rioting.[75]

28 August 1829 and 13 October 1830, particularly Acland's series of public letters, 'To the Bread-Eaters of Bristol'. Bath corporation's insistence that that financial assistance for cooperative projects was the responsibility of central government is complained of in TNA, HO 42/52, Caulfield Lennon to Duke of Portland, 5 Oct. 1800.

[74] Wendy Thwaites, 'Oxford Food Riots: A Community and its Markets', in *Markets, Market Culture and Popular Protest*, pp. 160–1.

[75] *Bristol Gazette*, 28 March 1811; *Annual Register*, 55 (1812), Chronicle, p. 55; BA, Corporation letter book, Mayor of Bristol to Ryder, 13 April 1812.

8

Naval Impressment in Bristol, 1738–1815

Bristol was a city of spires and masts. Alexander Pope was struck by the hundreds of ships at Broad Quay and the Backs, 'their masts as thick as they stand by one another, which is the oddest and most surprising sight imaginable'. 'The streets are as crowded as London', he remarked, 'but the best image I can give of it is, Tis as if Wapping and Southwark were ten-times as big, or all their people run into London.'[1]

It was the 'swarming vessels', to echo Richard Savage, that particularly attracted the Admiralty. Swarming vessels meant seamen, and seamen, especially experienced topmen, were what the navy needed to man its ships in wartime. Between 1738 and 1815 Britain was at war roughly two in every three years, and as fleets grew in size, her demand for men was insatiable. At the beginning of the war of Jenkins' Ear in 1738, 23,000 men were borne by the navy; that is, registered on the ships' books. That number rose dramatically in subsequent wars peaking at 85,000 in the Seven Years' War, over 100,000 in the American, and at an amazing 140,000 towards the end of the Napoleonic wars. This was a six-fold increase in the space of roughly seventy-five years, and it could only be sustained by appropriating seamen from the merchant marine, whose own numbers could only be sustained by relaxing the official requirements of the Navigation Acts, which insisted on British and colonial ships managed by a high proportion of home-grown mariners. Because wages in the merchant marine were always higher than those of the royal navy, and appreciably higher in wartime, men had to be coerced into joining His Majesty's fleets. Precisely how many men were pressed into service is impossible to say. The figures are fragmented and fraught with problems. The best we currently have, derived from the Shelburne papers for the American war, suggests that 37.5 per cent of all seamen enlisted on land were impressed, and probably 34 per cent of the 235,000 men recruited ashore and

---

[1] George Sherburn (ed.), *The Correspondence of Alexander Pope* (5 vols, Oxford, 1956), IV, 204–5.

afloat.[2] As the historian who compiled these figures admitted, some of those who technically 'volunteered' for the navy did so under duress. It was either a case of come quietly and accept the bounty for a volunteer; or be pressed and be damn'd.

Whether for volunteers or pressed men, Bristol was an important port; the premier Atlantic port at the beginning of the century, surpassed only by Liverpool in the period after 1760. In 1787, 2838 seamen signed articles in Bristol, of whom 2470 (87 per cent) gave Bristol as their place of residence. This meant that roughly 5 per cent of the Bristol population were merchant seamen in the late 1780s; in terms of the adult male population, somewhere in the region of 15 per cent. In addition there was a rich variety of quayside trades that the Admiralty deemed impressible: shipwrights, ropemakers, sail-makers, ferrymen, bargemen, even the odd cooper.[3] This was because the Admiralty had a capacious view of whom it could enlist: those that 'used the sea' or as press warrants declared, 'seamen, seafaring men and such persons whose Occupations and Callings are to work in vessels and Boats upon rivers'. This meant that when homecoming fleets arrived back in port, a quarter of Bristol's male adults between the ages of eighteen and fifty-five were likely vulnerable to impressment. When privateering was the rage, the proportion would be higher still, for over 6000 men crewed for those ships at the beginning of the Seven Years' War.[4]

Impressment in Bristol happened at two principal sites. It could take place in the centre of the city, near the quays and pubs around Marsh Street where seamen would congregate to talk, drink and play. But it also occurred at the estuary of the Avon, in the cove of anchorage called Kingroad off Portishead Point, or slightly further upriver at Hung Road or Broad Pill. Kingroad was where the tenders lay to take men south to Plymouth, where recruits would be assigned a berth on a vessel. It was also the place where tenders would lie in waiting for the homecoming fleets, especially from the West Indies and Virginia, which made up roughly three-quarters of the Atlantic traffic into Bristol. In the case of the Jamaica trade, with its cargoes of sugar, thirty to forty ships would arrive annually at the estuary of the Avon during the mid century years, manned, at least officially, by crews of twenty-two to twenty-eight men. Tobacco ships from the Chesapeake were somewhat smaller, and

---

[2] Ronald G. Usher, 'Royal Navy Impressment During the American Revolution', *Mississippi Valley Historical Review*, 37:4 (1951), 667–9. J. Ross Dancy offers considerably smaller figures for the 1790s, but his figures are suspect because of the way they are calculated and because of the problematic category of the 'volunteer'. See *The Myth of the Press Gang* (Woodbridge, 2015), and review by Nicholas Rogers in the *Journal of Military History*, 80:2 (2016), 541–3.
[3] TNA, Adm 1/1735 D215, 9 July 1813. See also Nicholas Rogers, *Manning the Royal Navy in Bristol: Liberty, Impressment and the State, 1739–1815*, Bristol Record Society, 66 (Bristol, 2013), no. 572.
[4] Latimer, II, 320–1. In 1756, 74 ships are listed as privateers, of which 42 (57 per cent) offer sizes of crews. The total crewmen for these 42 privateers was 5500.

their fleet was half the size of the Jamaican, but between them they brought in a potentially rich harvest of recruits. In the Seven Years' War crews from these destinations would annually average 1200 men in total, an enticing prospect for frigates or third-rate men-of-war.[5]

Prior to the Seven Years' War, impressment in Bristol was intense but sporadic. The demands of the navy could generally be met from the home-coming ships in London, which meant that the Downs was the principal field of operations. The civic authorities in Bristol did occasionally order a general search for potential recruits, a sweep-up operation that would take in vagrants as well as straggling seamen. One of these occurred at the beginning of the war against Spain in 1739, when over the course of three days and nights, constables committed some two hundred men to Bridewell, of whom seventy were deemed appropriate for the navy. These civic searches, a standard procedure for impressing men in previous eras, became rarer in the eighteenth century although the mayor and magistracy continued to recruit in this manner into the American war.[6] From the 1740s onwards the Admiralty tended to recruit its own men directly, concentrating their operations on Kingroad in the first instance, with press-gangs occasionally venturing upriver to pick up men at the port.

Impressment at the estuary of the Avon was not without its problems. Captains quickly realised that seamen were being dropped off on the north Somerset shores and ships were arriving at Kingroad with skeletal crews. As Captain Robert Fytche observed in September 1740, 'It is impossible to get any [seamen] here, the Pilots' Boats meeting the Ships below the Holmes & putting their Men ashoar before any Boats can board them.'[7] Fytche sent tenders to Ilfracombe and Lundy to prevent this early exodus, but the upshot was sometimes that naval resources in the Bristol region were sorely stretched. Tenders that served both Liverpool and Bristol were not always available, with the result that local captains had trouble holding onto men. Captain Frogmere, who succeeded Fytche at Kingroad, told the Admiralty that 'if there was two or three Tenders employed at the port it would very well answer ye Purpose of raising men'. In his next letter a week later, he informed the secretary he had heard 'nothing of my own Tender, and that ordered from Whitehaven is not yet arrived, [so] that [I] am at a loss how to dispose of my supernumeraries', that is, his recruits.[8]

These frustrations led to some bloody confrontations. In March 1742, Lieutenant James Roots of the *Russell* tender espied the surgeon and a few sailors leaving the *Queen Mary*, a Jamaica-bound boat that was licensed as a privateer. He thought the men were deserting ship and likely evading

---

[5] Figures derived from Kenneth Morgan, *Bristol and the Atlantic Trade in the Eighteenth Century* (Cambridge and New York, 1993).

[6] *Bonner and Middleton's Bristol Journal*, 2 Nov. 1776.

[7] TNA, Adm 1/1780, fol. 317.

[8] TNA, Adm 1/1780, fols 266–7.

impressment, just as some crew members of the *Jefferies* had done before. Roots hailed the *Queen Mary* men to bring to, and when they ignored his call, he ordered his press-gang to fire a warning shot over the bow and then at the boat. One bullet whistled through the boatswain's hat, but another hit a seaman through the groin and knee, shattering the man's knee bone, and crippling him for life. Lieutenant Roots and William Ferrier, whose shot injured the seaman, were arrested by the Bristol authorities and committed to Newgate. The Bristol merchants and owners of the *Queen Mary*, Clarke and Thomas, demanded such high bail that Roots and Ferrier remained in prison for six months. When they came to trial at the Bristol assizes in September 1742, they faced the wrath of Justice Denison, who

> seem'd much inclined against the Defendants and told the Jury, that although a regard was due to the King's Ships, yet that great care ought to be taken by the officers in the execution of their Duty so as to not injure the rest of the King's subjects. And that he knew of no Authority that a man of war's crew had of firing Balls upon mariners belonging to Merchant ships in order to oblige them to bring to, and there was no evidence to prove the assertion.[9]

The jury awarded the crippled seaman 120 guineas, and a further £40 to Jenkin Thomas, who was also injured during the skirmish. The fines were too high for Lieutenant Roots and seaman Ferrier to pay, and so without Admiralty aid they remained in prison. In fact Roots died in jail in February 1743 after 'a tedious and lingering illness'.[10]

The *Queen Mary* affair put relations between the Admiralty and the city of Bristol on edge. Press-gangs were not only firing on open boats, they were interfering with outward-bound vessels and legitimate commercial enterprises. Within two months of Roots's death, another incident compounded matters. This time a press-gang boarded the *Bremen Factor*, a homeward-bound ship, off the Holms. A few of the crew hid in the hold fearing they would be taken up, and when members of the press-gang came to look for them, Alexander Broadfoot warned them off, brandishing a blunderbuss full of swan shot and demanding to see the lieutenant in charge. The press-gang ignored this warning and so Broadfoot fired, killing Cornelius Callahan and wounding another ganger. Broadfoot was consequently indicted for murder at the Bristol assizes, but during the trial it became clear that the press warrant had been irregularly administered, for the lieutenant should have been present when the press-gang boarded the vessel. Consequently the charge against Broadfoot was reduced to manslaughter and he was burnt in the hand, the minimal sentence for such offences.

In directing the jury to this verdict, the Recorder Michael Foster was nonetheless anxious to uphold the legality of impressment, even if it had been inappropriately executed in this instance. In a precedent-making

---

[9] TNA, Adm 1/1780, fols 45–6, 181–3.
[10] TNA, Adm 1/1780, fols 181–3. See also Rogers, *Manning*, nos 26–9.

judgement he insisted that impressment was 'a prerogative inherent in the Crown, grounded upon common-law, and recognised by many Acts of Parliament'. Framed in this manner, Foster tried to deflect the argument that naval impressment was a feudal prerogative incompatible with the political zeitgeist of the post-1688 era, or a violation of rights enshrined in the Great Charter. These were topical critiques of impressment, voiced especially in James Oglethorpe's *Sailors Advocate*, a six-penny pamphlet that ran through eight editions between 1728 and 1777. That tract described impressment as an 'Unwarrantable Violence ' upon the liberty of the subject, incompatible with Magna Charta, and indeed with some rulings in the seventeenth century by Lord Chief Justice Holt.[11] Clearly Foster was troubled that these two press-gang affrays in Bristol waters would inflame hostility to impressment, nationally, and in the West Country in particular.

The wars of the forties did little to clarify the rights and righteousness of impressment in Bristol. Merchants wanted convoys and seemingly cooperated with the Admiralty's recruiting drives. Yet they staunchly defended the pilots when the regulating officers tried to impress them, arguing that they were essential to the commerce of the city, despite the fact that pilots regularly helped seamen evade the clutches of the gang. Mayor John Foy did so in March 1747, reminding the Admiralty that there was a standing order 'against impressing Pilots and others immediately employed in the care and management of ships in Port'.[12] Anxious to shield their own topmen from the navy, merchants also decried any high-handed tactics the Admiralty might use to fill its ships. Those complaints would have struck a chord with a marine population that detested the presence of press-gangs at the Avon estuary and at port. Many would appreciate Oglethorpe's comments on the seaman's predicament: forced service in the navy, with no possibility of seeing his family for the duration of the war. 'How can it be expected that a man should fight for the Liberty of others, whilst he himself feels the pangs of Slavery, or expose his life to defend the property of a Nation when his dearest pledges [his family] are pining away with want?'[13]

The struggle against the press-gangs intensified during the Seven Years' War when the Admiralty extended its operations to sixty towns, an intervention that was accompanied by efforts to reconcile the needs of the state with those of commerce by allowing 'protections', that is exemptions, to specified trades and select members of crews. In Bristol the early recruiting drives were conducted by captains from Kingroad in conjunction with the city authorities, who provided the constables for the general searches of pubs and also

---

[11] [James Oglethorpe], *The Sailor's Advocate* (London, 1728), p. 4. On Oglethorpe's pamphlet in the context of his other philanthropic ventures, see Julie Anne Sweet, 'The British Sailor's Advocate. James Oglethorpe's First Philanthropic Venture', *Georgia History Quarterly*, 9:1 (2007), 1–27.

[12] BA, Mayor's letter book, 5 March 1747.

[13] *Sailor's Advocate*, pp. 6–7.

offered top-ups to the royal bounties offered volunteers. Some concern was registered that the press-gangs were operating arbitrarily; there was 'consternation in the city' when the gangs stripped boats of all hands, and then sifted out those that were protected. Complaints arose that mercenary constables were cashing in on the enterprise.[14] These incursions were sometimes resisted. In March 1755 three men escaped from the constables as they were escorting impressed men to the Gibb. A month later, the crew of a Bridgewater slip on the Backs defied the gangs and precipitated a bloody skirmish in which two of its members were eventually taken.[15] Consequently the establishment of a rendezvous in the port in the early spring of 1756 was met with a frosty reception from the mayor, who told the first regulating officer, Captain Samuel Graves, that 'there was not a man to be got at Bristol unless we took from protections'.[16]

Conflicting chains of command between the port and the estuary also complicated matters. Captain John Evans of the *Prince Edward*, an experienced recruiter who was in charge of the tenders at King Road, disliked any suggestion that he was subordinate to Graves and was piqued when Graves did not return men he had lent him to recruit in the city. This tension did not last long, because Graves was removed from his post in a matter of months, working out of Plymouth by June 1756. Precisely why his tenure at Bristol was so short is unclear. Graves is alleged to have used his press-gang as a bruising militia for the Whig party in the March 1756 by-election, intimidating Tory voters as they went to the hustings. He was also accused of taking up a freeman blacksmith named James Matthews to prevent him from voting. Graves vehemently denied these charges. 'I defy the whole party who made the Complaint to prove one instance where either myself, Officers or Press Gang ever interfer'd in an Election', he pleaded with the Admiralty.[17] But a cloud of suspicion hung over him, and when the election return was contested, the Tory John Brickdale threatened to have him brought to the bar of the Commons to explain his conduct. This did not happen, as the Whigs abandoned their petition against the return of Jarrit Smith, the Tory candidate.[18] Nonetheless the publicity did not endear him to the Admiralty. Nor did a bungled attempt to impress a victualler and 'considerable dealer' named Thomas Dennison, whom Graves suspected was an ex-seaman. The Whig corporation advised Graves to discharge Dennison, as the opposition party would make 'a great disturbance in the town' over the affair; but Graves refused to do so, with the result that one of Graves's lieutenants became embroiled in a lengthy law

---

[14] *FFBJ*, 3–10, 17–24 May 1755; *Bath Journal*, 19 May 1755.
[15] *FFBJ*, 15 and 29 March 1755.
[16] TNA, Adm 1/1833 (Samuel Graves), 29 Feb. 1756; see also Rogers, *Manning*, no. 34.
[17] TNA, Adm 1/1833 (Samuel Graves), 11 March 1756; see also Rogers, *Manning*, no. 36, and *FFBJ*, 13–20 March 1756.
[18] JHC, 27 (1753–7), 550–1, 97; Bristol petition, 30 March 1756, 7 May 1756; TNA, Adm 1/1833 (Samuel Graves), 1–2 May 1756; see also Rogers, *Manning*, no. 40.

suit with Dennison over trespass, assault and damages.[19] At the Bristol assizes in the summer of 1757, the offending lieutenant Peter Rawlings and one of his seamen, Benjamin Ryan, were found guilty on a King's Bench information and became virtual fugitives from the law, for Dennison was still chasing down Rawlings in 1765 and had him arrested in Exeter.[20] The Admiralty had defended Rawlings and Ryan, but their lordships doubtless resented the bother to which Graves had put them.

The result was that Bristol had no appreciable press-gang presence on the quays until 1759, when a severe shortage of manpower forced the Admiralty to try again to establish a rendezvous there. In the interim, sailors tried to keep the Kingroad gangs at bay. On 1 July 1758 Captain Thomas Saumarez reported that he had

> sent the Boats up the River and upon Impressing some men ... a great number of Seamen and the Mob of Bristol Arm'd themselves and marched severall places in order to find the Officers or any of the people belonging to His Majesty's Ships, swearing they wou'd Murder all of them they shou'd meet with, and haul the Boats up into Town and burn them.

Between three- and four hundred men went to the lodgings where the officers were staying and searched it, threatening to pull it down and take Saumarez hostage.[21] Not finding any officers, they marched to Hotwell armed with pistols, cutlasses, and large 'faggot sticks' in the hope of confronting the press-gang officers.

This rough reception did not bode well for the new regulating captain, Captain Thomas Gordon. He quickly found himself confronting three hundred riotous seamen when he began recruiting in February 1759. They wounded his drummer and threatened 'Death and Destruction of the officers, searching for them everywhere'.[22] Against such a formidable force, Gordon's two gangs of thirteen men each had no chance, at least not without civic support;[23] and the corporation was loath to back press warrants after the rough ride Saumarez had experienced, advising Gordon to concentrate his efforts at Kingroad. Mayor Henry Muggleworth and several aldermen even recommended that the Admiralty bring in troops; the large number of armed seamen demanded it. Once the word got out that this might happen, the seamen assembled again, 'vowing destruction to us', reported Gordon, 'and bidding defiance to the magistrates'.[24] Gordon managed to get a few recruits aboard the *Caesar* tender, many of them debtors or vagrants, but he quickly met the wrath of the seamen. His gangs were assailed with 'vollies of small

[19] TNA, Adm 1/1833 (Samuel Graves), 7 April 1756; Adm 1/3677, fols 104, 108, 113. Rogers, *Manning*, nos 37, 69–71.
[20] TNA, Adm 1/3678, fol. 383; Rogers, *Manning*, no. 72.
[21] TNA, Adm 1/2472 (Thomas Saumarez), 1 July 1758; Rogers, *Manning*, no. 81.
[22] TNA, Adm 1/1834 (Thomas Gordon), 1 Feb. 1759; Rogers, *Manning*, no. 99.
[23] Each gang had a lieutenant, two petty officers and ten men.
[24] TNA, Adm 1/1834 (Thos Gordon), c.6 April 1759.

shot'. Several were wounded in a Marsh street affray. 'As the seamen are in general well armed', he observed, 'we have been very fortunate to escape so long [with relatively few injuries] as we have had many Broyles.'[25]

Eventually these broils took their toll. Lieutenant Stephen Hammick fell ill of fatigue, spitting 'a vast Quantity of Blood.' Gordon's key ganger and recruiter, a prize fighter and ex-sailor named Cornelius Harris, was brutally tortured by privateers while searching for seamen on the Long Ashton Road.[26] Dumped on the side of the road, his head mangled and his hands fingerless, he died a few days later. Some of his assailants were cornered in a Marsh Street pub and surrendered after a rooftop shoot-out. Even so, the momentum of resistance in Bristol scarcely abated. It was complicated by quarrels with the military quartered in the city, making cooperation between the press-gang and the army difficult. Gordon sent some of his men into the country until tempers cooled and the military departed, but eight of them were attacked and wounded by the Kingswood colliers, who resented their appearance in the chase. 'I have not one Man in the Gangs but what is wounded or recovering of their wounds', Gordon dolefully reported in mid June. Without reinforcements, 'the [King's] Duty cannot be carried on in this large and Populous City where we have everything to contend with'.[27]

These words proved to be prophetic. By the end of 1759 recruitment in Bristol had become a major challenge to the Admiralty. Within the city and its environs, efforts to impress seamen, especially privateers, continued to be routinely violent. One distiller in Marsh Street even invited Gordon to visit his establishment to see the swivel guns he had mounted for his gang's reception.[28] For his part Gordon lamented that his gangs were frequently overpowered by bands of armed seamen, leaving a trail of wounded men and three fatalities. One such encounter involved Lieutenant Crosbie, who had managed to corner eight privateers in a country pub, only to find that a hundred colliers and seamen came to their aid, forcing him 'to retreat with a few slightly wounded'.[29] Incidents like this prompted Gordon to keep his men well armed, he reported, 'or else quit the City'.[30] Quitting the city was what the Bristol merchants wanted. They had never been happy about a portside rendezvous, especially those who had magisterial responsibilities for law and order. Consequently when such a concession was offered Liverpool, where relations between the regulating officer and corporation had seriously deteriorated, they pushed hard for the same favour. In January 1760, the Admiralty agreed. It ordered Gordon to break up the rendezvous in Bristol and focus his operations on Kingroad.

---

[25] TNA, Adm 1/1834 (Thos Gordon), 10 May 1759.
[26] TNA, Adm 1/1834 (Thos Gordon), 21 May 1759. This affray made the news, see *London Evening Post*, 12–15 May 1759; *FFBJ*, 12 and 26 May 1759; *Bath Journal*, 14 and 21 May 1759. For Hammick, see Adm 1/1834 (Thos Gordon), 1 May 1759.
[27] TNA, Adm 1/1834 (Thos Gordon), 17 June 1759.
[28] TNA, Adm 1/1834 (Thomas Gordon), 22 Oct. 1759; Rogers, *Manning*, no. 140.
[29] TNA, Adm 1/1834 (Thomas Gordon), 15 Sep. 1759; Rogers, *Manning*, no. 135.
[30] TNA, Adm 1/1835 (Thos Gordon), 7 Jan. 1760.

This was easier said than done. Captain Gordon no longer had the jurisdictional problems that confronted Graves, for he was now indisputably the senior officer on the river, but he faced the same problems of evasion that plagued his predecessor. Ships frequently dropped off impressible seamen before they reached Kingroad, sometimes with the help of the Pill pilots, who were too indispensable to the city to be disciplined effectively for their collusive activities. Gordon hired a skiff to track the movements of men from Ilfracombe to Kingroad, but he didn't have enough men to crew the boat efficiently and as winter approached some of them deserted. The return at Kingroad was in any case uneven. The Leeward Island ships were sometimes crewed by apprentices and foreigners, both exempted from the press. As for the Jamaican ships, they openly defied the press boats, as did the *Hanoverian Planter*. With five carriage guns and fifty armed men, she positively refused to allow the gangs to board her and sailed off to Milford Haven. Gordon sent the *Devonshire* tender in pursuit; but in the meantime the Jamaica fleet landed seventy men on the coast, of whom only twenty were secured. The result was that Gordon's catch was unspectacular. Between October 1759 and October 1760 his gangs brought in 164 men, substantially less than smaller ports like Gravesend and Dover and no more than 40 per cent of the return in Newcastle-upon-Tyne.[31]

During the Seven Years' War the Admiralty's press-gangs faced formidable opposition in Bristol and can hardly be said to have secured a firm footing in the port. In the brief mobilisation that accompanied the Falkland Islands crisis of 1770, Captain John Nott sought to repair this fractured situation by closely collaborating with the corporation. He persuaded the Common Council to raise the bounty for volunteers so that crimps might be better disposed to handing over their men.[32] He also obtained some seamen from the jails for the service, including John Cummings who had been prosecuted for perjury in a murder case aboard a slaver in Old Calabar and was lingering in a debtors' prison because of his inability to pay court fees and charges.[33] This policy brought in a fair crop of volunteers, both seamen and landlubbers. Of the 579 men raised in 1770, roughly two-thirds were volunteers. Of the men taken up by Nott's gangs, who were really only active in the month of December, only 20 per cent were impressed men. Even during the hot press of 21 December, when Nott was ordered to sweep the quays and ignore protections, the return was meagre.[34] He only raised twenty-five seamen, largely he said, because 'all the Men here belonging to the Ships are gone into Kingswood among the

[31] William L. Clements Library, Ann Arbor, Michigan, Shelburne MS, 139, no. 64.

[32] Crimps are people who ensnare sailors in debt and threaten them with imprisonment unless they agree to enter the navy or specific merchant ships. Crimping was used to recruit men for slave-trade voyages.

[33] TNA, Adm 1/2220 (John N. P. Nott), 3 Nov. 1770; Adm 1/3679/342–4, 306–7.

[34] A hot press is a radical form of impressment in which governmental exemptions from impressment are ignored. On these occasions press gangs normally swept up every likely sailor and discharged only those who had statutory protections.

Colliers, where we dare not go after them'.[35] Indeed, the proximity of the Kingswood pits to Bristol meant they were likely to be a near-permanent sanctuary for straggling seamen who wished to evade the press-gang. What also improved the seamen's chances of eluding the gangs was the fact that some crimps were supplying the tars with provisions and arranging mercantile berths for them. In this respect Captain Nott's hope that high bounties might crack the crimping trade in Bristol had not proved very successful.

The ability of seamen to elude the gangs continued to plague Bristol's regulating officers. There were plenty of places on the Somerset coast where sailors could decamp before reaching the estuary of the Avon. 'It has always been the practice for the homeward bound ships to land their Men to the Westward', reported Captain William Hamilton in 1779, a refrain familiar to other captains assigned to Bristol duty. Particularly aggravating to the regulating officers was the prominent role played by the pilots of Pill in these ventures. Their westward sailings took them as far as Ilfracombe and Lundy, leaving them plenty of opportunity to transfer impressible men to their skiffs and have their mates drop them off on the shore. For these activities and on their own account, pilots thought themselves immune from the press. They knew they were essential to the economy of the city; without them no traffic could navigate the muddy labyrinthine river to the town. Press-gangs complained continually about their obstructive attitude and threatened to take them in, but the stand-off between the gangs and the pilots usually moved to the latter's advantage, as the merchant elite quickly intervened so that Bristol commerce would continue to flow. In 1777, for example, Lieutenant Carlyton impressed several pilots whom he knew had helped straggling seamen evade the gangs, with the result that the river ground to a halt. The Merchant Venturers immediately protested, and Captain Hamilton could do little but accede to the requests for the pilots' discharge.[36]

Like Captain Gordon before him, Hamilton persuaded the Admiralty to hire a skiff or two to track the homecoming fleets as they came up the Bristol Channel and accompany them to Kingroad.[37] Yet he also recognised that these scouting vessels would need reinforcements if runaways from the homeward-bound fleets were to be impressed; ideally, an armed sloop off the isle of Lundy. One tender at the estuary would not be satisfactory. 'Most of the ships from this port now are ships of force [privateers]', the captain declared, 'and the men are resolute. It would therefore require a superior force to prevent bloodshed'.[38]

Hamilton did register some modest success in preventing the premature departure of homecoming seamen, or so he reported in May 1781.[39] But the

[35] TNA, Adm 1/2220 (Nott), 22 Dec. 1770.
[36] TNA, Adm 1/1903 (William Hamilton), 25 April 1777. See also Adm 1/1905 (Hamilton), 25 June 1779.
[37] TNA, Adm 1/1905 (Hamilton), 18 Nov. 1779.
[38] TNA, Adm 1/1905 (Hamilton), 12 July 1779.
[39] TNA, Adm 1/1906 (Hamilton), 12 May 1781.

bigger ships continued to defy his officers. In the same month he reported that the crews of three ships had fired at his skiffs and had successfully disembarked their men off Bridgwater Bay. Hamilton advised the Admiralty to establish a gang in that vicinity to handle these seamen, to no avail. The result was that Bristol's regulating officers had to tolerate a continual drain of potential recruits as seamen routinely landed on the Somerset shore and tramped through the countryside to places like Kingswood, or perhaps to Clutton and Radford in the north Somerset coalfield, where they might find temporary work before landing new berths. Captain Thomas Hawker complained in 1793 that seamen were flying to Kingswood in droves and a decade later it was still considered the sanctuary of hundreds who 'bid defiance to the gangs'.[40] Not that the coalfields were the only places of refuge. Hawker advised the Admiralty to send gangs to Bridgwater, or further up the Severn to Chepstow, and Newnham, on the edge of the Forest of Dean, all places where seamen lurked.[41] The latter was a resort of the Severn trowmen, who were threatened with impressment for obstructing the service, and it was not surprising that deep-sea sailors ventured there as well.[42]

Press-gangs simply had to live with the disappearance of many seamen before the homecoming fleets reached Avonmouth. It was a fact of life that aggravated searches at the estuary, especially when crews might throw six-pound shots into press-gang boats and even fire on boarding parties.[43] In August 1777, for example, crews from the Jamaica fleet attempted to by-pass the *Fanny* tender and scramble ashore near Hungroad. As their boats were making for the shore, the press-gang fired on one of them, killing James Reynolds, the boatswain of the *Friendship*. Recognising that this might inflame Bristolians and only add to the press-gang's unpopularity, Hamilton prevailed on the coroner to hold the inquest on the *Rose* tender rather than in Bristol itself. He also promised to pay the appropriate charges for the change of venue and ordered that the body of Reynolds be buried in a decent manner at St George's, Pill.[44] Even so, the coroner's inquest returned a verdict of willful murder and demanded that the master of the tender, Thomas Harrison, be brought into custody. This sent the Admiralty scrambling to find legal counsel for Harrison, whose actions the government thought merited a strenuous defence, since the seamen had been warned to bring to.[45]

[40] TNA, HO 42/71/96–7.
[41] TNA, Adm 1/1910 (Thomas Hawker), 28 April 1793; Adm 1/1912 (Hawker), 2 March 1795.
[42] TNA, Adm 1/581/117–27.
[43] TNA, Adm 3/85, Letter of Captain Hamilton, 17 July 1778; Adm 1/1906 (Hamilton), 12 May 1781; *Bonner and Middleton's Bristol Journal*, 6 June 1778; *Bristol Gazette*, 4 June 1778; Peter Marshall, *Bristol and the American War of Independence* (Bristol, 1977), p. 15.
[44] TNA, Adm 1/1903 (William Hamilton), 17 Aug. 1777; *General Evening Post*, 14–16 Aug. 1777.
[45] TNA, Adm 1/3680, fols 244, 303.

Hamilton's response to this incident points to the sensitivity of impressment at a time when many Britons believed they were regrettably engaged
in a civil war with their cousins across the Atlantic. In the City of London
efforts were being launched to make the city a press-free zone in an effort to
scupper the war effort, and Hamilton had no wish to be embroiled in a similar
controversy in Bristol. Unlike Liverpool, where the corporation was basically
loyal during the American war, Bristol's elite was divided. In 1775 Edmund
Burke and the Rockingham Whigs had encouraged the Merchant Venturers
and merchants outside the elite circle to petition parliament to consider
American grievances, but by the end of the year, as support for coercive
measures increased, the hawks and doves were more evenly matched, with
each side mustering more than nine hundred signatures for their respective
petitions.[46] This polarization continued for the rest of the war, both in the
corporation, at Merchant Hall, and among the public at large. It forced
the press-gang officers to tread warily least their indiscretions became part of
the political battle about the ends and means of the war effort.[47] The differences were especially marked over the politics of the navy, where the corporation under the leadership of John Durbin offered the freedom of the city to
the Earl of Sandwich, the controversial First Lord of the Admiralty who was
the principal war minister in the Lords. A year later, during the demonstrations in favour of Admiral Augustus Keppel, who was acquitted of all charges
for his actions off Ushant, Hugh Palliser, one of Sandwich's protégés, was
derisively paraded in effigy through the principal streets.[48]

The situation became especially acute in the summer of 1779, when the
advent of the French and Spanish into the war meant Britain now faced two
European enemies as well as its former colonists. Desperate for seamen, the
Admiralty issued an order to press from all protections, statutory as well as
administrative, in order to re-man the fleet. In the first dramatic hot press of
that summer, the Bristol gangs picked up 640 men, an intake that surpassed
that of Hull but was less than Liverpool.[49] This big sweep occurred at a time
when the Whigs and Tories were battling for the advantage in city councils,
and it inevitably proved controversial. Merchant Hall demanded the return
of some pilots, and the mayor, Sir John Durbin, told Captain Hamilton to
release a freeman sailmaker named William Lewis for fear that his impressment would compromise the Tory motion for a loyalist address in Common

---

[46] James E. Bradley, *Popular Politics and the American Revolution in England* (Macon, GA,
1986), pp. 22–3, 65. For the continuation of conflict over America, see Marshall, *Bristol
and the American War of Independence*, pp. 17–23.

[47] Latimer, II, 440.

[48] *Worcester Journal*, 5 Feb. 1778; *Morning Post*, 22 Feb. 1779.

[49] See Christopher Lloyd, *The British Seaman, 1200–1860* (London, 1968), appendix II;
see also *Ipswich Journal*, 3 July 1779, where it would seem that Bristol moved quickly to
impress, for the early returns suggest that it did better than Liverpool, and even temporarily surpassed London.

Council.[50] Hamilton reluctantly complied with this request, but hard on the first press one of his gangs seized James Caton as he was conducting business at the Exchange. Caton was a well-known merchant and former skipper with American sympathies. In 1778 he had subscribed five guineas towards the upkeep of American prisoners of war.[51] He was probably taken up to settle some personal political score in the city, with the press-gang an accomplice to this malice. Certainly the affair fuelled protests against the press-gang, for Caton wrote of his experiences, which were published in the newspapers and replicated in a small tract. Caton's detention 'engages the conversation of all ranks of people in this city', remarked several newspapers, and there is even evidence to suggest it resonated in the 1780 general election.[52] According to his own account, Caton was thrown into the insanitary lock-up in Prince Street, Bristol and later hurried off to the tender in Kingroad. All requests from his friends to visit him at Kingroad were denied. Fortunately, Bristol's MP Edmund Burke and its Recorder, John Dunning, took up his case and quickly secured his release with a habeas corpus at King's Bench.[53] Caton subsequently sued Captain Hamilton and Lieutenant Michael Lane for false arrest and imprisonment, claiming he had served as a master of a vessel and was therefore legally exempt from the press. According to the *Annual Register*, Caton asked for £5000 damages, an enormous sum even for four days' confinement and the disruption of his business and reputation.[54] At the Bristol Guildhall before Justice Nares in August 1780, Caton was awarded only £50, but Hamilton and his lieutenant still had to face costs of over £300.[55] Hamilton hoped that the Admiralty would pay his expenses. 'I beg leave to assure their Lordships', he wrote, 'that in this affair I was neither actuated by private pique, nor wantonness of malice, but did it with a sole view of serving my Country.'[56] One wonders what the Admiralty thought of his loyalty.

The Caton affair was but one of a series of onshore incidents in which the press-gangs were entangled during the American war. In 1777 a local woollen draper raised a mob to rescue a man from the press-gang, beating up the

---

[50] TNA, Adm 1/1905 (William Hamilton), 25 June 1779.

[51] *FFBJ*, 10 Jan. 1778.

[52] *London Evening Post*, 13–15 July 1779; *St James's Chronicle*, 15–17 July 1779. Caton's *Plain Narrative* was published in the London newspapers. The only surviving copy of the tract is in the Bristol Reference Library. It is not included in Eighteenth-Century Collections Online (ECCO). See also Rogers, *Manning*, nos 244–6. There is a flyer about the Caton affair in a collection of election broadsides, 1774–90, in the Bristol Reference Library, B 6979.

[53] *Bath Journal*, 19 July 1779; *London Evening Post*, 17/20 July 1779; Marshall, *Bristol and the American War of Independence*, pp. 15–16.

[54] *Annual Register*, 23 (1780), Chronicle, p. 223.

[55] TNA, Adm 1/1906 (William Hamilton), 5 Feb. 1780, 21 Dec. 1780; see also Latimer, II, 440. The total bill, with damages, was £376-15-5d.

[56] TNA, Adm 1/1906 (William Hamilton), 21 Dec. 1780; Rogers, *Manning*, no. 266.

midshipman in the process. Two years later a press-gang leader and crimp, a Mr Farrell who kept the *Shakespeare* at the Gibb, was fatally wounded while searching out men at the *Boar's Head* on Redcliff Hill.[57] In the summer of 1781 sailors responded to an attempt to impress a brother tar from his sanctuary in Kingswood by marching on the rendezvous at the Drawbridge, rescuing the man and stealing the gang's colours.[58] These confrontations signalled that onshore hostility to the gangs persisted, although they were never as frequent or bloody as the affrays at Kingroad and the mutinies on the tender, where conditions on board were fetid and feverish if the ship lingered in the estuary.[59]

Compared to the previous war, press-gang violence declined during the American hostilities. In the period 1755–63 there were twenty-seven serious affrays that were reported to the Admiralty or to the press. In half of these, men, and in two cases landladies, were either killed or seriously wounded. This is a higher quotient of violence than nationally, where just over a third (36.7 per cent) were injured in a press-gang affray. During the American war, the number of reported affrays fell to fourteen, although the level of violence remained high, with eight fatal incidents and two occasions when men were seriously wounded (71 per cent), conspicuously higher than the national average (32 per cent). Evidence such as this is admittedly a little crude. Many rough-ups causing minor injuries went unreported, and conversely some serious ones went untreated and likely eluded contemporaries. But newspapers did take a keen interest in the random violence of press-gang encounters, it was part of the critique of impressment, and so the figures do offer a rough guide. What those figures suggest is that resistance to the press-gang in Bristol was highest during the Seven Years' War, when the gang's presence was for the first time conspicuously intrusive. Forty-seven per cent of all serious affrays in the years 1739–1815 occurred during this period, 24 per cent during the American fighting. Thus 71 per cent took place in the mid-century wars, declining noticeably during the French wars at the turn of the century. Instructively, the period of high violence against the gangs was also the golden era of privateering in Bristol, with no fewer than 209 prizes taken by Bristol-based ships in the years 1756–63, and 173 from 1776–83. Hyper-masculine seamen, armed to the teeth and eager for the spoils of war, were not likely to take kindly to press-gang interventions, particularly to a hot press where protections were customarily ignored.

Begrudgingly, Bristolians adjusted to the presence of press-gangs on their streets. Seamen for their part opted to evade the press rather than confront

---

[57] *Bath Journal*, 15 Feb. 1779; *Morning Chronicle*, 16 Feb. 1779; *Ipswich Journal*, 20 Feb. 1779; TNA, Adm 1/1905 (William Hamilton), 12 Feb. 1779; Marshall, *Bristol and the American War of Independence*, p. 15; *Aris's Birmingham Gazette*, 2 Nov. 1778; TNA, Adm 1/1903 (Hamilton), 12 July 1777.

[58] *Bath Chronicle*, 12 July 1781; *Oxford Journal*, 14 July 1781.

[59] During the American war there were nine affrays or mutinies at Kingroad, and six anti-press-gang incidents ashore.

the gangs directly, a practice no doubt welcomed by the gangs themselves
after the bloody, bruising encounters of the mid-century decades. In this new
era of measured disengagement the regulating officers did chalk up some
successes. During the American war Bristol raised an average of 480 men per
year, three times what Captain Gordon had raised in 1759–60, at the height
of the Seven Years' War. This put Bristol high in the provincial league tables:
fourth after Dublin, Cork and Liverpool, just ahead of Newcastle. London
predictably towered over the others. With its seven gangs it brought in ten
times the number of recruits raised in Bristol, no less than a third of all men
enlisted in the British Isles.[60]

Over time, however, Bristol's record proved disappointing. An Admiralty
survey for the years 1803–05 reveals that the port was still raising a commendable number of men, 677 seamen and landsmen in eighteen months, 779
if one included boys.[61] But the port had fallen in the league tables. The
Irish ports were not included in the enquiry, but of those on the mainland
Bristol now lagged behind Liverpool, Leith, Tyneside, Deal, Gravesend,
Hull, Swansea and Greenock. Within this group Bristol's recruiting practice
was one of the more expensive, calculated at just over £3 per recruit. This
was comparable to Greenock and Swansea, but substantially more than the
others, with Liverpool and Leith recruiting at a cost of £1.1 and £1.4 per
head. In terms of impressing seamen, Bristol's record was also poor. Of the
seamen recruited only 36 per cent were actually impressed, compared to 50
per cent in Liverpool, 66 per cent on the Tyne, and a formidable 78 per cent
in Swansea.

In subsequent years Bristol's naval recruitment plummeted. In 1811,
Captain John Philips, brought in to pump up the numbers, raised 320 recruits,
compared to an annual return of 450 at the resumption of the Napoleonic
wars. In the next year his gangs could only raise 237, of which a third were
boys, some of them street urchins delivered by the magistrates of Bath, who
wanted to relieve the fashionable visitors of these little predators. This
decline prompted the Admiralty to consider its costs, particularly the £3000
a year it was expending on the *Enchantress*, the tender in Kingroad. It also
considered opening a rendezvous at Newport, aware that south Wales now
seemed a more dynamic recruiting ground.

Why did Bristol's recruiting performance decline so dramatically? Part
of the explanation might be Bristol's economic decline, the fact it was no
longer the vibrant port it once was. After the American war, when the Bristol
merchants invested heavily in privateering, Bristol's transatlantic trade slowed
relative to other western ports. Bristol had already lost ground to Liverpool
and Glascow in the slave and tobacco trades, and lacking the kind of access

---

[60] National Maritime Museum, MID.7/3/2, cited in Roger Morriss, *The Foundations of
British Maritime Ascendancy* (Cambridge, 2010), pp. 236–8, table 6.2.
[61] TNA, Adm 1/581, fols 86–9. These are Admiral Philips's figures from his tour of the
ports. The list is in rank order, calculated by average annual returns.

Liverpool had to the new areas of industrial growth, its merchant elite opted for the safe and still profitable sugar trade as its principal source of wealth.[62]

Yet economic decline is not a sufficient explanation for Bristol's recruitment failure. That decline was not so precipitous as to account for laggard recruitment; Irish and Spanish trades remained buoyant, and while there was a decline in the number of ships entering the port by the nineteenth century, from 485 in 1787 to 386 in 1801, that fall, when one considers higher tonnage and larger crews, was not that dramatic.[63]

One critical reason was that over the long term Bristol's seamen, with the help of pilots, colliers, crimps and even merchants, successfully evaded the gangs. Press-gangs discovered fewer men without protections as ships entered Kingroad. They increasingly had to venture into the country to find straggling seamen. As enlistment levels dropped, regulating officers tried to tap sources that had hitherto been off-limits: shipwrights from the yards; carpenters who occasionally took an oversea voyage, perhaps to supervise the building of a planter mansion or sugar mill in the Caribbean; Severn trowmen, some of whom were undoubtedly ex-seamen; Pill pilots and watermen. In 1806 Captain George Barker managed to bully the owners of the Severn trows into delivering 10 per cent of their workforce to the navy in return for protecting the rest. It proved harder to win over the other trades. Shipwrights mustered in their hundreds to rescue their brethren from the gangs. Pill pilots threatened to close down the river when their men were taken. In May 1803, the Pill villagers, angered by the impressment of some of their pilots, prevented the Cork packet from sailing up the river to show their displeasure. It was not until 1813, late in the day, that the regulating officer was able to negotiate further quotas, and then very much against the wishes of the merchant-dominated corporation. As Captain Man Dobson observed in February 1814, tempers smouldered over the niggardly way in which the Admiralty chipped away at customary exemptions from the press. 'The raising of men at this port having been nearly lost', he remarked, 'all persons concerned feel the alteration so much the more.'[64]

In the twilight of Bristol impressment, regulating captains struggled with the legal complexities of evasion. Press-gang officers were irritated by the appearance of the silver oar, the emblem of civic power, and the bailiff who would demand the return of a seaman with a dubious debt. 'Every able and ordinary seaman' that we have impressed recently, mourned Captain Thomas Hawker, has been 'immediately arrested [for debt] by the Sheriff's Officers, both from the Rendezvous and with the Silver Oar from the Tenders.' Midshipman John Wakefield was similarly piqued that Richard Higgins, a deserter from HMS *Boadicca*, evaded service this way, and even had the audacity to work at his

---

[62] See Morgan, *Bristol and the Atlantic Trade*.
[63] Minchinton, *Trade of Bristol*, pp. 180–1.
[64] TNA, Adm 1/1737 D71; Rogers, *Manning*, no. 596.

former trade as a coach-spring maker while in Newgate.[65] Apprentices were a constant source of irritation because, while apprentices of two years' standing were technically exempt from impressment, masters frequently abused the privilege by having experienced seamen pose as novices. William Mansfield's indenture stated his age was thirteen; his parish register revealed he was actually eighteen years of age and on further enquiry Lieutenant Pitman discovered he had already been on two voyages.[66] This was enough to refuse his discharge.

Particularly troubling was the hazy documentation on mates and masters by which crews sought to elude impressment. In April 1811 Lieutenant Rowe impressed a 28-year-old seamen named John Millard, who on two voyages to the West Indies in the *Avon*, had switched back and forth from mate to master. 'There is hardly a Ship' arriving in port, observed Captain Philips in his discussion of the case, where the captain did not endorse the register over to the mate, by which means the navy was 'deprived of a Number of Men'.[67] Beyond this there was a regular trade in protections, where the brief description on the back scarcely matched the visage and stature of the holder; or where crew members simply impersonated protected seaman.[68] One Thomas Jones, impressed out of a Newport brig, claimed he was a mate of two years' standing, although the lieutenant thought he was Irish not Welsh, and suspiciously young for a mate. He was retained when it became clear from the documentation obtained from Newport that he was an impostor.[69] These practices bred cynicism among press-gang officers, who sometimes openly doubted the veracity of affidavits thrust upon them. In September 1813 Man Dobson remarked of two dubious claims, both made by Welshmen, 'how little dependence is to be placed in affidavits made by that class of people in that part of the Empire'.[70]

Entangled in red tape and confronted with declining enrolment, the impress service in Bristol became increasingly hard-nosed in its application of the rules; rules that had been honed from the small body of impressment law that had emerged from applications for habeas corpus at King's Bench.[71] Masters were forced to show that apprentices had no prior sea experience; mates were impressed if they ventured from their boats, even to supervise the loading of cargoes on the quays. This happened to Charles Carville, who was managing the loading of the outward-bound cargo of the *Edward* and popped into a nearby pub for a quick pint.[72] Old seamen were taken up; one, William

[65] TNA, Adm 1/1924 H 174; Adm 1/1738 D 444.
[66] TNA, Adm 1/1736 D 377.
[67] TNA, Adm 1/2339 P 505.
[68] TNA, Adm 1/1739 D 146.
[69] TNA, Adm 1/2341 P143; Rogers, *Manning*, no. 536.
[70] TNA, Adm 1/1736, D 346, 463.
[71] Kevin Costello, 'Habeas Corpus and Military and Naval Impressment, 1756–1816', *Journal of Legal History*, 29:2 (2008), 215–51.
[72] TNA, Adm 1/2340 P772; Rogers, *Manning*, no. 529.

Lawton, aged fifty-five with a wife and five children, had already served ten years and had been previously discharged at the Peace of Amiens. If he had been retained until the end of the war, it would have meant another seven years' service.[73] Runaway apprentices were not necessarily returned to their masters if they volunteered, a reversal of earlier policies. Men were entered who were dubiously fit to serve. William Lee, a 22-year-old lad, who fractured his skull when falling off a building in Manchester, was found to be a 'stout healthy young man' by the surgeon at the rendezvous, even though his mother pleaded he was not 'in his proper senses' and feared he might endanger himself or others 'in his Frenzy'.[74] A cooper with a cataract in one eye and poor sight in the other, who had been rejected by the militia, was recruited into the navy.[75]

Where the Admiralty felt there were extenuating circumstances in an application for releasing a young man from the navy, the bar for liberation was often set high. In days when men routinely bought themselves out of service by finding substitutes, for the militia or the navy quota of 1795–97 for example, the Admiralty started asking for double substitutions and buy-outs as high as £80. A boatswain with a large family and an aging mother had to find as many as four landsmen to get his discharge.[76] A topman in a collier, caught without a protection, had to find £66 to be released from the navy, an enormous sum for a man of that social class. An apprentice who had two years' experience at sea prior to his indentures was also taken up. His mother, Ann Morgan, petitioned for his release, saying she already had two sons in the service and had provided others in previous years. A poor woman with a large family, she said her friends could contribute £40 for his discharge. The Admiralty initially rejected this offer, but ultimately settled for £60, again a formidable sum of money.[77]

In the final decade of the Napoleonic wars petitions requesting that impressed men be discharged from the navy appear more frequently in the Admiralty records. This might simply be an accident of survival, but it may also register a growing and no doubt begrudging recognition of the navy's right to impress. If this was the case, it did not necessarily enhance the Admiralty's popularity, which remained an unpredictable Leviathan, often merciless in its decisions. A plasterer named John Adams recklessly entered the navy as a landsman after a night of drinking with his mates. His wife, who had two small children and was pregnant with another, could not get him released, even though he was the sole breadwinner.[78] A consumptive cabinet-maker who had left the navy through ill health was dragged back in

[73] TNA, Adm 1/1540 B62; Rogers, *Manning*, no. 233.
[74] TNA, Adm 1/1737 D 35; Rogers, *Manning*, no. 597.
[75] TNA, Adm 1/1735 D 215; Rogers, *Manning*, no. 572.
[76] TNA, Adm 1/1534 B 251; Rogers, *Manning*, no. 422.
[77] TNA, Adm 1/1735 D 128, 158; Rogers, *Manning*, nos 562–3.
[78] TNA, Adm 1/1531 B78.

again, without a reprieve, even though his employer vouched he was a 'very sober workman' and offered four guineas towards finding a landsman in his stead.[79] The Admiralty was an officious taskmaster, and no great respecter of rank. Their Lordships deferred to the Duke of Beaufort, who managed to get a popular ferry-boy out of the navy; they also did a favour for Justice Harford, who had inadvertently frightened two local lads into joining the navy and on behalf of their poor parents had requested their discharge, although this was likely because Harford was a strong advocate of the war, with one of his relatives an officer in the navy.[80] The same courtesy was not, however, extended to Edward Protheroe, the conservative Whig MP for Bristol between 1812 and 1820, even where the claims for a discharge were strong. Of the three petitions he endorsed, only one found favour with the Admiralty, and that involved Charles Harris, the second mate of the *Trelawney*, who also happened to be the grandson of a former mayor and alderman. To extricate this eighteen-year-old from the navy, he was picked up on an outward-bound trip to Jamaica, and his family had to find two able-bodied substitutes.[81]

Where impressments were contestable in law, Bristolians could threaten litigation or apply for writs of habeas corpus to have sailors removed from the navy. Habeas corpus applications at King's Bench increased substantially after 1750. Paul Halliday has estimated that perhaps 1000 applications were made in the second half of the century, a seemingly substantial number until one realises that 200,000 men were likely impressed in the same period.[82] Such applications took time and money, somewhere between £10–20 in fees and costs, and they had to be made quickly, for naval officers adopted delay tactics to move men from ship to ship, and even defied the orders, especially when the application was filed out of term. Judging from the applications made at the onset of the French wars, from 1793–97, such applications were often made by employers anxious to get apprentices out of the navy, or perhaps experienced seamen such as first mates. Geographically they were skewed towards the eastern ports and the London coal or provisions market, to concerns where access to justices and King's Bench would not seriously disrupt the ordinary course of business.[83] How many emanated from Bristol is unknown. Certainly the city had some local attornies who specialised in impressment cases, just as other ports. One was John Cranidge, a schoolteacher in Taylors Court, who was the 'scribe and lawier for all the seamen who are impressed', claimed Lieutenant Campbell. He was 'notorious for his violent democratick

[79] TNA, Adm 1/1534 B 252; Rogers, *Manning*, no. 423.

[80] TNA Adm 1/1534 B 261, 1/2338 P 399 and 432; Latimer, II, 500.

[81] TNA, Adm 1/1531 B 102. For the other petitions, see Adm 1/1739 D 59 and 91.

[82] Paul D. Halliday, *Habeas Corpus from England to Empire* (Cambridge, MA, 2010), p. 115, 380n.

[83] Philip Woodfine, '"Proper Objects of the Press": Naval Impressment and Habeas Corpus in the French Revolutionary Wars', in *The Representation and Reality of War. The British Experience*, ed. Keith Dockray and Keith Laybourn (Stroud, 1999), pp. 39–60; Costello, 'Habeas Corpus', 215–51.

principals', a man who supported Henry Hunt in his brief foray into Bristol politics and 'the advocate of every disaffected person'.[84] He handled the case of the American black jack John Randall, a cook aboard the *New Kingston* West Indiaman, who was impressed in July 1813. Randall had already been discharged from the navy on account of a leg injury, and he had evidence of his American citizenship from the consul in Plymouth. But because he was married to an English woman residing in Bristol, the Admiralty refused to discharge him.

Taking on the navy in such cases became an uphill task, particularly during the French wars, when the Admiralty developed a growing confidence in challenging habeas corpus applications before a sympathetic judge, Lord Kenyon.[85] Not surprisingly hostility to impressment could erupt in more conventional ways. At the resumption of the French wars in 1803, a riot broke out at the Rownham ferry. On 23 March, Captain William Prowse of HMS *Ceres* was ordered to help the regulating officer remove some impressed men from the guardroom of the 1st Regiment of Dragoons and put them aboard a tender bound for Plymouth. Prowse sent his lieutenant to do the job, but upon his arrival, Lieutenant Norman encountered a crowd in an ugly mood, 'huzzaing and using language of the most inflammatory kind'. The previous night soldiers had lined the bridges of Bristol while a press-gang scoured the streets and quays looking for possible recruits. Two hundred stragglers were reportedly taken up in this nightly raid and those considered fit for service were ready to be escorted to Rownham, where the tender awaited them. Norman did not like the look of the crowd, and requested a detachment of dragoons to help him escort the men to the quayside, expecting trouble. 'A Multitude of People variously armed with Bludgeons repeatedly attempted to rescue the impressed men', Prowse reported. Consequently Lieutenant Norman ordered the troops to fire over their heads of the people to intimidate them. This only had the opposite effect. 'The mob became outrageous and closely assaulted the party', Prowse continued, and the marines, jostled and bruised, retaliated by firing on the crowd halfway along the Hotwell Road, killing a boy and wounding several other people.[86] Norman succeeded in getting the impressed men to the boat, but a warrant was issued for the arrest of him and his party. Norman was not detained very long, nor were the two privates who shot the demonstrators. A coroner's inquest decided that the death of the lad was justifiable homicide. But the incident was a bad start to the new wave of recruiting that began as the Peace of Amiens crumbled and the war against Napoleon resumed.

[84] TNA, Adm 1/1735 D 221; Rogers, *Manning*, no. 574.
[85] Costello, 'Habeas Corpus', 215–51.
[86] TNA, Adm 1/2326, Captain Prowse to Sir Evan Nepean, 28 March 1803. See also *Bristol Gazette*, 31 March 1803; *Bonner and Middleton's Bristol Journal*, 2 April 1803; *The Times*, 30 March 1803; *Sussex Weekly Advertiser*, 4 April 1803; *Reading Mercury*, 4 April 1803.

Subsequent efforts to take up straggling seamen also met with violent resistance. One of Captain Barker's recruiting parties was harried out of Bath by an angry mob, and another, in pursuit of men in Ilchester, was attacked near Shepton Mallet by 'a number of Men with Sticks and Knives'.[87] Compared to other ports, Shields, Whitby and Poole, the Bristol protests were brief and modest in this period. Yet the threat of physical resistance to impressment was ever-present, at the rendezvous and in the street. As late as January 1814 a lieutenant and his ganger were swarmed in the streets when they attempted to take up a straggling seaman, and when they were challenged on what authority they did this, the crowd spirited the man away. Prominent among the ringleaders was the master of a Minehead sloop, Henry Forrest, and a well-known ironmonger named Richard Hunt. It was Hunt who demanded the lieutenant show his credentials: 'what right have you with this Man?' he declared. The impress service retaliated by impressing Forrest on the grounds that he was irregularly registered as master of his vessel. It also wanted to nail Hunt. Captain Man Dobson advised the Admiralty that if no notice were taken on his intervention it 'would destroy the service of raising Men in this place.'[88]

Despite this remark, Bristol never required a reputation as a formidable site of resistance to the press-gang over the course of the eighteenth century. It was not a notorious no-go area, like the whaling port of Whitby on the north Yorkshire coast. Difficult to reach overland, and not easy to enter in North Sea gales, Whitby was a tough, resourceful port whose returns for the navy were abysmal. The whalers were intrepid seamen and the population at large was implacably hostile to the press-gang's presence. On one occasion the populace literally ran the gang out of town in a publicly humiliating manner, telling the recruiting captain that if he and his men returned 'they must not expect to live'.[89]

Whitby's confrontation with the gangs was immortalised in Elizabeth Gaskell's historical romance, *Sylvia's Lovers*.[90] Bristol had no novelist to commemorate its dealings with the press and its history was more prosaic. Yet as in Whitby, geography played an important role in how press-gang relations were played out. Whitby was impenetrable, a veritable fortress of a port, isolated on the North Sea. It could only be tamed by a permanent military presence. Bristol was accessible, but its approaches offered seamen opportunities for eluding the press on the Somerset Levels or perhaps further along the coast near Minehead. The persistent refrain of recruiting captains at Kingroad was the difficulty of finding men to recruit from vessels piloted into the estuary with skeletal crews. Captains hired skiffs to try to monitor

[87] TNA, Adm 1/1528 B 42 and 43; Rogers, *Manning*, nos 383–4.
[88] TNA, Adm 1/1737 D 24, 26, 42.
[89] TNA, Adm 1/579, fols 86–9; *Newcastle Courant*, 3 March 1793.
[90] On Whitby and Gaskell's novel, see Nicholas Rogers, *The Press Gang. Naval Impressment and its Opponents in Georgian Britain* (London, 2007), pp. 127–32.

the movements of men; they tried to discipline pilots who openly abetted the escapes to the shore. Yet in the end the return of men from this port was unimpressive, the exception being the American war when the dislocations of transatlantic trade reduced the possibilities of finding work in the merchant marine and left more seamen vulnerable to impressment. Instructively, it is only in the American war that the returns of able seamen, the men the navy really wanted to handle the topsails, were noticeably high.[91] In hard times Bristol could recruit landsmen, but experienced seamen were difficult to find. Although much has recently been made of the navy's ability to recruit able seamen in British waters, Bristol was very much an exception.[92]

Bristol was not without its periods of noteworthy anti-press-gang violence. The first attempts to establish a rendezvous in the port was met with heavy resistance and was successful in marginalising the press-gang presence for the duration of the Seven Years' War. Even during the American, affrays between the press-gangs and privateers kept the quotient of violence dangerously high. Whereas Bristol recruited 3.4 per cent of all men in the British Isles in the period 1775–83, it was responsible for 8 per cent of all serious affrays. After that, the contest with the press was less confrontational and more evasive. Refractory populations, in Pill and in the coalfields, for example, helped make seamen elusive. And the wear and tear of locating and enlisting men took its toll on the press-gangs, some of whose members were themselves pressed into service: men like Hugh Jones, impressed out of a Welsh sloop, who had lost one eye through small pox; or William Jones, aged fifty, pressed from a Guinea-man and well worn, for the lieutenant of the gang commented, 'how far a tedious voyage may alter a man's appearance, I will not pretend to say'.[93] They were likely warned that collusions with seaman would put them on the tenders to Plymouth.

Over time the press-gangs seem to have opted for an easy life of low-level recruiting. At Kingroad most of the officers aboard the *Enchantress* tender were sleeping on shore by 1813, a matter that bothered Captain Man Dobson because it encouraged lethargy among crews as well as officers.[94] This low-level recruitment suited the Bristol merchants. In offering bounties to volunteers and boats for hire, the merchants appeared to support the recruiting drives of the navy, enough to stay on the right side of the Admiralty, whose convoys were important to Bristol's shipping. At the same time the merchants seem to have shielded their topmen from impressment, and through the auspices of the council and Merchants' Hall, protected vital lines of supply, protesting when gangs impressed coastal trowmen or pilots whose skills were needed to ferry boats to the port. In the triangulated relationship between Admiralty,

---

[91] TNA, Adm 1/1903 (William Hamilton), figures for January 1777.
[92] Denver Brunsman, *The Evil Necessity. British Naval Impressment in the Eighteenth-Century Atlantic World* (Charlottesville, VA, 2013).
[93] TNA, Adm 1/1903 (William Hamilton), 28 Dec. 1776.
[94] TNA, Adm 1/1735 D 122; Rogers, *Manning*, no. 561.

seamen and merchants, the latter seem to have successfully kept their options open, at least until the final years of impressment when the recruiting captains insisted on quotas from what were anachronistically 'enumerated' populations. Then recruiting captains would complain that 'the Corporation and Merchants of Bristol will not do anything towards raising men for His Majesty's Navy but what they are obliged to do'.[95]

[95] TNA, Adm 1/1736 D 312; Rogers, *Manning*, no. 576.

9

Bristol and the War of American Independence

The rise of Bristol to a position of commercial prominence was very much bound up with the transatlantic economy, so that any long-term transformations to that economy inevitably affected its status. The war with America and the eventual declaration of independence wrought significant changes in Bristol's relationship with the North American colonies; by extension it also altered the dynamic of its trade with the West Indies. In the decade after the Seven Years' War Bristol's American trade grew spectacularly. From September 1763 until September 1764, eighty-one ships entered Bristol from British North America, carrying 6798 tons of merchandise; the corresponding figures for 1774–75 were 175 ships and 20,561 tons, a three-fold increase in tonnage and two-fold in ships. In 1775, the first year of the war, the number of ships entering Bristol from America fell to 125; in 1780 it was just 1. The corresponding figures for ships clearing Bristol for North America were 57 and 9. Vessels entering Bristol from the West Indies also showed a decline, from 85 to 66 over the same period, so that the overall volume of incoming transatlantic trade was seriously affected by war. According to Ken Morgan's figures, it fell from an average of 21,202 tons in 1772–73 to 12,326 tons in 1778–80, the lowest level of trade since the War of Austrian Succession in the 1740s.[1]

The result was lay-offs and higher poor rates. Without reciprocal trading, local businesses came under attack. Some serge and stuff-manufacturing firms collapsed; tobacco-pipe making for the American market disappeared. With a credit crisis in America and the reneging of many debts by American merchants and planters, bankruptcies also took their toll. There were over five hundred during the course of the war, at a rate three times as high as

---

[1] Walter E. Minchinton, *The Trade of Bristol in the Eighteenth Century*, Bristol Record Society, 20 (Bristol, 1957), pp. 177, 181; Latimer, II, 414–15; Kenneth Morgan, *Bristol and the Atlantic trade in the Eighteenth Century* (Cambridge, 1993), p. 25; Ronald H. Quilici, 'Turmoil in a City and an Empire: Bristol's Factions 1700–1775' (Unpublished PhD Thesis, University of New Hampshire, 1977), tables H6 and H7, pp. 335–8. These figures include trade with Canada and Newfoundland.

Liverpool.[2] These included a number of leading Bristolians: Sir James Laroche, the master of the Merchant Venturers in 1782 and MP for Bodmin in Cornwall, 1768–80; the Farr brothers, prominent Presbyterian merchants from the Lewin's Mead chapel, one of whom (Thomas) was the mayor in 1775 while his brother (Paul) was the master of the Merchant Venturers.[3]

It is possible to exaggerate the depth of the economic crisis, at least at the top of the merchant hierarchy. Confronted with non-importation agreements among American merchants angry about British policies, Bristol merchants did sometimes manage to diversify. A few such as Samuel Span secured military contracts to supply rum and bread to the troops. Several snapped up temporary supplies of tobacco from the Dutch islands of St Croix, St Thomas and St Eustatius and shipped them to Britain. In this respect, at least, Bristol fared better than Liverpool and competed favourably with London, importing over 1 million tons of tobacco in 1779 and 2.5 milllion in 1780.[4] In 1775, at the onset of the conflict, Richard Champion still thought trade was 'tolerably good' because of new manufacturing markets in Poland and Russia.[5] And for those merchants and shipowners who were sceptical of such opportunities, there was always privateering. Over two hundred vessels were commissioned during the course of the war and together they secured eighty-eight prizes. Indeed, one newspaper calculated that by the spring of 1779 privateers from Bristol and Liverpool had earned £6.5 million in profit; a wildly optimistic estimate one suspects, but certainly indicative of the handsome windfalls that could be made.[6] Overall, Bristol managed to stay afloat. It sustained a healthy coastal trade to over fifty-five ports, and via canals, to places like Leeds and Nottingham.[7] It continued to trade to Ireland, Newfoundland and southern Europe, which in terms of tonnage constituted 45 per cent of its foreign trade at the beginning of the war.[8] Bristol's ongoing trade to the West Indies also survived the vicissitudes of war. It remained the leading British outport for the value of goods received; its gross customs receipts were £243,370 in 1781, just ahead of Liverpool. The trade dislocations wrought by war were serious, not catastrophic. Bristol's trade with North America recovered after the war,

---

[2] A search in the London Gazette produces nearly six hundred for the years 1775–83, although this includes some bankruptcy proceedings held in Bristol. Using Sketchley's trade directory, 1775, we have estimated the rate as 1 to every 60 eligible businessmen. The comparable rate for Liverpool was 1:200. See Julian Hoppit, Risk and Failure in English Business 1700–1800 (Cambridge, 1987), p. 83.

[3] Minchinton, Trade of Bristol, p. 189, appendix G; James E. Bradley, Religion, Revolution and English Radicalism. Nonconformity in Eighteenth-Century Politics and Society (Cambridge, 1990), pp. 197, 377.

[4] Morgan, Bristol and the Atlantic Trade, pp. 26–7.

[5] G. H. Guttridge (ed.), The American Correspondence of a Bristol Merchant 1766–1776. Letters of Richard Champion (Berkeley, 1934), p. 60.

[6] St. James's Chronicle, 1–3 April 1779.

[7] Morgan, Bristol and the Atlantic Trade, p. 99.

[8] Quilici, 'Turmoil in a City', pp. 104, 337.

although over time it became clear that the American war had slowed its momentum of growth.

Long-term trends should not, however, disguise the deep sense of anxiety that Bristolians felt about the American crisis. It was its imponderability and uncertainty that bothered people. Even a merchant-manufacturer as well informed as Richard Champion talked of the conflict as a 'calamity' and wondered where the unfolding crisis would end. He considered it 'as big with Importance as any ever known in the Annals of this Country'.[9] The struggle not only affected ledgers and pocketbooks; it posed important questions about the nature of empire, authority, and political governance in America and in Britain. 'Since America has been in a State of Resistance', reflected Champion, 'great Confusion has reigned in the Counsels of the Ministry.'[10] It was a confusion that spilled onto the streets and hustings of Bristol.

Bristol's first exposure to the American conflict occurred over the Stamp Act of 1765. This statute formed part of a series of fiscal measures implemented by the British ministry of George Grenville to address the escalating size of the national debt, which had grown from roughly £72 million in 1755 to over £129 million by 1764 as a result of the Seven Years' War. The act imposed a tax on all legal documents including newspapers. Such a measure had been in place in Britain for decades, but its extension to the colonies was unprecedented. It was challenged by the North Americans on the grounds that such a tax could only be made by their own assemblies. In effect, Americans argued the measure was unconstitutional, a taxation without consent and a violation of their cherished English liberties. For the first time the colonies mobilised collectively to oppose the measure, creating a Stamp Act Congress to coordinate the boycotting of British goods. These protests spilled over onto the streets of ports like Boston and New York, with Sons of Liberty burning stamps and intimidating collectors. Such demonstrations were not only confined to the American seaboard but erupted in the West Indies as well. Islanders in St Kitts and Nevis, where the Pinney family had plantations, burnt stamps and pillaged royal property.[11]

Bristol merchants were understandably troubled by the disruption of trade caused by this resistance, and alongside their counterparts in Liverpool, York and many manufacturing towns petitioned for a repeal of the Act. On 11 January 1766 members of the Society of Merchant Venturers drew up a petition for repeal, fearing the serious economic repercussions that might result from a prolonged dislocation of trade. A further petition was launched the same evening by merchants and gentlemen outside the Society and signed by the mayor, aldermen and principal inhabitants.[12] No official endorsement of

---

[9] Guttridge (ed.), *American Correspondence*, p. 39.

[10] *Ibid.*, p. 45.

[11] *London Evening Post*, 22–25 Feb. 1766. For examples of interventions by the Sons of Liberty in New York, Charlestown, Connecticut, see *New York Gazette*, 2 and 9 Dec. 1765.

[12] *St James's Chronicle*, 11–14 Jan. 1766.

repeal came from the corporation because it laboured under the embarrassing predicament of having presented the freedom of the city to the author of the act, George Grenville, very probably at the behest of its own MP, Robert Nugent, who was a warm supporter of Grenville and his policies. Even so, the opposition to the Stamp Act was widely supported within the merchant community and the city at large. The corporation had the bells of the city rung to celebrate its repeal, and in the evening there were 'uncommon bonfires' and illuminations. According to one account, 'the Merchants trading to that Quarter of the World generously threw Money to the Populace'.[13] A few weeks later the Merchant Venturers thanked Lord Rockingham for removing an act 'injudicious and detrimental to the colonies as well as to the trade and manufacturers of the mother country'.[14]

Within a decade the merchants and Bristol trades were divided over America. By 1774 the North ministry had implemented a series of acts to punish the Americans for their continued recalcitrance to British policy, particularly in the wake of the Tea Party of 1773, when Bostonians dumped over three hundred chests of tea into the harbour as a protest to the continuation of the Townshend Revenue Act of 1767 and parliament's willingness to allow 17 million lb of surplus tea owned by the East India company to be sold in American markets. Massachusetts' charter was suspended; Boston's port was closed; troops occupied the city.

Conventional wisdom has it that Britons were angered by the Boston Tea Party and willing to back North's coercive policy.[15] Yet Bristolians were divided over America. In January 1775 the Society of Merchant Venturers split evenly over a motion to petition parliament for more conciliatory measures, with the presiding Master casting a negative vote. The pro-American faction regrouped to force the petition through at the next meeting, and so a petition from Merchants' Hall criticising government policy reached the Commons along with one from the Whig-dominated corporation. A subsequent set of petitions, drawn up after the war had begun, found the Bristol public as divided as the merchant elite. On 18 September loyalist merchants attempted to force an address commending government policy through the Common Council, only to have their motion blocked by lack of a quorum.[16] A counter-petition outlining the disastrous effects of coercion quickly followed. Organised by Richard Champion and Paul Farr under the guidance of Edmund Burke, the newly elected MP for Bristol, it eschewed the heavy anti-ministerialism of the City of London, whose previous petitions not only advocated a change in policy but the dismissal of the North ministry and a

---

[13] *New Hampshire Gazette*, 25 April 1766.

[14] Latimer, II, 371.

[15] P. D. G. Thomas, *Tea Party to Independence: The Third Phase of the American Revolution, 1773–1776* (Oxford, 1991); F. P. Lock, *Edmund Burke. Volume I, 1730–1784* (Oxford, 1998), ch. 10.

[16] *FFBJ*, 30 Sep. 1775, 7 Oct. 1775.

measure of parliamentary reform. In contrast, the Bristol petition concentrated on the economic impact of the war, both nationally and locally, hoping to win over many moderates who might have been estranged by the strident tone of the metropolitan demands. It managed to collect 978 signatures, with Champion apparently going door-to-door to rustle up support. This petition was quickly followed by a pro-ministerial address that mustered over nine hundred supporters.[17] Its architects were disappointed they did not win the official endorsement of the corporation, although the outgoing mayor, Charles Hotchkin, certainly tried.[18] Their address was presented to court by a bevy of Bristolian MPs. They included Richard Combe, MP for Alborough, and the son of a former mayor; Alderman James Laroche, MP for Bodmin, soon to be knighted for his loyalist activities; and Matthew Brickdale, the MP for Bristol between 1768 and 1774.

The petitioning campaign of October 1775 delved deeply into the Bristol population. The number of men who signed the two documents was equivalent to 47 per cent of the resident electorate, although most of them, some 52 per cent of the total, were not in fact enfranchised voters.[19] Assuming the total population of Bristol was in the region of 55,000 in 1775, this would mean that about 20 per cent of the adult male population (over twenty years of age) in the city was directly involved in this agitation. Both of these petitions were framed at meetings in Guildhall and then left at taverns for people to sign. Both were also published in London newspapers, in the case of the ministerial address, with signatories.'[20] These very public statements inevitably prompted speculations about how such support was mustered and how much pressure was put on ordinary freemen.[21]

Why did Bristolians become so polarised over America by 1775 when they were seemingly unanimous in 1765? The economic situation was perilous but not dire. The conciliatory petition of 1775 even emphasised the importance of recent imports of American wheat for the local market as well as 'the great quantity of other valuable commodities essential to our navigation

---

[17] James Bradley, *Popular Politics and the American Revolution in England* (Macon, GA, 1987), table 3.1, p. 65. John Phillips's figures are somewhat different: 800 for the address, 1200 for the petition. See John Phillips, 'Popular Politics in Unreformed England', *Journal of Modern History*, 52 (1980), 617–20. He misdates the petition, which was 1775 not 1776.

[18] *Sarah Farley's Bristol Journal*, 30 Sep. 1775.

[19] Phillips, 'Popular Politics', 611. Phillips calculated that 41 per cent of the addressers were not franchised and 62 per cent of the petitioners.

[20] G. H. Guttridge (ed.), *The Correspondence of Edmund Burke* (Cambridge, 1961), III, 221. See also Bradley, *Religion, Revolution and English Radicalism*, pp. 330–3; *London Evening Post*, 10–12 Oct. 1775; *London Gazette*, 3–7 Oct. 1775.

[21] *London Evening Post*, 17–19 Oct. 1775; *General Evening Post*, 21–24 Oct. 1775, comment by a 'Lover of Truth'. On the organisation of the 1775 petition see Bradley, *Religion, Revolution and English Radicalism*, pp. 332–5, and *Popular Politics*, pp. 117–18. Champion said he had been unable to get an account of the addressers' actions printed in the London newspapers in a letter to the Duke of Portland, 5 October 1775, but his subsequent actions may have been successful.

and commerce'.[22] It did so to underline the potential losses Bristol might suffer if the political situation deteriorated any further. Even so, there was no straightforward relationship between attitudes towards America and the fortunes of business. One could just as easily attribute the catastrophe to the reckless resistance of the colonists as to government intransigence. Those who switched their assets to accommodate wartime contingencies were not necessarily war-hungry ministerialists either. Among the owners of privateers, for example, eight of the top fifteen were very visible ministerial supporters. They included Lowbridge Bright, a merchant banker on Queen Square; Richard Tombs, a shipwright from St Nicholas; Richard Meyler and John Maxse, both West India brokers at the Exchange. Yet John Noble, the sheriff in 1775 and a prominent privateer, signed the conciliatory petition in September 1775, and voted for pro-American candidates in 1774. Similarly Richard Bright, the co-partner of the *Renown* with his cousin Lowbridge, remained an active oppositionist. He was a prominent member of the Whig Union Club and agitated for a change of ministry at Merchants' Hall in 1779.[23] Clearly perspectives on the war were influenced by whom one might blame for the conflict as the possibilities for reconciliation diminished.

Disagreements over America were political as well as economic because the struggle opened up new vistas, disturbing the customary ways in which British politics had been practised. To begin with, the American conflict forced contemporaries to define the lines of authority in an empire that had grown incrementally, with different charters, rights and privileges. Britain was so habituated to a notion of an empire of trade that when it inherited vast tracts of America from the French after the Seven Years' War, it stumbled into the problem of governing a continental empire.[24] For the new men who came to power under George III, this was an opportunity to push for a more centralised, authoritarian concept of imperial rule, something that had been advocated since the late 1740s.[25] As the American conflict unfolded, they insisted on an unqualified parliamentary sovereignty over the colonies, a notion that some of their parliamentary opponents found difficult to dislodge. Lord Rockingham's circle, for example, played an important role in the repeal of the Stamp Act, yet it supported a declaratory act endorsing parliamentary sovereignty. Once the war began, it found it difficult to sustain this position and address American grievances sympathetically, especially as the colonists insisted upon the rights of assemblies to tax themselves. The Bristol

---

[22] *London Evening Post*, 10–12 Oct. 1775.
[23] For the privateers, see TNA, HCA 26/33–4; *The Bristol Contest* (Bristol, 1781), p. 4. For the amendment, see *General Advertiser*, 7 July 1779.
[24] Nicholas Rogers, 'From Vernon to Wolfe: Empire and Identity in the British Atlantic World of the Mid-Eighteenth Century', in *The Culture of the Seven Years' War*, ed. Frans De Bryn and Shaun Regan (Toronto, 2013), pp. 26–58.
[25] Sarah Kinkel, 'The King's Pirates? Naval Enforcement of Imperial Authority, 1740–1776', *William and Mary Quarterly*, 71:1 (2014), 3–34.

MP Edmund Burke only did so by advocating an overriding but 'sleeping sovereignty'.

Ministerial allies exploited this vulnerability. Prior to the loyalist address in Bristol, John Wesley wrote a trenchant pamphlet describing the pro-Americans in Britain as crypto-republicans ready to sow anarchy through civil war. Wesley offered no concessions to the colonial assemblies, which he regarded as corporations whose authority flowed from the king. In his eyes, parliamentary sovereignty had real substance. The king in parliament, as Wesley conservatively framed it, could tax all subjects, whether formally represented in parliament or not. Claims about no taxation without representation were irrelevant. So were arguments vindicating consent through social contract theory, one Americans adopted through a radical reading of John Locke.[26] No one existed in a state of nature, Wesley insisted. When British emigrants ventured to the American wilderness they did so as subjects of the crown, to whom they still owed allegiance. Republican independence, Wesley assured his American brethren, would not give them greater liberty than they already enjoyed.[27] Indeed, the existence of slavery within the colonies and the rough treatment handed out to loyalists exposed the hypocrisy of Americans who carped about liberty but acted tyrannically.

Wesley's *Calm Address* sold very well; according to his own account, forty thousand copies in the space of three weeks.[28] It was part of his new offensive against pro-American sentiment, which he feared was undermining respect for the king and frustrating a resolution of the crisis. In letters to the Earl of Dartmouth and Lord North he compared the current situation to the 1640s; rising disaffection and distress at home could explode into republican anarchy. 'As I travel four or five thousand miles every year', Wesley told North,

> I have an opportunity of conversing freely with more persons of every denomination than any one else in the three kingdoms. I cannot but know the general disposition of the people – English, Scots, and Irish; and I know the majority of them are exasperated almost to madness, Exactly so they were throughout England and Scotland about the year 1640; and in a great measure by the same means – by inflammatory papers which were spread, as they are now, with the utmost diligence in every corner of the land.[29]

As the title suggests, the *Calm Address* was designed to dissipate this bubbling ferment.

[26] T. H. Breen, *American Insurgents, American Patriots. The Revolution of the People* (New York, 2010).
[27] John Wesley, *A Calm Address to our American Colonies* (Bristol, 1775).
[28] John Wesley to Thomas Rankin, London, 20 Oct. 1775, in John Telford (ed.), *The Letters of John Wesley* (8 vols, London, 1931), VI, 182. See also Kenneth E. Rowe, 'Charles Wesley's Letter Sheds Light on John Wesley's Activism during the Revolutionary War', *Methodist History*, 45:3 (2007), 190.
[29] *Letters of John Wesley*, VI, 155–64, quote 163.

Wesley's opponents saw things differently. To them the *Calm Address* was anything but. It was inflammatory, provocative and signalled a complete volte-face on the part of the Methodist celebrity. This was important because Wesley had a strong following in Bristol, preaching to thousands of the lower and middling ranks at public, open-air sermons.[30] The city was also the site of the first permanent Methodist chapel and a distribution point for the many tracts the sect promoted.[31] In the circumstances Wesley's new position on the war could not be ignored.

One of the first into the fray was Caleb Evans, the Baptist minister of Broadmead chapel. He accused Wesley of switching sides in the hope of preferment. Writing as 'Americanus' in the *Gentleman's Magazine*, Evans charged Wesley with having 'one eye upon a pension and another upon heaven; one hand stretched out to the K—g, the other raised up to God'.[32] In subsequent letters Evans reminded Wesley that he had previously recommended a pro-American tract to people in Bristol, among them James Rouquet, the curate of St Werburgh and a trustee of Wesley's will of 1770. Wesley even gave his pro-American tract to William Pine, his former publisher, who extracted it in the *Bristol Gazette*.[33] Evans also accused him of plagiarism, of lifting large sections of Samuel Johnson's *Taxation no Tyranny* without attribution. Both of these charges, of plagiarism and political caprice, made Wesley squirm. They resulted in denials and half-hearted recantations. Yet the one thing Wesley refused to admit was that he had supported the American Henry Cruger in the 1774 Bristol election, a matter that would have cemented his reputation as a political turncoat.[34]

Evans was not only interested in impugning Wesley's reputation; he marshaled some familiar Lockeian arguments to buttress his critique. Taxation by consent inhered from man's social contract with society; it was 'the very soul and vital spirit' of freedom, confirmed by parliament despite its imperfect representation. Evans reminded Bristolians that Americans were not represented in the British parliament, even notionally; their property rights were guaranteed by their assemblies, and for over a century successive British governments had accepted this. Although Evans never emphasised

[30] Andrew Oliver (ed.), *The Journal of Samuel Curwen, Loyalist* (2 vols, Cambridge, MA, 1972), pp. 400, 402.
[31] Jonathan Barry, 'The Press and the Politics of Culture in Bristol 1660–1775', in *Culture, Politics and Society in Britain, 1660–1800*, ed. Jeremy Black and Jeremy Gregory (Manchester, 1991), pp. 49–81.
[32] *Gentleman's Magazine*, 45 (1775), p. 561.
[33] For the will, see 'John Wesley's 1770 Will', *Proceedings of the Wesley Historical Society*, 54 (2003), 29–38.
[34] Henry Abelove, 'John Wesley's Plagiarism of Samuel Johnson and its Contemporary Reception', *Huntington Library Quarterly*, 59:1 (1996), 73–9. For Wesley's retraction, see *Gazetteer*, 13 Dec. 1775, reprinted in *Letters*, VI, 194–5. For Evans's accusations about Wesley, the plagiarist and turncoat, see Caleb Evans, *A Letter to the Reverend John Wesley occasioned by his Calm Address to the American Colonies* (Bristol, 1775).

the constitutional authority of colonial assemblies to tax themselves as much as his contemporary Americans, [35] he was adamant that Americans could rightly reject British taxation without appropriate representation. Wesley's insistence on the ubiquity of royal power struck him as dangerously authoritarian. Consensual taxation was enshrined in the Magna Charta, recognised in various statutes and jurisdictions, and consolidated by the revolution settlement of 1688, when a Convention Parliament replaced one monarch with another. The people as represented by parliament were the real source of power, and so both historically and practically taxation was a matter of consent.

Political disagreements over America had domestic ramifications. The debate over America's lack of representation in the British parliament raised the question of who else was unrepresented. If taxation implied consent, should not all taxpayers be represented? Should taxpayers include women, at least women whose legal personality was not subsumed in their husbands? Caleb Evans recognised the defects of British representation, but thought the existence of a potwalloper franchise established the principle that tax-paying male householders were entitled to the vote. Wesley, by contrast, was not at all troubled by the social inequities of the vote. Most people were rightfully denied the franchise because they were either too ignorant, idle, or dependent, women included. For the leader of the Methodist movement, whose followers were principally women, the issue of a female franchise was simply off the agenda.[36] Yet in the preface to the second edition of his tract, Wesley inadvertently opened up the question of the female vote by ridiculing Evans as a fictional Montesquieu who would confer the franchise on all who have free will, including women.[37] Wesley clearly thought this idea preposterous, but the idea was picked up in the Bristol press. 'How far the Ladies have really a will of their own', wrote one correspondent of *Sarah Farley's Bristol Journal*, 'is a point that perhaps Mrs. Wesley can better determine than her husband.' As far as this writer was concerned, it was a defect in the constitution that spinsters and widows could not vote, and he/she invited readers to ask the sisters of gentlemanly associators whether indeed they had free will.[38]

This debate revealed how difficult it was to control the parameters of the debate over political citizenship once the issue of no taxation without representation had been aired. As the conflict with America deepened and pro-Americans confronted a parliament intransigently committed to war, or at least to war-based bargaining positions, so the issue of America and

---

[35] On this theme, see Eliga Gould, 'Liberty and Modernity: The American Revolution and the Making of Parliament's Imperial History', in *Exclusionary Empire. English Liberty Overseas, 1600–1900*, ed. Jack P. Greene (Cambridge, 2010), pp. 112–31.

[36] Wesley, *Calm Address*, p. 6; Evans, *A Letter to Wesley*, pp. 8–9.

[37] Wesley, *Calm Address*, 2nd edn (London, 1775), pp. v–vi; see also John Fletcher, *A Vindication of the Reverend Mr. Wesley's Calm Address* (London, 1776), pp. 16–17.

[38] *Sarah Farley's Bristol Journal*, 2 Dec. 1775.

parliamentary reform became increasingly intertwined. This was a blessing and a curse. A blessing in that the political agenda expanded; a curse in that it was difficult a mobilise public opinion around one consistent goal. Many believed the first impediment to American reconciliation was a corrupt Commons, but there were various solutions to how this might be redressed: by reducing the sinews of clientage; by more frequent elections; by extending the franchise or eliminating its more exclusive features; by redistributing parliamentary seats; or by finding ways to make MPs more accountable to their constituents. The range of options generated disagreements as the subsequent history of the Association movement revealed. It also bedevilled Bristol politics, where proposals to enhance the independence of the Commons ranged from reducing court influence to universal manhood suffrage, the latter advocated by 'A Real Friend of the People' in 1781.[39]

Certainly the American conflict generated demands for a more capaciously open politics. Americans themselves drew inspiration from John Wilkes, who exploited the desire for a robust, libertarian politics by challenging the questionably legal forms of action by which governments muzzled criticism of their policies. General warrants, narrow definitions of libel law, informations, that is, affidavits generated with a view to prosecution but not linked specifically to an indictment, were all challenged as violations of liberty. So was Wilkes's own exclusion from the House of Commons, despite having been elected by the Middlesex voters in 1768. This exclusion generated mass protests and a petitioning campaign that anticipated those of 1775. Organised through clubs, committees and associations, it challenged the conventional channels by which political issues were marshalled and managed.[40]

As a large freeman borough with a vibrant press, Bristol was party to these challenges. In March 1769 an Independent Society was founded by the merchant Samuel Peach to promote radical activism, 'unconnected with Party, and uninfluenc'd by ministerial Power'.[41] This was accompanied by efforts to invigorate parliamentary reform. Extracts from the writings of radical Whigs such as Algernon Sydney were printed in the newspapers. Much store was laid on developing political literacy through clubs and associations, particularly on mobilising the good sense of craftsmen and shopkeepers. As one manifesto boldly insisted, there was 'often more real publick wisdom and sagacity in shops and manufactories than in the Cabinets of Princes'.[42]

As Wilkes's battle for Middlesex was unfolding, Bristol instructed its MPs, Matthew Brickdale and Lord Clare, to support measures to make the legal

---

[39] *The Bristol Contest* (Bristol, 1781), p. 104.

[40] On these themes, see George Rudé, *Wilkes and Liberty* (Oxford, 1962); John Brewer, *Party Ideology and Popular Politics at the Accession of George III* (Cambridge, 1976); Kathleen Wilson, *The Sense of the People: Politics, Culture and Imperialism in England, 1715–1785* (Cambridge, 1995).

[41] *FFBJ*, 5 Nov. 1768, 25 Feb. 1769, 11 March 1769, 21 Oct. 1769; on Peach as the founder of the Independent Society, see *Burke Correspondence*, III, 3.

[42] *Burke Correspondence*, II, 398.

system and parliament more accountable to the citizenry, the latter through trimming patronage in the Commons and promoting frequent elections.[43] In the wake of the Townshend revenue acts of 1767, electors also asked their MPs to repeal import taxes on British manufacturing goods to America, and generally to promote better relations between Britain and its American colonies. These demands were followed by a petition to the crown in July 1769 which deplored the deteriorating situation in America and the persecution of John Wilkes. It drew 2245 signatories, more than any other petitioning borough save London and Westminster. Its sponsors clearly hoped Bristol would emulate the City of London as a major site of radical opposition. One self-styled Atticus hoped 'the rotten foundations of Bribery and Corruption' would be shaken by such activism.[44]

Mass petitioning on this scale was unprecedented in Bristol, but instructions to MPs were not. The Merchant Venturers had been privately instructing MPs on matters of trade for decades, and publicly instructions had been issued in 1733, 1742 and 1756, alerting MPs to pressing matters within the constituency. On the last two occasions they featured demands for parliamentary reform that were not so very different from those voiced in 1769.[45] So there was some continuity between the instructions of the mid-century decades and those of the Wilkite era. Both implied a theory of representation in which MPs were essentially 'attorneys of the people', delegates who were supposed to represent the popular will of their constituencies.[46] In 1769, however, the issue of delegatory representation came to a head because Robert Nugent, Lord Clare, denied he was bound by it. He declared he would only take advice with an eye to the 'character, situation, abilities and temper of mind' of his constituents, a supercilious remark that smacked of elitism. Consequently, when Bristolians presented a mass petition to the throne on the Wilkes imbroglio, they denounced Clare for ignoring their instructions and declared he had lost their confidence.[47]

This vote of non-confidence was important because it upset the electoral arrangement reached by the two leading factions in Bristol to share the constituency. Negotiated in 1761, this agreement was supposed to last for three successive general elections to allow the leading merchants to cast aside old political and sectarian rivalries and focus on issues pertinent to Bristol's commercial prosperity.[48] Such a patrician deal suited the oligarchs; but it denied ordinary freemen the right to choose their MP, offering them only a bumper electoral dinner at the expense of the two leading caucuses. This

---

[43] *FFBJ*, 11 March 1769; *Bath Journal*, 13 March 1769.

[44] *FFBJ*, 8 July 1769, cited by Rudé, *Wilkes and Liberty*, p. 112. For signatories, see appendix VII.

[45] *FFBJ*, 11 Dec. 1756; Rogers, *Whigs and Cities*, p. 300.

[46] *Craftsmen*, 22 Dec. 1739; Rogers, *Whigs and Cities*, p. 242.

[47] *Bath Journal*, 24 July 1769; for Clare's remarks, see *London Chronicle*, 18–21 March 1769.

[48] On the growing rapprochement between elite Whigs and Tories, see Rogers, *Whigs and Cities*, pp. 290–303.

might suit client voters but it was certainly unacceptable to the well-meaning middling men of a predominantly Dissenting persuasion who constituted the reformist wing of Bristol electors. One 'independent elector' denounced such compromises as 'dangerous and destructive to the liberties of this city' and reminded Bristolians that it meant a narrow group of no more than a dozen men, a joint committee of the Steadfast and Union Societies, determined the representation of the city.[49]

The final election in which the two principal caucuses carved up the constituency should have been in 1774, at least under the 1761 agreement. It came unstuck because of Clare's deepening unpopularity. Not only did Clare flout the wishes of the new Whigs over the 1769 instructions; he was thought to be a time-server in high politics and a flunkey for office, particularly lucrative ones in Ireland. To cap everything he had seconded George Grenville's motion for the Stamp Act of 1764 and supported coercive measures against the colonists, actions that pro-Americans in Bristol found particularly hard to swallow. While Clare still had his supporters among the mercantile elite, it quickly became apparent that he lacked popular support. A poll in his name was kept open in 1774, but it became very obvious that his candidature was a non-starter.

A space thus opened up for another Whig candidate in 1774, yet there was no consensus as to who that might be, as the radical wing of the party was hostile to electoral compromise. Its candidate was Henry Cruger, an American merchant from New York, who had chaired the meeting to instruct MPs in 1769 and prior to that had delivered the petition for the repeal of the Stamp Act to Bristol's representatives in parliament. His candidature had been on the cards since 1772, when he and his father-in-law, Samuel Peach, arranged a visit of John Wilkes to Bristol and organised a new set of instructions to MPs, demanding shorter parliaments. Cruger's nomination was formally ratified by the Independent Society in June 1774, while the American was on a business trip to New York.[50] It was backed by John Wilkes and other radicals at a London rally of the Bristol out-voters in October 1774. There resolutions were tabled pressing for parliamentary reform and the repeal of North's Coercive Acts.[51]

Moderates within the Whig party were troubled by this development. Richard Champion, a Quaker and porcelain manufacturer, disliked the radical tone of the Independents and feared its activities might prove a tonic to the kinds of resistance exemplified by the Boston Tea Party. He acknowledged there was 'a great Discontent in the town against the present Members' and resolved to promote two reformers, the Rockingham protégé Edmund Burke

---

[49] *FFBJ*, 19 March 1768.
[50] P. T. Underdown, 'Henry Cruger and Edmund Burke: Colleagues and Rivals at the Bristol Election of 1774', *William and Mary Quarterly*, 51:1 (1958), 17–18; *Bristol Gazette*, 9 Jan. 1772; *FFBJ*, 22 Feb. 1772.
[51] *Gazetteer*, 11 Oct. 1774. See also a broadside by 'Smoke'm' dated 18 Oct. 1774, in BRL, Electoral broadsides, 1774–1790.

and John Dunning, the Recorder of Bristol and a follower of Lords Shelburne and Chatham. Dunning declined, leaving Champion to consider Burke. Yet in the summer of 1774, Champion still thought Clare a plausible candidate; he would not commit himself to pairing Burke with Cruger until that reality stared him in the face. 'We are in a state of confusion and uproar', remarked one commentator, 'the Patriots, with the Almighty Mob, are determined to turn out the old members. They have sent to Mr. Burke to beg he will come down and join Mr. Cruger.'[52] How enthusiastic Bristolians were for this pairing is debatable. When Burke was nominated on the second day of the poll there were shouts of 'Cruger only'.[53] Between the equivocations of Champion and the reservations of radicals, the pairing was loose, to say the least. Each candidate had their separate committees, agents, taverns and managers, with Cruger's attorney, Thomas Symonds, operating as a liaison between the two groups. There was no joint election programme, merely a few broadsides that linked the two Whig candidates as a desirable pairing in this two-member, two-vote constituency.

The 1774 election was a long, hard-fought contest between three candidates: Matthew Brickdale, the Tory incumbent, Henry Cruger and Edmund Burke. Bristol voters were deluged with squibs and broadsides impugning the character of the candidates and their fitness to represent Bristol.[54] Matthew Brickdale was depicted as a dullard out of depth in the current crisis, a man propelled into national politics on the reputation of his father, one of the founders of the Steadfast Society. Henry Cruger was cast as a mercantile libertine, a Yankee entertaining women of easy virtue at his party headquarters. Edmund Burke was seen as the silver-tongued orator, a smooth operator under the clientage of Lord Rockingham, whose primary allegiance would always be to his aristocratic faction.

Amid this scurrility, the American conflict cast a shadow over the whole campaign. Although historians have sometimes argued that the conflict in America was a marginal issue in the 1774 election, this was certainly not true of an Atlantic port like Bristol.[55] Cruger was accused of being puffed up with 'American patriotism and politicks'.[56] He was a 'Bill of Rights Man', claimed

---

[52] Cited in G. E. Weare, *Edmund Burke's Connection with Bristol, From 1774 till 1780* (Bristol, 1894), p. 25.

[53] *The Bristol Poll* (Bristol, 1774), p. 4.

[54] F.P. Lock, *Edmund Burke*, pp. 375–6, cites about one hundred different handbills from BRL, 'Bristol Election 1774' (B 18197) and 'Bristol Elections, 1774–1790' (B 6979).

[55] Bernard Donoughue, *British Politics and the American Revolution* (London, 1964), pp. 177–200. Frank O'Gorman states that only fourteen of the sixty-nine boroughs contested in 1774 revealed divisions on the American issue, although he stresses the importance of the issue in the petitions and addresses, following Bradley. See Frank O'Gorman, *Voters, Patrons and Parties. The Unreformed Electoral System of Hanoverian England 1734–1832* (Oxford, 1989), p. 294.

[56] Kenneth Morgan (ed.), *The Bright-Meyler Papers: A Bristol–West Indian Connection, 1732–1837* (Oxford, 2007), p. 470.

one customs officer, an appellation that conjured up the Wilkite agitation and by extension the waterfront protests in North America by the Sons of Liberty. 'In the present unhappy disagreement between England and America it is the duty of every elective body in the Kingdom to send up to the next Parliament men cool and dispassionate, of honest hearts and sound under-standing', declared one ministerial spokesman.[57] By this criterion Cruger was too much of a firebrand to merit election, although his own supporters coun-tered this accusation by stressing his commercial expertise and his personal stake in reaching a settlement with the Americans. Burke, by contrast, was praised for his role in repealing the Stamp Act, and for opposing the Quebec and Boston Port Acts, the latest enactments of Lord North's ministry. His steadfast stand on the latter, thought one 'Freeholder', at least offered the prospect of arresting 'the Sinking Commerce of this opulent City'.[58]

Brickdale's attitude towards America was regarded by his opponents as dogmatically authoritarian, and one squib threw in some local history to sully his credentials. It reminded voters that Matt's brother was none other than 'Don John Brickdale', a reference to his controversial role as a turnpike commissioner at Don John Cross in 1749 and to his aggressive response to the colliers in 1753. In this electoral satire all 'Catholic' voters were invited to Clifton to meet Don John himself, and to defeat 'the dissenting Hereticks of all denominations', a sly reference to the High Tory credentials of the Brickdale family, and to Matthew Brickdale's endorsement of the Quebec Act, which officially sanctioned Catholicism as the religion of the Canadiens and threatened to revitalise it within the empire. This notion of a Catholic revival, encouraged by an authoritarian ministry of which Brickdale was a minion, was a potent fiction that simmered throughout the American war and would precipitate riots in Glascow and Edinburgh in 1779 and more dramatically in London the following year. It was an issue that mobilised many Quakers and Protestant Dissenters against the ministry.[59]

National issues were certainly raised at the Bristol hustings in 1774, yet the length of the contest, an unprecedented twenty-three days, gave all parties the opportunity to create freemen and mobilise new voters. As we have seen earlier, generating new voters after the writ of the election had been issued was hardly new to Bristol. However, it reached new highs in 1774.[60] No fewer than 1100 new freemen were admitted from the issue of the writ to the

---

[57] Weare, *Edmund Burke's Connection*, p. 69. On Cruger as the 'Bill of Rights' man, see Quilici, 'Turmoil in a City', p. 243, citing BA, Samuel Lowder Papers, 11 and 28 Oct. 1774. For the ideological concordance of Wilkite and American radicalism, see Pauline Maier, *From Resistance to Rebellion. Colonial Radicals and the Development of American Opposition to Britain, 1765–1776* (New York, 1972), chs 6–7.

[58] Weare, *Edmund Burke's Connection*, p. 66.

[59] Charles William, Earl Fitzwilliam and Sir Richard Bourke (eds), *Correspondence of the Right Honorable Edmund Burke* (London, 1844), I, 466.

[60] In 1754, for example, 889 freemen were admitted in March and April, but the admis-sions fizzled out a week before the election.

nomination of the candidates, a mere seven days, and a further 900 freemen were admitted during the actual poll. By any criterion this was completely illegal. A total of 2080 freemen were created in a matter of weeks, as many as 39 per cent of the number of voters. According to contemporary accounts, party agents arranged for these men to obtain burgess certificates, corralling them in small groups of five to ten at a time. Tagged with party cockades, they were then marched to the hustings to cast their votes and then they were provided with polling money, about seven shillings and sixpence, to spend at local taverns.[61] One way to obtain a freedom in Bristol was to marry the daughter or widow of a former freeman. An astonishing six hundred voters appear to have obtained the freedom in this manner, likely exposing some to charges of bigamy, unless contemporaries took these 'electoral marriages' extremely lightly. The devious arts of creating voters was practised by all candidates, with the 'radical' Cruger being the most culpable. He secured 42 per cent of all these new voters, compared to Burke's 35 and Brickdale's 23 per cent. Of Burke's total number of voters, 43 per cent were newly admitted freemen; the corresponding figure for Brickdale was 31 per cent.[62] Ultimately Brickdale, the defeated candidate, was unable to prove his malpractices were less serious than others, although it is instructive to note that he was only 251 votes behind Burke, whose agents registered 258 more admissions after the writ was issued. Had their success in enrolling freemen been reversed, Brickdale would have narrowly defeated Burke.

Does this electoral chicanery vitiate any conclusions we might want to make about the meaning of the 1774 election beyond reducing it to a matter to superior electoral organisation? It is a question worth asking, for it has seldom been confronted in the literature. Curiously, the Namierite historians who studied Bristol were never really interested in the nitty-gritty of client politics; their analyses stopped with people like Richard Champion, in the archival evidence of the major political players.[63] There is an ongoing assumption in their work that voters can be manipulated like marionettes. As for historians interested in the issues that spiralled around America and the social divisions these revealed, the creation of new freeman is certainly acknowledged. James Bradley notes the flood of freemen before the elections, but he uses it as a coordinate of partisan behaviour, measuring these voters against those who were more experienced. He assumes the new voters were self-motivated, not bought. Older historians like G. E. Weare zone in on the venality, but largely for Hogarthian colour. Only Elizabeth Baigent, an urban geographer, addresses the issue directly, arguing that this dependent vote

---

[61] HC, *Parliamentary Papers, Select Committee on Bribery* (1835), pp. 377–8; Weare, *Edmund Burke's Connection*, p. 84.

[62] HC, *Parliamentary Papers, Bribery*, pp. 377–8; Weare, *Edmund Burke's Connection*, p. 118.

[63] Ian R. Christie, 'Henry Cruger and the End of Edmund Burke's Connection with Bristol', *Transactions of the Bristol and Gloucester Archeological Society*, 74 (1955), 153–70.

complicates, if it does not confound, a class analysis of electoral behaviour in Bristol politics.[64]

On the face of it the election was won by the agents who managed these new voters. At least they made a major contribution to the result. Yet one should not assume all new voters were necessary dependent ones, for what is remarkable about this election is the high number of new voters from London, where Cruger was able to exploit his Wilkite connections to advantage. Overall, the electoral geography of 1774 suggests a landslide vote for Henry Cruger. He won virtually every parish by a wide margin, including some High Church parishes where one would have expected Brickdale's interest to have prevailed. Although the clergy overwhelmingly sided with Brickdale, Cruger defeated Brickdale in every parish save two, All Saints and St Michael. He was really only decisively defeated in the latter, where the rector was Samuel Seyer, the master of Bristol Grammar School. Cruger scored spectacularly in those parishes where the Dissenting interest was well placed, such as St James, where he gained 625 votes to Brickdale's 323, winning the support of 73 per cent of the total vote there. The same was true of St Philip and St Jacob, an industrial parish that had many Presbyterians and Quakers. Here Cruger won 478 votes to Brickdale's 170, some 82 per cent of the vote in that locality. A more discriminating analysis, taken from a sample of the registers of nonconformist chapels, reveals that Cruger won over 80 per cent of the Presbyterian vote, over 82 per cent of the Baptist, and 73 per cent of the Quaker. Particularly noteworthy was the turnout from the Broadmead Baptist church, where Caleb Evans was a mobilising force.[65]

Cruger's support from the Dissenters of Bristol was important in one other respect. Richard Champion predicted the American would fare badly among them because of his womanising ways. Champion thought Cruger a 'generous good natured Man – but one, who has not only given himself a Loose in the Youthful Follies of Life, but has at the same time preserved no Appearances. This in a City, whose inhabitants devoted chiefly to Trade, have a severe Cast of Manners, has subjected him to great disadvantages.' Particularly, Champion added, to 'the graver sort among the Dissenters'.[66] Yet Cruger's libertinism did not prove a handicap, probably because the Dissenters, like

---

[64] Weare, *Edmund Burke's Connection*; Bradley, *Religion, Revolution and English Radicalism*, pp. 223–4; Elizabeth Baigent, 'Economy and Society in Eighteenth-Century English Towns: Bristol in the 1770s', in *Urban Historical Geography: Recent Progress in Britain and Germany*, ed. Dietrich Deneke and Gareth Shaw (Cambridge, 1988), pp. 122–4. It is noteworthy that Baigent does not make much of the dependent vote in her later article with James Bradley, even though the evidence they produce on the social dimensions of electoral behaviour suggests it was an important factor. See Elizabeth Baigent and James E. Bradley, 'The Social Sources of Late Eighteenth-Century English Radicalism: Bristol in the 1770s and 1780s', *English Historical Review*, 124 (2009), 1075–1108.

[65] Bradley, *Religion, Revolution and English Radicalism*, pp. 235–8.

[66] Burke, *Correspondence*, III, 46–7. See also *The Bristol Contest*, p. 80, where Cruger is accused of having an 'immoral character'.

many other Bristolians who were not under the thumb of electoral managers, voted for measures not men. Cruger was the preferred candidate because he had a personal stake in resolving the American conflict and because his family connections in New York might prove extremely useful, especially since the possibilities of reconciliation were still high and formal war had still to be declared. 'Philanthropos' recommended Cruger because he knew something about the currency crisis in America where the restrictions on paper credit had resulted in long-term indebtedness to British merchants, to the tune of £2 million. Cruger would enrich the 'mercantile and manufacturing interest' of parliament, he opined; right now it was regrettably 'filled with a set of hare-brained Nimrods whose property is chiefly in land' and 'who understand commercial advantages just as much as they do ... squaring ... the circle'.[67]

Burke came in second because he had a proven pro-American record and could be relied upon to use his oratorical talents to engage the government's increasingly coercive stance against the colonists. He was 'the Man that boldly stood forth against that vile Boston Act', wrote a 'Freeholder'.[68] To be sure, some voters were troubled by his distaste for radical politics, particularly his refusal to be bound by constituency instructions as had Clare. They were probably among the small group who plumped (or voted only) for Cruger, in all some 6 per cent of Cruger's total vote. More were likely troubled by Burke the interloper, a rising star from an aristocratic faction, parachuted into Bristol politics by two Quakers, Richard Champion and Joseph Harford; a man who was angling for any urban seat, sounding out the possibilities of standing for the City of Westminster while negotiating over Bristol. This explains why 19 per cent of Cruger's voters paired him with the Tory Matthew Brickdale rather than Burke.[69] They were known entities, commercial men, members of Common Council, active in local politics. Yet in the end the overwhelming majority of opposition voters paired Burke with Cruger in a search for a suitable solution to the America crisis. One spokesman writing as 'the Jovial Huntsman' thought they would work to repeal 'those cursed acts that are so lately made';[70] that is, the Coercive Acts, and the Quebec Act, which denied Canadiens a representative assembly and officially tolerated Catholicism, a retrograde step in the eyes of those contemporaries who equated popery with despotism.

Even allowing for the venal vote, the 1774 election was an assertion of the need for a conciliatory approach to the American conflict. The North ministry was put on notice that its policies were unacceptable to England's

---

[67] Cited in Weare, *Edmund Burke's Connection*, p. 71.

[68] BRL, B 6979, 'Bristol Elections 1774–1790, Addresses, Squibs, Songs', 87, cited in Bradley, *Religion, Revolution and English Radicalism*, p. 214.

[69] The figures are calculated from Weare, *Edmund Burke's Connection*, p. 75. For the poll, see *The Bristol Poll Book* (Bristol, 1774). For Burke's hopes for Westminster, see *Burke Correspondence*, III, 51–3, 58–9.

[70] 'Bristol Elections', 171, cited in Bradley, *Religion, Revolution and English Radicalism*, p. 214.

second city. Yet six years later, in the general election of 1780, Burke resigned before polling began and Cruger went down to a crushing defeat, castigated as a damn Yankee. How did this happen? Why did Bristol become more loyalist over time?

A year after the 1774 election Bristolians were evenly divided over the merits of the government's coercive policy towards America. The pro-government address and anti-ministerial petition in large part reflected the state of play during the election itself. Of the petitioners who voted in 1774, over 90 per cent had cast their ballots for Burke and Cruger. Of the addressers, 74 per cent had cast their ballots for Brickdale, again showing considerable continuity. Yet the voting pattern among the addressers does show some movement towards the ministerial camp, because it also reveals that one in four addressers had in fact switched sides, having voted for the anti-ministerial candidates a year earlier. Perhaps the outbreak of war had posed problems of allegiance; perhaps some had become disenchanted by opposition rhetoric, which could appear opportunistic and self-serving. As *Bonner and Middleton's Journal* stridently put it in March 1776: 'Of all the wretches that ever disgraced the name of Patriot, none come up to those pests of society, those murderous enemies of Britain, our *Anglo-Yankies*, that is, the English abettors of American rebels.'[71] Or perhaps the addressers were persuaded that the actions of the Americans in destroying property (the chests of tea in Boston harbour, for example) and defying government had reached intolerable limits; that the Americans, for all their professions of loyalty to the crown, were really seeking independence. As one correspondent in the *Morning Chronicle* exclaimed, 'whatever their declarations may be, it is from their actions too plain that they mean war – war, I say – for the purpose of Independency'.[72]

The shift to loyalism was nonetheless protracted and uneven. On the Bristol Common Council, for example, there was continuing contention over America and efforts to push through pro-ministerial addresses met with continued opposition. In 1777, in the wake of the military successes of Sir William Howe and his brother in Long Island and New York, the motion for an address congratulating George III on these victories passed by only one vote. Two years later, on the entry of France into the war, efforts to pass another loyal address were frustrated by the lack of a quorum within a Whig-dominated council.

Outside of the closed corporation, however, there were signs of growing antipathy towards the Americans. After the victory at Long Island, there were celebrations on Brandon Hill and an effigy of Washington was tarred and feathered at Pill and then hanged and burnt. Around the same time, effigies of Hancock and Adams were tarred, feathered and then burnt before the American coffee house near the White Lion Inn, the headquarters of

[71] *Bonner and Middleton's Bristol Journal*, 23 March 1776.
[72] *Morning Chronicle*, 19 April 1776.

the Bristol Tories.[73] These pro-ministerial celebrations were not as vigorous as those in Manchester and the West Riding of Yorkshire, where military contracts scarcely made up for the loss of the American market, but they were testimony to the growth of popular loyalism.

Among religious Dissenters there was still a hard core of pro-American sentiment and a deepening frustration with Lord North's policies.[74] Just before the American Declaration of Independence reached British shores, the Baptist preacher Caleb Evans warmly endorsed Richard Price's demand for American self-government in his *Observations on the Nature of Civil Liberty*, a tract that sold 60,000 copies within a few weeks and quickly went into five editions.[75] In his own pamphlet, *Political Sophistry Detected*, the charismatic leader of the Broadmead chapel described the American quest for liberty as 'one of the best causes of the world'.[76] It was his congregation and others like it, people who hailed from the middling classes, whom Samuel Curwen identified as 'warm Americans' in his travels through the south-west and Midlands.[77]

Evans believed that government was fundamentally for the benefit of the people, 'who are left therefore to chuse for themselves that form of government which they judge to be most for their good'.[78] To Church-and-King men this was political apostasy of the first order, especially so when the publication of Evans's tract happened to coincide with the Declaration of American Independence. It must have confirmed their suspicions that American sympathisers were crypto-republicans, subversives within the British state. These misgivings fitted with the constant refrain that flowed from loyalist petitions and tracts about the corrupting influence of 'patriot', pro-American discourse.

Early in 1777, loyalists on Common Council attempted to pass a congratulatory address to the king on his military successes in America, only to fail for lack of a quorum. An effort was also made to mobilise the freemen in support of an address, but the turnout proved disappointing.[79] A week later, however, loyalism received a dramatic boost when Bristol suffered several outbreaks of arson at the waterside. On 15 January 1777, fires broke out on three separate merchantmen, the *Savanna la Mar*, the *Fame* and the *Hibernia*, and also at the warehouse of James Morgan in Cypher Lane near Corn Street. Because the fires appeared at different locations within a short space of time, the mayor, Andrew Pope, believed they were the act of several saboteurs whose

---

[73] Latimer, II, 392; *Bonner and Middleton's Bristol Journal*, 19 Oct. 1776.

[74] Baigent and Bradley, 'Social Sources of Late Eighteenth-Century Radicalism', 1103–5. A few rich Presbyterian merchants had switched to the loyalists.

[75] Robert E. Toohey, *Liberty and Empire. British Radical Solutions to the American Problem 1774–1776* (Lexington, 1978), p. 100.

[76] Caleb Evans, *Political Sophistry Detected* (Bristol, 1776), p. 35. For references to Richard Price see pp. 30–1, 33–4.

[77] *Journal of Samuel Curwen*, p. 74.

[78] Evans, *Political Sophistry*, p. 17.

[79] *Sussex Weekly Advertiser*, 20 Jan. 1777.

'Design was to destroy the whole city'.[80] The secretary of state, Lord Suffolk concurred: it was 'a Design of the blackest Nature'. He offered a pardon to any accomplice who could provide evidence of the plot and a £1000 reward, a huge sum by eighteenth-century standards, complementing those more typical rewards of £50 or £100 that were offered by the corporation, the Merchant Venturers, the fire wardens, Morgan, and some loyalist merchants who owned the ships.[81] On 19 January, as troops were marching from Gloucester, further fires broke out along Quay Lane at the back of Small Street. The damage was not great: several thousand pounds' worth of Spanish wool and materials, together with three warehouses. Yet the firemen spent four hours quenching the flames, fearing the blaze might spread to Broad Street and Small Street. As it was, the malt house next to St John's had to be pulled down to preserve the church; and the Bell tavern caught alight on five occasions.[82]

Arson threw Bristol into a panic. The mayor talked of people 'under the utmost Terror'. Another wrote of 'incendiaries that surround us. 'Tis out of the power of my pen to depict the horrible situation of the whole city.'[83] Gentlemen patrolled the streets all night; recruiting parties lent a hand; and the king's messenger arrived to confirm the government's resolution to get to the bottom of the business. In the aftermath of the scare, more evidence of a potential conspiracy came to light. Some combustibles were discovered in barrels of oil; a crude bomb was found in a warehouse, a 'globular machine' the size of a 6lb cannon ball, made of wire, filled with inflammable materials and covered with brown paper, pitch and rosin. Several people were taken up: one, an American sailor named Perry; another a deranged exhibitionist who told the constable 'he would discover something of moment' and fished out of his pocket a tinderbox and gunpowder, saying it was intended for an alderman's residence.[84] Most suspects were quickly released, but further fires were reported in early February, along with anonymous letters. One directed to Mr George Hannaford was found on St John's Bridge, Lewin's Mead, near Caleb Evans's congregation. It apologised for the 'ill success' of the venture, but urged comrades to

> be of good Courag & fear not, wee must stand or fal together. You rem[em]ber what our good Chief sayd when we saw him last that 'heel [he'll] go to hellgate but heel [he'll] turn the Constutione [Constitution] & raise the Wegs [Whigs] up again. Pray god the day may come for tho we don't prosper to our wishes in America, I beleev our scemes [schemes] here. There's a general plot laid & we nid [need] not fear.[85]

---

[80] TNA, SP 37/12, fols 5–6, 8, 12, 14,

[81] *London Gazette*, 18 Jan. 1777.

[82] SP 37/12, fol. 18; *Bath Chronicle*, 23 Jan. 1777.

[83] *Bath Chronicle*, 23 Jan. 1777; SP 37/12, fol. 18v.

[84] *St James's Chronicle*, 16–18 Jan. 1777, cited in Jessica Warner, *John the Painter. Terrorist of the American Revolution* (New York, 2004), p. 157.

[85] TNA, SP 37/12, fol. 37; also quoted in Warner, *John the Painter*, p. 159.

The mayor found this note troubling enough to send to the secretary of state. It might involve some nationwide conspiracy, he suggested. Certainly it implied a 'patriot' conspiracy, for there was corroborating evidence of a man who drifted through Bristol, a dark-haired, hollow-eyed man in a brown or pompadour coat, 5 feet 7 inches high. He was later identified as James Aitken, aka John the Painter. He had lodged at the Pithay, had burnt a shirt for tinder, and disappeared after one night's stay, leaving behind Richard Price's pamphlets on American liberty and Voltaire's *La Henriade*, an epic poem on the religious fanaticism and civil discord that informed the Siege of Paris of 1589.[86]

Soon after the Bristol fires Aitken was captured in Odiham, Hampshire, and taken to London to be interrogated by Sir John Fielding, the Bow Street magistrate. Fielding tried to discover his American connections, asking Aitken outright whether he knew General Washington. Aitken remained evasive, even taciturn, but he was eventually induced to open up to a fellow painter who had also been to America, one John Baldwin. Aitken confessed to Baldwin that he had had an interview with the American envoy in Paris, Silas Deane, who had given him money for his enterprise. Some newspapers elaborated on this, claiming Aitken had been given a bill of exchange worth £300, to be redeemed with a London merchant of Deane's acquaintance. This was untrue. Aitken had been given a very modest sum from Deane, nothing more than travelling expenses, yet Deane had not discouraged Aitken's plan to burn the dockyards and shipping in major ports, even if he probably thought the solo project a vain endeavour. Deane had even arranged for Aitken to have a passport signed by the French foreign minister, the Comte de Vergennes, and he also advised Aitken to visit Deane's former pupil and friend, Dr Edward Bancroft, when in London. Aitken did this, calling at Bancroft's home a few doors from Lord North's house on Downing Street. There he received a cool reception from this specialist in tropical medicine because Bancroft was actually a double agent, feeding the British government information about Franco-American relations and the very real possibility of an alliance. In the revelations that followed Bancroft was kept out of the picture; he was simply used by the government to draw out Deane so that there might be enough evidence for his extradition from France. Bancroft's name never surfaced in Aitken's trial at Winchester for attempting to burn down the ropeyard at Portsmouth, although it did appear in Aitken's printed confession before his execution.[87] At the trial, Baldwin, the star witness for the crown, made as much as he could of the American connection, and the loyalist press embellished this with reports that Aitken had sailed from America with none other than Benjamin Franklin, whose pamphlets were among the reading material the arsonist had left behind in Bristol. Again this was untrue. Franklin arrived in France with Arthur Lee,

---

[86] *Bath Chronicle*, 23 Jan. 1777; Warner, *John the Painter*, p. 153.
[87] *London Evening Post*, 15–17 March 1777.

joining Deane to solicit French military aid and win them over to American independence. Yet Aitken had mentioned Franklin's name to Baldwin and it was not implausible that Franklin was privy to Aitken's plan; at least the possible connections between Aitken and Franklin through the mediation of Deane were sensitive enough for Thomas Jefferson to buy Deane's letter book from a French blackmailer in 1788 and destroy it. It was the sort of shady evidence that tarnished the grand narrative of American liberty.[88]

Confronted with these plausible links, the loyalist press had a field day. Aitken's name-dropping, especially of Washington and Franklin, was deliciously exposed. Deane's endorsement of Aitken's plan was emphasised. The *London Evening Post* pleaded with the public to reserve judgement until Deane had a chance to respond to the accusations of complicity voiced at the Winchester trial, suggesting that Baldwin had been encouraged by the ministry to make extravagant claims.[89] But it was alleged (wrongly) that Deane left for the United States as soon as he was incriminated and in any case the narrative of American perfidy made better press. Certainly America's shadowy machinations made all talk of conciliation hollow. In one fictive report of Aitken's speech before the scaffold, the pro-American saboteur became a poor penitent painter wishing success to British arms 'against a set of rascally and villainous Rebels now in America'.[90] The paper gloatingly remarked that administrative vigilance had upset many domestic 'patriots' who privately sympathised with John the Painter. They did 'not happen to rank so high as honest John in the active part of patriotism, yet, in the theory and sentimental part of things, their souls are nevertheless perfectly congenial'.

It was talk like this that certainly troubled Burke. He had already witnessed a loyalist address in Bristol in early 1777 congratulating the king on the success of arms in New York and Long Island. Drafted just a day before the first outbreaks of arson, it drew 1270 signatures, over 300 more than in 1775.[91] Burke thought of mustering a counter-address, but then had second thoughts. It might backfire. The loyalist tail was up. As a deliberate snub to Burke and Cruger, this address, and two others, one from the Merchant Venturers and another from the corporation, were presented to the king by conservative MPs associated with Bristol. They were not presented by the incumbents, as would customarily have been the case.[92] Commentators maliciously suggested that the overwhelming success of the petitions might inspire pro-Americans to act revengefully. 'We live in continual dread of having our

---

[88] See Warner, *John the Painter*, *passim*, for the reconstruction of this fascinating story.

[89] *London Evening Post*, 8–11 March 1777.

[90] *General Evening Post*, 11–13 March 1777.

[91] *Berrow's Worcester Journal*, 30 Jan. 1777.

[92] *London Gazette*, 21–25 Jan. 1777. One address from the mayor, burgesses and commonalty of Bristol was presented by Sir James Laroche; the one from the Merchant Venturers by Richard Combe; and the third, from the freeholders, clergy and inhabitants, by Thomas Tyndall. On Burke's responses and discussion with his friends in Bristol, see *Burke Correspondence*, III, 317–20.

Houses in Flames while we are asleep', wrote one correspondent. 'It was an ill-judged Thing to present an Address to his Majesty on the Success of his Arms at this critical Time, for we have a Number of Americans among us, Men of capital Fortunes, who strongly opposed the Address.'[93] Burke disliked these innuendos and the anonymous letters spawned by the arson, which discredited pro-American sentiments. He urged the Town Clerk, Sir Abraham Isaac Elton, to do some damage control and protest against the scapegoating of pro-Americans. Jokes or comments about pro-American sympathisers, he insisted, 'cause great Uneasiness Doubts and Suspicions, to the great disadvantage and discredit of our City'.[94] He was angry when Lords Sandwich and Suffolk were given the freedom of the city of Bristol for their role in the prosecution of John the Painter. At a time when American privateers were marauding Bristol ships in the Bristol Channel, he thought these commendations ridiculous, particularly to a first Lord of the Admiralty. He feared the Bristol elite had been swept away by loyalist rhetoric: 'So totally negligent are they of every thing essential; and so long, and so deeply affected with Trash the most low and contemptible.' He thought there was still 'a little more life' in Bristol Whiggery, he told Charles James Fox in October 1777, but he feared a high tide for loyalism, buoyed by a 'heavy lumpish acquiescence in Government'.[95] Events in the next few months confirmed his fears. Early in 1778 Burke hoped to galvanise the Bristol opposition to again petition for peace, but he learned from Paul Farr this would be a great challenge given the 'languor, or timidity or prudence or caution, or what ever else you may please to call it of the Whigs of this City'.[96]

The episode of John the Painter was a pivotal event in the consolidation of Bristol loyalism. It was not seriously undermined by the military reversals of Saratoga and beyond or the entry of France and Spain into the conflict in 1778 and 1779. Not even the contemptible, politically charged court martial of the Whig admiral Augustus Keppel, whose acquittal was greeted throughout the country with anti-ministerial jubilations, did much to reverse the tide.[97] Bristolians burnt Keppel's arch-enemy Hugh Palliser in effigy, but the illuminations in honour of the admiral were singularly muted in compared to Bath.[98] Moreover, when political disillusion with the war did begin to generate a movement for change in late 1779 and early 1780, Bristol's response was tepid. Burke remarked on Bristol's 'coolness' in January 1780, when nationwide efforts were made to push for an enquiry into the war and some measure

---

[93] *Public Advertiser*, 25 Jan. 1777.
[94] *Burke Correspondence*, III, 325–7.
[95] *Ibid*, III, 381–2.
[96] Wentworth-Woodhouse, Burke Papers, Farr to Burke, 31 Jan. 1778, cited in Charles R. Ritcheson, *British Politics and the American Revolution* (Norman, OK, 1954), p. 245.
[97] Nicholas Rogers, *Crowds, Culture and Politics in Georgian Britain* (Oxford, 1998), ch. 4.
[98] *Bath Chronicle*, 18 Feb. 1779; *Morning Post*, 22 Feb. 1779.

of reform. So, too, did Thomas Mullett, an important local politician in the Cruger camp, who complained to Wilkes of Bristol's 'want of spirit'.[99]

Loyalism became a formidable force in Bristol politics during the American war. Its tone was intransigent and beleaguered; its supporters were embittered by the prospect of a fragmented empire and outraged by the whiffs of radicalism that emanated from Bristol's journeymen population. The victim of this political climate was Henry Cruger. He was one of the Americans with 'capital fortunes', and it is worthwhile mapping his political fortunes as a weathervane to Bristol sentiment in this troubled era.

Cruger is an underexplored figure in Bristol politics, overshadowed by Burke, despite the fact that Cruger contested four elections in the period 1774–90 and served two terms to Burke's one. This preference for Burke has a lot to do with his stature in British politics, to the historical record itself, to a conservative strain in historical scholarship, and to a provincial deference in Bristol towards a renowned orator in Westminster.[100] It is as if Bristol is collectively embarrassed that it lost Burke after one term. There is a statue of Burke; a plaque to Cruger. Yet Cruger offers better clues to the shifting terrain of Bristol politics during the American war and beyond.

Cruger is frequently typecast as a 'hot Wilkite', a term attributed to him by Lord North.[101] At one level this is true enough. Under the influence of his father-in-law Samuel Peach, Cruger was an active player in Whig-radical politics. He advocated shorter parliaments and the notion of the MP as a delegate to his constituents. He pushed for a reconciliation with America and recoiled at government incursions against liberty-loving citizens. In 1775 he criticised the conciliatory petition framed by Burke because it was too strong on parliamentary sovereignty. Yet like his father-in-law, Cruger was a patrician radical, and if Thomas Chatterton is to be believed, there was a lot more of the patrician in him than the radical.[102] He hailed from a well-heeled mercantile family that had been active in New York politics for three generations. His grandfather, father and uncle had held civic or provincial office in what was then a rising Atlantic port, with a population less than half the size of Bristol's during the American war, running at approximately 23,600 in 1780.[103] Cruger's uncle John, had been a New York delegate at the Stamp Act

---

[99] BL, Add. MS 30,872, fol. 180, cited by Herbert Butterfield, *George III, Lord North and the People* (New York, 1968 reissue), p. 198; *Burke Correspondence*, IV, 200.

[100] See, for example, Patrick McGrath (ed.), *Bristol in the Eighteenth Century* (Newton Abbot, 1972), p. 8: 'If Bristol failed to re-elect Burke ... it made at least one lasting contribution to civilized life which counter-balanced its pre-occupation with money making. In 1764 the Theatre Royal, Bristol, began its long and remarkably varied existence.' Should we measure Bristol's rejection of Burke by the standards of Kenneth Clark's big C 'Culture'?

[101] Sir John Fortescue (ed.), *The Correspondence of King George the Third* (6 vols, London, 1927–28), III, 137, no. 1518.

[102] [Chatterton], *The Squire in his Chariot, passim*.

[103] New York City's population was 21,803 in 1771 and 23,614 in 1780. Bristol's population was about 55,000 in 1775.

Congress in 1765 and helped set up the New York Chamber of Commerce in 1768. His own father was a member of the provincial assembly until 1759 and from that year until 1773 a member of the state's governing council, when Henry's eldest brother, John Harris Cruger, took his place. So the Cruger family was extremely well placed in New York's politics. Linked to the De Lancey clan through politics and marriage, the Crugers were familiar with the open, populist waterfront politics of New York. Cruger's father, Henry senior, helped organise a mass petition against the Stamp Act, and his uncle, as a New York Assembly man, had received a set of instructions on that issue.[104] This probably explains why Henry Cruger junior had little difficulty adjusting to the Wilkite politics of the late 1760s and 1770s, even though his father and uncle disliked the rabble-rousing that accompanied more open systems of politics. His uncle, in fact, had been instrumental in tempering the New York protests against the Stamp Act, dissuading mobs from hazing Stamp Act commissioners and placating protesters by storing the unpopular stamps in City Hall.[105] Quite ironically, Henry Cruger's father and uncle opposed the American 'Wilkes' in New York politics, Alexander McDougall. They would have looked askance at Cruger's radical associations in Britain.[106]

At the same time Henry Cruger commanded respect from Bristol's mercantile elite, with whom he did business.[107] Indeed, it is noteworthy that in all the elections for which poll books survive during this era, 1774, 1781 and 1784, he always mustered some support from the overseas merchants. His immediate family was part of a transatlantic trading network that covered Bristol, Jamaica, the Danish island of St Croix, the Dutch island of Curacao, as well as ports in Holland. They provisioned of the plantation complex in the Caribbean and America, transporting everything from furniture to food to staves for sugar refineries, importing in return sugar, coffee, grain and timber into Britain and Europe. They had an investment in slavery and slave-based products. Henry's younger brother Nicholas, organised several shipments of slaves in the 1770s and Cruger himself defended slavery as 'the practice of every civilised nation'.[108] In 1789 he advised the Merchant Venturers on how

---

[104] *New York Gazette*, 2 Dec. 1765.

[105] Philip Ranlet, *The New York Loyalists* (Knoxville, 1986), pp. 21–3; Carl L. Becker, *A History of Political Parties in the Province of New York, 1760–1775* (Madison, 1909), pp. 32–4.

[106] On McDougall, see Maier, *From Resistance to Rebellion*, pp. 192–4, 221, 277.

[107] Among the merchants with whom Cruger negotiated insurance policies in 1766 were William Reeve, James Laroche, George Champion, Thomas Easton and Isaac Elton Jnr. See 'Commerce of Rhode Island, 1726–1774', in *Collections of the Massachusetts Historical Society*, 7th series, 9 (Boston, 1914), p. 145.

[108] *FFBJ*, 21 May 1789. Cruger introduced pro-slavery petitions to parliament. He favoured a gradual abolition of the slave trade and a handsome compensation for planters if emancipation was on the cards. See Peter Marshall, 'The Anti-Slave Trade Movement in Bristol', in *Bristol in the Eighteenth Century*, ed. McGrath, pp. 201–2. On Nicholas Cruger, for whom Alexander Hamilton was a clerk in St Croix, see Ron Chernow, *Alexander Hamilton* (London, 2005), p. 31.

they might defend slaving interests.[109] He saw no contradiction between a libertarian radicalism, the defence of property and legal rights before an intrusive state, which could only be kept in check through a broader representation in the legislature, and chattel slavery; presumably because Africans in bondage were denied subjecthood. St Croix and Curacao, where Cruger's brothers Telemann and Nicholas were located, were important entrepôts for trade to the French West Indies and the so-called neutral islands. The Crugers wanted it every way. They worked around the regulatory machinery of the British navigation acts, like many other American-based firms.[110] They were against the tighter regulations introduced after 1763 and actively protested the Stamp Act. They supported non-importation agreements in an effort to bring the British government to desist from internal taxation. They remained, however, advocates of a loosely coordinated, decentralised empire.

When Cruger entered parliament in 1774, he did not automatically identify with Wilkes and the radicals. He was well aware that he was the only American-born member in the Commons of 1774 and took it upon himself to represent the colonial voice, having a regular correspondence with merchants and kin on the other side of the Atlantic. 'You may rely upon it', he confided to his brother-in-law Peter Van Schaack, 'I will connect myself with none of the violent parties, but endeavor to temper my fire with prudence.' In his first speech to parliament on the subject of America, he deplored the violence of some Americans but claimed that 'a people animated with the love of liberty, and alarmed with apprehensions of its being in danger, will inevitably run into excesses'.[111] His position on America was somewhat different from Burke's. He acknowledged parliamentary sovereignty, but he thought it should be 'justly and adequately exercised' to accommodate colonial reservations about internal taxation. On this critical issue he took a tougher line than Burke, who would have regarded the exclusion as simply efficacious. Quickly recognising that even moderates in New York found this position unpalatable, Cruger seems to have shifted to a Chathamite solution of the crisis, one that recognised parliament's sovereignty over trade but not taxation, which should be left to the colonial assemblies, or, in a federated union, to the continental congress. As that vision ebbed, he found himself in no man's land between an intransigent government and an impotent, point-scoring opposition. Neither offered any help to the moderate loyalism of his family, some of whom tried to distance themselves from the polarising politics of America by moving to upper-state New York, as did his uncle and brother-in-law. Two of his brothers, in fact, took the plunge into revolutionary politics: Nicholas on the American side, John Harris Cruger on the British.

[109] Roger Hayden, 'Caleb Evans and the Anti-Slavery Question', in *Pulpit and People. Studies in Eighteenth-Century Life and Thought*, ed. John H. Y. Briggs (Eugene, 2009), pp. 162–3.
[110] See Thomas Truxes, *Defying Empire* (London and New Haven, 2008), *passim*.
[111] Henry Van Schaack, *Henry Cruger, the colleague of Edmund Burke in the British Parliament* (New York, 1859), pp. 13, 52–3.

Increasingly Henry Cruger wanted to dissuade the ministers and their advisers from the reckless course they were taking, not by strident opposition in parliament so much as by private communications with ministers. In November 1775, Cruger's father had an audience with Lord North at Downing Street, pressing him to consider opening peace talks in the light of the conciliatory petitions from Congress and Pennsylvania, and offering his views on the likely reaction of loyalists to an expeditionary force in New York. Henry Cruger junior followed suit. As the war continued he sent missives to Charles Jenkinson, a politician who had the ear of the king. In May 1777 he warned him not to be complacent about American resistance, for 'the War is not so near an end as we could wish'. Cruger also provided some private intelligence from New York to supplement the official accounts that Jenkinson was receiving and offered his own evaluation of the currency crisis that beset wartime America.[112]

One might imagine that Cruger was really abetting the government with much needed intelligence, and it may well be that he was trying to keep his own and his family's options open while the war was in the balance. Burke suspected that Cruger was consorting with the enemy, and to a degree this was true. On one occasion he did receive a small pension for his intelligence.[113] Yet Cruger was not a government spy or patriotic turncoat. In December 1777 he supported Wilkes's motion to repeal the Declaratory Act as a means of opening up the possibilities of reconciliation between Britain and America, optimistically insisting that 'independence is not yet the great object of the majority of the people'.[114] At the same time he was deeply suspicious of the Rockinghamites, believing their interest in America was opportunistic, little more than a means of embarrassing the North ministry. 'To get in is what we all want', Cruger reflected, 'and patriots in one station are great tyrants in another. America has long been made a cat's paw.'[115]

Cruger was very late in recognising the inevitability of American independence. Only in May 1780 did he explicitly do so, responding to General Conway's proposals for reconciliation with the Americans by insisting that independence was now the only realistic option for concluding the war and charting a new course of commercial prosperity.[116] By then he was already caricatured as an American republican and firebrand. Bristol Tories put it out that Cruger had written a letter to Peter Wickoff of Philadelphia in

---

[112] BL, Add. MS 38209, fols 120, 178; Henry Cruger Van Schaack, 'Diary and Memoranda of Henry Cruger', *Magazine of American History*, 7 (1881), 359–63.

[113] BL, Add. MS 37,836, fol. 63,

[114] *London Chronicle*, 11–13 Dec. 1777.

[115] Van Schaack, *Henry Cruger*, p. 19. On the increasingly untenable strategy of the Rockinghamites, see Frank O'Gorman, 'The Parliamentary Opposition to the Government's American Policy 1760–1782', in *Britain and the American Revolution*, ed. H. T. Dickinson (London and New York, 1998), pp. 115–16.

[116] John Almon, *Parliamentary Debates*, 17 (1780), pp. 658–9; *Morning Chronicle*, 6 May 1780.

July 1774 championing American resistance. Cruger vigorously denied the charge, but it would not go away. Bristolians were led to believe he was the kind of Anglo-Yankee responsible for the imperial crisis, one that by 1779 threatened not only trade with America but valuable interests in the West Indies as well. To press home the point, the Tories distributed five thousand copies of Wesley's *Calm Address*, which insisted that malevolent domestic 'patriots' were leading Americans astray. They were 'Ahithophels' who sought not only American independence but the subversion of the British state. When Bristol Tories created a volunteer force during the invasion scare of 1779, they refused to allow the Whigs to join because of their presumed disaffection.[117]

The 1780 election went badly for the Whigs. Cruger and Burke were distant, querulous partners whose time in parliament together repaired nothing. Cruger thought Burke aloof and condescending, even though Burke had been an agent for New York and had secured a council seat for Henry's eldest brother, John Harris Cruger, on the retirement of Cruger senior. He also believed Burke was 'so cursedly crafty and selfish that no-one can possibly receive the least benefit from a connection from him'.[118] Burke, for his part, found Cruger vain, tetchy and unpredictable in his politics: he 'never once intimated to me what line of Politicks he intended to take', he confided to Champion.[119] Their relationship got off to a bad start over misunderstandings about Cruger's formal introduction to parliament, and it never improved. In a letter to the Duke of Portland, just before the 1780 election, Burke described Cruger as 'a man of no sort of Parliamentary value, of very indifferent Character, on whose word no man has a reliance'.[120] He disliked the fact that Cruger had raised 'Jealousies and heartburnings' over his opposition to shorter parliaments in May 1780. So quite apart from political differences about parliamentary reform, parliamentary sovereignty, and the best strategy for unlocking the imperial crisis, there were personal antipathies that made their continued pairing problematic.

Burke was already in trouble with his constituents long before the election was called. He favoured a liberalisation of Irish trade, which cut into some vested interests in Bristol. He supported the Catholic Relief Act in a constituency where 'no popery' still meant something. He favoured a better deal for debtors in prison, to which many merchants were averse. And basically he was ill-suited to do the dog work of lobbying on behalf of the mercantile class that was expected of a Bristol MP. In this respect his remark that he often felt more like a ship's broker than an MP was extremely telling.[121] His

---

[117] *Burke Correspondence*, IV, 122.

[118] *Burke Correspondence*, II, 428, 465–7. Van Schaack, *Henry Cruger*, p. 16.

[119] *Burke Correspondence*, III, 86.

[120] *Ibid*, III, 268.

[121] Cited by Ernest Barker, 'Burke and his Bristol Constituency, 1774–1780', in *Essays on Government*, 2nd edn (Oxford, 1951), p. 195.

supporters initially hoped to repair this damage by resorting to the electoral arrangements of previous decades whereby each party nominated one candidate to stand for parliament. John Noble, one of Burke's managers, believed Cruger might be fobbed off with £2000 and the payment of his existing electoral expenses, allowing Burke to run in an uncontested election with the Tory Matthew Brickdale.[122]

Given Cruger's commitment to open politics, this was never on the cards, and it made any subsequent arrangement between the two men impossible. Ultimately Burke decided to abandon the poll, leaving his parliamentary fate in the hands of Lord Rockingham, who returned him in his pocket borough of Malton. With Burke gone, Cruger stood in Bristol with his father-in-law Samuel Peach, but before a revivified Tory party he gave up after ten days. Cruger attributed his failure to Church-and-King prejudice, and certainly the slogan a 'virtuous King' resonated from the hustings. Militant loyalism and flagrant anti-Americanism made Cruger's contest a painful and violent one. Rival mobs rampaged the streets, culminating in an attack on the Tory headquarters at the White Lion. One gentleman described the city as 'a scene of lawless riot and outrage'.[123] Cruger's scribes, angered by the machinations of Burke's allies and the nativism of the hustings, consoled themselves by printing a mock playbill 'for the benefit of a weak Administration'. Matthew Brickdale was billed as 'Orator Mum' and his partner, Sir Henry Lippincott, as 'Dupe'. In an entr'acte entitled 'The Poll Books, or a new method of securing a majority', Sir Henry was to play the role of 'Close 'em', a reference to his partiality as sheriff in the Gloucestershire by-election of 1776, when he terminated the election after eleven days to thwart supporters of the Berkeleys.

Within four months of the general election, another was called upon the death of Sir Henry Lippincott. Once more the Whig Union Club sought an electoral arrangement with the Tory Steadfast Society, but this time the Tories were in a position to dictate the terms. They declared they would take the vacant seat and allow the Whigs the next option. This cosy deal was pre-empted from below. A group of small masters and journeymen at the Three Queens declared against caucus politics and canvassed for Cruger, and eventually the Union Club was shamed into promoting him as well. Cruger's opponent was George Daubeny, a merchant and banker with investments in sugar refinery and glass manufacture, who had been on Common Council since 1769 and had worked aggressively for the war effort, raising money for recruiting troops in 1778 and 1779. On this last occasion he had clashed with Cruger, who deprecated the attempt to use corporation money to fund a losing war. Consequently the election promised to be fiercely partisan, an

---

[122] *Burke Correspondence*, III, 273; IV, 238.
[123] *London Chronicle*, 9 Sep. 1780.

anti-war American facing a robust warmonger.[124] Cruger's party attempted to mobilise anti-Catholic sentiment by casting Daubeny as a man whose loyalty to the crown was virtually Jacobite, a line of argument that gestured towards the jure divino sentiments attributed to high Tories like Wesley, and to the Catholicising impulses of George III, which had surfaced during the Gordon riots. In June 1780 the Bristol corporation had feared anti-Catholic fervour would spill onto its streets, and Cruger's campaigners were quite prepared to exploit such intolerance three months later.[125] In reply the Tories castigated Cruger as a foreigner, a Yankee, a rebel, with the clergy leading the chorus of calumny. Edward Barry described them as firebrands 'plying the people with such fictious perils as may make them believe their religion, their church, their all are at stake'.[126] In one election print Cruger is projected as a Yankee victor whose carriage is drawn by supporters trampling on the crown and the scales of justice. This mock chairing is accompanied by the devil and a chimney sweep, familiar sentinels in anti-Jacobite and later anti-Painite effigy-burnings. Behind Cruger is an American sailor riding a John Bull and waving an American flag with the thirteen stars of the colonies. Cruger carries a flag as well, this one with the inscription, 'The Voice of REBELLION is a Supreme Law which passeth all Understanding.'[127]

Indeed, flags featured prominently in this election, for the Tories provocatively flew the American standard from church steeples and ship masts to highlight the rebel in their midst. The gesture created an uproar and Crugerites clambered to remove them.[128] The captain of a Swansea merchantman on Welsh Back refused to remove his flag from its mast, and when the crowd on the quay insisted he do so and began to board his boat, he ordered his crew to turn their swivel guns on the trespassers, killing two and wounding eleven. The coroner's inquest judged the action self-defence, a verdict that enraged Cruger's supporters. They carried black banners at the funeral of the two men, Thomas Webb and William Fokes, and placed a plaque in Temple churchyard to their memory, stating they had been 'inhumanly murdered'. The captain and crew were subsequently indicted for murder, but they were acquitted at the September assizes.[129]

---

[124] Debrett, *Parliamentary Debates*, V, 44, cited by I. R. Christie in his biography of George Daubeny in *House of Commons, 1754–1790* (London, 1964), accessible online <http://www.historyofparliamentonline.org>. On 27 November 1781 Daubeny made an impassioned speech in favour of continuing the war and claimed that the citizens of Bristol 'were willing to sacrifice half their fortune in the prosecution of it'.

[125] Ernest Barker, *Burke and Bristol* (Bristol, 1931), p. 92.

[126] Edward Barry, *A Serious Address to the Citizens of Bristol* (Bristol, 1781), p. 14.

[127] BM print no. 1868,0808,4786, entitled, *The Virtuous and Inspir'd State of Whigism in Bristol, 1781*. See figure 7.

[128] Descriptions suggest the merchant flag of the time, the thirteen red and white stripes, not the stars and stripes adopted by Congress in 1777.

[129] *FFBJ*, 3 March, 29 Sep. 1781, 6 Oct. 1781; *Gentleman's Magazine*, 51 (1781), p. 142.

11 *The Virtuous and inspir'd State of Whigism [sic] in Bristol, 1781.*

Cruger narrowly lost the 1781 by-election by some 342 votes. This was partly attributable to the fact that Daubeny had a deeper purse, replenished with secret service money from the government. He was also able to mobilise the pauper vote at the last minute, having control over the Bristol Corporation of the Poor. Cruger did well among the corporation, where Whigs had retained a majority since 1778. He excelled among the London out-voters, where he polled 427 votes to Daubeny's 148. He also polled well in the populous parish of St Philip and St Jacob where the Dissenting interest was strong, although not in St James, where some of the noteworthy Dissenting chapels were located, including the Presbyterian chapel at Lewin's Mead. This probably reflected the unease and disenchantment of the more affluent Nonconformists with Cruger's candidature. Even so, all seven Dissenting ministers who voted in this election opted for Cruger.

Predictably Daubeny fared well among the clergy, gaining thirty-one votes to Cruger's twelve. He also commanded the support of Bristol's upper crust, gaining the genteel vote by a ratio of two to one. He secured the majority of the merchants, professions, yeomen and genteel trades as well; so, despite his poor showing on the corporation, the wealth of Bristol essentially backed him. What is also noteworthy is that he commanded considerable support further down the social scale. Although much was made in the election about Cruger's support from journeymen and 'vagabond tradesmen' he did not in fact gain a majority among the more populous trades, or among the labourers and mariners. Cruger seems to have gained the vote of those that prided themselves on their independence, small masters and journeymen who would not be browbeaten into voting as their masters dictated.[130] This disposition fits nicely with the claim that Cruger held on to the Nonconformist vote. Daubeny clearly mustered a sizeable dependent vote, but one should not discount the fact that Bristol loyalism did have some popular appeal. He won every parish save three, Castle Precincts, St Leonard, and St Philip and St Jacob. His support was particularly robust among the maritime trades hit by the war, and he penetrated trades such as the coopers, shoemakers and tailors, who had previously been firmly in the pro-American camp.

After two successive defeats and some major losses in the American war, one would have thought Cruger's fortunes in Bristol had totally collapsed. Yet he made a comeback in 1784, even though he was in America at the time of the election and did not personally canvass Bristolians. This remarkable event requires some explanation, especially since it is marginalised in political narratives of the era that fixate on Burke. How did a man vilified as an American in 1781 win an election three years later when in America?

The answer to this question has everything to do with the changing political prospect. In 1781 Bristolians were in a grim mood. The war in America was dragging on and the West Indies was threatened. The islands of St Vincent and Grenada had fallen to the French and the jewel in the plantation economy, Jamaica, was under attack. Only Rodney's fleet stood between survival and disaster, and in 1780 he had fought a long inconclusive battle against the French admiral, De Guichen, off Martinique, which gave rise to all sorts of speculations about naval mismanagement at the top and threatened to produce recriminations on a par with Keppel's engagement off Ushant in 1778. Rodney followed this up with the capture of St Eustatius, a Dutch island that tolerated and profited from all sorts of underhand commerce. Rodney regarded the property there as a legitimate war prize, to howls of protest from merchants in London, Bristol and Liverpool who had been exploiting the island's neutrality to salvage some profit from a war-ridden economy. First America, now the Caribbean: from a mercantile perspective, the prospect was bleak.

By the spring of 1782 Britain had lost four of the Caribbean islands it had gained during the Seven Years' War as well as the older islands of St Kitts and Montserrat. This prospect tarnished Bristol's enthusiasm for war. The critical change came in January 1782, less than a year after Cruger's defeat in the by-election. Moderate Whigs John Noble and Joseph Harford asked Cruger, who was the mayor at the time, to call a meeting to consider a petition to end the war and negotiate with the Americans. The Whig-dominated council

---

[130] *The Bristol Contest* (Bristol, 1781), pp. 17–18. Cf. Bradley, *Religion, Revolution and English Radicalism*, p. 246, table 7.7, where his sample has Cruger commanding proportionately more artisan votes than Daubeny. The fundamental problem is unpacking artisan votes, which include both masters and journeymen, and conceal rather than disclose wealth.

doubted that a petition to the king would change anything, given his open dislike of the opposition, and so Harford drafted a petition to the Commons calling for peace and a change of ministry. This was not opposed by the Tories, who recognised that the threat to West Indian trade was dire and of serious concern to the whole mercantile class.[131] A more broadly based petition echoed these sentiments a few days later, part of a concerted campaign nationally to topple the North ministry. This did not immediately succeed, but within months Bristol joined other towns and county associations in congratulating the king on appointing Lord Rockingham and the Whig lords Shelburne, Richmond and Grafton to head a new government. In Bristol the meeting was opened by Cruger, who commended the king for appointing men who embraced 'in their collective capacity ... all the political virtue in the kingdom'. With their appointment, Cruger continued, 'the blessings of peace, commerce and liberty may be expected' and Britain could look forward to recovering her former prosperity and 'reuniting with America'.[132]

Precisely on what terms such a reconciliation might be accomplished was left open, but the push for peace received a substantial boost from Admiral Rodney's victory over De Grasse at the Battle of the Saints on 12 April 1782. The victory destroyed French plans to invade Jamaica and went a long way towards securing British naval supremacy in Caribbean waters. 'No British Admiral since the reign of Charles II has rendered his country such signal services', chirped the *Bath Journal*. 'Great Britain has regained her former *Ardour*, snatched *Glory* from the French', it continued. 'By this victory, our superiority in the West Indies is decided, and opportunity offers a recovering some of our lost possessions there.'[133] In Bristol there were two days of celebrations, with bells, illuminations and a *feu de joie* in honour of the admiral; and when Rodney returned to do a triumphal tour of the country, nowhere was he fêted so magnificently as in the metropolis of the west. Here merchants staged a procession that featured Britannia, a beef-eating John Bull, an emaciated Frenchman, the god Mars, and a Minerva figuratively protecting his majesty. To the swirl of banners proclaiming the 'valiant and glorious Rodney' his country's saviour, a cavalcade conducted the hero of the hour through the principal streets of the city and round Queen Square. Later that evening, at the Merchants' Hall, the Bristol elite toasted Rodney along with Lords North and Sandwich, before concluding the day with a brilliant ball at the Assembly Room. The poorer sort were regaled with beer and victuals before a bonfire on Brandon Hill.[134]

The Rodney junket was a bi-partisan affair, although judging from the toasts the Bristol Tories tried to score points against the new Rockingham ministry, which had controversially recalled Rodney because of his behaviour

---

[131] *FFBJ*, 26 Jan. 1782, 16 Feb. 1782.
[132] *FFBJ*, 20 April 1782.
[133] *Bath Journal*, 27 May 1782.
[134] *FFBJ*, 25 May 1782, 16 Nov. 1782.

over St Eustatius. Raising glasses to North and Sandwich must have been a disagreeable gesture for Bristol Whigs, who had recently offered the Rockinghamites the freedom of the city.[135] Yet all recognised that Rodney's victory cleared the way for a genuine negotiation to end the war, one in which American independence would likely be recognised and the empire in the Caribbean secured. From a Bristol point of view this was not a bad solution to the American conflict. It shored up crucial commercial assets in the West Indies and it offered the possibility of renewed trading links with America in a freer market economy, something that conservative Whigs like Josiah Tucker had been arguing for since the war began.

Within this context, Henry Cruger staged a comeback in Bristol politics. As mayor of Bristol 1781–82, he had patched up his differences with Noble, Harford and other Burke supporters. Becoming president of the Whig Anchor Society in 1782 was one measure of this. Another was that he did not press for more radical changes in parliamentary representation, as happened in London and even in Somerset,[136] but went along with the Burkean proposal for economic reform; that is, advancing the independence of the Commons by cutting government patronage and the civil list. In effect, he shelved his former radical proclivities in the interests of Whig unity and personal ambition. He proved to be a trimmer.

In other respects, Cruger's candidature looked like an asset not a liability. He retained important contacts in New York, a port that was to feature very prominently in the maritime economy of the new republic. He could not be accused of profiting from the war. Along with many other Bristol merchants he had lost trade and credit, including some £20,000 in unredeemable debts. And his family had paid the price of their loyalty to the British empire. His father had retired from New York politics and died in Bristol, a broken man. His elder brother, John Harris Cruger, had distinguished himself fighting for the British in South Carolina and Georgia, and had lost all his American assets as a result. The Crugers could hardly be typecast as victorious Americans, even if one of Henry's brothers, Nicholas, successfully negotiated the shoals of revolutionary politics in the new republic.[137]

Of course there were those in 1784 who wanted to play the American card. It was circulated that on one of his visits to New York Henry Cruger had stood alongside General Washington and had torn down the British flag, replacing it with the thirteen stripes of the Union. Voters were again reminded of the Wickoff letter.[138] These rumours were dismissed as hearsay

---

[135] *FFBJ*, 20 April 1782.

[136] *FFBJ*, 29 June 1782. At the county meeting at Wells there were petitions passed at different meetings calling for economic and parliamentary reform.

[137] Nicholas Cruger was accused of abetting the rebels by the Tory printer John Rivington in New York. He was twice imprisoned during the war for his rebel affiliations and emerged afterwards as a strong supporter of Washington.

[138] *FFBJ*, 10 April 1784.

and the 'Yankee Doodle' tag lacked the appeal that it had three years earlier. The most substantial objection to Cruger concerned his citizenship. Now that America was independent, was not Cruger an alien, legally incapable of sitting in the Commons? Had he in fact sworn allegiance to the United States, especially since he still held property in America and had no trouble returning in 1784? Cruger's brother, John Harris, denied his brother was an American citizen, and this seemed to satisfy voters as it did a Commons' committee that looked into his candidature.[139] Legally Cruger was born in the British empire and remained British as long as he did not permanently reside in the United States.

There were other factors that helped Cruger. One ironically was loyalism. With Henry absent in America, John Harris Cruger was called in to canvass for him, and his loyalty to the British crown was unquestioned. He had fought with British forces in Georgia and Carolina and risked his fortune. Furthermore, in the controversy over the 1784 election, Cruger sided with the king and his new minister William Pitt, convinced that Fox and North intended to augment their patronage in the newly proposed legislation for the East India company. In effect, he supported the king's decision to defy the Whig majority in the Commons and choose Pitt as his first minister. In this regard, Cruger had an unlikely ally in Josiah Tucker, a conservative Whig who had voted against him in three successive elections.[140]

By contrast, Cruger's opponents found it more difficult to distance themselves from the constitutional controversy of 1783/4. Until the battle over the East India Bill broke, the incumbent MPs, Brickdale and Daubeny, were widely expected to be re-elected.[141] Then both political parties in Bristol were caught off guard by the groundswell of opinion in favour of the king, which resulted in two pro-prerogative petitions that together mustered almost five thousand signatures.[142] Sensing the mood of the populace, the Whig party in Bristol decided to endorse Cruger, whose radical associates in the City of London viewed the East India Bill as an issue of sinister political patronage. Brickdale, who had regularly voted for the administration under North, declined to vote on the East India Bill. He was propitiously ill during the crisis and kept a relatively low profile. But Daubeny emerged from it as a conniving politician who supported the Fox–North coalition and then tried

---

[139] *FFBJ*, 10 and 24 April 1784; JHC, 40, 9 Feb. 1785, p. 506; P. J. Marshall, *Remaking the British Atlantic. The United States and the British Empire after American Independence* (Oxford, 2012) p. 221. See also *St James's Chronicle*, 14–16 March 1786, and *General Advertiser*, 18 March 1786, where Cruger's citizenship is discussed.

[140] *FFBJ*, 6 March 1784.

[141] Mannaseh Dawes, *Observations on the mode of electing representatives in parliament for the City of Bristol* (Bristol, 1784), pp. 31–3.

[142] *London Gazette*, 17–21 Feb. 1784, 2–4 March 1784. The first, organised by the maverick conservative, David Lewis, at Taylors' Hall, produced 1097 signatures; the second, launched from the Guildhall by Alderman William Miles, produced 3879 signatures. See also *FFBJ*, 7 and 28 Feb. 1784.

to jump onto the King George bandwagon, presenting one of the Bristol petitions along with crowd-pleasers like Lord Rodney. Although the Bristol elite backed Daubeny, the broader electorate despised his weathervane tactics, with the result that Cruger sneaked in, in what was essentially a three-candidate contest. Cruger's father-in-law Samuel Peach picked up only 373 votes and was widely regarded as an outlier. Unlike 1781, Daubeny failed to mobilise enough dependent votes to pip Cruger at the post, even though nearly a thousand new freemen were admitted during this contest.[143] Cruger's victory was a narrow one; only sixty-eight votes separated him from Daubeny, who had built up a powerful local interest. Sixty-three per cent of Cruger's supporters were in fact plumpers, but enough voters paired him with Brickdale to deny Daubeny a seat.[144] So ultimately Cruger benefitted from Bristol loyalism. His pedigree was not a liability in an idiosyncratic election where conventional political configurations were scrambled: the Whig Union Club backing a Pittite; the Loyal and Constitutional, candidates who supported the Fox–North coalition.

The vote for Cruger in 1784 could be seen as an effort to restore the equilibrium between the parties. One 'Freeman' argued as much.[145] It could also be seen as a vote for a fresh start in America. In terms of incoming traffic, Bristol trade with North America did expand after the war, although the tobacco trade never recovered its pre-revolutionary levels. In terms of outgoing traffic Bristol could never compete with Liverpool and its network of canals to the industrial heartland. After the war it exported less hardware and pottery and faced increasing competition with Ireland in the export of glass to New York.[146] A Virginia merchant predicted that Bristol's American trade would 'not be of sufficient importance to take the attention of a Capital House',[147] and essentially he was correct. Bristol trade increasingly concentrated on the West Indies. In the end Rodney's victory mattered more than Cruger's, for Bristol's North American trade never recovered from the war.

As for Cruger, he did not stay in Britain long enough to see out his second term. In March 1783, upon the conclusion of peace, he had written to John Hancock congratulating his countrymen on their independence. He informed the former president of Congress that he would continue to trade in Bristol 'in the American business, where I hope by receiving fresh marks of their favour and by redoubled industry to redeem the time lost in this accursed war'.[148] Yet following the death of his father-in-law, Samuel Peach, in May 1785, Cruger

[143] *General Advertiser*, 20 March 1786.
[144] Bradley, *Religion, Revolution and English Radicalism*, p. 226.
[145] *FFBJ*, 10 April 1784.
[146] Walter E. Minchinton, 'The Port of Bristol', p. 131; Morgan, *Bristol and the Atlantic Trade*, pp. 27–8.
[147] Morgan, *ibid.*, pp. 28–9.
[148] *New England History and Genealogical Register*, 25:51, cited in *Commons 1754–1790*, ed. Namier and Brooke, in biography of Henry Cruger, accessible online at <http://www.historyofparliamentonline.org>.

transferred his commercial concerns to the port of London. Unable to restore his commercial fortune, he fished for a consular position in the United States. Such an appointment, he told Pitt, would 'give great Satisfaction in America, as well as to <u>many</u> respectable friends in this Country. I am willing to resign my Seat in Parliament, and my zealous endeavours should be exerted to further the Election of any Candidate at Bristol that you would recommend.'[149] Pitt was not interested, however, and within six months Cruger had departed for New York, just before the 1790 general election. Quite remarkably, he was elected to the New York senate in 1792 despite claims from his opponents that he was British. A man who straddled both worlds, Cruger was anchored in the end to his New York lineage, unlike his first son, who adopted the name of Peach and remained in Gloucestershire as a country gentleman. Cruger's time in Bristol, nonetheless, tells us a lot about the tortured politics of the American crisis in England's second city: the interconnections between local and international politics; the timbre of its radicalism, both patrician and popular; the persistence, even resurgence of sectarian rivalries over America; and the undertow of electoral venality in a constituency on the cusp of popular political consciousness.

[149] TNA, PRO 30/8/127, fols 170–1.

10

A Loyal City? The Diversity of Dissent in Bristol in the 1790s

The relatively low visibility of popular radical organisations at Bristol in the decade following the French Revolution has led historians of the city to conclude there was little support for them. Mark Harrison, for example, notes that although the 'public expression of loyalism was abundant' in a welter of anti-Jacobin addresses forwarded by the corporation to the throne, the radicalism to which it was opposed remained 'spectacularly absent'. It is not easy to disagree. Compared to well-known radical centres in smaller towns, like Norwich, Sheffield and Manchester, Bristol appears disproportionately quiet.[1] For an explanation we may look partly towards the familiar arguments about the city's introspective concern with its own civic affairs, where issues over corruption and accountability in a relatively open electoral franchise centred more readily on the exclusive activities of the corporation. In these years, the corporation, its merchant allies and the political elite attracted more hostile public attention than ever before through their energetic attempts to further increase their own executive and judicial powers and to control the election of the city's representatives, nullifying the impact of the city's generous freeman franchise.

It is certainly no coincidence that in 1790, at the first English general election after the fall of the Bastille, a challenge was launched at Bristol against the by now customary pact agreed by the Tory candidate, the Marquis of Worcester, and the Whig candidate, Lord Sheffield. The Reverend Edward Barry revived the city's Independent Society of Freemen, claimed he had attracted 1500 men to join him, and called for a third independent candidate to step forward to uphold the right of election. 'It was neither men nor party they assembled for', declared Barry, 'but the CAUSE; to protect their common rights'. A candidate was duly found in the merchant David Lewis, but the opening days of the poll were not encouraging and Lewis withdrew with just twelve votes to his name. With the remaining two candidates elected and chaired, Lewis, who according to the local press could have 'nothing to complain of but the perfidy of his promising friends', made his way to the

[1] Mark Harrison, *Crowds and History: Mass Phenomena in English towns, 1790–1835* (Cambridge, 1988), p. 274.

Bush and consoled himself over dinner with Sheffield and the Whigs. Barry blamed Lewis for not trying hard enough, and Lewis blamed Barry for falsely claiming he had 1500 freemen ready to cast an independent vote. 'Yours were the heroes of independence, who all promised me their votes, interest and support; but soon discovered that two gallons of ale per day and other bribery would be much better for them than keeping their promises as honest men.'[2] The outcome was welcomed by the local press. 'Nothing can surpass the cordiality now subsisting between the two parties, nor the peace and good-will that prevail throughout the city', noted one paper; and another, 'Instead of rancour, riot and every excess, nothing is to be seen but countenances of satisfaction and pleasantness.'[3]

These comments were wide of the mark. Suspecting perhaps that Lewis's candidature had been a cynical Whig ruse to break the pact and return members for both seats, a three-hundred-strong Tory mob left the White Lion after the poll closed on 17 June, attacked the houses of several prominent Whigs with iron bars and threatened to 'have a stroke at the Bush' as well. A number of men were taken up and two prosecuted for riot.[4] Public announce-ments of civic consensus and 'cordiality', it would seem, were premature, a point acknowledged by some political observers as the dust settled in the following months. By the end of 1792, Tory supporters were becoming increasingly indignant at what they saw as the Whigs' habit of filling every vacancy on the Common Council with members of their own party. The impartial were afraid both sides would use it as an excuse to have the city 'plung'd again into the miseries of a contested election' at the next oppor-tunity and that membership of the White Lion Club was being boosted by a suspicion that Sheffield's supporters were already planning to seize both seats. The corporation, it was said, 'who ought to be the preservers of unanimity' had now become 'instrumental' in its negation.[5] However keen the corpora-tion was to scotch these rumours and publicly distance the affairs of the city from factional politics of any kind, a sustained and increasingly combative public critique of political exclusivity would continue to develop during the decade, provoked not only by issues over rights of election, but by a general belief that the corporation habitually conferred unlawful powers upon itself. The hostility that greeted the corporation's efforts to obtain a new Gaol Act was evidence enough. The need to replace Newgate with a modern prison was generally accepted, yet the corporation's intention was to meet the entire cost by arbitrarily levying an annual county rate. Roughly drawn lampoons

---

[2] David Lewis, *A Letter to the Rev. Edward Barry M.D.* (Bristol, 1790), p. 9.
[3] *Bath Chronicle*, 24 June 1790; *Bristol Gazette*, 25 June 1790; Rev. E. Barry, *Coalitions and Compromises* (Bristol, 1790); *Genuine Letters and Other Official Papers from the Original Manuscripts of the Independent Society of Freemen* (Bristol, 1790).
[4] BA, JQS/P/121, Information of John Weeks, Thomas Bowcott, Thomas Appleby and Onesiphorus Norman, 19 June 1790.
[5] Correspondence in *Bonner and Middleton's Bristol Journal*, 17 Nov. 1792.

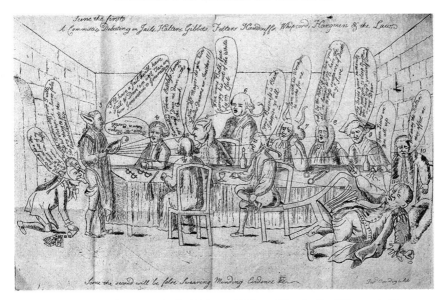

12 *A Committee Debating on Jails, Halters, Gibbets, Handcuffs, Whipcord, Hangmen and the Law*, 1792.

like *A Committee Debating on Jails, Halters, Gibbets, Handcuffs, Whipcord, Hangmen and the Law*, framed public opposition around a remote and self-interested corporation conducting business behind close doors. In this print (Fig. 12) members of the corporation, some of them in their cups, form a motley group before Major John Noble, whose hind quarters are licked by two men seeking preferment. 'I will have a Jail and Dam 'em, we'll Tax 'em from Generation to Generation', says Noble. 'Bravo, Mr Mayor', replies an Alderman. 'Have a Bastille'.

More formally, a city-wide committee of delegates drew up a lengthy list of objections, particularly 'to the powers given ... to the Mayor, Aldermen and Common Council to determine every year what sum or sums of money they shall think necessary to be assessed and raised'. Although the corporation countered each objection in turn, it was clearly impractical to push ahead in the face of public opinion, and so Newgate was not finally replaced until the close of the Napoleonic wars. More damning still, the corporation's use of military intervention against an unarmed crowd protesting tolls on Bristol Bridge in September 1793 left a deep scar on local memory. It was recollected nearly forty years later during the reform riots of 1831.[6]

Connecting these local issues to the universal suffragist agenda of the popular reform movement is not straightforward. Nevertheless links were made, as the controversy over the corporation's Gaol Bill revealed. As an

[6] *Bristol Gaol Bill, August 4th 1792: Objections to an Act lately obtained for building a new gaol within the city of Bristol, and for other purposes* ... (Bristol 1792), p. 1.

intemperate pamphlet from John Rose, one of the corporation's most consist-ent critics in the 1790s, put it,

> It is an indisputable truth that the universally acknowledged inequality and corruption in the reputation of this country, is in a great measure to be attributed to corporations and their undue influence: If, therefore, they were all to be abol-ished, it would be one grand step towards a desired reformation.

Rose contrasted local government at Bristol with the system in the City of London and argued that they were 'almost as striking as night and day'. While there were 'some rays of light' in London, Bristol was enveloped in 'total darkness'. Whereas London's councillors acted as 'servants of the public', Bristol's acted 'as rulers'.

> As their authority now stands, all the disapprobation of their fellow citizens is set at defiance; and, sheltering themselves under the perpetuity of their offices, they frown at the murmurs of the people and treat their inquietudes with contempt: – they add insolence to oppression, and carry themselves with such an haughtiness towards the inhabitants, it renders them odious and disgusting.[7]

Loyalist panegyrists leapt to the city's defence. Bristol's virtues lay in 'HONOUR, JUSTICE and a thirst for TRADE', insisted the poet Romaine Joseph Thorne in 1794; it was a haven for 'CHARITY' where the 'liberal hand provides the needy old' under the watchful legacy of 'Immortal COLSTON'. Moreover, since 'discord now and civil wars are 'o'er', its citi-zens were unequivocally focussed on resistance to infidel France. Thorne's verse provoked an immediate reaction, not least from fledgling pantisocrats like Robert Lovell, who responded with a lengthy tribute of his own, in which 'sordid wealth', and mercantile heritage are recast as nurseries of corruption, slavery and 'Avarice'. Behind it all, lurks the corporation:

> While heedless magistrates recline in peace,
> Content to mumble o'er the good Police
> But ne'er essay its blessings to secure,
> Nor stretch the hand to help the suppliant poor
> Suffice to them the *name*, the important air,
> The *Fur-Clad Gown* and *Magisterial Chair*.

> Oppression, frequent as the varying hour,
> Still marks this mighty *self elected* power;
> To them the exclusive charter'd powers belong,
> 'The right' and privilege of 'doing wrong'.[8]

---

[7] John Rose, *Free Thoughts on the Offices of Mayor, Aldermen and Common Council of the City of Bristol, with a Constitutional Proposition for their Annihilation* (Bristol, 1792), pp. 9–13.

[8] Romaine Joseph Thorne, *Bristolia: A Poem* (Bristol, 1794); Robert Lovell, *Bristol: A Satire* (Bristol, 1794), lines 15–20, 306–9. Lovell's response to Thorne is discussed in greater detail in Robin Jarvis, 'In Search of Robert Lovell: Poet and Pantisocrat', *Journal for Eighteenth-Century Studies*, 40:1 (2017), pp. 120–1.

Bristolian introspection frequently blurred distinctions between local and national issues, but however strong the temptation, it would be overly simplistic to assume popular indifference to the wider politics of reform.

One reason it has been difficult to trace formal radical societies on the London Corresponding Society (LCS) model after 1792 is that the corporation rarely forwarded information to Whitehall about the strength of radicalism or took overt judicial measures against it in the courts. This may, of course, have been because there was nothing substantive to report, yet evidence of the corporation's introspective attitude at this time is nevertheless easy enough to find. At a time when Church-and-King propagandists were quick to associate dissent with disloyalty, corporate bodies with a strong Dissenting tradition had nothing to gain by drawing public attention to social and political divisions in communities nominally under their care. As the corporation was well aware, dissent could still present public order anxieties; indeed it had done so at Bristol in the immediate aftermath of Birmingham's anti-Dissenting 'Priestley riots' in 1791. That summer, the mayor, John Harris, a prominent Baptist with abolitionist sympathies, received at least five anonymous letters threatening the destruction of 'your fine manchin house and your fine Baptist meating and not your meating only but Prisperterines likewise and Romands and all your Decenters houses'. Harris passed the information to Henry Dundas at the Home Office, but expressly requested no reward notices in the *London Gazette*, for 'an idea going abroad of the apprehension of a disturbance might excite in the common people a disposition to do that which it is both our inclination and duty to prevent'. Harris requested military aid as a safety measure, but for this was criticised by the Tory alderman, George Daubeny. 'If any (tumult) should arise', Daubeny advised the Home Office, 'it is my real opinion that it will be produced in consequence of the attention of the multitude being excited by the means taken to prevent it.'[9] A similarly cautious approach was adopted by more lowly Dissenters as anti-Jacobin feeling surfaced the following year. In December 1792, two men disrupted a service at the Swedenborgian New Jerusalem Chapel on St James's Back by running in and throwing phosphorus on the ground. Although a prosecution was started, it was quickly dropped when the accused offered to make a public apology.[10]

Despite loyalist attacks, there is little evidence that the city's Dissenting chapels harboured conclaves of advanced radicals at this time, and it is equally difficult locally to test E. P. Thompson's suggestion that the suppression of radicalism correlated with a Methodist 'great awakening'. Circuit membership at Bristol fell by three hundred between 1793 and 1797, against a national trend of steady growth, but this may have been the result of a serious schism amongst Bristol's Methodists in 1794. This dispute did have

[9] BA, TC/Adm/Box/42/28, bundle 27, Anonymous letters to the Mayor; TNA, HO 42/19, John Harris to Henry Dundas, 21 July 1791, 25 July 1791; George Daubeny to Evan Nepean, 25 July 1791.
[10] *Bonner and Middleton's Bristol Journal*, 5 Jan. 1793.

radical undertones for it was over the contested right of individual chapels to permit non-ordained men to administer the sacrament during communion. A confrontation during a service at the conservatively run New Room prompted a third of members to leave, all of them 'lower class' according to one account, and to relocate at the recently completed Portland Chapel. The majority (819 of the 1000 members who attended the consequent emergency District Meeting), backed the liberal view against the conservative leadership, but any suggestion that they held wider democratic views should be treated with caution. Samuel Bradburn, perhaps the most prominent Sacramentalist minister, broadcast his own views about 'Equality' in a sermon at the New Rooms at the beginning of the year. It was controversial in its advocacy of an unspecified reform of government, but otherwise a call for Methodists to disavow republicanism and lend support for property, hereditary privilege and 'natural' hierarchy.[11] More radical currents than Methodism can be detected but the numbers involved were tiny and their influence questionable. The millenarian herbalist William Bryan, a later disciple of Richard Brothers, had made Bristol his home by 1794 for instance, where he attracted some attention with eschatological prophecies, but not the interest of the city bench. 'Woe to this city of Bristol!', he declared in a critique of the slave trade and the 1793 military massacre on Bristol Bridge, 'The cry of innocent blood is against it: it shall be shaken and fall.'[12]

It was not just Dissent that drew cautious and introspective responses from the city bench. In the tense atmosphere surrounding an unprecedented wave of strikes affecting many of the city's artisan industries, George Munro, military commander of the Western District, criticised the inactivity of the magistrates. The assistance of soldiers might once again become necessary, the mayor conceded in response, 'but to prevent any confusion from the report of military aid being requested, I write this letter in the most private manner and I earnestly request it may be as private in your office'.[13] John Harris was succeeded as mayor by John Noble, another Whig merchant reluctant to raise the alarm. As he stepped down at the end of the year, he would only admit that his mayoralty had been marked by hostile handbills, paragraphs, anonymous threats and incendiary letters', all of which he ignored as the work of minority malcontents 'beneath his notice'. The familiar pattern was repeated once again in January 1793 when the mayor of Liverpool, who had received

---

[11] E. P. Thompson, *The Making of the English Working Class* (London, 1963), pp. 419, 427; C. Garrett, *Respectable Folly: Millenarianism and the French Revolution in England and France* (Baltimore, 1975), pp. 147–8; T. S. A. MacQuiban, 'The Sacramental Controversy in Bristol in the 1790s', *Bulletin of the Bristol Branch of the Wesley Historical Society*, 60 (1991); BA, Bristol Methodist Society class lists, 1796–99; Samuel Bradburn, *Equality. A sermon … preached at the Methodist chapel, Broadmead, Bristol, February 28, 1794* (Bristol, 1794).
[12] Garrett, *Respectable Folly*, pp. 175–8.
[13] TNA, HO 42/21, George Munro to Henry Dundas, 9 Aug. 1792; HO 42/23, Thomas Mudge to Henry Dundas, 8 Dec. 1792; BA, Corporation letter book, John Noble to Henry Dundas, 13 Aug. 1792.

an anonymous threat to fire shipping on the town quay, wanted to know if anything similar had arrived at Bristol. Henry Bengough, the new mayor, replied in the negative, and said nothing about the anonymous threatening letter he had in fact forwarded to Henry Dundas in January, several weeks after its discovery. Bengough's covering note included the usual plea against publication in the *Gazette* and an assurance that the corporation could handle the situation, and Dundas was disinclined to take action anyway since so much time had elapsed since its delivery.[14]

These are the contexts in which we should consider any correspondence from the corporation assessing the strength of popular reform societies. In September 1792, Dundas asked Noble for 'the number and extent of the Associations which have been formed at Bristol', as 'their proceedings should be carefully attended to ... [and] every good citizen and well-wisher to our excellent constitution should unite in pursuing every legal means of suppressing them'. To reinforce the message, a London solicitor, Thomas Mudge, was despatched to the west of England in December to report on the situation. No response has survived, either from Noble or Mudge. Yet when the Bristol Recorder, Richard Burke, asked the Grand Jury a similar question in April 1793, they told him that 'attempts' to spread democratic ideas in the city had been 'ineffectual ... and we rejoice in the general disposition of the inhabitants which has left us with nothing out of the usual course to present'.[15]

But things were not necessarily as quiet as they appeared on the surface. There is some evidence for the existence of a Corresponding Society in 1792 and by December at least one bookseller had been reported for promoting and selling copes of the *Rights of Man*. 'Notwithstanding His Majesty's loyal proclamation and the late circular letter', it was alleged, 'his windows continue filled with inflammatory publications, the most imprudent caricature prints, heads of the principal disturbers of our country, etc'. Correspondence survives between the LCS and a Bristol Constitutional Society (BCS) in October the following year, although, if the twelve copies of an LCS publication they requested are anything to go by, the BCS was modest both in number and ambition. An *Address*, outlining constitutional reforming principles was published in the spring of 1794. Its phrasing was so carefully considered that even 'our enemies acknowledge there is something very fair and reasonable' about it. They were not over-confident. As they put it themselves in letters to the LCS, there were in the city, 'many strong prejudices to combat', and 'we are candid enough to confess that the circumstance does not appear to us in the most favourable point of view'. A copy of the *Address* was forwarded by an anonymous loyalist to the Treasury solicitors for legal opinion, but no prosecution followed.

---

[14] BA, Corporation letter book, Henry Bengough to mayor of Liverpool, 16 Jan. 1793; Bengough to Dundas, 7 Jan. 1793; *Sarah Farley's Bristol Journal*, 6 Oct. 1792; BA, TC/Adm/Box/44/13, Henry Dundas to Henry Bengough, 7 Jan. 1793.
[15] TNA, HO 42/21, Henry Dundas to John Noble, 12 Sep. 1792; BA, JQS/P/130, Declaration of the Grand Jury, April 1793.

Yet there may have been more to the BCS than this. In response to the suppression of the 'British Convention' at Edinburgh in December 1793, and the arrests and transportation orders that followed, popular radical societies planned to reconvene the Convention in London. In May 1794, a large open-air meeting of northern reformers from Leeds, Sheffield and other Yorkshire manufacturing towns resolved to back a plan for a mass gathering of national delegates 'preparatory to a General Convention' and to hold it in Bristol.[16] Within days, Pitt's ministry moved decisively against the reform movement, suspending habeas corpus, and in London issuing warrants for high treason against fifteen prominent LCS members, six members of the Society for Constitutional Information, and, as an obstruction to inter-regional collabo-ration, a further three at Sheffield. Charges were prepared against all of them, for 'the object of assembling a pretended general convention of the people, in contempt and defiance of the authority of parliament'.[17] These measures swiftly dashed any hopes of a delegate meeting at Bristol, but such a meeting could hardly have been agreed upon in the north without the knowledge and cooperation of Bristol radicals. If they were in a position to host it, their ineffectiveness should not be overplayed.

If the low public profile of radicalism at Bristol was anomalous, so too was its counterweight, Church-and-King loyalism. Although several loyal addresses to parliament and the king were promoted following the Royal Proclamation against sedition in November 1792, including one from the corporation and magistrates, no official encouragement was offered for the formation of loyalist societies. Indeed, Bristol was the only urban centre of any size in the coun-try not to form a public body modelled on John Reeves's Association for the Preservation of Liberty and Property Against Republicans and Levellers, in London. The corporation met privately to adopt a loyal address, then hosted a public meeting in the Guildhall at which a series of loyal resolutions were approved and copies distributed to vestry rooms for general signing. No further action was contemplated beyond a general encouragement to support the magistrates in keeping the peace and opposing sedition.[18] In common with many other towns, innkeepers were prevailed upon to make public displays of loyalty by adopting a joint resolution not to allow radicals to hire their rooms for meetings. The staunchly loyalist publican at the Bush, John Weeks, was happy to comply. Weeks convened a meeting of Bristol innkeepers, who resolved not only to refuse the hire of rooms for radical meetings, but to keep a

---

[16] *Annual Register*, 35 (1792), Chronicle, p. 153; BL, Add. MS 16927, John Reeves Papers, Brunswick to Moore, 5 Dec. 1792; BL, Add. MS 27812, Francis Place Papers, Journal of the London Corresponding Society, 31 Oct. 1793; TNA, TS24/2/13, *Address of the Bristol Constitutional Society* (Bristol, 1794); HC, *Parliamentary Papers*, Second Report of the Committee of Secrecy, Appendix H, 1794, letters from Bristol 28 Jan. 1794, 24 April 1794, and Sheffield, 11 May 1794.

[17] Mary Thale (ed.), *Selections from the Papers of the London Corresponding Society, 1792–1799* (Cambridge, 1983), p. 167.

[18] *Bonner and Middleton's Bristol Journal*, 15 Dec. 1792.

close watch on their customers, 'to disclose and make known any treasonable or seditious expressions which may come to our knowledge, in order that the guilty persons shall receive just punishment'. A total of 630 innkeepers signed this resolution. In addition, the corporation and political establishment did their best to prevent reform meetings in any of the city's public buildings.[19] This strategy was part of the struggle over public space in English towns to which Katrina Navickas has recently drawn our attention. The Seditious Meetings Act of 1795, in particular, determined 'what constituted a legitimate public meeting' and 'where and when such meetings could take place'. In Bristol the struggles over rights of assembly would focus upon access to the symbolic landscapes of Brandon Hill and Queen Square in the early nineteenth century, but the smaller reform movement of the 1790s was more concerned with the hiring of tavern rooms or civic spaces like the Guildhall.[20]

The lack of a formal loyalist association in Bristol generated frustration in several quarters, not least in the pages of *Felix Farley's Bristol Journal*. Surely 'a city with so much consequence both for riches and number of inhabitants as Bristol will not be backward in showing that spirit', reasoned a correspondent. The Duke of Brunswick took the same view, lamenting to the secretary of the parent association in London, 'I very much regret we have no Association here'. In January 1793, an attempt to form one at a pub in Dowry Square, Clifton, came to nothing, and so eighty-one disappointed members of the True Briton Society pledged action against local Jacobins. This society was not formed specifically to tackle the radical clubs. It was a convivial drinking club, already in existence when the proclamation was published, and for whom the libertarian constitutional maxim, 'May a subject never be above a King nor a King above Law and Liberty', was no less urgent than suppressing the *Rights of Man* and harassing Jacobins. As one of their own songs had it after an evening of toasting in November,

> True Britons their title – not troubled with spleen
> They drink a good health to the King and the Queen
> For *getting* the Prince and success to the Nation
> No more of excise and much less of taxation
> Derry down etc.[21]

---

[19] *Gloucester Journal*, 14 Jan. 1793. For later interference, see for instance Coleridge's allegation in 1795, that 'within the last three weeks, a circular letter has been sent to the publicans of this city, requiring them to exclude from their houses certain gentlemen whose names are underwritten and whom the letter styles "damned Jacobin pests of society" etc. etc.,': S. T. Coleridge, *An Answer to 'A Letter to Edward Long-Fox M. D'.* (Bristol, 1795).

[20] Katrina Navickas, *Protest and the Politics of Space and Place, 1789–1848* (Manchester, 2016), pp. 52–8; Steve Poole, '"Til our liberties be secure": Popular Sovereignty and Public Space in Bristol, 1780–1850', *Urban History*, 26:1 (1999), 40–54.

[21] BL, Add. MS 16927, John Reeves Papers, Duke of Brunswick to Moore, 5 Dec. 1792; *FFBJ*, 8, 15 and 22 Dec. 1792, 12 Jan. 1793, 2 Feb. 1793; *Bonner and Middleton's Bristol Journal*, 1 Dec. 1792. For the Clifton Association, see *Bristol Mercury*, 10 and 17 Dec. 1792.

In the days following the Guildhall meeting, effigies of Tom Paine, 'with the Rights of Man in one hand and a pair of stays in the other', were publicly paraded and burnt on bonfires on Redcliff Hill, Brandon Hill and in Old Market. The newspaper reporting of these effigy-burnings was minimal, despite the 'thousands' that purportedly attended them.[22] The one exception was the anti-Painite demonstration of the Kingswood colliers, reported in *Felix Farley* a few months later. Beginning in Kingswood, it traversed public space in an almost time-honoured fashion, parading through the streets of Bristol with horsemen, Sunday School children, a mock priest, devil, and bands thumping out 'God Save the King'.[23] Whether magistrates sanctioned these events, as they did in other places, is unclear. If they did, the demonstations would certainly have been carefully supervised. By 1780, the corporation had become increasingly intolerant of the popular use of bonfires and fireworks to mark loyalist anniversaries. Even the junketing on the 1788 centenary of the Glorious Revolution had been restricted to a military cannonade on Brandon Hill and the placing of an illuminated patriotic canopy over the statue of William III in Queen Square. 'Illuminating houses and throwing fireworks', it was ruled, 'may be productive of dangerous consequences', and were accordingly forbidden. Each November on the anniversary of the Gunpowder Plot, efforts were made to restrict commemorations to a civic procession to the Cathedral for divine service, and to fine anyone caught firing squibs in the streets. In 1790, *Felix Farley's Bristol Journal* explicitly urged the local bench to take preventative measures against the annual 'riots and disorders' still sporadically disrupting the city on November the fifth. Things did get seriously out of hand in 1792, just as the fashion for burning effigies of Paine was about to take off. In that year, the first for over a decade in which the magistrates allowed the building of public fires, a crowd of young men looking for tinder violently sacked two Tower Lane brothels. Furniture and fittings were plundered and dragged to the pavement outside the Exchange and there set alight. This serious disturbance, 'an act of wantonness committed in the face of Magistracy', as *Felix Farley* put it, was the cause of two prosecutions for unlawful entry, destroying property and riot. Heard at the city assize the following spring, one of them returned a capital verdict.[24] Without a push from the corporation – common policy in many other south-western towns – popular loyalism lacked leadership and financial support. Without any noticeable effort by the city bench to bring local radicals before the courts on charges of sedition, loyalists lacked the will and encouragement to be vigilant. In stark contrast to attitudes in other South Western centres, no prosecutions

[22] *Bristol Gazette*, 20 Dec. 1792; *Bonner and Middleton's Bristol Journal*, 22 Dec. 1792.
[23] *FFBJ*, 2 March 1793.
[24] For the Revolution jubilee, see *FFBJ*, 1 and 8 Nov. 1788; *Bonner and Middleton's Bristol Journal*, 8 Nov. 1788. For the later disturbances, see *FFBJ*, 6 Nov. 1790, 10 Nov. 1792, 13 April 1793; BA, JQS/P/129, Information of Alice King, Isabella Hines, Sophia Taunton, Mary Davis, Elizabeth Nelson and others, 10 Nov. 1792.

of local democrats and reformers for seditious offences were contemplated at Bristol until the second half of the decade.[25]

The so-called Bridge Riot of September 1793 finally put paid to any lingering possibility that the corporation might have a role to play in forging loyalist unity at Bristol.[26] While these events were not in themselves directly connected to the politics of reform, the public image of local government in the city was irreparably damaged by them; indeed they ensured a broad coalition of public disdain for the corporation that cut right across arguments between 'loyalists' and 'Jacobins'. That the Bridge affair blew up just a few short months after a temporary settlement in the row over the Gaol Act was salutary in itself. Once again, financial integrity was at issue, this time over the calculation of costs for building the new town bridge back in 1768. The bridge had been in the offing since the late 1750s but wrangling within the elite similar to that over the turnpike trusts inhibited any easy consensus about how it might be financed. Initially the trustees hoped that the bridge might be financed by a house tax and wharf duty, but the spiralling cost of the bridge, which reached £49,000, demanded other sources of income. To help recover the investment made by the bridge trustees, a toll on horses and carriages was agreed upon, with the proviso that it ceased once all debts were paid and a reserve of £2000 had been reached to cover maintenance costs. Officials on the council led Bristolians to believe that this target would be reached by Michaelmas 1793, and as trade recession and bank failures took hold on the outbreak of war with France, causing nearly fifty notable Bristol bankruptcies, such news was especially welcome. It meant lower transportation costs for traders on the Somerset side of the river and potentially lower rents. But the trustees unexpectedly announced that the tolls would be let for another year, claiming that the current balance could not redeem the debt and support further maintenance. 'Surprise sat on every countenance', wrote John Rose, 'whilst murmurs and renewed calculations were heard in every street and in almost every company. Even those who had little or no immediate concern in the business felt an indignation at the deception.'

It seemed that the trustees, several of whom were councillors and Merchant Venturers, were up to their old tricks, feathering their own nest at the expense of the ratepayers. Consequently, a few 'public spirited gentlemen' did a deal with the outgoing lessor, Abraham Hiscoxe, to relinquish his lease nine days before it expired, on the assumption that the hiatus in tolls would make it impossible for the tolls to be legally demanded again without a new

---

[25] For comparative figures in the region see Steve Poole, 'Pitt's Terror Reconsidered: Jacobinism and the Law in Two South Western Counties, 1791–1803', *Southern History*, 17 (1995).

[26] Full summaries of the Bridge affair will be found in Mark Harrison, 'To Raise and Dare Resentment: The Bristol Bridge Riot of 1793 Re-Examined', *Historical Journal*, 26:3 (1983); Harrison, *Crowds and History*, pp. 271–88; Philip. D. Jones, 'The Bristol Bridge Riot and its Antecedents', *Journal of British Studies*, 19:2 (1980); Michael Manson, *'Riot!' The Bristol Bridge Massacre of 1793*, 2nd edn (Bristol, 2013).

act of parliament. As a result, the gates were thrown open and passengers went over the Bridge toll-free for the first time on the evening of Thursday 19 September.[27]

To press the point, 'a number of indiscreet persons' pulled down the gates and the toll-board and publicly burned them. On 28 September, when the nine days were almost up, the trustees announced they were still carrying a debt of £2500, erected new gates and instructed a new renter to begin taking tolls again. Like the corporation, the bridge trustees were secretive about their finances, publishing annual returns but not an accumulating total. They were not widely believed but, in any case, many people had convinced themselves that the nine-day rule made a resumption illegal. A crowd quickly gathered in protest and the offending gates were taken down and burned. The magistrates arrived, read the Riot Act and summoned the Herefordshire militia. The crowd did not disperse so the militia fired on them, wounding several and killing one spectator, John Abbott, a 55-year-old tiler and plasterer.[28] The following day a much larger crowd gathered in protest when a renewed attempt was made to collect tolls. There were scuffles and a few arrests, but in the afternoon the authorities managed to enforce the toll with the presence of the Herefordshire militia. That evening they retired, distributing two thousand handbills warning the populace not to resist the new imposts. On the third day, 30 September, the tolls were once again resisted and magistrates made a more concerted attempt to clear the bridge and restore order. The Riot Act was read three times in the morning and the militia summoned. Stalemate ensued for some hours before the militia were withdrawn again, but shortly after that, a renewed attack was made on the toll-houses, according to Rose, by 'about twenty boys who had taken it into their mischievous heads to make a bonfire'.[29]

The testimony of apprentice William James, however, suggests the attack on the toll-houses drew wider support. He talked of 'several of the Populace calling out for fire' and demanding a load of faggots from the Back. When the faggots arrived 'they began to huzza & immediately set fire to them', placing them strategically around the temporary gates.[30] At this point a small party of the Herefordshire were ordered to return, but withdrew again under a shower of stones and oyster shells. According to James, 'the officer and many of the soldiers had their hats struck off their heads & were otherwise ill-treated'. As the crowd increased in the fading evening light, a larger party of soldiers was marched back in, accompanied by the magistrates and constables, 'not to a grave and solemn but to a very brisk tune'. When stones were thrown this time, the acting magistrate John Noble ordered the soldiers to

[27] John Rose, An Impartial History of the Late Disturbances in Bristol (Bristol, 1793). For bankruptcies, see Latimer, II, 499–500.

[28] Rose, An Impartial History, p. 15.

[29] Ibid., p. 11.

[30] BRL, B 13065, Committee for investigating the Bristol affairs, p. 45.

fire volleys in several directions without warning and without any new reading of the Riot Act. The diarist, William Dyer, whose nephew witnessed the
fusillade, recorded the soldiers forming themselves into a defensive square
and so opening fire in all four directions, 'towards Bristol Back, Bridge Street,
High Street, and in front, straight forward over the Bridge towards St Thomas
Street, and 'tis reported, fired incessantly during 15 minutes'.[31] 'Men, women
and children flew on all sides', Rose reported, 'and whilst the press which it
occasioned impeded the progress of their fight, it gave the military an opportunity to practice the science of street-firing with astonishing adroitness;
the people being brought down by the musquetry in almost every direction.'
Many were wounded by gunshots, and dinners were abruptly disrupted by
bullets ricocheting off walls.

The shooting took the public by surprise. It was expected that the magistrates would give due warning of military action and no one thought Riot
Act readings at midday would still be in force in the evening. On the following morning, Tuesday 1 October, there were revenge attacks on corporation property. Both the Council House and the Guildhall, where the militia
were temporarily quartered, had their windows shattered. Peace was finally
restored that night by the removal of the Herefordshire and the introduction of a party of dragoons from Salisbury and two new militia regiments
(the Monmouthshire and the Brecon) from Wells. The former protected the
Herefordshire militia from reprisals as it retreated to the riding school near
Hotwells. Peace in the longer term was secured by a group of 'truly philanthropic gentlemen' whose offer of nearly £2000 for the lease on the tolls was
accepted by the trustees. They had no intention of collecting tolls to recover
their investment however, so, although the magistrates thought it 'neither
wise or salutary', no further charges were ever made on Bridge traffic.[32] In the
ensuing months, the corporation rejected every demand for a public inquiry.

Dr Edward Long-Fox, a reforming physician ventured to launch one, but
he was unable to secure a suitable meeting place from the corporation, or from
the Assembly Rooms, whose owners were intimidated by the threat of losing
their licences. His committee pushed ahead with the inquiry nonetheless
and recovered some telling evidence about the constables' aversion to military intervention and the poor handling of the riots by the city magistrates.
Fox and company considered the possibility of using the coroner's foreman
to probe further into the indiscriminate fire by the military, but their legal
counsel advised against this and warned that the corporation might sue for
libel if the inquiry hinted at any dereliction of duty on its part.[33] Predictably
the corporation accepted no responsibility for the casualties. Indeed George
Daubeny had the council pass a resolution commending Lord Bateman and

---

[31] BRL, Manuscript diary of William Dyer, 2 vols, 1744–1801, p. 280.
[32] Rose, *An Impartial History*, p. 14.
[33] BRL, Committee for investigating the Bridge affairs, pp. 59–71.

his militia for manfully doing their duty. A hundred guineas were thrown the militia's way to lubricate the violence.

Just how many were killed and injured in the Bristol Bridge riots? There were troublesome accounts in the press of militiamen dumping bodies in the water. Several corpses surfaced in the course of the week, including that of a gentlemen from out of town, who had clearly not been mugged because he still had his watch and a £10 note on his person. John Rose went door to door to discover the casualties. He estimated that ten men and a woman were killed outright and about fifty more wounded. They came from a wide spread of parishes, not simply those contiguous to the bridge, and included master shoemakers and bakers, an accountant and auctioneer, and one gentleman from Castle Cary in Somerset. They ranged in age from 14 to 55, with an average age of 29 and a modal age of 22. Thirty-eight per cent were aged 25 years or under, and 14 per cent were women. The radical young poet, Robert Lovell, put the number of casualties a little higher and like many other Bristolians registered his indignation at what he clearly saw as a vindictive act against a largely curious not riotous public. 'The killed and wounded on this fatal day amounted to upwards of seventy. Their names will remain an eternal monument to the infamy of those who ordered the Militia to fire; and to the disgrace of the inhabitants of this city, who have neglected to support an investigation of the cause of so horrid a massacre.'[34] As a military atrocity against unarmed civilians, the events on Bristol Bridge may not have been unique but they were certainly significant. Sixty-three casualties were named; rather more than at St George's Fields in 1768 but considerably fewer than the estimated 400 sabred or shot during the Gordon Riots in 1780 and the 654 killed or wounded at Peterloo in 1819.[35]

A single conviction drove the crowd on Bristol Bridge; the resumption of tolls was legally and morally wrong. As the chief constable of St Stephen remarked to the inquiry, 'the People had no other view but the suppression of an arbitrary tax'.[36] That the perceived avarice of the Bridge Trustees should place an unjustified tax on trade at a time when the city's economy was in deep recession only strengthened the case. Historians have been interested in the extent to which eighteenth-century crowd disturbances were underpinned by a legal and moral 'legitimising notion', strong enough to overcome customary levels of deference and sufficiently resolute to command support from the wider community. The idea was first applied by E. P. Thompson to crowd actions relating to the unjust and uncustomary marketing of essential foodstuffs – an affront to a 'moral economy', framed by both custom and

---

[34] Lovell, *Bristol: A Satire*.

[35] For the Gordon Riots, see Adrian Randall, *Riotous Assemblies: Popular Protest in Hanoverian England* (Oxford, 2006), p. 203, and Nicholas Rogers, *Crowds, Culture and Politics in Georgian Britain* (Oxford, 1998), p. 152. The figures for Peterloo are taken from Michael Bush, *The Casualties of Peterloo* (Lancaster, 2005).

[36] BRL, Committee for investigating the Bridge affairs, p. 70.

law. Thompson was extremely cautious about stretching the term into other areas of social and economic life, and Mark Harrison has examined the case for a 'moral economy' of bridge tolls at Bristol and found it unconvincing.[37] Nevertheless, the readiness of a respectable Bristol crowd to obstruct the taking of tolls for a couple of days, to either assist in the firing of toll-booths or stand by while it happened, and to refuse to disperse when confronted by armed soldiers under the Riot Act, invites some pertinent questions about deference and notions of 'right'. As we have seen, the corporation had sanctioned the killing of civilians during riots before, in 1730 and 1753, when the dead were weavers and colliers from 'without the gate', and the perpetrators armed citizens rather than soldiers. In those cases, inquest findings of homicide were overruled by the mayor with the support of the Attorney General. In 1793, coroner's inquests returned nine verdicts of 'Wilful Murder by person or persons unknown', although in the case of William Powell, the foreman of the jury had advised a verdict against 'the person who ordered the military to fire'.[38] No prosecutions followed these verdicts. Clearly, bringing the corporation to account now was no easier than it had been sixty years earlier. Indeed, there were some who feared the whole matter might yet be lost to future generations. 'However strange', noted one incredulous pamphleteer, 'it appears to be almost probable that the Facts and Merits of the late Disastrous Transactions are in danger of passing into oblivion without any proper Exertion to have them clearly ascertained and fully committed to record!'[39]

True to form, very little attempt was made by the magistrates to advise central government about what had happened. On the second day (29 September), Henry Bengough wrote to Dundas requesting military aid, but the letter conveyed little of the seriousness of the situation and Bengough was in no hurry to write again a day later when eleven people lay dead. Dundas did learn something of the massacre but not from the mayor. The London daily papers reported the first deaths on 2 October, and by 3 October they were carrying colourful and detailed reports of events. As the *St James's Chronicle* had it, soldiers had been permitted to fire

> in three different directions, which took a fair sweep up High Street, down the Back and over the Bridge. The dead bodies were carried about the streets on hand barrows for a considerable time this morning. There were supposed to be killed and wounded about 40; 24 of whom were carried to the infirmary before eight o'clock. Several letters have been picked up on the Bridge, declaring vengeance against some of the Aldermen and soldiers. The city is in a very alarming state.[40]

The Home Office also received an anonymous letter from Bristol that morning, alleging streets 'filled with Murdered bodyes', one 'poor labourer …

---

[37] Harrison, *Crowds and History*, pp. 271–88.
[38] BRL, Committee for investigate the Bridge affairs, p. 23.
[39] Veritas, *Inquisition for Blood Shall be Made: To the Inhabitants of Bristol and Parts Adjacent* (Bristol, 1793).
[40] *Lloyd's Evening Post*, 2 Oct. 1793; *St James's Chronicle*, 3 Oct. 1793.

murdered by a bayonet being thrust into his bowels', and blaming everything on the corporation.[41] Dundas immediately fired off a letter to the mayor, making no attempt to conceal his irritation:

> Reports having been circulated in town since I heard from you last that riots of an alarming nature had taken place at Bristol, I could have wished that you had sent me the earliest intelligence of the extent of the same and of the measures which have been taken to oppose them in order that I might have been able to form a judgement of the real situation of your town and in case the force stationed with you had not appeared sufficient, which I hope was not the case.[42]

Mayor James Morgan replied on 7 October in a guarded response assuring Dundas that 'the magistrates are using their utmost endeavours to discover and bring to justice the instigators of the disturbance who (there's too much reason to fear) had other objects besides putting a stop to the collection of the Bridge Toll'. Inasmuch as the continuance of the bridge toll was considered symptomatic of corrupt and unaccountable local government, Morgan was possibly right. Those pressing most loudly for an end to tolls in the weeks preceding the massacre included David Lewis, for instance, the first lease-holder of the toll, the defeated independent candidate in 1790, and a strong critic of the Bristol establishment. He was not alone in his criticism of the management of the bridge. Satirical broadsides and panegyrics were quick to link the bridge, the corporation and the controversy over the Gaol Bill. Predictably, the corporation responded by pressing the panic button and crying conspiracy. John Noble, one of the most active magistrates in the riots, publicly labelled every demand for an independent inquiry as 'seditious'. Richard Burke believed the whole affair had been 'raised by a conspiracy'. He was anxious about the impact of 'seditious libellers continually inciting (the crowd) to new attempts, and now to revenge'. One of many that came to the corporation's attention was the London *Star* newspaper, which had been expressly critical of the magistrates. Characteristically, a suit for libel was only briefly considered, for 'as matters are dying away, better let all prosecutions drop'. No arrests ensued, either of libellers or rioters, and Morgan contented himself with a request that the soldiers Dundas had sent into the city to replace the 'bloody blues' be retained for the winter, 'to prevent any further disturbances taking place'.[43]

---

[41] TNA, HO 42/26, Anon to William Pitt, 3 Oct. 1793.

[42] TNA, HO 42/26, Henry Dundas to Henry Bengough, Oct. 1793.

[43] BRL, Holograph letter B18588, Richard Burke to John Noble, 25 Nov. 1793; John Noble, *To the Citizens of Bristol* (Bristol, 1793); TNA, HO 42/26, John Morgan to Henry Dundas, 7 Oct. 1793, 11 Nov. 1793. On an objection from the commanding officer that it would mean dividing his men and keeping them from more urgent postings, Morgan happily acquiesced (19 November 1793). For hostile association between the gaol, the bridge and the corporation, see Lovell, *Bristol: A Satire*. For satirical commentary on the re-emergence of Lewis, see *The Lamentation of Bristolia: or the First Chapter of the Chronicles of Judas and Haman* (Bristol, 1793).

Radical Constitutionalism in Bristol

Aside from the efforts of the Bristol Constitutional Society to overtly agitate the city for parliamentary reform, radical constitutionalism emerged publicly through a loose circle of professional men, including the Romantic poets Coleridge, Lovell and Southey, the Quaker physician Edward Long-Fox (who established an 'unofficial' committee of investigation into the bridge killings), the Foxite Whig William Coates, the bankers Joseph Edye and John Savery, the merchant Richard Bright, the publisher John Rose, and Dr Thomas Beddoes, experimental scientist and Coleridge's physician. Beddoes, whose involvement with the Hotwells pneumatic institute and vocal opposition to quackery was notorious, is perhaps better remembered today for the radicalism of his medicine than for his politics. He was, as Roy Porter once put it, 'a mere bit player in Britain's cultural history', but he produced a steady flurry of radical pamphlets while at Bristol, from the self-explanatory *Where Would Be the Harm of Speedy Peace?* (1795) and *A Word in Defence of the Bill of Rights Against Gagging Bills* (1795) to the slightly less obvious, but highly critical, *An Essay on the Public Merits of Mr Pitt* (1796).[44]

On the periphery of this group hovered a shifting crowd of unlikely sympathisers like the merchant Azariah Pinney, a friend of Beddoes who dubbed the group 'Coleridge's Party', although their preferred term was the Friends of Peace.[45] From 1795–97, this party of liberal thinkers clashed frequently with the corporation over the city's support for the Pitt ministry's attempts to silence the Corresponding Societies through the so-called Gagging Acts of December 1795, and the government's continuing commitment to war with France. When pressed, this circle always denied any connection with formal radical societies, but they certainly lent them support. Coleridge, who earned himself a reputation as a powerful Opposition speaker in Bristol at this time, announced in the prospectus for his own radical journal, *The Watchman* (1796), that he would cooperate with the Whig Club to oppose the Gagging Acts, as well as the 'Patriotic Societies', to obtain a 'right of suffrage, general and frequent'.[46]

The Friends of Peace (FoP) first raised their profile through noisy interventions on loyalist platforms. The immediate cause of the Gagging Bills was the mobbing in London of the king's state coach as he went to open the new session of parliament at the end of October, and in common with local elites in many urban centres over the following days the corporation announced

[44] Mike Jay, *The Atmosphere of Heaven: The Unnatural Experiments of Dr Beddoes and his Sons of Genius* (New Haven, 2009); Roy Porter, 'Thomas Beddoes and the Bristol Enlightenment' (Unpublished paper, 1991), p. 13; Roy Porter, *Flesh in the Age of Reason* (London, 2003), pp. 412–15.

[45] University of Bristol Library, Special Collections, Pinney Family letter book, 1795–6, Azariah Pinney to Wiliam Wordsworth, 26 Nov. 1795.

[46] See L. Patton (ed), *The Collected Works of Samuel Taylor Coleridge 2: The Watchman* (Cambridge, 1970).

a public meeting in the Guildhall for the adoption of a loyal address to the throne. Rose, Coates, Fox, Lovell and Coleridge led a party of objectors into the hall and moved an amendment, that 'the insult would never have been offered if the People had not been rendered outrageous by their sufferings under the present cruel, sanguinary and calamitous war'. Fox and Lovell were shouted down, but Coleridge was more successful. In a 'most eloquent, most pathetic and most sublime' speech, he tied the assault, the bills and the war together, asserting that 'the very means which government had taken to prevent what were called popular and Jacobinical principles were calculated to produce them'. Unsurprisingly, the amendment was not adopted, but the FoP had drawn attention to themselves in the press and were now in a position to announce a meeting of their own to address the king and contest the bills. Despite initial objections from Mayor James Harvey, this meeting went ahead in the same rooms three days later. Loyalists did not attempt any physical disruption, although the FoP accused the corporation of ordering the military to beat to arms outside the Guildhall doorway while the meeting was in progress. Inside the building then, division was caused only by an argument over who should be called upon to present a petition against the bills. Coates and Coleridge wanted the prominent national figures, Sheridan and C. J. Fox to do it since both of the city's MPs had already expressed support for the bills, but this was rejected to avoid 'any obloquy that might be attempted to be thrown on the meeting and petition by the Minister and his adherents'. But entrusting it to Sheffield and Somerset, Rose pointed out, would not amount to 'approbation of their past conduct'. According to Sheridan, the Bristol petition gathered four thousand signatures and was finally presented by Sheffield, 'although the noble Lord has not made any observation upon it'.[47]

Coleridge's political career was effectively launched by these two meetings in Bristol. It continued a few days later with a public lecture on the bills at the Pelican Inn in Thomas Street, quickly published as *The Plot Discovered*, and a spirited defence of Edward Long-Fox, who had been attacked anonymously in print for joining with 'a few factious aliens to scatter among them the seeds of discord and sedition'. Coleridge's response, 'I glory that I am an alien in your city', is a reminder of the longevity of the familiar Bristol axiom that it was outsiders, whether geographical or philosophical, who most often disrupted local polity.[48] His *Watchman* appeared for the first time in March 1796 but ceased publication after just two months after failing to identify itself very

---

[47] *The Star*, 23 Nov. 1795; Thomas Beddoes, *A Word in Defence of the Bill of Rights Against Gagging Bills* (Bristol, 1795); S. T. Coleridge, *An Answer to 'A Letter to Edward Long-Fox, M.D.'* (Bristol, 1795).

[48] S. T. Coleridge, *The Plot Discovered, or An Address to the People against Ministerial Treason* (Bristol, 1795); A. W., *A Letter to Edward Long-Fox, M.D.* (Bristol, 1795); Coleridge, *An Answer to A Letter to Edward Long-Fox*.

clearly either as a journal of radical reform or as a critic of the corporation.[49] It failed, ironically enough, just as a new alliance between the reforming wing of the Bristol Whig party and leading Dissenters in the city was forming to contest another Tory/Whig coalition at the 1796 parliamentary election.

The sitting Whig MP, Lord Sheffield, was regarded by the Party's Foxite wing as a supporter of both the slave trade and the Gagging Acts, and his re-nomination in 1796 was conducted, to their considerable annoyance, at a meeting to which they were not invited. The radical Whigs therefore met separately and nominated a rival candidate, Benjamin Hobhouse, for an election that, unusually for Bristol, was now entered by two more independent candidates, a Mr Thomas and the redoubtable David Lewis. As some Bristol radicals openly acknowledged, the chances of any of these three breaking the mould were extremely slender. The real problem, argued the publisher, John Rose, was a persistent and erroneous belief amongst electors that dividing the representation of the city between two equal interest groups created an equitable balance of power when, in practice, it produced nothing but factional bickering and popular discontent. Rose's solution was radical. Writing as 'a Constitutionalist and One of the People', he proposed a convention of delegates, chosen by parish meetings and organised on similar lines to the campaign against the Gaol Bill in 1792; a non-partisan electoral college that would rationally select two virtuous men to represent the public interest, and then back them in numbers at the poll. The suggestion was not taken up.[50]

In the contest that followed, Hobhouse was promoted by his supporters as 'a native, and a member of the Society of Merchants', and, such was the ignominy in which Sheffield was held, overtures were even made to the Tories by some Whigs for a Bragge and Hobhouse joint ticket. There was nothing particularly radical about Hobhouse, a Dissenter who had publicly attacked the corporation in 1794 for hypocritically refusing to oppose the Test Acts and who, it was claimed, had been briefly associated with an unidentified reform society at Bath in 1792–93. Coleridge attacked him for his vulgar attitude to purchasing votes, alleging he had spent 'about £2000 in beer and cockades. That is – making the mob filthy and fine', and he certainly attracted a boisterous crowd. At the close of the first day's polling an attack was made on the Whig committee rooms at the Bush, the Mansion House and the Council House, and consequently, anxious to dissociate himself from disorder and already trailing badly, Hobhouse pulled out of the contest that night. The Bragge and Sheffield camps made much of his failure, branding him, somewhat unfairly, as a hapless Francophile revolutionary. 'The *British Lion* is roused and the *Jacobin Hobhouse*, alarmed at his Roar, has skulked off like a Spy', trumpeted one handbill; another, 'Spurn, as you value your Rights

[49] S. T. Coleridge, *The Watchman, 1796*, facsimile edn (Poole, 1998).
[50] *An Address to the Electors of the City of Bristol on the Approaching General Election* (Bristol, 1795).

and Liberties, the Democratical – Jacobinical – Soup-meagre – Frenchified Englishman – Benjamin Hobhouse!'[51]

The FoP reconvened to challenge the loyalist consensus over continuing support for the war in 1797 but without Coleridge, who had left Bristol for Nether Stowey, and without Lovell, who had died in 1796. Fox, Coates and Edye attended a February meeting called by the mayor to adopt another loyal address to the throne, and tried in vain to pass an amendment calling on the king to dismiss his hawkish ministry. In April they requested that the mayor convene a town meeting to pass a motion of censure against the war and calling on the king to dismiss his ministers. He refused but allowed them to call a meeting of their own in the Guildhall at which motions were passed blaming the war for the parlous state of the national finances. As a consequence, it was argued, 'The manufacturing poor ... are daily dismissed from their employments to penury; and from penury to a premature grave.' A petition was accordingly drawn up. Within a week, the mayor had convened a loyalist meeting at the Guildhall 'to declare our dissent from the proceedings of some of our fellow citizens' and a loyal address was adopted for presentation to the throne.[52]

Beneath the respectable activities of the FoP however, political conflict of a more robust nature was also making its mark. Although the corporation made little obvious effort to identify and prosecute plebeian radicals at any point during the 1790s, the combative atmosphere surrounding the passage of the Gagging Acts in 1795 prompted a small surge of activity. Magistrates were alarmed to find handbills 'of the most treasonable kind' pressed upon privates of the Hampshire Fencibles when they arrived in the city to disperse striking hatters and colliers in November, and a seaman named John Chossoll was taken up for it. Mayor James Harvey was suspicious of Chossoll's acquaintance with several members of the LCS and held him for several days while crown solicitors' advice was sought on a possible prosecution. He was released without charge but Harvey ordered 'a trusty person to keep an eye on him'. At about the same time, the Bristol Moravian Society refused admission to a man named Thomas Powell, who had 'joined or been intimate with the members of certain societies suspected of being seditious'. But Powell was not prosecuted either, and we hear nothing more of the sort of societies of

---

[51] Lewis polled four votes at the close, and Thomas two. BRL, untitled election handbill, 25 May 1796; *Huzza! Huzza! Huzza! Bragge and Sheffield Forever!!!*, and *Attend Men of Bristol!*, undated handbills [May 1796]; L. Griggs (ed.), *The Collected Letters of Samuel Taylor Coleridge* (6 vols, Oxford, 1956), I, 219, Coleridge to John Fellows, 31 May 1796; *Bristol Mercury*, 30 May 1796; Benjamin Hobhouse, *Thoughts Humbly Offered to the Mayor and Sheriffs of Bristol* (Bristol, 1794). Hobhouse was elected for Bletchingly in 1797, opposed the war and Pitt's domestic policies in parliament and was approached by the Wiltshire shearmen's union as a potential ally during the hard fought dispute of 1802. See *Public Characters of 1807* (London, 1807) pp. 101–36.

[52] *Bristol Mercury*, 6 Feb. 1797; *Bristol Gazette*, 20 and 27 April 1797, 4 May 1797; *Courier*, 27, 28 and 29 April 1797.

which he may have been a member until 1797.[53] This does not mean they had ceased to operate. The BCS was unlikely to advertise its meetings in the Bristol newspapers, and for its part, the press was clearly not interested in drawing attention to it. In January 1797, for instance, the LCS received two communications from a society at Bristol and the BCS held a 'numerous and respectable meeting of the Friends of Freedom' at its own rooms in Union Street, to mark the first anniversary of the acquittal of the London radical, Thomas Stone. However, the meeting was recorded only in the London *Courier*, a paper sympathetic to the Corresponding Societies, while the Bristol press ignored it.[54]

Harvey became most active following the alarms caused by the unexpected landing and defeat of French troops in Pembrokeshire at the end of February 1797. On 2 March, a rumour that a second landing had taken place threw the city into a state of feverish excitement. 'The confusion occasioned here was almost unprecedented', declared a newspaper, as the drums beat all billeted soldiers to arms. The Sussex Fencibles, the Royal Bucks militia and a company of the 13th Foot were marched down to the quay and loaded onto boats to Wales and the Volunteers sent to Stapleton to guard the French prisoners of war, before it became clear that it was a false alarm.[55] A day later, a crowd of rural labourers marched into Bristol from Rowberrow in Somerset to offer their services in the city's defence, stood by the Exchange and sang 'God Save the King'. 'Instead of alarm, fear or despondency appearing in our streets, they were crowded by tens of thousands of people, all burning with the utmost zeal and impatience to face the common enemy', trumpeted *Felix Farley*.[56] And it was in this heady atmosphere that Harvey apprehended a 'low fellow' named William Bennett for distributing radical handbills outside the Exchange and held him for a breach of the peace. Before Bennett could be committed, John King,[57] author of the handbills and owner of the property in Union Street where the BCS held its meetings, came to the Guildhall and accused Harvey of acting unlawfully. King's solicitor had advised him not to offer bail for Bennett but to let Harvey proceed with the case in the expectation that it would fail for want of evidence. Harvey reluctantly thought it

[53] BA, Corporation letter book, James Harvey to Duke of Portland, 2, 7 and 11 Dec. 1795; Bristol University Library, Special Collections, Moravian Congregation finance committee minutes, 12 Dec. 1795 (our thanks to Madge Dresser for this reference); TNA, HO 43/7, John King to James Harvey, 5 Dec. 1795.
[54] TNA, Privy Council (PC) 1/41/A138, LCS treasurer's accounts, Jan. 1797; *Courier*, 3 Feb. 1797.
[55] *Bonner and Middleton's Bristol Journal*, 4 March 1797.
[56] FFBJ, 4 March 1797.
[57] This was probably Dr John King, a young surgeon of radical views who began working with Thomas Beddoes and Humphry Davy at the Pneumatic Institute in Hotwells in 1799. He may also have become a follower of the prophetess Joanna Southcott by 1806. Jay, *The Atmosphere of Heaven*, p. 218; J. F. C. Harrison, *The Second Coming: Popular Millenarianism, 1780–1850* (London, 1979), pp. 128, 252, n.47.

best to let Bennett go, 'though such discharge, I fear, would occasion no small clamour in the town'.[58] This prediction turned out to be correct. Three weeks later, Bennett was set upon by a loyalist crowd for selling radical newspapers outside the Exchange. They 'rolled him in the ken[n]el' and relieved him of his papers and hat, then dragged him to the Guildhall and handed him over to Harvey, who this time bound him over to appear at the quarter sessions for assaulting a member of the crowd. King arrived again and bailed Bennett out, but as they left they were chased down Wine Street and into King's house in Union Street. A siege commenced. King sent a message to Harvey appealing for assistance and a few constables were despatched to advise him to lock his doors. In the early evening, twenty members of the BCS arrived and there were scuffles as they pushed through the crowd and went inside. When the constables left at 8.00p.m., the crowd tried to force an entry and shots were fired from a window by a member of the Society 'in hope of intimidating them'. King sent once more for assistance from the Council House and at 9.00p.m. Harvey arrived, confiscated the gun and advised King that the crowd would disperse if the members of the BCS left the building. As they filed out, Harvey allegedly turned to the crowd and said, 'Gentlemen, I thank you for your loyalty – I own he is a bad subject, but this is not the way to punish him – leave him to us.' Then he left. At 9.30p.m., a final assault was made on the front door, which gave way, and the crowd broke in and stole food and furniture before King was able to disperse them with a sword.

The crowd gathered again the following day, and King tried three times to persuade both Harvey and Alderman George Daubeny

> to endeavour if possible to rescue my family and property from the most daring set of rioters ... I have had two of my windows broke and they are still increasing in number ... It is now growing dark and I have every reason to suppose as night comes on the house will be demolished.

At 8.30p.m., after another series of assaults on BCS members, Harvey appeared with a small force of constables to protect the building. He then rounded on King, blaming him for inflaming the crowd with his seditious pamphlets, and left. Shortly afterwards a constable arrested two stone-throwers, and the crowd, realising the game was finally over, quietly dispersed. Both detainees were released without charge the following morning. Clearly, this was a fairly serious loyalist riot against a society of Bristol reformers, yet no mention was made of it in any of the Bristol newspapers until King was able to bring a prosecution for riotous assembly against one member of the crowd, James Latham, at the August quarter session five months later. The jury acquitted Latham after ten minutes' deliberation because, as *Felix Farley* saw it, King had picked on Latham, 'well knowing he is a very loyal and inoffensive man'. But for the survival of a single copy of King's own published

---

[58] BA, Corporation letter book, James Harvey to Vicary Gibbs, 3 March 1797.

account of events, all detailed knowledge, not only of the riot, but of the existence of a radical society, would now be lost.[59]

Despite the attack on his premises, King continued using it as a point of contact for local radicalism. In May, Harvey intercepted a package of five hundred handbills from the LCS, addressed to King in Union Street, and sent them to the Home Office.[60] The London society was appealing to all provincial reformers to join them in staging mass outdoor meetings on 31 July, in defiance of the Gagging Acts, or rather by careful observance of their provisions. Most histories of radicalism in this period record only that Nottingham answered the call. In fact, Bristol democrats had every intention of holding a meeting as well but, as Harvey told the Duke of Portland the following day, 'a stop was put to it'. Harvey believed the notorious democratic orator, John Thelwall, had been engaged as a speaker and, if so, it would have been the last speech he ever made as an LCS lecturer and on an openly radical platform. It is certainly possible but it would require a revision of Thelwall's own account of his political retirement. 'Prescribed and hunted – driven like a wild beast – and banished like a contagion from society', Thelwall declared himself in retreat from formal politics in late June when he left London on foot for Nether Stowey, in search of poetic solace with Coleridge. A series of physical attacks on his meetings by loyalist crowds, not only in London but at Stockport, Yarmouth, Norwich, King's Lynn, Wisbech and Derby, had apparently taken its toll. Thelwall, as he put it himself, 'tho unchanged in his opinions, renounced all connection with public affairs ... He perceived ... that from the fury with which he was pursued, every effort he made, instead of producing the Reason he loved, only irritated to the Violence he abhorred.' On 12 July, he left Bristol for the final stretch to Nether Stowey after spending several days walking the city and enjoying the company of several friends there, one of whom was very probably Thomas Beddoes. He promised to return again 'before I quitted that side of the country'. At the end of the month, unable to remain any longer in Somerset, Thelwall secured a smallholding beside the Wye in Herefordshire and travelled north to take it up.

On 1 August, however, Harvey informed the Home Office that Thelwall had arrived in Bristol again with the intention of lecturing, but that 'steps' had been taken and 'a stop was put to the seditious meeting intended for yesterday'. Harvey was nevertheless apprehensive that a second attempt would be made, and wrote again to the Home Office for advice. Portland was astonished that a provincial society like the BCS would be in any mood

[59] This account is taken predominantly from the only detailed source for it, John King, *A Statement of the Facts Relative to the Riot in Union Street, Bristol, with some Free Observations on the Conduct of the Civil Power on that Occasion* (Bristol, 1797). A scanty report appeared after a trial hearing five months later in *FFBJ*, 19 Aug. 1797. See also BA, TC Adm Box/50/19, John King to James Harvey, 28 March 1797, and BA, JQS/P/153, Information of Jeremiah Marshall King, 12 April 1797.

[60] BA, Corporation letter book, James Harvey to Duke of Portland, 20 May 1797; TNA, HO 43/9, John King to Harvey 23 May 1797.

to persevere after the national failure of the 31 July meetings scheme, but noting the 'alarm' in Harvey's tone he advised the mayor to adopt the same preventative measures used in London, where six exemplary arrests had been made of platform speakers for an unspecified 'conspiracy' and the crowd dispersed by a heavy show of military force. Characteristically, Harvey was loathe to introduce soldiers and assured Portland that the magistrates could handle it. 'I am under no apprehensions of any serious evil that can arise from the disaffected of this place who, with confidence, I acquaint your grace are, comparatively speaking, very few indeed.' Although the city remained quiet after this, evidence that popular radicalism in Bristol was stronger than we have been led to believe – and strong enough to draw Thelwall from his proclaimed retirement – is compelling.[61]

The fate of any second attempt to stage a public meeting may in fact have been sealed by the arrest at Bath on 11 August of William Bennett, by now well known to the authorities at Bristol, and a journeyman tailor named Thomas Robins. These two had been under surveillance there for keeping company with 'about six journeyman shoemakers and a journeyman smith', distributing radical handbills and making 'parole declarations' in Bath alehouses. They were, however, discharged with a 'severe reprimand' at the borough sessions in October.[62] Bennett's importance to the local popular movement is only hinted at and very little is known of him. He appears to have joined the LCS in 1796 as a member of the more reckless Friends of Liberty who believed that 'the Corresponding Society, having great connections, can furnish them with arms on Emergency'.[63] As Roger Wells and others have persuasively shown, radicals turned increasingly to more confrontational and secretive strategies after the passage of the Gagging Acts, the silencing of Thelwall and the Naval mutinies of 1797, ushering in closer cooperation with the insurrectionary United Irishmen and French Directory. The south-west was particularly sensitive to these developments after it became known that the French planned an intervention in Ireland and hoped to prevent English reinforcements sailing to combat them by sending a raiding party up the Avon by night to fire Bristol. The abortive French landing in Pembrokeshire in 1797 only heightened the tension, and the government was well aware by

[61] Jenny Graham, *The Nation, the Law and the King, Reform Politics in England, 1789–1799* (2 vols, Lanham, 2000), II, 808–28; Nicholas Roe, *Wordsworth and Coleridge: The Radical Years* (Oxford, 1988), pp. 234–6; John Thelwall, 'Prefatory Memoir' and 'A Pedestrian Excursion', in *Selected Political Writings of John Thelwall*, ed. Robert Lamb and Corinna Wagner, vol. 3 (London, 2009), pp. 53, 55, 78, 81. Thelwall does not directly name Beddoes but records 'an interesting conversation on subjects of literature and science at Dr _____'s', following a walk around the Gorge and Downs; TNA, HO 43/9, Duke of Portland to James Harvey, 7 Aug. 1797; BA, Corporation letter book, James Harvey to Duke of Portland, 1 and 8 Aug. 1797.
[62] TNA, 42/41, Jefferies to Duke of Portland, 11 Aug. 1797; HO 43/9, John King to Jefferies, 16 Aug. 1797; *FFBJ*, 12 Aug. 1797.
[63] Thrale, *Selections from the Papers of the London Corresponding Society*, pp. 245, 346.

1798 that frustrated sections of the Corresponding Societies were beginning to splinter into insurrectionary groups of United Englishmen and United Britons, meeting clandestinely and gathering arms in support of the French in the event of invasion.[64]

In the spring of 1798, then, Bennett, together with another strong advocate of physical force, Dr Robert Watson, were tasked by LCS secretary, Thomas Evans, to take 'a certain quantity of pikes' to Bristol, 'in order to plant a society there of United Britons'. Watson was a veteran revolutionary who had fought the British in America and been on intimate terms with Lord George Gordon during the latter's incarceration at Newgate following the London riots of 1780. He spent two years in Newgate himself for playing a major role in the London Crimp House riots of 1794 and was frequently in dispute with the LCS executive over his reckless and argumentative behaviour.[65] If he and Bennett were gathering pikes at Bristol, there can be little doubt of the intention, but progress was nipped in the bud by a series of government raids on radical strongholds, the sudden suspension of habeas corpus and numerous arrests of known activists. No raids were carried out in Bristol, but a meeting of the LCS General Committee in London was targeted on 19 April and among those taken up was William Bennett, who had gone there to discuss the allocation and purchase of Bristol pikes. Samples of these were found on the table by Bow Street Runners and Bennett was questioned for nine hours, kept in custody until 28 April, then released without charge.[66]

There is no surviving record of Bennett's examination by the Privy Council, but the evidence suggests that the government spymaster, William Wickham, who considered him a pretty small fish, offered to drop charges on condition that he became an informer. Bennett allegedly accepted, and on the day after his release, Wickham sent him a 'generous loan'. Bennett left two notes at Wickham's house on 30 April, confirming his mission to Bristol and promising 'a great deal of information' if granted a further interview. But Wickham abandoned him, possibly after reading a letter from Bennett's uncle warning Wickham that Bennett had a loose tongue and had been openly calling himself 'secretary to the Corresponding Society at Bristol'. Watson, meanwhile, was a wanted man at Bristol, vulnerable to the 'nightly patrols' of Volunteers pledged to root out all 'traitors and incendiaries' in the city following the arrests in London. A warrant for high treason was issued against him in May, but he evaded capture by obtaining passage on a ship variously

---

[64] Roger Wells, *Insurrection: The British Experience, 1795–1803* (Gloucester, 1983), especially chs 6 and 7.

[65] TNA, PC 1/42/A140, William Bennett to William Wickham, 30 April 1798; *Morning Chronicle*, 15 Nov. 1794; *Courier*, 17 Nov. 1794.

[66] For the outline circumstances of Bennett's arrest, see TNA, PC 1/42/A140, William Bennett to William Wickham, 30 April 1798, and PC 1/44/A161, List of prisoners taken and the dates of their release, 1798 and 1799.

described as bound for New York, London or Stockholm, and disguised, so it was said, as a Polish Jew.[67]

This is the last we hear of radical initiatives at Bristol in the 1790s. Although the city's reformers faced a more actively hostile magistracy under Mayor Harvey than they had under men like Bengough and Morgan, judicial interference remained piecemeal and relatively mild. If Morgan had feigned ignorance when asked about the strength of Jacobin societies, Harvey at least knew about the Constitutional Society, had visited its rooms, had interviewed and even arrested its key personnel, prevented at least one public meeting and interfered with its mail. But, like Morgan, he was disinclined to share his knowledge with Whitehall and never reported the arrest of Bennett or the results of his questioning, or even the two-day riot outside the BCS's rooms in Union Street. Harvey's attitude to radical disturbance was not, therefore, at odds with custom and practice in the city. Aside from Bennett and Chossoll, neither of whom were actually prosecuted, the only other arrests made at Bristol for seditious offences during this period came in 1803. Ann Watkins, a publican, was investigated for making 'unguarded expressions to militiamen', and two men, one unnamed, the other George Pollard, were taken up for seditious words. Pollard was reported for drinking a toast to Bonaparte in a pub in Lime Kiln Lane whilst 'in liquor'.[68] None of these three were prosecuted either. Despite John Weeks's determination to ensure that any seditious remarks overheard in the taproom of any one of Bristol's numerous inns would result in 'just punishment', there was no appetite amongst Bristol's rulers for a loyalist legal offensive. Since the Duke of Portland was quite unaware of the activities of men like Bennett and King, or of the arrival of Watson, the Home Office was unable to take any initiatives of its own at Bristol and unlikely to probe for further information. Silence has been interpreted by historians as absence, but, as we have seen here, this is not necessarily an accurate picture.

---

[67] TNA, PC 1/42/A140, James Major to William Wickham, 30 April 1798; William Bennett to William Wickham (two letters), 30 April 1798; *FFBJ*, 28 April 1798. Conflicting stories of Watson's escape appear in *The Times*, 26 May 1798, and in his obituary in *The Times* 22 and 23 Nov. 1838. See also Marianne Elliott, *Partners in Revolution: The United Irishmen and France* (New York, 1982), pp. 141–2.

[68] TNA, HO 42/72, John Noble to Lord Pelham, 8 Aug. 1803 with (enclosure) information of John Baker and Thomas Skyrme, 8 Aug. 1803; *Bath Journal*, 21 Feb. 1803.

11

Hunt and Liberty: Popular Politics
in Bristol, 1800–20

When the politics of opposition reappeared openly in Bristol in the first decade of the nineteenth century, it was driven once again by local issues, but also by the fortuitous arrival of Henry 'Orator' Hunt on the eve of the general election in 1807, who took a house in fashionable Bellevue, Clifton, while settling his business interests in the Jacobs Wells brewery. Hunt had developed an appetite for arguments about electoral independence through a series of noisy interventions in the contest for Wiltshire the previous year, and now saw Bristol as an ideal place in which to further develop his ambitions. Partly through Hunt's influence then, conflicts over local corruption and the right of franchise came to dominate the language of opposition in the city in this period, once more making the corporation and the local party system the principal focus of discontent.

The Bristol newspapers had loudly congratulated the Whig and Tory clubs for getting their candidates elected without the trouble of a poll after the general election of November 1806, but the collapse of the resulting ministry after just six months raised the issue again in the late spring of 1807.[1] Soon after the new election was called, it was announced in Bristol that an independent candidate, Sir John Jarvis, had unexpectedly come forward to oppose the customary coalition. Jarvis was the commander of the city's Volunteer rifle corps, an unlikely candidate, and Hunt was highly suspicious of him. In the first place Hunt believed Jarvis to be a Tory and in the second Jarvis appeared to have nobody in place to nominate him. Suspecting that Jarvis was actually a paper candidate, produced by the coalition to dissuade the freemen from putting forward a genuine independent candidate of their own, Hunt accompanied Jarvis to the Guildhall. There he tried to nominate Jarvis himself, but was debarred since he was neither a freeman nor a freeholder in the city and since nobody else stepped forward to do it, the Whig Evan Baillie and the Tory, Charles Bragge-Bathurst were elected without a contest. Jarvis's farcical non-candidature raised tempers that had already been sorely tested in 1806, and public animosity towards Bathurst in particular led to serious disturbances, the immediate causes of which remain unclear. A letter in the *Mercury* from

---

[1] *FFBJ*, 1 Nov. 1806.

'a hard working Bristolian' alleged that the candidate had visited a factory on election day and told workers that 'six shillings a week was enough to support a working man and his family'. For that, he was 'assailed on all sides', claimed the writer, and 'threats of what they would do to him were he in their power followed, of course'. Others ascribed the animosity to Bathurst's vocal support for the corporation's Dock Bill, but whatever the cause, the response was certainly violent. 'Never, we will venture to say, was there a mob assembled that proceeded to such acts of violence as this did', complained *Felix Farley*, as a 'lawless and ferocious banditti' several thousand strong targeted Bathurst's chairing ceremony with 'volleys of stones ... oyster shells and mud', forcing him to abandon his chair and retreat into the White Lion.[2]

In his own later account, Hunt claimed the crowd were sufficiently incensed to kill Bathurst to force a re-election, and that a number of prominent Tories were severely hurt in the fighting. According to Hunt however, the complete destruction of the White Lion was prevented only by his own intervention as he took control and led the crowd onto Brandon Hill where he announced his own intention to stand for election in Bristol at the next opportunity.[3] With this promise, Hunt began an association with Bristol that would last for the next ten years; a connection that would be instrumental in turning the rhetoric of independence in the city into one of radical reform.

At the time of his arrival, there had been little change since the campaigns of Barry and Lewis in 1790. In 1807, Bristol's most vociferous local propagandist for the right of election was the surgeon, Thomas Lee, a man with no interest in organising a coherent political platform. 'Much has been said respecting the formation of a club to oppose the factions', he declared. 'This would be becoming a faction yourselves. The man who wants numbers to back him before he will advance will follow numbers when they retreat. No clubber is or can be independent. The moment a man becomes one, that moment he is shackled.'[4] Encouraged by the surprise victory of Sir Francis Burdett at Westminster however, and now convinced that Bristol had been 'reduced to a level with the rottenest of rotten boroughs', Hunt formed a Bristol Patriotic and Constitutional Association at the Lamb and Lark in Thomas Street, pledged to combat coalitions at all future elections. This society, modelled on the well-organised Westminster Committee in London, caused such a rupture with Lee that the surgeon left the city for good amid some absurd accusations from Hunt that he was a member of the United Irishmen.[5]

[2] FFBJ, 11 May 1807; *Gloucester Journal*, 11 May 1807; *Bristol Mercury*, 25 May 1807.
[3] *Memoirs of Henry Hunt, Esq.* (3 vols, London, 1820), II, 119–20.
[4] Thomas Lee, *Eyes to the Blind! An Address to the Electors of Bristol, Vindicating their Elective Franchise Against the Endeavours of the Corporation and of Certain Clubs* (Bristol, 1807), p. 30.
[5] *Memoirs of Henry Hunt*, II, 127; John Belchem, *'Orator' Hunt: Henry Hunt and English Working-Class Radicalism* (Oxford, 1985), pp. 20–2. The UI allegations are referred to in the *Bristol Mirror*, 18 June 1808.

Hunt had no interests to pursue in Bristol until the next election and he busied himself in Bath, London and in Wiltshire, but his influence may be detected in the calling of a public meeting of freeholders at the Guildhall in May 1809, to censure government in the wake of the Duke of York's exposure for trafficking commissions and contracts. This meeting, chaired by the veteran radical banker William Coates, moved quickly from the condemnation of corruption to resolutions for reform to 'restore the constitution to its original purity as moulded and established by Magna Carta, the Bill of Rights and the Act of Settlement'. Parliament, it was alleged, was nothing but 'an assembly of persons styling themselves the representatives of the people' but where 'the influence of public opinion is unblushingly condemned and its legitimacy openly denied'.[6] Support for Burdett also continued in Hunt's absence, partly because the city Recorder, Vicary Gibbs, was instrumental in sending the radical baronet to the Tower for breaching parliamentary privilege in 1810. When Gibbs arrived to open the Bristol assize in April, he was greeted by wall chalkings proclaiming 'Burdett for ever' and 'No Gibbs', and a number of 'incendiary handbills' on walls and lamp-posts. In the evening, the key institutions of corporation authority came under attack, as windows were smashed at the Guildhall, Mansion House and Council House and seventeen arrests were made before the crowd could be brought under control.[7]

Since both Bragge-Bathurst and Baillie had intimated that they would stand down at the next election, and Hunt's independent candidature was widely forecast, it was clear not only that there would be a contest for the first time since 1796 but that the selection of candidates to oppose Hunt was likely to be controversial. Hunt's opportunity arrived in the summer of 1812 when Bragge-Bathurst's appointment as Chancellor of the Duchy of Lancaster prompted a by-election for one of Bristol's two seats. The Tories produced Richard Hart Davis as Bathurst's replacement and the Whigs amiably agreed not to stand against him, so it was to be a straight contest between Davis and Hunt.

It was extraordinarily violent. According to Hunt, Davis mobilised 'upwards of four hundred mock constables or bludgeon men', drawn from 'the greatest ruffians that the city of Bristol and the neighbourhood of Cock Road and Kingswood could furnish'. They were armed with twenty-four-inch staves and battle commenced for the possession of electoral territory. But Hunt was a more determined and able independent candidate than either Hobhouse or Lewis had been and he took the fight to the Tories with a vengeance. After the nomination ceremony, when Hunt's crowd were bettered by Davis's, the Tory vanguard doubled in size and 'became so outrageously brutal that it was absolutely necessary to put them down', reasoned Hunt. Consequently he openly sanctioned arming his own supporters with bludgeons. 'If they once begin to knock down the people', he declared, 'let them without ceremony be

[6] *FFBJ*, 27 May 1809.
[7] *FFBJ*, 21 April 1810.

driven out of the city.' Hunt announced himself 'the staunch friend of Radical Reform and the enemy of oppression'. He made the Talbot Inn his headquarters and established a recognised public arena for the campaign outside the Exchange, a commanding position at the centre of Bristol's electoral theatre in which huge crowds could be addressed.

The physical and symbolic control of public space in these crowded thoroughfares was of vital importance as polling continued over the next few days. One key battleground was the confined area outside the Guildhall in Broad Street where polling took place; it was almost opposite the White Lion, and where Davis's men had been 'stopping up all access'. Hunt's newly armed crowd now ousted the Tory mob from Broad Street and quickly took command of public space both there and in Corn Street, attacking Davis's committee rooms, the British Coffee Room and the White Lion, which was left without a single intact window. This was followed by a foray to Berkeley Square where the home of the prominent Tory alderman and West India merchant, Thomas Daniel, was targeted. The crowd then sallied to Clifton where Davis's own house was pelted and his garden ransacked. Attacks on the Council House, centrally positioned at the junction of Corn and Broad Streets, were common enough during civil disturbances at Bristol, but here they were more sustained and vicious than usual. As tension increased, the mayor and magistrates were only able to maintain control of the city centre at night by summoning troops to patrol the central streets when the polls closed each evening. With forty people taken up for riot and sent to Newgate, the scale of the disorder was without precedent at a Bristol election. In fact, Hunt believed there was more at stake now than a seat in parliament, for it had become 'evidently a contest between the rich and the poor'. Certainly, as Mark Harrison and John Belchem have shown, the majority of Hunt's supporters were artisans and small tradesmen. 'I had no allies but the people; of *them* indeed, I had the great mass with me, but thought I had well-wishers in all the richer classes, there was scarcely a single man beyond the rank of a journeyman who had the courage to openly give me any countenance or support.'[8] The Bristol establishment did what it could to obstruct Hunt's campaign, even forwarding copies of his handbills to the Home Office with a suggestion that he be prosecuted for seditious libel.[9]

Hunt kept the polling open for fifteen days but was roundly defeated by 1907 votes to 235. The turnout was surprisingly low given the length of the contest and the attention it received, and Hunt felt he would have done better if the 'hundreds upon hundreds' who were 'anxious' to vote for him

[8] *Memoirs of Henry Hunt*, II, 243, 247, 259, 264, 273; Mark Harrison, *Crowds and History: Mass Phenomena in English Towns, 1790–1835* (Cambridge, 1988), pp. 205–15; Belchem, *'Orator' Hunt*, pp. 26–30. Harrison and Belchem's appraisal of Hunt's support is based on the list of his voters published by the Tories after the election and then republished by Hunt himself in his *Memoirs* (III, 5–7).

[9] TNA, HO 43/21, John Beckett to W. Taylor, 8 July 1812.

had not felt intimidated by the Establishment. 'All the merchants, tradesmen and masters of every denomination openly vowed vengeance against all their dependents and connections if they voted for me', he claimed. 'I believe there never was anything equal to the threats and intimidation that took place in that city during that election.' It was equally likely of course that Whig voters had simply stayed away from the polls by choice, but there may be some truth in Hunt's allegations. The Tory Steadfast Society later published a list of all those who had voted for Hunt. Most of them hailed from the populous parishes of Bristol and featured a good smattering of shoemakers, carpenters, tailors and masons, occupations well known for their radicalism. The Tories intended 'to injure them in their business by pointing them out', Hunt claimed, and not without cause perhaps, because, as everybody knew, this contest had only been a dress rehearsal for the general election to be called in the autumn.[10]

That election was complicated because the Whigs had fallen out over the selection of their candidate. Their first choice had been the experienced parliamentarian, libertarian legal reformer and abolitionist, Sir Samuel Romilly, but some found his politics altogether too radical and plumped for a local traditionalist, Edward Protheroe. He hailed from one of the elite families who made their fortune in the West Indian trade, and he was well placed on the corporation, having been its sheriff in 1797 and mayor in 1804. With the Whig vote thus split, Hunt may have thought himself in with a chance if Whig voters could be persuaded to back Romilly and himself against Protheroe and Davis, but Romilly, who knew he could secure a much easier constituency elsewhere, gave up after a week. He was mismatched with Hunt from the start, with the latter sniping at him for not being a supporter of Burdett, and the two of them having diametrically opposed views about popular campaigning. Romilly gave every indication that he found crowd politics vulgar and disliked appearing on public platforms, whereas Hunt courted street politics at every opportunity. Romilly also made an ill-judged appearance with John Noble, the alderman most associated with the Bristol Bridge riots. When the results were declared after ten days and the conservative Davis/Protheroe coalition duly elected by a sizable majority, Hunt had at least doubled his vote to 456 but he had failed to cement an alliance with Romilly, who polled 1685 before retiring. The complexity of the contest and its shifting alliances mitigated against a repeat of the crowd trouble that marked Hunt's earlier intervention in the summer, though there was a short fracas between his supporters and some shipwrights working in the yard of the prominent Tory shipbuilder, Abraham Hillhouse, on the Hotwells road.[11]

In the end Hunt secured only a tenth of the electors who voted in the general election of 1812. The great bulk of his support came from the artisanal parishes to the south and east of the city; over half in fact from St James,

[10] *Memoirs of Henry Hunt*, II, 266, III, 3; Harrison, *Crowds and History*, p. 215.
[11] Harrison, *Crowds and History*, pp. 215–18.

St Philip and St Jacob, and the new parish of St Paul's. It was composed predominantly of the industrial crafts and trades: tailors, turners, tilers, masons, carpenters, cabinet-makers and blacksmiths. Shoemakers, above all, favoured Hunt, as they did among the out-voters of greater London, where the flamboyant radical secured 43 per cent of the electors who had trekked the Great West Road, including the radical shipwright John Gast from Deptford.[12]

Winning over voters was not Hunt's only objective. He was also on a consciousness-raising mission, exposing the nefarious tactics of the Bristol elite, drawing their ire and forcing electoral irregularities. On this score he did chalk up some successes. Bringing in troops at elections was irregular; so, too, was the positioning of two brass six-pound cannons at the front of the Exchange, the response of the civic authorities in the general election to the purported threat of radical theatrics. Both of these incidents were picked up by William Cobbett in his *Political Register* and reiterated in Hunt's petitions against electoral graft. Hunt also criticised the pork-barrel tactics of his opponents whose expenses in the general election – for treating, purchasing freedoms and so on, amounted to £15,000 apiece, whereas Hunt's own expenses amounted to a meagre £30. He also delved into the civic mismanagement of charitable bequests, obtaining access to the corporation's books by virtue of a Speaker's warrant. Hunt knew he could not break the grip of the big clubs in Bristol politics, at least not immediately. But he was an expert in the politics of exposure, drawing attention to the disreputable system of electoral management that had for so long kept Bristol freemen in thrall. In his contests, Hunt recalled, 'the people of Bristol had an opportunity of hearing more bold political truths than they had ever heard before; both the factions of Whigs and Tories were exposed, and their united and unprincipled efforts to deceive and cajole the people were freely canvassed'.[13] For all his flamboyance, conceit and opportunism, Hunt recognised that the only way to challenge Bristol's oligarchy was to take it to the streets.

Hunt continued to make sporadic visits to Bristol over the next four years. He was at a public meeting in the Guildhall protesting the property tax in 1815 for example, unsuccessfully proposing amendments against all 'war taxes'.[14] If Hunt tried to call public meetings of his own, it often prompted anxious letters from the mayor to the Home Office requesting cavalry to maintain

---

[12] *Bristol Poll Book*, 1812. Hunt did secure the vote of four gentlemen and five accountants. Shopkeepers were in short supply, presumably because they feared the loss of custom. Among the food trades Hunt did win over four butchers, two grocers, a baker and a cheese factor, and men like these also featured as members of Hunt's crowd, though not necessarily as voters. Of the thirty-six men taken up for rioting in Hunt's favour, three were bakers, one a fishmonger and another, a butcher. Most of the rest were artisans: shoemakers, coach-makers, blacksmiths, carpenters, glassmakers and cabinetmakers. Two were seamen and one a Kingswood collier. BA, TC/Adm/Box/63/14, List of prisoners in Bridewell.

[13] *Memoirs of Henry Hunt*, III, 16.

[14] *FFBJ*, 21 Jan. 1815.

order. Outside of election periods there was little real cause for alarm however, although an afternoon spent haranguing crowds from his usual pitch outside the Exchange in 1813 did culminate in a small section of the crowd running off to Portland Square and pulling down the centrepiece statue of George III with a rope. A maltster's servant named John Harris, heard shouting 'Hunt forever' as he sprinted away, was committed to the quarter session and gaoled for a year.[15] Occasional signs of popular opposition over the next three years are detectable but they remained isolated, piecemeal and politically incoherent. Bonfires were lit on Brandon Hill to celebrate the failure of the government's property tax in 1816, for instance, and an effigy of Richard Hart Davis tossed onto the flames for good measure, not by any coherent group, but by 'an assemblage of boys'.[16]

Hunt's most keenly anticipated reappearance at Bristol came in December 1816 when the post-war recession was at its most serious and the orator's national reputation was on the rise. In London, Hunt had been persuaded to take a leading role that Autumn as a platform speaker at a series of radical reform rallies at Spa Fields, as attempts were made to establish Hampden Clubs to agitate reform throughout the country. Hunt was flattered by the attention and seemingly unflustered by the radical core of the Spa Fields committee which was dominated by insurrectionary Spenceans. He would speak, Hunt confirmed, on condition that the purpose of the meeting to peacefully petition the Regent for universal suffrage and relief from poverty was absolutely clear and no attempt would be made to introduce Spence's 'chimerical and fanatical' plan for public landownership. The first meeting in November went well enough; indeed Hunt's performance sealed his reputation as the national movement's most dynamic new figurehead and established the strategic principle of mass platform, outdoor public meetings for reform. At the second meeting, on 2 December, however, an 'unofficial' Spencean platform was established elsewhere on the field and used to engineer a crowd attack on East End gunshops and a half-hearted attempt to take the Tower and the Royal Exchange. The rising took the government completely by surprise and took a day to suppress; and although Hunt's vehement denial that he knew anything about it was probably genuine, his self-promotion as 'Spa Fields Hunt' did not make him look any less dangerous to the authorities.[17] If Hampden Clubs were now to be established in the West Country, Hunt was the obvious choice for a speaker, and meetings to consider how to respond to

---

[15] *FFBJ*, 27 March 1813; *Bristol Mercury*, 29 March 1813; BA, Corporation letter book, Mayor of Bristol to General Cumming, 22 March 1813, and to Lieutenant Colonel Middlemore, 22 March 1813.

[16] *Bristol Mirror*, 23 March 1816.

[17] Belchem, 'Orator' Hunt, pp. 42–54; Iain McCalman, *Radical Underworld: Prophets, Revolutionaries and Pornographers in London, 1795–1840* (Oxford, 1993), pp. 106–12; David Worrall, *Radical Culture: Discourse, Resistance and Surveillance, 1790–1820* (Detroit, 1992), pp. 97–113.

the Regent's refusal to accept the Spa Fields Address were therefore proposed at Bath and Bristol.

It is difficult to assess the strength of radical organisation in Bristol at this time. In November, the Tory press could boast that whatever the scale of 'disaffection and discontent' elsewhere in the country, 'the city of Bristol appears to stand aloof from the infection, and where the partisans of Mr Hunt might naturally be supposed to abound the most, we are unusually temperate and quiet ... Hampden Cubs are names unknown amongst us'.[18] Radical newspapers were certainly feeling the squeeze. Cobbett's *Register* was banned from the Commercial Reading Room in 1815 and refused shelf space by 'one of our principle news vendors' a year later. Although still on sale in the street outside the Exchange, its customers 'do not exceed fifty in a population of 48,000'.[19] But behind the bluster, JPs were anxious. Hunt remained locally popular; indeed he gathered a crowd of eight- to ten thousand at Bristol when he returned to the Exchange in July 1816 for an impromptu street celebration to mark the fourth anniversary of the 1812 election.[20] Now he applied to the mayor to use the Guildhall for a public meeting. John Gordon and the West India merchant Thomas Daniel were worried about the unprotected state of ammunition dumps near the city, 'Mr Hunt being of Bristol notoriety'. The Town Clerk of Bath, worried that trouble might spread to his own city, shared their belief that a substantial military presence would be needed if the meeting went ahead. 'There is little doubt if the insurgents are successful in London all provincial towns and cities will follow their example', he advised Lord Sidmouth, 'Bristol assuredly will require all the military aid in its neighbourhood to be on that ground.' Sidmouth sent orders for all arms to be moved to a safer place, and offered the mayor a small detachment of irregular cavalry, but the increasingly paranoid Daniel emphatically assured him it would not be enough: 'You have no idea of the ferocity of a Bristol mob.' Whatever the Tory press was saying publicly, Daniel believed a radical committee was holding regular meetings at the Bath Barge in Queen Street. The mayor and aldermen, 'do not think themselves justified in searching for their papers', he wrote, and appealed to Sidmouth to send down some London officers to do it. Daniel, who sensed the 'Spa Fields gentry' everywhere, was even suspicious of 'a person of mean attire' seen purchasing large quantities of coloured ribbons in a Bristol shop. The city's night watch was instructed to keep a look out for the 'chalk authors' who had been leaving 'incendiary inscriptions' on buildings for more than a fortnight and if possible make some exemplary arrests.[21]

[18] *FFBJ*, 30 Nov. 1816.
[19] *Cobbett's Political Register*, 30 Dec. 1815; *FFBJ*, 30 Nov. 1816.
[20] *Morning Chronicle*, 19 July 1816.
[21] TNA, HO 42/156, John Gordon to Lord Sidmouth, 6 Dec. 1816; Thomas Daniel to Sidmouth, 6 Dec. 1816; Phillip George to Sidmouth, 6 Dec. 1816; TNA, HO 42/157, Thomas Daniel to Lord Sidmouth, 19 and 22 Dec. 1816; *Bristol Mercury*, 23 Dec. 1816.

The magistrates began by closing down and seeking to control public space, refusing Hunt permission to hold any meeting at the Guildhall. Unperturbed, Hunt switched the venue to Brandon Hill, chose Boxing Day to maximise the crowd and prompted reaction on an extraordinary scale. Four troops of lancers were drafted from barracks at Weymouth and Trowbridge, 478 men from the North Somerset Yeomanry and 96 from the 35th Regiment of Foot in Castle Cary and Dorchester, yet even this sizable military force was outnumbered by the enrolment of 2000 special constables, including Hillhouse's shipwrights who had clashed with Hunt in 1812. Hunt's Bristol committee, which included John and Thomas Cossens and Thomas Pimm, were warned by the magistrates against erecting any 'illegal' hustings on the top of the Hill. The newspaper press urged Bristolians to stay away and encouraged employers to withdraw Christmas boxes from any of their workers seen on the Hill. Many of them, according to Cobbett, went further, publishing handbills threatening workers with dismissal and making them 'guilty of a conspiracy to obstruct petitioning'. R. B. Thornhill, commanding a troop of yeomanry, announced his intention to spoil Hunt's arrival from Bath by stationing his men on Totterdown Hill, 'where you may depend upon it that Mr Hunt and his guides will be properly dealt with'. On the radical side, handbills counselled against intimidation. The right to meet and petition was 'solemnly assured and guaranteed … It is a right which you hold under the law and not under the indulgence or sufferance of the magistrates', ran one.[22]

On the morning of the meeting the weather was atrocious and there were soldiers everywhere. 'The streets were lined with troops, drenched in rain', recalled Hunt. At midday the weather improved and Hunt estimated some ten thousand people came to hear him move resolutions for annual parliaments, universal suffrage and vote by ballot. The resulting petition attracted 20,700 signatures. 'These resolutions and this petition', declared Hunt, 'were carried by a meeting of unarmed citizens, assembled upon Brandon Hill, which was surrounded by armed troops, drawn up within sight, and some of them within hearing … the appearance of the city was more like a besieged fortress than anything else'.

Both sides claimed victory. John Scandrett Harford, son-in-law of Richard Hart Davis and owner of Blaise Castle, thought the 'prompt and vigorous measures' of the magistrates had saved the city from 'serious consequences … A very small number were assembled to hear the Orator who went away quite discomforted and chopfallen.'[23] Mayor John Haythorne also insisted that Hunt's audience had been 'few and contemptible', but he was disappointed

[22] FFBJ, 28 Dec. 1816; Bristol Mercury, 23 and 30 Dec. 1816; Cobbett's Political Register, 'Address to the Men of Bristol', 11 Jan. 1817; BA, TC/Adm/Box/67/15, R. B. Thornhill to mayor of Bristol, 25 Dec. 1816; Addington to Thomas Daniel, 7 Dec. 1816; BRL, Jefferies Collection, vol. 9, To the Citizens of Bristol (Bristol, 1816); Memoirs of Henry Hunt, III, 218–19.

[23] BA, Harford Papers, 28048 c.62, J. C. Harford to J. Harford, 6 Jan. 1817.

to learn that a number of his constables had since signed the reform petition, and he thought the danger far from over. Sidmouth was urged to convert the former French prison at Stapleton into a barracks and to retain three or four troops of horse in the city. Haythorne had received a number of anonymous threatening letters from 'disappointed villains' and he was convinced 'there exists a correspondence between the agitators here and those of Spa Fields'.[24]

War was now waged on the vendors of unstamped radical newspapers. In January 1817, Abel Dagg Cook and John Bullen were both gaoled for two months under the Hawkers and Peddlers Act for selling copies of Cobbett's *Political Register* outside the Exchange. Some loyalists feared repression might backfire. 'I think it will be found to be a fact that *Cobbett's Register* has been read by Hundreds in this city who would not look at it prior to this commitment', warned one. But Haythorne thought prosecution had 'much impeded' the circulation of 'infamous and blasphemous papers ... industriously circulated' in the city, and moved next against the Narrow Wine Street printer, Joseph Arnold, who had been publishing copies of Hone's satirical *Political Litany* and the *Sinecurist's Creed*. Although convicted and fined, Arnold continued printing Hone's pamphlets and was reported again to the Home Office in the summer.[25] Loyalist handbills were posted in London, apparently at the behest of the Middlesex bench, proclaiming 'Mr Hunt Hissed out of the City of Bristol', but, typically, Hunt found the means to turn the smear to his advantage. Learning that a seventeen-year-old youth named Thomas Dugood had been arrested and confined in Cold Bath Fields by a magistrate for pulling one of these handbills from the wall in a London street, Hunt secured his release and exposed the behaviour of the local bench as arbitrary and scandalous. The case attracted a good deal of attention in the news media.[26]

Since neither Davis nor Protheroe would agree to support it, the Brandon Hill reform petition was presented to parliament by Lord Cochrane at the end of January 1817. It was ordered to lie on the table. Its presentation, together with a large number of similar Hampden Club reform petitions from other provincial towns, was timed to coincide with the state opening of parliament, but this proved a catalyst for serious disorder following the outright rejection of all but a handful of them. As the hugely unpopular Prince Regent left the Lords at the close of the ceremony, his coach was attacked by the crowd that been lobbying MPs in Palace Yard, its windows broken and its panels dented by stones. Davis dissociated himself from the Bristol petition entirely, rising in the Commons to deny the legitimacy of the meeting that produced it and

[24] TNA, HO 42/158, John Haythorne to Lord Sidmouth, 5 Jan. 1817.
[25] *Morning Post*, 23 Jan. 1817; *Bath Chronicle*, 29 Jan. 1817; TNA, HO 42/159, John Haythorne to Lord Sidmouth, 8 and 9 Feb. 1817, C. McDowell to Sidmouth, 8 Feb. 1817; TNA, HO 42/160, John Haythorne to Sidmouth, 21 Feb. 1817; TNA, HO 42/166, C. Carr to Sidmouth, 10 June 1817; BA, TC/Adm/Box/68/4, R.F.M. to John Haythorne, n.d. [Feb. 1817].
[26] *Memoirs of Henry Hunt*, III, 237–42.

'protesting against its being received as the Petition of the People of Bristol'. Meanwhile the Tory press sniped from the sidelines. 'It is a fact', grumbled *Felix Farley's Bristol Journal*, 'that the charity children of Temple parish repeatedly signed that petition on their return to and from school'. The best response, given the events in Palace Yard, the paper insisted, would be a non-party declaration of loyalty to the Regent, and the Tories busied themselves with its promotion in the ensuing days. This Declaration of Principles was widely canvassed and intended as a public statement of hostility to Hunt and everything he stood for. Each week, the names of the growing list of subscribers were publicly printed in the paper, a tactic which will have

> convinced the nation that in this city and its vicinity, the revolutionary opinions of the day … have found no countenance or support amongst the portion of its citizens who have a stake in the country worth preserving. The document … will become a memorial in the annals of Bristol to which our posterity will refer in testimony to the loyalty and patriotism which their forefathers displayed in these times of national peril and alarm. In Bristol we conceive that this declaration must have set at rest all apprehension of disturbance and misrule and that the energies and attention of the Administration are at liberty to be directed to the suppression of those symptoms of dissatisfaction which are occurring in other places.

In essence the Declaration was to be understood as a representation of non-party feeling; a rallying point for the civic establishment and its right to govern the city as it always had. The Tory, J. M. Gutch was anxious to point out that it was possible to sign it and still wish for reasonable reforms, for even 'the best friends of government can scarcely think it immaculate'. Some Bristol radicals complied by using it as a platform for sending further democratic messages to parliament. The Castle Street hatmaker, John Cossens, for example, who had travelled to London with Hunt as a delegate to present the Bristol petition, signed the Declaration but he added that he was, 'a staunch advocate for the constitution in all its purity, a friend to parliamentary reform, universal suffrage, annual parliaments and voting by ballot'. *Felix Farley* declined from printing these amendments, but they were revealed by the *Mirror*. The *Mercury* and the *Gazette*, meanwhile, considered the document a Tory measure at root and kept their distance.[27]

In London, the government was alarmed not only by the physical attack on the Regent and the spread of the radical press but by continuous reports of arming and industrial disturbance in the north, which culminated in the Pentrich rising. In this context ministers fought to constrain the awakening radical movement. Habeas corpus was suspended and a Seditious Meetings Act passed to once again restrict 'tumultuous' assemblies. In a bid to outsmart

---

[27] *FFBJ*, 1, 8 and 15 Feb. 1817, 15 March 1817; *Bristol Mirror*, 15 March 1817; *Bristol Mercury*, 17 Feb. 1817; *Bristol Gazette*, 22 Feb. 1817. For the presentation of petitions and the attack on the Regent's coach, see Steve Poole, *The Politics of Regicide in England 1760–1820: Troublesome Subjects* (Manchester, 2000), pp. 142–58.

any attempts by the government to interfere with mass petitioning, the reform petitions of 1818 were smaller in signatories but greater in quantity, a strategy designed to maximise the length of time required in parliament to consider and reject them. Although democratic organisations in Bristol remain shadowy in this period, Davis, Protheroe and Samuel Romilly were kept busy in the spring of 1818 presenting at least ninety-eight short reform petitions from the city, each signed by no more than twenty people. Davis told the Commons to expect 'several hundred' altogether and that as many as one thousand might be in preparation, but assured them the documents did not reflect the true feelings of his constituents.[28]

By this time, Hunt had relaxed his connection to Bristol, although he was still frequently referred to as '*Bristol* Hunt' in the national press. He had initially intended to offer himself for election a third time in Bristol, but he was embroiled in London politics when the next general election was called in 1818, and so he stood at Westminster instead. Without success. Meanwhile, the election in Bristol began farcically, with divisions amongst the Whigs. The more radical wing regarded Protheroe as a candidate for the 'coalition of the Blue interest', and consequently they made it clear they would not be backing him. Unwilling to face a contest with a third candidate, Protheroe announced his withdrawal. Consequently Evan Baillie's son, Hugh Duncan, was proposed in his place, but Protheroe's supporters persuaded him to stand after all. This caused Baillie in turn to back off until he, too, was prevailed upon to reconsider, finally forcing the contest both Whig candidates had hoped to avoid. Protheroe emerged the easy victor, despite complaints from Baillie's supporters that the mayor had closed the poll too early and denied London freemen time to get to Bristol and vote. Even so, the division within the Whig party was clear. Baillie's supporters sported slogans reading 'No Coal Tax! No Gaol Tax! No Property Tax! No Protheroe!' and the sitting MP was forced to defend his parliamentary record at every turn. 'It is not a delegate, gentlemen, that you send to parliament', chided Protheroe, 'but a representative'. The election was not without crowd violence, but Baillie was no Hunt and the disturbances were restricted to 'crowds of disorderly fellows throwing stinking fish, dead cats, dogs, rats and other offensive missiles' at people making their way through Clare Street to vote, as well as a customary attack upon the windows of the White Lion. Order was quickly restored by ward constables, and toasts were drunk at the conclusion of Davis's chairing ceremony wishing 'confusion to all revolutionary meetings whether held at Spa Fields or on Brandon Hill'.[29]

The radical failure of 1818 spurred the creation of a new independent society, the Friends of Freedom of Election in January 1819. It was not a universal suffragist Hampden Club and its committee was drawn from professional men who, like most partisans of independence, were already enfranchised as

[28] *Bristol Gazette*, 5 March 1818; *Bath and Cheltenham Gazette*, 11 March 1818.
[29] *Bristol Mirror*, 20 and 27 June 1818.

Bristol freemen. Unlike earlier independent societies, the FFE was avowedly reformist, pledging to returning only MPs who would help to abolish the Septennial Act and rotten boroughs, and advocating 'an extension' of the franchise. Its well-heeled core members included C. H. Walker, the Clare Street solicitor who some twelve years earlier had been briefly gaoled during a dispute with the corporation. He was one of Hunt's backers in 1812 and would remain a propagandist for reform until he left the city in 1831. Others included the attorneys Thomas Stocking, Wintour Harris and John Winter, who had been connected to independence campaigns since at least 1809.[30]

Disputes over the legitimacy of petitioning practices were common in the early nineteenth century. They were closely associated with the development of mass platform politics. The standard eighteenth-century practice had been to restrict a petition to the 'principal inhabitants' of a town, although the mass petitioning of the 1770s and beyond saw a broadening of the base as more non-voters signed. By the early nineteenth century, the now customary practice of gathering multiple signatures from across the social divide invariably prompted disagreement over definitions of the city's voice. On the one hand, quantity had been made to appear at least as important than quality, but on the other the practice invited accusations of corrupt canvassing and suggestions that some signatories – especially women and children – were not valid citizens. Unsurprisingly then, when the FFE submitted a petition to parliament against Protheroe's election, *Felix Farley* asserted not only that the number of signatories was derisorily low but that 'many of them were apparently written by the same hand'. At the same time, a Tory petition against the speedy resumption of cash payments was decried by the Whigs as unrepresentative because it was produced 'at a meeting of the (West India) club of which Alderman Daniel was chair, and signed by its members, and now it was being promoted as a petition of the inhabitants of Bristol'.[31]

In the wake of the Peterloo massacre in August 1819, the FFE was superseded by a Concentric Society modelled on the better-known pro-reform club of the same name in Liverpool, and led once again by Stocking, Walker and Winter. Although devoted to 'freedom of election and a constitutional reform of parliament', the society was not populist and its radicalism was comparatively lukewarm. Membership was by invitation only and voting rights restricted to members (mostly freemen) paying at least a guinea a year in subscriptions. On the matter of parliamentary reform, the society's objectives were vague. It declared only that it was 'advisable that the elective franchise should be extended'.[32]

Nevertheless, the society held a Brandon Hill meeting in September, demanding justice for all those 'hewn down and trampled upon by yeomanry cavalry acting under the direction of magistrates' at Manchester. It resolved

[30] *Bristol Mercury*, 25 Jan. 1819.
[31] *FFBJ*, 6 Feb. 1819.
[32] *Copy of Resolutions Passed at the Formation of the Bristol Concentric Society* (Bristol, 1819).

to invite Hunt back to Bristol to give a public first-hand account of the massacre. The Clare Street shoemaker, Thomas Williams, sent the invitation but Hunt was far too busy in London preparing the legal case against the authorities to make provincial tours. The Concentric Society pressed ahead nevertheless with plans for a second Peterloo meeting and ended up back on the Hill in October, as the mayor had characteristically denied them either the Guildhall or the Assembly Rooms. A petition of outrage was adopted and left for signing at the Mercury's offices in Clare Street. 'The Hustings was covered with black cloth', it was reported, 'and the Orators appeared in deep mourning.' Estimates of the attendance varied. The openly hostile Felix Farley counted 1500 if 'women and boys' were included; the Observer accepted 4–5000, but derided them as mostly 'hobble-dee-hoy boys ... throwing tufts of grass at each other ... and females of the lowest description'. Walker claimed 10,000 and The Times, which had been forthright in its condemnation of the Manchester magistrates, reported 15,000. Whatever the figure, wrote Thomas Cole to Lord Sidmouth, 'it is of some satisfaction to know that there was scarcely a respectable person on the hill. The chairman is an insignificant character.' Yet if the strength of public support for radicalism is difficult to calculate, support for the political establishment is certainly questionable. While the Concentric Society canvassed names for the Brandon Hill petition, the mayor presided over a loyalist meeting at the Guildhall that adopted a 'Patriotic Declaration' against 'those enemies of the State who are plotting the subversion of all civil government'. Despite the socially powerful voices behind it, the Declaration attracted just three thousand signatures. The Mercury was scornful of this unimpressive tally. 'In some parishes', alleged the paper, 'the vestry hawked it from door to door and, of course, the lower orders of parishioners were neither influenced nor dragooned into signing what they felt to be the very reverse of their wishes and opinions.'[33]

Brandon Hill was now the central point of Bristol's radical topography. In an age where rival claims to public space led inevitably to associations between landscapes, buildings and politics, the appropriation of Brandon Hill as a place for popular radicalism is unsurprising. The city's only other large open space was Durdham Down, but its geography made it more suitable for carriage rides for Clifton swells and peripheral Gloucestershire executions than for meetings of the working classes. Brandon Hill, by contrast, gifted to the city by Elizabethan charter and managed by the corporation for public benefit, was situated midway between the fashionable houses of Berkeley Square and the poor, densely populated streets closer to the river and along the Hotwell Road, making it accessible to all social classes in the

[33] Bristol Mirror, 18 Sep. 1819; FFBJ, 18 Sep. 1819, 2 and 16 Oct. 1819, 20 Nov. 1819; Bristol Gazette, 16 Oct. 1819; Bristol Mercury, 11 Oct. 1819, 22 Nov. 1819; Belchem, 'Orator' Hunt, p. 87; A full, true and particular account of the Meeting on Brandon Hill (Bristol 1819); TNA, HO 42/196, Thomas Cole to Lord Sidmouth, 5 Oct. 1819.

city. It had been used in the early eighteenth century for Jacobite revels and by striking seafarers in 1745, but it came into its own as a popular forum for opposition groups when the nineteenth-century authorities began refusing them the use of public buildings. Henry Hunt had made use of the street outside the Exchange because of its situation at the epicentre of electoral geography, midway between the Tory White Lion and the Whig Bush Tavern. Pro-coalition speeches made from the upper windows of these buildings now had to contend with Hunt's disruptive salvos a mere stone's throw away. But the Hill's legendary open status made it impossible for the corporation to restrict access, and the natural gradient of its twenty unimproved acres meant uninterrupted views of an orator's wagon for vast numbers of people. As Thomas Stocking put it in 1819,

> although the Chief Magistrate had refused the respectable citizens of Bristol (who had signed the requisition) to call the meeting or give them the grant of the Guildhall, he conceived the refusal rather benefitted than injured the cause for which they had met, as thousands then assembled would not have had an opportunity of hearing the mournful tales that would fall from the lips of the various gentlemen then assembled concerning the late bloody deeds at Manchester.

The sustained resort to the Hill by anti-coalitionists and political radicals in 1807, 1816, 1818, 1819 and 1820 had now made it 'famous for political meetings' in the view of the *Bristol Mirror*. According to the Freemen's campaigner, Edward Kentish, it was Bristol's 'Folkmote'.[34]

It should not be assumed that the solidarity expressed towards the victims of Peterloo by the Concentric Society betrayed much sympathy for their politics. The society's radicalism was questioned by *Felix Farley* in February 1820 when an election was called and the Whigs once more found themselves divided over a suitable choice of candidate. Their first choice was the merchant Henry Bright, son of Richard, but the Concentric Society faction thought him insufficiently committed to reform and pushed to have another member of the Baillie family, James Evan, nominated instead, or in addition. As in the previous election, these disagreements in the Whig ranks resulted in both candidates being nominated, forcing the sitting Tory member, Davis, into a contest. Baillie, a reluctant candidate all along, withdrew on the fourth day with 115 votes and Davis and Bright were duly elected. But in the fallout from the campaign, Gutch and Thomas Stocking began a public row in the columns of Gutch's newspaper (*FFBJ*). Stocking was infuriated when Gutch referred to him as a man of 'radical notoriety' and moved swiftly to put him right. 'A radical, sir, as you must know, with your party, is a term synonymous with a revolutionist and it is seldom used by anyone without being intended

---

[34] Steve Poole, '"Till our liberties be secure": Popular Sovereignty and Public Space in Bristol, 1750–1850', *Urban History*, 26:1 (1999), 43–5; *Full, true and particular account of the Meeting on Brandon Hill*; Edward Kentish, *Narrative of the Facts Relative to the Bristol Election as Connected with the Meeting on Brandon Hill* (Bristol, 1818).

to convey the idea of an advocate for the doctrine of universal suffrage.' On the contrary, insisted Stocking, he had never been a supporter of anything more progressive than a household franchise.[35]

If there were any more actively democratic popular organisations in Bristol at this time, they remained inconspicuous. However, the discovery of the Spencean-led Cato Street conspiracy in London in February 1820 kept provincial magistrates alert to any evidence of a revolutionary underground. In March, a Bristol lodging-house keeper reported one of her tenants to Mayor William Fripp for using seditious expressions. James Board, a journeyman carpenter, who passed regularly between London and Bristol, allegedly let slip that he knew the conspirators Davidson and Thistlewood, had attended Spencean meetings and knew all about the plot to assassinate the Cabinet. Moreover, he told her, 'if they had succeeded, it would have been for the good of the country'. Fripp ordered Board's arrest, examined him and took depositions from his landlady; he then forwarded the paperwork to Sidmouth with a recommendation that he be prosecuted at government expense. But irregularities in the preparation of the case caused its abandonment and Board was released without charge.[36]

These were not advantageous times for open radical organisation. Government intolerance towards the continued growth of constitutional public assembly and petitioning had been loudly signalled by Peterloo and the passage of the Six Acts, and clandestine planning had been rendered impossible by the heavy infiltration of Spencean networks by government spies. The clear involvement of unscrupulous agents provocateurs in the Cato Street affair exposed the vulnerability of even small group meetings to interference from Whitehall.

In this respect at least, popular support for the claim on the throne of 'Queen' Caroline towards the end of the year, was a gift. Support for the Regent's estranged wife was widespread, not because Caroline was popular in herself; she was barely known until the death of George III triggered her status as 'consort in waiting' to the new George IV. Rather, the Queen's cause presented all opposition parties with a platform on which to campaign against the government's determination to prevent her re-entering the country and disrupting the coronation, on the grounds that she had adulterously consorted with her valet cum secretary, Bartolome Pergami. The Regent, loathed in radical circles for expressing his satisfaction over the carnage of Peterloo and associating himself with a highly repressive Tory ministry, was more broadly unpopular for his marital ungallantry and profligate life style. This, in turn, widened the participatory threshold for the signing of petitions and addresses of support for Caroline to include women, who deprecated the Regent's moral double standard. Tory loyalists would take no such step themselves and consequently found themselves at a disadvantage in the battle to

---

[35] *FFBJ*, 26 Feb. 1820, 11 and 18 March 1820.
[36] TNA, HO 52/1, William Fripp to Lord Sidmouth, 4 and 11 March 1820.

procure the greater number of signatures of support. As recently as 1819, a correspondent of *Felix Farley* had excused the comparatively low number of signatures on Bristol's post-Peterloo loyal address on the grounds that more than half the city's population was female, and women 'never sign loyal addresses though they do sometimes sign radical ones'.[37] In Tory circles, the charge that 'women and boys' had been present at a public meeting or, worse still, added their names to an address, remained clear evidence of its illegitimacy and unrepresentative nature. By September then, Bristol had begun several addresses of support for Caroline. One from the 'ladies and female inhabitants', organised by the radical Elizabeth Cranidge, accrued fourteen thousand signatures. The 'females of Clifton and Kingswood' followed suit in October.[38]

While radicals attached themselves to the Queen's cause as a viable way of organising opposition to government, the broad nature of her support made it more difficult than usual for the corporation to close down public space. Meetings were therefore permitted in the Guildhall on both sides of the question and although Concentric Society stalwarts like Wintour Harris still attempted to press radical amendments to resolutions proposed at Loyalist meetings. For once, the Guildhall was not restricted to the Tories and reformers did not have to resort to Brandon Hill. The corporation and the vestries produced a string of loyal addresses as a counterweight to Queenite petitions and did what they could to obstruct pro-Caroline illuminations as the attempt to incriminate her in a Bill of Pains and Penalties faltered in the Lords. After a partial illumination in October ended with a few Tory windows getting broken by 'a crowd of mischievous boys', the Town Clerk took firmer action, summarily seizing and prosecuting a printer named Bennett for omitting his name as publisher from an illumination handbill. Bennett fought back by issuing the Town Clerk with a writ for assault and the mayor had to step in quickly to quash the conviction. It was, nevertheless, a clear signal that the corporation wished to stymie opposition to the king.[39]

Even so, it proved difficult to contain the broadly based support for the Queen. When the bill against her was finally abandoned by the ministry in the face of stiff resistance by both Houses of parliament, Richard Bright, the father of the Bristol MP, chaired a meeting at the Guildhall to congratulate Caroline on surviving a legal process that was 'derogatory to the crown and to the rights of the people'. Bristolians responded by celebrating the event for two nights, despite the fact the magistrates advised against it. Among the illuminations was a picture of Britannia trampling on a Green Bag inscribed Conspiracy, a reference to the secret manner in which the government had assembled evidence of Caroline's adultery. Out of the bag tumbled obsequious Tory newspapers including *Felix Farley's Bristol Journal*, whose editor

[37] *FFBJ*, 20 Nov. 1819.
[38] *Bristol Gazette*, 21 Sep. 1820, 16 Oct. 1820.
[39] *Bristol Gazette*, 16 Oct. 1820, 23 and 30 Nov. 1820, 7 Dec. 1820.

J. M. Gutch had characterised Caroline as a 'mass of guilt and pollution'. The illumination also depicted Britannia crowning a bust of the queen on a pedestal inscribed 'Public Opinion, the Liberty of the Press'. She brandished a caduceus, the mythic staff of Hermes, which unfurled a copy of the *Bristol Mercury* with the motto 'The Liberty of the Press is the Palladium of the Rights of Englishmen'.[40]

Radicals hoped the Queen Caroline Affair might prompt a powerful reform initiative. Charles Walker, among others, capitalised on the sympathy for the queen and protested her exclusion from the coronation, when George IV hired a posse of bruisers to keep Caroline's entourage from entering Westminster Abbey. Chairing a meeting of the Concentric Society in July 1821, Walker urged Bristolians to show their displeasure on coronation day and some indeed did so. One illumination in Frogmore Street featured the motto 'Vivant Rex and Regina', a pointed reference to the queen's exclusion from the ceremony. It also displayed the pledge of the king 'to hold my Crown in trust for the good of the people', a promise that rang hollow for many reformers in the light of the king's suppression of the reform movement. Alongside this loyalist irony, 'the Queen, the Queen' was the prevailing cry on the street, and many houses refused to light candles in their windows. These celebrations, like those of the accession of George IV a year earlier, only emphasised the huge gap that had opened up between the bulk of the population and the ultra-Tory corporation and its allies among the elite. The *Mercury* dismissed the civic procession at the coronation as a 'spiritless pageant'; nothing could rouse 'the cheerless despondency of the people'.[41] Yet in the end little political traction could be derived from the Caroline affair, which at various points along its tortured narrative threatened to degenerate into a farce between two royal incorrigibles.[42]

There was a moment when it might have prompted another reform initiative, for one month after the coronation, Queen Caroline died of peritonitis. Metropolitan radicals wanted to transport her coffin through the City of London on its way to the Duchy of Brunswick; they wanted to pay their respects in person and remind the public of the strong support she had received there. They wanted to command critical public space. To do this Queenites had to deflect the official cortege from taking her carriage through the suburbs by blocking streets and erecting barricades. Troops confronted pro-Caroline crowds about this at Cumberland Gate in Hyde Park and in the affray that followed two demonstrators were killed. At the inquests one of them, George Francis, was deemed to have been murdered by unknown guardsmen, and London radicals used this verdict to rally the pro-Caroline

---

[40] *Bristol Mercury*, 20 November 1820.
[41] *Bristol Mercury*, 21 July 1821.
[42] On this aspect of the affair, see Thomas Laqueur, 'The Queen Caroline Affair: Politics as Art in the Reign of George IV', *Journal of Modern History*, 54 (1982), 417–66.

forces and expose ministerial oppression.[43] The *Bristol Mercury* was caught up in this metropolitan episode, hailing the diverted procession as a victory of the people, and reporting the inquests and subsequent rally on behalf of the victims in considerable detail. 'We are beginning to reap the baleful harvest of Ministerial Misrule', it declared.[44] But at the time the story broke Walker and Stocking were absorbed with a suit at the Bristol assizes, and nothing came of it. The opportunity for a possible breakthrough in the local political landscape passed. At the next general election in 1826, Charles Walker, disillusioned by the tepid reformism of Henry Bright, was even prepared to return to the conservative Whig Edward Protheroe senior, in an effort to break the grip of caucus politics in Bristol. His plight epitomised that of the reforming middle class in Bristol, who had become profoundly alienated from the city's elite.

[43] On this incident, see Iorwerth Prothero, *Artisans and Politics in Early Nineteenth-Century London* (Folkstone, 1979), pp. 147–53.

[44] *Bristol Mercury*, 1 Sep. 1821. See also the *Mercury* of 8 September 1821, where C. H. Walker sued a livery-stable keeper in Clifton for fatally mistreating his horse after a vigorous ride to Bath in a phaeton. Thomas Stocking was a witness for the prosecution. Walker lost the case.

'This is the blaze of Liberty!' The burning of Bristol in 1831

They are the people who have no common interest with their fellow men, who have no stake in the country, who labour hard for insufficient food for their families, with no other prospect than the poor house before them. They are, however, powerful, and, like the mighty hurricane, are now sweeping everything into one common destruction before them.[1]

Let us call to mind that not one personal injury was either intended or perpetrated – that wherever 'property' was threatened, life was spared – and that the only victims of their intemperance were themselves.[2]

Neither historians nor heritage professionals have found it easy to come to terms with the extraordinary popular uprising of October 1831. There is, to this day, no commemorative monument to the several hundred unarmed men and women killed by direct and merciless military intervention on 31 October. We do not even know the number. As at Peterloo twelve years earlier, where the death toll was much smaller and the outcry greater, there was no public enquiry and only a few inquests, none of which asked particularly searching questions and city coroners were in no mood to be critical. The Whig mayor, Charles Pinney, was put on trial and acquitted; not for murder but for failing to bring the crowd to book more quickly. Military commanders boasted with impunity of the slaughter they had overseen while a Special Commission tried 114 rioters, convicted 81, transported 26 and executed 4. The earliest attempts at historical analysis, and much popular writing on the subject since, tended to coalesce around themes of public alienation, whether it be from the structures of central or local government, or simply from the principles of civilised social order. As one popular account put it, 'Whenever such convulsions take place in a community, they will almost always be traceable to one cause, namely an unnatural state of society, arising from misgovernment.'[3] Specifically, it is argued, the people and their rulers were out of touch.

[1] 'Terrific Riots at Bristol', *Radical Reformer*, 4 Nov. 1831.
[2] *Poor Man's Guardian*, 12 Nov. 1831.
[3] Originally from J. K. R. Wreford, *Curiosities of Bristol and its Neighbourhood* (1854); reproduced in George Pryce, *A Popular History of Bristol, Antiquarian, Topographical and Descriptive* (Bristol, 1861), p. 467.

13 *Bristol from Brandon Hill on the Night of 30th October 1831.*

Government was out of touch because the Recorder, Sir Charles Wetherell, had been foolish enough to claim to his parliamentary colleagues that there was little interest in reform at Bristol. The corporation was out of touch because it was remote, corrupt and unaccountable. These popular analyses located the cause of the riots in the institutional failures of the local state and a breakdown in civilised behaviour amongst a degenerate working class.

The Bristol crowd, insofar as it has been ascribed any agency at all, has emerged as little more than a locus for plunder and destruction, prefiguring perhaps former Prime Minister David Cameron's judgement on the London riots of 2011 as a case of 'criminality, pure and simple'.[4] Cameron's pejorative language was intended to steer public hand-wringing over the disturbances well clear of any suggestion that the perpetrators were poor, socially and economically excluded, or dysfunctional consumers, urged to express their citizenship by the acquisition of material goods yet unable to comply with the financial requirements that go with it. Something similar happened in 1831 and the effect has been to rob the crowd not only of rationalism and agency, but of public sympathy and understanding. As testified by numerous attempts by contemporary illustrators to capture the essence of the riots, it was often easier to represent the incendiary spectacle of a burning city than to suggest any kind of meaning or purpose behind the activities of the crowd (Fig. 13).

---

[4] Cameron's assessment has been much quoted and commented upon. See for instance, Tim Hope, 'Riots Pure and Simple?', *Criminal Justice Matters*, 87 (2012).

It is true that the two most scholarly modern analyses, by Mark Harrison and Jeremy Caple, have disputed earlier assumptions that the riots had little or nothing to do with the politics of reform, and Caple in particular sees the assault on the gaols as an attempt at 'tearing down symbols of authority which, to a large degree, were erected to discipline the working class and labouring poor'. Yet even here, traditional views prevail. 'Used as an ideologically unifying slogan, reform was the initial impetus for the demonstration', he believes, but, 'shorn of such interest, it merely served as an excuse appropriated to cover excessive behaviour and plunder'.[5] By this measure, expropriation and attacks upon private property cannot be read as political acts in themselves and so tend to be interpreted as acts of hooligan excess.

What are we to make of these disturbances? This chapter looks for answers less in the recounting of familiar narratives of popular outrage than in the rather less familiar actions of the judiciary and the military. The means used to restore order and reassert proper authority, it will be argued here – the selection of evidence and the conduct of the trials, and the attitudes displayed by the soldiery under a virtual declaration of martial law – reveals as much about the rationale of the crowd as it does about the corporation. As has been pointed out many times, few of those who took part had any direct material interest in parliamentary reform. As we know, Bristol in 1831 was not a rotten borough but a city with a broad and comparatively large electoral franchise. Moreover, the Reform Bill that Wetherell had been so ill-advised to oppose, contained nothing of direct advantage to the men and women who forced him from the city on 29 October and then fired the gaols, the bishop's palace, the Customs House, several warehouses, the toll-houses and two sides of select residential properties in Queen Square.

Some consideration is necessary of the social and economic conditions that lay behind both the events themselves and the attitudes underpinning public discourse about them. Certainly, there was no shortage of divisive language as the search began for scapegoats on 1 November, and the depth of conservative unease about the city's own social constituency quickly became plain. 'The composition of the populace of Bristol is of a description very easily worked upon by mischievous persons', considered General Jackson, sent by Whitehall to oversee military operations against the crowd. 'Mobs are easily collected from a population so ill-composed and so uncontrolled by authority.'[6] The principal agents of this 'ill-composure', it was repeatedly asserted, both in private correspondence and the press, were not necessarily native Bristolians.[7] 'We have been informed by several of the sufferers that the band consisted almost entirely of the lower order of Irishmen, with women and

---

[5] Mark Harrison, Crowds and History: Mass Phenomena in English towns, 1790–1835 (Cambridge, 1988), pp. 289–314; Jeremy Caple, The Bristol Riots of 1831 and Social Reform in Britain (New York, 1990), pp. 141, 145.

[6] TNA, HO 40/28, General Jackson to Lord Melbourne, 15 Dec. 1831.

[7] TNA, HO40/28, Gore to Lord Melbourne, 3 Nov. 1831.

boys of the same country', reported the *Gazette*. 'We should be sorry to raise a prejudice against any class, but the immense mass of plunder which has since been recovered from Marsh Street … goes to confirm the supposition.'[8] The discovery of looted property in these areas in the immediate aftermath of the riots produced plenty of alarmist rhetoric about the living conditions of the Irish poor. A city solicitor warned Lord Melbourne of the

> state of extreme filth in which many parts of the city now are, particularly those spots inhabited by the lower orders of Irish labourers in Host Street and Marsh Street, where the apparently accumulated dirt of many years is to be seen many feet deep. This horrible nuisance consists of ordure, dead cats, dogs and rabbits, pig dung, cess pools of stagnant water, decayed putrid vegetables and other such-like dangerous substances.[9]

And this writer, for one, considered the expulsion from the city of the 'real portion' of the Irish, was now the only solution to the problem. 'In Host Street, up to two waggon loads of furniture were found in one house', ran one account,

> Marsh Street, St James's Back, the Pithay and the Dings, and in fact almost all the lowest and dirtiest parts of the town were also filled with plunder of various descriptions … Numberless are the instances in which property has been thus found upon the lowest and most abandoned wretches … From the quantity of goods found in the habitations of the lowest class of Irishmen, it is clear that a considerable number of them were employed in the work of plunder, if not of incendiarism.[10]

There is some evidence to support these claims, if only because magistrates made a beeline for migrant districts the minute they began the work of recovering stolen goods. Constables sealed Marsh Street at both ends to prevent any escapes, then systematically raided each house in turn. This enabled the arrest of poor women like Margaret Dwyer, a labourer's wife, who was caught with a single linen sheet concealed under her bed, which she admitted buying from a boy in the street the previous evening.[11] A similar search in Lewin's Mead led to the arrest of fourteen-year-old Daniel Doyle and his widowed mother, for having several stolen items in their room, including a watch that Daniel had picked up in the ruins of the Bridewell. Plunder is, perhaps, too strong a word for expropriation on such a modest scale as this, but prejudice against the poor Bristol Irish ran deep.[12]

---

[8] *Bristol Gazette*, 3 Nov. 1831.

[9] TNA, HO40/28, N. Tomlins to Lord Melbourne, 6 Nov. 1831.

[10] *Trials of the Persons Concerned in the Late Riots before Chief Justice Tindal …* (Bristol, 1832), p. 22.

[11] *The Examiner*, 6 Nov. 1831; TNA, ASSI 6/3, Information of William Barrell, 5 Nov. 1831.

[12] *Trials of the Persons Concerned in the Late Riots before Chief Justice Tindal*, pp. 141–2.

This was built partly on resentment that Irish migrants rounded up and expelled from London were commonly given passage to Bristol and 'thrown *en masse* upon the city to be sent home'. In a city of over 100,000 people, already 'suffering unusual depression, both in its manufactures and commerce', the accommodation of transitory vagrants, 'a burthen upon the city of Bristol, which gains no advantage from the influx', was unlikely to be popular. 'The injustice of such an arrangement is strongly felt', it was reported, and 'the question was asked, how far it is politic or consistent with sound principles thus to send over persons to underwork an already superabundant population.' As the 1833 Parliamentary Commission on the Poor Laws heard, the costs of these arrangements were not inconsiderable. Annual poor law expenditure was already £28,000, but that included an additional cost of £1,127 in the previous year for the repatriation of Irish vagrants at eight shillings a head. This figure was kept high by the determination of St Peter's Hospital not to grant any relief to Irish vagrants without a settlement. Those who applied and wished to remain in Bristol were set to work on the roads as paupers, and to evade that, they had either to scratch an impoverished living on the streets and on the margins of petty crime, chance a return to London, or accept repatriation and take rooms in an overcrowded Marsh Street or Host Street lodging house at threepence a night while awaiting passage. 'In some cases, full fifty are lodged in the same room', it was reported to the commission, 'the beds touch each other and the scene is described as beggaring description. When a batch arrives, the lodging housekeepers swarm around the work-house to tempt them to their houses.' Most, it was believed locally, never returned to Ireland.[13]

The Irish poor are unlikely to have harboured much sympathy for city elites. Little had been done to protect them in 1825 when Marsh Street lodging houses were attacked by an English crowd during a dispute over the undercutting of wages in the Bedminster tannery by a number of Irish labourers.[14] And in 1829, Irish lodging houses and a chapel had again been attacked by a Protestant mob during disturbances over the 1829 Catholic Emancipation Bill. Importantly, this crowd had initially gathered to cheer Sir Charles Wetherell as he came to open the assize, for his opposition to the bill as Attorney General under Wellington. Wetherell had urged restraint and requested no demonstrations, but nothing was actively done to prevent the crowd greeting him with orange and blue ribbons. The city magistrates

---

[13] HC, *Parliamentary Papers*, 'Report from His Majesty's commissioners for inquiring into the administration and practical operation of the Poor Laws' (1834), pp. 460–1, 513A. The relief and suppression of vagrancy at Bristol following the reforms of 1834 is discussed and placed within a national framework in Brian O'Leary, 'A Reluctant Response to Vagrancy: The Evolution of Poor Law Casual Relief in England and Wales, 1834–1919' (PhD Thesis, University of Exeter, 2014). For the mayor and magistrates' establishment of a Refuge for the Houseless Poor in 1847, as vagrant numbers continued to escalate in the wake of the Irish famine, see pp. 390–1.

[14] *Bristol Mercury*, 12 July 1825.

were widely criticised at the time for their inactivity in protecting property and bringing the perpetrators to justice, not least in the pages of the
liberal *Bristol Mercury*. Indeed, 'because their opinions seemed to coincide
with the Magistrates', the mob seemed to believe they might be guilty of all
kinds of excesses with impunity'. For two nights, windows were smashed in
Host Street and Marsh Street and at the chapel in Trenchard Street. 'All
this occurred within five minutes walk of the Council House', reflected the
Mercury, a clear indication of magisterial indifference. In fact a small number
of arrests were made, but these led only to the conviction, as ringleader, of
One-eyed Dick, the chimney sweep Richard Jobson, under the Trespass Act.
Jobson was ordered to pay twenty shilling's damages and a five shilling fine
but these were both paid on his behalf by 'some gentlemen'. Memories of
Alderman Fripp's role in these events – that he had 'refused protection to the
Bristol Catholics' – were still freely circulating in 1835.[15]

Poverty was certainly grinding in some parts of the city, but it was
not restricted to the Irish. As in any seaport, the demand for labour was
tightly bound to the supply of shipping, and in relative terms at least, the
harbour's trade was shrinking. 'Is there much fluctuation in the employment
in Bristol?', an owner of rented housing was asked in 1838. 'There is', he
replied. 'The coming in and the going out of ships?' 'Yes.'[16] The out-parishes
of Bedminster, St Philip and St George, which together held a population
as big as that of the city, were a particular cause for concern, partly because
they were so poorly policed. The fabled 'Cock Road Gang' on the borders of
Gloucestershire may have been tamed by the close of the Napoleonic wars
through the combined efforts of Methodist missionaries and the Kingswood
Prosecution Association, but Bristolians were still inclined to imagine themselves under siege. 'The outskirts of Bristol receive and retain, in readiness to
pour upon that city whenever a fitting opportunity offers, all the refuse of a
larger population which has been thrown off or taken refuge in these places
and is pent up there, ready for action', claimed the Reverend Henry Bishop
in his testimony to the Commission. 'It was not so much to be wondered at
that on one occasion, the population burst like a torrent upon Bristol as that
a winter should pass without such an occurrence.' The population of these
parishes was certainly poor. In St Philip, the number of persons receiving
relief, *in the summer*, had risen from 51 in 1827, to 131 in 1831, and 169 by
1832. Two-roomed lodging houses predominated, built small to evade the £10
rateable value imposed by the Sturges Bourne Act, and mostly 'in a damp,
unhealthy situation, where the cholera broke out, and inhabited by the refuse
of society', according to the Commission. St George and Kingswood, now a
distressed mining and industrial out-parish on the fringes of St Philip, was in

---

[15] *Morning Chronicle*, 10 April 1829; *Bristol Mercury*, 14 April 1829; TNA, HO 52/29,
Anonymous 'appeal', n.d. [1835].
[16] HC, *Parliamentary Papers*, 'First report from Select Committee on Rating of Tenements;
with the minutes of evidence, and appendix' (1837–8), p. 193.

similar straits. Miners earned little and were subject to seasonal fluctuations in pay and employment. Although they had thrown off their former disorderly reputation to become 'religious, orderly and peaceable', in the eyes of some at least, the local economy had been hard hit by the recent failure of the spelter works, leaving the population 'very poor' and their employment 'precarious and irregular'.[17] There is no evidence that colliers from these parishes played any significant part in the riots but, as we shall see, military commanders thought them guilty by association and believed they had been effectively dispersed on the final morning. Was it any wonder, queried the *Poor Man's Guardian*, that the poor had grown to resent the luxuries of the wealthy? 'And, add to these feelings the knowledge that we, who are destitute and who starve, have produced the very abundance which those who so excessively enjoy it have done nothing to produce ... Such are some of the considerations which teach us to make allowances for the destruction of property by the poor and the plundered'.[18]

Riot

However we calculate the individual benefits proffered by the bill at Bristol, Wetherell's badly timed, anti-reform declaration was absurdly wide of the mark, and his presumption, as an outsider, had been widely publicised for some weeks in the Liberal press. It was true that the corporation, so long a stronghold of Whiggery, had been dominated by anti-reform Tories for more than a decade, but that only made its distance from public opinion plainer than ever. In the spring of 1831, both parliamentary seats had been won without opposition by two moderate reforming Whigs, J. E. Baillie and Edward Protheroe, and since its formation in May, the Bristol Political Union (BPU) had been marshalling large crowds at public meetings – two of them in Queen Square – calling for the Reform Bill to be made law as a matter of urgency. Then, in the wake of rioting in Derby and Nottingham after the Lords rejection on 8 October, some twenty-six thousand Bristolians put their names a new petition demanding the Lords accept the bill. As the same time, however, the Recorder, a quixotic, intemperate lawyer of unbounding ambition, had been assuring parliamentarians that enthusiasm for reform in Bristol was waning.

[17] 'Administration and practical operation of the Poor Laws', pp. 514, 891. The Commission was at pains to point out the difference between the coal miners and retailers. 'Though for many years living so near a large city and in fact inhabiting a part of it, their habits and manners seem to have raised a barrier between them and the rest of the world, but although uncivilised and ignorant, they appear to be neither immoral nor disorderly. Although "the colliers" indeed are generally spoken of with dread and even in Bristol are regarded as very formidable', they were often lumped together with unscrupulous small vendors in coal and this had sullied their reputation.

[18] *Poor Man's Guardian*, 12 Nov. 1831.

Wetherell more or less threw down the gauntlet, challenging Bristolians to voice their political opinions. This was embarrassing to the Tory-dominated corporation because it exposed the corporation's lack of concord with the majority of citizens. The Bristol Tories attempted to rustle up a bodyguard for Wetherell's impending visit to open the assize, fearing trouble. Captain Claxton of the Royal Navy tried to enlist the support of sailors and ship-wrights to defend the irascible Recorder, but, with some prompting from the BPU, they refused to be a 'cat's paw' of the corporation.[19] The corporation even had the audacity to try to inveigle the BPU into guarding Wetherell, on the grounds that it had a vested interest in maintaining order in the city, but vice-president William Herapath rejected such complicity. The BPU was not prepared to be annexed by the corporation; even later on, when it did offer help in a deteriorating situation, it wanted to maintain its autonomy as a new force in Bristol politics, to project itself as an emblem of a new reform order. As Herapath later declared, his organisation 'would not fight the Magistrates' battles'.[20] If the magistrates could not maintain order, perhaps they should resign their commission and allow for popular elections in their stead. The BPU would refrain from disorder, Herapath declared, but the union could not prevent Bristolians expressing their disapproval of the Recorder.

This Reformist position was shared by the majority of the middle-class ratepayers, who at this stage were not prepared to assist the corporation in their predicament. In relation to the corporation the veteran London radical, Francis Place, remarked there was only 'distrust, apathy and disgust.'[21] Consequently the corporation sent a deputation to Lord Melbourne to request troops for Wetherell's visit, a move that the reform MP Edward Protheroe thought unacceptable and unprecedented. Melbourne met the corporation halfway; he offered ninety-nine men, the majority from the 14th Regiment of riot-hardened soldiers. This was a very modest number for a city of Bristol's size; it was a gesture that hardly resolved the corporation's problem. In the end, the troops were held in reserve, and the corporation scrambled to enlist three hundred special constables drawn from the Tory clans and reputedly from some of their rougher hirelings. This relatively small force was under-standably regarded as 'Tory bludgeon men' in pro-reform quarters, and their behaviour when called to action did nothing to dispel the notion. Pinney knew it an insufficient force and can have been in no doubt that hostility to the Recorder was now quite likely to get out of hand. There were some suspicions, voiced after the riots were over, that the corporation had been perfectly prepared to accept a manageable amount of disturbance so that the Political Union might be blamed and reform associated with disorder. 'Most

---

[19] BL, Add. MS 27,790, fols 130–3; [John Eagles], *The Bristol Riots. Their Causes Progress and Consequences* (Bristol, 1832), pp. 54–5; Caple, *Bristol Riots*, p. 8.

[20] BL, Add. MS 27,790, fol. 155.

[21] BL, Add. MS, 27,790, fol. 118. See also Richard Volger, *Reading the Riot Act: The Magistracy, the Police and the Army in Civil Disorder* (Milton Keynes, 1991), pp. 35–6.

of our magistrates are anti-reformers', noted Joseph Fry, 'and there is no doubt would not have disliked a moderate proportion of row.'[22] Thomas Manchee certainly regarded the magistrates' decision to parade the soldiers in public each day after their arrival on 26 October as an act of provocation, 'calculated only to irritate the feelings of the whole and to incite the insolence of those who were inclined to outrage'.[23] It was acts like these that deterred many middle-class parishioners from collaborating with the corporation until the eleventh hour.

After a predictably boisterous entry procession on 29 October, Sir Charles Wetherell tried in vain to open the assize in the Guildhall but was forced to abandon it after repeated disruptions. He and the mayor then beat a hasty retreat to the Mansion House in Queen Square for the scheduled civic dinner, although not without a shower of stones descending on the mayor's coach. By early afternoon they found themselves besieged there by several thousand people, booing, jeering and throwing missiles. Pinney dispatched his staff-wielding constables to disperse them and make some arrests, but no magistrates went with them and their antipathy to the crowd soon led to a great deal of skirmishing and a renewed assault upon the Mansion House amid shouts that Wetherell should leave town. Realising now that the assize would have to be postponed and Wetherell removed from the city, Pinney tried to disperse the crowd by reading the Riot Act. He called on Lieutenant Colonel Brereton, the resident field officer, to bring some of the soldiers into the square. Wetherell meanwhile disguised himself and escaped over the rooftops, travelling post-haste to Newport. There was no sense in using a small military force to attack such a vast and agitated crowd so Brereton exercised his judgement, riding carefully amongst them and urging them to go home. This calmed the crowd to an extent, but matters deteriorated when a section of it went off at midnight to attack the Council House in Corn Street. The 14th Dragoons galloped after them but were pelted with stones and mud from small, narrow side streets where their horses could not enter. They retaliated with gunfire and a bystander, Stephen Bush, was killed at the Pithay.

This quietened things for the time being and the soldiers returned to their billets, but Bush's shooting proved cathartic. Crowds reconvened the following morning and made a fresh attack upon the Mansion House, this time forcing an entrance and sacking the ground floor from top to bottom. Although protesting crowds had broken its windows on more than one occasion, the Mansion House had never before been overrun and the magistrates' failure to prevent it happening was a key turning point. As Manchee

---

[22] Joseph Fry to Caroline Bowley, 31 Oct. 1831, reproduced in *Eyewitness! Five Contemporary Accounts of the 1831 Bristol Reform Bill Riots*, Frenchay Village Museum Chronicles No. 8 (Bristol, 2004), p. 15.
[23] T. M. Manchee, *The Origins of the Riots of Bristol and the Causes of the Subsequent Outrages*, 2nd edn (Bristol, 1832), p. 12; Harrison, *Crowds and History*, pp. 289–91.

put it, 'if ever a moment was to arrive when severity was justifiable, it was then'.[24] Instead, Pinney had little choice but to abandon the building, leaving Alderman Hillhouse to read the Riot Act and Brereton to recall the 14th Regiment.

This made matters worse. Popular anger over the killing of Bush the previous evening ensured a rough reception for the soldiers and they were roundly pelted. Brereton responded by ordering them back out again, but they were now pursued by a section of the crowd who jeered them and hurled stones. At the drawbridge on the Quay, the soldiers turned and fired, shooting a second man dead on the spot, and repeated their action twice more as they retreated across College Green. Tempers were now severely frayed. Realising that the 14th had become a serious liability, and frustrated that the magistrates could give him no clear directions for the restoration of order, Brereton made the critical decision to send them out of the city to Keynsham. The removal of two-thirds of his men at such a moment must have fully convinced the crowd that the authorities were in retreat and that they had little left to fear from military intervention. Moreover, most of the constables who had fought with them outside the Mansion House on Saturday had now deserted their posts. From this point onwards, neither the magistrates nor the military had any means of controlling events.

The attacks on the gaols that followed that afternoon may initially have been conceived as acts of conclusion, since their first purpose was probably to set free all those taken prisoner since the previous morning. The liberation of prisoners was nonetheless quickly followed by the burning of the treadmills and the firing of the gaols, which indicated that the intervention had moved beyond its immediate goal to protest against the new prison discipline of redemption by unremitting labour. Rioters also invaded the Gloucester County Gaol beyond Lawford's Gate, and released debtors from a nearby lock-up, actions betraying broader social opposition to the micro-management of the poor.

With Queen Square now as much a centre of bacchanalian carnival as riot, Sunday's incursions were effectively as much a new beginning as a climactic end. As the surrounding houses were burned and looted, the Custom House sacked and sorties launched against selected targets, a cap of Liberty was symbolically placed on the head of William III's equestrian statue and the crowd took to celebratory dancing. According to one eyewitness, they 'cleared a circle in the middle of the Square and went round hand in hand, prisoners in their prison dresses (drunk with the delight of having been set free), and women of the worst description'. It was these vivid scenes that left the most lasting impression on contemporary commentators, now repulsed by the forces their earlier inactivity appeared to have unleashed. Francis Place, for one, struggled for adequate words:

[24] Manchee, *Origins of the Riots*, p. 16.

Groups of drunken men and women, and boys and girls, were seated on the ground and on pieces of furniture in the open spaces of the square, where they committed the most atrocious and abominable excesses, such indeed as would be a disgrace to the most debased of mankind in any age and in any country however barbarous were its people. Such as could be practiced by none who were not degraded and debauched below anything it is possible to suppose could have taken place in England.[25]

Certainly these final scenes in Queen Square bore little resemblance to the methodical liberation of the gaols that marked the previous day. Some believed it was not even the same crowd. The gaols, the Mansion House and the bishops palace had been systematically targeted by people with an identifiable set of politically inspired objectives; they levelled their aim against an intransigently Tory corporation, an ultra-Tory Recorder, and a bishop whose vote in the Lords frustrated reform. The firing and looting of Queen Square, by contrast, was more readily read as an act of misrule, a pillage of the rich, an expropriation of wealth and privilege by an underclass from the poorest rookeries, well beyond the reach of political rationale. 'There was a difference between the drunken, stupefied, diminished mob (in the Square) … and the active, vigorous, infuriated thousands whom Colonel Brereton endeavoured to soothe', reasoned one of the London papers.[26] Although critics of the corporation quickly blamed the incompetence of the magistracy for the victory of the crowd that Sunday afternoon, the brunt of the criticism was reserved for military commanders who failed to engage them. One was Captain Codrington, who arrived in the square with the Dodington Yeomanry on Sunday evening to find half the houses on fire and the crowd freely helping themselves to food, drink and other property. Unable to find a magistrate to sanction any action, he simply withdrew. But chief amongst the scapegoats was Colonel Brereton, with whom Melbourne was furious for sending the 14th out of town. Brereton defended his decision as best he could. 'Between an overpowering, infuriated mob and a magistracy from whom no essential aid could be procured, I was left in a very unenviable condition', he wrote:

Supposing we had shot many of them and dispersed them for the instant, they would have reassembled with considerable augmented numbers, which I could not have prevented for I had not Force to occupy the many outlets of this large city. Men and horses would have been exhausted and so exasperated were the Mob previously that they had determined to attack all the houses for arms to destroy the dragoons in their quarters when they went to refresh. Would it have been right under such circumstances to Hazard the troops being repulsed, for if they had, the Mob, flushed with their victory would have had possession of the whole city and fired the shipping. Of this intention they made no secret, nor of their plan to attack the Banks and then throw all of the surrounding country into confusion.[27]

[25] Harrison, *Crowds and History*, pp. 292–7; *Life and Correspondence of Robert Southey* (6 vols, London, 1850), VI, 168; BL, Add. MS 27790, fol. 160.
[26] *Evening Mail*, 9 Dec. 1831.
[27] TNA, HO 40/28, fols 70–4, Lieutenant Colonel Brereton to Fitzroy Somerset, 3 Nov. 1831.

Brereton's fear that a renewed offensive by the 14th might have made matters far worse was perfectly credible. Even Digby Mackworth, who would take a leading role in the bloody suppression the next morning, was sympathetic: 'They might have effected a few charges and cleared the streets again and again, but unless supported by some other description of force, they would have done no permanent good and they would soon have been so exhausted as to leave the whole city defenceless.'[28] However, Brereton's insistence that the crowd had designs on shipping and the banks was alarmist and made with little evidence. There were reports that the crowd who parleyed with members of the Political Union before destroying the Dock Gates had threatened to 'ransack the banks' and the proprietors were consequently warned of it, but after the departure of the 14th, there was nothing to prevent such an attack and none took place.[29] Brereton's assertions do prompt some very necessary questions however: What *did* frame the consciousness of the crowd during those three days in October? And what, if any, were the wider, popular meanings of 'reform' expressed through crowd action during these events?

If we listen to the language of the crowd in the days that followed Wetherell's arrival and ejection on 29 October, it becomes clear that, in the minds of a significant section of the Bristol poor at least, there was very much more to 'reform' than an extended franchise. The group of rioters who built a bonfire in the yard of the New Gaol, dumped the prison's linen sheets onto it and cried, 'Here goes! Reform!' as they did so, saw no disconnection between the two. Neither did the small crowd who went with James Coleman to demand £4 from his former employer, Thomas Blethyn in alleged wage arrears. Blethyn paid up and Coleman told them not to hurt him for he was 'a good fellow', but they nevertheless made him raise his hat and shout 'Reform!' before letting him go. Clearly for some, reform meant getting even with mean-spirited employers; it also meant getting even with the authority of the Established Church. 'Damn him, we'll have down the bloody parsons of St Stephens', William Reynolds was said to have declared, as the Queen Square residence of the Reverend Charles Buck was put to the torch. For others, it was the institutions of law that needed reform. 'Damn my bloody eyes', shouted Matthew Worry, running from the burning Bridewell, 'it was we that set fire to that!' And for some, like the apprentice ceramicist, Edward Arbon, it was the institutions of employment. Threatening to fire his master's workshop, Arbon shouted, 'Damn my eyes and Damn my blood if I don't burn the bloody place down and put an end to plate making.' When a deputation from the Political Union tried to reason with the crowd outside the newly liberated gaol, 'they were listened to with considerable attention', but they would not be 'deviated from their purpose', which was now to 'destroy the Dock Gates, saying that since the erection of the Gates, labour had become more scarce and wages had been lowered'. And as Christopher Davis made

[28] *Morning Post*, 22 Nov. 1831.
[29] BL, Add. MS 27790, fol. 153.

his way back over Princes Bridge the same evening, 'an Irishman came up to him and, pointing to the blaze at the Gaol, said, "This is the blaze of Liberty, Davis", to which Davis replied, "indeed it is, and I wish I could have had one hundred such men as you are with me last night"'. As many witnesses testified in fact, Davis had a great deal to say about the meaning and purpose of the uprising. 'Now, damn, won't we have reform', he shouted at the storming of the gaol, 'This is what ought to have been done years ago.' The word, 'reform', or just the idea of it, lent shape and meaning to every action of the crowd; it did not require close definition. A man struggling with a sack of stolen grain asked for help from an assumed reformer. 'Is that a reform table?', asked Thomas Gregory of a man carrying a looted table from one of the burning houses in Queen Square on the Sunday night. The looter confirmed that it was and Gregory cheerfully let him pass. Pointing out that men like these had nothing to gain from the Reform Bill will not aid our understanding of this extraordinary three days of mayhem and expropriation.[30] As we shall see however, solicitors for the crown preparing cases for the subsequent Special Commission, understood the situation well enough. And so, too, did the military commanders charged with restoring order in the city once Brereton's inadequacies had become clear.

Massacre

After two days of virtually unopposed crowd activity, hard line military intervention began in earnest at daybreak on 31 October. The tone for this was set, not by any of those officially in command, but by an off-duty veteran of the Napoleonic wars, Major Digby Mackworth, a self-appointed adviser to the magistrates who had helped Mayor Pinney escape from the Mansion House on Saturday night. Mackworth had fought with distinction at Talavera, Albuera and Waterloo, but his most recent posting had been to the Forest of Dean in June, where thousands of miners and foresters had risen against enclosures. Frustrated by having too small a force at his disposal in the Forest, Mackworth had been unable to prevent the destruction of several miles of fencing and embankments, so he may thus have considered himself amply qualified to offer advice on taking firmer action now if Bristol was to be preserved.[31] What he was doing in Bristol in October is unclear. He was a member of the personal staff of General Lord Hill, commander-in-chief of the British army, and a magistrate for the county of Monmouth, but far outside his jurisdiction and he had no current military command. Rumours began

---

[30] Bristol Mercury, 17 Jan. 1832; TNA, HO 40/28, Information of Catherine Shea, 15 Nov. 1831; Trials of the Persons Concerned, pp. 35, 41; TNA, ASSI 6/3, Information of Isaac Lyons, 9 Nov. 1831; Information of Samuel Shipstone, 14 Nov. 1831; Information of John Harvey, 9 Jan. 1832; BL, Add. MS 27790, fol. 188; Examiner, 13 Nov. 1831.

[31] For Mackworth's posting to the Forest from Merthyr, see Hereford Journal, 15 June 1831.

to circulate that his real mission was to maintain surveillance upon Bristol's reformers during the assize.[32] Whatever his credentials, the sheer scale of the slaughter that followed was without domestic precedent. And it was backed, at last, by the enrolment of hundreds of members of the public, some of them armed with guns, who offered themselves as constables to aid the military.

Mackworth entered Queen Square just in time to witness what he later claimed was a fresh attempt to set fire to some houses on a corner close to the Quay. Fearful of the flames spreading to destroy the shipping, he assumed command of a patrol of the 3rd Dragoon Guards, who had come into the square under Brereton, and ordered a charge with drawn swords. There was little need. According to Manchee, 'The master spirits ... had disappeared ... Thousands had retired to their homes, inebriated, or to protect and conceal the plunder they had carried off. Those that remained were, many of them, rolling on the ground in such a beastly state of drunkenness as to be incapable of further mischief.'[33] Mackworth was untroubled. 'It was no longer time to consider numbers or to await magistrates' orders ... I called out, "charge, men, and charge home!"... Numbers were cut down and ridden over; some were driven into the burning houses, out of which they were never seen to return.'[34] This action was 'repeated several times as they reassembled', he reported, 'with a loss (I should imagine) of about 120 killed or wounded'. One soldier was shot in the arm, though it is not clear by whom, and Mackworth claimed several of his men 'received smart contusions', but it is unlikely they met with very much resistance. Manchee thought it likely the wounded soldier had been hit by 'a random shot of the constabulary' and that Mackworth's order was 'uncalled for, unauthorised, and, under the circumstances, cruel if not illegal'.[35] Regardless of the necessity however, Brereton now agreed to recall the 14th from Keynsham to finish the job and Mackworth galloped off to fetch them.

They returned at 10.00a.m., anxious to prove themselves after Sunday's undignified and humiliating retreat. No new reading of the Riot Act appears to have taken place, but Mackworth's force now joined a company of the 44th under Major Beckwith and recently arrived from Gloucester. Beckwith was unable to get a magistrate to accompany him back to Queen Square, but these combined military forces now fell upon anyone unfortunate enough still to be out of doors. These soldiers, 'in the most spirited manner, cut down all the mob they met with'. It was 'effectually done', according to Mackworth:

> Probably about 250 of the mob were sabred in these operations but no fire arms were used. This I particularly desired, both from humanity, however undeserved, and from the fear of teaching the mob to look for similar weapons – which from

[32] *Evening Mail*, 30 Nov. 1831; *Satirist*, 4 Dec. 1831.
[33] Manchee, *Origins of the Riots*, p. 35.
[34] *Morning Post*, 22 Nov. 1831.
[35] Manchee, *Origins of the Riots*, p. 35.

14 J. Catnach, *Riots at Bristol. Great Numbers Killed and Wounded.*

the facilities afforded them in so large a city, might have turned seriously to our disadvantage.[36]

The army may indeed have gone in without firearms, but the same discipline could not be guaranteed from the ad hoc *posse commitatus* that now convened itself to assist them. As the accountant, Henry Downman, later testified, the magistrates, 'could not give any orders for the use of arms but it was the duty of every man to arm himself in the best manner he could on such an occasion. I thought it my duty to arm myself with pistols. I knew that several were so armed.' The recruitment of this unofficial force began on Sunday night. James George, Tory brewer and alderman, was in the Commercial Rooms that evening, where he 'requested several Gentlemen to assist', and he wrote directly to others he thought reliable on Monday morning. One of these was Captain James Lewis of King Square, 'a gentleman possessing considerable property and of highly respectable connections' who had previously served as a special constable in 1830. A labourer named John Harper met him in Queen Square before eight o clock, when he 'pulled a pistol part of the way from under his great coat and said, "this is for some of ye"'. Shortly after that, Lewis took out the pistol and fired it, ostensibly to intimidate a drunken man who refused to disperse. 'If you don't go away, I'll make ye', he is supposed to have said, but he shot a fourteen-year-old onlooker, Thomas Morris, instead. Morris subsequently died of his wounds and became the subject of the riot's best-recorded inquest. 'In the excitement of that morning, seeing property

[36] TNA, HO 40/28, fols 16–19, Digby Mackworth to Fitzroy Somerset, 31 Oct. 1831; *Morning Post*, 22 Nov. 1831.

burning in all directions, I should certainly have felt myself justified in firing if I had met with any resistance', admitted Henry Waldo, but 'we did not meet with sufficient resistance to render the use of arms necessary'. Whether it was necessary or not, Lewis did not face any criminal charges.[37]

On Tuesday morning, Beckwith was less certain about the number of casualties than Mackworth had been. 'I can give no idea', he told Melbourne. 'On Monday everything was done at a gallop and with the sword, and in consequence, for one that was killed a hundred were wounded.'[38] A few days later, Mackworth revised his estimate. 'I have reason to think the numbers of killed and wounded by the Dragoons, which I estimated in a former letter at 400, is considerably under the truth. So many killed have been ascertained that, especially in an "arms blanche" business, would amount to almost double that number.'[39] *Arms blanche* was an accurate enough description for, as even the published and very incomplete casualty lists and inquest reports testify, the army's intention was not simply to disperse, but to maim and kill all those with whom they came into contact. Nor was the carnage restricted to Queen Square. Although no crowd activity was recorded anywhere else in the city that morning, those who fled the square were pursued and hunted down in several of the principal streets. And although the magistrates published hand-bills later in the day, warning everyone to stay at home or risk being mistaken for a rioter, several innocent bystanders were cut down. One was Daniel James, who died after being sabred in the head. He was 'cut at by a soldier who was riding up Corn Street, with others, cutting at all they met – the trumpet having sounded to the charge'. Another was a 23-year-old mason named John Howman, who was 'standing in the crowd, looking on', when 'his head was nearly severed from his body by one of the soldiers with his sabre'.[40]

'The troops cut at everyone they met with indiscriminately', wrote the editor of the *Mercury*, W. H. Somerton. Members of the *posse commitatus* and the Political Union, worried that they may not be recognised, wrapped strips of white calico around their arms, 'as a protecting badge', but some of these men too were injured. By this time, Somerton believed, the cavalry were quite beyond control. 'In some cases they rode their horses upon the pavement and aimed at terrified individuals who had sought refuge in some corner, and this was the case not only in the streets adjacent to Queen Square but in every part of the city. One man had his arm nearly severed from his body near the New Church at Lawford's Gate'. Mackworth, it would be said afterwards by defenders of the corporation, led the dragoons into no less than eleven 'heroic charges' against unarmed civilians that morning, upon which

[37] *The Observer*, 6 Nov. 1831; TNA, ASSI 6/3, Inquest into the death of Thomas Morris, Information of James George, Henry Downman, John Harper, Henry Waldo and John Angle.

[38] TNA, HO 40/28, fols 53–60, Major Beckwith to Fitzroy Somerset, 2 Nov. 1831.

[39] TNA, HO 40/28, Digby Mackworth to Fitzroy Somerset, 4 Nov. 1831.

[40] *The Observer*, 6 Nov. 1831.

'hung, at that time, the destinies of the country. He it was who saved it.' Somerton was less forgiving: 'The sight of this useless piece of duty – this act of cruelty it may justly be called – was particularly distressing. On every side were to be seen unoffending women and children, running and screaming while several men, apparently on their way to work, were deliberately cut at'.[41]

Without exception, all thirty-one men treated at the infirmary for sabre wounds had received cuts either directly to the head, to raised wrists and arms as they tried to protect themselves, or, in one case, to the shoulder. Sabre blows were delivered with savage force. Sixteen-year-old Samuel Vains took a sword to the face, 'dividing the skull'; Robert Thompson (sixty) suffered a wound that 'nearly detached the front of his nose', and David James (forty-five) was 'wounded across the front of the head, dividing the skull and penetrating the brain'. The youngest surviving sabre victim was Charles Manning, just eleven years old. Of a further fourteen, the source of whose wounds was less certain but 'probably sabre wounds', eight had taken blows to the head and face. And despite the assurances of Mackworth and Beckwith that no firearms were used, ten men were also treated for gunshot wounds.[42] The infirmary figures are certainly low, given the very high estimates of wounded recorded by military commanders. But as the authorities turned their attention to rounding up suspects for committal to the assize, attending the infirmary to have wounds dressed carried a clear risk of arrest. This was the experience of John Jones, who was seen to be wearing a stolen military jacket under his coat when he attended to have a sabre wound to his head dressed by a surgeon. Armed guards were placed on the doors and no in-patients were permitted to leave until examined by a magistrate.[43]

Meanwhile, Whitehall ordered General Sir Richard Jackson to Bristol to take command for the coming weeks, with a formidable army of reinforcements, including a six-pound field gun and a twenty-four-pound howitzer, to be held in readiness at Bath.[44] On 2 November, crowds reassembled in Queen Square, according to Beckwith, 'to view the mangled remains of some of the poor wretches who were cut down and burnt on Monday and whom they were dragging out from the ruins'.[45] Somerton was appalled by these scenes. 'Heads without bodies, trunks without members and broken fragments of limbs were successively exposed to the public gaze', he recorded.[46] But Mackworth thought it salutary. They were in 'a dreadfully mutilated state' but it was 'no bad thing that the public should see a little of them – most of them were burnt through their own drunkenness and impudence and some driven into

[41] *Hereford Journal*, 18 Oct. 1852; W. H. Somerton, *A Narrative of the Bristol Riots* ... (Bristol, 1831), p. 33.

[42] From a list published in the *North Devon Journal*, 17 Nov. 1831.

[43] *Bristol Mirror*, 5 Nov. 1831; TNA, ASSI 6/1, Information of Emelius Scipio Mayor, 10 Nov. 1831.

[44] TNA, HO 40/28, fols 33–4, Fitzroy Somerset to General Jackson, 31 Oct. 1831.

[45] TNA, HO 40/28, fols 68–72, Major Beckwith to Fitzroy Somerset, 2 Nov. 1831.

[46] Somerton, *Narrative*, p. 34.

the burning houses by the charge of the third dragoon guards. These never came out again alive.'[47]

Once it became clear that he had the upper hand, Jackson began a gradual process of demilitarisation. At the same time he assured the Home Office he'd keep enough soldiers on hand not only to police the coming assize, but because 'it would be very desirable, if a fair opportunity offers, to give a lesson to the colliers of Kingswood'.[48] There is in fact no evidence that the colliers had anything much to do with the riots, but suspicion of outside agents persisted as usual, and Mackworth for one thought miners had been fleeing the city on the final morning. In fact, he claimed to have 'pursued with one troop the Kingswood colliers, who had been very active in the riots, some miles on the Gloucester Road'. And Beckwith insisted, 'The greater number of our opponents did not belong to Bristol, as was evident from the number of broken heads that were seen on almost every road leading from the town.'[49]

There was no public enquiry into the actions of the military; indeed, the city's entire military forces were drawn up in the ruins of Queen Square in November and congratulated personally by General Lord Hill, commander of the entire British army. Hill took the opportunity to publicly announce his particular pleasure at the role played by Mackworth, as a member of his own personal staff. Others took a contrary view. The *Satirist* dubbed Mackworth 'the Bristol Butcher' and a 'savage and cowardly braggart', and called on the War Office to distance itself from him. 'Would any brave and generous hearted man have talked of his men "rejoicing with all their hearts" at the prospect of "cutting down all they met with" in "a mere despicable mob" of fellow creatures and fellow countrymen whom low wages, want of work, starvation and despair had driven to intoxication and crime?'[50]

Trial

With the streets relatively calm again, judicial retribution followed fast on the heels of massacre. The Special Commission, which opened on 2 January 1832 under Lord Chief Justice Tindal and Justices Taunton and Bosanquet, had itself been a source of some controversy. Firstly, the magistrates, as well as Wetherell, were unhappy with Melbourne's refusal to allow them to try the rioters themselves at a regular court of oyer and terminer. Yet given the strength of public criticism at the way the magistrates had conducted themselves during the riots, it would have been foolhardy to allow them to

[47] TNA, HO 40/28, Digby Mackworth to Fitzroy Somerset, 3 Nov. 1831.
[48] TNA, HO 40/28, fols 60–6, General Jackson to Fitzroy Somerset, 2 Nov. 1831.
[49] *Morning Post*, 22 Nov. 1831; TNA, HO 40/28, fols 53–60, Major Beckwith to Fitzroy Somerset, 2 Nov. 1831.
[50] *Bristol Mirror*, 19 Nov. 1831; *The Satirist*, 4 Dec. 1831.

run the trials.[51] Many believed it would have been a matinée of vengeance. Secondly, concerns remained that the commission might provoke a renewed outbreak of unrest unless skilfully handled. It was, after all, the first attempt to reconvene the law courts since Wetherell's disastrous entry in October, and rumblings of discontent were easily read in the anonymous graffiti chalked on walls 'in many places' around the city, threatening 'a House for a Neck!' in the event of exemplary executions.[52] Jackson was afraid the lower orders were only 'held in awe by the presence of a military force' and that the constables, already depleted by about half from the 1700 who flocked to his assistance on 31 October, would simply melt away if the soldiers were removed. 'Without soldiers', he bluntly advised Melbourne, 'there will be no constables.'[53]

This in turn raised questions about the security of the judges and the safe conduct of prisoners from the gaol to the Guildhall. Too strong a military presence might give an unfavourable impression that the trials were being conducted under martial law, and antagonise the crowd instead of merely intimidating them. A fresh drive to recruit additional constables was therefore made. Their task was visibly to keep order on the streets and to guard the prisoners, but with an assurance of military support if called for. By the time the commission opened, 1390 special constables had been enrolled, and expert advice received from the Metropolitan Police. Soldiers from the Royal Fusiliers, the 75th, the 52nd, the 3rd and the 14th were ordered under arms but kept out of public sight at various strategic points close to the route. The prisoners would be marched to the Guildhall through streets by which 'the narrow and crowded parts of the Quay will be avoided'; a special body of constables were to be posted to Marsh Street, which would be barricaded at each end to keep the Irish at bay. Gunners armed with hand grenades were ordered in three places along the route, and another stock of grenades was delivered to the gaol for the use of the governor should trouble break out there. Further soldiers were posted at Clifton, and regular patrols ordered along the approach roads from Hot Wells, Bath and Bedminster to guard against any unwelcome incursions from outsiders. These men were to act only if required by the magistrates, but were to do so 'with promptitude and energy until the restoration of power' if anything went wrong.[54] In the event, it did not.

---

[51] Caple, *Bristol Riots*, pp. 197–8.

[52] TNA, HO 40/28, Abraham Bagnall to General Jackson, 27 Dec. 1831. Wetherell was not called upon to open another Bristol assize until March 1835, but even then Mayor Charles Payne sent an apprehensive message to the Home Office requesting assistance, since 'it is impossible to conjecture what effect his presence may produce': TNA, HO 52/26, Charles Payne to Henry Goulbourn, 25 March 1835.

[53] TNA, HO 40/28, General Jackson to Lord Melbourne, 15 and 25 Dec. 1831.

[54] Caple, *Bristol Riots*, pp. 196–200; TNA, HO 40/28, Charles Pinney to Lord Melbourne, 27 Dec. 1831 and 1 Jan. 1832, Memorandum, 1 Jan. 1832, Details of sheriff's duty, 2 Jan. 1832.

Opening the case for the crown, Attorney General Sir Thomas Denman carefully instructed the jury on the business before them. The charges levelled against the defendants were for riot, plunder and the destruction of property. The crowd had completely destroyed the Bridewell, he reminded them, but 'Whether they imagined there were any persons charged with rioting confined there, or whether it was a general hatred of all gaols that induced them to proceed to these acts of outrage, it is not for me to determine. With such motives I have nothing at all to do.' Some in the crowd were leaders, others were led, and some merely bystanders, he added, but, 'Even if they were present, and never lifted a hand or uttered a word, they are all equally guilty – this is the law – this must be the law of every civilised country, and will be made awfully known in this city.'[55] Thus forty-two men and women were charged with simple theft or receiving stolen goods, many of them of little value. William Lee had been arrested for trying to pawn a stolen silver teaspoon, and John Jones for the military jacket he had 'picked up' in Queen Square and which he was wearing under his coat when he went to have his wounds dressed in the infirmary. John Simmons had been caught carrying home two spirit measures and some fire tongs and Hannah Reeves was taken up simply for carrying a bundle of linen she could not account for. Fourteen-year-old Daniel Doyle who, it will be remembered, had been apprehended during a search of Lewin's Mead for stealing a watch from the ruins of the Bridewell, was sentenced to six months with hard labour and a whipping, while his mother Eleanor narrowly escaped conviction for receiving after declaring her intention to surrender their stolen goods at the Guildhall.[56] Amongst labouring poor people like these, crimes of this kind were hardly exceptional. Indeed, Eleanor Doyle was back in court several times for petty thefts and public order offences between 1833 and 1836, and Daniel was eventually transported for seven years in 1835 for stealing lead from a boat on the Quay.[57] Another of the Irish detainees, James 'Jemmy' Donovan had his case for looting wine from the Mansion House cellars thrown out, possibly because the jury regarded him as a notorious but largely harmless drunkard. Between 1829 and 1862, he made numerous court appearances for a wide variety of petty offences, most of them committed while drunk.[58]

[55] *Trials of the Persons Concerned*, p. 2.

[56] TNA, ASSI 6/3, Information of Robert Moggeridge, 7 Dec. 1831 and information of Ella Smith, 8 Nov. 1831; *Trials of the Persons Concerned*, pp. 141–2; *Bristol Mirror*, 14 Jan. 1832.

[57] *Bath Chronicle*, 9 May 1833; *Bristol Mercury*, 4 July 1835, 1 Oct. 1836; *Bristol Mirror*, 14 Feb. 1835, 2 May 1835, 18 April 1835.

[58] The long and pitiful criminal career of Jemmy Donovan, the 'leading man in Bacchus's assembly' (*Western Daily Press*, 20 July 1859), is easily followed in Bristol's police courts through the pages of the city's newspaper press.

A further sixty-five prisoners faced charges for destroying buildings, and seven were simply charged with riot.[59] Here, the crown pursued its objective with ruthless determination. Reviewing depositions sent to them for opinion by the Bristol bench, the Law Officers found, 'clear proof of the crimes of arson, riotous demolition of houses, plunder, premediated or at least aggravated riots'. They added: 'We think it necessary that some examples should be made for each of these', and charges brought for 'the highest crimes which the evidence can bring home to them'.[60] Given such an unforgiving strategy, the execution of four defendants as instigators, and transportation orders for a further thirty-four were only to be expected, and the determination of prosecuting counsel to drive charges home, sometimes on the sketchiest evidence, was made perfectly clear. Selection seems to have had nothing to do with previous convictions although several defendants were already well known to the authorities. Cornelius Hickey, for instance, who had served a six-month sentence in the New Gaol for theft in 1829, was now convicted of burning houses in Queen Square, and was transported. Robert Ponchard, accused of taking part in the attack on Bridewell, was a former prisoner of it and so was identified by the turnkey, but was acquitted.[61] However, the crown had set its sights most keenly on a small number of men whom it regarded as the most culpable, whether active rioters like William Clarke or non-combatants like Christopher Davis. The prosecution of these two individuals, the first for physically leading the crowd and the second for encouraging them, was crucial to the crown's construction of events.

Clarke was seen many times and in many places over the course of the riots. Witnesses placed him in Queen Square handing out stolen goods to passers-by, shouldering a large iron bar in the streets and calling on the crowd to follow him. More than any other figure, Clarke epitomised the extraordinary self-confidence and bravado of the crowd as they progressed through the city unopposed on Sunday evening. At the Black Horse on College Green, he ordered a first round of drinks for everyone without payment, then willingly paid a shilling for the second. The landlady tried to persuade him to go home but he just showed her 'five very large keys' seized from Lawford's Gate prison and added, 'their work was not half finished and that I should see the Palace on fire in half an hour ... He asked me if I should know him again and said, "My name is William Clarke, commonly called Bill Clarke"'. They drank for half an hour, then went to the bishop's palace and set light to it. But the prosecution's main emphasis was placed on the leading role Clarke played in the attacks upon the city gaols, his part in breaking down the doors, in taking the keys from each, and in shouting that they would have 'liberty'. The symbolic value of the great keys to the gaol should not be underestimated. Clarke had

[59] Caple, *Bristol Riots*, p. 209.
[60] TNA, HO40/28, Thomas Denman to mayor of Bristol, 22 Nov. 1831.
[61] *Bristol Mercury*, 18 March 1829; *Bath Chronicle*, 7 May 1829; TNA, HO40/28, Information of John Phillips, turnkey, 30 Oct. 1831.

shown them off as trophies in several different alehouses the same evening. At the Horse and Groom in Lime Kiln Lane, he ordered drinks, then

> took from his coat pocket a large bundle of keys and said, 'Here you Buggers, this is the keys of the bloody gaol'. He then pulled out of his other pocket a very large key and holding it up said 'This is the Father of all of them and there shan't be a bloody gaol standing in a fortnight'.[62]

Clarke's counsel was none other than Charles Holden Walker, the reforming lawyer and critic of the city's incestuous judicial system, who had been locking horns with the corporation since 1807 and who had memorably taken up the case of Mary Milford against Sir Henry Lippincott in 1809 (see Chapter 2). The task before him was an unenviable one; and prospects for success little improved by the staunch refusal of the judges to allow him a jury list from which to challenge selection. 'Not forgetting where this prosecution was to be tried and from what body the panel was comprised, I applied for a copy – I urged the necessity of my having it – but I urged in vain. I neither had it, not was I permitted to see the original.' Neither was Walker made aware that the crown was preparing a string of supplementary capital indictments against Clarke in addition to the offence for which he was initially committed, aiding and abetting the destruction of the gaol.[63] As far as that charge was concerned, Walker suggested, prisons were no ordinary buildings, and Clarke could as easily have been tried for treason as destroying property, but the judges were not prepared to risk the case by raising the charge. Walker's efforts were to no avail and Clarke was convicted.

Christopher Davis's case was perhaps the most singular and it was reserved until last. As a businessman of some property, he was a comparatively well-known figure in the city and easily recognised by numerous witnesses at every stage in the riots. Although charged with destroying several buildings, including the gaol, the actual evidence against him was restricted to his encouragement of the crowd and his use of inflammatory language to urge them on. William Harvey recalled meeting Davis near the Drawbridge on Sunday night. 'The damned bishops have been the cause of this', Davis told him, and, 'it was a damned shame for one bishop to have £40,000 per year while so many were starving'. Richard James met Davis in Marsh Street. 'Damn your eyes, James', he exclaimed, 'this is glorious, this is the sort of thing we want.' Some witnesses, like Hugh Wickham, heard him actively addressing the crowd: 'The mob were assembling round him. I heard him say, "Down with those churches; the stones will do to mend the roads". He pointed with his umbrella.' John Parker offered similar testimony. He had seen Davis waving

---

[62] Evidence of Robert Trickey, Mary Anne Coper, in *Trials of the Persons Concerned*, pp. 4, 10; TNA, ASSI 6/3, Information of Mary King, 19 Nov. 1831 and Robert Harding Trickey, 24 Nov. 1831.
[63] C. H. Walker, *The Petition of William Clarke, Convicted at the Late Special Commission at Bristol ... with Prefatory Observations* (Bristol, 1832).

his hat and calling to the crowd, 'Go it my boys; hurrah!' Although some witnesses also suggested that Davis expressed regret about the violence and the freeing of prisoners from the gaols, the prosecution rested on his failure to assist the constables in bringing the riots to an end,

> not assisting in preserving peace, not watching to identify persons, not in preserving property but in encouraging the rioters, not only by his presence but by his language and gestures, which will be proved to be infamous and inciting to the last degree, and when addressed to such persons, by a man of his station in life, possessing property, and a father to a family, could not fail to be highly encouraging to the rioters ... putting his hat upon an umbrella as if it was a cap of liberty.[64]

Concerted attempts were made to save Davis's life too. He was an alcoholic, it was said in his defence, and always volatile when drunk. It was to no avail.

The three more men were initially selected for execution: Thomas Gregory, Joseph Kayes and Richard Vines. Although Caple concludes that all five were 'perceived as leaders', very little evidence was produced to suggest that these three were anything of the kind although the case against Gregory and Kayes, who were hanged, was considerably weaker than the case against Vines, who was granted an eleventh-hour reprieve.[65] These three men were not tried individually. Like many of their fellow defendants, they were arraigned as part of a small group against whom a collective charge had been prepared; in this case, destroying houses in Queen Square. The individual evidence against each of them was far from overwhelming. Vines, twenty-one years old, made a living as a hobbler, hauling boats into the harbour from Pill, and was convicted for burning and plundering the Reverend Charles Buck's house in Queen Square. He had no attorney to represent him and he offered very little in his own defence. Passing sentence, the judge distinguished Vines as a rioter who was heard 'calling the mob on' and seen feeding the flames in Buck's living room, but very similar evidence had been produced against Vines's co-defendant, William Reynolds, who was not selected for hanging.[66] After sentence had been passed however, a firm of Bristol lawyers, Estlin and Ball, took up his case. A number of people who knew Vines came forward to save his life. All of them were agreed: Vines was an idiot and not responsible for his actions. 'He was the sport and laughing stock of the boys in his neighbourhood and easily prevailed on to do anything he was put up to do', wrote one petitioner, 'whether right or wrong, and that he went by the name of Foolish Dicky or Silly Dick amongst the said boys.' He was incapable of regular employment, deeply impressionable and his father too was 'simple and half-witted'. The judges were sympathetic and Vines was saved for life transportation.[67]

---

[64] *Trials of the Persons Concerned*, pp. 105–12.

[65] Caple, *Bristol Riots*, p. 210.

[66] *Trials of the Persons Concerned*, p. 115.

[67] A number of petitions on Vines's behalf were forwarded to the Home Office. See for example, TNA, HO 17/68, Affidavits of William Earle, Richard Lessey, John Williams, William Merryfield and Henry Davis.

Thomas Gregory, the fourth man to be condemned, was identified by two witnesses breaking into houses, stealing candlesticks and carrying a lighted brand, and he made no defence. However, concerns were raised after the trials were over that at least one of these testimonies was flawed and some concerted efforts were made to save him. Thomas Roberts, a Baptist minister, began collecting evidence of his own in the days following and established that the principal witness in the case, a shoemaker called John Allen, had been overheard by his landlord saying 'a considerable time since that he would do everything in his power to get Gregory transported'. Allen had asserted in court that he had known Gregory in Bristol for two or three years; longer, Gregory claimed, than he had even been living in the city. Gregory believed Allen held a grudge against him. Moreover, Allen told Thomas that he had been in company that night in Queen Square with the attorney, William Harmer, but when Roberts questioned Harmer he found the two witnesses' recollections quite different. 'Harmer swears that he saw the prisoner go in and out of the house', Roberts informed the Home Office, 'but that he saw no fire in his hand going in, nor did he perceive any plunder in his possession coming out. If Allen could see the fire in Gregory's hand, why could not Harmer'? But such petty distinctions were of no interest to the crown and Thomas was ignored.[68]

Joseph Kayes, a decently dressed gentleman's groom, was charged with burning two houses, one the home of the sherriff's officer, Charles Bull. His conviction rested upon testimonies from five witnesses that he was on the scene, even though the building was 'full of people' and it was very dark.[69] In contrast to Gregory, no evidence, however questionable, was offered that Kayes had either looted or set fire to anything. One prosecution witness, Martha Cross, was openly rewarded for her evidence with a gratuity of £10 by the judge at the conclusion of the case and Kayes, who 'shrieked' his innocence from the bar ('I am not guilty! My wife! My children! Murder! I am murdered!') was convinced the witnesses had perjured themselves at the behest of a corrupt constable who harboured a grudge against him, and been well rewarded for their compliance. 'It is plain to the knowledge of every man that they do receive payment for so doing', he declared from the condemned cell, 'for they would not bring persons to swear to a man if they did not profit and get satisfaction for their trouble.' Kayes had not gone into hiding in the days following the riots but returned openly to work and offered no resistance to arrest. He was, it would seem, hanged on comparatively weak identificatory evidence, simply for being present, and as an example to his class.[70]

His was no isolated misfortune either, as the equally weak conviction of the 23-year-old baker, and transportee, Stephen Gaisford, would confirm. Gaisford

---

[68] TNA, HO 17/69, Thomas Roberts to Sir Thomas Denman, 24 Jan. 1832.
[69] Evidence of Isaac Bull and others, in *Trials of the Persons Concerned*, p. 82.
[70] *Trials of the Persons Concerned*, p. 114; *Incidents in the Life of Joseph Kayes who was Executed at the New Gaol ...* (Bristol, 1832), p. 11.

was arraigned alongside George Andrews, Patrick Bernard and Benjamin Broad for burning down William Cross's house in Queen Square the same night. As the Attorney General had already argued, a very large crowd had taken part in this attack 'and it was impossible to apprehend all of such an assemblage', so the jury would 'consider the testimony of the respectable witnesses' against the men at the bar and act accordingly. Cross had gone into the house himself while it was being ransacked, trying to salvage his property, issuing instructions to his servants by candlelight and was 'a little confused, certainly'. He thought he saw Gaisford there, although it was for no more than a minute and 'I am not positive' it was he. John Manning saw Gaisford go in and out of the house, but for most of the time he was 'standing about' with Broad and 'not doing anything'. Cross-examined moreover, Manning admitted he had only 'guessed Gaisford was there, and that he had been pressed to identify him by Oatridge, the governor of Lawford's Gate prison, who was not in Queen Square that night but who knew both Broad and Gaisford from his past record. Indeed, according to Gaisford, Oatridge had already declared his life 'not worth a farthing'. 'But for that bloody Oatridge outside the Gate', Manning is supposed to have said, 'he would not have to swear against them.' Although several other witnesses, including Cross's servants, were able to identify Andrews and Bernard, none of them had any recollection of Gaisford. For his part, Gaisford admitted being in the square with Broad in the early evening but that he'd been asleep in a lodging house by a little after midnight, an hour or so before Cross's house was set alight. The keeper of the house, John Crowley, confirmed Gaisford's story. However, the prosecution turned on Crowley, questioning his reputation and forcing an admission of several previous convictions for 'rows' and disorderly conduct. And although neither Broad nor Gaisford had been clearly identified committing a capital felony, Gaisford's reputation was further sullied by his friendship with Broad who, it was suggested, was a brothel keeper. Moreover, one of Broad's defence witnesses, John Heards, was alleged to be a frequenter of brothels himself, and a man against whom charges of theft from a prostitute had previously been laid. In short, the evidence against Stephen Gaisford was highly questionable and his conviction unsafe. His parents were quick to petition for clemency. As they pointed out, the jury had found him and Broad 'less guilty than the other two'. But it was to no avail and all four of the accused were sentenced to transportation for life.[71]

Contemporary opinion on the conduct of the trials was divided and the pro-reform papers were, unsurprisingly, the most critical. 'When we look at the sentences, we certainly do wonder at their injustice', commented the

[71] Case details from *Trials of the Persons Concerned*, pp. 52–60; TNA, HO17/69, Petition of the parents of Stephen Gaisford, n.d.; HO 40/28, Examination of Stephen Gaisford, 7 Nov. 1831. Gaisford's case will not have been helped by his own criminal record. He had received a month's hard labour as a rogue and vagabond in November 1828 and been before the bench on several occasions after that. See *Bristol Mirror*, 29 Nov. 1828, 2 May 1829 and 10 July 1830.

Mercury, 'and we cannot help reiterating our ignorance of the principle on which they have been regulated.' There was, the paper concluded, neither rhyme nor reason to the setting of examples on the one hand and the extension of mercy on the other, but this simply drew attention to the fact that there was no discernible policy behind either the crown's prosecution strategy or the Special Commission's sentencing beyond the desire to secure an adequate number of convictions and set a memorable example.[72]

Retribution

While the condemned men awaited execution at Newgate for the next thirteen days, stringent efforts were being made to save them, principally by liberal critics of the corporation. A clemency petition with ten thousand signatures was submitted to Whitehall, arguing firstly that nothing the convicts had done had been premeditated and that they had shown no intention of harming anybody, and secondly that they had only been able to commit outrages against property in the riots' latter stages because the magistrates had failed to do their duty at the outset. Particular efforts were made on behalf of Davis, who had committed neither theft nor criminal damage, and of Clarke, the crown's principal scapegoat, against whom some of the most contradictory evidence had been admitted. Charles Walker presented fifteen 'exculpatory' affidavits to the Home Office on Clarke's behalf, and a separate petition from six hundred residents of Bedminster testifying to the condemned man's good character. If his behaviour had been intemperate during the riots, his friends insisted, it was attributable to mental damage from an old industrial injury to his head and the consequent ill effects of alcohol on his capacity for reasoned thought.[73] There was some expectation that all this activity would bear fruit, at least in the cases of Davis and Clarke, but when a solitary reprieve arrived for Vines on the eve of execution, it quickly became clear that the fate of the other four was sealed. Presumptions of 'idiocy' would serve, it seemed, but not of drunkenness.

On 27 January, the date fixed for the executions, a strategic decision was reached to keep the military away from public view but to pack the road between the gaol gatehouse and the New Cut with between 6–700 special constables. This left little space for the crowd to gather on the Cut's northern bank and effectively confined spectators to a relatively distant position on the southern side. There was scant public appetite for this final act of retribution however and many stayed away, leaving one reporter to observe that, 'in the aggregate, there were fewer persons present than were on the same ground on the Sunday when the gaol was broken open'.[74] Many Bristolians, like Walker

---

[72] *Bristol Mercury*, 17 Jan. 1832.
[73] Walker, *The Petition of William Clarke*.
[74] *A Full Report of the Trials of the Bristol Rioters before the Special Commission ... with the Sentences and Executions Subsequent Thereon* (Bristol, 1832).

15 *Trials and Execution of the Unhappy Rioters at Bristol.*

and the liberal press, considered the trials arbitrary and improperly conducted and the sentences unnecessarily harsh. The magistrates, it was repeatedly alleged, were no less culpable than the poor men sent to the gallows, for it was their inertia during and following the protests against Wetherall's arrival on 29 October that had allowed the situation to spiral out of control so rapidly.[75] The denial of mercy to Clarke, in the teeth of so much popular feeling in his favour, was especially galling to Walker,

> taking into account the criminal apathy – the *self-preserving* qualities which so pre-eminently distinguished the conduct of the Magistrates of Bristol throughout the late riots – their abandonment of their duties – their giving up the city, as it were, to fire and pillage – the excitement to crime which such conduct gave rise to... and the flat contradiction of the most important facts deposed to on the part of the prosecution, upon which a sense of aggravated guilt must rest, if it rest at all, is a question upon which high legal authority has already decided.[76]

A crowd estimated at 4–5000, large enough but smaller than expected, witnessed the executions in silence, then quietly dispersed. 'We had hoped that a well-timed mercy would have been shown to reconcile the violently opposed interests of the rich and poor', commented the *Poor Man's Guardian*; 'but in future, the latter will look upon the former as their worst enemies'.[77]

Ex-officio informations were lodged against Mayor Pinney and several of the magistrates for neglect of duty, but only Pinney came to trial, and he was

---

[75] See for example, *The Magistrates of Bristol Brought to the Bar of Public Opinion* ... (Bristol, 1832).

[76] Walker, *The Petition of William Clarke.*

[77] *Poor Man's Guardian*, 4 Feb. 1832; A. Layman, *Narrative of Conversations held with Christopher Davis and William Clarke, who were Executed January 27th, 1832* ... (Bristol, 1832).

honourably acquitted in November. The case was weakly presented and the verdict unsurprising, but the trial and its outcome exposed more clearly than ever the irreparable nature of the rift between citizens and corporation. The liberal press was convinced of one thing at least. 'The trial of the Mayor of Bristol ... had revealed to the public the deadly hostility whch exists between the corporation and the inhabitants of that ancient city', declared *Bells Life in London*:

> Common protection and common interest demand a harmony between the magistrates and the people, which can only be obtained by giving the people the power to elect their own magistrates ... The self-election system, the narrow and exclusive system, the routine system, the junta system are all usurpations, and Corporations as we know them must either be reformed or destroyed.

Regardless of the outcome, Pinney's trial seemed only to highlight the obsolescence of authority that was electorally unaccountable. 'The Corporation of Bristol is what a close Corporation in the midst of a great city may be expected to become', argued *The Globe*, 'very odious, very inefficient and, as standing in the way of some better government of the place, very mischievous.'[78]

> The children cry, my father dear,
> The mother cries, my son,
> The wife laments and tears her hair,
> Crying, 'oh! I am undone',
> Oh! such a scene in Britain's Isle
> Was never seen before,
> For the fate of those unhappy men
> Some thousands does deplore.[79]

---

[78] *Bristol Mercury*, 10 Nov. 1832. With evident satisfaction, the paper noted a selection of responses in the London press, all urging the reform of local government in the light of Pinney's acquittal.

[79] From *The Sorrowful Lamentation of the Unhappy Men of Bristol who Receivd Sentence of Death for the Late Riots* (London, 1832).

Postscript

The Bristol riots hit the news. Detailed reports of the riots were blazoned in the press, in London, Dublin, Edinburgh, and in many provincial towns in England. As part of the reform crisis a lot was at stake in how the riots were interpreted. They became something of a litmus test of reform. For *Blackwood's Magazine*, an ultra-Tory monthly, the Bristol riots gave the public a 'foretaste of democracy'.[1] Extending the franchise would only result in more scenes of appalling degeneracy, scenes of deluded mobs and manipulative demagogues, whose real intent was revolution. For reformist newspapers, the lesson learned from the riots was the decadent state of local government in Bristol, emblematic of Old Corruption, a portrait of self-selected politicians irresponsibly clinging onto power and privilege in the face of public mistrust and resentment, allowing a turbulent but manageable crisis to spiral out of control. As we have seen, this opinion gathered force after the trial of Mayor Charles Pinney in November 1832, leading the *Examiner* to declare 'let us set about municipal improvement with all the speed we may'. As the *Reading Mercury* opined a year earlier: 'The great bulk of the inhabitants, including sensible persons of all parties, are sick of the self-elected system and anxious it should be abolished.'[2]

For radical commentators the riots were regrettable because they would be used as a pretext for denying the vote to the bulk of the male population, keeping 'all their fellow labourers in their present tyrannical subjection'. The real culprit, said the *Poor Man's Guardian*, was the local oligarchy, which had reduced offenders 'to such a state of mental ignorance and degradation'. Francis Place believed the Bristol riots underscored the benumbing influences of religious prejudice and class on political consciousness. Church-and-King bigotry and 'the contempt of all who are able to live without working for all who do work' had rendered life brutish and miserable for the majority. Until there was some relief from the daily struggle for survival, which cramped people materially and intellectually, the degradations of a Bristol riot would continue.[3]

---

[1] *Blackwood's Magazine*, 31:192 (March 1832), 483.
[2] *Reading Mercury*, 14 Nov. 1831.
[3] BL, Add. MS 27,790, fols 173–5; *Poor Man's Guardian*, 5 Nov. 1831.

In the larger scheme of things, the Bristol riots do pose some interesting questions for historians from below, if only because of the range of action they generated, from demonstrations for reform to scenes of spectacular vandalism and drunkenness. Early historians from below were primary interested in revolutionary crowds, or those that anticipated in some way the popular contentions of the industrial era; crowds that made a perceptible political difference in new social formations. In George Rudé's work they ran along a progressive–radical vector and were by definition quite exclusive, omitting electoral mobs, crowds gathered on ceremonial occasions, street gangs, and even some forms of collective criminality: smuggling, wrecking, poaching, for example. This was stacking the deck for the revolutionary crowd. Even Edward Thompson, whose ambit of crowd enquiry was more capacious in that it was embedded in customary economies and plebeian counter-theatres, would sometimes rate crowd or mob actions according to their radical potential, or their potential for opening up radical space. Both of these historians, in fact, wrote off the Bristol riots as regressive. Rudé dubbed them a 'hangover from the past', while Thompson compared 'the persistence of older, backward looking patterns of behaviour' in Bristol with 'the self-disciplined patterns of the new working class movement' at Peterloo.[4] This type of classification tended to terminate analysis rather than open it up. It was driven by a meta-narrative of modernity. Bristol was disappointing because it didn't measure up.

What one sees in the Bristol riots is the co-existence of different kinds of popular protest, some of them off the political register. It warns us against reifying the crowd; it teaches us that crowd actions often involved changeable coalitions of workers with different objectives.[5] The slogans for 'Reform' and 'King and Reform' that were voiced at Sir Charles Wetherell's entry into Bristol and at the assize can be linked back to the formal petitions in favour of parliamentary reform that circulated in 1831 and to the agitations of the newly-formed Bristol Political Union. Following the rejection of the second Reform Bill by the Lords on 8 October, the BPU had organised a mass meeting in Queen Square, mustering support for parliamentary reform and applauding the king's resolution to proceed with the bill. That meeting ended with the leaders of the BPU being drawn through the streets in triumph – a familiar ritual for the people's 'champions' – and a mass enrolment of new members of the association in Broadmead.[6] At the meeting some of the language of constitutional defiance was employed by the speakers. Reformers moved to 'enforce the restoration of the just rights of the People'. They were exhorted to organise nationally through the auspices of the Birmingham Political

[4] George Rudé, *The Crowd in History* (New York, 1964), pp. 149n, 240; E. P. Thompson, *Making of the English Working Class* (London, 1963), p. 75.
[5] On this point, see Perry Anderson, *Arguments Within English Marxism* (London, 1980), p. 42.
[6] *Bristol Mercury*, 11 Oct. 1831.

Union, who were to assemble a convention of delegates to press for parliamentary change. This was read by paranoid conservatives as a pitch for an anti-parliament or provisional government. Bristolians were also urged to be firm and patient – 'the people are too strong to require violence' – but the patience came with the warning that further resistance to reform might well open the gates to social anarchy. One of the motions passed at the meeting asserted that the Lords' rejection of the Reform Bill had created a public feeling 'likely to subvert the existing relations of society'.[7]

That language of menace clearly fuelled efforts to oust Wetherell from Bristol on the grounds that he was an improper and unworthy law officer for the city, defiant of popular opinion and protected by a narrow corporate elite, itself a 'local aristocracy' in whom authority and trust had evaporated.[8] Consequently, the disruption of the assize and the trashing of civic festivities became desirable goals, leading on the one hand to the rescue of demonstrators in the city gaols and on the other to the raiding of the civic cellars and a general bacchanalia. The course of the riot became centrifugal. Like the Gordon Riots it pushed outwards to embrace other targets and aspirations. These included the destruction of toll-houses at Prince Street bridge and elsewhere, which were long-standing grievances.[9] It featured attacks on corporate property in Queen Square, much of it leased to private families, and it involved the destruction of government property such as the Excise and Customs House. These especially were fonts of electoral patronage and sites of unwelcome surveillance to the informal grey economy of petty smuggling and perquisites that was carried on at the waterside. It also featured a sustained attack on Bristol's prisons, which in the 'reforming' era of John Howard had become more systematic instruments of detention and punishment. And it prompted demands for festive doles 'in every direction of the city', particularly free beer for the wrecking bands from neighbouring pubs.[10] Some of these activities were not pretty. They may well have involved petty extortion and the settling of personal scores that left no trace in the legal record. Mobs usually served notice on corporate lessees that they were going to bring down and burn their habitations. But not always. Rioters set fire to a house in Prince Street where a Mrs Jones was lying-in, forcing her to leave her bed expeditiously. They trampled on a popular comedian, Mr Woulds, as he attempted to recover some of his personal effects, leaving him very vulnerable to the fire.[11] As we have

[7] Bristol Mercury, 11 Oct. 1831.

[8] On the language of menace and constitutional defiance, see Joseph Hamburger, James Mill and the Art of Revolution (New Haven and Yale, 1963), pp. 48–111 and James A. Epstein, 'The Constitutional Idiom: Radical Reasoning, Rhetoric and Action in Early-Nineteenth Century England', Journal of Social History, 23:3 (1990), 553–74.

[9] Leeds Mercury, 5 Nov. 1831; Morning Post, 2 Nov. 1831.

[10] Bristol Mercury, 8 Nov. 1831.

[11] Norfolk Chronicle, 12 Nov. 1831; Bury and Norwich Post, 9 Nov. 1831; John Bull, 7 Nov. 1831.

seen, some drunken rioters perished in the fires, or staggered horribly from scorching buildings, burnt beyond belief.

Contemporaries focussed on the degradation of the riots. It made better copy; it was guaranteed to excite middle-class curiosity, if not rage; it made political capital as a commentary on the political inadequacy or immaturity of an incipient working class. As Ian Haywood has noted, dating from 1780 the theme of degeneracy was applied to unruly disturbances, forming part of a Romantic trope in which infernos, fiends, drunken wildness and wanton destruction touched the sublime and unnerved the propertied.[12] Writers of pulp fiction got in on the act. 'Close at hand, with a terrible surging roar, the peril of riot and outrage was upon them', ran one moralising novel, and 'in another minute they were in the midst of a shouting, rushing crowd of the roughest and vilest of the people'.[13] *Blackwood's* talked of 'rapine, sack and burning'; the *Bath Chronicle* of the 'cold-blooded malignity' of the 'demons' of the night. 'I lay in bed contemplating the awful red glare of the hemisphere', remarked an onlooker from Clifton.[14] Newspaper accounts were saturated with such images. They tended to underplay the rough-and-ready logic of crowd actions for the spectacular and anecdotal. They zoned in on immediate causes, whether that meant the unpopularity of the Recorder, magisterial neglect, military indecision, or even radical subversion.[15] Some comparisons were made to the Gordon riots, particularly with respect to the lethargy of the mayor and the destruction of the gaols. And like those riots, rumours spread like wildfire. 'It is impossible to describe the consternation which prevailed, as it had been ascertained that the leaders of the mob had taken an oath to destroy the whole of the city', remarked the *Chester Chronicle*.[16] The *Annual Register* believed that the 'dense masses of the lower orders' who 'poured out from St Phillips and Lawfords Gate' to greet Wetherell at Totterdown were bent on firing the shipping. Stories circulated that the mob was 'determined to have all the colliers in to their aid and threatened that if they would refuse they would burn them in their pits'.[17] To complete the picture of social anarchy, it was reported that Merchants' Hall in Prince Street, the citadel of merchant power, had been burnt to the ground, and that navies, sailors and country people had swarmed into the city to top off the urban destruction. Among those responsible for the destruction of the bishop's palace were 'men

---

[12] Ian Haywood, *Bloody Romanticism: Spectacular Violence and the Politics of Representation 1776–1832* (New York, 2006), pp. 216–22.

[13] Emily M. Lawson, *Through Tumult and Pestilence: A Tale of the Bristol Riots and the Cholera Time* (London, n.d.), pp. 64–5. See also A Country Parsons Daughter [Elizabeth Holmes], *Scenes in Our Parish* (New York, 1833), pp. 240–56.

[14] *Bath Chronicle*, 10 Nov. 1831; *Blackwood's Magazine* 31:192 (1832) 473; *Northampton Mercury*, 5 Nov. 1831.

[15] On radical subversion, see the *Morning Post*, 2 Nov. 1831; *Blackwood's Magazine*, 31:192 (March 1832), 465–83, and 32:202 (Dec. 1832), 956–67.

[16] *Chester Chronicle*, 4 Nov. 1831.

[17] *Newcastle Courant*, 5 Nov. 1831.

from the country with blackened faces'.[18] It was a nightmarish recall of earlier disturbances, particularly the turnpike riots of the mid century, projected onto 1831. Such images of mayhem allowed *Blackwood's Magazine* to build a phantasmagoria of conspiracy. William Herapath of the BPU, usually viewed as a peacemaker, was suspected of trying to entrap mobs on the spit of the New Gaol so that they would destroy Alderman Hilhouse's shipping yard. He and his fellow travellers from Birmingham were intent on fomenting anarchy so that foreign revolutionaries from France or Ireland could take over the city and establish a provisional government, a move comparable to the recent coup in France.[19]

Such fears betrayed deep social anxieties in the highly charged reform crisis of 1831. Yet despite the ghosts of the past that haunted accounts, no sustained or measured attempt was made to situate the riots on a continuum of crowd interventions in Bristol during the long eighteenth century. The riots of 1831, after all, were not the only occasion when mobs took temporary possession of Bristol's civic spaces or damaged corporation property. There had been significant occupations of the centre of Bristol before and angry confrontations with magistrates at the Guildhall. Crowds had attacked buildings and disrupted celebrations in Queen Square in 1714 and 1735 during the 'Jacobite' disturbances of those years. Anti-impressment mobs swept through the nearby quays in the early years of the Seven Years' War. Turnpike rioters threatened to pull down the Exchange and rescue comrades from Newgate in 1749. Kingswood colliers descended upon the Council House in an attempt to hold down food prices four years later; they rescued demonstrators from Bridewell, and took hostages from the Bristol elite. One very prominent woollen draper, John Brickdale, a leading light in the Steadfast Society, was forced into hiding for three months for his role in suppressing turnpike and food riots in 1749 and 1753. Like Wetherell, he understood his popular rating and wisely made himself scarce.

Of course the scale of the 1831 riots was greater, both in numbers and destructive power. And there was arguably more at stake in 1831 than in the earlier confrontations. In the early stand-offs, right down until the 1790s, there was some expectation that confrontation would be part of a continuing dialogue with the local patriciate over social provision, wage regulation, and tax impositions like tolls at turnpikes and bridges. Indeed, it could be argued that if plebeian crowds did not always get what they wanted, or if they were sometimes bought off by electoral largesse, they did help curb the pretensions of power at the apex of Bristol society. They kept the magistrates on their toes over labour disputes; they delayed heavier tolls on coal and market produce for over two decades. They forced the elite to subsidise food supplies in times

---

[18] *Norfolk Chronicle*, 5 Nov. 1831.
[19] *Blackwood's Magazine*, 32:202 (Dec. 1832), 956–67. Three hundred members of the BPU, out of a total of over 2900, eventually joined the specials in suppressing disorder. See Hamburger, *James Mill*, p. 169n.

of dearth and to mediate the confrontations of tars, pilots and trowmen with the Admiralty. That rough-edged paternalism began to dissolve in the final years of the century, coincident with a significant slowing of Bristol's economy, an unhealthy concentration on the Caribbean trades, and a noteworthy retreat of the social elite to the suburbs and beyond. After 1790 magistrates became harder to find to mediate local disputes; they were socially remote. They were also harder nosed, increasingly unwilling to intervene in the market, tougher on social provision, particularly for migrants, and arrogant in their management of civic trusts. As part of the corporate elite, they were prickly about their chartered privileges, unwilling to share the management . of the city with new statutory bodies or to consult with other groups over tax levies. The repressions of 1793 over the tolls on Bristol Bridge signalled this tougher stance. As regards law and order, magistrates played it by the book, but at considerable cost in terms of public trust and good will, and in 1810 and 1812 crowds continued to signal opposition by laying siege to the Council House, Guildhall and Mansion House, breaking windows and refusing magistrates' orders to disperse. After the Napoleonic wars, a huge distance had opened up between the patriciate and the rest of the population. Bristol's growing middle class, consigned to a client status, was unable or unwilling to mediate the distance. Why should it, when, despite a long-standing tradition of civic independence and some success in sustaining religious diversity in the city, it was continually denied a parliamentary voice and sidelined on many projects to improve the city's economy. The 1831 riots reflected the deepening alienation and anger of different marginal groups in Bristol society whose only common ground was a disgust, if not hatred, for the patriciate who continued to dictate Bristol's destiny. As the *Globe* remarked, 'the magistrates were so unpopular as a body with the mass of the citizens, that even men, the most interested in the preservation of the peace, would not co-operate with them till the danger of property had been proved by the actual destruction of a part of the city'.[20] And we could add, proved beyond doubt in a leading site of corporate power, with the possibility that it would threaten shipping, the lifeblood of the port. Triggered by the reform crisis and the arrogance of the Recorder, the riots registered the fissures and interclass tensions of a stagnant society.

The mutuality that once mediated tensions between the privileged elite and the labouring poor was in tatters by the summer of 1832. The punitive, unpopular executions and transportation orders handed down by the January Special Commission, cheered on by a cholera outbreak that ripped through the city's poorest districts in the summer, had arguably done quite enough damage on their own. But the true extent of the divide was perhaps best illustrated by events on Brandon Hill in August, when the Whig Party and its supporters gathered to celebrate the passing of the Reform Act by honouring 'the trades'. Refused permission to hold a subscription banquet

---

[20] Cited in the *Bristol Mercury*, 10 Nov. 1832.

either at the new cattle market or on Durdham Down by a corporation still smarting from the blame heaped upon it for the riots, the Whigs did what reformers had been doing at Bristol for more than a century – they conjured the liberties of Brandon Hill as public space from which they could not be excluded by the oligarchy. Indeed, the Hill had hosted a mass meeting of some five thousand working-class reformers a few short months earlier during the tense 'May days'.[21]

Things took a turn for the worse however, when the Whigs tried to restrict access to the Hill. Tickets at 2s 6d a head were issued to six thousand respectable tradesmen, vetted by their benefit societies, with tables set out on the grass overlooking the city, and 'barricadoes' erected around the perimeter to exclude the unwanted. But while favoured ticket-holders waited patiently to be shown to their seats, a crowd twice the size, composed of 'hungry men, women and children' overran the barricadoes, occupied the slopes and re-appropriated the feast. 'The most troublesome of this class', noted the *Mercury*, were the poor women, of whom we saw dozens with reticule baskets collecting scraps of every description.' Grandees on the top two tables could do little but look on as 'a number of men and women of a very low description took possession of the other tables and conducted themselves in a most disorderly manner. On the fourth or fifth table from the chairman, a woman was seen dancing.' Waiters were punched and a remonstrating tradesman was stabbed in the neck. As the city's two Whig MPs hurriedly abandoned the scene, barrels of beer were rolled away towards the tenement dwellings of the Hotwells road, where a covered wagon full of puddings was also commandeered.[22]

'It is said that "coming events cast their shadows before"', railed the *Morning Post*.

> May not the Grey ministry behold the shadow of their own fate in this act of the Bristol harpies? May they not see that the mob power, which it cost them so much trouble to set in motion, will, like the rolling stone, overrun the limits which they have assigned to it and find that the first injury it inflicts will be upon those men who made it feel its own power?[23]

An evening display of fireworks did go ahead as planned, and the fences were removed to ensure no spirit of exclusion remained, but this too ran into trouble as a number of respectable celebrants complained of 'rabble' gangs picking their pockets and stealing their hats.[24] The wages of reform, it must have seemed to some at least, had now been paid in full: deference was at an end and Bristol's once vaunted civic consensus had received an overdue *coup de grace*.

---

[21] *Bristol Mirror*, 12 and 19 May 1832.
[22] *Bristol Mercury*, 18 Aug. 1832.
[23] *Morning Post*, 17 Aug. 1832.
[24] *Bristol Mercury*, 18 Aug. 1832.

Bibliography

Primary Sources

Manuscript

Bath Guildhall Record Office
Assize of Bread records, May 1801

Bodleian Library
MS Gough, *Somerset*

Bodleian Library
Harleian MS 3782

British Library
Add. MS 11275, Letters to Dr Nathaniel Forster
Add. MS 16927, John Reeves papers
Add. MS 27790 and 27812, Francis Place papers
Add. MS 27951, 'Itinerarium Bristoliense'
Add. MS 32719–32, Newcastle papers
Add. MS 37836, John Robinson papers
Add. MS 61609, Blenheim papers

Bristol Record Library
B 6979, Election broadsides, 1774–90
B 10162, Minutes of the Society for the Reformation of Manners 1699–1705
B 13065, Committee for investigating the Bridge affairs, 1793
B 18588, Holograph letter, Richard Burke to John Noble, 25 Nov. 1793
Bristol poll books, 1722, 1734, 1754, 1775, 1781, 1784, 1810, 1830
Election handbills, 1796
Jefferies MS
Manuscript diary of William Dyer, 2 vols, 1744–1801
Weare MS 19841

Bristol Archives
04350/5 & 6, Assize of Bread books 1795–96 and 1800–01
04351, Assize of Bread Grain returns, 1790–1823
04353/5, Register of Apprentices, 1724–40

04359/8–9 and 16, Burgess books, 1732–43, 1780–86
04379, Mayor's letter book, 1746–52
05158, Common Council letter book
05158, Town Clerk's letter book
11168/70/a–b, Bright papers
Abstract of the Articles of Agreement of the Bristol Flour and Bread Concern (1801)
Bristol Methodist Society class lists, 1796–99
F/Au/1/85 [1716] and F/Au/1/131 [1761], Corporation audits
JQS/BW/1–2, Burials in wool
JQS/C, Summary Convictions registers
JQS/D, Quarter Sessions docket book
JQS/P, Quarter Sessions papers
M/BCC/CCP, Common Council proceedings
MS 6687, Lewin's Mead minute book, 1710–14
MS 09701/26, Correspondence of Richard and Thomas Haynes
MS 28048, Harford papers
MS 44785/1–10, Edward Southwell papers
MS 12144, Steadfast Society: election proceedings, 1806–12
Petty Session convictions, 1728–95
P.St LB/OP/13, St Luke's, Brislington, vagrancy examinations
SMV/2/1, Society of Merchant Venturers, Hall books
SMV/8/2, Steadfast Society records
SMV/8/3, West India Association
TC/Adm/Box, Town Clerk's papers

Dr Williams Library, London
John Evans MS 34.4

Gloucestershire Record Office
D 1799, Blathwayte papers

Somerset Heritage Centre
DD/AH/59/12, Acland papers
Q/SR, Quarter Sessions, sessions rolls

The National Archives
Adm 1, Captains' in-letters to Admiralty
Adm 3/85, Correspondence to Admiralty Board, 1778
ASSI 2, Assize records, Western circuit, gaol delivery
Assi 6/3, Criminal depositions, Bristol riots 1831
ASSI 23, Assize records, Western circuit, gaol books
CO 5, Colonial papers, North America
E 179/116/541, Hearth tax 1670
E 190/1214/3, Port books, Bristol, 1738–39
HCA 26/30/147 and 26/32/45, Letters of marque
HO 17/68, Criminal petitions, 1821–39
HO 40, Home Office papers, disturbances

HO 42, Home Office papers, general correspondence
HO 43, Domestic entry books
HO 52, Correspondence with magistrates and municipalities
 KB 33/5, King's Bench, Crown side, precedents and miscellanea
PC 1/42, Privy Council's enquiry into corresponding societies and treason
PRO 30/8, Chatham papers
PROB 11/1191/198, Will of Mary Elton, 1789
SP 35, State Papers Domestic, George I
SP 36, State Papers Domestic, George II
SP 37, State Papers Domestic, George III
SP 44, State Papers, entry books
T 47/8, Register of tax on male servants, 1780
T 54/23/2, Treasury, entry books of warrants
T/90 Sheriff's cravings
TS 11/944, The king against John Vint for a libel
TS 11/961/2567, Papers of the Society of Constitutional Information
TS 24/2/13, Address of the Bristol Constitutional Society (Bristol, 1794)
WO 1, War Office, in-letters

University of Bristol Library
Special Collections, Pinney Family letter book, 1795–96

William L. Clements Library, Ann Arbor
Shelburne MS 139

Printed Primary

Almon, John, *Parliamentary Debates*, 17 (1780).
Anon., *An account of the proceedings against the rebels … tried before Lord Chief Justice Jefferies*, 2nd edn (London, 1716).
Anon., *An Account of the Riots, Tumults and other Treasonable Practices since his Majesty's Accession* (London, 1715).
Anon., *Address of the Bristol Corresponding Society for Parliamentary Reform, to the people of Great Britain* (Bristol, 1794).
Anon., *An Address to the Electors of the City of Bristol on the Approaching General Election* (Bristol, 1795).
Anon., *The Bristol Contest* (Bristol, 1754).
Anon., *The Bristol Contest* (Bristol, 1781).
Anon., *Bristol Gaol Bill, August 4th 1792: Objections to an Act lately obtained for building a new gaol within the city of Bristol, and for other purposes …* (Bristol, 1792).
Anon., *A Collection of Sundry Messages and Warnings to the Inhabitants of the City of Bristol*, 2nd edn (Bristol, 1728).
Anon., *Collections of the Massachusetts Historical Society* 7th series, IX (Boston, 1914).
Anon. *The Colliers of Kingswood in an Uproar, Or, an Account of their present Mobbing, and Preventing Coal being brought to this City …* (Bristol, 1738).
Anon., *Copy of Resolutions Passed at the Formation of the Bristol Concentric Society* (Bristol, 1819).

Anon, *A dialogue between the Member of Parliament and a commander of a ship, about encouraging the seamen of Great Britain and the speedy manning the navy without impressing* (London, 1709).

Anon., *A Full Report of the Trials of the Bristol Rioters before the Special Commission … with the Sentences and Executions Subsequent Thereon* (Bristol, 1832).

Anon., *A full, true and particular account of the Meeting on Brandon Hill* (Bristol, 1819).

Anon., *Genuine Letters and Other Official Papers from the Original Manuscripts of the Independent Society of Freemen* (Bristol, 1790).

Anon., *Incidents in the Life of Joseph Kayes who was Executed at the New Gaol …* (Bristol, 1832).

Anon., *The Lamentation of Bristolia: or the First Chapter of the Chronicles of Judas and Haman* (Bristol, 1793).

Anon., *A letter to a Member of Parliament from a Gentleman of Bristol, containing a Particular and True Account of the Extraordinary Proceedings relating to the late Election of Members of Parliament for that City*, 2nd edn (London, 1715).

Anon., *The Life of Nicholas Mooney* (Bristol, 1752).

Anon., *A List of All the Names that Sign'd the Two Petitions against Thomas Coster, esq* [1735? Bristol?] copy in BRL (B 15163).

Anon., *The Lives and Trials of Cornelius York, George Masters and John Millard* (Bristol, 1740).

Anon., *The Magistrates of Bristol Brought to the Bar of Public Opinion …* (Bristol, 1832).

Anon., *Public Characters of 1807* (London, 1807).

Anon., *The Seaman's Groans* (London, 1702).

Anon., *Some Particulars Relating to the Life of William Dillon Sheppard* (Bristol, 1761).

Anon., *The Sorrowful Lamentation of the Unhappy Men of Bristol who Received Sentence of Death for the Late Riots* (London, 1832).

Anon, *Thoughts on education, union of classes and co-operation suggested by the late riots in Bristol* (London, 1831).

Anon. *Three letters upon the subject of the Gin Act and common informers* (London, 1738).

Anon. *The tradesman's and traveller's pocket companion, or the Bath and Bristol Guide* (Bath, 1753).

Anon. *The Trial of Samuel Tout and Robert Westcott* (Taunton, 1801).

Anon., *Trials of the Persons Concerned in the Late Riots before Chief Justice Tindal …* (Bristol, 1832).

Anon., *The Tryals of the Rioters at Bristol* (Bristol, 1714).

Barrett, William, *The history and antiquities of the City of Bristol* (Bristol, 1789).

Barry, Edward, *A Serious Address to the Citizens of Bristol* (Bristol, 1781).

Barry, Rev. Edward, *Coalitions and Compromises* (Bristol, 1790).

Batt, Rev. William, *Union and Loyalty Recommended: A Sermon Preached at the Mayor's Chapel, 15th September 1754* (Bristol, 1754).

Beddoes, Thomas, *A Word in Defence of the Bill of Rights Against Gagging Bills* (Bristol, 1795).

Benezet, Anthony, *Some historical account of Guinea*, 2nd edn (London, 1788).

Boyer, Abel, *Political State of Great Britain* (38 vols, 1711–40).

Bradburn, Samuel, *Equality. A sermon … preached at the Methodist chapel, Broadmead, Bristol, February 28, 1794* (Bristol, 1794).

Brome, James, *Travels over England, Scotland and Wales* (London, 1700).

Catcott, Alexander S., *The antiquity and honourableness of the practice of merchants* (Bristol, 1744).

Chauncy, Ichabod, *Innocence vindicated* (London, 1684).

Chapman, Richard, *New Year's Gift; Being a seasonable call to repentance, as well upon the account of some threatening incendiaries, as of the more threatening vices of the resent age ... in a poem, moral and divine* (London, 1731).

Chatterton, Thomas, *The Squire in his Chariot* (London, 1775).

Clarke, Edward Daniel, *A tour through the south of England* (London, 1793).

Clarkson, Thomas, *The History of the Rise, Progress and Accomplishment of the Abolition of the Slave Trade* (2 vols, London, 1808).

Charlesworth, Andrew. *An Atlas of Rural Protest in Britain 1548–1900* (Philadelphia, 1983).

[Chatterton, Thomas], *The Squire in his Chariot* (London, 1775).

Coleridge, Samuel T., *An Answer to 'A Letter to Edward Long-Fox M. D.'* (Bristol, 1795).

Coleridge, Samuel T., *The Plot Discovered, or An Address to the People against Ministerial Treason* (Bristol, 1795).

Collins, Emmanuel, *The Saints Backsiding: or, The Remarkable Case of a Late Reverend, Holy, Anabaptistical Preacher belonging to Their Meeting in Bristol* (Bristol, c. 1756).

Combe, William, *The Philosopher in Bristol* (2 vols, Bristol, 1775).

Dawes, Mannaseh, *Observations on the mode of electing representatives in parliament for the City of Bristol* (Bristol, 1784).

Defoe, Daniel, *A tour thro' the whole island of Great Britain*, 2nd edn (4 vols, London, 1753).

Dunton, John, *The Neck Adventure: or the Case and Sufffferings of John Dunton* (London, 1715).

Dunton, John, *The Shortest Way with the King* (London, 1715).

[Eagles, John], *The Bristol Riots. Their Causes Progress and Consequences* (Bristol, 1832).

Evans, Caleb, *A Letter to the Reverend John Wesley occasioned by his Calm Address to the American Colonies* (Bristol, 1775).

Evans, Caleb, *Political sophistry detected* (Bristol, 1776).

Fletcher, John, *A Vindication of the Reverend Mr. Wesley's Calm Address* (London, 1776).

Foote, Samuel, *The Genuine Memoirs of the Life of Sir John Dinely Goodere* (Bristol, 1741).

Goldwin, William, *A Poetical Description of Bristol* (Bristol, 1712).

Gutch, J. M., *Letters on the impediments which obstruct the trade and commerce of the city and port of Bristol* (Bristol, 1823).

Heath, George, *The new history, survey and descriptions of the city and suburbs of Bristol* (Bristol, 1794).

Heath, George, *The New Bristol Guide* (Bristol, 1799).

Hobhouse, Benjamin, *Thoughts Humbly Offered to the Mayor and Sheriffs of Bristol* (Bristol, 1794).

[Holmes, Elizabeth], *Scenes in Our Parish* (New York, 1833).

Hooke, Andrew, *Bristolia, or Memoirs of the City of Bristol, both Civil and Ecclesiastical* (Bristol, 1749).

Howell, Thomas, *A Complete Collection of the State Trials* ..., vol. 24 (London, 1818).

Hunt, Henry, *Memoirs Of Henry Hunt, Esq.* (3 vols, London, 1820).

Jenkins, John, *An Exact Representation of the Manner of Conducting the Scheme for Supplying the Poor with Bread in the Cheapest and Best Manner...* (Bristol, 1772).

Johnson, James, *An Address to the Inhabitants of Bristol on the Subject of the Poor Rates with a View to their Reduction* (Bristol, 1820).

Kentish, Edward, *Narrative of the Facts Relative to the Bristol Election as Connected with the Meeting on Brandon Hill* (Bristol, 1818).

King, John, *A Statement of the Facts Relative to the Riot in Union Street, Bristol, with some Free Observations on the Conduct of the Civil Power on that Occasion* (Bristol, 1797).

Kington, John Barnet, *Thirty letters on the trade of Bristol* (Bristol, 1834).

Lawson, Emily M., *Through Tumult and Pestilence: A Tale of the Bristol Riots and the Cholera Time* (London, n.d.).

Layman, A., *Narrative of Conversations held with Christopher Davis and William Clarke, who were Executed January 27th, 1832* ... (Bristol, 1832).

Lee, Thomas, *Eyes to the Blind! An Address to the Electors of Bristol, Vindicating their Elective Franchise Against the Endeavours of the Corporation and of Certain Clubs* (Bristol, 1807).

Lee, Thomas, *White Lion Club, late Riot and Dock Tax* (Bristol, 1807).

Lewis, David, *A Letter to the Rev. Edward Barry M.D.* (Bristol, 1790).

Lovell, Robert, *Bristol: A Satire* (Bristol, 1794).

Macaulay, Thomas Babington, *The History of England from the Accession of James II*, 12th edn, Vol 2 (London, 1856).

Macky, John, *Journey through England* (London, 1724).

Manchee, T. M., *The Origins of the Riots of Bristol and the Causes of the Subsequent Outrages*, 2nd edn (Bristol, 1832).

Matthews, William, *Matthews's New Bristol Directory for the year 1793–4* (Bristol, 1793).

[Oglethorpe, James], *The Sailor's Advocate* (London, 1728).

Oldmixon, John, *The Bristol Riot* (London, 1714).

Oldmixon, John, *A Full and Impartial Account of the late Disorders in Bristol* (London, 1714).

Oldmixon, John, *The history of England during the reigns of King William and Mary* ... (London, 1735).

Paddock, R., *The Rencontre: A Poetic Tale (Founded on Fact) descriptive of the late violent Proceedings in the City of Bristol* (Bristol, 1801).

Pope, Alexander, *The Correspondence of Alexander Pope*, ed. George Sherburn (5 vols, Oxford, 1956).

Pope, Alexander, *Works* (2 vols, London, 1735)

Prudent Man's Friend Society, *First Report* (Bristol, 1813).

Reynell, Carew, *Two Sermons Preached Before the Mayor, Aldermen and Common Council of the City of Bristol* (Bristol, 1729).

Robertson, Archibald, *A topographical survey of the great road from London to Bath and Bristol 2 volumes* (London, 1792).

Rose, John, *Free Thoughts on the Offices of Mayor, Aldermen and Common Council of the City of Bristol, with a Constitutional Proposition for their Annihilation* (Bristol, 1792).

Rose, John, *An Impartial History of the Late Disturbances in Bristol* (Bristol, 1793).

Savage, Richard, *London and Bristol Compar'd – a Satire written in Newgate, Bristol* (London, 1744).

Seyer, Samuel, *Memoirs historical and topographical of Bristol* (2 vols, Bristol, 1823).

Somerton, W. H., *A Narrative of the Bristol Riots ...* (Bristol, 1831).

Southey, Robert, *Life and Correspondence of Robert Southey* (6 vols, London, 1850).

Stuckey, John, *A compleat history of Somersetshire* (Sherborne, 1742).

Sullivan, R. J., *Observations Made During a Tour Through Parts of England* (London, 1780).

Swift, Jonathan, *Works* (12 vols, London, 1765–75).

Thistlethwaite, James, *Corruption* (London, 1780).

Thorne, Romaine Joseph, *Bristolia: A Poem* (Bristol, 1794).

Tucker, Josiah, *A brief essay on the advantages and disadvantages which respectively attend France and Great Britain*, 2nd edn (London, 1750).

Veritas, *Inquisition for Blood Shall be Made: To the Inhabitants of Bristol and Parts Adjacent* (Bristol, 1793).

W., A., *A Letter to Edward Long-Fox, M.D.* (Bristol, 1795).

Walker, C. H., *Letters on the Practice of the Bristol Court of Requests on Judicial Sinecures in Bristol* (London, 1820).

Walker, C. H., *The Petition of William Clarke, Convicted at the Late Special Commission at Bristol ... with Prefatory Observations* (Bristol, 1832).

Walker, Charles Houlden, *An Appeal to the Public on the Conduct of David Evans Esq, late Mayor, and John Noble and James Harvey Esqs, Aldermen of Bristol* (Bristol, 1807).

Walker, Charles Houlden, *A Report of the Trial of Sir H. C. Lippincott, Bart., on a Charge of Rape Committed on the Person of Mary Milford, Spinster, Aged 17 Years* (London, 1810).

Wesley, John, *A Calm Address to our American Colonies* (Bristol, 1775).

Edited Primary Sources

Beaven, Alfred, *Bristol Lists. Municipal and Miscellaneous* (Bristol, 1899).

Barry, Jonathan and Kenneth Morgan (eds), *Reformation and Revival in Eighteenth-Century Bristol*, Bristol Record Society, 45 (Stroud, 1994).

Butcher, E. E. (ed.), *Bristol Corporation of the Poor*, Bristol Record Society, 3 (Bristol, 1932).

Calendar of State Papers Domestic (1692–1701).

Copeland, Thomas W. *et al.* (eds), *The Correspondence of Edmund Burke* (10 vols, Cambridge, 1958–78).

Eyewitness! Five Contemporary Accounts of the 1831 Bristol Reform Bill Riots, Frenchay Village Museum Chronicles No. 8 (Bristol, 2004).

Fortescue, Sir John, *The Correspondence of King George the Third* (6 vols, London, 1927–28).

Griggs, L. (ed.), *The Collected Letters of Samuel Taylor Coleridge* (6 vols, Oxford, 1956).

Guttridge, G. H. (ed.), *The American Correspondence of a Bristol Merchant 1766–1776. Letters of Richard Champion* (Berkeley, 1934).

Historical Manuscript Commission, Stuart Papers

House of Commons, *Parliamentary Papers*

Journals of the House of Commons

Lamb, Robert and Corinna Wagner (eds), *Selected Political Writings of John Thelwall* (3 vols, London, 2009).

Lamoine, G. (ed.), *Bristol Gaol Delivery Fiats, 1741–1799*, Bristol Record Society, 40 (Bristol, 1989).

Minchinton, Walter E., *The Trade of Bristol in the Eighteenth Century*, Bristol Record Society, 20 (Bristol 1957).

Morgan, Kenneth (ed.), *The Bright-Meyler Papers: A Bristol-West Indian Connection, 1732–1837* (Oxford, 2007).

Oliver, Andrew (ed.), *The Journal of Samuel Curwen, Loyalist* (2 vols, Cambridge, MA, 1972).

Patton, L. (ed.), *The Collected Works of Samuel Taylor Coleridge 2: The Watchman* (Cambridge, 1970).

Ralph E. and M. Williams (eds), *The Inhabitants of Bristol in 1696*, Bristol Record Society, 25 (Bristol, 1968).

Ralph, Elizabeth, 'Bishop Secker's Diocese Book', in *A Bristol Miscellany*, ed. Patrick McGrath, Bristol Record Society, 37 (Bristol, 1985).

Rogers, Nicholas (ed.), *Manning the Royal Navy in Bristol: Liberty, Impressment and the State, 1739–1815*, Bristol Record Society, 66 (Bristol, 2013).

Second Report of the Commissioners for Inquiring into the State of Large Towns and Populous Districts (London, 1845).

Thale, Mary (ed.), *Selections from the Papers of the London Corresponding Society, 1792–1799* (Cambridge, 1983).

Wesley, John, *The Journal of the Reverend John Wesley*, ed. Nehemiah Curnock (8 vols, London, 1909–16).

Wesley, John, *The Letters of John Wesley*, ed. John Telford (8 vols, London, 1931).

Newspapers and periodicals

Annals of George I
Annual Register
Aris's Birmingham Gazette
Bath and Cheltenham Gazette
Bath Chronicle
Bath Journal
Bath Herald
Bonner and Middleton's Bristol Journal
Blackwood's Magazine
Bristol Gazette
Bristolian
Bristol Mercury
Bristol Mirror
Bristol Oracle
Bristol Weekly Intelligencer
British Journal
British Weekly Mercury
Bury and Norwich Post

Chester Chronicle
Cobbett's Weekly Political Register
Courier
Craftsman, or Country Journal
Daily Advertiser
Daily Courant
Daily Gazetteer
Daily Journal
Daily Post
Echo, or Edinburgh Journal
Evening Mail
Examiner
Farley's Bristol Advertiser
Farley's Bristol Newspaper
Felix Farley's Bristol Journal
Fog's Weekly Journal
Flying Post
General Advertiser
General Evening Post
Gentleman's Magazine
Gloucester Journal
Grub Street Journal
Hampshire Chronicle
Hampshire Telegraph
Hereford Journal
Historical Register
Ipswich Journal
John Bull
Kentish Gazette
London Evening Post
London Chronicle
London Gazette
London Journal
Mist's Weekly Journal
Monthly Chronicle
Morning Chronicle
Morning Post
New York Gazette
Newcastle Courant
Norfolk Chronicle
Northampton Mercury
North Devon Journal
Observer
Old England
Oxford Journal
Poor Man's Guardian
Post Boy

Public Advertiser
Radical Reformer
Reading Mercury
Read's Weekly Journal
St. James's Chronicle
St James's Evening Post
Sarah Farley's Bristol Journal
Satirist
Sherborne Mercury
Sussex Weekly Advertiser
Taunton Courier
The Times
Town and Country Magazine
Watchman
Weekly Journal
Weekly Packet
Western Daily Press
Western Flying Post
Whitehall Evening Post
Worcester Journal

Secondary sources

Abelove, Henry, 'John Wesley's Plagiarism of Samuel Johnson and its Contemporary Reception', *Huntington Library Quarterly*, 59:1 (1996), 73–9.

Albert, William, 'Popular Opposition to Turnpike Trusts in Early Eighteenth-Century England', *Journal of Transport History*, 5:1 (1979), 1–17.

Albert, William, *The Turnpike Road System in England 1663–1840* (Cambridge, 1972).

Alford, B. W. E., 'The Economic Development of Bristol in the Nineteenth Century: An Enigma?', in *Essays in Bristol and Gloucestershire History*, ed. Patrick McGrath and John Cannon (Bristol, 1976).

Anderson, Perry, *Arguments Within English Marxism* (London, 1980).

Archer, John, *By a Flash and a Scare: Arson, Animal Maiming and Poaching in East Anglia, 1815–1870* (Oxford, 1990).

Aspinall, A. (ed.), *The Later Correspondence of George III 3: 1798–1801* (Cambridge, 1967).

Atkinson, B. J., 'An Early Example of the Decline of the Industrial Spirit? Bristol Enterprise in the First Half of the Nineteenth Century', *Southern History*, 9 (1987).

Ayers, J. (ed.), *Paupers and Pig Killers: The Diary of William Holland, a Somerset Parson, 1799–1818* (Gloucester, 1984).

Backscheider, Paula R., *Daniel Defoe. His Life* (Baltimore and London, 1989).

Baigent, Elizabeth, 'Economy and Society in Eighteenth-Century English Towns: Bristol in the 1770s', in *Urban Historical Geography: Recent Progress in Britain and Germany*, ed. Dietrich Deneke and Gareth Shaw (Cambridge, 1988).

Baigent, Elizabeth and James E. Bradley, 'The Social Sources of Late Eighteenth-Century English Radicalism: Bristol in the 1770s and 1780s', *English Historical Review*, 124 (2009), 1075–1108.

Barker, Ernest, *Burke and Bristol* (Bristol, 1931).

Barker, Ernest, 'Burke and his Bristol Constituency, 1774–1780', in *Essays on Government*, 2nd edn (Oxford, 1951).

Barry, Jonathan, 'Bourgeois Collectivism? Urban Association and the Middling Sort', in *The Middling Sort of People*, ed. Jonathan Barry and Christopher Brooks (London, 1994), pp. 84–112.

Barry, Jonathan, 'Bristol Pride: Civic Identity in Bristol, c. 1640–1775', in *The Making of Modern Bristol*, ed. Madge Dresser (Bristol, 2005), pp. 25 –47.

Barry, Jonathan, 'Chatterton, More and Bristol's Cultural Life in the 1760s', in *From Gothic to Romantic. Thomas Chatterton's Bristol*, ed. Alistair Heys (Bristol, 2005).

Barry, Jonathan, 'Civility and Civic Culture in Early Modern England: The Meanings of Urban Freedom', in *Civil Histories. Essays Presented to Sir Keith Thomas*, ed. Peter Burke, Brian Harrison and Paul Slack (Oxford, 2000).

Barry, Jonathan, 'The Politics of Religion in Restoration Bristol', in *The Politics of Religion in Restoration England*, ed. Tim Harris, Paul Seaward and Mark Goldie (Oxford, 1990).

Barry, Jonathan, 'The Press and the Politics of Culture in Bristol 1660–1775', in *Culture, Politics and Society in Britain, 1660–1800*, ed. Jeremy Black and Jeremy Gregory (Manchester, 1991).

Beattie, J. M., *Crime and the Courts in England, 1660–1800* (Oxford, 1986).

Belchem, John. *'Orator' Hunt: Henry Hunt and English Working-Class Radicalism* (Oxford, 1985).

Bennett, G. V., *The Tory Crisis in Church and State. The Career of Francis Atterbury, Bishop of Rochester* (Oxford, 1975).

Bogart, Dan, 'Turnpike Trusts and Property Income: New Evidence on the Effects of Transport Improvements and Legislation in Eighteenth-Century England', *Economic History Review*, 62:1 (2009), 128–52.

Bohstedt, John, *The Politics of Provisions* (Farnham, 2010).

Bradley, James E., *Popular Politics and the American Revolution in England* (Macon, 1986).

Bradley, James E., *Religion, Revolution and English Radicalism. Nonconformity in Eighteenth-Century Politics and Society* (Cambridge, 1990).

Braithwaite, William, *The Second Period of Quakerism* (Cambridge, 1961).

Breen, T. H., *American Insurgents, American Patriots. The Revolution of the People* (New York, 2010).

Brewer, John, 'The Number 45: A Wilkite Political Symbol', in *England's Rise to Greatness, 1660–1763*, ed. Stephen Bartow Baxter (Berkeley and Los Angeles, 1983).

Brewer, John, *Party Ideology and Popular Politics at the Accession of George III* (Cambridge, 1976).

Brewer, John, *The Pleasures of the Imagination: English Culture in the Eighteenth Century* (London, 2013).

Brown, Christopher, *Moral Capital: Foundations of British Abolitionism* (Chapel Hill, 2006).

Brunsman, Denver, *The Evil Necessity. British Naval Impressment in the Eighteenth-Century Atlantic World* (Charlottesville, 2013).

Burke, Peter, Brian Harrison and Paul Slack (eds), *Civil Histories: Essays presented to Sir Keith Thomas* (Oxford, 2000).

Bush, Graham, *Bristol and its Municipal Government 1820–1851*, Bristol Record Society, 29 (Bristol, 1976).

Butterfield, Herbert, *George III, Lord North and the People* (New York, 1968 reissue).

Campbell, Lord John, *Lives of the Lord Chancellors* (10 vols, Jersey City, 1885).

Caple, Jeremy, *The Bristol Riots of 1831 and Social Reform in Britain* (New York, 1990).

Chase, Malcolm, *Early Trade Unionism: Fraternity, Skill and the Politics of Labour* (Aldershot, 2000).

Christie, Ian R., 'Henry Cruger and the End of Edmund Burke's Connection with Bristol', *Transactions of the Bristol and Gloucester Archeological Society*, 74 (1955), 153–70.

Clark, Anna, 'Queen Caroline and the Sexual Politics of Popular Culture in London, 1820', *Representations*, 31 (1990), 31–88.

Clark, Anna, *The Struggle for the Breeches: Gender and the Making of the British Working Class* (Berkeley and Los Angeles, 1997).

Clark, Peter, *The Cambridge Urban History of Britain 2: 1540–1840* (Cambridge, 2008).

Costello, Kevin, 'Habeas Corpus and Military and Naval Impressment, 1756–1816', *Journal of Legal History*, 29:2 (2008), 215–51.

Cruickshanks, Eveline, *Political Untouchables: The Tories and the '45* (London, 1979).

Dancy, J. Ross, *The Myth of the Press Gang* (Woodbridge, 2015).

Davidoff, Leonore and Catherine Hall, *Family Fortunes: Men and Women of the English Middle Class 1780–1830* (London, 1987).

Devereaux, Simon, 'Recasting the Theatre of Execution: The Abolition of the Tyburn Ritual', *Past and Present*, 202 (2009), 127–74.

Dobson, C. R., *Masters and Journeymen: A Prehistory of Industrial Relations, 1717–1800* (London, 1980).

Donoughue, Bernard, *British Politics and the American Revolution* (London, 1964).

Drescher, Seymour, *Capitalism and Anti-Slavery* (London, 1986).

Drescher, Seymour, *Econocide. British Slavery in the Era of Abolition*, 2nd edn (Chapel Hill, 2010).

Dresser, Madge, *Slavery Obscured* (London and New York, 2001).

Dresser, Madge (ed.), *Women and the City* (Bristol, 2016).

Earle, Peter, *Monmouth's Rebels* (London, 1977).

Estabrook, Carl B., *Urbane and Rustic England* (Manchester, 1998).

Elliott, Marianne, *Partners in Revolution: The United Irishmen and France* (New York, 1982).

Epstein, James A., 'The Constitutional Idiom: Radical Reasoning, Rhetoric and Action in Early Nineteenth-Century England', *Journal of Social History*, 23:3 (1990), 553–74.

Epstein, James, 'Understanding the Cap of Liberty: Symbolic Practice and Social Conflict in Early Nineteenth-Century England', *Past and Present*, 122 (1989), 75–118.

Farge, Arlette, *Fragile Lives. Violence, Power and Solidarity in Eighteenth-Century Paris*, trans. Carol Shelton (Cambridge, MA, 1993).

Fritz, Paul S., *The English Ministers and Jacobitism between the Rebellions of 1715 and 1745* (Toronto and Buffalo, 1975).

Garrett, Charles. *Respectable Folly: Millenarianism and the French Revolution in England and France* (Baltimore, 1975).

Gerard, Kent and Gert Hekma (eds), *The Pursuit of Sodomy: Male Homosexuality in Renaissance and Enlightenment Europe* (New York, 1989).

Gorsky, Martin, 'James Tuckfield's "Ride": Combination and Social Drama in Early Nineteenth-Century Bristol', *Social History*, 19:3 (1994), 319–38.

Gorsky, Martin, *Patterns of Philanthropy. Charity and Society in Nineteenth-Century Bristol* (Woodbridge, 1999).

Gould, Eliga, 'Liberty and Modernity: The American Revolution and the Making of Parliament's Imperial History', in *Exclusionary Empire. English Liberty Overseas, 1600–1900*, ed. Jack P. Greene (Cambridge, 2010).

Graham, Jenny, *The Nation, the Law and the King, Reform Politics in England, 1789–1799* (2 vols, Lanham, 2000).

Greaves, Richard L., *Secrets of the Kingdom. British Radicals from the Popish Plot to the Revolution of 1688–1689* (Stanford, 1992).

Griffin, Carl, *The Rural War: Captain Swing and the Politics of Protest* (Manchester, 2012).

Habermas, Jürgen, *The Structural Transformation of the Public Sphere*, trans. Thomas Berger (Cambridge, MA, 1989).

Halliday, Paul D., *Habeas Corpus from England to Empire* (Cambridge, MA, 2010).

Hamburger, Joseph, *James Mill and the Art of Revolution* (New Haven, 1963).

Hadfield, Charles, *British Canals*, 5th edn (Newton Abbot, 1974).

Hadfield, Charles, *The Canals of South and South Eastern England* (Newton Abbot, 1969).

Harrison, Mark, *Crowds and History: Mass Phenomena in English towns, 1790–1835* (Cambridge, 1988).

Harrison, Mark, 'To Raise and Dare Resentment: The Bristol Bridge Riot of 1793 Re-Examined', *Historical Journal*, 26:3 (1983), 557–85.

Hay, Douglas *et al.* (eds), *Albion's Fatal Tree: Crime and Society in Eighteenth-Century England* (London, 1975).

Haywood, Ian, *Bloody Romanticism: Spectacular Violence and the Politics of Representation 1776–1832* (New York, 2006).

Hindle, Steve, Alexandra Shepard and John Walter (eds), *Remaking English Society. Social Relations and Social Change in Early Modern England* (Woodbridge, 2013).

Hitchcock, Tim, *Down and Out in Eighteenth-Century London* (London, 2004).

Hitchcock, Tim and Robert Shoemaker, *London Lives: Poverty, Crime and the Making of a Modern City, 1690–1800* (Cambridge, 2015).

Holman, J. R., 'Orphans in Pre-Industrial Towns – The Case of Bristol in the Late Seventeenth Century', *Local Population Studies*, 15 (1975), 42–4.

Hope, Tim, 'Riots Pure and Simple?', *Criminal Justice Matters*, 87 (2012).

Hoppit, Julian. *Risk and Failure in English Business 1700–1800* (Cambridge, 1987).

Hunt, William. *Historic Towns: Bristol* (London, 1887).

Jackson, Gordon, 'Ports 1700–1840', in *The Cambridge Urban History of Britain 2: 1540–1840*, ed. Peter Clark (Cambridge, 2000).

Jarvis, Robin. 'In Search of Robert Lovell: Poet and Pantisocrat', *Journal for Eighteenth-Century Studies*, 40:1 (2017), 111–26.

James, Reginald, 'Bristol Society in the Eighteenth Century', in *Bristol and its Adjoining Counties*, ed. C. H. MacInnes and W. F. Whittard (Bristol, 1955).

Jewson, C. B., *The Jacobin City* (Glasgow and London, 1975).

Jones, Francis, 'Disaffection and Dissent in Pembrokeshire', *Transactions of the Honorable Society of Cymmrodorion* (1946–7), 206–31.

Jones, J. R., *The Revolution of 1688 in England* (London, 1972).

Jones, Philip D., 'The Bristol Bridge Riot and its Antecedents: Eighteenth-Century Perception of the Crowd', *Journal of British Studies*, 19:2 (1980), 74–92.

King, Peter, 'Edward Thompson's Contribution to Eighteenth-Century Studies: The Patrician–Plebeian Model Re-Examined', *Social History*, 21 (1996), 215–28.

Kinkel, Sarah, 'The King's Pirates? Naval Enforcement of Imperial Authority, 1740–1776', *William and Mary Quarterly*, 71:1 (2014), 3–34.

Langton, John, 'Residential Patterns in Pre-Industrial Cities: Some Case Studies from Seventeenth-Century Britain', *Transactions of the Institute of British Geographers*, 65 (1975), 1–27.

Laqueur, Thomas, 'The Queen Caroline Affair: Politics as Art in the Reign of George IV', *Journal of Modern History*, 54 (1982), 417–66.

Latimer, John, *Annals of Bristol* (3 vols, Bristol, 1887–1900: reprint, Bath, 1970).

Leech, Roger H., *The Town House in Medieval and Early Modern Bristol* (Swindon, 2014).

Linebaugh, Peter, *The London Hanged: Crime and Civil Society in the Eighteenth Century* (London, 1991).

Lloyd, Christopher, *The British Seaman, 1200–1860* (London, 1968).

Lock, F. P., *Edmund Burke*, 2 vols (Oxford, 1998 and 2006).

Longmore, Jane, 'Civic Liverpool: 1680–1800', in *Liverpool 800: Culture, Character and History*, ed. John Belchem (Liverpool, 2006), 113–69.

Mackeson, John F., *Bristol Transported* (Bristol, 1987).

MacQuiban, T. S. A., 'The Sacramental Controversy in Bristol in the 1790s', *Bulletin of the Bristol Branch of the Wesley Historical Society*, 60 (1991).

Maier, Pauline. *From Resistance to Rebellion. Colonial Radicals and the Development of American Opposition to Britain, 1765–1776* (New York, 1972).

Malcolmson, Robert W., '"A set of ungovernable people": The Kingswood Colliers in the Eighteenth Century', in *An Ungovernable People: The English and their Law in the Seventeenth and Eighteenth Centuries*, ed. J. Brewer and J. Styles (London, 1979).

Manson, Michael. *'Riot!' The Bristol Bridge Massacre of 1793*, 2nd edn (Bristol, 2013).

Marcy, Peter T., 'Eighteenth Century Views of Bristol and Bristolians', in *Bristol in the Eighteenth Century*, ed. Patrick McGrath (Newton Abbot, 1972).

Marshall, John, *John Locke, Toleration, and Early Enlightenment Culture* (Cambridge, 2006).

Marshall, Peter, *The Anti-Slave Trade Movement in Bristol* (Bristol, 1968).

Marshall, Peter, *Bristol and the American War of Independence* (Bristol, 1977).

Marshall, P. J., *Remaking the British Atlantic. The United States and the British Empire after American Independence* (Oxford, 2012)

McCalman, Iain, *Radical Underworld: Prophets, Revolutionaries and Pornographers in London, 1795–1840* (Oxford, 1993).

McCormick, Ian (ed.), *Secret Sexualities: A Sourcebook of 17th and 18th Century Writing* (London, 1997).

McKenzie, Andrea, *Tyburn's Martyrs: Execution in England, 1675–1775* (London, 2007).

McGrath, Patrick (ed.), *Bristol in the Eighteenth Century* (Newton Abbot, 1972).

McGrath, Patrick and Mary E. Williams (eds), *Bristol Inns and Alehouses in the Mid-Eighteenth Century* (Bristol, 1979).

Miller, John, *Cities Divided: Politics and Religion in English Provincial Towns, 1660–1722* (Oxford, 2007).

Minchinton, Walter E., 'Bristol: Metropolis of the West in the Eighteenth Century', *Transactions of the Royal Historical Society*, 5th series, 4 (1954), 69–89.

Monod, Paul K., *Jacobitism and the English People 1688–1788* (Cambridge, 1993).

Morgan, Gwenda and Peter Rushton, *Eighteenth-Century Criminal Transportation: The Formation of the Criminal Atlantic* (Basingstoke, 2004).

Morgan, Kenneth, *Bristol and the Atlantic Trade in the Eighteenth Century* (Cambridge, 1993).

Morgan, Kenneth, 'The Bristol West India Merchants', *Transactions of the Royal Historical Society*, 3 (1993), 183–208.

Morgan, Kenneth, 'Liverpool's Dominance in the British Slave Trade, 1740–1807', in *Liverpool and Transatlantic Slavery*, ed. David Richardson, Suzanne Schwarz and Anthony Tibbles (Liverpool, 2007).

Morriss, Roger, *The Foundations of British Maritime Ascendancy* (Cambridge, 2010).

Navickas, Katrina, *Protest and the Politics of Space and Place, 1789–1848* (Manchester, 2016).

Namier, Sir Lewis, *The Structure of Politics at the Accession of George III*, 2nd edn (London, 1957).

Nash, Gary, 'The Social Evolution of Preindustrial American Cities, 1700–1820. Reflections and Directions', *Journal of Urban History*, 13:2 (1987), 115–46.

Neale, Matt, 'Crime and Maritime Trade in Bristol, 1770–1800', in *A City Built Upon the Water. Maritime Bristol 1750–1900*, ed. Steve Poole (Bristol, 2013), 76–93.

Neale, Matt, 'Making Crime Pay in Late Eighteenth-Century Bristol: Stolen Goods, the Informal Economy and the Negotiation of Risk', *Continuity and Change*, 26:3 (2011), 439–59.

Nicholas, Donald. 'The Welsh Jacobites', *Transactions of the Honourable Society of Cymmrodorion* (1948), 467–74.

Nichols J. F. and J. Taylor, *Bristol Past and Present 3: Civil and Modern History* (Bristol, 1882).

O'Gorman, Frank, 'The Parliamentary Opposition to the Government's American Policy 1760–1782', in *Britain and the American Revolution*, ed. H. T. Dickinson (London and New York, 1998).

O'Gorman, Frank, *Voters, Patrons and Parties. The Unreformed Electoral System of Hanoverian England 1734–1832* (Oxford, 1989).

Pawson, Eric, *Transport and Economy: The Turnpike Roads of Eighteenth Century Britain* (London and New York, 1977).

Petrie, Sir Charles, 'The Jacobite Activities in South and West England in the Summer of 1715', *Transactions of the Royal Historical Society*, 18 (1935), 85–106.

Phillips, John A., *Electoral Behavior in Unreformed England 1761–1802* (Princeton, 1982).

Phillips, John A., 'Popular Politics in Unreformed England', *Journal of Modern History*, 52 (1980), 617–20.

Phillips, John A., 'The Structure of Electoral Politics in Unreformed England', *Journal of British Studies*, 19:1 (1979), 79–100.

Plumb, J. H., *The Growth of Political Stability in England 1675–1725* (London, 1967).

Poole, Steve, '"Bringing great shame upon this city": Sodomy, the Courts and the Civic Idiom in Eighteenth-Century Bristol', *Urban History*, 34:1 (2007), 114–26.

Poole, Steve (ed.), *A City Built Upon the Water. Maritime Bristol 1750–1900* (Bristol, 2013).

Poole, Steve, 'For the Benefit of Example: Crime Scene Executions in England, 1720–1830', in *A Global History of Execution and the Criminal Corpse*, ed. Richard Ward (Palgrave, 2015), 72–8.

Poole, Steve, 'A Lasting and Salutary Warning: Incendiarism, Rural Order and England's Last Scene of Crime Execution', *Rural History*, 19:2 (2008), 163–77.

Poole, Steve, *The Politics of Regicide in England 1760–1820: Troublesome Subjects* (Manchester, 2000).

Poole, Steve, 'Scarcity and the Civic Tradition: Market Management in Bristol 1707–1815', in *Markets, Market Culture and Popular Protest in Eighteenth-Century Britain and Ireland* (Liverpool, 1996).

Poole, Steve, '"Till our liberties be secure": Popular Sovereignty and Public Space in Bristol, 1780–1850', *Urban History*, 26:1 (1999), 40–54.

Pressnell, L. S., *Country Banking in the Industrial Revolution* (Oxford, 1956).

Prothero, Iorwerth, *Artisans and Politics in Early Nineteenth-Century London: John Gast and his Times* (London, 1979).

Pryce, George, *A Popular History of Bristol* (Bristol, 1861).

Randall, Adrian, *Riotous Assemblies: Popular Protest in Hanoverian England* (Oxford, 2006).

Randall, Adrian and Andrew Charlesworth (eds), *Markets, Market Culture and Popular Protest in Eighteenth-Century Britain and Ireland* (Liverpool, 1996).

Ranlet, Philip, *The New York Loyalists* (Knoxville, 1986).

Reclus, Élisée, *The Earth and its Inhabitants: The Universal Geography* (6 vols, London, 1878–94).

Richardson, David, *Bristol, Africa and the Eighteenth-Century Slave Trade*, Bristol Record Society, 38–9, 42, 47 (4 vols, Gloucester, 1986–96).

Richardson, David. 'Slavery and Bristol's "Golden Age"', *Slavery and Abolition*, 26:1 (2005), 35–54.

Richardson, Ruth, *Death, Dissection and the Destitute*, 2nd edn (Chicago, 2001).

Ritcheson, Charles R., *British Politics and the American Revolution* (Norman, 1954).

Roberts, Penny, 'Arson, Conspiracy and Rumour in Early Modern Europe', *Continuity and Change*, 12 (1997).

Rodger, N. A. M., *The Command of the Ocean* (London, 2004).

Roe, Nicholas, *Wordsworth and Coleridge: The Radical Years* (Oxford, 1988).

Rogers, Nicholas, 'Burning Tom Paine: Loyalism and Counter-Revolution in Britain, 1792–3', *Histoire sociale/Social History*, 32:64 (1999), 139–72.

Rogers, Nicholas, *Crowds, Culture and Politics in Georgian Britain* (Oxford, 1998).

Rogers, Nicholas, 'From Vernon to Wolfe: Empire and Identity in the British Atlantic World of the Mid-Eighteenth Century', in *The Culture of the Seven Years' War*, ed. Frans De Bryn and Shaun Regan (Toronto, 2013).

Rogers, Nicholas, 'Popular Protest in Early Hanoverian London', *Past and Present*, 79 (1978), 70–100.

Rogers, Nicholas, *The Press Gang. Naval Impressment and its Opponents in Georgian Britain* (London, 2007).

Rogers, Nicholas, 'Riot and Popular Jacobitism in Early Hanoverian England', in *Ideology and Conspiracy: Aspects of Jacobitism, 1689–1759*, ed. Eveline Cruickshanks (Edinburgh, 1982).

Rogers, Nicholas, *Whigs and Cities. Popular Politics in the Age of Walpole and Pitt* (Oxford, 1989).

Rogers, Pat, 'Daniel Defoe, John Oldmixon and the Bristol Riot of 1714', *Transactions of the Bristol and Gloucestershire Archaeological Society*, 93 (1973), 145–56.

Rudé, George, *Wilkes and Liberty* (Oxford, 1962).

Rudé, George, *The Crowd in History* (New York, 1964).

Sacks, David Harris, *The Widening Gate. Bristol and the Atlantic Economy, 1450–1700* (Berkeley and Los Angeles, 1991).

Sharp, Buchanan, *In Contempt of All Authority. Rural Artisans and Riot in the West of England, 1586–1660* (Berkeley and Los Angeles, 1980).

Sheldon, Richard, 'The London Sailors' Strike of 1768', in *An Atlas of Industrial Protest in Britain, 1750–1990*, ed. Andrew Charlesworth *et al.* (London, 1996).

Shelton, Walter, *English Hunger and Industrial Disorders: A Study of Social Conflict During the First Decade of George III's Reign* (Toronto, 1973).

Sjoberg, Gideon, *The Pre-Industrial City, Past and Present* (Glencoe, IL, 1960).

Souden, David, 'Migrants and the Population Structure of Later Seventeenth-Century Provincial Cities and Market Towns', in *The Transformation of English Provincial Towns 1600–1800*, ed. Peter Clark (London, 1984).

Speck, W. A., *Tory and Whig: The Struggle in the Constituencies 1701–1715* (London, 1970).

Sweet, Rosemary, *The Writing of Urban Histories in Eighteenth-Century England* (Oxford, 1997).

Thomas, P. D. G., 'Jacobitism in Wales', *Welsh Historical Review*, 1 (1960–63), 279–300.

Thompson, E. P., 'Eighteenth-Century English Society: Class Struggle without Class?', *Social History*, 3 (1978), 133–65.

Thompson, E. P., *The Making of the English Working Class* (London, 1963).

Thompson, E. P., 'The Moral Economy of the English Crowd', *Past and Present*, 50 (1971), 76–136.

Thompson, E. P., 'Patrician Society, Plebeian Culture', *Journal of Social History*, 7 (1974), 382–405.

Thompson, E. P., *Whigs and Hunters: The Origins of the Black Act* (London, 1975).

Toohey, Robert E., *Liberty and Empire. British Radical Solutions to the American Problem 1774–1776* (Lexington, 1978).

Truxes, Thomas, *Defying Empire* (London and New Haven, 2008).

Underdown, P. T., 'Henry Cruger and Edmund Burke: Colleagues and Rivals at the Bristol Election of 1774', *William and Mary Quarterly*, 15:1 (1958), 14–34.

Usher, Ronald G., 'Royal Navy Impressment during the American Revolution', *Mississippi Valley Historical Review*, 37:4 (1951), 667–9.

Van Schaack, Henry, *Henry Cruger, the Colleague of Edmund Burke in the British Parliament* (New York, 1859).

Van Schaack, Henry Cruger, 'Diary and Memoranda of Henry Cruger', *Magazine of American History*, 7 (1881), 359–63.

Volger, Richard, *Reading the Riot Act: The Magistracy, the Police and the Army in Civil Disorder* (Milton Keynes, 1991).

Ward, J.R., *British West Indian Slavery, 1750–1834* (Oxford, 1988).

Ward, J. R., *The Finance of Canal Building in Eighteenth-Century England* (Oxford, 1974).

Ward, J. R., 'Speculative Building at Bristol and Clifton, 1783–1792', *Business History*, 20:1 (1978), 3–19.

Warner, Jessica. *John the Painter: The First Modern Terrorist* (London, 2004).

Weare, G. E., *Edmund Burke's Connection with Bristol, From 1774 till 1780* (Bristol, 1894).

Wells, Roger, *Insurrection: The British Experience, 1795–1803* (Gloucester, 1983).

Wells, Roger, *Wretched Faces: Famine in Wartime England, 1793–1801* (Gloucester, 1988).

Wells, Roger and John Rule, *Crime, Protest and Popular Politics in Southern England, 1740–1850* (London, 1997).

Wilson, Kathleen, *The Sense of the People: Politics, Culture and Imperialism in England, 1715–1785* (Cambridge, 1998).

Woodfine, Philip, '"Proper Objects of the Press": Naval Impressment and Habeas Corpus in the French Revolutionary Wars', in *The Representation and Reality of War. The British Experience*, ed. Keith Dockray and Keith Laybourn (Stroud, 1999).

Worrall, David, *Radical Culture: Discourse, Resistance and Surveillance, 1790–1820* (Detroit, 1992).

Wreford, J. K. R., *Curiosities of Bristol and its Neighbourhood* (Bristol, 1854).

Wrigley, E. A. and R. S. Schofield, *The Population History of England 1541–1871* (Cambridge, 1981).

Zook, Melinda, *Radical Whigs and Conspiratorial Politics in Late Stuart England* (University Park, 1999).

Unpublished Theses

Baigent, Elizabeth, 'Bristol Society in the Late Eighteenth Century' (Unpublished DPhil Thesis, University of Oxford, 1985).

Davies, Julian Paul, 'Artisans and the City: A Social History of Bristol's Shoemakers and Tailors, 1770–1800' (Unpublished PhD Thesis, University of Bristol, 2003).

Pearce, Trevor, 'A Divided Elite: Governance and Prison Reform in Early Nineteenth Century Bristol' (Unpublished PhD Thesis, University of the West of England, 2009).

Quilici, Ronald H., 'Turmoil in a City and an Empire: Bristol's Factions 1700–1775' (Unpublished PhD Thesis, University of New Hampshire, 1977).

Underdown, P. T., 'The Parliamentary History of Bristol, 1750–1790' (Unpublished MA Thesis, University of Bristol, 1948).

BIBLIOGRAPHY

Web-Based Sources

The History of Parliament, *The House of Commons, 1690–1832*,
  <http://historyofparliamentonline.org>.
University College London, Legacies of Slave-Ownership,
  <http://www.ucl.ac.uk/lbs/>.

Index

STUDIES IN EARLY MODERN CULTURAL, POLITICAL AND SOCIAL HISTORY